KT-160-398

THE
FIGHT
OF THE
CENTURY

THE
FIGHT
OF THE
CENTURY

Jack Johnson, Joe Louis,
and the
Struggle for Racial Equality

Thomas R. Hietala

PARK LEARNING CENTRE

UNIVERSITY OF GLOUCESTERSHIRE

PO Box 220, The Park, Cheltenham, GL50 2QF

Tel: (01242) 532721

M.E. Sharpe
Armonk, New York
London, England

Copyright © 2002 by M. E. Sharpe, Inc.

The author gratefully acknowledges these publishers and right holders for permission to reprint excerpts from the following works: *The Collected Poems of Langston Hughes*, copyright © 1994 by The Estate of Langston Hughes. Used by permission of Alfred A. Knopf, a division of Random House, Inc.; The Poetry of Claude McKay, Courtesy of the Literary Representative for the Works of Claude McKay, Schomburg Center for Research in Black Culture, the New York Public Library, Astor, Lenox and Tilden Foundations; *The Invisible Soldier: The Experience of the Black Soldier, World War II*, compiled and edited by Mary Penick Motley, copyright © 1975 by Wayne State University Press, Detroit, Michigan; *Untold Tales, Unsung Heroes: An Oral History of Detroit's African American Community, 1918–1967*, compiled and edited by Elaine Latzman Moon, copyright © 1994 by Wayne State University Press.

All rights reserved. No part of this book may be reproduced in any form without written permission from the publisher, M. E. Sharpe, Inc., 80 Business Park Drive, Armonk, New York 10504.

Library of Congress Cataloging-in-Publication Data

Hietala, Thomas R., 1952-
   The fight of the century : Jack Johnson, Joe Louis, and the struggle for racial equality / Thomas R. Hietala.
    p. cm.
   Includes bibliographical references and index.
   ISBN 0-7656-0772-0 (alk. paper)
   1. Johnson, Jack, 1878-1946. 2. Louis, Joe, 1914-3. African American boxers—Biography. 4. Boxing—United States—History—20th century. 5. United States—Race relations—History—20th century. I. Title.

GV1131 .H64 2002
796.83′092′2—dc21   2001049165

Printed in the United States of America

The paper used in this publication meets the minimum requirements of American National Standard for Information Sciences Permanence of Paper for Printed Library Materials, ANSI Z 39.48-1984.

BM (c)   10   9   8   7   6   5   4   3   2   1

Contents

THE
FIGHT
OF THE
CENTURY

Introduction

"Many Thousand Gone"

> No more auction block for me,
> No more, no more,
> No more auction block for me,
> Many thousand gone.
>
> —*Negro Spiritual*

Inspired by the revolutionary ideal of liberty and justice for all, some African Americans have fought for freedom with their fists while others have done battle with their pens. In the summer of 1908, just months before Jack Johnson became the first black to win the heavyweight championship of the world, Richard Wright was born in Natchez, Mississippi. Wright's father abandoned the family when Richard was a young boy; his mother struggled with illness and a series of debilitating strokes. So Richard spent his youth in an orphanage and with relatives in Mississippi and Arkansas. He moved to Memphis in 1925, the year before Joe Louis Barrow and his family left Alabama for Detroit. Wright, like Jack Johnson and Joe Louis, eventually settled in Chicago, where he gained renown for his prolific and poignant writings about race and place in his native land.

In Memphis, Wright had rented a room on Beale Street and worked at an optical company. Before work each day he watched "the morning ritual" of a black man who would "mop until he sweated" and lament, "Ahm still working for white folks!" "He hated his job," Wright observed, "and talked incessantly of leaving to work in the post office." In this same building, a "round, yellow, fat elevator operator" nicknamed Shorty also caught Wright's atten-

3

tion. "Psychologically he was the most amazing specimen of the southern Negro I ever met," Wright noted. "Hardheaded, sensible, a reader of magazines and books, he was proud of his race and indignant about its wrongs." Among whites, however, "he would play the role of a clown of the most debased and degraded type."

Wright watched Shorty wheedle money from his white passengers. Singing, "smiling, rolling his eyes," Shorty looked at a familiar rider and pleaded, "I'm hungry, Mister White Man. I need a quarter for lunch." Ignored by the man, Shorty warned he would not budge the elevator until he got the money. "If you don't take me to my floor," the white man blustered with a smile, "you will die." Now partners in a perverse ritual of power and pretenses, the men acted in a way that disgusted Wright. "[T]his black sonofabitch sure needs a quarter," Shorty repeated as he "sang, grimacing, clowning, ignoring the white man's threat." "Come on, you black bastard," the man grumbled. "I got to work." Shorty again demanded two bits. He threw the lever, raising the car to a point just shy of its destination. "What would you do for a quarter?" the white man asked. "I'll do anything for a quarter," Shorty replied. "You can kick me for a quarter." The man laughed, jingled some coins in his pocket, and tossed a quarter on the floor. "Shorty stooped to pick it up and the white man bared his teeth and swung his foot into Shorty's rump with all the strength of his body," Wright recalled. "Shorty let out a howling laugh that echoed up and down the elevator shaft." He resumed the ascent and stopped at the right spot. After witnessing this strange routine many times, Wright chided Shorty for exchanging his pride and dignity for silver. "Listen, nigger," Shorty snapped, "my ass is tough and quarters is scarce."

With more exposure to the intricacies of race relations in Memphis, however, Wright learned how deceptive appearances could be. He soon realized that blacks habitually misled whites to mollify them, bowing and scraping before them but resenting and ridiculing them behind their backs. Whites acted out their own peculiar racial masquerade. Shorty was not alone in hiding behind a mask, for Wright began to notice disturbing contradictions in his own mind and manners. Weary of whites who expected deference from blacks as part of some preordained natural order, Wright decided to move north. He told his white boss and fellow workers, however, that he had to leave Memphis to care for his infirm mother in Chicago. "I lied as earnestly as possible," Wright confessed. "I did not want to lie, yet I had to conceal what I felt." Shorty knew Wright's real motives and dropped his own mask at the news. "Sometimes I get so goddamn mad I want to kill everybody," Shorty fumed at Wright. "I'll never leave this goddamn South. I'm always saying I am, but I won't. . . . I'll die here. Or maybe they'll kill me."

Wright shared Shorty's frustration. This repressive society forced them to purchase a modicum of physical safety at the price of sublimating natural psychological impulses and reactions that might provoke conflict and bloodshed. The constant specter of white violence, however, was but one aspect (though an important one) of a system that compelled blacks to serve white needs and not their own. Wright particularly resented the whites' mantra that they alone knew what was best for his people. "The white South said that it knew 'niggers,' and I was what the white South called a 'nigger,'" Wright explained. "Well, the white South had never known me—never known what I thought, what I felt."[1]

Over several generations, African Americans devised many methods to evade and endure white oppression. In the days of the whip and auction block, slaves sometimes mocked their masters, abused tools and animals, feigned illness, and pilfered food to supplement meager rations. More desperate chattel resorted to arson or arsenic, risked maiming or even death by defying owner, overseer, or patroller, or left loved ones behind to follow the drinking gourd to freedom. More typically, slaves found solace in scripture, tales, and songs. After emancipation, blacks enjoyed more freedom of movement, greater choice in place and terms of employment, some prospect for upward mobility, and, for a brief period, a federal commitment to civil rights and a fair franchise. But southern whites wanted to retain segregation and subordination. Whatever their abilities and ambitions, blacks discovered, as Shorty did, that quarters were scarce and only an "ass [that] is tough" could sustain them through the travails of a caste system so firmly set in its biases. Wright and others realized that whites had to attain much greater sensitivity and courage to remedy the nation's racial ills. After living in Chicago for nearly two decades, Wright defined the challenge ahead. "For white America to understand the significance of the problem of the Negro will take a bigger and tougher America than any we have yet known," he advised in 1944. "I feel that America's past is too shallow, her national character too superficially optimistic, her very morality too suffused with color hate for her to accomplish so vast and complex a task." Perhaps too pessimistic about the prospects for better race relations, Wright knew his people had little choice but to acquiesce to "color hate"—the risks of defiance seemed so high relative to the scant likelihood of any real advances. Yet Wright understood that African Americans paid dearly for wearing the mask. The key, then, was to alleviate black suffering and rage, find ways to awaken the white conscience, and foster change without incurring the wrath of extremists who might brandish rope and fagot to uphold the racial status quo. In the first half of the twentieth century, Jack Johnson and Joe Louis became important symbols to Wright and others in this struggle to advance the black minority without provoking retribution from the white majority. While virtually all black

Americans had to acquiesce to racial proscription and stifle their urges to strike back, the African American champions provided vicarious thrills in their socially sanctioned punishment and defeat of white hopes.[2]

Despite the white racists' claim that all blacks look, think, and act alike, African Americans have often disputed the best methods for protesting their condition and improving their lot. At times a tiny but impassioned minority has opted to leave the United States to "return" to Africa. Other activists have also distanced themselves from whites, but instead of crossing the Atlantic they formed race towns stretching from Eatonville, Florida, to Boley, Oklahoma, and Allensworth, California. Some leaders, Booker T. Washington in particular, advocated manual training in agriculture and industry to effect gradual progress through economic advances. Still hopeful for reform through litigation and legislation, black professionals and their white allies formed the National Association for the Advancement of Colored People (NAACP) in 1909. Others launched newspapers, established fraternal orders, promoted unions, or wrote appeals exhorting Americans to live up to their democratic ideals. When the nation went to war in 1861, 1898, 1917, and 1941, African Americans demanded the right to fight for their country, hoping that sacrifices on the battle field would secure rights on the home front. Whatever tactics they preferred, black Americans agreed that the future must be better than the past.

Blacks believed that prominent individuals as well as key organizations could fight prejudice and assist the race, so Jack Johnson and Joe Louis filled an important niche in African American history. In the short term, achievements by an exceptional person could provide some solace to those routinely denied opportunity and equality. Moreover, gains by race pioneers might portend broader progress for the masses. Such high hopes imposed an added burden on black celebrities who attained prestige, wealth, and power denied to the less fortunate. The realities of race relations made it impossible for those who surged ahead to ignore those they left behind.

This hope for collective gains through individual achievement pervaded African American thought in the age of jim crow. Fannie Barrier Williams, a founder of the National Association of Colored Women (NACW) in 1896, for example, wrote, "Among colored women the club is the effort of the few competent in behalf of the many incompetent . . . for the social uplift of the race." Like Williams, Mary Church Terrell urged elite black women to organize and lead. "We have always been equal to the highest emergencies in the past," Terrell, the first president of the NACW, noted, "and it remains for us now to prove . . . we are a unit in all matters pertaining to the education and elevation of our race." The NACW expressed this spirit in its telling motto, "LIFTING AS WE CLIMB."

Even Booker T. Washington and W.E.B. DuBois agreed that striving by a select few could secure substantial gains for the many. "We can safely say that at least six thousand men and women from Tuskegee are now at work in different parts of the South," Washington boasted in 1901, "who, by their own example or by direct effort, are showing the masses of our race how to improve their material, educational, and moral and religious life." In addition, Tuskegee graduates with "common sense and self-control" were promoting "better relations . . . between the races." Wary of Washington's emphasis on economics and his relative silence on voting and civil rights, DuBois nevertheless agreed that a black elite—the "Talented Tenth"—could improve race relations. "The function of the Negro college, then, is clear," DuBois argued in 1903. "It must maintain the standards of popular education, it must seek the social regeneration of the Negro, and it must help in the solution of problems of race contact and cooperation." Many black editors stressed how closely tied the individual African American was to the entire race. "We can climb no higher," C.W. Posey of the *Pittsburgh Courier* sighed, "than the lowest among us."

As Terrell, DuBois, Wright, and others contemplated "problems of race contact and cooperation," Joe Louis graduated from Golden Gloves to the prize ring and seemed destined to win the title if allowed to compete for it. Cheered by his rapid rise and stellar reputation, black writers stressed his vital role in the struggle for equality. A 1935 editorial in *The Crisis*, the journal of the NAACP, for instance, cautioned the race not to "hitch its wagon to a boxer" like Louis or measure its "achievement on the . . . speed and power of his left hook." Yet the writer advised readers not to underestimate his impact: "We don't think, however, that the feat of Louis ought to be minimized, and we don't think it fair or accurate to state that his success as an individual will have no effect on the fortunes of the rest of his race." Louis had "a double duty to perform," Cecil Craigne maintained in the *Chicago Defender* in 1936, "one to himself, the other to his race." Both Johnson and Louis recognized the demands of this "double duty," but the first black champion found it much more difficult than the second to meet such high expectations.[3]

In a society that denied most blacks the franchise, civil rights, due process of law, and equal opportunity in education and employment, Johnson and Louis attained a substantive and symbolic importance that transcended sports. Their subversive potential concerned white racists. "I think one of the most disgraceful things that we tolerate in American life," Senator Theodore Bilbo of Mississippi proclaimed in 1945, "is prize fights between Negroes and white men." Bilbo feared that blacks would parlay their recent military service into civil rights advances when the war ended. He wanted to send them to Africa instead, and until their complete removal he advocated strict segregation and subordination. A popular African American champion with a multiracial following did not serve Bilbo's purpose of maintaining white over black.[4]

Potent symbols of inversion and redemption, Johnson and Louis loomed large in the aspirations of their people and endure as major figures in black folklore. They also merit attention because they raise and clarify vital issues of race, regionalism, national identity, and foreign policy during the first half of the twentieth century. As great *black* hopes, Johnson and Louis won individual distinction and fame while also carrying an entire race on their shoulders. They played the anomalous role of breaking barriers of color and caste in a society in which rights and opportunities were often apportioned on the basis of origin and race. In a culture that defined peoples of African and Asian origin in group terms rather than by individual traits, a black champion's achievements had ramifications for the entire race. Similarly, his private life had public consequences because of the white tendency to view the black celebrity as a representative of the whole group. So a black champion could do much good with success and proper behavior, great harm with failure and unsavory conduct. For African Americans, the championship title became a surrogate public office, with lines blurred between private and public, individual and communal.

The first chapter of *The Fight of the Century* examines the social, cultural, and political context of Jack Johnson's rise to prominence during the Progressive era. It delineates the climate of opinion by examining major works of ethnology, history, and fiction that provided the rationale for racial inequality and proscription. Two crucial fights—Johnson's victories over champion Tommy Burns and challenger Jim Jeffries—loom large in this chapter as rare occasions when a lone black man challenged the legitimacy of the nation's race hierarchy and its expression in discrimination at home and colonialism abroad. Johnson's personal life is the focus of Chapter 2, especially his defiance of racial taboos in his sundry relationships with white women. This section analyzes the federal investigation and sensational trial of the black champion on a "white slave traffic" charge. It reviews public reaction to the case and traces the transformation of Johnson from a symbol of black redemption to the embodiment of pernicious racial stereotypes.

The third chapter assesses Johnson's demise in the historical context of a rising tide of racism and nativism in the nation during the Progressive era. Anxious whites called for greater restrictions on immigration, further limitations on black suffrage, and legislative initiatives to separate the races and prevent mixed marriages. Tensions sparked a spate of lynchings and riots, and the mounting intolerance found artistic expression in D.W. Griffith's pathbreaking film, *The Birth of a Nation*. In this climate of reaction and repression, Johnson fled the country and sought refuge abroad as a fugitive from justice. After losing his title to Jess Willard in 1915, he tried but failed to improve his reputation and prospects by joining the United States Army in France. When President Woodrow Wilson summoned Americans in 1917 to "make the world safe for democracy," Johnson and other skeptical blacks hoped that the nation would also make life safe for them. Chapter 4 evaluates Johnson's legacy and his place in black folklore. It recounts his return to the United States and his surrender to federal agents in the aftermath of World War I. Blacks realized that the Wilsonian rhetoric about democracy and human rights had little relevance to the home front, as whites weary of sacrifice and war longed for a return to "normalcy."

Joe Louis emerged as a contender in the long shadow of Jack Johnson during the mid-1930s. Chapter 5 reveals how his able managers depicted him as the very antithesis of the first black champion. The Louis entourage felt a sense of duty to the entire race, and black fans reciprocated with an intense devotion to their great black hope. Later, when Louis beat Max Schmeling of Nazi Germany and joined the army during World War II, he attained the rank of national hero. The sixth chapter shifts focus from Louis and his immediate circle to the society and nation and the state of race matters during the Depression and World War II. Drawing on a wide array of "top rail" as well as "bottom rail" sources, this section assesses the great migration, the hard times, and the evolution of the urban ghetto with its characteristic high unemployment, poverty, crime, violence, and decay. If Louis gave his people cause for optimism, then other factors suggested reason for despair—the scourge of lynching, police brutality, the tenacity of jim crow, and the ordeal of the Scottsboro boys. The attack on Pearl Harbor in late 1941 then placed the racial struggle at home into the wider context of the war against aggressive enemies abroad.

The life and legend of Joe Louis became entwined with global politics between 1935 and 1945 (the subject of Chapter 7). The international tensions that sparked World War II made three of Louis's bouts particularly important at this time—his fight with Primo Carnera of Italy in 1935 and his two matches against Max Schmeling of Germany in 1936 and 1938. Even more crucial was Louis's service to the nation during the war, transforming him into an icon of loyalty and sacrifice to a crusade beyond color. Yet the persistence of jim crow in the military dramatized the disparity between rhetoric and reality. Chapter 8 ponders the legend of Joe Louis, contrasting his private life with his public image. It also recounts his eclipse by Jackie Robinson, when baseball surpassed boxing as the new frontier of rising black expectations. A brief epilogue ponders the impact of African American celebrities on race relations and points out some of the enduring enigmas of color and caste in American history.

Among the most prominent African Americans between the end of the first Reconstruction and the beginning of the second, Johnson and Louis help bring into focus the general contours as well as the specific details of American society, culture, politics, and diplomacy in their time. To capture the vital themes as well as the instructive nuances in this action and reaction between lone champion, his group, other races, and the nation as a whole, *The Fight of the Century* utilizes diverse sources emanating from the famous and the obscure. In addressing questions of race and identity, the text quotes presidents, senators, literary giants, journalists, and celebrities, but it also provides a soapbox to soldiers, sharecroppers, blues singers, and slum dwellers often seen but not heard. Political speeches, memoirs, news articles, editorials, and court records help tell this story, but so do other sources often neglected in narrating and interpreting the past—novels, poems, movies, photographs, advertisements, folklore, music, jokes, and cartoons. This wide spectrum of evidence helps make this study interdisciplinary and integrative, bringing highbrow and lowbrow, mainstream and margin into the story of a nation and a people engaged in a constant struggle to define and direct their destiny.

The text often takes the reader inside the ropes to re-create the epic fights between Johnson, Louis, and their white opponents. It also ventures well beyond the scene of sweat, blood, and leather, since interracial contests during the first half of the twentieth century involved much more than boxing talent and technique. The ring became a national (and sometimes international) stage, and the dramatic confrontation between the two protagonists sometimes provoked a curiosity and reaction reminiscent of a crucial election, a major battle, or a natural disaster. The stark competition between black and white moved interracial boxing from the realm of sports into the arena of cultures, races, ideologies, and nations in conflict.

Jack Johnson and Joe Louis epitomized group striving and achievement in their time. Whether in boxing or business, baseball or the ballot box, the concert halls or the halls of Congress, African Americans wanted no more and no less than full equality and justice. They relished those rare moments when one of their own shattered white pretensions to superiority; they took to the streets to demonstrate their solidarity and sense of vindication when their black hope smashed a white rival to the canvas. The two champions joined the ranks of race heroes who turned the tables on the dominant whites and provided vicarious satisfaction to the oppressed, in the proud tradition of the plantation trickster who outsmarted the master, the rebellious slave who risked life for liberty, the legendary John Henry who pitted his humanity against the modern machine, and the "ba-ad nigger" who defied racist pro-scriptions and wreaked vengeance against "the man." The black champions made a fortune inflicting humiliation and pain on white men—there is no sweeter retribution than getting one's licks in and getting paid for it. The reversal of roles in the ring offered some recompense for black folks who lacked Johnson's and Louis's boxing skills but shared their color. With Jack and Joe on top, the slaves now held the whip in their hands, the whites panted under the hot sun in the fields, and the black folks reposed in the shade on the veranda of the big house.

Johnson and Louis affected the nation and its people far beyond the ring and long past their prime. Many black Americans identified strongly with "the Big Smoke" and "the Brown Bomber," yet most actually had very little in common with them beyond skin color and all the presumptions that went with it. But shared pigmentation was no small matter in the land of the lash, blackjack, and lynch rope. African Americans who cheered their champions understandably wanted, like Shorty in Memphis, to live in peace in a country where quarters would not be so scarce, where one's ass did not have to be so tough to survive another day.

1

"A Retribution Seeks"

White Repression and Black Redemption

> The night is darkest near the dawn,
> The voice of nature speaks;
> The blood that's from the Negroes drawn
> A retribution seeks.[1]
>
> —*Lizelia A. J. Moorer, "Retribution," 1907*

Of all the annual picnics celebrated on the Fourth of July by Ruby Berkley Goodwin's family and kin in DuQuoin, Illinois, the one in 1910 seemed the most memorable to her. Ample food—fried chicken, barbecued ribs, sweet corn and tomatoes, potato salad, cakes and pies—lively conversation, and a sing-along generally marked the yearly summer festival. But 1910, when Halley's Comet streaked across the sky, turned out to be a year like no other for blacks in DuQuoin and across the nation. In body the relatives gathered for their traditional rite of summer; in spirit, however, they dwelled two time zones away in Reno, Nevada. "Today . . . the grownups all seemed preoccupied," Goodwin recalled. "If a question was asked, it had to be repeated two or three times." One question, however, always received "a quick reply"— the adults knew what time it was out West. Usually good for three or four drumsticks, two slices of lemon pie, and a bad case of indigestion, Uncle Charlie could not eat. The tension that sapped his appetite even "made itself felt among the children."

What "preoccupied" Ruby's kin was a distant event that should have had little relevance to their daily lives as respected African Americans in a racially and ethnically mixed coal-mining town. "Black was a mark of distinction," Ruby learned from her elders, "not of condemnation." Still, Ruby's relatives knew that most blacks in the nation did not enjoy the familiarity and tolerance that prevailed in DuQuoin. The recent race riot in Springfield, a mere 150 miles to the north, had served as a vivid reminder of the volatility of race relations. Only two years after the Springfield horror, racial tensions again threatened to wreak destruction and bloodshed across the land. Just one spark might ignite an interracial conflagration, and this Fourth of July might provide that spark.

Like an estranged couple seeking a quick divorce, James Jeffries and Jack Johnson ventured to Reno in 1910 to contest custody of the heavyweight title. Jeffries had retired undefeated in 1904. The son of former slaves, Johnson had defeated Tommy Burns to win the crown in 1908. Several prominent whites, including former champion Jim Corbett and writer Jack London, however, persuaded Jeffries to try to recapture the crown for their race. They viewed Johnson as a usurper, a king without legitimacy. Some 10,000 fans and 300 reporters (virtually all white) ventured to Reno to watch "the battle of the century" between the black champion and "the great white hope."

Ruby's father Braxton had once watched Johnson defeat six opponents in a battle royal. Johnson had entered the event to enhance his prospects for becoming the first black heavyweight champion. After his victory Johnson mingled with Braxton and other black fans. "If I ever get a chance at Jeffries," he advised them, "you put every penny you can get on me. I'll bring home the bacon." Now with Jeffries and Johnson about to fight for the title, blacks in DuQuoin found few whites willing to wager on the white hope. "But there was more at stake than just a few dollars," Goodwin explained. "The fate of an entire race hung in the balance. Today, one lone black man had the power to make us a race of champions."

The mood at the picnic also pervaded the pool hall where Braxton supplemented his miner's wages by tending a lunch counter. Ruby's mother sent her and her sister to see if their father could leave to join the family for dinner. "When we reached the pool hall all the tables were idle," Ruby recalled. "Dad and all the men stood on the sidewalk near the door." Pondering Johnson's chances, one fellow favored him in a fair contest. "A white man is the biggest coward on the face of the earth," he proclaimed. "In the South it takes two or three hundred of 'em to lynch one unarmed nigger." When asked if he had sold his food and could leave, Braxton replied, "I ain't sold nothing. Nobody's got any appetite. Everybody's waiting to see how the fight comes out." When Ruby quizzed her father about the match, he called Johnson "a clever boxer" who was "shifty and hard to hit." Conceding that Jeffries was "strong as a bull" with "a mean wallop," Braxton predicted, "My boy will win." The two girls repeated their father's assurance when they returned to the picnic. Uncle Tobe, "a soft-spoken, mild-mannered little fellow," agreed. "I believe if they let 'em stand up there toe to toe and fight it out . . . Johnson will win," he observed. "A black man is as good as a white man any day." Others joined the refrain. "The white man knows you're as good as, if not better than he is," grandma declared. "He just don't want you to find it out."[2]

Rights and Opportunity—for Whites Only?

Jack Johnson's fate mattered to black Americans because, over the past generation, the national government, the states, most whites, and even a few prominent blacks had retreated from the ideals of equality and justice that had emerged during Radical Reconstruction. By the time Jack Johnson was born in Galveston, Texas, in 1878, for example, President Rutherford Hayes had terminated the federal army's role in the South, removing troops who had protected the ex-slaves and restoring home rule to former masters and their political allies. Without the federal sword and shield and the watchful eye of Freedman's Bureau agents, former slaves were at the mercy of southern whites determined to remove any vestige of power or influence from federal bureaucrats, "carpetbaggers," "scalawags," and blacks who sought basic rights and economic opportunity. By the time Johnson fought Jeffries, southern legislatures, with the complicity of every branch of the federal government, had relegated blacks to a status not far removed from their previous subordination as slaves. Deprived of the vote, abandoned by the courts, denied equal education, shunted to inferior facilities, and confined to menial jobs, black Americans paid dearly for the reconciliation of Cavalier and Yankee. Completion of the transcontinental railroad, the conquest of the Plains Indians, the Compromise of 1876, and the successful war against Spain in 1898 symbolized national reunification and marked the emergence of the United States as a global power. Such rapid progress, however—like the levers for advancement, comfort, and convenience in the Deep South—seemed to be "for whites only."

The opening decades of the new century seemed an inauspicious time for Jack Johnson to win the title. In the summer of 1906, for example, tensions between black troops and white police and civilians in Brownsville, Texas, came to a climax with a deadly shoot-out involving black soldiers and armed white civilians. In September white mobs in Atlanta terrorized blacks during a riot of unusual scope and severity. "Atlanta's was a horrible butchery of innocents absolutely without cause," editor Harry Smith wrote in the *Cleveland Gazette*, "for which a just God will surely punish her." The savagery in Atlanta that caused the deaths of eighteen blacks and one white (and perhaps more) was, Smith contended, "a natural outcome" of Hoke Smith's recent race-baiting gubernatorial campaign. W.E.B. DuBois, a professor at Atlanta University, noted that the riot revealed blacks to be "a mobbed and mocked and murdered people" without refuge, for neither North nor South granted safety or sustenance to African Americans. He implored God to "show us the way and point us the path" in "a godless land!"[3]

Ben Davis, editor of the *Atlanta Independent*, lost hope for any real advancement for the black American in Atlanta or elsewhere in Dixie. "The trend of legislation in the South is to degrade him and confine his possibilities," he objected in 1907. "In politics he is disfranchised; in transportation, hauled about like cattle; and in education, outrageously discriminated against. He is excluded from every industry where the supply of white labor will admit it." Even though Davis had echoed Booker T. Washington's view that blacks had brighter prospects in the South than the North, he, like Washington, failed to persuade southern whites to provide even minimal safety and opportunity to blacks. "The white man believes that he is the South," Davis grumbled, "and the ten millions of the Negroes among them are no part or parcel of it, and have no rights under the law that deserve protection." But "the Negro is as much a part of the South," he insisted, "as the South is a part of the nation."[4]

Such exhortations failed to convince southern whites to change their ways. Caught in a tangled web of sharecropping, tenantry, debt, and convict-lease labor, former slaves and their offspring realized that whites in Dixie intended to maintain their antebellum monopoly over wealth, power, and privilege. These conditions inspired a protest song popular among rural southern blacks at this time:

> Well, it makes no difference how you make out your time.
> White man sho' to bring a nigger out behin' . . .
> Lemme tell you, white man, lemme tell you, honey,
> Nigger makes de cotton, white folks gets de money.[5]

Davis denounced "the little peanut politicians" who resorted to "prejudice and cheap demagogy" to win office. "The reign of lynching, night riding, murder and arson that is now sweeping over this country . . . is directly traceable to the Southern politician's propaganda of race hatred and prejudice," Davis complained. "The seat[ing] of these men in congress and the governor's office" had "cost the South millions of wealth and countless treasures in life, sorrow and character."

Davis was correct in noting the increase in prejudice and violence. In Nashville in 1907, for example, "a white brute . . . without provocation" assaulted two black women walking to work. "He hacked up their faces with a large knife until the sidewalk was covered with blood and they were faint with weakness," the *Nashville Globe* reported. Yet neither the white police nor the white press showed much interest in the vicious attack. "Had the perpetrator been black and the victims white," the *Globe* complained, "he would have been apprehended before his tracks were cold." Police made no arrests in the case. The white newspapers "with all their facilities for gathering news could not learn anything about this assault," the *Globe* noted, but "if a Negro steals a rotten egg they have it before he cracks the shell." J.C. Battle, the *Globe* editor, considered local police an even greater menace to blacks than white brutes and biased reporters. He hinted that "their annual target practice" had begun when a white officer shot a black man and claimed "self-defense . . . the same old tale."

In a harrowing incident that year, Frank Mills, distraught over the sudden death of his wife, ventured out after midnight to summon an undertaker. A policeman confronted and beat him for no reason. "I cannot go out on the streets to make preparation to bury my dead wife," Mills grieved to a reporter, "without being assaulted by an officer of the law." A month later, the *Globe* noted, a patrolman shot and killed a black man for "purloining a ham." The thief, the officer insisted, had attacked him with an iron bar. Battle countered that the man died from a bullet in his back. Nashville's police, Battle maintained, shot blacks "on the smallest pretext" for "the most petty offenses." They acted like "armed terrorists" shielded behind their badges.

Thomas Heflin, an Alabama congressman, made national news when he confronted a group of blacks drinking liquor on a Washington, DC streetcar in early 1909. Determined to eject the blacks from the car, Heflin drew his revolver and fired twice, hitting a black passenger in the head and a white passenger in the leg. Heflin had demonstrated his fitness for the Nashville police force, J.C. Battle wryly observed, where "the accepted theory" held that an officer "always shoots in the air at a man who is advancing upon him—even when the ball enters the back of the victim." Heflin did not leave Congress to join the Nashville squad, but he did want to separate blacks from whites on district streetcars. He introduced bills in 1909 and 1911 calling upon transit firms to provide segregated coaches. Perhaps separation would protect innocent commuters from Heflin's errant shots whatever their color.[6]

By the time Johnson rose to prominence, some black Americans had become so discouraged by their prospects that they embraced the panacea advocated by many white racists—emigration to Africa. Less drastic but still telling, others formed all-black towns in Boley, Oklahoma, Allensworth, California, and elsewhere to escape the ravages of racism. These migrants had good reason to flee from whites. In 1901, when Johnson fought his first important professional fight, for example, lynch mobs took the lives of 107 black men. Denied due process of law, these victims died horrible deaths that often turned into public spectacles. By the time Johnson fought Jeffries in 1910, white vigilantes had lynched some 2,275 black citizens—making racial murder a crucial component in the enforcement of a caste system that placed little value on African American lives.

The lesson was not lost on Jack Johnson. In late 1909 he bought a spacious home for his mother and siblings at 3344 Wabash Avenue in the heart of black Chicago. Like millions of other southern blacks, the Johnsons joined the great exodus from the South to the burgeoning industrial and commercial cities of the North. In addition to their light satchels of meager belongings, these migrants brought vivid memories of racial injustice, dreams of a better tomorrow, and cultural resources including fervent religion, spirituals, folk tales, and the soulful lyrics, notes, and rhythm of the blues. Pushed by deep disappointments and pulled by high expectations, black migrants left what DuBois labeled a land of "blood" for a land of "greed." This exodus changed American society, culture, and politics in irreversible ways.

This vast migration of poor blacks and a massive influx of impoverished immigrants from southern and eastern Europe alarmed whites with older and deeper roots in northern soil. Even well-established blacks in northern cities worried that this flood of newcomers would create insurmountable problems in the congested urban centers stretching from New York City to Chicago. Intense competition for jobs and housing augmented racial, religious, and ethnic tensions. Ghettos confined blacks to congested and deteriorating neighborhoods while raising anxieties among nearby whites. Even smaller cities such as Wichita, Springfield, Illinois, and Denver faced new problems because of rising racism and nativism. "In America this seems to be the age of discrimination," editor W.N. Miller lamented in the *Wichita Searchlight* in 1907. While Japanese immigrants met growing disdain and proscription in California, Miller noted, blacks in Kansas encountered new efforts to impose jim crow. The Wichita school board instituted segregated classrooms in the fall of 1906, for example, just two weeks before the Atlanta riot. This policy, Miller complained, amounted to "penning the colored children off" like "wild animals." Miller grew even more apprehensive as whites denied jobs to blacks that had previously been open to all and sought racial separation in many public facilities. "It does not take a prophet or the son of a prophet," he warned in 1907, "to see that in Wichita the color line is being more closely drawn between the whites and colored people." By 1908 "colorphobia" had so infused the city "that her cemetery association has established a line for burying the dead." An undertaker had recently called a cemetery worker to prepare a burial site for a deceased infant without specifying the child's race, Miller explained. When the black parents and minister arrived for the interment, a sexton told them they must wait for a new grave to be dug because the plot just prepared lay in the "white" section. "American prejudice," Miller sighed, "goes even to the grave."[7]

The Springfield Massacre

In Springfield, Illinois, job competition and an alleged rape of a white woman by a black man triggered a savage antiblack pogrom in August 1908. A *Nashville Globe* headline described the scene: REIGN OF TERROR IN SPRINGFIELD—ILLINOIS CAPITAL IN HANDS OF A RAVING MOB—INNOCENT NEGROES LYNCHED AND SHOT TO DEATH. In Springfield, however, blacks retaliated—some consolation to Harry Smith of the *Cleveland Gazette*. "Our people of that city fought the mobs most creditably," he noted, "killing and wounding a number of the white brutes." If white police would not protect all citizens, then blacks must protect themselves. "Every Afro-American home should possess at least one Winchester and plenty of ammunition," Smith counseled. "In times of peace prepare for the mob!"[8]

From a black business convention, Booker T. Washington pleaded for an end to the rampant violence. "Within the past 60 days 25 Negroes have been lynched in different parts of the United States," he observed. "Of this number, only four were even charged with criminal assault upon women." Washington had no desire to shield actual criminals from prosecution. "No legal punishment is too severe for the brute that assaults a woman," he advised, but "there is no way of distinguishing the innocent from the guilty except by due process of law. That is what courts are for." He recommended two steps to halt lynching. "All people at all times and all places" deserved "a fair trial," he noted, and "all good citizens" should work together to rid their cities of "the idle, vicious, and gambling element." Ben Davis urged "the press and the pulpit" to denounce the wanton racial violence. "Mob law anywhere is without reason or excuse," he stated, "uncalled for and barbarous without regard to section." He wanted the death penalty imposed on mob murderers who routinely killed blacks but evaded prosecution or conviction. Editor Thomas Fortune of the *New York Age* complained in late 1908 that every single white in Springfield charged "with riotous conduct and murder" had been acquitted.

To Ida B. Wells, the whites' excuses for the Springfield massacre sounded both familiar and false. In 1892, for example, Wells had defended the character of three black lynching victims in Memphis. Their sole offense, she protested, had been their able management of a popular grocery store that competed with a rival business owned by a white merchant. Wary of reports that sex crimes had provoked the Memphis lynchings, Wells investigated the victims' lives and reached a different conclusion. "Of the [e]ight Negroes lynched since last issue of *Free Speech*," she announced, "three were charged with killing white men and five with raping white women. Nobody in this section believes the old thread-bare lie that Negro men assault white women." Besides, some white women freely consorted with black men, she added, just as white men crossed the color line for intimacy with black women. Her refutation of racist clichés infuriated whites. Like others who preferred flight to a terribly lopsided fight, Wells fled Memphis for Oklahoma. A mob ransacked and destroyed her newspaper office. But Wells did not quit. She carried her antilynching crusade to the North and to Great Britain. After the Springfield tragedy and additional murders by white mobs in Cairo, Illinois, she wrote a rebuttal reminiscent of her Memphis days. Whites had again punished innocent blacks for no reason. "Three Negroes were lynched under the shadow of Abraham Lincoln's tomb during those three days," she wrote. "Not one of them had any connection whatever with the original cause of the outbreak."[9]

The Clansman

The repression and violence that marked the era between Jack Johnson's birth in 1878 and his fight with Jim Jeffries in 1910 arose amid an increasingly racist drift in politics, the arts, entertainment, and sports. Many forms of popular culture romanticized the antebellum South, vilified Reconstruction, and traduced African Americans. Thomas Dixon, author of *The Clansman*, a 1905 novel later adapted to stage and screen, epitomized this trend. In Dixon's portrayal of the Civil War and its aftermath, the menace posed by former slaves—not the secession or intransigence of southern whites—most imperils the nation. President Lincoln, Dixon wrote, intends to colonize all blacks after the war. "We can never attain the ideal Union our fathers dreamed, with millions of an alien, inferior race among us, whose assimilation is neither possible nor desirable," Lincoln tells Austin Stoneman, a radical congressman. "The nation cannot now exist half white and half black, any more than it could exist half slave and half free."

Dixon depicted a noble South ravaged by Union soldiers, federal agents, carpetbaggers, and ex-slaves who inflict every species of crime upon helpless whites. "Black hordes of former slaves, with the intelligence of children and the instincts of savages, armed with modern rifles, parade daily in front of their unarmed former masters," a southern doctor laments to Stoneman. "A white man has no right a negro need respect." Whites have been "made subject to the black spawn of an African jungle"; never before have a people "been so basely betrayed, so wantonly humiliated and degraded!" No white southerner would submit "to be the slave of a slave." The country had become "great," the doctor argues, "because of the genius of the race of pioneer white freemen who settled this continent, dared the might of kings, and made a wilderness the home of Freedom." The future depends upon maintaining "the purity of this racial stock." Prospects seem bleak, for former servants now ruled as masters. The African, the doctor tells his guest, "lived as his fathers lived—stole his food, worked his wife, sold his children, ate his brother, content to drink, sing, dance, and sport as the ape!" A bloody war and a punitive peace have ruined a formerly civil society.

In the climax of Dixon's novel, an ex-slave elevated to the rank of a militia captain and three fellow blacks enter a cabin in the Carolina foothills, bind a white mother to a bedpost, and beat her into silence. The officer then rapes her daughter. Too distraught to live, mother and daughter flee their home and leap to their deaths from a nearby cliff. The rape and suicides provoke local whites to create the Ku Klux Klan, for, in Dixon's view, "the time for words has passed, the hour for action has struck." A mob identifies the rapist, kills him, and dumps his body into a black preacher's yard. The Klan disbands all Negro militia units in the state. On Dixon's final page, whites learn that the Klan has carried elections in six states of the old Confederacy and celebrate the good news with crosses aflame on hills across Dixie. "Civilization has been saved," a Klansman proclaims, "and the South redeemed from shame."

This redemption created a new order, Dixon believed, one spared the onus of slavery but still committed to white supremacy. Dixon's drama of the decline and resurgence of the white South had considerable staying power. A decade after the book appeared, he and D.W. Griffith transformed the novel and subsequent play into the innovative full-length feature movie, *The Birth of a Nation*.[10]

Dixon was not alone in his apologia for racial repression. Shortly after the Civil War, whites had enacted black codes to control the former slaves. These laws sought to confine blacks to manual labor and domestic service, to deny them land ownership, to require proof of employment, to keep weapons from them, to preclude their testimony against whites in court, and to curtail their freedom with curfews and vagrancy laws. Vigilantes also enforced white dominance. "The restrictions in respect to bearing arms, testifying in court, and keeping labor contracts were justified by well-established traits and habits of the Negroes," Professor William A. Dunning of Columbia University argued in 1907. "And vagrancy laws dealt with problems of destitution, idleness, and vice of which no one in the midst of them could appreciate the appalling magnitude and complexity."

When Reconstruction challenged white rule by empowering former slaves, Dunning recalled, they proved unready as well as unworthy. "The negro had no pride of race and no aspiration or ideals save to be like the whites," Dunning argued. "With civil rights and political power not won, but almost forced upon him, he came gradually to understand and crave those more elusive privileges that constitute social equality." Either "consciously or unconsciously," blacks sought "a more intimate association with the other race." Blacks demanded mixed schools, integrated facilities, even full sexual liberty, Dunning added, which led to "the hideous crime against white womanhood which now assumed new meaning in the annals of outrage."

When a special commission awarded the contested election of 1876 to Hayes, Dunning noted, leaders North and South had resolved their major differences. Republicans abandoned the ex-slaves and their few white allies, and Democrats accepted Hayes. "Let the reforming Republicans direct the national government," Dunning recalled of the bargain, "and the southern whites may rule the negroes." This resolution satisfied him. "[President] Grant in 1868 had cried peace," Dunning concluded, "but in his time, with the radicals and carpetbaggers in the saddle, there was no peace. With Hayes peace came."[11]

Just as Dunning stressed black incapacity and white capability, Dr. Robert Bean provided graphic evidence of African Americans' innate inferiority and the need to proscribe them. A professor of anatomy at the University of Virginia, Bean conducted various statistical tests on crania from whites, blacks, and people of mixed races. Not only were African Americans' brains smaller, he contended, but they were deficient in lobes associated with the higher functions of cognition, moral sense, and creativity. "The Caucasian, and more particularly the Anglo Saxon," Bean wrote in 1906, "is dominant and domineering, and possessed primarily with determination, will power, self-control, self-government, and all the attributes of the subjective self, with a high development of the ethical and esthetic faculties and great reasoning powers." In other words, whites possessed the traits most conducive to success in modern society. What whites had in abundance blacks woefully lacked. "The negro is primarily affectionate, immensely emotional, then sensual, and under provocation, passionate," Bean contended. "They are imitative rather than original, inventive, or constructive. There is instability of character incident to lack of self-control, especially in . . . the sexual relation." Bean offered scientific "proof" to explain the lascivious and brutal behavior of blacks such as the militia captain in Dixon's novel. "The Caucasian and the negro," Bean concluded, "are fundamentally opposite extremes in evolution." Ill-suited to a struggle for survival in which only the fittest would survive, blacks (like Indians) might evoke contempt or pity in whites. But these works gave whites little reason to feel any empathy or identification with blacks. The races might as well have been distinct and hostile species.[12]

To many whites, African Americans of Jack Johnson's era seemed little removed from Tom Dixon's fictional characters. In response to chronic complaints about problems in educating black children, sociologist Howard Odum of the University of North Carolina echoed Bean's pessimism about black aptitude. "He has no pride of ancestry, and he is not influenced by the lives of great men," Odum argued. "The Negro has few ideals and perhaps no lasting adherence to an aspiration toward real worth. He has little conception of the meaning of virtue, truth, honor, manhood, integrity. He is shiftless, untidy, and indolent." Black people, Odum added, roamed aimlessly and lacked restraint and reason. "The Negro is improvident and extravagant; lazy rather than industrious, faithful in the performance of certain duties, without vindictiveness, he yet has a reasonable amount of physical endurance," Odum observed. "But he lacks initiative" in addition to being "often dishonest and untruthful" and "over-religious and superstitious." He was, in other words, best suited to be a servant or drudge for paternalistic whites, an inference Odum left to the reader.

Deficient in cognition, blacks had libido to spare. "Their lives are filled with that which is most carnal; their thoughts are most filthy and their morals are generally beyond description," Odum maintained. "Physical developments from childhood are precocious and the sex life begins at a ridiculously early period." Such "sex development" precluded "mental growth." To Odum, blacks lacked family ties, notions of social responsibility, and respect for work. "There is little paternal and filial affection, and little abiding solicitude for the welfare of members of the family . . . little respect and care for the aged and infirm," he wrote. "There are few high ideals of woman, wife and mother, and little thought of individual chastity and of the purity of the home." Blacks viewed labor "as an evil necessity," often sinking into vagrancy or poverty. Odum prescribed restraint, hard work, and acquisitiveness. "Race prejudice will continue with an increasing tendency but the races will come to a more complete understanding," he predicted. "When the Negro has proved himself, the world will make way for him."[13]

A pattern emerged in these works. Dixon, Dunning, Bean, Odum, and others stressed supposed group traits while ignoring individual variations in character, education, socialization, and income. Their evidence was scanty, often anecdotal, and hardly objective or reliable. They emphasized ineradicable genetic traits rather than historical and environmental factors. If blacks did not learn, create art, or work hard, biological inheritance and not lack of opportunity or training accounted for their deficiencies. Rather than explore the real reasons for the racial divide, these authors tended to justify the existing caste system. Almost without exception, whites from senators to slaughterhouse workers blamed blacks and not their own prejudices for racial tensions. Whatever the intentions of Dixon, Bean, and other race theorists, they fostered a climate of opinion in which foibles or failures of individual blacks were interpreted as proof of group weakness and incapacity. This proclivity of whites to use any instance of black misconduct to indict the entire race placed a heavy burden on prominent African Americans to walk the straight and narrow.

Teddy Roosevelt and the "Black Battalion"

President Theodore Roosevelt defied custom and public opinion when he invited Booker T. Washington to dine with him in 1901. While southern whites railed at the move, African Americans welcomed the gesture as a sign that Roosevelt intended to include them in the "square deal" he promised the nation. But high hopes later turned to dismay when Roosevelt hastily discharged three full companies of soldiers from the "Black Battalion" in late 1906—167 men, six of them Medal of Honor winners. Black soldiers and white civilians had exchanged shots on the night of August 13–14 in Brownsville, Texas, leaving one white person dead and another wounded. "From 9 to 15 or 20 of the colored soldiers took part in the attack," Roosevelt noted. When the innocent men refused to identify the guilty, Roosevelt explained, he discharged them all, even though he regarded dismissal as "utterly inadequate" for "mutineers and murderers" and those who "aided and abetted mutiny and murder and treason by refusing to help in their detection." Angered by criticism of his blanket discharge, Roosevelt objected that any accusation of racial bias in his course was "utterly without foundation." "Precisely the same action would have been taken had the troops been white," he insisted. "Indeed, the discharge probably would have been made in more summary fashion."

Roosevelt noted his opposition to lynching, then compared the soldiers who fired the shots and those who concealed them to a lynch mob. "If the colored men elect to stand by criminals of their own race because they are of their own race," he warned, "they assuredly lay up for themselves the most dreadful day of reckoning." He thought "the most important lesson" for all was "the duty of treating the individual man strictly on his worth as he shows it." Roosevelt argued that he had adhered to this principle. "In the North as in the South I have appointed colored men of high character to office, utterly disregarding the protests of those who would have kept them out of office because they were colored men," he noted. "So far as was in my power, I have sought to secure for the colored people all their rights under the law."

Treating each man "strictly on his worth" was a laudable rule, but Roosevelt violated it in his dismissal of the black soldiers. The shootings occurred near midnight, and many of the men likely knew little or nothing about the incident. Moreover, Roosevelt and the white commanders at Fort Brown admitted that no more than twenty soldiers, probably fewer, had done the firing. Others might have known or suspected who the marauders were, but how many knew and just what they knew had not been ascertained. Roosevelt might well have acted similarly if white troops had confronted hostile civilians, as he stated to the Senate, but he probably would have considered more carefully the repercussions of a blanket discharge of so many white soldiers. Besides, he had ignored black soldiers' complaints about the insults and dangers in places where local whites resented their presence. Roosevelt's promise of equal treatment and impartial justice missed a vital point: white soldiers never had to endure the contempt and provocation black troops did, particularly in the South. Even Booker T. Washington, who remained loyal to the president in public, confided to an associate that he had tried but failed to persuade Roosevelt to delay. The discharge, Washington wrote, was "a great blunder."[14]

War Department investigators found "contradictory evidence" to explain the Brownsville incident but concluded that the chief cause was "the resentment of certain of the townspeople at the proximity of a Negro battalion." From the moment black troops had arrived, "unfortunate differences" had arisen between them and local whites. "The instances of friction were numerous and notorious enough," Secretary of War William Howard Taft reported in late 1906, "to be the cause of much discussion in the barracks rooms of the three companies." The soldiers frequently encountered hostile whites in the city. Prior to the melee, Taft explained, "it was reported in Brownsville that a white woman was seized by the hair by a colored soldier and dragged on the ground," a rumor that "caused great bitterness and excitement of feeling" among whites. Worried about rising tensions, white officers "sent patrols into the town to bring back their [black] soldiers to the fort." Around midnight, however, the shooting began, and black soldiers were immediately blamed for the outbreak. Despite his own doubts, Taft defended Roosevelt's course. "The fact of their color and the racial feeling aroused between them and the citizens of Brownsville," he argued, "may have been the cause and furnished the motive, but certainly not a justification, for the plot to murder men, women, and children." Any charge of bias against Roosevelt, Taft concluded, "hardly merits notice."

Washington urged the administration to devise "some plan" that would "do something that may change the feeling the colored people . . . have regarding the dismissal of the three colored companies." He warned Taft that he could not recall "a time when the entire people have the [adverse] feeling that they now have" toward an administration. "The race is not so much resentful or angry," he explained, as "hurt and disappointed." While "not excusing or justifying this feeling," Washington felt compelled to convey it to Taft. "This order came at a time," he added, "when the race was experiencing deep trial on account of the Atlanta riots and when there was much to discourage the race in the atmosphere."[15]

Thomas Fortune of the *New York Age*, formerly a staunch supporter of Roosevelt, called the discharge "executive lynch law." W.N. Miller of the *Wichita Searchlight* initially urged that Roosevelt be given the benefit of the doubt. "In almost every act dealing with the Negro aside from this," Miller noted, "Roosevelt is admitted by friend and foe to have acted in fairness to the Negro, and it will not be amiss to listen for future explanations before going too fast now." The Military Affairs Committee headed by Senator Joseph Foraker of Ohio uncovered ample evidence of rampant racism in Brownsville and recurring insults aimed at black soldiers. Moreover, the committee noted that War Department investigators had failed to uncover solid proof against any particular members of the battalion. Miller now doubted the local whites' explanation for the confrontation. "Texas will prove her case against the colored soldiers," he cautioned, "no matter how many lies are necessary." Nor did Miller find persuasive the "future explanations" he had awaited from the White House. "The Negro should vote against every interest of Theodore Roosevelt in the political side of our republic," Miller advised in mid-1907. "He has proven untrue to the great trust and confidence reposed in him by the Negroes and his every defeat should be the delight and aim of every Negro." Challenged by Foraker, black editors, and opposition Democrats—even notorious race-baiter Ben Tillman argued that the soldiers deserved formal proceedings to determine their fate—Roosevelt decided he would reinstate some of the men if they could prove their innocence. Taft endorsed the plan. Senator Foraker protested, and so did Miller. "The vilest horse thief, the most dangerous burglar, or the bloodiest murderer," Miller objected, "would not be required either to prove his innocence or to submit to a trial with a judge who had even in the most casual way expressed the opinion that the defendant was guilty."

Roosevelt's course outraged black leaders, among them Harry Smith, longtime editor of the *Gazette* and a member of the Ohio legislature. "Those 3,200 printed pages of evidence taken by the Senate Committee on Military Affairs," Smith argued, "clear our soldiers of the criminally disgraceful charge of 'shooting up' Brownsville." Yet Roosevelt and Taft "still stubbornly persist in their refusal to make . . . amends." Smith again chastised the two men a month later, noting that "the intense feeling" against them had increased because of "their persistent refusal to right . . . the terrible wrong done our soldiers." As the 1907 elections approached, Smith urged voters to "remember Brownsville and rebuke Roosevelt!" When the Cleveland mayoral candidate endorsed by the White House lost, Smith cheered.[16]

Roosevelt's hasty dismissal of the black soldiers came, as Washington reminded Taft, only six weeks after the Atlanta riot. That outbreak had claimed the lives of at least ten blacks and two whites, while over fifty blacks and ten whites had been injured. Mobs stormed black enclaves and looted and torched scores of homes and businesses. The outbreaks in Atlanta and Brownsville disturbed Roosevelt, who used his annual message of 1906 to bemoan "the prevalence of crime among us, and above all . . . the epidemic of lynching and mob violence" sweeping the nation. "A great many white men are lynched, but the crime is peculiarly frequent in respect to black men," he noted. "The greatest existing cause of lynching is the perpetration, especially by black men, of the hideous crime of rape—the most abominable in all the category of crimes, even worse than murder." But lynch mobs avenged "in bestial fashion a bestial deed" by lowering themselves "to a level with the criminal." Yet Roosevelt seemed confused. After citing rape as "the greatest . . . cause of lynching," he later remarked that "two-thirds of the lynchings are not for rape at all."

Roosevelt was either muddled in thought or haphazard in his language when he linked mob murder to sexual assault. He failed to distinguish alleged from actual rape, nor did he point out that only due process—not frenzied mobs or their genteel defenders—could determine whether the evidence sustained the charge. Besides, if rape and not race concerned the vigilantes most, why were white rapists spared the lynch rope? Perhaps even more telling, why did white mobs not avenge black women assaulted by men of either race? Since whites controlled the police, the courts, and the major media throughout the nation, a black man who raped a white woman had little if any chance of avoiding prosecution and conviction. Lynching, then, was a ritual of terror aimed at a group, not a condign punishment for an actual criminal. Many whites accepted mob murder because of prevailing negative images of black men. Often depicted as a seldom used but salutary form of punishment, lynching represented the ultimate expression of white over black.[17]

Roosevelt advised Americans to "reward or punish the individual on his merits as an individual." Neither color, creed, nor status, he added, should compromise "even-handed justice." But Roosevelt proceeded to remind blacks of their collective duty to help apprehend suspects among them. "Every colored man should realize that the worst enemy of his race is the negro criminal, and above all the negro criminal who commits the dreadful crime of rape," he explained. "For a colored man to fail to help the officers of the law in hunting down with all possible earnestness and zeal every such infamous offender" constituted "an offense against the whole country, and against the colored race in particular."

In a private letter Roosevelt accused blacks of habitually harboring criminals and thereby aggravating racial tensions. He had sent an advance copy of his message to Silas McBee, editor of *The Churchman*. Grateful for McBee's praise, Roosevelt returned to the lessons of Brownsville. "I have been amazed and indignant at the attitude of the negroes," he confided, "and of short-sighted white sentimentalists as to my action." To him the issue was "one of naked right and wrong." Roosevelt grumbled that northern politicians who criticized him cared mainly about "the negro vote." Sensitive to public opinion in policy matters, he objected that a president sometimes had to put principle above politics. "In that part of my message about lynching . . . I speak of the grave and evil fact that the negroes too often band together to shelter their own criminals, which action had an undoubted effect in helping to precipitate the hideous Atlanta race riots," Roosevelt noted. "I condemn such [an] attitude . . . for I feel that it is fraught with the gravest danger to both races." Unable to do anything in Atlanta, Roosevelt had decided to act quickly in Brownsville. "Here, where I have power to deal with it, I find this identical attitude displayed among the negro troops," he explained to McBee. "I should be recreant to my duty if I failed by deeds as well as words to emphasize with the utmost severity my disapproval of it."[18]

Thomas Fortune found Roosevelt's analysis of lynching no more persuasive than his explanation for discharging the black troops. "I am sorry that the President did not let you blue pencil his message, as far as it relates to us," Fortune informed Booker T. Washington. "His advice that Afro-Americans who know nothing of their criminals shall help to hunt them down and his adoption of the lynch law method of slaying the innocent with the guilty are vile propositions calculated to do us great injury." Roosevelt, Fortune complained, "has forfeited the confidence and good esteem of the Afro-American people and largely of the American people by the adoption of Southern ideas and methods of dealing with us."

W.E.B. DuBois described Roosevelt as "a man who will stand up for a thing when he is right and will stand just as stubbornly when he is wrong." Roosevelt had erred in dismissing all 167 soldiers, DuBois insisted, when only a few had done the shooting. Certainly "a considerable number, fifty, perhaps a hundred" knew nothing about who had fired at the whites. In addition, the administration had not punished the white officers who commanded the black troops. DuBois objected to the president's charge that "in some indirect way the best class of Negroes were responsible for Negro crime."

Roosevelt had, DuBois observed, "deliberately and repeatedly wronged the most helpless eighth of his country." Moreover, support for the administration from "certain Negroes" for their own purposes could not hide its many errors. Insisting upon "justice to the soldiers," DuBois blamed "Negro crime . . . primarily upon the injustice done black men in the South," since "no nation or race can righteously or justly be restricted to the career of making themselves footstools for their enemies."[19]

Jack Johnson, the Great Black Hope

In this context, Jack Johnson's eminence in the prize ring prompted discussion of the relative merits of different peoples and what his success portended for race relations. Even though the 1910 match between Johnson and Jeffries provoked more violence and inspired more vivid memories, as Ruby Berkley Goodwin's memoir shows, the fight between Johnson and Tommy Burns for the title in late 1908 also mattered deeply to Americans. The overtones of race pride and prejudice that surrounded the championship fight in Australia made it a cultural event that transcended sports. Had it been held in the states, it would have aroused more interest and meant even more to Americans.

Burns did not rank among the greats of his sport, but he was white and the champion, and that mattered to many fans. The challenger, however, did not think pale skin could compensate for paltry skills in the ring. Capable and confident, Johnson grinned, bantered, and taunted Burns from the start of the fight to its finish, a display that deeply offended Jack London, who covered the fight for the *New York Herald*. "The gong sounded and the fight and monologue began," London noted. "'All right, Tommy,' said Johnson with exaggerated English accent, and thereafter he talked throughout the fight when he was not smiling." Burns also baited Johnson, London added, but his "verbal punches" ceased when his opponent answered them with a flurry of jabs and uppercuts. "Johnson play-acted all the time. His part was the clown, and he played with Burns from the gong of the opening round to the finish of the fight," London observed. "Burns was a toy in his hands." Johnson teased the white champion. "'Hit here, Tahmy,'" he told him, then exposed "his unprotected stomach." When hit, he "would neither wince nor cover up." Johnson invited Burns to try again. "'Now here, Tahmy,'" and when Burns put leather to dark skin, Johnson continued "to grin and chuckle and smile his golden smile." Johnson had reason to smile—he took the title from Burns and knocked out the notion that no black man could beat a white man. London conceded Johnson's wide edge over Burns in the ring, but London's tribal loyalty overshadowed his sportsmanship: "Personally I was with Burns all the way. He is a white man, and so am I. Naturally I wanted to see the white man win. Put the case to Johnson and ask him if he were the spectator at a fight between a white man and a black man which he would like to see win. Johnson's black skin will dictate a desire parallel to the one dictated by my white skin." London attributed Johnson's triumph to his "bigness, coolness, quickness, cleverness, and vast physical superiority." But Johnson had not just defeated Burns, he had humiliated him, a reversal of race privilege that irked London and other whites. Shamed by Johnson's easy win, London ended his dispatch to the states with a plea. "But one thing remains," he implored. "Jeffries must emerge from his alfalfa farm and remove that smile from Johnson's face." For London and others who remained unreconciled to a black champion, Jeffries became "the great white hope."[20]

After the fight, Lester Walton of the *New York Age* predicted that all blacks would gain from Johnson's victory even though whites understandably deplored it. "The white sporting world does not relish the spectacle of a Negro being the champion fighter of the world," Walton explained. "Every Negro, from the lad large enough to sell papers to the old man who is able to read the papers . . . is happy today, but it is not natural that the white man should be." When whites recovered from their initial dismay, they would see the significance of Johnson's triumph. "Every time Johnson knocked down Burns a bunch of prejudice fell," Walton argued, "and at the same time the white man's respect for the Negro race went up a notch." An *Age* editorial predicted that Johnson's win would help break down "the barriers of colorphobia." J. Bernie Barbour, a songwriter in Chicago, thought Johnson had proved that under the skin "all men are the same in muscle, sinew and in brain":

> Thereby records on history's page,
> An honor unknown to this age,
> A Negro champion now the rage.
> The Black Gladiator![21]

Comedian Bert Williams told an *Indianapolis Freeman* reporter that "Negroes are proud of Johnson" for having demonstrated exceptional physical and mental skills. "He is fast on his feet, has a world of strength and knows how to keep his brain clear when in action," Williams noted. "He is the best fighter the black race has ever produced, and I think even the white followers of the ring are disposed to give him credit. I am ready to back him against any white fighter."

Early in 1909 Johnson called on Frank Lewis, an old friend and "the main squeeze" at the Railroad Inn at Fifty-first and Armour in Chicago, not far from the new champion's home. "The people residing in the neighborhood were just crazy to see Jack Johnson," Julius Taylor of the *Broad-Ax* reported.

Fans filled the inn "to the brim" and "kept on coming until they extended out into Fifty-first street, blocking the street car traffic." Johnson received a similar reception in New York City. He arrived, the *Age* reported, "amidst the plaudits of assembled thousands of fight fans." The new champion "dressed soberly and unaffected," but the reporter felt some concern about Johnson's fame because he might do something to embarrass or harm his people. Johnson assured fans he recognized "the responsibilities of his championship" and the fact that "thousands" wanted to "shove him down." "Slip up now, Mr. Johnson," the writer warned, "and you will find that it won't take so many, and they will use a rougher method, too." Lester Walton also understood that prominence had its perils, not just for Johnson but for his people. "Johnson is the most widely known and thoroughly discussed Negro in America today," Walton noted. "It behooves him to act the part of a champion out of the ring as well as in," since writers were eager to find "a bit of information on which they can construct a sensational article that will tend to ridicule and degrade the champion of champions, as well as reflect discredit on the race of which he is a member." Johnson must avoid trouble. "Let him . . . make discretion his motto," Walton advised, "and act accordingly."

Emmett Scott, Washington's aid at Tuskegee, encouraged Frank Wheaton of Harlem to discuss correct mien and conduct with Johnson. "As a fellow Texan, I am not only interested in his achievements, but proud of him as well," Scott informed Wheaton. "I want him to do the absolutely proper and dignified thing." Scott hoped Johnson would grant "as few interviews to the newspapers as possible" and "refrain from anything resembling boastfulness." Scott also urged Wheaton to persuade Johnson to rehire Sam Fitzpatrick, his well-respected former manager. "I was just a bit disturbed by Fitzpatrick's statement that Johnson was hard to manage after winning a fight," Scott confessed, "simply and only because I do not like white men to feel that Negroes cannot stand large prosperity."[22]

"Success in All Vocations"

To the Reverend Reverdy Ransom, Johnson's ascent signaled a rising tide against white domination at home and abroad. "The darker races of mankind, and the black race in particular," he predicted in 1909, "will keep the white race busy for the next few hundred years throughout the world in defending the interests of white supremacy." Johnson's success, Ransom added, "will be more and more the ambition of Negroes in every domain of human endeavor." Jackson Stovall saw a similar parable in Johnson's story. "There is not a patriotic Negro in America today, no matter what his views may be in regard to the prize ring and its principals, who is not proud of the fact . . . that one of his race reigns supreme in his vocation, though it be from a pugilistic standpoint," Stovall asserted. "Supremacy in one vocation begets supremacy in another." Johnson had inspired all his people, not just boxers. "While pugilism does not compare favorably with the intellectual forces of mankind," Stovall explained, "yet the same pluck, patience, perseverance and stick-to-itiveness characterized by the colored champion is essential to success in all vocations."[23]

Johnson, then, symbolized what his race might achieve in a society more attuned to potential and performance than color. This hope inspired a wide spectrum of black Americans, from Braxton Berkley to Bert Williams, Uncle Tobe to Reverdy Ransom, Lester Walton, Ida B. Wells, and W.E.B. DuBois. Boxing, not the church, government, business, the army, or higher education, had become the harbinger of a more democratic society freed from the dead hand of a racist past. Whatever one thought of the ring, it had clear rules and an ethic of fairness that allowed the better man to win solely on the basis of ability. This bloody business appalled many people outside the fistic fraternity, yet boxing gave Johnson an equal opportunity denied to blacks in virtually every other endeavor in American life.

At times in American history a crucial event has defined a pivotal moment in race relations, when festering tensions have escalated from minor vexations to horrible violence and death. The Stono Rebellion in South Carolina in 1739, for example, dramatized the rising rancor and heightened prospects for bloodshed in an increasingly repressive society in which a small white ruling class exploited a black slave majority. Plantation owners coveted cheap slave labor, but too many slaves jeopardized white security. Nat Turner's Rebellion in 1831 reminded southern whites of their vulnerability to hostile slaves, and the violence in "bleeding Kansas" during the late 1850s and John Brown's raid on Harpers Ferry revealed the widening rift between North and South over "the peculiar institution." The Civil War and Reconstruction forced Americans to confront the plight of the tenth of the nation long enslaved and oppressed. What would replace the old order of "unrequited toil" and proscription in the South? Would whites experience "a new birth of freedom" and extend full civil rights to blacks throughout the nation?

With the end of Reconstruction and the failure to resolve the old dilemma of achieving national concord amid racial diversity, other problems vied for the nation's attention. These stemmed from industrialization, urban growth, class conflict, massive "new" immigration, and intense global competition for colonies, markets, and overseas bases. The nation meddled more frequently abroad despite its own inability to ease tensions between myriad groups at home. If the nation could not provide security and civil rights to diverse peoples within its own borders, how could it fulfill a mission to uplift, in President McKinley's telling phrase, the "little brown brothers" in distant lands?

This incongruity between racism at home and missionary imperialism abroad vexed W.E.B. DuBois. Not long before Jack Johnson began his professional boxing career, the United States had crushed the final Native American resistance in the West. At the time he fought his first professional bouts, the United States went to war with Spain, annexed Hawaii, conquered the Philippines in 1898, then suppressed a Filipino revolt after the war. The nation joined an expedition to quell the Boxer Rebellion in China and demanded an "open door" for its merchants and missionaries there. McKinley, Theodore Roosevelt, John Hay, and other "large policy" advocates had few doubts about their nation's destiny to extend its influence and control. DuBois, however, saw this new empire from another angle. "The problem of the twentieth century is the problem of the color-line," he observed in 1903, "the relation of the darker to the lighter races of men in Asia and Africa, in America and the islands of the sea." The ordeal of secession, civil war, and reunion in the United States had been a mere page in world history, DuBois contended, another manifestation of the struggle between light oppressors and dark subjects. "It was a phase of this problem," he noted, "that caused the Civil War." Forty years after the war whites still held most blacks in virtual bondage. "For this much all men know," DuBois concluded, "despite compromise, war, and struggle, the Negro is not free."

> In the backwoods of the Gulf States . . . he may not leave the plantation of his birth; in well-nigh the whole rural South the black farmers are peons, bound by law and custom to an economic slavery, from which the only escape is death or the penitentiary. In the most cultured sections and cities of the South the Negroes are a segregated servile caste, with restricted rights and privileges. Before the courts, both in law and custom, they stand on a different and peculiar basis. Taxation without representation is the rule of their political life.

DuBois detected a further decline in blacks' status a few years later but reiterated his determination to secure full rights for all. "In the past year the work of the Negro-hater has flourished in the land," he told a gathering at Harpers Ferry in 1906. "Step by step the defenders of the rights of American citizens have retreated." Disfranchisement and discrimination had increased, he complained, but "we will not be satisfied to take one jot or tittle less than our full manhood rights." He invoked the legacy of rebellious slaves and abolitionists. "And we shall win," DuBois declared. "The past promised it, the present foretells it."

Addressing a conference in New York City in 1909, DuBois warned whites that they would pay for their prejudice and proscription. "The cost of liberty," he advised, "is less than the price of repression." A few months before Johnson fought Jeffries, DuBois warned that racists who tried to keep people of color "in a place of permanent inferiority" were "handling dynamite." *"There is in this world no such force,"* he proclaimed, *"as the force of a man determined to rise."*[24]

Jack Johnson vs. Jim Jeffries: Symbolism vs. Substance

If a contemporary needed validation of DuBois's view that "the color line" would loom large in the twentieth century, that person need have looked no further than Reno, Nevada, on July 4, 1910. Never before (or since) has a sporting event so starkly reflected an era, a place, a mood, and a people. From the time Johnson beat Burns in late 1908 until July 4, 1910, the forces and events that brought Johnson and Jeffries together unfolded in a manner worthy of an Aeschylus or a Sophocles. Jack London had called for a white knight to restore the throne to his race, and Jim Jeffries seemed right for the crusade. Former champion Jim Corbett shared London's concern, but he urged promoters and fans to give Jeffries ample time to prepare for Johnson. "I have seen Jeffries within the last few weeks, and it is my honest opinion that he should not think of facing Johnson in less than a year and a half or two years," he advised in early 1909. "There is too much at stake—a Negro has the championship and it must be won back by a white man, to whose race it belongs." John L. Sullivan, another ex-champion, pledged $75,000 to promote Jeffries against Johnson. A Seattle millionaire wired Jeffries with an offer of a $100,000 fight purse, 70 percent for the winner and 30 percent for the loser. To bolster Jeffries' confidence, the man offered to stake $25,000 on him. A prospective match against the black champion raised Jeffries' stock among boxing promoters and booking agents. Jeffries, like Johnson, used the mounting interest in a possible showdown to draw large crowds on vaudeville.

But Jeffries had qualms about meeting a younger (and darker) fighter. In Chicago in March he admitted his reluctance to forsake retirement to return to action. Despite the lure of money and acclaim, he stressed the perils in boxing the black champion. "If I were to whip Johnson, I realize that I would be hailed as the greatest champion in pugilism's history," Jeffries reflected. "I know that it would mean more fame than ever fell to any fighter's lot, and that it would make me a rich man. But I also realize that to lose to Johnson would make me a dog. . . . I simply won't fight unless I know I am good enough to knock out Johnson. You don't catch Jim Jeffries losing to a colored man."

Jeffries decided he could beat both Father Time and the black champion. At age thirty-four he began his comeback to regain the title for his race. For sixteen months he trained while fans monitored his progress. Rex Beach, hired by the *Atlanta Constitution* to cover the match, visited the white hope's quarters a week before the fight. "I saw that which I never expected to see— a man who has come back," Beach cabled from Reno. "Jeffries has renewed his youth. DeSoto should have gone west in his search for that fabled fountain, the waters of which he believed could roll back the years from human shoulders. . . . I believe Jeffries to be the most dangerous and most rugged fighter the world has ever known."

The next day Beach visited Johnson's camp. While Jeffries had regained his youth, Johnson seemed to have dissipated his. "At Rick's road-house, where Johnson lives, you find yourself in a honky tonk," Beach reported. "A pair of muscular pianists and a fiddler poison the air with ragtime. There are two roulette tables going constantly, drunken men abound. The rooms, the porches, the yards, are packed with all classes and conditions of people." Yet Johnson remained "serene, smiling, unconcerned" amid "the distracting bedlam." This romp-and-stomp setting validated many unflattering traits whites ascribed to African Americans—their aversion to discipline and training, an insatiable appetite for amusement, an inability to grasp the significance of a big event.

Helping to prepare Jeffries for the upcoming mill, Corbett exuded confidence. "There is no doubt in my mind that Jeffries will have an easy time defeating Johnson," he assured Richard Sims of the *Atlanta Constitution* on July 2. "As I have always said, Johnson (and all negroes, in fact) are imbued with a traditional yellow streak." Jeffries would, Corbett predicted, knock Johnson out "around the twelfth round." Others echoed this optimism. Despite his own thrashing by Johnson, Tommy Burns predicted a Jeffries win. "Take it from me," he told a *New York Times* correspondent. "Johnson has not got a chance." The *Constitution*'s staff drew the obvious conclusion. "Jeffries has been strictly temperate," a writer observed on the eve of the fight. "But how the punch will fly when he gets into the ring."[25]

Like Rex Beach and Richard Sims, Jack London roamed around Reno for news of interest to fans back east. In announcing Jack Johnson's arrival, London took his cue from Dr. Robert Bean on the cranial deficiencies of blacks and the consequent puerile behavior they displayed. "Johnson is happy-go-lucky in temperament, as light and carefree as a child," London suggested. "He is easily amused. He lives more in the moment, and joy and sorrow are swift passing moods with him. He is not capable of seriously adjusting his actions to remote ends." Jeffries, on the other hand, did grasp the significance of the event and had followed a "heroic course" of sustained conditioning that "put him in the superb condition he is in today." "This fight does not mean to Johnson what it does to Jeff," London added. "If Johnson loses the fight, he won't be worried much. If Jeff loses, it will almost break his heart" because of "a race pride of which he is intensely self-conscious." Johnson lacked such pride, however, and seemed oblivious to any transcendent purpose. "If I whip that white man, he never will forget it," Johnson announced. "If that white man whips me, I'll forget it in about fifteen minutes."[26]

The relative fitness of the two rivals was just one of many topics that aroused interest in the fight. Reporters from across the nation flocked to Reno to cover the event, and a boxcar full of telegraphic equipment and trained hands from Chicago to install and operate it provided news to fans near and far. "Monday one hundred and fifty thousand words went out from here over the wires and the fight was a week away," Rex Beach marveled. "The fall of Port Arthur [during the war between Russia and Japan in 1905] did not take one-quarter that number of words to tell and every day it is the same. In other words, two novels are written every twenty-four hours, dealing entirely with the question of individual superiority." A city of 15,000 people, Reno swelled to more than double its size by the Fourth of July. Pullman cars stretched down the railroad tracks for miles and faded to dots on the horizon. Visitors scrambled, often unsuccessfully, for meals and lodging. Money changed hands rapidly at the gambling halls. Cash evaporated like water in the desert as fans awaited the showdown at high noon. For a time Reno reverted to its Wild West ways, a boom town giddy with fortunes quickly won and lost in mining claims on the Comstock Lode. Hustlers, vagabonds, betting fans, and local entrepreneurs seized the moment, hoping to strike gold one more time.[27]

The stakes involved both pocketbooks and pride. When Johnson had left Oakland for Reno, some 500 black fans assembled to bid him goodbye and good luck. "I want to advise every one of you to bet on me," he told them. "Just get your money down that I will bring home the bacon and then sit back and wait until the time comes to cash in." To friends in Galveston Johnson wired, "Bet all you have and all you can borrow on me. I will win sure." In Little Rock, Walter Campbell, a black barber, bet a white funeral director that "if Jeffries won the undertaker was to get free shaves as long as they both lived, but if Johnson won, the barber was to be given at his death the most expensive funeral the undertaker could provide." In Omaha a man "mortgaged his household goods for $100" and bet on Johnson "at odds of 2 to 1." Young black men pooled "a pot of $2,000" and wagered it on Johnson "at odds of 10 to 6." Lincoln Grant, "colored," put up $5,000 against $7,500 from rancher Barney Duell. In DuQuoin, Illinois, "you couldn't find much Jeffries money," Ruby Berkley Goodwin recalled. "What few dollars the white men were willing to wager to uphold their belief in white supremacy was quickly snapped up by the Negroes and Italians." Blacks who bet on Johnson, a white Atlanta reporter asserted, provided further proof of their inherent folly. No whites would bet on Johnson. "Odds as great as 3 to 1 on Jeffries were offered in the city yesterday," the writer noted, "with few if any takers."

> Local sports have decided that there isn't anything to the big fight but the white man all the way along and even large odds fail to tempt them to risk their coin on the smoke. Among the white sports there is hardly to be found a single man who wants the Johnson end of a wager. Practically all of what little coin there is floating around waiting for Jeffries' takers is being furnished by negroes, whose race pride stands out above their judgment.

In other words, when blacks bet on Johnson they displayed a typical racial weakness. Emotions (an erroneous "race pride") and not reason ("judgment") made them squander their money on Johnson when any intelligent person knew that Jeffries would surely win.

Les Walton of the *New York Age*, on the other hand, surmised that whites and not blacks would pay for *their* foolish pride. "There is going to be thousands of dollars placed on the Johnson–Jeffries fight on purely sentimental grounds," Walton predicted, "and the money will not be bet and lost by Negroes, either." Barron Wilkins, a hotel proprietor in New York City and a friend of Johnson's, sent him $20,000 pooled by local blacks to bet on him at prevailing odds. In Reno, according to a *New York Times* report, the mutual betting board on its first day (July 2) had eighty-eight wagers on Jeffries, and only thirty-five on Johnson. Arthur Ruhl of *Collier's* noted that "the betting was 10 to 6 or 7 on Jeffries and the talk about 1,000 to 1." Even though fans occasionally crossed the color line to wager, the correlation between race and bet was high, creating a situation fraught with danger. If Jeffries won, blacks would lose money, the title, and all it symbolized. If Johnson won, whites would suffer a severe blow to their bank accounts as well as their race pride.[28]

The day of decision finally arrived. City police and Nevada Rangers patrolled the gates of the new amphitheater to prevent spectators from entering with firearms.[29] A small contingent of women entered the arena and took seats in the screened balcony boxes that promoter Tex Rickard had provided for their comfort. Other women mixed with men in the general audience. A brass ensemble performed while fans arrived and mingled. The band had intended to play "All Coons Look Alike to Me," but Rickard or one of his assistants had persuaded the conductor to play "Dixie" instead. Perhaps some whites on the scene longed for "the land of cotton," but Jack Johnson and the few black spectators there did not share that nostalgia for the Old South. For them "old times there . . . not forgotten" meant enslavement, jim crow, and terrorism associated with white supremacy. Johnson and others had left the South because they preferred not "to live and die in Dixie." With the band's last number, the announcer introduced five former heavyweight champions to the excited crowd—John L. Sullivan, Bob Fitzsimmons, Jim Corbett, Tommy Burns, and, of course, Jim Jeffries. In compliance with Jeffries' wishes, he and Johnson did not pose for pictures before the fight, nor did they shake hands. At 2:44 mountain time, Rickard, now acting as referee, cleared the ring and signaled for the opening bell. Some 20,000 fans in the arena and millions across the country, including those at the Berkley family picnic, turned their attention to the "white hope" and "big smoke."

Those who backed Jeffries suffered a fate reminiscent of speculators who had sought fast fortunes in Nevada mining claims. Their expected bonanza became a colossal bust. Beyond Jeffries, his family, and friends, no one wanted the former champion to regain the title more than Jack London. But just as hope had never brought pay dirt to a prospector's pan, desire alone could not capture the crown. "The greatest battle of the century," London observed, "was a monologue delivered to twenty thousand spectators by a smiling negro who was never in doubt and who was never serious for more than a moment at a time." The "monologue" consisted of Johnson's countless unanswered punches. A dialogue of sorts did take place, however, between Johnson and ringside hecklers. Early on, Jeffries tried to immobilize the champion's long arms in a clinch. "Ah, Jeff," Johnson chided him, "don't love me so!" In round five, Johnson taunted Corbett in Jeffries' corner: "Ain't so easy, am I?" Before the sixth, Johnson leaned over the ropes and teased John L. Sullivan: "John, I thought this fellow could hit." When Jeffries managed to land a punch, a white spectator shouted at Johnson, "Why don't you smile now?" Johnson glanced at him and grinned. After round seven, Johnson addressed Corbett again. "Too late now to do anything," Johnson chortled. "Jim, your man's all in." Corbett encouraged his flagging white hope. "It only takes one or two, Jim!" Corbett shouted. "Promptly Johnson landed two stingers," then a third, London reported, and he turned to Corbett and bragged, "See that?"

By now Jeffries's face was bleeding profusely. "Make that big stiff fight," Corbett urged as the ninth began. "That's right," Johnson retorted. "That's what they all say." Punished by another flurry of Johnson's jabs, Jeffries tried to cover by crouching even more. "I will straighten him up in a minute," Johnson announced. "He will straighten you up, nigger!" a white onlooker screamed. Johnson knew how to counter his opponent's moves. He gazed at Corbett and advised, "Watch me straighten up the famous crouch." Landing an uppercut with the force of a kick from a prospector's mule, Johnson lifted Jeffries to his toes. Discouraged and desperate, Jeffries clinched often. Johnson winked at Corbett over Jeffries's shoulder, using lulls to instruct reporters on what to send over the wires. "Why don't your man fight?" Johnson asked Corbett during the twelfth round, the round in which Corbett had predicted that Jeffries would knock Johnson out. In the waning minutes, a frantic Corbett tried to rile Johnson in hopes he would lose his head and throw away his title. "Why don't you do something?" Corbett sneered while Johnson fought defensively during round fourteen. "Too clever," Johnson answered, "too clever, like you."

Corbett must have suffered the torments of the damned. He had engaged a stenographer to record his remarks during the fight, and a reporter for the *Nashville Globe* overheard a few of his comments. "Look at the Negro nodding and bowing to the crowd," Corbett noted early on. "He's grinning now, but will he keep it up?" Johnson was, Corbett later admitted, "making a sucker" out of Jeffries. When Johnson landed a devastating left on Jeffries's jaw in the thirteenth round, Corbett winced and turned away. "That punch," he conceded, "would have killed an ox." After the fourteenth, Corbett noted that Jeffries "can't see out of the right eye." In the fifteenth and final round, Corbett realized the end was near. "I don't want to look at it," he sighed. Tex Rickard stopped the fight. Jack London did look but deplored what he saw. "He who had never been knocked down was knocked down repeatedly," London wrote. "He who had never been knocked out was knocked out. Never mind the technical decision. Jeff was knocked out. That is all there is to it. An ignominy of ignominies, he was knocked out and through the ropes by the punch he never believed Johnson possessed—by the left and not by the right." The punch did indeed fly, as the *Atlanta Constitution* had predicted, but Jeffries, not Johnson, had tasted the leather. While Corbett and his crew tended to Jeffries, a dozen armed men escorted a spry Johnson from the ring without incident.[30]

Johnson vs. Jeffries: The Aftermath

When the fight ended, Rex Beach noticed a woman at ringside "said to be a wealthy ranch owner who ran her own cattle business." Weeping and disoriented, she turned to a man seated nearby and pleaded, "Please show me the way out, Mister. I'm crying so I can't see." Just as upset, rancher "Bull" Montana replied, "Madame, you'll have to lead me out for I'm crying harder than you are." Beach saw the mood of the white crowd change during the fight. Before the opening bell, "hats waved, flags fluttered, feeling ran high, patriotism was riot." Ninety minutes later, spectators filed out "in a funeral gloom." Despite their chagrin, "nowhere in the crowd was there the least disturbance," Beach added, for "an undertone of fairness and good fellowship ran through it all." Some fans, hoping to recoup gambling and betting losses, returned to the tables and lost even more. Now stranded in Reno, they could not afford train tickets. "At last accounts there were many who will have to wire home for money," Beach reported on July 5. "The financial conditions of hundreds, hit by the fight and the games, is desperate."

Ruby Berkley's kin reacted quite differently when telegraphic reports to the office of the *DuQuoin Call* brought the news. "The Negroes were jubilant," she recalled. "Everybody wanted to buy someone else a dinner, a glass of beer, or a shot of whiskey. Jerome Banks, who had lost his leg in a mine accident, came down the street waving one of his crutches and his short stump in the air. The older people laughed and cried, and the children danced around and knocked each other about in good fun." Grandma Thompson, ninety-seven years old, "stood under the grape arbor and raised her quivering voice in song. We all joined in: 'Hallelujah, hallelujah, the storm is passing over, Hallelujah!'" Only in retrospect might it seem strange that an elderly black woman born in slave days would invoke a Negro spiritual to express her elation over a black boxer's triumph in the secular and masculine world of prizefighting. Johnson "had delivered," Ruby concluded. "We were now a race of champions!" To many blacks in DuQuoin and around the nation, it was the ultimate vicarious thrill, a moment of deliverance second only in importance to the day of jubilee in 1865.

Reno underwent an instant transformation. Before the fight it had been "the wildest, liveliest town in America," a correspondent noted, but afterward "it was almost like a city of the dead," its streets resembling "a lane in a cemetery." With "nine out of ten" men wearing "the look of those who return from a funeral," the exodus seemed "like one from a city afflicted." Jack Johnson quietly and quickly left by train, and other blacks, similarly subdued, followed his cue. "Not a drum was heard, not a clarion note," Harris Lyon reported. "As far as the black race was concerned in Reno that night, the Arabs had nothing on them when it came to tent-folding." Two or three hundred blacks "silently stole away," Lyon noted, "up back alleys and side streets, at a good, ground-gaining lope." They took no chances; discretion reduced the odds of a racial confrontation. Reno failed to confirm the stereotype of a wild western town filled with drunken, trigger-happy desperadoes. Just one shooting disturbed the general calm on fight day. A miner shoved a wad of bills into his pocket and accidentally dislodged his pistol, which discharged and sent a bullet into his own back.[31]

Elsewhere in the nation, however, whites and blacks clashed after the fight—with far deadlier results than in Reno. On a streetcar in Houston, an exuberant black fan announced Johnson's victory and enraged a white passenger. The white man drew a knife and slashed the black man's throat from ear to ear. A black man in Roanoke suggested Johnson's success might bring some repose to his people. "Now," he remarked, "I guess the white folks will let the negroes alone." A white man who heard him retorted "No!" The two scuffled, inciting several brawls that caused multiple injuries and arrests. "Six negroes with broken heads, six white men locked up, and one white man . . . with a bullet through his skull," read a wire in the *New York Times*. To avert further bloodshed, the police chief ordered all saloons closed at 9:30 that night. From Norfolk came news that a mob of angry white sailors from the naval yard had "attacked negroes wherever they met them." In Washington, DC, "many fistic encounters" erupted between the races. Two black men died when whites in Little Rock went on a rampage to avenge the humiliation of Jeffries.

Interracial violence occurred in Atlanta, New Orleans, and Wilmington, Delaware. In Uvalda, Georgia, tensions ran high even before Johnson and Jeffries entered the ring. A July 4 dispatch printed in the *New York Times* reported "three negroes were killed and many wounded in a clash with whites at a construction camp near this place today." Blacks had "been insolent in their remarks about Jeffries for some time . . . boasting that Johnson would kill the white man." Their drinking and gibing, the report added, "enraged" whites, who formed a mob "to clean out the camp." Whites alleged that gunfire came from the site, but none were wounded in a very one-sided confrontation.[32]

The mayhem was not confined to the South. A report out of Omaha noted "a dozen fights" with "many arrests" and "one negro . . . killed." In Pittsburgh, "Greeks and Russians, who had been quarreling with the blacks for weeks, were the main cause of the uprising." To celebrate Johnson's win, blacks in Pittsburgh boarded streetcars, ejected riders, and scuffled with whites. Meanwhile, in Philadelphia, "Lombard Street, the principal street in the negro section, went wild in celebrating the victory and a number of fights in which razors were drawn resulted."

In Clarksburg, West Virginia, whites took the offensive. "A posse of 1,000 white men organized," a report noted, "[and] drove all the negroes off the street." Police dispersed a mob that had already placed a noose around a black man's neck. Clashes occurred throughout New York City. "Gangs of men and boys formed apparently for the sole purpose of beating up whatever negroes they could get their hands upon," the *New York Times* noted, "and in many instances the negroes retaliated." One brave white man stopped white assailants who were using a lead pipe on a black man. Not all violence was interracial. A black constable in Mounds, Illinois, lost his life when he tried to arrest four blacks who intended "to shoot up the town in honor of Jack Johnson's victory." Chicago fared better, according to Cary Lewis, an *Indianapolis Free-man* correspondent. Whites "were made the butts of black folks' boisterous wit," he recounted, but "all replied in a happy and responsive vein."[33]

Black observers blamed sullen whites for most of these incidents, and candid whites agreed. "The white ruffians showed their teeth and attacked almost every colored person they saw upon the public streets," Calvin Chase, editor of the *Washington Bee*, complained. "The city was a scene of the most bitter race feeling. The police could not handle the mob." But Chase did not lump all whites together. "The more thoughtful white people," he added, "took in the situation as they would take in anything else." A report from New York City pointed out that "the mob spirit seemed to rise wherever a negro cheered for Johnson . . . or permitted his exultation over the victory to grow to an extent that made it offensive." Reporter Welborn Jenkins stood in a mixed crowd in Atlanta awaiting news from Reno. When an announcer declared Johnson the winner, "a group of young white men hurl[ed] a stone at a janitor who was loudly cheering from a window above the street." Sixty years after the fight, Benjamin Mays, the son of former slaves and later president of Morehouse College, recalled two events from his youth that impressed upon him the virulence of racism. The first was the bloody Atlanta riot of 1906, the second the 1910 battle in Reno. Almost sixteen years old at the time of the fight, Mays realized that whites in his hometown of Greenwood, South Carolina, feared the repercussions of Johnson's supremacy in the ring. "White men in my county could not take it," he reflected. "A few Negroes were beaten up because a Negro had beaten a white man in far-away Nevada." Blacks did not discuss Johnson's victory "in the presence of whites," for it "was hard on the white man's world." Black elation and white animus after the fight became a staple of African American folklore. In Evansville, Indiana, the "colored people" celebrated Johnson's victory with "all-night-long parties" despite white disapproval. The next day Open Mouth Rainey, a "smart-ass little colored boy," sauntered into a local grill and ordered "a cup of coffee as strong as Jack Johnson, and a steak beat up like Jim Jeffries." The white owner slapped "Open Mouth" and grabbed a pistol from under the counter. Rainey went for his gun too, but the owner had the edge and shot him five times. In Brooklyn a black man ordered a dog he called "Jeffries" to lie down. "Why don't you call it Johnson?" a white man nearby asked. "Because Johnson is black," the man replied, "and this dog is yellow."[34]

Black journalists welcomed Johnson's triumph but disagreed on its importance. Calvin Chase, for example, suggested that blacks in all fields could duplicate Johnson's success if whites would drop discriminatory barriers. "The colored man is the equal to the white man in every particular," Chase asserted, "and he will demonstrate his equality on educational and other lines if he is given the same opportunity as Johnson was given." Les Walton of the *New York Age* did not see Johnson's personal achievement as a sign of black superiority, but he did expect his success to benefit the entire race. "The case of Jack Johnson shows the superiority of individuals, irrespective of color, and by defeating Jeffries we are bound to be more highly respected," Walton argued. "From now on the white man will not generally underestimate us as he has been guilty of doing heretofore." Even though the fight had incited violence, Walton doubted the casualties had exceeded those typical of a divisive national election. On the first anniversary of the match, Walton repeated that all blacks had gained from their champion's achievement. "Jack Johnson's victory has caused the white race to entertain a higher respect for the Negro," Walton maintained. "Before the Johnson-Jeffries fight the white brother, in general, seemed to be puffed up with the idea that color alone counted." But Johnson had proved that "ability" and not race "is the chief factor in any struggle for superiority."[35]

This plea by Walton that "ability" and not "color" should count challenged deeply entrenched white beliefs in innate racial traits and the need to keep the races separate and unequal. Like other black intellectuals and activists, Walton sensed that whites and not blacks possessed the greater measure of race consciousness; whites, not blacks, refused to distinguish between the unique traits of an individual and the purported characteristics of an entire race. Because whites often generalized about blacks on the basis of a single person's misdeeds, black journalists urged white editors to stop their practice of emphasizing race in glaring headlines and stories about black criminals. Since white editors virtually ignored blacks except in cases of lurid crime, they conveyed the impression that African Americans raped, robbed, and murdered at a rate grossly disproportionate to their numbers. But the press could not ignore Jack Johnson. His ascendance provided an antidote to the usual adverse publicity in white publications.

During the race riots in New Orleans, Atlanta, and Springfield, Illinois, for example, white mobs had responded to real or alleged crimes by blacks by lashing out indiscriminately at random persons whose only offense was their color and misfortune in being in the wrong place at the wrong time. Similarly, those who justified lynching insisted that swift public torture and execution of black suspects deterred other blacks from committing similar heinous crimes. Only "Judge Lynch," apologists maintained, could protect white women from black men. Ida B. Wells, Walter White of the NAACP, and researchers at Tuskegee proved that alleged or actual rape accounted for fewer than a quarter of the lynchings from the mid-1880s to World War I. But facts could not change opinion or practice when so many whites were predisposed to see all black men as incipient rapists.

The outbreak in Brownsville, the pogroms in Atlanta and Springfield, and a spate of lynchings had heightened President Roosevelt's fears about disorder and lawlessness. The interracial violence after Johnson beat Jeffries also disturbed him. That bout, Roosevelt observed, "provoked a very unfortunate display of race antagonism." Formerly an amateur boxer himself, Roosevelt noted that "a number of professional boxers, including several ring champions," were "among the men whose friendship and regard" he "really valued." He heartily endorsed "boxing as a sport." But "enormous" purses, "the betting and gambling," and racial unrest had turned him against the prize ring. He hoped "public sentiment" would make the Johnson–Jeffries bout "the last prize fight" in the nation. He also recommended that "some method . . . be devised to stop the exhibition of the moving pictures" of the recent fight.

What Roosevelt left unsaid revealed more than what he did say. He might have chided blacks for being boisterous after Johnson's victory and scolded whites for attacking blacks in a fit of racial pique. Rather than urge Americans to uphold fair competition and equal opportunity—ideals that transcended boxing—Roosevelt evaded the challenge implicit in Johnson's recent victory and his status as a national, indeed international, champion in his profession. Roosevelt could have praised Johnson for winning the title and defending it against Jeffries fair and square. He might have denounced bias that posed barriers in other fields. Instead, Roosevelt put boxing in the same category as tainted meat, narcotics, liquor, child labor, and prostitution— evils that should be eliminated through enlightened legislation. Perhaps Roosevelt's reversal after Jeffries lost to Johnson was pure coincidence, since he did not blame the ensuing violence on blacks. Yet a ban on boxing in 1910 would have deprived Johnson and his people of the considerable prestige inherent in the title. Besides, the timing made Roosevelt's conversion seem more prejudiced than principled. A call for a prohibition on boxing before the Reno fight would have been less suspect.

The *Atlanta Constitution* also proposed a ban on prizefighting after Johnson beat Jeffries. "The best brute won!" the paper proclaimed. "The twentieth century and the twentieth century newspaper should not be the forum for the staging of such aboriginal outrages." The *Constitution*'s writers had not been so critical when anticipating a Jeffries triumph. Had the white hope won, Roosevelt and the *Constitution*'s staff would hardly have described prize fights as "aboriginal outrages" inimical to the spirit of the age. Reformers had good reason to find boxing repulsive, and many surely had motives beyond racial bias to urge an end to the blood sport. But the timing of the crusade had an odor to it. The demise of the only viable white hope and the prospect of a black champion's extended reign gave whites added incentive to ban boxing. For his part, Johnson felt no ill will toward Roosevelt for turning against prizefighting. "The former president and I met several times," Johnson recalled. "Roosevelt displayed not only keen interest in sports but he could discuss them intelligently, and he had a fund of knowledge concerning ring events that surprised me."[36]

Relegated to the bottom rail, black Americans understandably viewed Johnson and his title differently than Roosevelt and other whites viewed Jeffries. Even those blacks who found boxing repugnant saw Johnson's achievement as a valuable racial asset, a precursor to substantial progress in all fields. Harry Smith, for example, conceded boxing was "barbaric" but maintained that Johnson had "rendered all the people of this country a signal service." The integrated ring and Johnson's supremacy within it had shown whites that blacks had aspirations and talents quite similar to their own.

Some blacks suffered injury, even death, after the epic battle in Reno. However lamentable the casualties, the past suggested that real progress in race relations seldom occurred without strife and even the loss of life. "It was a good deal better for Johnson to win and a few Negroes to be killed in body for it, than for Johnson to have lost and all Negroes to have been killed in spirit by the preachment of inferiority from the combined white press," William Pickens of Talladega College contended. "It is better for us to succeed, though some die, than for us to fail, though all live." White writers "were ready to preach insulting homilies to us about our inferiority," Pickens surmised. "Many . . . editors had already composed and pigeonholed their editorials of mockery and spite—and we shall not conceal . . . our satisfaction at having these homilies and editorials all knocked into the waste basket by the big fists of Jack Johnson." Calvin Chase agreed. "The white man cannot expect always to be in the front rank without competition," he observed, "and we all should look at things this way."

Less analytical and eloquent than Pickens and Chase, the black masses expressed joy in Johnson's undisputed claim to the crown in other ways. "Chicago's Black Belt bedlam was good natured," Carey Lewis reported after Johnson defeated Jeffries. "Women were as wild as men, and children copied their elders. The uproar started in a hundred places at once." In New York City, Les Walton remarked, "the results of previous presidential elections have never aroused the interest manifested by millions of Americans of all races and color." Blacks sustained their sense of vindication by reading about Johnson's victory. "I have never seen so many colored people reading newspapers as since the fight," Walton noted. "Then again, never have I seen so few white people read the papers as within the past few days."[37]

After his win, Johnson journeyed east with his white friend Nat Fleischer, a sportswriter who had covered the fight. "I shall never forget the sight that greeted us in New York," Fleischer reminisced. "Thousands of Negroes crowded the streets, parading, shouting, shooting off fireworks, and carrying on in hilarious fashion." George Schuyler of the *Pittsburgh Courier* remembered how black Syracuse reacted to Johnson's triumph. "I rode around the streets of my home town on a bicycle selling newspapers like hot cakes," he recalled, "and, like most Negroes, bursting with pride and enthusiasm." In Nashville a cigar dealer displayed "a few of the Johnson-Jeffries pictures in his show window," the *Globe* noted. "It takes one policeman all of his time to keep the sidewalk clear." Johnson, Ruby Berkley Goodwin observed, "had no idea of the magic he was sprinkling over the entire Negro population."[38]

Johnson himself thought his victory in Reno had redefined a national holiday for a tenth of the people. At a Chicago theater in 1912, Johnson told patrons that "he used to see white folks celebrating on July 4, but that the colored people never had much to rejoice over or to touch off fireworks." His triumph, however, "changed things for them and gave them an equal chance to make merry on that big day . . . when one great athlete of the colored race defeated a white man." Whites had Lexington and Concord, the Battles of New Orleans and Chapultepec, the victory over the Spanish Fleet in Manila Bay. Blacks had emancipation day in 1865 and July 4, 1910, when Johnson vanquished Jeffries and subverted the notion, at least in a preliminary way, that the white majority had an indisputable right to reign in the ring and the entire world beyond.

After beating Jeffries, Johnson stood proudly at the summit, and, symbolically, millions of African Americans stood beside him. For Johnson and his people, the championship seemed a partial but promising fulfillment of their collective hopes and dreams, a portent of a future brighter than their troubled past and present. For better or worse, the champion was bound closely to his race, and it to him. The *New York Age* discerned the tie and worried about it. "We hope Mr. Johnson will conduct himself in a modest manner," the *Age* advised. "He can hurt the race immeasurably just now if he goes splurging and making a useless, noisy exhibition of himself." Already well known for his fast cars and daring driving, Johnson should avoid arrests for "speeding" or "any charge." Though he alone had won and defended the title, any abuse of his high office would have repercussions for millions who shared his skin color but not his celebrity. "Any undue exhibition on the part of Mr. Johnson will hurt every member of the race," the *Age* warned. "On the other hand, becoming modesty and self-control will win him many lasting friends."[39]

Johnson soon learned, however, that those who reach the loftiest heights also risk the steepest descent. At the pinnacle in mid-1910, the champion stayed there for an unexpectedly brief time. Initially a symbol of black potential, pride, and progress, Johnson by late 1912 would become a painful reminder of a rare opportunity squandered and a dream denied. To the chagrin of those who hoped that Johnson might open new doors for his race, he instead became the provocation for even greater restrictions. Whether villain, victim, or both, disclosures about his unseemly private life would show that neither "becoming modesty" nor "self-control" defined his character. When the black champion tumbled from the top, a whole race suffered the bumps and bruises of his rapid fall.

2

"A Tempest of Dispraise"

From Black Hope to Black Burden

Ah, Douglass, we have fall'n on evil days,
Such days as thou, not even thou didst know . . .
We ride amid a tempest of dispraise.[1]

—Paul Lawrence Dunbar, "Douglass," 1903

Americans, George Jean Nathan and H.L. Mencken observed in their 1920 book, *The American Credo*, thought neither wisely nor too well. "Collected into herds," the masses, they noted, "gather delusions that are special to herds." "The essential," Nathan and Mencken explained in their preface, "may be hidden in the trivial." They then listed 488 popular and seemingly trifling notions that actually revealed important elements of the national creed and character. So what did Americans of this era believe? "That the real president of the United States is J.P. Morgan. . . . That all Chinamen smoke opium. . . . That many soldiers' lives have been saved in battle by bullets lodging in Bibles which they have carried in their breast pockets. . . . That a jury never convicts a pretty woman." Nathan and Mencken did not explore the origins or validity of these ideas. Rather, they stressed that the beliefs themselves, not their merits, revealed the popular mind.

Aware of intense race consciousness among whites, the authors listed many intriguing majority beliefs about blacks. "That all male negroes can sing" was a widely held opinion, as was the impression "that every negro who went to France with the army had a liaison with a white woman and won't look at a nigger wench any more." If military service abroad had not spoiled African Americans, then schooling at home did. "Whenever a negro is edu-

48

cated he refuses to work and becomes a criminal" was a popular perception. So was the belief "that the moment a nigger gets eight dollars, he goes to a dentist and has one of his front teeth filled with gold." Black veterans who had been spoiled in France were not the only African American men who coveted white women. "That all negro prize-fighters marry white women, and that they afterward beat them" was included in the authors' catalog of truths dear to the American herd.[2]

Not long after *The American Credo* appeared in 1920, former champion Jack Johnson surrendered to federal agents at the border between California and Mexico. Having jumped bail in 1913 after being convicted of a felony, Johnson had resided abroad for many years, a fugitive from justice who chose exile in Europe and Mexico over incarceration in a federal prison. If it was "lonely at the top," as folk wisdom maintained, Johnson learned it was even lonelier at the bottom. For it was he who had inspired the belief that black fighters "marry white women" and "afterward beat them." In addition, Johnson had "one of his front teeth filled with gold," gold all too conspicuous in the big smile that vexed Jack London and others desperate for a white champion.

Johnson had cause to protest his fate, but for the most part he was the primary agent of his own undoing. He lived by his own code, making choices that disturbed and often enraged whites and many blacks as well. Johnson followed his own "credo," not that of Nathan and Mencken's "herds." Johnson knew, for example, that the laws of Illinois permitted mixed marriages. So he regarded his choice of a wife as no one's business but his own. He would wear no one's harness, not one fashioned by blacks and certainly not one forged by whites. His fierce independence disturbed peoples of all hues, though his color made his conduct particularly reprehensible to white men who viewed white women as their exclusive preserve.

The Progressive Era and the Impulse to Reform

By the time Johnson found himself in deep legal trouble and in danger of losing his freedom, reformers had defined the prize ring as an intolerable blight on American civilization. Like prostitution, liquor, and gambling, boxing undermined morals and tainted the society that sanctioned it. In 1910, when reform groups and religious organizations in California lobbied against hosting the bout between Johnson and Jeffries, Governor James Gillette decided to ban the fight from his state. Tex Rickard then secured a site in Nevada, a state already in disrepute among progressives for its reputation as a haven for hasty marriage, quick divorce, casual sex, gambling, and drinking. Unable to prevent the bout itself, reformers demanded that the films of the fight be suppressed and urged new laws against boxing. Editors Lyman Abbott and Hamilton Mabie of *The Outlook*, for example, reminded readers that the recent Johnson–Jeffries fight had incited "race riots in many parts of the country." "This sequel to the degrading exhibition at Reno was bad enough," they argued, "but there seems likelihood that the race conflicts will be renewed and extended if the moving pictures portraying the fight are exhibited throughout the country." The editors praised leaders in several cities who had pledged to ban the films if the law allowed it. "The United Society of Christian Endeavor," some 4 million members strong, was waging "a determined fight against the display of the moving pictures in every city and town," *The Outlook* noted. "An aroused and united public opinion" would shrink the audience for this "degrading spectacle." Amateur boxing could continue but prizefighting must end:

> If it is right to prohibit indecent pictures because they stimulate to vice, it ought to be right to prohibit brutal pictures because they stimulate to brutality. If it is right to prohibit prize fights within a State, it ought to be right to prohibit graphic representations of prize fights. And the same public opinion which has put an end to prize fighting in almost every State of the Union ought to put a stop to the exhibition of moving pictures of prize fights.

Former president Theodore Roosevelt supported the ban and hoped that the Johnson–Jeffries bout would be the last of its kind. "It would be an admirable thing," he added, "if some method could be devised to stop the exhibition of the moving pictures taken thereof."

The editors of *Vigilance*, a journal formed to fight the traffic in women for commercial vice, placed fight films in the same category as dance halls, theaters, and amusement parks for their deleterious effects on the morals of youth. "The respect for decency and the desire for clean living are both likely to be lowered in the minds of many who see the moving pictures, who have no interest and little sympathy with a prize fight," the journal warned. "To brutalize the taste of the impressionable in a community is to offend the moral law today, and impair moral impulse and purpose tomorrow." Many cities had banned the films, the editors reported, and they urged "every self-respecting town and city" to do the same.[3]

The call for federal action to suppress the fight films drew support from unexpected sources. "There are always those to invoke the academic argument of states' rights," the *Atlanta Constitution* editorialized a week after Johnson beat Jeffries. "But states' rights do not extend as a protecting shield to defend a shameless rotten borough state in its willingness to disgrace the whole country for a few dollars. If there is not law enough in Nevada to protect her from her own shame, then the law should be found by the nation!" The *Constitution* asserted a national interest in preventing interracial prizefights and chided Nevadans for crassness. If the state could not "avoid the temptation to swap decency for dollars," the *Constitution* argued, "its feet should be set in the narrow path by outside coercion, if that is necessary." With virtual unanimity, southern whites opposed any federal initiative against lynching. But the greater menace of two men of different races fighting fairly for the title warranted intrusion by federal authorities.[4]

This crusade against boxing and fight films right after Johnson beat Jeffries seemed suspicious to many blacks and whites alike. Blacks sensed that Johnson's color, not his calling, was the real rub. Les Walton of the *New York Age*, for instance, called the effort to ban the films "the most childish and idiotic crusade . . . for some time. Had Jeffries won there would have been no opposition to showing the pictures." The *Nashville Globe* detected "inconsistency of the rankest nature" in efforts to suppress the films. "When *The Clansman* was staged a few years ago the doors of every theatre in the country were thrown open," the *Globe* recalled. "Billboards were covered with pictures that were of a nature . . . to create a hatred toward a helpless people, but no city forbade the show being exhibited; but when a Negro prize fighter defeats a white prize fighter, a great howl is set up about race riots, race domination, and the like."

Julius Taylor, editor of the *Chicago Broad-Ax*, denounced the "religious organizations . . . preachers, and the press" that opposed the films. Those same groups, he complained, "have never in the past attempted to suppress *The Clansman*, which depicts a Negro raping a white woman." Nor had they denounced "blood-thirsty anarchists, half devils and half savages," like Ben Tillman, James Vardaman, Tom Dixon, and others whose chief aim was "to stir up race hatred and prejudice—to uphold mob and lynch law." Two weeks later Taylor belittled the "holy horror" expressed at the films. Had Jeffries won, he would have been hailed "as divine evidence of the superiority in every respect of the white race over the black race." Juli Jones of the *Indianapolis Freeman* ridiculed the plea that children be spared from seeing these films. "The child must not see this horror, yet they have seen *The Clansman*, heard the great Tillman lecture, read for years what Vardaman had to say, and know the art of burning Negroes at the stake by heart," Jones protested. Had Johnson lost, "these same persons would have advocated that these pictures be shown in the public schools every Friday in order to show . . . the superiority of the white man over the black man." If a white hope emerged who could beat Johnson, the fight would be staged on the Capitol grounds, Will Foster predicted in the *Freeman*, and American officials would invite diplomats from "every government under the sun" to attend. Films of a Johnson defeat "would be shown in every church, Sunday school, and day school on the globe, [and] to the savages in Africa" to demonstrate white ascendance over black.[5]

Sarcasm aside, the fact that Johnson handily defeated Jeffries augmented many whites' disdain for professional boxing, particularly interracial bouts. They viewed Johnson's fame and fortune as dangerous deviations from the natural order. Besides, had Jeffries won, large crowds would have feted him everywhere and rushed to see the films. Sincere critics, of course, would have followed the same course regardless of the outcome on July 4. But Johnson's victory gave added incentive to Roosevelt and others to join those who had long urged a ban on boxing, and the agitation gave white governing bodies needed cover to prohibit prizefights. Racism alone did not prompt this movement, but bias played a major role in it. To a man, the best heavyweights in 1910 were black—not just Johnson but also Sam Langford, Sam McVey, and Joe Jeannette. With the demise of Jeffries, the remaining "white hopes" were not great and inspired little hope. Whether intentional or coincidental, the crusade against boxing mainly jeopardized the futures of able black fighters.[6]

Debate about an integrated ring, however, was a trifling matter compared to the furor over the integrated bedroom. While Johnson regarded his intimate relations with women as strictly a private concern, the "herds" thought otherwise. In 1898, before his days of fame, Johnson had married Mary Austin, a black woman from Galveston, his hometown. But a 1901 divorce ended the union. Johnson then carried on a long but stormy romance with Clara Kerr, another black woman. They also split, but Johnson kept trying. Now a well-known boxer, he appeared on the same stage as singer Ethel Waters and asked her to dinner. She refused, a rebuff Waters thought "intrigued" Johnson. "I don't think he had met one other colored girl since becoming famous," she reflected, "who didn't try to track him down." Over the years they became "good friends." One of their conversations stuck with Waters. "I like colored women, I could love a colored woman," Johnson told her. "But they never give me anything. Colored women just won't play up to a man the way the white girls do. . . . You fluff me off. No matter how colored women feel toward a man, they don't spoil him and pamper him and build up his ego." Waters, aware of her own fierce independence, did not deny it. She thought that black prostitutes, for example, were feistier than white ones. "Pimps very seldom had trouble with the white girls in their stables," she recalled of life in the tenderloin. "The white girls almost always did as they were told." But "brown skin whores" raised "all the hell, were the rebellious and independent ones, and showed they had minds and wills of their own."

Waters avoided the perils of the vice district where she lived because "several paternal-minded sporting men," among them Jack Blackburn, a fine boxer, kept an eye on her. Blackburn and his friends, she believed, "would have slapped me from Independence Square to West Philadelphia if they saw me doing anything they thought would hurt me." Forced to grow up fast in the "Bloody Eighth" ward but talented enough to move up and out, Waters fared no better with men than Johnson did with women. "Whenever I mixed up romance and my bank account I seemed to end up with no dough and even less of a love affair," she lamented. "I never could learn to fuss over any man. . . . Jack Johnson was right about that."[7]

After the "heartaches" with Austin and Kerr and the snub from Waters, Johnson befriended Hattie McClay, a white prostitute of Irish descent. They traveled to Europe and Australia, where Johnson defeated Tommy Burns for the title. Annoyed by her heavy drinking, Johnson left McClay for another white woman, Belle Schreiber from Milwaukee, a manicurist turned prostitute. In San Francisco with Schreiber, Johnson had to contend again with McClay, who sought a reconciliation. Johnson evaded her with a deft rope trick. "My most successful method of leaving and entering my room," he recalled, "was by means of a rope which I let down from a window when I was leaving, and which on my return was lowered to me when I signaled." Jack managed to keep Hattie and Belle apart, but the love triangle was a portent of more serious problems to come.

Johnson's personal life attracted more attention when he became champion, but the additional scrutiny did not deter him from his customary recklessness with cars, money, and women. Early in 1909, for example, white officials and black residents in Galveston considered holding a celebration for the hometown hero who had once toiled as a stevedore on the local docks. But city leaders abandoned the idea when they heard that Johnson had recently married a white woman while in Australia. With rumors rife of the mixed marriage, prominent white Texans lost ardor for their native son. Rather than welcome him home, officials warned they would prosecute him for violating the state law against mixed marriages if he and his wife came to Texas and stayed together, even for a brief visit.

The gossip about Johnson's marriage angered some prominent blacks as well, editor J.D. Crenshaw of the *Nashville Globe* among them. "If the persistently circulated report of his marriage is true, he has made a fatal mistake and subjected himself to the just contempt of every member of his race," Crenshaw warned. "If it is true, he stands before that awful and dread bar, public opinion, a defendant without defense." Any black man who married outside his race was "a fawning, cringing, worthless rascal," since "a worthy and congenial companion" could easily be found among "millions of honorable, intelligent" black women. Harry Jackson of the *Indianapolis Freeman* reported that Johnson intended to stay with his wife in Texas for as long as they pleased. "It does not seem possible for prosecution in Johnson's case, as he did not marry his white wife in that state," Jackson noted. "But the courts down there seem to think that they can prevent the two from living together."

Then the plot (and confusion) thickened. A stringer for the *Freeman* in Chicago reported that "Johnson emphatically denies that his wife is a white woman." Johnson's spouse, the story noted, "is three-quarters colored blooded." "I did not marry her in Australia," Johnson explained to the reporter. "Her maiden name was Hattie Smith, and we were married in Mississippi about two and a half years ago. She went to Australia from London with me." Julius Taylor of the *Chicago Broad-Ax* announced that Johnson had wagered $1,000 that no one could prove his wife was not "colored."[8]

Johnson's gambit worked, largely because ascertaining "race" in the United States involved a greater degree of clairvoyance than science. The color line was not as clear as ethnologists and segregationists liked to believe. Racial identity had an element of choice beyond genetics and appearance—a fact apparent in the phenomenon of "passing." Moreover, Johnson used the word "wife" loosely; he was not legally married to Hattie "Smith." But Johnson bought time and regained favor with his denial. An *Atlanta Independent* columnist welcomed the news: "Jack Johnson squared himself with the colored people alright when he said his wife was a colored woman," and he made his point when "he offered $1000 to anyone who could prove that she was not a member of the colored race." Johnson had temporarily "postponed his visit to Texas," the writer continued, "to accept a flattering offer" to box exhibitions instead. Ben Davis, the *Independent*'s editor, also welcomed Johnson's explanation. A staunch proponent of self-help, separatism, and black pride, Davis condemned mixed marriages and advocated harsh penalties for interracial sex. "The *Independent* is uncompromisingly opposed to the amalgamation, the miscegenation, or any kind of mixing of the races," he declared. "Not for sentimental reasons, but because we believe the intermarriage of the races is a crime against nature and the spirit of the Bible."[9]

The press might have misquoted Johnson. Hattie "Smith" was really Hattie McClay, Johnson's traveling companion but not his lawful wife. According to the prevailing racial and ethnic categories at the time, she was "white," not "three quarters colored." Johnson told the truth when he said she had ventured to England and Australia with him. But her lineage and marital status were only two parts of the puzzle. To make matters worse, journalist Harry Jackson reported that "Johnson's first wife, who is a colored woman, declares that he was illegally married to his second wife, and he did not get a legal divorce from her." That he had not obtained a "legal divorce" was moot, since he had not contracted a legal marriage to Hattie. In his autobiography, Johnson did not repeat his claim that he had married Hattie "Smith." In 1909, however, he lied because he wanted to retain his liaisons with white sporting women without losing his earning power in the boxing arena or on stage. Adept at feinting inside the ring, Johnson found deception useful outside of it as well.

At a horse track in New York later in 1909, Johnson met Etta Terry Duryea, a white woman who apparently did "pamper him" and "build up his ego." They traveled, lived together, and then married in early 1911 at Frank Sutton's hotel in Pittsburgh. In a now common pattern, Johnson lavished attention and money on Etta but neglected Hattie and Belle. McClay gave up and drifted away, but Schreiber and Johnson could not cut the Gordian knot that bound them. That knot, Johnson soon learned, formed part of a noose that Belle would eventually slip around his neck.

In late 1909 Johnson's finances improved and a semblance of calm marked his personal life. He signed a lucrative contract to fight Jeffries. He purchased and furnished a stylish brick house on Chicago's South Side, and his mother Tiny and brother Henry moved from Galveston in time to celebrate Christmas as a reunited and far more affluent family in the promised land. Johnson also bought a custom-built $10,000 roadster, more expensive than the house on Wabash. He cruised the city without a driver's license and registration and collected traffic tickets—a giddy time for him. Over the holidays Johnson invited S.H. Dudley, a comedian and musician who had been his partner in a saloon venture, for a ride in his new car. Comedian though he was, Dudley found little to laugh at as Johnson tore around the city. "A hundred times they missed a trolley car, a wagon, or an excited pedestrian by the narrowest margin, each time leaving Dudley's nerves in a more shattered condition," the *Indianapolis Freeman* reported. "Dudley begged, pleaded, and prayed to Jack to slow down and use more precaution. . . . Jack only smiled and drove the car more recklessly."[10]

Jack's recklessness was not confined to the road. He continued his dalliance with white prostitutes after marrying Etta. He angered theater managers when he reneged on contracts. At times he scuffled with fans and photographers. Despite his fast and loose ways, he trained well enough to beat Jeffries and retain the title. With the white hope disposed of, Johnson seemed destined to reign a long time—a prospect that delighted many African Americans but also raised concerns about how whites would react to a black monopoly on top for years to come. A month after the Reno fight, Jim Corbett announced his intention to find a new and better white hope. "Corbett says he will never rest until he develops a white man who can lick Jack Johnson and restore the championship to the Caucasian race," the *Freeman* noted. "Jim is going to get mighty tired before his resting period sets in." Corbett's desire was no personal quirk, for many whites regarded the title as a public office and race entitlement. These matters of color transformed Johnson from a private citizen into a public figure.[11]

Johnson became prominent at a time when growing numbers of reformers and politicians viewed government—the federal government in particular—as a potent agent for improving the health and morals of an increasingly urban, industrial, diverse, and divided nation. During the Progressive Era, Congress passed laws to regulate food and drugs, to restrict labor by women and children, to improve safety for industrial workers, and to prohibit liquor after many states had already gone "dry." Private and public agencies created programs to uplift juvenile delinquents, drinkers, unwed mothers, and new immigrants. Reformers in many states banned prizefighting. They fought prostitution and fretted over dance halls, amusement parks, movie theaters, lotteries, saloons, and gambling dens. Progressives sought to improve city government, professionalize municipal services, and close urban vice districts. They also sought to elevate private behavior.

Johnson appeared in court frequently in early 1910 to contest various charges of rape, unpaid debts, traffic violations, broken contracts, and assaults on various men who had purportedly insulted him or his wife. One man sued over an alleged attack by Johnson's bulldog. "The lives, liberty, and happiness of over nine million Negroes," Rad Kees of the *Freeman* warned, "are being antagonized and jeopardized by his folly." Samson, Goliath, and Gulliver had all met their match, Kees observed, and unless Johnson put "a quietus to his wild methods, the strong hand of the law is apt to chain him down." Johnson seemed to spend more time in his cars and in court than in the gym. Editors urged greater restraint. Besides losing his crown, he might humiliate the whole race and provoke reprisals against it.

Johnson continued to see Belle Schreiber despite his wife's objections. While he collected traffic fines and critical editorials in early 1910, Congress debated how to combat the so-called white slave trade. Even though the Immigration Act of 1907 had included a provision against traffic in women for commercial sex, the importation of alien women for prostitution persisted. An Immigration Commission report in 1909 told lurid tales of foreign girls and women enticed to the United States by promises of good jobs or marriages to wealthy men, only to end up whores and virtual slaves to procurers who misled and abused them. The white slave trade, the commission noted, was one of "unspeakable brutality manifested in deception, threats, physical cruelty, even to the point of criminal assaults, and in the demands for submission to degrading practices even worse than that of ordinary prostitution." In addition, many alien women with "loathsome diseases" passed them on to their patrons who then infected innocent wives and children. Even more disturbing, investigators learned that procurers enticed young and naive white women to leave their rural and small-town homes for large cities to engage in sex for money. Convinced that cities and states could not halt the traffic alone, reformers sought federal legislation under the guise of regulating commerce. "A despairing and desperate womanhood, herded into miserable districts, have come to be the most terrible of all enemies," one reformer cried, "more dangerous by far to our national life than an invading army of many times their number." This peril allowed legislators to direct their paternalistic concern for young and vulnerable women to the larger cause of upholding precious village values against the corrosive effects of modern urban life. The fear of infected foreign prostitutes further heightened nativist disdain for "new" immigrants. Even many southern lawmakers with states'-rights principles could not resist this federal call to arms.[12]

The Mann Act

President Taft called for action in late 1909. He advised lawmakers that recent research by the Bureau of Immigration indicated an "urgent" need for new laws "and greater executive activity to suppress the recruiting of the ranks of prostitutes from the streams of immigration into this country." A bill against "the transportation of persons for purposes of prostitution across national and state lines," Taft counseled, would be both constitutional and moral. Congress proceeded to debate and devise a bill to remedy this undeniable evil.[13]

Legislators seeking stringent penalties against the interstate and international transport of women for prostitution could imagine no better use of federal power. John Burnett, a congressman from Alabama and a member of the House Committee on Immigration and the Immigration Commission, told his colleagues in early 1910 that recent inquiries into the white slave trade had revealed "the same deplorable conditions" for both native-born and alien prostitutes. Acknowledging that some lawmakers preferred that the states and not the federal government take the initiative against this "matter that is immoral in itself and fraught with evils direful and portentous," Burnett reminded colleagues that the Supreme Court had upheld the right of Congress to prohibit the transit of lottery tickets across state lines. If Congress could restrict lotteries, it certainly could legislate against the white slave traffic. "I am a strict constructionist of the Constitution," Burnett observed, "but God forbid that I should construe it so strictly as to say that we must sit with hands folded and let this cankerworm gnaw at the moral vitals of our Republic." He urged a more punitive bill against the traffic. "We have legislated to give people pure food," he declared amid applause from the gallery. "Now let us legislate, so far as we can, to give them pure morals."

Oscar Gillespie of Texas had doubts about "the constitutional power of Congress to enact this legislation," yet he endorsed a sweeping bill to combat "the crime of crimes." "The meanest, the blackest crime that was ever instilled into the human heart by the devil himself," he told the House, "is this crime of trafficking in the virtue and chastity of women." He urged Congress to exercise its regulatory power "over the telegraph, over the mails, [and] over the railways" to suppress both prostitution and gambling.

The sponsor of the bill, James Mann of Illinois, regarded this sex "slavery" as even worse than black servitude in the antebellum South. "The white-slave traffic, while not so extensive, is much more horrible than any black-slave traffic ever was," Mann argued, and he exhorted Congress to use "its constitutional powers" to abolish the trade and punish its merchants. Adolph Sabath, Mann's colleague from Illinois, conceded that the pending bill was "a stringent and a drastic measure" but concluded that Congress had no choice:

> We cannot go too far to protect the thousands of innocent, virtuous, and simple alien girls who come to this country as strangers, incapable of understanding our language, and in many instances without maternal or paternal protection, and sometimes without either, no one to guide them in the path of rectitude and away from the numberless pitfalls, thus making them easy prey for the vampires and parasites on womanly virtue. This bill ... will also protect our own girls, who unknowingly might be transported from one State into another for immoral purposes, as is so often done.

How could anyone oppose efforts to protect the "innocent" and "virtuous" from "vampires and parasites?"

Gordon Russell of Texas endorsed the bill, noting that "no nation can rise higher than the estimate which it places upon the virtue and purity of its womanhood." Emphasizing the perils to native-born women, Russell estimated that "65,000 daughters of American homes each year [are] conscripted into the great army of prostitutes." Moreover, he pointed out that white prostitutes had black as well as white clients. "More than forty years ago this country was drenched in fraternal blood and offered up the lives of nearly a million of the very pick and flower of its citizenship in the struggle to abolish the slavery of the black man," Russell proclaimed. "In God's name, can we do less now than pass this bill, which will be a step toward abolishing the slavery of white women?" The House passed a bill on January 26, 1910, "to further regulate interstate and foreign commerce by prohibiting the transportation therein for immoral purposes of women and girls." The Senate approved the bill five months later, on the final day of the session.[14]

The debate over the Mann Act showed that many legislators who admired its intent doubted both its legality and practicality. Was a woman traveling between states, whatever her purpose, really a form of interstate commerce? If a legislator assisted a female constituent stranded in Washington by paying for her train trip home and she became a prostitute, had he committed a felony? Should ticket agents query every woman passenger about her profession, morals, and purpose? Why punish the person who paid the fare but not the person who traveled? The train, not the ticket, carried the passenger across state lines. Was the rail company liable for passengers' behavior after their journey? What if a relative or friend loaned money to a woman who traveled to a new state to enter a brothel? As James Mann himself admitted, it seemed unfair that naive alien women deceived and exploited by native vice merchants should face deportation under the new law when their debauchery stemmed from others' nefarious acts. To many lawmakers, the Mann Act seemed a bad bill hastily drawn for a good purpose.

Even before passage of the measure, the United States Attorney for the Northern District of Illinois had shown particular zeal in enforcing the 1907 law against the traffic in women. Led by Edward Sims and Harry Parkin, the Chicago office had earned rave reviews from reformers across the nation. Sims summarized his staff's success in a 1909 report to the Immigration Commission. "Of a large number of persons who a few months ago were actively engaged in the importation of alien women and girls for immoral purposes," he noted, "some are serving sentences of imprisonment, others have forfeited bail and fled, and . . . no inconsiderable number have become so frightened at the prosecutions that they have abandoned their practices, left the city, and gone into other business." As a result of this crackdown, Sims noted, "the value of the establishments in the Chicago red-light districts" had "depreciated 50 per cent."[15]

In this climate of rising race consciousness, nativism, and moral rearmament, virtually any white woman who consorted with or married a black man might be seen as a "white slave." And slaves of any color, Americans knew, sometimes took desperate measures to escape their bondage. A few months after Jack and Etta Johnson opened the "Café de Champion," an interracial cabaret on Chicago's South Side, Etta lifted Jack's revolver to her temple on the night of September 11, 1912, and squeezed the trigger. She died shortly after. Johnson was not in the apartment above the club when Etta shot herself—a fortunate fact, Robert Abbott of the *Chicago Defender* observed. "Like wolves the reporters for the city papers tried in every way to have someone say that Jack was in the room at the time of the shooting," Abbott complained. White dailies hoped to "brand him as a wife murderer." Nowhere near the scene, however, he had "many alibis" to prove his innocence. "When the count of nine came," Abbott gibed, "Jack was on his feet and ready to strike the body blow to Mr. Lie." The Chicago dailies suggested that racial bias prompted the suicide because "Negroes hated Mrs. Johnson." Never fully accepted by blacks, Etta had also been ostracized by whites for marrying Jack. Two months before her death, Etta, the *Chicago Broad-Ax* reported, described her plight to a friend: "I am a marked woman. I cannot go any place and am given no consideration as a human being. Once I was a well known woman. I was liked by everybody. Now, because my husband is a black man, I have become a recluse—a social outcast. I wish I had never married Jack." A report from Chicago in the *Philadelphia Tribune* confirmed the cause of Etta's despondency. "I have all my misery for marrying a colored man," she told a black woman who lived nearby. "Even the colored race doesn't respect me; they hate me. I intend to end it all."

Editor Chester Franklin of the *Denver Statesman* called the white press "a veritable scandal-monger" for sensationalizing the suicide and making a fuss over the minuscule number of mixed marriages. Harry Smith agreed, complaining that never in his thirty years as editor of the *Cleveland Gazette* had he read so many "malicious lies" as those in the white press about the suicide. "Those were tremendous efforts they made to increase prejudice against mixed marriages and the race," Smith reflected. "Mrs. Johnson's tragic death was most unfortunate from every viewpoint. The race will suffer the harrowing results, and not Jack Johnson." Harry Smith's prophecy proved half right— both Johnson and his people would "suffer the harrowing results" of his relations with white women.[16]

A Private Life, Public Concerns: Progressive Moralism and Jack Johnson

This white obsession with mixed marriages might have ebbed had Johnson acted discreetly after his wife's death. With speculation still rife over what had happened to Etta and why, Johnson faced another charge for allegedly abducting Lucille Cameron, a white woman he had hired months earlier as a "secretary." The relationship was hardly secretarial—Cameron had left a house of prostitution in Minneapolis for the brighter lights of a bigger city. She met Jack Johnson and, as in a romance novel, it was love at first sight. Lucille's mother, however, saw her daughter playing a lead role in a horror story, not a romance, and rushed to Chicago to retrieve her. Prodded by federal officials, she filed a complaint for abduction against Johnson, who was arrested and then released on bail. Federal agents questioned Lucille about her move to Chicago and her tie to the champion. They detained her in various places on a bogus disorderly conduct charge to keep her from her "abductor." The agents wanted to shackle Jack Johnson, not liberate Lucille Cameron. Unlike the scheming agents, Lucille's mother expressed her motives with unabashed candor: "I would rather see my daughter spend the rest of her life in an insane asylum than see her the plaything of a nigger." Johnson had a "hypnotic influence" over Lucy, she muttered, and she signed papers declaring her daughter insane. When Johnson went to his bank to get money to pay Lucille's bond, a white mob backed him against a wall and threatened to lynch him. The drama drew national attention. Nothing on the vaudeville stage or new silver screen could match it.[17]

Any story varies, of course, with the viewpoints of its characters. Much to the surprise of officials, Lucille Cameron's statement to federal agents led Johnson not to the penitentiary but to the altar. Agents Martin Lins and Bert Meyer escorted Cameron to the local Office of the Bureau of Investigation and questioned her on October 20. Cameron told them she had met Johnson the night he had returned to Chicago after successfully defending his title against Jim Flynn on July 4, 1912. "She said she immediately fell in love with Johnson and went to the cafe frequently thereafter, and finally went to work for him as a stenographer, also as a companion to his wife who has since committed suicide," Lins informed his bosses in Washington. "Her attitude was at all times defiant, and she would divulge nothing against Johnson, declaring in every breath that she loved him, wanted to marry him, and would do so immediately on being given the opportunity."

Lins thought Cameron lied when she denied being "intimate" with Johnson, but he did believe she had acted on her own volition and was no "white slave" to a black master. "No information could be obtained from her," he admitted, "which would tend to establish the fact that Johnson was instrumental in having her or any other girl brought here for immoral purposes." Agent Meyer confirmed that Cameron met Johnson after she arrived in Chicago. "She now insists on marrying him," Meyer noted, "regardless of the pleas of her mother who has come here from Minneapolis." Agents found no violation of the Mann Act. "I ascertained that she came to Chicago in April, 1912, of her own accord," Lins acknowledged, "[and] paid her own transportation from Minneapolis to Chicago."[18]

Agents brought Cameron out of seclusion to testify before a grand jury on October 24. She "made a clean breast of the whole affair," Lins reported, "admitting her acts of prostitution with Johnson." After an hour on the stand "she collapsed and had to be carried out . . . and a physician called in attendance." Agents took daughter and mother to a nearby hotel "without the knowledge of the Johnson crowd and [the] horde of newspaper men and curiosity seekers in the vicinity of the grand jury."

Martin Lins doubted a viable Mann Act case could be made against

Johnson, but Bert Meyer persisted. "It appears that Lucille Cameron was induced to come from Minneapolis . . . directly or indirectly by Jack Johnson," Meyer suggested on October 25, "and that persons carrying out this act were agents of Johnson." Meyer pounded the pavement in the tenderloin, interviewing people about Johnson's private life and how white prostitutes like Cameron found their way to Chicago. Meyer informed headquarters that he had learned about a woman named Catherine Dorsey who had "operated an assignation house in Minneapolis" and made "the acquaintance of Lucille Cameron there." Dorsey then moved to Chicago, "and it is supposed that Jack Johnson . . . a patron of her house, requested her to induce Lucille to come to Chicago." Whatever Johnson's exact role in Cameron's relocation, agents checked out rumors about his penchant for white sporting women. "There is a great amount of information coming in," Meyer added, "that Jack Johnson for the past three years has been taking different white girls on his trips over the country for immoral purposes." Such "information" might lead to a Mann Act indictment, but Lucille Cameron would not provide it. Three days later Lins confirmed "beyond doubt" that Cameron had lived in Chicago "at least three months" before meeting Johnson. So the prospect that he had "aided in any way in her transportation" seemed "very remote."

Stymied in the Cameron inquiry, Harry Parkin of the District Attorney's Office instructed Lins and his agents "to secure evidence as to illegal transportation by Johnson of any other woman for an immoral purpose." Meyer reported on November 1 that "plenty of evidence" proved that "Cameron practiced prostitution with Jack Johnson," but he found "little or no evidence as to interstate features" in the case. Still searching for other leads, agent G.N. Murdock questioned conductors and porters about rumors of Johnson's frequent travels with white women. He informed his superiors on November 2 that T.D. Culleny, a porter on the Chicago–Los Angeles line, recalled that "on two different occasions Johnson had white women on the train"—once when he had traveled to sign the contract to fight Jeffries and again when he headed west to train for the fight. Culleny "says that the [Johnson] crowd drank a great deal and caused lots of disturbance," Murdock related. "On several occasions" the travelers "quarreled and the men beat the women but . . . nothing was done beyond reporting it to the train conductor."[19]

White reporters learned many details about the investigation, and sensational headlines and stories soon filled the dailies across the country. With tiny staffs, leaner budgets, and little or no access to leaks from white officials, the black press proceeded more cautiously in its coverage. Black editors detected a certain lynch mob spirit behind the probe. Still, they had nothing to gain in defending Johnson if the rumors about him were true. They deplored how the white press treated blacks, especially men, but they did not want to compromise their credibility by blindly siding with Johnson, who, it seemed, had violated certain taboos even if he had not broken any law.

Johnson had received "some sympathy" for his wife's "tragic death" but seemed likely to "forfeit all that and more" because of "his entanglement with another white woman," Chester Franklin noted in the *Denver Statesman*. "If he were just white, so that no criticism might attach to our race for what he does, we would not be so interested." But since whites tended to judge all blacks by the deeds of a few, Franklin grumbled, Johnson had become "a distinct burden to us in our struggles." Those "struggles" were many and growing, and Franklin worried that a scandal involving Johnson would augment bias against black workers in Denver. "The accident of color has linked us all together so that the incapacity of some is the excuse for the refusal of us all by white employers," he observed. "Where the employers do not discriminate against us, labor does." Two weeks later, Franklin accused whites of "a deliberate conspiracy" to drive blacks from employment. "We are herded into unsanitary homes," he added. "Then when hunger forces us to steal, we are declared criminal, and when disease fastens upon us we are the weaker race." He blamed whites for "shameless hypocrisy" in sending missionaries to Africa while relegating American blacks to "charnel houses and schools of crime."

Les Walton of the *New York Age* thought Johnson's "numerous escapades" since his win over Jeffries had diminished his stature among "both black and white." Johnson acted with "unadulterated brazenness and utter disregard" for public opinion. "Although he is the world's champion physically," Walton maintained, "his conduct has shown him to be a weakling mentally." Johnson's notoriety also alarmed editor C.W. Posey of the *Pittsburgh Courier*. He knew that whites often punished the entire black race for a single person's error. In late 1911, for example, a white hotel manager in the city had fired all forty of his black waiters after one was arrested. "The lesson has been brought home to us with renewed emphasis," Posey wrote. "We can climb no higher than the lowest among us." This seemingly inescapable law of racial gravity prompted Posey to scold Johnson for having "disgraced" his title. "He has flouted white outcasts in the face of his people," Posey complained, and deserved censure even if Cameron had "sought him like a lioness for prey." Johnson was, Posey lamented, "a failure as a representative of the race."

Others also sought to isolate Johnson from the race. The *Nashville Globe* saw "nothing [in] common" between them. "He has placed a great gulf between himself and his people," the *Globe* stated. "He has no respect for black women, and black people despise his name." Billy Lewis of the *Indianapolis Freeman* viewed Johnson's entanglement with Cameron as "very, very bad."

Like others, Lewis knew Johnson's private life could affect his race's reputation and prospects. "This is no time to advocate individual emancipation," Lewis advised, "when the entire race is looked on as a unit." He faulted Johnson for defying "the unwritten laws" against "racial amalgamation," noting that such mingling was "almost as strongly opposed by our own race as by the white people." A *Freeman* editorial advised the couple not to marry. "If Lucille Cameron becomes Lucille Johnson," the *Freeman* warned, "that moment she is as good as mourned as dead by her own kind, and she will be without cordial reception elsewhere." Etta's suicide foreshadowed the ordeal Lucille would face should she "step foot across the color line" to marry Jack.[20]

Amid this outcry Johnson met with some hundred prominent blacks at the Appomattox Club in late October. Dr. George Hall stated that no other African American in Chicago over the past half-century had aroused such opprobrium, and he reminded Johnson of his duty to his race. Johnson denied press reports that he had bragged he could "get as many white women" as he wanted, and he insisted that he alone must decide what was best for him. "I am not a slave and . . . I have the right to choose who my mate shall be without the dictation of any man," he declared. "I have eyes and I have a heart, and when they fail to tell me who I shall have for mine I want to be put away in a lunatic asylum." This "right" was absolute, Johnson insisted, "so long as I do not interfere with any other man's wife." People opposed his making "his own choice," he protested; "that is where the whole trouble lies." In response to Johnson's appeal, George Hall, Julius Taylor, and other leaders issued a statement urging fairness toward the champion and advising "the public and press alike" not to "indict the entire Negro race for any infraction of the law by an individual member of the race."

Taylor pondered the motives for the vendetta against Johnson. He suspected that "the vast majority of the owners and managers of the daily newspapers" with their "unfair and unjust hearts" simply could not bear a black champion. For that reason they depicted him "as the most repulsive and the most heinous black monster that has ever trodden upon the face of the earth." Robert Abbott agreed that most white editors relished the salacious rumors about Johnson. In late October, for example, the Chicago dailies reported that Ada Banks-Davis, a singer in Johnson's club, had shot him in the leg during an argument. They also speculated that Johnson had pursued her and caused a rift between the singer and her husband. Banks-Davis, however, told a *Defender* reporter that she was estranged from her husband not because of Johnson but because "she has long been the breadwinner of the family, providing everything." The dailies would not correct their errors. "I have tried to get the reporters to publish the facts," she complained, "but you know that they are only looking for a new sensation."

Which "new sensation" the papers exposed seemed to depend on the subject's skin color. Abbott noted, for example, that the white Chicago editors so preoccupied with Johnson and "sex slavery" had "entirely overlooked" a recent story of a poor black girl, only fifteen, who had just had a baby. A white attendant at the Cook County hospital had seduced the girl. Chicago's black press also noted that even though the city's main vice district was on the South Side, its patrons came from white neighborhoods as well as black. Whites committed crimes every day, but headlines in the dailies did not make an issue of their race or ethnicity.[21]

By late October, federal officials knew that Cameron would not turn state's evidence against Johnson, even if her course estranged her from her mother. But Johnson had accumulated enemies like traffic tickets, and many craved the sweet taste of revenge. One of them anonymously advised the district attorney "that the sooner the country is rid of him the better protected our women shall be." In a long, detailed letter dated October 28 from Buffalo, New York, this informant supplied crucial leads about Johnson's past. He must have once been very close to him, for he divulged specific names, dates, and places to direct federal agents to people with evidence needed to indict Johnson.

In 1908, George Little, Johnson's former manager and "the so-called master of the tenderloin," the writer recalled, had introduced Johnson to several prostitutes at the famous Everleigh Club, the best little whorehouse in Chicago. There Johnson met "Belle Gifford" as well as two other women who later slipped away from the club to have sex with him, an escapade that prompted their dismissal by the Everleigh sisters. With bookings "in numerous cities" arranged by Little and Abe Abrahms, Johnson toured with Gifford and "passed her off as his wife." Gifford had even sent her former "sweetheart" in Chicago "a photograph taken from a Boston newspaper of Jack Johnson and herself, sitting in an automobile." The caption read JACK JOHNSON AND HIS PRETTY WHITE WIFE. Jack and Belle traveled "from city to city and from state to state," until "he finally after abusing her and mistreating her, cast her aside for another victim." The informant noted that Belle Gifford, "a name assumed by her," had grown up in Milwaukee under "good parentage" and had worked at a local hotel as a stenographer. After traveling with Johnson, Gifford "returned to Chicago under the name of Mrs. or Miss Jacques Allen" and maintained "a questionable flat in the Ridgewood Apartment building" at Twenty-eighth and Wabash, just a few blocks from Johnson's Southside home. In closing, the informant (identified only as "Chicagoan") urged the district attorney "to gather sufficient additional evidence" from these leads "to send this nigger to jail for the balance of his life."

The "Smoking Gun"

Within days of the informant's letter to the district attorney in Chicago, a former madam in the tenderloin phoned Bert Meyer and assured him she knew ample details about Johnson's personal life. She sent in her place James "Duffy" (aka "Duncan"), who told Meyer about a strange relationship between Johnson and one "Belle Baker." In his next report, Meyer called Duffy "an ex-post office safe blower and all-round crook . . . familiar with all the workings of the underworld," who had "very valuable information." Meyer learned that "Belle Baker" was now a prostitute in Washington, and he urged headquarters to find her. Agents combed the vice district until T.S. Marshall located the woman at a D Street brothel. He persuaded "Belle Allen, whose right name is Belle Schreiber," to accompany him to the main office of the Bureau of Investigation to tell her tale.

Shreiber confirmed agents' suspicions by detailing her troubled life with Johnson. Her words packed a wallop far greater than Jeffries' punches in Reno. Not only did she hand federal agents the proverbial smoking gun they needed, she gave them a veritable shooting gallery. The Justice Department now had a white hope who could inflict considerable damage on the champion. "Johnson sent me money through George Little, his manager, for me to go to New York" in 1909, Schreiber told agents. After a week at a hotel there, she "went to an apartment over the Savoy Cafe" where she and Johnson lived "as man and wife" and "he beat me repeatedly." The next year she left a Pittsburgh brothel and rented an apartment at 2730 Wabash in Chicago. "Under an understanding with Johnson" he paid the first month's rent and gave her $1,250 for furnishings. Then two other women "came and stayed with me there at my solicitation and turned in to me money collected from the sale of liquor and money for their room and board. . . . I conducted the business of this place where they prostituted themselves." Belle maintained, however, that she "had no relations personally with anyone other than Johnson."

Belle and Jack continued to travel together. "At almost every place we visited," she recalled, "Johnson beat me and mistreated me." She swore that she "conducted the business" of prostitution with Johnson's "full knowledge" from October 1910 well into the following year. "I personally, as well as the girls, stayed with various of my men friends who called to see me," Schreiber admitted. "And although I cannot positively state that Johnson knew of any particular act of sexual intercourse performed by me with anyone else, still the circumstances were such that he must have known that I was engaged in the business for which this place was conducted." In March 1911, Johnson had given Schreiber money to leave Chicago, and she went to Washington. Temporarily reunited later that year in Chicago, Johnson "proposed opening up another resort, similar to the one I had conducted before," but she "declined his proposition." She returned to Washington, where agents found her. She added that she had "not heard from Johnson" since early 1911.[22]

The statement had flaws. In one breath Schreiber claimed "no relations" with anyone but Johnson; in another she admitted she "stayed with various . . . men friends" and assumed Johnson "must have known" she engaged in sex for money in the apartment he furnished for her. Nor did she accuse Johnson of being a procurer or pimp—rather, she accepted his aid and did not give him any proceeds from her trade. In other words, Johnson had sex with Schreiber but did not obtain any money from her business. Whether such distinctions would save Johnson was unclear, since Congress had enacted a vague and elastic bill. Officials in the Justice Department hoped they could stretch the law just enough to put Johnson behind bars.

To secure Schreiber prior to her testimony in court, a bureau agent accompanied her from Washington to Chicago. To spare her exposure and embarrassment, officials announced that the grand jury would convene at 2:00 on November 7. Under this cover, agents sneaked Schreiber into the federal building an hour early to testify. The ruse worked, shielding her from photographers and reporters. That evening at 5:00 the grand jury indicted Johnson for violating the Mann Act, and police arrested him. The Bureau of Investigation whisked Schreiber off to New York City and placed her in protective custody. Officials feared that Johnson's friends would try to locate her and persuade her not to testify at trial or bribe her to flee the country. If all else failed, Johnson's desperate minions might even murder her and silence her forever.[23]

Johnson posted a hefty bond of $30,000 on November 18 and called upon United States Attorney James Wilkerson. Johnson stated his willingness to plead guilty and "to pay any fine imposed," agent Meyer noted, if only "he could escape a prison sentence." Johnson doubted he could win in court. But Wilkerson refused to bargain. He and his staff wanted Johnson to do time.

Nervous about Schreiber's reliability, prosecutors urged the presiding judge to begin the trial promptly. This melodrama required a good girl gone bad, a victim of Johnson's insatiable lust and hot temper. The reality, however, was more complicated. Schreiber exhausted the patience and expense accounts of those who guarded her. Agent Pigniulo, for example, requested reimbursement for personal funds he had tapped to amuse Schreiber. "I beg to state that during the entire time I had charge of Miss Schreiber her extremely nervous and crochety temperament made her a very difficult person to handle," he pleaded to Chief Bielaski. "She required constant humoring and pampering and, if thwarted in the slightest wish, immediately 'went up in the air'

and threatened to become an adverse witness." In letters to friends intercepted by agents, Schreiber groused about her quarters: "Regular prison bars
on the windows—no papers to read—no fire and cold indoors—This is a
place for wayward girls—girls in the family way and witnesses also for the
government—food awful." Lights went out at 9:00 and wake-up time was
6:30 in the morning—a schedule ill-suited to a career whore. "I am almost
crazy," she complained, "and so unhappy." "I . . . cannot sleep at all," she
wrote a friend in Washington. "But believe me I am on my way—as soon as
I can escape." Agents stepped up their surveillance and security. William
Offley, superintendent of the New York Office of the Bureau, warned Bruce
Bielaski, his superior in Washington, DC, that Schreiber was "very restless"
and likely to cause "some trouble." Schreiber objected that agents had "no
right to hold her" and insisted she be moved to "some hotel in New York City
or elsewhere."

The strange hours, bland food, and lack of sleep and privacy were only
part of Schreiber's problem. Offley surmised on November 23 that Schreiber
was sick and irritable "from the reaction following her inability to indulge in
the usual amount of liquor." Agent Emma Rosen tried to amuse Schreiber
with shopping trips, restaurant outings, movies, and car rides, but the bureau's
white hope remained petulant and sullen. Agent Raymond Horn, ignoring
ample evidence to the contrary, encouraged Schreiber that all would go well
"so long as you continue to be the good little girl that you have been." Satisfied that "half the battle is over," Horn praised Schreiber for her sacrifices.
"You will soon have rendered your country a service such as few are ever
fortunate enough to duplicate," he noted, "one that will go a long ways toward wiping out those acts of your past which I know you are not particularly desirous of reflecting upon."

Agents near Schreiber, however, did not see the "good little girl" Horn
flattered or a contrite woman eager to start anew. Accompanying Schreiber
on a visit to a New York City madam, agent Rosen saw her charge whisper-
ing to a housekeeper. Wary of Schreiber's intentions, Rosen advised her to
speak up. Schreiber had asked the woman if the madam would hire her after
she testified at Johnson's trial—and not for purposes of cooking and clean-
ing. When Schreiber refused to return to her quarters after an outing in mid-
December, agents mollified her by promising to take her back to Washington.
"She did not see why she should be detained as a prisoner," agent J.A. Poulin
reported, "when the culprit, Johnson, was out on bail and at his liberty." On
the train to the capital, Schreiber, according to agent G.C. Craft, "accosted
one Jerry Moore, a passenger on the train, whom she remembered as a former
patron of hers while she was an inmate of the Sinclair house of prostitution
in Washington." Her identity and destination compromised by the approach

to Moore, Schreiber was detained in Baltimore and placed in a home for unwed mothers. There she acted as she had in New York, and agent J.J. Grgurevich found himself at wit's end to please her. Piqued at the high expenditures to placate Schreiber, Bielaski ordered Grgurevich to take her out "at considerably greater intervals than heretofore." The chief instructed other agents to limit outings involving "any considerable expense" to "once or twice a week." Deprived of drugs and liquor, subjected to constant surveillance, restrained from her trade, and estranged from a previous source of diversion and largesse in Jack Johnson, Schreiber again threatened to bolt. Were she to flee and not testify, prosecutors feared that they would not be able to win a conviction against Johnson.

On December 4, 1912, the day after Horn called Schreiber a "good little girl" and assured her "half the battle is over," Jack Johnson and Lucille Cameron married in Chicago. No one in Cameron's family attended the wedding, but they could have read ample details about the event in the press. Schreiber "has learned from the newspapers of the marriage of Johnson," William Offley reported on December 5, "and is very bitter toward him in consequence." She was not alone in her "very bitter" reaction to the news.[24]

Known for superb pacing within the ring, Johnson proved quite inept in his timing outside of it. The moment was not auspicious for a mixed marriage between a black prizefighter under a Mann Act indictment and an outcast white prostitute declared insane by her mother. Speaking at an Irish Fellowship luncheon in Chicago, Dr. Frank Lydston, a proponent of eugenics, denounced the interracial mingling he saw in the city. "Jack Johnson," he fumed, "instead of roaming the streets, should be in the morgue." As bureau agents combed the vice districts of several cities for additional evidence against Johnson, Americans elected Woodrow Wilson president, the first southern Democrat to win the White House since James K. Polk in 1844. Though many blacks had become disillusioned with Republicans Roosevelt and Taft, they had good reason to distrust the party that included race-baiting southern politicians such as Ben Tillman, Tom Heflin, Cole Blease, and novelist Tom Dixon.

At the annual National Governors' Conference in Richmond, for example, South Carolina Governor Cole Blease defended lynching. On the day Johnson married Cameron, Blease told fellow governors, "I will never order out the militia to shoot down their neighbors and protect a black brute who commits a crime against a white woman." In his state, he observed, "all that is needed is that they get the right man, and they who get him will neither need nor receive a trial." Advised that he should pledge to uphold the Constitution, Blease screamed, "To hell with the Constitution!" "When the Constitution steps between me and the defense of the white women of my state," he explained, "I will resign my commission and tear it up and throw it to the breezes." Blease did not speak for most governors, of course, or for most white Americans. But as the *New York Times* noted, Blease had more partisans than he deserved. "There are Bleasers in the North," the *Times* admitted, "as well as in the South." The *Times* concluded that "this is not an age for Blease and his like."[25]

Whether or not the age belonged to "Blease and his like," Johnson's marriage to Cameron so soon after Etta's suicide and his "white slave" indictment riled the majority race. "The simple fact that a Negro has chosen for his wife a friendless white girl," Robert Abbott noted, "has stirred the country from center to circumference." Why? Abbott blamed "the demon of prejudice." To Abbott and others, marriage was a matter of individual choice; neither public opinion nor law should interfere in so private a matter. Other Americans, especially southern whites and northern Negrophobes, disagreed. Many states in the South enforced laws against mixed marriage. Several northern and western legislatures also debated bills against marriages between whites and blacks (and sometimes between whites and Asians) at this time. The journal of the National Association for the Advancement of Colored People (NAACP), *The Crisis*, reported in April 1913 that lawmakers in New York, New Jersey, Michigan, Minnesota, Illinois, Wisconsin, Ohio, Iowa, Kansas, and Colorado had recently introduced bills against intermarriage, with penalties ranging "from imprisonment to enforced surgical operation."

Authorities discouraged interracial contact in other ways. In New York City and Pittsburgh, for example, athletic boards banned interracial boxing. Legislatures in California and Colorado considered separate schools for children of European, African, and Asian descent. Missouri had joined other southern states in discouraging black voting; Blease's South Carolina had petitioned the federal government to repeal the Fifteenth Amendment that had extended the franchise to adult black males. Delaware and Washington, DC, debated segregation on streetcars. Lynchings took the lives of sixty-three black men and women in 1912, the NAACP reported, allegations of sexual assault, the usual excuse, surfaced in only seventeen cases. Investigators for the NAACP found several motives for the mob murders defended by "Bleasers." Three black men died because of "labor troubles and insulting remarks" in Arkansas; a Louisiana boy perished for "writing letters to ladies"; a man was executed for "testifying against liquor sellers" in Mississippi; another in Tennessee lost his life for "refusing to dance." Two black women were lynched on suspicion of murder, one in Texas and the other in Georgia.[26]

With the recent precedent of rapid action against the white slave trade, lawmakers urged immediate federal legislation against intermarriage. Seaborn Roddenbery, a Georgia Democrat, introduced a constitutional amendment on December 11, 1912, stipulating that marriage between "all persons of African descent" and "Caucasians" be "forever prohibited." Only a week had passed since Johnson's nuptials in Chicago. Roddenbery alluded to recent reports on the "enormity" of the white slave trade in New York and "its appalling extent . . . in Chicago." Most "revolting" was that Illinois law had allowed "a white girl of this country" to become "the slave of an African brute." The news out of Chicago infuriated him. "The newspapers . . . announce that Jack Johnson again marries a white woman," Roddenbery seethed. "Thank God such an outrage is impossible anywhere in the Southland."

Roddenbery condemned northern laws that permitted "the fiendish" Johnson to marry outside his race. The South acted more wisely. "No brutality, no infamy, no degradation in all the years of southern slavery," he exclaimed, "possessed such villainous character and such atrocious qualities" as intermarriage. Dixie had always shielded its white women from black men. Roddenbery expressed "gratification" as a southerner "to observe with what fairer vision, with what greater intelligence" northerners "now view and appreciate the difficulties and struggles our southern people went through when we came from the crucible of war to meet and solve the negro question in the ashes of poverty."

In stressing "the negro question" rather than slavery and secession as the source of his region's problems, Roddenbery took his cue from Tom Dixon's *Clansman*. In describing Jack Johnson he could just as well have been referring to the novel's main villain. This tactic dated back to antebellum days, when southern spokesmen such as John C. Calhoun, James Hammond, and George Fitzhugh had defended race slavery as a preferable system of labor and social control to the North's "wage slavery." Yankees had never quite understood: Dominion over the inferior and dangerous black population concentrated in the South, not the wealth produced by slave labor, had always been the southerners' paramount concern.

Roddenbery thought a federal law against intermarriage would reduce discord between the races and sections. "It is detrimental to the highest welfare of both races," he argued, "for such a condition to exist." If northern whites and blacks continued to marry, notions in favor of such unions "would begin to creep into the heads of negroes" in the South, or, new European immigrants unfamiliar with racial mores in Dixie might settle there and marry blacks, undermining segregation and white supremacy. Any such challenge, Roddenbery warned, might "bring annihilation to that race whom we have protected in our land for all these years." As in 1861, the nation faced a severe test in 1912. "This is a time for the American Congress to intervene," he advised, "and decree that forever the dominant race in this country shall preserve its veins from even the taint of African blood."

Alabama's Tom Heflin interrupted Roddenbery to point out that Abraham Lincoln had denounced mixed marriage in his debates with Stephen Douglas. Roddenbery added that many "leading patriots of the retreating past" had opposed "this debasing, ultrademoralizing, un-American, and inhuman leprosy." The nation must unite against intermarriage to avert another civil war. "It is abhorrent and repugnant to the very principles of a pure Saxon government," he pleaded. "It is subversive of social peace. It is destructive of moral supremacy. Ultimately this slavery of white women to black beasts will bring this Nation to a conflict as fatal and as bloody as ever reddened the soil of Virginia or crimsoned the mountain paths of Pennsylvania."[27]

A Man and Race Under Indictment: Johnson's Decline and Fall

Informed observers could not dismiss Roddenbery, Blease, and their kind as mere aberrations. By the time Jack Johnson married Lucille Cameron, anti-black sentiment was intense, the racial rift was widening, and whites were considering new laws to take away remaining rights and opportunities from blacks. President Taft had "bent the supple hinges of the knee to the wishes of the democrats of the South," Christopher Perry of the *Philadelphia Tribune* protested, and had acquiesced to "race segregation along all walks of life." From the army base in Brownsville to the Treasury Building in Washington, blacks faced mounting disdain and exclusion. The press also seemed more hostile. "It is hard to find a more implacable foe of the black American than the daily press," editor Chester Franklin complained in the *Denver Star*. "It plays the game all the time of piling up our infractions of good breeding and law" while "suppressing our accomplishments." Ben Davis of the *Atlanta Independent* cited two topics "eternally discussed in America: rich men and Negroes. The latter more cussed than discussed." Explaining the decision of the NAACP to begin publishing a monthly journal on race issues, W.E.B. DuBois noted the negligence of "the regular periodical press" toward "the Negro problem . . . unless the black man is vilified and traduced." Nearly all white sources, he argued, "have assumed, and for the most part firmly believed, that the Negro is an undesirable race destined to eventual extinction of some kind." He did not welcome "chronicling ten mob murders a month" and "a dozen despicable insults" besides, but he believed the NAACP had to do it because no one else would.[28]

Charles Anderson, a federal employee in New York City and a prominent black Republican, reminded Booker T. Washington in April 1913 that many state assemblies had taken up new discriminatory bills since Woodrow Wilson's election. "Jim-Crow car bills, segregation bills and marriage restriction bills have whitened the legislative chambers in almost every state in the union," including an intermarriage bill pending in Albany, he noted. "The penalty proposed for concubinage between the races is one so horrible that it cannot be expressed in language, even between man and man." The state athletic commission had banned interracial bouts, Anderson added, and though he did not mind the exclusion of Jack Johnson from the ring he thought it "most unfair" to other boxers and "a ruthless violation of justice and of decent public sentiment." Anderson worried that the repression would worsen. "If we are not very careful and vigilant," he cautioned, "we will wake up some bright morning to find that many of our most precious rights have been destroyed."

Wilson's administration moved quickly to replace blacks in the federal service with whites. The purge seemed to fulfill Chris Perry's prophecy that Wilson's candidacy had signaled that "what was lost" in the Civil War would be recovered by "the return to power of those who believe in the absolute elimination of the black man." Perry doubted that former slaves and their progeny had advanced much since 1865. "While Lincoln broke the chains of slavery," he reflected in 1913, "the colored man is obliged to drag the clanking irons with him wherever he goes."

Discriminatory bills contained no exemptions for individuals. Even W.E.B. DuBois, the first black recipient of a doctorate from Harvard, could not vote in Georgia after disfranchisement in 1908, nor could he draw books from the "public" library in Atlanta even though he had authored many seminal scholarly works. Bert Williams, a gifted black comedian, amused white audiences as well as black, but theater managers often shunted him off to a dingy dressing room and told him to stay away from white entertainers on the same bill. Williams frequently had to ride the freight elevator and dine alone. One night Williams and Eddie Cantor, his white friend, strolled into a bar and ordered Scotch. The bartender served Williams his drink but growled, "That'll be fifty dollars." Williams plucked three $100 dollar bills from his wallet and replied, "I'll take six, if you please."

Ethel Waters endured similar insults. One of the first black artists from the North to tour the South, she could not comprehend how whites treated black stars. "We found ourselves applauded by the ofays in the theater," she noted, "and insulted by them on the streets." She bickered with white theater managers who did not give her the consideration she deserved. Onstage a star was a star, but on the street a black celebrity was just another "nigger." No black man or woman, however talented, could escape the cruel realities of color in America, especially in the South. Blues singers conveyed their dismay in their tunes. "Why do they call me black," they sang, "when I'm so blue?"[29]

Nor could the race escape censure and reprisals for one man's foibles. Jack Johnson's marriages—in fact, his overall conduct as champion after 1908—put black leaders in a bind. They knew he acted within his rights when he married white women and they doubted the merits of the white-slave charge against him. Yet they knew that their race was tethered to Johnson and would suffer for his indiscretions. His rise had provided a psychological lift but few tangible gains beyond the easy money from betting. His disgrace, however, would mean significant losses for all his people.

After the abduction charge against Johnson in the fall of 1912, the *Nashville Globe* contended that blacks had identified with him in only a limited way. "Negroes who have common sense have never been affected by the victories of Jack Johnson to an extent to make them forget themselves," the *Globe* argued. "And when he married a white woman, right thinking Negroes lost all respect for him." A few days after Johnson and Cameron married, the *Globe* labeled him "the black man's burden," comparable to Cole Blease, "an equal grievance" to decent whites. After Blease defended lynching and wished aloud he could get his hands on Johnson, the editor proposed "a capital idea": "Put them in a ring . . . ten by ten. Gee, what fun!" Fred Moore of the *New York Age* found "no fault" in Johnson's marriage, "an individual matter." But "no sensible person," he noted, "can fail to foresee that Jack Johnson is piling up trouble every day for himself and for the race." Since whites bought most fight tickets, Johnson could ill afford to alienate white promoters and fans. "Besides," Moore added, "we must face the inevitable fact that there is a lot of race prejudice in this country against intermarrying."

Billy Lewis of the *Indianapolis Freeman* observed that "the Negroes of Chicago have suffered very much on account of Jack Johnson," including those fired by resentful white employers. But "race prejudice," not Johnson, was the cause. "It was no crime to marry the white woman," Lewis argued. "The opposition to it was a thing of sentiment," and Johnson chose to ignore it, "that's all." Grant Williams of the *Philadelphia Tribune* agreed that Johnson had committed no crime in marrying Cameron. He stressed the absurdity of holding all blacks accountable for Johnson's behavior. "Would it be fair for us to judge all white women by the actions of Lucille Cameron?" he queried. "Johnson represents the lowest type of the sporting element among the colored race and his present wife certainly does not represent the best class of white women, hence both are equal." Former champion John L. Sullivan "was a regular bully," Williams recalled, and "hardly a day passed that he did not get drunk and assault some man or woman." Sullivan did not represent his group; nor did Johnson with his ardor for "automobiles, white women, and diamonds" reflect his. Whites applied a double standard. Certain traits in an Irish American fighter made him a likable rogue, but those same traits in an African American boxer made him a public menace.[30]

Initially sympathetic to Johnson, Ida B. Wells watched the events of late 1912 with chagrin. She regretted his opening a cabaret, arguing that he should have provided a public gymnasium for black youth instead. "Johnson chose to open a saloon to cater to the worst passions of both races," she wrote. "When he was not on the road, he spent most of his time there, entertaining the wildest of the underworld of both sexes and especially of the white race." Despite her distaste for the club, she defended Johnson against the Mann Act charge. After conferring with Gilchrist Stewart, an attorney who reviewed the case for the Constitution League, a group devoted to equal justice and due process of law, Wells advised the *Gazette*'s Harry Smith that "not a scintilla of evidence" justified the prosecution of the champion. Johnson's marriage to Cameron disturbed Wells because of the bride's reputation, not her race. Other blacks shared this sentiment. On New Year's Eve, Johnson, without an invitation, brought his new wife to the annual ball of a black Illinois National Guard regiment. Guests hissed loudly at the couple, and officers politely but firmly told them to leave. It was an "unfriendly and hostile demonstration," eyewitness Julius Taylor reported, caused by Lucille's "past reputation" and "the wide publicity" given the recent marriage. "They must both learn," Taylor counseled, "that once in a while there are some things in this old wicked world that they cannot buy with all their money."

In another letter to Harry Smith, Wells praised those who had expelled the couple. "It has done more than any other one thing to win back some of the respect for the race which Jack Johnson's conduct has lost for it," she maintained. "It was something of an eye opener to the white man who believed that all Negroes were falling over themselves to associate with white people, especially white women, to realize that there were those who did not feel this a compliment and who did not propose to tolerate white women of unsavory reputations among them." The incident had opened Johnson's eyes as well, for he had assumed that "his money could take him to any function of Colored people" regardless of "his scandalous conduct."

Other eminent blacks joined the fray. Certain that "prejudiced and asinine daily newspaper sports writers" were "eager to filch from Jack Johnson a championship they can find no white man . . . to win," Harry Smith nevertheless agreed that bias against Johnson was no excuse for his boorish behavior among his own. With a bill to ban mixed marriages before the Ohio legislature, Smith alluded to his earlier warning. "As the *Gazette* predicted," Smith wrote, "our people of the north, particularly, are paying dearly for Jack Johnson's escapades."[31]

While black journalists bemoaned Johnson's "scandalous conduct" and "escapades," federal investigators pried further into his personal life, pursuing new leads and locating more witnesses for the upcoming trial. Officials wanted the court to act quickly because Belle Schreiber remained a problem. "The principal witness in the case is being cared for at considerable expense to the government, and there is constant danger that she may be located and tampered with by representatives of the defendant," J.A. Fowler, an aid to the attorney general, noted. "Now she is a willing witness," but "continued brooding over the probable notoriety and consequent embarrassment" from her upcoming testimony might make her forsake the prosecution.

Agents uncovered evidence that led to additional indictments for "sexual perversion." Anthony "Yank" Kenney, Johnson's former trainer, confided to investigators that he had once occupied a room next to Johnson and Schreiber in a cottage at Cedar Lake, Indiana, in 1909. Screams late in the night awakened Kenney. "Don't beat me anymore," he had heard Schreiber beg Johnson, "and I will do it, or do anything." Kenney, according to Chicago bureau chief Charles DeWoody, suspected that Johnson was "attempting unnatural practices."

Agents in Chicago watched Johnson closely. From coast to coast, investigators scrutinized old hotel registers, telegraph logs, and newspaper photographs. They searched for other people who knew about Johnson's interstate travels with white women. Agent Charles Sterling found the owner of the Chicago apartment building where Schreiber had set up her flat for prostitution. "Johnson paid the rent," the landlord recalled, and he remembered evicting Schreiber because "Johnson was creating too much disturbance by coming around under her window and honking his automobile horn whenever he wanted her to go out with him." In mid-March, Bruce Bielaski, acting director of the bureau, sent photographs of Schreiber to agent Frank Garbarino in Philadelphia to assist him in his interviews. He advised that the pictures "be carefully preserved" because Schreiber seemed "very fearful that they may get into the hands of newspaper men and be published."

Agent C.J. Scully questioned R.E. Patton, manager of a New York City burlesque show, who recalled some "trouble" with Johnson because of his "advances toward some of the girls of the chorus." In Philadelphia, the son of a former madam told an agent that his mother had fired a woman named Hattie McClay in 1908 "on learning that the girl was having intercourse with Johnson." He also disclosed Johnson's "intimate relations with a white girl named Ethel Perry . . . whom he was transporting from city to city and from state to state."[32]

Johnson's last hope for a dismissal disappeared when the Supreme Court upheld the constitutionality of the Mann Act in *Hoke and Economides v.*

United States and three related cases on February 24, 1913.[33] On March 12, Johnson met with Charles DeWoody and offered to plead guilty if he could pay a "substantial fine" but avoid prison. Johnson argued, DeWoody noted, that "his color" made it "impossible for him to secure a fair trial." Johnson explained that he had never received money from the prostitutes he knew. Citing precedents in which defendants had paid fines in lieu of prison terms for pleading guilty in similar cases, Johnson implored DeWoody to settle for a fine in return for his sparing the government expenses for a trial. DeWoody would not deal.[34]

Trials and Tribulations

Johnson went on trial before a jury of twelve white men in early May. But the court of public opinion had already convicted him. Did "his color" preclude "a fair trial," as he feared? Yes and no—his race handicapped him, but also working against him were the broad scope of the Mann Act, its ambiguity, the Supreme Court's willingness to sanction a poorly conceived law, and his own disregard for prevailing "sentiment among the herds." In *Athanasaw and Sampson v. the United States*, for example, the Court reviewed the case of two theater managers who, through an agent, had provided a railway ticket from Atlanta to Tampa for seventeen-year-old Agnes Couch. She had responded to a newspaper ad for singers and dancers at the managers' club. Couch did not have sexual relations during her brief stay in Tampa. She did, however, as she testified in a lower court, have a shock when she met young theater employees her first day who "at lunch . . . were all smoking, cursing, and using such language I couldn't eat." She also accused one manager of kissing and caressing her in her room. The Court sustained the men's convictions for violating the Mann Act, finding them guilty of bringing a "girl" of "modesty" into a setting "which might ultimately lead to that phase of debauchery which consisted in 'sexual actions.'" In other words, even though the managers had not seduced the girl or lured her into prostitution, they had exposed her to temptations conducive to sexual activity. The verdict stood because the 1910 law made the transport of any white female "for the purpose of prostitution or debauchery, or for any other immoral purpose" a crime. The Mann Act, the Court argued, was not limited to commercial vice, since its intent was "a more comprehensive prohibition." The Court upheld the sentences—thirty months in prison for Athanasaw, fifteen for Sampson.[35]

Jack Johnson also ran a club where drinking, smoking, and dancing were the usual fare—a setting that "might ultimately lead" to "prostitution or debauchery" or "other immoral purpose." With the precedent set by the Athanasaw case, a jury might find Johnson guilty even if the prosecuting attorneys proved only that he had paid to transport a dancer, singer, waitress, or private secretary across a state line to work for him who then engaged in any "immoral practice" in Chicago. Moreover, Johnson's cabaret was even more suspect because of its interracial clientele and the champion's frequent presence there.

The law as interpreted by the courts cast a wide net, and Johnson was a big fish. The police and courts acted within a cultural milieu of extreme race consciousness, pervasive racial and ethnic stereotypes, legal and casual discrimination, and rising fear. With Johnson's trial immanent, Justice Department officials had directed agents to do background checks on the jurors. A report by George Bragdon on William Ullrick of Evanston captured the climate of the time. Ullrick, agent Bragdon noted, had lived in Evanston "about 10 years" and held an interest in "two of the leading jewelry stores" there. "Well fixed financially," he owned "considerable real estate on the North Shore." A Republican of "Progressive tendencies" and "a strict churchman" (Episcopalian), Ullrick was "not inclined toward sports of any sort." Like "most of the residents and property-owners" in Evanston, Ullrick was "strongly prejudiced against negroes," for he suspected that their migration to the city had "cause[d] real estate to depreciate materially in value." Married with one child, "his reputation for honesty is of the best." Bragdon found no fault with Ullrick's views on race and property. On the contrary, he greatly admired him. "In brief," he assured his superiors, "Juror Ullrick would make an excellent juror from the point of view of the government."[36]

The prosecution's strategy emerged in Harry Parkin's opening statement. Rather than accuse Johnson of any blatant violation of the Mann Act, he condemnned him for transgressing basic standards of decency. Less obvious but equally important, Parkin noted that Johnson had habitually defied white preferences regarding black behavior. With his case so dependent on a career prostitute and forsaken mistress who had been the defendant's intimate companion for years, Parkin had to convince jurors that Johnson was capable of the most despicable deeds, including the interstate transport of women for prostitution and "debauchery." The white press, of course, had already helped prosecutors make that point. Parkin relied heavily on inference and innuendo, attacking Johnson's character more than his crime. Such an approach seemed likely to sway William Ullrick and his peers.

Parkin might not have read the antiblack writings of Professors Robert Bean and Howard Odum, and novelist Tom Dixon, but he held similar views. Blacks showed "instability of character," Bean had observed, and "lack of sexual control, especially in . . . the sexual relation." Odum had described blacks as "most carnal," with "thoughts . . . most filthy" and "morals . . . beyond description." Black males, Dixon hinted, had no greater ambition than to ravish white women. Parkin depicted Johnson as the epitome of such awful traits. "Upon one occasion in one city the defendant had three different white women, each of whom he was entertaining and having sexual intercourse with at the same time while he was exhibiting himself in that city," Parkin told the court. "He took these three women from various cities across the country at the same time, sometime in the same train." Parkin reminded jurors that Johnson was "a prize fighter" who used his ring skills in a peculiar way: "Very many times, when he either had a fit of anger," or when "these women who he carried about the country with him" refused to "do some of the obscene things which he demanded of them, that he practiced the manly art of self defense upon them." Often "blacking their eyes and sending them to hospitals," Johnson paid their medical bills "until they recovered from the wounds which he had inflicted upon the[ir] faces and bodies." Marriage meant nothing to him, for he continued to have sex with many white women even after he married, "some of them coming under the same roof where he kept his wife." Parkin let jurors connect the dots between Johnson's lechery and his wife Etta's suicide eight months earlier.

Consciously or unconsciously, Parkin demonized the defendant with pernicious stereotypes about blacks, particularly black men. These images were common in fiction, melodrama, advertising, and folklore. Like Dixon's former slaves who ran riot over their previous white guardians, Johnson defied nature when he beat white men and consorted with white women. Rather than use the word "entertain" or "perform" to describe Johnson's theatrical engagements, Parkin said Johnson had been "exhibiting" himself before mixed audiences, implying unseemly vanity and deviance. Skirting the ambiguous evidence of domestic abuse by Johnson, Parkin emphasized his resorting to violence "very, very many times" in "a fit of anger" or when he craved "obscene things" from his women. Like ethnologists who linked black "pathology" to small crania and arrested cognitive development, Parkin depicted Johnson as vain, volatile, lustful, and vicious. Similar to white historians who defended southern "redeemers" for having proscribed ex-slaves who seemed lazy, improvident, and amoral, Parkin stressed Johnson's unsavory profession, his unstable relationships, and his hedonism. He also alleged that Johnson had engaged in crooked fights. So he had not only cheated on his wife, he had cheated boxing fans as well. But his worst sins occurred behind closed doors and not in the open ring. He had carnal knowledge of many white women whom he forced to commit "the crime against nature." He violated, beat, and then discarded them. He was, in short, a savage.

Benjamin Bachrach, Johnson's counsel, tried to parry Parkin's opening statement, arguing that "it was no crime" for Johnson "to take a prostitute with him when he took a trip, to take her along and have intercourse with her on the train" prior to July 1, 1910, when the Mann Act became law. Yes, Johnson had furnished an apartment for Belle Schreiber in Chicago, Bachrach conceded, but that was no felony because Johnson did not intend for the flat to become a sporting house. Bachrach assumed that prosecutors would have to prove that Johnson knew that Belle Schreiber had intended to enter the skin trade and that he had paid her transportation for that very purpose. Since the initial target had been procurers and panderers, Bachrach thought that Johnson's guilt depended on whether he profited from Schreiber's business. As Bachrach well knew, Johnson gave money to Schreiber and did not receive it. At least in financial terms, the apartment at the Ridgewood was a loss to the champion, not a source of income extorted from white "slaves."

Following the opening statements, Parkin called his first witness to the stand. Lillian Paynter testified that Belle Schreiber had been a prostitute in her and her sister's Pittsburgh brothel in early 1910. "My sister put her out of the house because she heard that Belle was mixed up with a colored man," Paynter recalled, but she could not identify Jack Johnson as that man. Bertha Morrison, a Ridgewood resident also in the "sporting business," stated she had seen Johnson enter Schreiber's quarters "two or three times." Morrison and police officer John O'Halloran testified that the building housed many prostitutes. Leopold Moss, a merchant on Michigan Avenue, sold and delivered furniture worth $1,196.53 to "Miss Jacque Allen" in Ridgewood apartment 424. Jack Johnson, Moss remembered, paid the bill. (The invoice, submitted as evidence, included charges for four bed frames and four mattresses with springs. Johnson might have wondered why a single woman living alone needed four beds, but he apparently never asked.) These facts were obvious: Schreiber had crossed state lines to move to Chicago; she lived in a building well known for prostitution; Johnson had furnished her flat and called upon her there.

Prosecutors still needed Schreiber's testimony, however, to fill in their opening sketch of Johnson. To their great relief, he and his friends had never located her. After the bad pretrial publicity and Parkin's harsh portrayal, Schreiber needed only to supply the sordid details of her history with the defendant. She first saw Johnson, she recalled, when she was an Everleigh Club "inmate" in 1909, then later "met him frequently in New York, and had sexual intercourse with him." Johnson "paid the expenses of my trip," she added, "and my expenses in New York." The pattern continued in Boston, Providence, Rhode Island; Cedar Lake, Indiana; and Oakland, California. "In my travels with the defendant I went under the name of Mrs. Jack Johnson," Schreiber explained, "and registered at hotels under that name when I lived with him." But Johnson did not confine his attention to Schreiber—she remembered seeing him with "Hattie" in New York and again in Oakland. Johnson paid Schreiber's rail fare to Indianapolis, joined her there, and they proceeded to Pittsburgh. In various cities Johnson had one, two, even three white women with him. "This girl Hattie," Schreiber testified, "was living with him as his wife." Then Etta Duryea began to vie for Johnson's affections.

After Johnson defeated Jeffries on July 4, 1910 (three days after the Mann Act became law), he traveled to Atlantic City where he and Belle again shared a hotel room. They discussed the future. "He told me to come to Chicago, to look for an apartment; he said if I was sporting I might as well make the money for myself as to make it for others," Schreiber told the court. "He gave me the money to come to Chicago." Their peculiar partnership continued, even though "Etta Duryea was with the defendant" in Toronto. There Schreiber met Johnson "every day" for "the same relations." He gave her money to proceed to Montreal, where they reunited. Schreiber entered the Paynter sisters' brothel in Pittsburgh. Johnson later sent her $75, Schreiber stated, and she took the train to Chicago, found an apartment (Johnson paid the rent), hired "a sporting girl," and began to ply her trade. Johnson visited her there with predictable results.

Bachrach in his cross-examination probed Schreiber for details of a more complex relationship with Johnson than that of aggrieved white slave to cruel master, or even career prostitute to regular patron. While in New York "we became quite friendly," Schreiber admitted of her early days with Johnson. Bachrach then asked if she loved Johnson. "I don't know what love is," she replied in a line worthy of a blues singer. Schreiber conceded that she had sent a congratulatory telegram to Johnson after he beat Jeffries. "There was no reason for my sending him the telegram," she stated. "I did not want to bring myself to his notice again." But further queries revealed a good reason for keeping Johnson on a hook: She had, she confessed, phoned him "three or four times" for money when she was alone and desperate.

Upon dismissal from the Paynters' house, Schreiber had phoned Johnson for help. Johnson sent her a telegram and $75 to travel to Chicago, but she admitted she no longer had the telegram—or "any more friends" she could rely on for help: "I lost all my friends, and he was the only one I could turn to. I suppose I regarded him as my friend, too." A second time Bachrach asked if she loved Johnson. "I told you," she countered, "I did not know what love was."

Just as Parkin had tried to make Johnson repugnant to the jury, Bachrach now tried to smear Schreiber and show that her relationship with Johnson, however unsavory or immoral, did not make him a felon. In response to Bachrach's questions, Schreiber admitted she had been "in sporting houses in Chicago, New York, Pittsburgh, Washington, and Detroit." When pressed, she also disclosed that Bureau of Investigation agent Raymond Horn had conferred with her in Washington about her forthcoming testimony. Finally, she conceded that she had telegraphed Johnson again on September 14, 1912, to express condolences about Etta's suicide. Such a gesture also seemed inconsistent with her argument that she did not want to bring herself "to his notice again."

Parkin resumed his questioning, changing the focus from Schreiber's past and her feelings for Johnson to the champion's promiscuous and peevish ways. As Johnson discarded one woman for another, he reclaimed lavish gifts from the first to bestow upon the next. "The jewelry and the diamonds which the defendant Johnson gave me, he took them away from me," Schreiber recalled. "After he took them away from me, the next girl, Etta Duryea, was wearing them." Parkin asked if Hattie had also worn this jewelry. Bachrach objected that queries about Hattie were irrelevant, since that relationship had ended well before the Mann Act took effect. But Judge George Carpenter overruled. Schreiber then confirmed that Hattie had worn the very same jewels.

Parkin summoned Hattie "Watson" (McClay) to the stand, for no apparent reason other than to display yet another of Johnson's white whores to the court. Bachrach objected, but Carpenter overruled, granting Parkin "a right to show the general characteristics of the defendant along certain lines." When Parkin tried to elicit details about the relationship between Jack and Hattie back in 1907, however, Carpenter sustained Bachrach's objection—one of the few times the defense prevailed.

Johnson took the stand. "I did not, while in Atlantic City, tell Belle Schreiber that, inasmuch as she was engaged in the sporting business, it would be better for her to go into the business for herself," he objected, nor had he advised her "she should take an apartment and that I would furnish it for her in order that she might be in the sporting business." Moreover, "at the time I sent that $75.00," he explained, "I did not intend that Belle Schreiber should go from Pittsburgh to Chicago in order to engage in the business of prostitution. . . . I had no intention at all as to where Belle Schreiber should go from Pittsburgh, or if she should leave Pittsburgh at all. She didn't say where she was going, she said she was sick." Johnson estimated he had spent "between nine and ten thousand dollars" on Schreiber over the years, sometimes for gifts, often for expenses when they were together, occasionally for assistance when Schreiber was alone and in need. He added he had stopped "being attentive" to her in late 1910 because of his impending marriage to Etta.

Parkin asked Johnson if he had beaten Etta so badly that she needed hospitalization. He denied it. Parkin then asked if he and Schreiber had engaged in sex "in every town where you and she were together." "I don't remember," Johnson replied. "I never kept tab." Maybe Johnson did not keep "tab," but federal agents did. "Well, at one time, you had three of them together, didn't you?" Parkin taunted. "Didn't you have Hattie and Etta and Belle there [in Philadelphia in 1909] at the same time?" Johnson tried to evade the question by answering that he had known the witness "Hattie Watson" by the name "Anna McClay." Seeing the danger in Parkin's tactics, Bachrach protested against "the constant repetition about the women, and particularly the woman who was his wife and is now dead." He also objected to queries about Johnson's relationship with Etta prior to their marriage. The judge again sustained the prosecution. Parkin pressed his advantage. "The fact is that you had one or two or three women traveling around with you," he gibed, "and it didn't make much difference to you?" Johnson's counsel objected, again to no avail. Parkin then contended that the champion had knowingly participated in a fixed fight with Stanley Ketchel. Bachrach protested, and Carpenter sustained the objection. Then Parkin reared back and threw his knockout punch: "You had struck Belle on various occasions?" he asked. "Never in my life," Johnson replied. "Do you remember using an automobile tool on her?" Parkin asked. "Never in my life," Johnson repeated. Schreiber had informed agents of Johnson's insistence upon "perverted practices" and his resorting to "vicious beatings" to make her comply. Jack Kenna, a sparring partner, had also told federal agents of "a quarrel" in which "Johnson assaulted Schreiber."[37]

Parkin then questioned Roy Jones, a former saloonkeeper. Jones stated that Jack had beaten Etta and had asked him to go to the hospital to effect a reconciliation. Parkin asked Jones if Johnson had urged him to persuade Etta not to file assault charges. "Yes, sir," Jones replied. (Etta told nurses, however, that her bruises were the result of a nasty fall while climbing aboard a streetcar.)[38]

In his final plea Bachrach urged a dismissal on grounds that the Mann Act was unconstitutional. The states and not the federal government had the power to regulate vice. He also argued that prosecutors had failed to prove that Johnson himself had arranged Schreiber's travel to Chicago. Nor had he enticed Schreiber into the vice market in the city. And even though Schreiber had used money from Johnson to make her apartment into "a sporting house," she never shared her income with him. No evidence had surfaced that Johnson had lured other prostitutes to Chicago.

Judge Carpenter instructed the jury that "a colored man in the courts of this country has equal rights with a white man." As in all criminal cases, the defendant had a right to a "presumption of innocence" until proven guilty. "The prosecuting witness in this case is an abandoned woman . . . an unfortunate creature," Carpenter noted. "You might . . . call her the discarded mistress of the defendant." He then rendered his interpretation of the Mann

Act. "The law does not apply solely to innocent girls," he asserted. "It is quite as much an offense against the Mann Act to transport a hardened, lost prostitute as it would be to transport a young girl, a virgin." The judge stated that "pecuniary profit" from vice was not "an essential element at all" in determining guilt. The issue was whether Johnson "did cause the transportation" of Belle Schreiber across state lines in the autumn of 1910 for the purpose of prostitution or debauchery. Carpenter told the jurors to disregard the sexual perversion counts. The prosecution had withdrawn them for lack of evidence and squeamishness about delving into the more graphic details of Johnson's sexual practices.

On May 13, 1913, the jury found Johnson guilty on all seven remaining counts of the indictment. Three weeks later, Carpenter sentenced the champion to a year and a day in the penitentiary and a $1,000 fine. So a federal indictment, not a white hope's right hook, put Johnson on the ropes and knocked down the value of his title. Johnson could not fend off vengeful old enemies, tenacious bureau agents, determined prosecutors, and an aggrieved Belle Schreiber. Harry Parkin and federal agents had accomplished what Johnson's white opponents had failed to achieve. They had humbled the man with the golden smile and heavyweight crown.[39]

A few days after the trial, Martin Lins drove Belle Schreiber to the depot to catch a train to Pittsburgh. While Lins exchanged farewells with his key witness, a roadster carrying Jack Johnson roared up to the station. Lins initially feared that Johnson wanted revenge against Schreiber, but Lins then realized that Johnson was there to see off his good friend George Sutton, who had come to Chicago to help Johnson through his ordeal. Lins watched as Johnson walked beside the coaches and peered into the windows, hoping to catch a final glimpse of Schreiber and Sutton. Much to Lins's relief, Johnson did not board the train. Finally the engine kicked in and the train left the station, adding with each second physical space to the emotional distance between great white hope and grave black disappointment.[40]

Sutton and Schreiber both returned to Pittsburgh on that train—Sutton to resume managing his hotel where Julia Allen had first met Jack Johnson and Belle Schreiber and where Johnson had married Etta Duryea; Schreiber to put the sensational trial behind her and proceed with a life without Jack Johnson.

Interpreting the Champion's Conduct and Conviction

Johnson and Schreiber had stood in opposite corners in the court, but their professions gave them much in common. For both faced the looming prospect that younger rivals would soon take their business away. In the cruel

Darwinian world of prizefighting and prostitution, biology was indeed destiny, and Johnson, thirty-five, and Schreiber, twenty-six, did not have time on their side. Their livelihoods greatly influenced their lifestyles; their preoccupation with the present often made them foolhardy about the future. The strange relationship between them is best symbolized by Johnson behind the wheel of his roadster, Schreiber at his side, defying law and common sense by traveling down the road at breakneck speed in search of something neither could fully understand or explain. Their dubious callings and tastes epitomized the sporting life, a life inimical to solid and sober citizens, like William Ullrick, who maintained monogamous marriages, worked at unglamorous jobs for modest income, bought homes, raised children, went to church, obeyed the law, and admired temperance, restraint, and frugality. Many Americans would undoubtedly have preferred to see Schreiber as well as Johnson behind bars.

During and after the trial, black editors and columnists debated whether the government had prosecuted or persecuted Johnson. The lurid testimony had badly eroded his residual support in the black press. Some observers even detected a silver lining behind the cloud of his conviction, for incarceration would keep him from further indiscretions that would humiliate his race. Julius Taylor praised Judge Carpenter for being "more than extremely fair in dealing out justice" to Johnson. The *Chicago Defender* agreed, noting that it had only asked that Johnson receive "a fair and impartial trial." The paper expressed itself "satisfied" with the proceedings.[41]

But Harry Parkin caused second thoughts when he declared that the prosecution had been aimed at the whole race, not just Johnson. "This verdict will go around the world," Parkin gloated after the conviction.

> It is the forerunner of laws to be passed . . . forbidding miscegenation. This Negro, in the eyes of many, has been persecuted. Perhaps as an individual he was. But his misfortune is to be the foremost example of the evil in permitting intermarriage of whites and blacks. He has violated the law. Now it is his function to teach others the law must be respected.[42]

A startling admission, it raised doubts about just what "law" Johnson had "violated." The evidence on the Mann Act charge was inconclusive. But there was no denying Johnson had wed two white women, controversial but legal acts in Pennsylvania and Illinois. By crossing the color line for wives and paramours, Johnson had defied an unwritten "law" far more potent than those in the statute books. Prosecutors would take his freedom away so he could "teach others" about "the evil in . . . intermarriage."

The Reverend W.A. Byrd of Rochester, New York, labeled Parkin's statement "unworthy of a federal officer" and urged his dismissal. "He appears just as fit to be prosecuting federal attorney," Byrd added, "as Jack does champion of the world." Billy Lewis of the *Indianapolis Freeman* protested that Parkin's comments revealed that the case had little to do with "the charges preferred." Rather, "a race prejudice was the underlying motive of the prosecution . . . in the interest of the race division," an admission Lewis found "appalling." Writers at the *New York Age* felt more ambivalent. "There are no reasons," one writer counseled, "why we should waste any sentiment upon Johnson and the fate that has overtaken him." The disclosures about his "fast and loose" life disgusted the *Age* staff. "A man is entitled to one woman," an editorial noted, and "neither the law nor public opinion justifies him in having one woman and many prostitutes—a sort of lord of his harem." But when Parkin called the verdict an edict against race mixing, the *Age* took a new tack. Editorials now complained about "excessive bail," the haste in trying Johnson, and "the petty annoyances and persecutions" by bureau agents and the district attorney. "Johnson was a black and had no pull," the *Age* grumbled. "[T]he word went along, spoken or understood, to nail him to the indictment without delay or mercy, and it was done." Les Walton found plenty of blame to go around. "No race should be judged by the actions of a prize fighter," he protested, "but the Negro race has been unfortunately placed in such a position." The champion's "indiscretion" had "done his race much harm."[43]

For weeks newspapers across the nation printed articles and editorials about the trial and its lessons. Blacks had hailed Johnson as a symbol of racial redemption who epitomized their aspirations for excellence and their will and ability to achieve it. Now, however, he seemed a heavy burden to the race, a fallen idol who reinforced racist images rather than refuting them. Johnson had, as George Nathan and H.L. Mencken would observe a few years later, impressed upon the American mind that black prizefighters always married white women and then beat them. Johnson's trial and his conviction for "enslaving" white women symbolized the dreadful decline of African Americans in the white mind by the eve of World War I. The race had indeed, as Paul Lawrence Dunbar wrote in 1903, "fall'n on evil days," with Johnson and his people facing hostility and exclusion "amid a tempest of dispraise."

3

"Under the White Man's Menace"
Divisive Wars at Home and Abroad

For I was born, far from my native clime,
Under the white man's menace, out of time.[1]

—Claude McKay, "Outcast," 1922

With the august manner of a revered leader or war hero, the tall, imposing man stepped from the train to bask in the adulation of a large, enthusiastic crowd. Thousands of white men, women, and children strained to see him, while rambunctious admirers jostled one another to shake his hand and express their gratitude. It was April 1915, a half-century after the terrible swift sword of the Union Army had vanquished the Confederacy and slashed a pathway to freedom for the slaves. But the towering man at the station in Jacksonville, Florida, this spring day had not commanded troops in the Civil War. He had, however, shed his blood in a recent battle of great significance to the nation and its people.

A wealthy and eminent man approached the hero and patted him on the back. "Lincoln emancipated the Negro," he mused, "but you . . . emancipated the white man." The scene in Jacksonville was repeated in several cities. The victory train, a *New York Times* correspondent reported, met "one continuous ovation" as it traveled through Dixie. In Richmond, Virginia, "several hundred enthusiasts on the station platform" shook the man's massive right hand—the one that had recently decked Jack Johnson in Havana to win the heavyweight title. For a respite from the crowd, Jess Willard retired to his private berth. But fans boarded the train and found him. "Excuse me for not getting up," he explained as people filed by. "I am resting." A small boy understood. "You can rest," the boy assured him, "for the remainder of your life, Mr. Willard." Tired of shaking hands, Willard bandaged his fist and placed his arm in a sling. The new champion now felt the adulation that had eluded Jim Jeffries in 1910. By defeating Johnson, Willard had brought the era of "great white hopes" to an end. William Rocap, a reporter from Philadelphia, watched as effusive whites hailed Willard along the entire eastern seaboard. He predicted Willard would be "the most popular champion . . . ever."[2]

Whether Willard would fulfill Rocap's prediction remained to be seen, but there was little doubt that Johnson had become the least popular champion to date. Whites who resented his prominence and abhorred his conduct welcomed his fall. Many blacks had also turned against him, for the revelations about his personal life during his trial in 1913 had disgusted Americans of all hues. His loss to Willard also raised doubts about his boxing skills. Blacks had rejoiced at Johnson's ascent, but, ironically, many now felt relief at his fall. Some in the black press still blamed race prejudice for Johnson's defeats both in and out of the ring. Whatever the origin of Johnson's travails, there was no denying that white efforts to proscribe and punish blacks had intensified during his tumultuous reign.

Jack Johnson as Public Enemy

Johnson's "white slavery" trial had become a morality play on interracial intimacy and the supposed need to protect white women from black men, and Johnson's eclipse would make it more difficult for him to attract white women. "The stories of the women are pitiable," chief prosecutor Harry Parkin sighed. "Why they fell they cannot explain." Judge George Carpenter thought the court could use Johnson to serve a higher purpose. "The circumstances in this case have been aggravating," he observed. "The life of the defendant by his own admission has not been at all a moral one." Johnson was "one of the best known men of his race and his example has been far-reaching." By sending Johnson to prison Carpenter hoped to deter other black men from consorting with white women.

District Attorney James Wilkerson also depicted Johnson as a public enemy. Opposed to a reversal or any mitigation of the prison sentence, Wilkerson told the court of appeals that the lower court had shown "marked leniency" toward Johnson "under circumstances of great aggravation." Like Parkin, Wilkerson wanted the state to use the case to demonstrate its resolve to protect vulnerable citizens from predators like Johnson. His "parade around the country with this strumpet had been an open, brazen, defiant, bestial spectacle, offensive to public decency and destructive of every sense of public virtue," Wilkerson declared. "The fact that it was tolerated as long as it was reflects little credit on our civilization."[3]

Many white Americans felt their "civilization" imperiled at this time—by a deluge of new immigrants from southern and eastern Europe, by Asians settling in the West, and by blacks everywhere. Senator James Vardaman of Mississippi, for example, defended whites in California who wanted to prohibit Japanese Americans from owning land. Denying any "feeling of hostility toward the Japanese or the Negro," he did admit being "deeply interested in maintaining the purity of the Caucasian race and the preservation of Anglo-Saxon civilization." No amount of Asian trade could compensate for racial mixing. "Race purity is indispensable to Caucasian supremacy," Vardaman argued in 1913, "and the only way to maintain that supremacy is to prohibit by law the comingling of the races."

Some westerners echoed the southerners' pleas for "race purity" and "Caucasian supremacy." When a crisis emerged over the segregation of children of Japanese descent in the San Francisco schools, Senator Francis Newlands of Nevada stressed the need "to maintain this country as the home of the white race." In 1909 Newlands had noted that Americans were "finding it difficult to assimilate even the immigrants of the white race" from Europe. To make matters worse, the nation had "drifted into a condition regarding the black race which constitutes the great problem and peril of the future." To the west lay Asia, "with nearly a billion people . . . who, if there were no restrictions, would quickly settle upon and take possession of our entire coast and intermountain region." Both "race amalgamation" and "race war and mutual destruction" threatened the nation's well being. To ensure "self-protection and self-preservation," Congress should allow "existing treaties" to expire, Newlands advised, then pass laws to restrict immigration to "the white race" only, with minor exceptions for "international commerce, travel, and education."

At the Democratic Convention in 1912, Newlands introduced a plank to the party platform "declar[ing] our purpose to maintain this as a white man's country" by adopting "a constitutional amendment confining the privilege of voting to the white race" as well as "legislation prohibiting the immigration to this country of all peoples other than those of the white race." Newlands wanted to send blacks back to Africa. "Our whole policy regarding the blacks since the war has been a mistaken one," he argued, for "their sudden elevation from . . . slavery to . . . political sovereignty was a cruel injury both to them and to the white race." Blacks in 1865 had been "entitled to vocational training and to intelligent and humane assistance in emigration from this country to the land of their origin" but nothing more. The postwar failure to colonize blacks, Newlands complained, had enabled them to grow to some

12 million, "whose constantly increasing numbers threaten our race integrity and our institutions." Republicans should have promoted black emigration, not civil rights. The disdain expressed by Newlands for Radical Reconstruction had become a common refrain among whites in all regions.[4]

The Democrats did not adopt Newlands's planks. But after the inauguration of Woodrow Wilson in early 1913, leaders moved quickly to diminish the clout and status of the nation's black population. Wilson and his advisers, for example, dismissed virtually all the prominent blacks who held federal patronage jobs and replaced them with whites. Wilson also sanctioned segregation in federal departments, most notably in the Postal Service under Albert Burleson of Texas and the Treasury under William McAdoo, Georgia born and a longtime resident of Tennessee. Dismay at the rapid purge of blacks in government temporarily united Booker T. Washington and W.E.B. DuBois. When Wilson removed Henry Furniss as minister to Haiti and nominated a former Missouri congressman to replace him, Washington called the administration "hopeless." He visited the capital to assess how his people felt about the impact of the Democrats' course. After "several days" in the city, Washington informed Oswald Garrison Villard that he had "never seen the colored people so discouraged and bitter." A staunch Republican, Washington reacted in a predictably partisan way. But DuBois, disillusioned with Roosevelt and Taft, had endorsed Wilson in 1912. Six months into Wilson's term, he realized that "the new freedom" would not include blacks. "Every enemy of the Negro race is greatly encouraged . . . every man who dreams of making the Negro race a group of menials and pariahs is alert and hopeful," DuBois wrote. "Vardaman, Tillman, Hoke Smith, Cole Blease and Burleson are evidently assuming that their theory of the place and destiny of the Negro race" was becoming the guiding principle of Wilson and his cabinet.[5]

Wilson's approach to blacks in the federal service accelerated a trend already begun by his predecessors. Roosevelt had hastily dismissed black soldiers for the Brownsville shooting in 1906 and sanctioned the move for a whites-only Progressive Party in the South in 1912. Taft had decided not to appoint persons to office who would be unacceptable to residents in the area where the official would serve, so the number of black appointees in the South had declined steadily during his term. Wilson took the process further, accelerating the dismissal of blacks and permitting his advisers to segregate the few that remained. The token patronage jobs previously available to blacks seemed doomed to extinction.

Now even more "discouraged and bitter," blacks interpreted Jack Johnson's plight in terms of this resurgence in racist ideas and policies. Though they might frown upon Johnson's conduct, they still had reason to view his conviction and sentence as prejudicial. Some skeptics doubted whether Johnson had violated the law and thought his stiff sentence hardly fit his "crime." Billy Lewis of the *Indianapolis Freeman* dismissed the indictment under the Mann Act as "an afterthought" and blamed Johnson's ordeal on "his known relation to white women." Recognizing the champion's symbolic importance, Lewis warned that his imprisonment would be "the biggest calamity to the race" since slavery. Editor George Knox agreed that prosecutors had used Johnson against his people. "As a Negro, a member of a despised race, he has been meted out a terrible punishment," Knox protested, "for daring to exceed what is considered a Negro's [proper] circle of activities." Judge Carpenter's decision to imprison Johnson seemed consistent with rising white animus and increasingly repressive racial policies. "The whole business," Lewis objected, was meant to remind "black folk" that they must accept their subordination. Still mulling over the case months later, Lewis explained that Johnson had committed a "trinity of unpardonables making for sin trip-licate": "His chief sin is being a Negro. Next he whipped a white man. Next he married a white woman."[6]

The *Chicago Defender*'s Robert Abbott objected to chief prosecutor Parkin's assertion that the white women linked to Johnson had been pure victims. "Note he doesn't say why they fell before they met Johnson," Abbott protested, "leaving the impression that they were veritable angels previous to that." As a matter of personal preference, Abbott frowned upon mixed marriages, but he opposed the Illinois legislature's efforts to ban them. Blacks must "demand the privileges accorded any other citizen," he advised, and should "fight to the bitter end any infringement of our rights."

The Reverend W.A. Byrd chastised Johnson for his "indecent career with women of the underworld" but also denounced Parkin for his prejudicial conduct. Fred Moore's *New York Age* doubted the impartiality of the Justice Department. A few weeks after the verdict, Attorney General Samuel McReynolds intervened to delay the Mann Act trial of Drew Caminetti, son of Antonio Caminetti, an immigration commissioner in San Francisco. Justice Department officials had pressed for a hasty trial for Johnson. The contrast between the two cases suggested that color, not crime, was the real issue. Unlike the Caminettis, Johnson had "no pull," the *Age* complained, so prosecutors sought to "nail him to the indictment without delay or mercy" and won a quick conviction. Les Walton believed that "the prevalence of Negrophobia" was Johnson's chief liability, although Walton did not absolve Johnson of blame. "Even had he not erred in judgment," Walton concluded, "his color . . . would have operated against him."[7]

In retrospect, Johnson thought his only "crime" had been winning the title, being assertive with white promoters, and beating Jeffries. "The search for the 'white hope' not having been successful, prejudices were being piled up against me," he wrote in his memoir. "And certain unfair persons, piqued because I was champion, decided that if they could not get me one way they would another." They resorted to "all sorts of efforts . . . to brand me as an undesirable character and to relegate me to obscurity." His indictment was "a rank frame up" based upon an "accusation . . . unfounded." His foes used "fraudulent practices" in a "bitter and intense . . . fight" to topple him. The vendetta appalled him. "My character and life were being torn to pieces in the newspapers," he complained. The calumny was "far worse than the prospect of the year in prison that awaited me." If the prospect of incarceration did not alarm Johnson, it nevertheless horrified his mother. "My mother told me," he recalled, "that she would rather that I die than that I go to prison." Johnson had occupied a municipal jail cell on occasion, but his mother viewed a long stint in the federal penitentiary as quite another matter.

Many blacks, including some former fans, wished that Johnson would simply go away. Julius Taylor of the *Chicago Broad-Ax* thought that the champion "sadly needs some kind of restraint or a guardian to prevent him from squandering his money upon white ladies whom no decent gentleman black nor white would wipe their dirty feet on." Taylor had heard that Johnson was the only black man ever to be entertained at the Everleigh Club. To gain entrée there, he had "flashed up and blew well onto two thousand dollars" so he could briefly be "on a social equality with the white ladies and gentlemen who frequented that high-toned club." In spite of his pending appeal, Johnson remained "a regular public pest" as he tore through Chicago "in his big touring car" and endangered "the lives of men, women and little children." Taylor advised Johnson to "establish his residence in some other city."[8]

Exile

Johnson decided by late June to flee the country. With long odds for a reversal, Johnson chose Paris over Joliet Prison. How he managed—whether by pure accident or secret agreement—to evade surveillance to purchase train and steamer tickets and flee from Chicago to Europe via Canada remains a mystery. Johnson's own tale varied with each telling. Bureau of Investigation records do not reveal how or why agents lost track of him. On June 27, 1913, Bruce Bielaski, the Bureau of Investigation director in Washington, informed Charles DeWoody, head of the bureau's Chicago office, that Canadian authorities, after consulting with the Justice Department, had decided not to hold or return Johnson, since present extradition treaties did not cover the Mann Act. Besides, Johnson possessed a ticket to Liverpool, so he was only a transient in Canada. Attorney General McReynolds asked United States Attorney James Wilkerson if Johnson's trip violated his bond agreement and what (if anything) could be done to retrieve him. Wilkerson thought Johnson could be detained as an "unfit subject" until returned to the states. But DeWoody replied that Johnson's bail agreement did not require him to remain within the court's jurisdiction. In the meantime, Johnson telegraphed the Chicago office and pledged to return for his appeal. The conduct of the Justice Department seems strange, to say the least. The government had devoted considerable time and money to investigate, prosecute, and convict Johnson. Yet officials showed surprisingly little curiosity about how Johnson had wiggled off the hook. In the absence of hard facts and reasonable explanations, speculation and rumors abounded.[9]

After interviewing Johnson in Paris in 1914, the *Chicago Examiner* accused federal officers of taking bribes and letting him escape. The *Examiner* printed facsimiles of checks from Johnson's friends to men handling his case, and the allegations forced Wilkerson to convene a grand jury to consider the matter. Jennie Rhodes, Johnson's sister, testified that her brother had complained about officials "bleeding him to death." The charge of abduction had been "a frame up," Rhodes argued, for Lucille Cameron's mother had been "induced to come here and make complaint against Jack to help the federal and state officials get some of his money." Johnson had paid her and her lawyer to drop the charges. Both Rhodes and Jack's mother swore that he and Sol Lewinsohn, his agent, had given thousands of dollars to federal officials during the Mann Act ordeal. "He said that the case cost him $60,000 and that the government got the most of it," Rhodes stated. "He was frequently called by telephone and would say that it was . . . DeWoody talking and that he had to go . . . see him." Upon his return, Johnson would mutter "that DeWoody or some other official was demanding money."

Jack and Jennie had gone to Lewinsohn's office a week before he fled to Canada. "Jack and Lewinsohn discussed the payment of $5,000 to Harry A. Parkin," Rhodes alleged, "in return for which Parkin was to permit Jack to leave the country without hindrance." Evalyn Kritzinger, who worked in the district attorney's office, testified that Jack and Lucille had told her "they were going to pay . . . officials what they wanted and would be permitted to escape because money was all the officials wanted." Attorney John Wayman "told me he and the government officials received $10,000," Kritzinger recalled. "He named Charles DeWoody as one of those who got part of the money." The grand jury, however, halted the probe and issued no indictments, accepting the explanation that the large "loans" from Lewinsohn to those close to the case were merely coincidental. Wilkerson advised McReynolds that there was "no ground" to punish any federal employee. He expressed "serious doubt" about the "mental responsibility" of those behind the allegations.[10]

At first Johnson did not link his escape to timely bribes to officials. He bragged that he had simply outsmarted them. Johnson bore a striking resemblance to Bill Gatewood of the Chicago American Giants, a Negro League baseball team. Posing as Gatewood, Johnson said, he boarded the train as the players departed for upstate New York via Canada on an extended road trip. Johnson reached Montreal safely, and Gatewood later caught up with his teammates. Both men had a bit of the trickster in them. During warm-ups, according to Negro League lore, Gatewood would stand by the dugout in full view of the crowd, raise a jug of corn whiskey to his lips, and drain it before swaggering to the mound. He would then pitch nine solid innings unfazed by his ritual. A rookie asked him about the jug. "This is only water," Gatewood chuckled. "The people think it's liquor, and they are amazed how I can still pitch. It's all for show."

Johnson also had a taste for humbug and a flair "for show." To deceive agents watching him, he explained, he had hired a man of similar stature to stay at his home, wear his clothes, and appear in the window and on the porch so agents would think he remained under wraps. Taking advantage of the mistaken identities, Johnson left his ringer in full view of agents while he sneaked to the train station. To avoid suspicion, his wife and friends remained behind. They reunited in Canada, then sailed across the Atlantic. Johnson had secretly shipped a few prized automobiles ahead so he would have familiar wheels abroad. The scheme unfolded just as he had planned. Having used his physical skills to defeat the white hopes, he now used his wits to foil his white oppressors.[11]

Johnson embellished his story over time, and the black press printed each new version as the truth. The lack of corroborative evidence, however, makes his explanation suspect. Most details about the ruse appeared in interviews Johnson gave in exile and in his selective and self-serving memoir. Johnson often exaggerated or invented tales to enhance his image or attain some advantage. Hoping for a pardon or leniency should he return home after World War I, for example, Johnson maintained that he had been a secret agent tracking German submarines at Spanish ports and off the Iberian coast. He claimed renown as a matador. Johnson also revised his story about his loss to Willard. In exchange for clemency upon his return, he forfeited the title. But like the escape from Chicago, Johnson's account of the fix in Havana lacked specifics on just who promised what to whom and why.[12]

What seems most probable is that officials on the case decided that Johnson in exile abroad was politically preferable to Johnson in prison at home. Even before the trial began, federal officials had wondered what Johnson might do. Charles DeWoody, for example, warned Judge Carpenter of rumors that Johnson intended to visit Canada. Carpenter replied that such a trip would not violate Johnson's bail agreement, but added that the champion might seek asylum abroad if the Supreme Court upheld the Mann Act in a pending decision. "I believe we all agree with the Court on the advantage to the Country if Johnson were to be exiled from it," DeWoody conceded, "but do not believe this is in justification . . . for allowing him to escape jurisdiction." Johnson had gone to trial, however, and lost.

But the mounting complaints in the black press about his harsh sentence must have concerned government observers. Woodrow Wilson and his advisers had already alienated black editors and activists. Since *Plessy v. Ferguson* in 1896, blacks had steadily lost faith in the federal courts. If black editors and columnists portrayed the trial as prejudicial and defined Johnson's prison sentence as an affront to the entire race, angry African Americans might unite in protest, perhaps even riot, when the door slammed shut on Johnson's cell.

Fears of racial violence were hardly far-fetched in 1913, since memories of Atlanta, Brownsville, and Springfield remained etched in leaders' minds. Even though Johnson had disappointed his people, he remained an important symbol to them. "We, the Negroes, have so little by way of triumph to make us merry over," Billy Lewis reasoned, "that we religiously cling to our lone pugilistic hero." When Johnson successfully defended his title against Frank Moran in Paris, a sportswriter for the *Philadelphia Tribune* admitted that 90 percent of "self-respecting colored citizens" deplored the champion's morals. Yet he urged blacks to "rejoice" in the victory because when Johnson lost the title whites would draw the color line. "We are compelled by force to share his faults," the writer advised, so "let us accept his virtues, even though they be questionable." Blacks derived some satisfaction from Johnson's exacting a measure of revenge in the ring. Inverting an aphorism captures Johnson's appeal: "If you can't join 'em, beat 'em."[13]

Fleeing abroad spared Johnson from a prison cell in 1913, but his exile was no triumphal tour. The big money in boxing was in the United States. Johnson's few bouts in Europe aroused scant interest. Other developments preoccupied the continent in 1913 and 1914, as intense imperial rivalries and deep ethnic divisions triggered a war of unprecedented magnitude and fury. For their part, Americans habitually ignored events overseas, whether diplomatic or athletic, and Johnson had become old news. "Now that Jack Johnson has gone," the *Defender* quipped, "perhaps President Wilson will get the front page of the papers."[14]

Johnson tried to emulate European aristocrats, but his tastes exceeded his income and status. Moreover, his reputation at home had influenced feelings about him abroad. Europeans, especially the British, had welcomed Frederick Douglass, Harriet Jacobs, and other former slaves who had espoused abolitionism—a receptivity that led African Americans to conclude that white Europeans lacked the harsh prejudices of their New World counterparts. But Johnson was no Douglass, and he soon wore out his welcome. Perhaps Europeans did judge Americans on character and not color, but whatever the measuring stick, British, French, and Russian officials all decided that Johnson and his entourage should live somewhere beyond their borders.

Johnson found Spain the most congenial refuge, but its people preferred bullfighting to boxing, and he made *poco dinero* there. Certain black newspapers romanticized his life as an expatriate, extolling the supposed freedom and equality Johnson enjoyed away from his racist homeland. The effusive reports on race relations and the exiles' happiness abroad contained as much fiction as fact, largely because Johnson or Gus Rhodes, his nephew, supplied them. Their dispatches from Europe usually functioned as indirect or explicit denunciations of their native land.

Yet Johnson discovered what other Americans of African ancestry realized for generations before and after him—the United States was home and his people had no other. "The land of the free and the home of the brave" was not fully free, nor particularly brave in resolving its racial problems, but by the time Johnson crossed the Atlantic in 1913 seven generations of his people had made the country their own. Laws in the South and custom in the North had often denied them ownership of the land, but over time the land had come to possess them. As slaves, subjects, and free people of color, Americans of African origin had played a vital role for nearly three centuries in the remarkable transformation of a struggling colony into a major world power.

Before abolition in 1865 and long after, Americans as dissimilar as Thomas Jefferson and Paul Cuffee, Abraham Lincoln and Martin Delany, Francis Newlands and Marcus Garvey, Theodore Bilbo and Afred Charles Sam advocated the relocation of the nation's black population to Africa or Latin America. But the colonization plans met firm resistance from most black leaders and their white allies who remained committed to a diverse and inclusive society. Despite the long history of hardships and dangers on American soil, few prominent blacks viewed the oppressive past as the inescapable future. Free blacks in Wilmington, Delaware, for example, had denounced the American Colonization Society in 1831. "That Africa is neither our nation nor home, a due respect to the good sense of the community forbids us to attempt to prove," they protested. "That our language, habits, manners, morals and religion are all different from those of Africans, is a fact too notorious to admit of controversy." Their petition recommended "education and improvement" for blacks instead of "any system of colonization that has been or can be introduced." Frederick Douglass also opposed black expatriation in 1862, dismissing calls for colonization as "the madness of the moment" that had "drowned the voice of common sense as well as common justice." Jack Johnson spoke ill of his country and its white majority early in his exile, but his experience abroad and the passage of time eventually softened his criticism of his native land.[15]

Upon arrival in Europe Johnson announced he would return to Chicago for his appeal. "I have done no wrong, the whole world is with me and I am over here to make some money," he told a *Defender* correspondent in France on July 10, 1913. "I have never had any idea of running away." But an August 5 dispatch carried a different message. "Johnson has publicly announced in Paris," the source observed, "that he has no intention of returning . . . to stand trial again." At a London hall later that month, Johnson "refused to perform under an American flag," a report noted. "He directed that it be removed and replaced with the French flag." Johnson told the audience he was innocent; his only crime was beating Jeffries. In September the Johnsons went to Vienna, where Jack boxed exhibitions and danced the tango with Lucille. "The audience goes wild," a dispatch gushed. "Johnson is in Europe to enjoy its freedom," a later wire from Budapest noted. "Who can blame him?"

Johnson issued a challenge to all remaining white hopes. "The public wants a white man to be my successor," he told Frank Young, the *Defender* sports editor. "I am ready to fight 'em all . . . at $30,000 apiece." Training to fight Frank Moran, Johnson assured fans that his trial and travels had not impaired his skills. "Johnson claims he is in the best condition of his ring career," a correspondent noted, "and he is telling his friends to bet their bankrolls upon him." But Young did not see much enthusiasm for Johnson in Chicago. "Few people bet on the fight and those who would have bet could get no takers without long odds," he explained. "Little money . . . changed hands." Johnson beat Moran on June 27, 1914, in Paris. Gus Rhodes reported that fans from Senegal, Dahomey, and the French West Indies had cheered heartily for Johnson. "The champion wore the colors of France," Rhodes stated. "French men and French women, who were present in great numbers, were with Jack Johnson."[16]

The roar of the guns of August captured Americans' attention, and with news of war came reports of one American's devotion to France. Johnson "has shown his allegiance to the French flag by offering his services to fight for that country," the *Defender* noted. "A letter received at this office today" reported that he "has been made colonel of a regiment of French soldiers." The letter lied; Johnson's only battle in France was against his waistline. Later that month, Johnson ventured to Moscow but fled because of the widening war. Billy Lewis urged Johnson to stay in Europe despite the growing perils. He had "saved the Negroes the deep humiliation that would have followed his imprisonment," Lewis observed. His persecution and exile had made him "a martyr to his people."

The ravages of war virtually halted prizefighting in Europe. Hoping to replenish depleted coffers, Jack, Lucy, and Gus headed for South America in early 1915. Addressing the Brazil Board of Commerce, Johnson resumed his anti-American tirade—a tune sure to please Latin Americans weary of "big stick" diplomacy and *Yanquí* exploitation of native riches. "Their lives are not their own," Johnson said of his people back home, "and when shot down by one man in the South the papers never speak of it, but when a mob lynches one the whole press, big and small, clap their hands for joy." His audience needed no reminders of *gringo* bias. From the Mexican War in 1846 to the interventions in Panama in 1902 and Nicaragua in 1912, American leaders had acted on the premise that peoples south of the Rio Grande lacked the genius to sustain stable governments and sound economies. Johnson broached the idea of starting a company that would purchase land and invite African Americans to resettle in Mexico—"the best place in the world for our people."[17]

Promoter Jack Curley hoped to match Johnson against Jess Willard, the most promising of the white hopes, in Mexico but found himself caught in the crossfire between rivals vying for power. Eager to gain United States aid in the struggle for control of the Mexican government, General Venustiano Carranza, a leader of one rebel faction, pledged that his troops would seize and remand Johnson to American officials if he crossed through territory under the general's control. "Will the champ risk his precious carcass by going to Juarez?" Billy Lewis asked. "I dare say he needs that additional $30,000 and extras. He lives in such a splendid state that his wad melts like snow in the summer time." Johnson coveted the money but wanted to avoid capture and extradition. Uneasy about the turmoil, Curley contacted people in Cuba about holding the fight there.[18]

Curley and Johnson were not the only Americans watching developments in Mexico and Cuba. Federal agents awaited a chance to nab him. Frederick Guy in El Paso, for example, warned bureau headquarters that Johnson might head for Juarez via southern Texas "disguised as a porter on a Pullman car." Agent L.C. Wheeler discussed Johnson's situation with Billy Birch, a sports editor at the *Chicago Herald* who expected to cover the fight. Birch told Wheeler that experts "in sporting circles" knew that Johnson was "about broke" after failing "to make any money" in Europe. Birch expected his next fight to be "a frame up," since he now needed money more than the title. Johnson was "heavily in debt," Birch observed, with prospects for lucrative fights abroad "very gloomy." Hinton Clabaugh, DeWoody's successor in the bureau's Chicago office, informed Chief Bielaski that he and Wheeler had "every confidence" in Birch and considered him "an excellent authority." To recoup his fortunes, Johnson intended to throw the fight for a "considerable" sum beyond "the stipulated percentage of the gate receipts." In addition, Johnson would win by losing because films of a Willard triumph would attract more whites to the theaters and earn much more money.

Johnson's plight made agents optimistic. "I believe somehow I can on one pretext or another," Clabaugh assured Bielaski, "get Johnson back on American soil and into custody." Bielaski replied that the bureau had "already taken steps to secure his return to the United States." Concerned about the "pretext" Clabaugh might use to snare Johnson, Bielaski "very much opposed . . . any agreement with this defendant whereby he would pay a fine with no jail or penitentiary sentence." Agent Robert Barnes in San Antonio encouraged Bielaski to keep him posted on Johnson's whereabouts. But when Curley gave up on Mexico and moved the bout to Cuba, he deprived agents in Texas of a chance to apprehend Johnson.

Cuban officials permitted Johnson to enter the country. Changing tactics, the Justice Department hoped to persuade authorities in Havana to expel Johnson as an undesirable alien. But Robert Lansing, State Department counsel, advised Attorney General James McReynolds that his department preferred to stay out of the matter. Cuban authorities were under no obligation to extradite a "white slaver," so the State Department had no diplomatic leverage to pry Johnson loose. Johnson again evaded capture and remained free—free to defend his title and free to lose it.[19]

Johnson had eluded Uncle Sam but could not evade Father Time. Sportswriters noted that youth had been in Johnson's corner when he fought Jeffries—Johnson was thirty-two, Jeffries thirty-five. But now Willard would possess that advantage. Deeply disappointed by Jeffries' loss in 1910, Rex Beach had mused about the odds against an older fighter. "The march of Time cannot be disputed," Beach wrote after the fight. "With some men he locks arms and trips swiftly down the path and with others he idles by the wayside like some love-shy maiden, but his feet are ever turned in the same direction; his progress may be slow, but it is sure." Gamblers in Reno had lost "little fortunes" in "gilded palaces," Beach reflected, but no loss at the tables "could have been like that of Jeffries when he called upon his youth and found that it had slipped away." Now, Johnson, at thirty-eight, had no youth to call upon as he faced Willard, who was twenty-seven.

Ring mavens still admired Johnson's skills but could not ignore his age and condition. Johnson faced the "hoodoo of years," wrestler Tex O'Rourke observed, for he had reached the point at which many champions had fallen to younger challengers. Johnson had defeated a few mediocre opponents in recent years, Billy Lewis argued, but Willard was better than they and had "almost an even chance to win." Tom Flanagan, who had trained and managed Johnson early in his career, noted that his fighter had generally taken "good care of himself." Yet Flanagan too expressed concern. "All the same age is age, and there is no elixir for it," he conceded. If Willard survived the early rounds, he stood "a great chance" of winning. "Time will tell," Flanagan predicted, for if Willard had "any real claim to being a first class man," his triumph would demonstrate again "that age is a more formidable rival than man in the ring game."

Johnson summoned Flanagan to Cuba to help him in his final days of training. Like the fans who had favored Jeffries in 1910, Flanagan now defied conventional wisdom and declared Johnson a formidable foe. "Willard cannot stand what Johnson has to offer in that first round," he bragged. "I am sure that he will win." Flanagan posted a $10,000 wager on the champion at 8 to 5 odds. Johnson exuded his usual confidence. White hopes had tried before and failed. "They say that I must win inside of an hour," Johnson scoffed on April Fool's day. "Baah! He can't last an hour!"[20]

Johnson vs. Willard

The Black Tenth Regiment had won distinction in its offensive against Spanish troops in Cuba in 1898, especially in the celebrated battle at San Juan Hill. But Johnson would find it hard to duplicate the feat of those "buffalo soldiers." Too old and too confident, Johnson at 6'1/2" and 235 pounds found himself on April 5 opposite a white hope of vast proportions and power—6' 6" tall, 245 pounds, a reach that exceeded the champion's by ten inches. Unlike the Spanish soldiers who capitulated quickly to the American troops in 1898, Willard had stamina as well as strength. And unlike Johnson's weaker rivals, Willard might withstand those legendary jabs while patiently wearing Johnson down. Time favored Jess over Jack, not only in age but also in Willard's capacity to recuperate between rounds and retain his punch if the fight became a marathon of pain.

The Mariano racetrack some ten miles from Havana hosted the bout. Cubans comprised most of the audience, with a smattering of Americans here and there. On the hillsides outside the track, Cubans unable to pay for tickets — some sharing Johnson's hue—gathered to watch the fight. Platforms near the ring held five movie cameras, three to film the bout and two spares in case of equipment failure. To shield the fighters from the crowd, squadrons of uniformed Cuban cavalry aligned their horses in formation near ringside. Other guards stood nearby with pistols and machetes. Willard entered the ring as the crowd favorite, wearing a belt with a stars and stripes motif. Unlike Jeffries in 1910, he shook hands with Johnson before the opening bell.

Early on, Johnson made Willard look awkward and inept, landing several blows for each punch landed by his opponent. Flashes of Johnson in his prime appeared as he backed Willard into the ropes, pinned him in corners, taunted him, and bantered with spectators and seconds. "Johnson, you will get yours today!" a man shouted. "Well," Johnson replied, "there is good money in it, isn't there?" During the sixteenth round, one of Willard's seconds gibed, "Jack, you run into Jess's right, we will pick you up right over here." Still on top at this point, Johnson answered, "Be sure you take good care of me." When another fan called Johnson an "old man," he retorted, "You just watch the old man!" He then stalked Willard and flailed him with several sharp jabs. Willard's upper body turned red from rope abrasions and Johnson's fists, but he was young and fit, advantages not enjoyed by Jeffries in Reno.

"Johnson's old time ring smile continued throughout these early rounds," a *New York Times* correspondent noted. "But as time sped" and his punches failed to topple the challenger, "the smile disappeared." The fading smile foreshadowed the loss of the title. By round twenty, Willard struck more often and with greater force; he gained confidence as Johnson's blows lost their sting. Willard used his substantial weight advantage and leverage to wear down Johnson and muffle his punches. Winded and weakened, the champion could not even clinch well. Realizing that his reign was about to end, Johnson told Flanagan to ask Jack Curley to escort Lucille from the track to spare her the anguish of his downfall. In the twenty-sixth round, Willard proved himself the greatest white hope when he dropped Johnson to the blood-spattered canvas with several body blows and the proverbial right cross to the jaw. The referee began the count.

Willard had worn down the champion with his tenacity and strength but had not rendered him senseless. Prostrate on the canvas and exhausted in the afternoon heat, Johnson managed to raised his arm to shield his eyes from the sun while the referee finished the ten-count. Johnson's action initiated a long debate in boxing circles. Why did he not get up and resume the fight? Why lose the title if one hard punch to Willard's chin might save it? Perhaps Johnson anticipated a lucrative rematch. To him, boxing was a business, and the bottom line mattered more at this moment than the color line.

By round twenty-six, Johnson had realized his chances were slim indeed. If he beat the count, he might endure a few more rounds of pain, but there was no career advantage in fighting longer in a losing cause. Johnson risked injury, even disability or death, if he persisted. Besides, Curley had guaranteed his usual take of $30,000, win, lose, or draw. Proceeds from the films would add even more. The referee's hand cleaved the hot and humid air one last time as he reached ten. "*Viva el Blanco!*" Cubans shouted. They flew white flags from their cars as they drove to Havana from the track.[21]

Each fighter initially reacted magnanimously to the outcome. "I never fought a cleaner man," Willard said of Johnson. "He never resorted to any foul tactics, but on the contrary tried to make it a good clean fight." Willard paid Johnson what passed as the highest compliment at that time. Johnson was "the most criticized champion that ever lived," Willard noted, "but certainly I found him a white man in the ring." Johnson admitted he had taken Willard too lightly. He predicted a long reign for Willard. "He is too tall and hits too hard for the rest of them," Johnson noted. "He is far cleverer than I had any idea of. . . . Youth had to assert itself, I guess." Despite the racial overtones in his remark that Johnson had been "a white man in the ring," Willard did not attribute his victory to color, nor did he make an issue of Johnson's past. Johnson for his part offered no excuses. He simply said the better boxer won and expressed his "one regret" that he was "not allowed to return" to the United States.[22]

Johnson changed his story in late July, alleging that he had agreed to take a fall in return for a large payment and a promise of leniency from authorities when he returned home.[23] Johnson did not specify who had spoken for the Justice Department. Nor did he admit any shame at the fix. He cast himself as a hapless victim, robbed of his title and swindled out of a fortune by anonymous scoundrels. Johnson either lied to excuse his loss or misconstrued hearsay remarks by journalists who had discussed his situation with federals agents. Writers might have hinted that Johnson would be treated kindly if he returned home without the title. The higher Johnson's status, the more he infuriated whites. Humbled and destitute, however, he would revert to his proper "place." Now it hardly mattered whether Johnson languished in prison or lived a free but forgotten former champion.

Johnson presented no hard proof of a fix. Two ring experts close to him who saw the fight, Tom Flanagan and Nat Fleischer, gave better reasons for the result. "The fight is absolutely on the level," Flanagan had assured fans prior to the bout. "There is not enough money in Havana to make Johnson lie down. He intends to retire champion of the world." After the match, Flanagan denied rumors of a fix. "Johnson proved too old to put up a good fight," he insisted. "That's all there is to it." Fleischer thought Johnson cried foul "to alibi himself." He had trained poorly and underestimated Willard.

Tom Jones, Willard's manager, announced that the new champion would not fight black challengers. Drawing the color line meant that Sam Langford, Joe Jeannette, and Sam McVey—like black folks in all other walks of life— would not get a chance to reach the top. Mixed bouts, Willard explained, caused "bad blood between the races." Johnson "did more to hurt his people," he argued, "than Booker Washington did to help them." Willard, however, blamed both "ignorant white men" and "ignorant colored men" for making an issue of interracial contests. Denying "any mean, petty little prejudice" in his decision, Willard stressed that character and intellect mattered, not race or origin. "A sober decent Chinaman looks better to me than a drunken bum of an American," he observed. "A Negro who uses his intelligence is a finer man than a white man who soaks his mind in a whiskey glass." Blacks ranked among "the greatest fighters in history," he added, and they were "as game and as square as white fighters."[24]

Tolerant for his time, Willard could have done even more had he put his principles into practice. Maybe whites did find Johnson's character and conduct more objectionable than his color. The real reason for white hostility would remain obscure, however, until another black champion with a different personality wore the crown. If a second black hope won favor in and out of the ring, then whites would affirm their principle that ability and mien, not race and national origin, mattered. The aftermath of the fight in Havana provided no pretext for avoiding other interracial contests. Blacks turned out to be better losers in 1915 than whites had been in 1910. And whites seemed reluctant to goad, insult, or provoke blacks over the reversal of fistic fortunes, a refreshing change from the way black fans had flaunted Johnson's win over Jeffries. Willard's declaration that race did not make the man was a reason for opening doors, not closing them.

Black journalists took Johnson's defeat in stride. They initially rejected rumors of a fix and denied that race determined the outcome. In reflecting on Johnson's reign, they saw advantages in his winning the title in 1908 and in losing it in 1915. The sports editor of the *Philadelphia Tribune*, for example, thought the country suffered from "too much Johnson" and dismissed his pathetic alibi. "If you laid down, Jack," he advised, "please play dead." Les Walton took the long view. "No race—white or black—has a lease for life or for even a long duration on the championship heavyweight title or anything else," he contended. "Johnson lost, not because he was black, but because Father Time and improper living had put him out of the running. Willard won, not because his face was white, but because he was a younger man and possessed more stamina than his adversary." In defeat, Johnson had gained "in popularity with the white public," making it "very likely" his prison sentence would be suspended. Were he to return, "he could exceed the speed limit as much as he desired and would not be molested," Walton joked. "And so kindly disposed are the white citizens toward him now that nothing would be said were he to go to Utah and take unto himself many wives."

James Weldon Johnson, associate editor of the *New York Age*, also waxed philosophical in assessing the turn of events. Although Jack Johnson had lost stature among "most of his own race," he had as champion been "something of a racial asset." J.W. Johnson drew a parallel between the black champion's reign and the sudden rise to power of Japan after it defeated Russia in 1905. "The white race, in spite of its vaunted civilization, pays more respect to the argument of force than any other race in the world," he asserted. "As soon as Japan showed that it could fight, it immediately gained the respect and admiration of the white race. Jack Johnson compelled some of this same sort of respect and admiration in an individual way." This pairing of an emergent Asian power and a black champion suggests the deep symbolism of interracial warfare and athletics at this time. James Weldon Johnson was not alone in welcoming Japan's challenge to white supremacy.[25]

Harry Smith was ambivalent about Johnson's fall. He regretted the defeat but expected "a lessening of race prejudice" because of it. Julius Taylor described Johnson as "a great menace to the colored race" who would now "drop out of sight" as "a thing of the past." Chris Perry of the *Philadelphia Tribune* also thought the result was "for the best." He advised Johnson to make further amends by returning home to do his time. "He has done the African people in all parts of the universe more injury since Reno, July 4, 1910," Perry complained, "than any other living man."

Robert Abbott had often chided white journalists for abusing Johnson. But he praised them for being "fairer to the defeated champion than was to be expected under the circumstances." Long an ardent boxing fan, Abbott now endorsed a ban on prizefighting. "All the authority and powers of governments" should be exerted to stop it, he urged, in order to maintain "public peace and welfare and the interest of both races." Since there were "enough unavoidable causes for friction and stirring up strife," it was best to eliminate those that could be avoided. Frank Young urged blacks to accept Johnson's loss as fair and square. "It was honestly fought," he argued, "honestly lost, honestly decided."[26]

Johnson's defeat evoked some sympathy on both sides of the color line. "Johnson fought a great fight. He showed no sign of the yellow streak . . . it was the fight of one lone black man against the world," James Weldon Johnson contended. "A great winner" in his prime, he had now proved himself "a good loser." Les Walton scoffed at allegations of a fix. He also scolded the police chief in New York City for stationing officers "in pairs at every corner in Harlem" on fight night. The move insulted Harlemites because "the colored man is a game sport and a good loser." Not blind to Johnson's faults, Walton still thought that the champion had been "maligned by the public, misrepresented by the press, and even persecuted by the United States Government." Tom Flanagan also complimented him. "He was a smiling, bighearted smoke, and I have known a lot of white men who did not have as white a heart as the burly black," Flanagan noted. "He may have had his faults but we all make mistakes, and Johnson made a lot of money in a hurry and that is likely to turn anyone's head." In Cuba the crowd had yelled "insulting remarks" and the men in Willard's corner had "badgered" him. Johnson showed more class in defeat, Flanagan argued, than whites had in victory.

Billy Lewis expected Johnson's defeat to "reduce race friction" but stressed that this "friction" had stemmed mainly from his controversial mixed marriages. Johnson, Lewis insisted, had the right to "his own judgment in matters where the individual judgment should rule." Lewis wondered how blacks could malign Johnson for marrying a white woman while they continually denounced jim crow. "Many who fought Johnson on the marriage score expect mixed schools, mixed theaters, mixed hotels, they expect no segregation," he protested. "They are condemned out of their own mouths." Since race leaders demanded equal access to public facilities, surely they could not deny the right to integrate the most basic and vital of institutions, the family. "I would advise staying on our own side . . . as a matter of expediency," Lewis counseled, for then "friction is avoided." But he admired Johnson's defiance. "As a man, and a citizen, I claim every right," Lewis declared. "If I do not get them it is simply because I am not strong enough to take them." Johnson, however, had been "strong enough," and that gratified many of his people. Under so many constraints, they derived some pleasure from Johnson's audacity.[27]

Others saw a different parable in Johnson's fate. Chris Perry chastised both the past and present champion. Johnson should have "kept his wind in his body for strength" rather than "talking it away in jibe and jest at his opponent," Perry contended. Had he "drunk more water and less rum" and "stuck to women of his own race," had he "bought more houses and fewer automobiles," he might have retained public respect as well as his title. Yet Johnson's mistakes did not justify Willard's drawing of the color line. "Before Mr. Willard can gain the respect of his own people," Perry argued, "he had better whip all of the black and white . . . hopes in sight." Segregation nullified the validity of any claim to superiority. "To be king of all," he maintained, "you must beat the best of them all."[28]

But Jess Willard had a more urgent cause than equal opportunity. Before Willard boarded the ship bound for Florida from Havana, Johnson approached him. Johnson lamented that he could not return to the states and blamed liquor for his misfortune. "It's tough, Mr. Willard, it's certainly tough," he confided. "They told me you never took a drink or smoked, and I put you down for a boob. Reckon I was the boob. Stay by the water wagon, boy. Only wish I had." Temperance advocates saw a vital lesson in Willard's triumph. At a revival in New Jersey, evangelist Billy Sunday welcomed the news.

"The result is great," he declared. "Every white man should be happy." Sunday's wife Helen knew why Johnson had lost. "Hurrah!" she shouted. "It's a case of too much booze and too much Paris." Johnson was twice damned in their eyes—he owned a saloon and enslaved white women. "The virtue of womanhood is the rampart wall of American civilization," Sunday preached. "Break that down and with the stones thereof you can pave your way to the hottest hell." The "dries" linked liquor to debauchery. "Booze is the parent of crime and the mother of sin!" Sunday exhorted in his standard prohibition sermon. "If you want to consort with the blackleg and the thief and the drunkard and the prostitute, go to the saloon." Willard agreed. "Drinking has done more than kill prize fighters," he noted. "It has made the profession disreputable." He hoped to redeem boxing. "If popularity depends upon hanging around saloons, buying drinks or letting drinks be bought for me, then I'll have to be unpopular," he explained. "I don't mean to be buried in whisky's graveyard of champions." The "dries" now had a towering symbol of strength and sobriety. Reports circulated that a temperance group had offered Willard $26,000 for the rights to his story. Willard had not only reclaimed the crown for the white race, he had quickly restored its lost luster.[29]

The Great White Hope and *The Birth of a Nation*

While Willard toured the nation, Johnson returned to exile in Spain. Hopes that his eclipse would mollify whites and reduce repression quickly faded, however, when another controversy arose that sharply divided the races. Reels of the recent fight were bound in red tape because Congress had banned the importation or interstate transport of prizefight films in 1910. But a dramatic new movie, *The Birth of a Nation*, aroused far more rancor than the films of the Johnson–Jeffries fight. Producer David Wark Griffith, who had helped stage *The Clansman* in 1906, based his film on the Tom Dixon novel that had inspired the play. Griffith secured the rights to the book and hired Dixon to help direct the movie.

Innovative and engrossing in its technique, the film was awful history, a selective and skewed view of the South during and shortly after the Civil War. The production told a tale of Yankee opportunists, federal officials, and bitter former slaves who had reduced white southerners to a bondage worse than black slavery. Like other revisionists of Reconstruction, Dixon and Griffith firmly believed that only southern whites understood African Americans. With that knowledge gained from long and painful experience, the Klan had emerged to restrain the former slaves and to restore white supremacy.

An unabashed bigot who hankered for power, Dixon had no use for art for art's sake. He sensed a chance to influence officials at the pinnacle of power, for he and Woodrow Wilson had been classmates at Johns Hopkins University and southern Democrats now prevailed in Washington. Dixon welcomed President Wilson's efforts to remove blacks from patronage jobs, for example, but in 1913 he sent a "passionate protest" to his former classmate for a recent deviation from that policy. He condemned the appointment of "a Negro to boss white girls as Register of the Treasury," since even one black boss was one too many. "The establishment of Negro men over white women employees of the Treasury . . . has in the minds of many thoughtful men and women long been a serious offense against the cleanness of our social life," Dixon advised Wilson. "I have confidently hoped that you would purge Washington of this iniquity." Urging Wilson to "withdraw the appointment," Dixon said he was one of Wilson's "best friends" and had "no axe to grind."

But Dixon did have an "axe to grind," its blade usually directed at blacks and liberals rather than southern Democrats. Dixon approached Wilson and Chief Justice Edward White in early 1915 to arrange a preview of *The Birth of a Nation* at the White House. The film, Dixon told Wilson, could mold public opinion. Griffith's crew toted the reels to Washington to instruct the powerful in the lessons of the past. "The real big purpose back of my film," Dixon later told Joseph Tumulty, the president's secretary, "was to revolutionize Northern sentiments by a presentation of history that would transform every man in my audience into a good Democrat!" But Dixon had even more in mind. Rolfe Cobleigh of *The Congregationalist* remembered that in a candid conversation Dixon had expressed his hope that the film would hasten the removal of all blacks from the nation. Pending this final exodus, Dixon wanted Wilson's party to attain the clout needed to repeal the Fourteenth and Fifteenth Amendments.

The son of a Confederate cavalry officer, D.W. Griffith also viewed his film as a radical reinterpretation of a misunderstood region. Five times wounded in the war and once left for dead on the battlefield, Jacob Wark Griffith, the film director's father, returned to his Kentucky home in 1865 and found his slaves gone, debts high, and his wife seriously ill. "One could not find the sufferings of our family and our friends—the dreadful poverty and hardships during the war and for many years after—in the Yankee written histories we read in school," D.W. Griffith recalled. "From all this was a burning determination to tell some day our side of the story to the world." With tales of his family "burned right into my memory," Griffith transformed Dixon's novel into a celluloid epic that "owes more to my father than it does to me."

After watching the 154 minutes of film, neither Wilson nor White commented publicly on the work. But exclusive screenings in the White House and other federal buildings helped promote the film and blunt efforts to suppress it. Distributors emphasized that esteemed and learned leaders had watched the movie without objection. In this way their silence became an endorsement.[30]

Not silent were blacks who regarded the film as a cinematic lynching. The movie made heroes out of vigilantes who restored white dominance in the name of saving their women from black men. By 1915, one of the articles of faith among H.L. Mencken's "herds" was that Reconstruction had been an abysmal failure spawned by northern malice, black insolence, and federal ineptitude. The film had many scenes and recurring images that conveyed this perspective. It was no coincidence that *The Birth of a Nation* drew full houses at the same time whites flocked to see Jess Willard. Griffith's film served to justify past oppression and legitimate new efforts to proscribe African Americans.

Speaking of the Pendleton, South Carolina, area where he lived as a boy, William Pickens, a dean at Talladega College, recalled "extraordinary good feeling" between the races back in the 1880s. "Race antagonism," he reflected, "seemed not to touch our world." But over the next generation whites became more hostile and repressive, not just in Pendleton but across the entire nation. "Race feeling was not nearly as combustible in Pendleton then," Pickens noted in 1911, "as it is in most places now." Others shared this view. Ben Davis of the *Atlanta Independent* decided that white officials did not really want to help blacks help themselves. Lynched with impunity, denied the vote and decent employment, and confined to unhealthy and dangerous slums, blacks in Atlanta lacked the minimal means to improve their lot. A devotee of Tuskegee, Davis had muted criticism of the white South. But by the time Jack Johnson went to trial, he could contain his frustration no longer. "If the Ku Klux Klan lives," he warned, "then the state must die." Whites "have segregated us, disfranchised us, jim crowed us and inveigled every description of inhumanity that human ingenuity could conjure up," he complained, and now Asian immigrants faced similar bias. "No country in the world," Davis concluded, "is as saturated with prejudice as the United States."[31]

As Pickens and Davis watched the rise of racism and nativism across the land, Pauline Schneider, a white woman in St. Louis, read W.E.B. DuBois's *The Souls of Black Folk*. She wrote to DuBois in 1914 to offer a "hand of sympathy and profound appreciation . . . across the color line." She lamented her "inability to contribute even a mite toward the removal of ignorance, injustice, and folly." Depressed by DuBois's bleak assessment in 1903, she wondered "whether the outlook has not brightened since the book was written." DuBois was ambivalent. The creation of the NAACP and "signs in the South of persons like you who will not consent to keep silent longer" seemed positive to him. Yet "race prejudice against Negroes has steadily increased in the last twenty years," he cautioned, "and is increasing."[32]

D.W. Griffith's epic appeared at this juncture of rising repression and despair amid scattered signs of hope. If this new medium had the influence Tom Dixon predicted, the film would certainly make race matters worse. Karl Brown, a cameraman with the Griffith studio, recalled hearing a shop rumor that his boss would turn Dixon's novel into a film. He rushed to the library for the book and read parts of it while riding home on the streetcar. "Terribly biased, utterly unfair, the usual diatribe of a fire-eating Southerner, reverend or no reverend," Brown, the grandson of a soldier in the Massachusetts Tenth, concluded. After he finished the book that night, he thought it "as bitter a hymn of hate" as he had ever seen, "an old-fashioned hell-fire sermon, filled with lies, distortions, and . . . the rankest kind of superstition." Known for his "thoroughness" and "fanatic concentration," Griffith would make the film "a thousand-fold more terrible than it could possibly be in print."

On the sets and through his camera lens, Brown watched the book become motion picture. After many weeks of filming, cutting, and splicing, Brown attended the preview in Los Angeles. He emerged a convert as a result of Griffith's stunning cinematography. "What unfolded on that screen," he confessed, "was magic itself." The artistic and technical brilliance of the film erased his previous misgivings about its message. "Every soul in that audience was in the saddle with the clansmen," Brown recalled, "and pounding hell-for-leather on an errand of stern justice." At the end, viewers "stood up and cheered and yelled and stamped feet" for Griffith. As he stepped out on stage, "wave after wave of cheers and applause wash[ed] over him like great waves breaking over a rock." The work "had been perfectly orchestrated" with "the instrumentation flawless," Brown concluded, a masterpiece by "a great composer of visual images instead of notes."[33]

Not all whites shared Brown's ardor. Jane Addams, the head of Hull House and a founder of the NAACP, for instance, called Griffith's portrayal of blacks "unjust and untrue." The film featured former slaves who jostled whites off walkways, swilled liquor in the statehouse while drafting a bill allowing mixed marriages, corrupted the ballot, and defiled white women. The film utilized many crude conventions of melodrama but implied a sincere effort to recreate the past. "It is claimed that the play is historical, but history is easy to misuse," Addams objected. "You can use history to demonstrate anything, when you take certain of its facts and emphasize them to the exclusion of the rest." The film represented "the most subtle form of untruth—a half truth."

The film also disturbed reviewer Francis Hackett, in part because "as a spectacle" he found it "stupendous." Griffith had taken cinema to a new level, but Hackett doubted that the impact of the film derived from its innovations. Like Addams, Hackett deplored its slant. However inspired Griffith's creative role, the film—particularly the part about Reconstruction—was vintage Tom Dixon in its "horrible" depiction of former slaves. Hackett called Dixon "a yellow clergyman" who, like "yellow" journalists, relied on caricature and sensationalism to sell stories. He also chided censors and viewers. "Whatever happened during Reconstruction, this film is aggressively vicious and defamatory," Hackett objected. "It is spiritual assassination. It degrades the censors that passed it and the white race that endures it."[34]

Whites not only endured the film, they embraced it. Griffith hit the mother lode—costs totaled about $100,000, the return some $18 million. Dixon earned $1 million in royalties alone, and chief cameraman Billy Bitzer became an instant millionaire from his $10,000 investment. "To those of us actually working in the Griffith studio," Karl Brown recalled, the major impact "was the sudden cascading of money, money, and yet more money into the studio itself." The film stirred debate, boycotts, bans, and even small riots, but few seats were empty when the Griffith trademark flashed on the big screen.[35]

Like the film itself, responses tended to be black and white. For Karl Brown, the conventions of melodrama Griffith used to convey his vision drained the rabid racism from Dixon's story. The characters in the film "were really caricatures," Brown contended, "and for that very reason became somehow inoffensive." But to DuBois and other critics, Griffith's "caricatures" were malicious as well as offensive, for they reified illusions and anxieties that spawned prejudice and discrimination. These images, DuBois argued, led whites to believe "that the chief industry of Negroes is raping white women." Griffith's film, DuBois warned, would further stigmatize and oppress blacks. The first half contained "marvelously good war pictures," but the remainder depicted the African American "as an ignorant fool, a vicious rapist, a venal and unscrupulous politician or a faithful but doddering idiot." DuBois noted that some NAACP branches had convinced local censors to expunge the interracial rape scene from the film. The national NAACP board, however, recommended that "the whole second half" be "suppressed."

Karl Brown erred when he argued that Griffith's blacks were "inoffensive" because they were "caricatures." The rub, of course, was that whites often viewed African Americans *only* as caricatures. Popular culture often portrayed the black person as "fool . . . rapist . . . idiot"—in lurid newpaper stories about black criminals, in advertisements featuring the grinning darky who pitched products from stove polish to molasses, and in plays and films in which black characters habitually snoozed, scratched, and shuffled between watermelon patch and chicken coop. Whites looked at blacks through a lens colored by both subtle and blatant biases. White journalists, for example, frequently depicted Jack Johnson this way—as a "fool" and "rapist" obsessed with speed and sex. By the time Johnson jumped bail and fled abroad, his public image resembled one of Dixon's and Griffith's fictional brutes.

Discerning observers knew that the racist caricatures in the film maligned the entire race. William Monroe Trotter, editor of the *Boston Guardian*, led a group of protesters to a premiere of the film. Fearing a disturbance might erupt if the blacks were admitted, the theater manager turned them away. When they objected, police arrested Trotter and one of his friends. Meetings and protests followed. "It is said not since the Civil War times have such demonstrations been seen here in Boston," Samuel Courtney, a local black lawyer, informed Booker T. Washington. "The Negroes are a unit in their determination to drive it out of Boston." Some whites joined them. Mary White Ovington, one of the founders of the NAACP, urged Boston Mayor James Curley to suppress the film. It "treated the Negro as a dangerous, half-insane brute," she objected, and might well "create antagonism, even violence." Curley agreed that the most incendiary scenes from the movie should be cut.[36]

Blacks in New York City greeted the film with hisses, boos, and rotten eggs when it opened on April 14, nine days after Willard beat Johnson. "On the anniversary of Lincoln's assassination," Cleveland Allen, the head of a news agency that served the black press, declared, "it is inappropriate to present a play that libels 10,000,000 loyal American negroes." Benjamin Mays recalled only one instance when he felt "physical fear" as a student at Bates College in Maine—when he and other black students ventured off campus to see Griffith's film. "It was a vicious, cynical, and completely perverted characterization of Negroes," Mays thought. "Even in Maine, the picture aroused violent emotions and stirred up racial prejudice," evoking "violent words and threats from the audience." Mays and his friends returned to campus safely, but half a century later he still remembered this sole encounter "with a prejudiced and hostile audience in Lewiston." In Chicago, Mayor William Hale Thompson banned the movie. Booker T. Washington thanked him, noting that the film "intensifies racial prejudice" and "misrepresents historical facts." Washington vowed that he and his followers planned to "do everything possible" to stop this "thoroughly harmful and vicious" movie.[37]

After Johnson beat Jeffries in 1910, various groups had pressured Congress to ban prizefight films. Now, in 1915, the National Board of Censors saw no reason to block *The Birth of a Nation*. For many black Americans, the whites' reaction the reels of Johnson–Jeffries, on the one hand, and

Griffith's movie, on the other, spoke volumes about their prejudices. Fans unable to travel to Reno had been denied a chance to watch the fight on film because whites feared that its dissemination might increase race tensions and incite riots. By all accounts, the fight had been fair and square. What the cameras filmed on July 4, 1910, was an actual event untainted by a screenwriter's or director's biases. Whites disliked Johnson's humiliation of Jeffries, but the celluloid images from Reno did not lie.

Just what the cameras had captured in shooting *The Birth of a Nation* was a more perplexing question. Griffith explored a vital subject in his film, one of much greater historical importance than the bout in Reno. But Karl Brown's camera recorded a past largely imagined by Tom Dixon and D.W. Griffith, not the complex issues and events of an actual era. The director reduced the most tumultuous period in American history—some fifteen violent, bloody, and divisive years—to about two and a half hours of film. Its aesthetic merits aside, the reels relied on gimmicks Dixon and Griffith had learned from the vaudeville stage and nickelodeon theater, where exaggeration and oversimplification ruled. Unlike boxing, Reconstruction was not simple. The ring could be accurately captured on film; the South during the Civil War and Reconstruction could not—at least not by D.W. Griffith. He never grasped this. Inspired by the blood-and-thunder western novel, Griffith applied its winning formula to the South. "Now I could see a chance to do this ride-to-the-rescue on a grand scale," he mused. "Instead of saving one poor Nell of the Plains, this ride would be to save a nation." The Klan would become Dixie's Buffalo Bill, rescuing imperiled white damsels from black savages.[38]

When Chris Perry suggested it was "best" that Johnson lost his title, he also faulted Griffith and Dixon for misnaming their film. "Dixon knows more about how to kill a nation," Perry argued, "than to give birth to one." Harry Smith found the film "mob inciting and vitally injurious" and urged Mayor Newton Baker to ban it from Cleveland along with another work called *The Nigger*. Smith thought these two productions were "infinitely worse from every decent viewpoint" than the 1910 fight films that had been banned in the city. Governor F.B. Willis agreed, ordering a suspension of *The Nigger* and closing Ohio to *The Birth of a Nation*.

Others entered the fray. George Knox of the *Freeman* thought the film promoted the "civil death" of black Americans. Booker T. Washington told Robert Abbott that the work was "fundamentally wrong" because it neglected "the substantial progress of the Negro race" and distorted "the cruel misunderstandings" of Reconstruction, "in which unfortunate individuals of both races figured." Dubbing the film *The Dirt of a Nation*, Abbott hoped it would end up on "the refuse heap." In the nation's capital, city commissioners had banned the fight films from Reno. The *Bee*'s Calvin Chase urged them to act quickly now because Griffith's film "intended to excite prejudice and hatred against the Negro" as a prelude to a repeal of the Reconstruction amendments and the "resubjection" of blacks "to servitude and ultimate extinction or expatriation." Chase hoped the local white clergy would show the same zeal against this film that they had demonstrated in 1910.[39]

Rumors persisted that Woodrow Wilson endorsed the film, a source of consternation among black Democrats. As the protests mounted, Wilson said he wanted to clarify his views on the matter when doing so would not appear a concession to "the agitation . . . stirred up by that unspeakable fellow," editor Monroe Trotter, who had previously met with Wilson to protest the imposition of jim crow on black federal employees. Wilson later directed his secretary, Joseph Tumulty, to confirm that the first family had watched the film at the White House, but that the president had been "entirely unaware of the character of the play before it was presented" and had not given "his approbation of it." The private screening was merely "a courtesy extended to an old acquaintance." Wilson walked a fine line between endorsement and denunciation, an understandable ambivalence. He wanted to mollify Tom Dixon without alienating black Democrats. On a more ideological level, Wilson shared many of Dixon's and Griffith's views. In his own history of this era, he had described former slaves as "easy dupes . . . taught to hate" their former masters by their "new masters"—"predatory" northern "carpet-baggers."[40]

The Rhetoric and Reality of Wilsonian Policies

Though annoyed by the furor over the film, Wilson remained riveted on foreign affairs. He pondered intervention in the civil war in Mexico and the widening war in Europe to protect American interests and ideals. These policy dilemmas raised perplexing questions about national identity and race and their impact upon foreign relations. If the president and Congress sent troops to fight in Mexico or France, would all races and ethnic groups serve in the armed forces as equals? By the time Griffith's film premiered in 1915, many black editors considered Wilson the worst president for their people since Andrew Johnson. Were Wilson to call for mobilization at home or intervention abroad, blacks might ignore his appeal. African Americans had fought and died in the Civil War, in the military campaigns against Native Americans in the West, and in Cuba in 1898. Yet their sacrifices had not secured them equal rights. Another war would undoubtedly spark intense debate about internal schisms and the American mission abroad.

During the election campaign of 1916, blacks assessed Wilson's first term and contemplated a second. "The administration . . . has almost completely undone what it took the Negro fifty years to accomplish politically," James Weldon Johnson complained. Defeating Wilson loomed as "the most vital question that has confronted colored voters . . . in twenty years." Having endorsed Wilson in 1912, DuBois now opposed him, but he spurned the Republican nominee as well. Wilson's pledge of "justice executed with liberality and cordial good feeling" for all had been "a lie, a peculiarly miserable campaign deception." Neither party cared about blacks. The Democratic Party could "maintain its ascendancy" only by relying upon "the Solid South," a region based on "hate and fear of Negroes." Consequently, it could not "effectively bid for the Negro vote." Republicans belonged to "the party of wealth and big business" and therefore were "the natural enemy of the humble working people who compose the mass of Negroes." Bishop Alexander Walters had also supported Wilson in 1912. Since then Wilson had been "personally . . . very kind" to him but had not lived up to the "fair promises and sweet-sounding phrases about justice and equal opportunity uttered in pre-election days." Editor Harry Smith of the *Cleveland Gazette* thought Wilson and Tom Dixon shared a peculiar nostalgia for the Old South. Wilson had "undone in three years the work of fifty years of Republicanism," Smith maintained. Wilson's patronage policy and his advisers' scorn for blacks who remained in government showed "nothing in Wilson's policy for the Afro-American, nor does he pretend there is." In addition to its specific acts, Smith lamented, the administration set an overall tone that was hostile to all blacks and inimical to their interests.[41]

Fifty-nine Americans perished in lynchings in 1916—fifty-five of them blacks. Of those fifty-five, three were women. A decline from eighty the previous year, the lynchings of 1916 made up in savagery for their drop in numbers. On January 20, Georgia vigilantes stormed a county jail, seized five black men, and hanged them. These peon laborers had resisted arrest, and in a melee one had shot a sheriff. This multiple lynching shocked even some southern whites. "We are being branded as barbarians not only North," the *Atlanta Independent*'s Ben Davis observed, "but the attacks and criticisms of our own neighbors and friends here at home are little milder than those that come from a distance." Editor George Knox of the *Indianapolis Freeman* called it a "wholesale lynching." Two alleged homicides and rumors of a rape incited three more lynchings in Georgia in February. "Negroes are now lynched," Davis grieved, "for any crime, no particular crime, even for suspicion."[42]

A mob in Waco, Texas, rushed into a courtroom on May 15 and seized seventeen-year-old Jesse Washington, just convicted of murder and condemned to death. A week earlier, a woman he worked for had scolded him for abusing the family's mules. He struck her with a hammer, sexually assaulted her, then killed her. When apprehended, he confessed to the murder. By prior arrangement, the sheriff left the courtroom to the mob. They stripped Washington, battered him with bricks and shovels, and cut him with knives. One man severed his ear and another castrated him. The mob tied a chain around him and dragged him behind a car. After starting a fire behind city hall, a few mob members wrapped the chain around the boy's neck, tossed one end over a tree limb, and hoisted him up. When Washington tried to remove the chain, his executioners cut off his fingers. Jerked aloft to cheers from a large crowd, the body was lowered into the flames, lifted, then dropped again to the mob's delight. The mayor and police chief watched the vigilante killing from city hall. Someone placed Washington's head on a prostitute's porch. Locals peddled his teeth and links of the hanging chain as souvenirs.

F.A. Gildersleeve, a local photographer, captured these dreadful scenes from a city hall window. He sold reprints until civic-minded residents convinced him that the grisly pictures were not good publicity for Waco. DuBois ran several photographs and eyewitness accounts of the lynching in *The Crisis*, calling it "perhaps the most horrible lynching" in American history. He expected criticism for his coverage but wanted to make a point. "Any talk of the moral leadership of this country in the world; any talk of the triumph of Christianity . . . is idle twaddle," DuBois insisted, "so long as the Waco lynching is possible in the United States." James Weldon Johnson concurred. Noting that American missionaries had failed to convert the Japanese, he proposed "Texas as a much nearer and a more needy field for their labors."[43]

Three months later whites went on a bloody rampage near Newberry, Florida. Boisy Long, accused of stealing hogs, resisted arrest and allegedly shot and killed a sheriff and wounded a doctor who had sworn to the warrant. While searching for Long, the mob murdered two of Long's neighbors, James Dennis and Josh Baskin, though neither was connected to the initial shootings. When Bert Dennis went to Newberry to purchase a coffin for his brother, whites jailed him. A second mob seized and jailed Boisy Long's wife Stella and Mary Dennis, who had adopted Boisey when he was a boy, for withholding information. With two innocent men already dead, the mob removed Stella Long and Mary and Bert Dennis from the jail and hanged them where Baskin had been slain. Stella Long had "four or five children." Mary Dennis had two and was expecting a third. Bert also had a family. Terrified by the killing spree, "Negroes came pouring from Newberry in to Gainsville for safety." Boisy's uncle, the owner of a large farm, was "terrorized" by a mob and turned his nephew over to a posse. Five innocent blacks died to appease angry whites—none a suspect in the initial fracas.[44]

That autumn a black woman suffered the wrath of an angry mob near Leary, Georgia. Mary Conley, who was sixty, worked shares on a white family's farm with her seventeen-year-old son Sam, and his wife. When Sam did not show up in the fields one morning, the owner found and scolded him and brandished a club. Mary implored him not to strike her son. He flailed her with the club and kicked her in the stomach when she fell. Sam picked up a peat and knocked the owner out. He carried his mother to their shack and fled, but officers nabbed him in Pretoria. In the meantime, the sheriff arrested and jailed Mary. Expecting that the sheriff might take her to a safe haven, a mob seized and shot her several times, then dumped her body on a highway. The employer died from Sam's blow, but Sam insisted he had intended to protect his mother and not kill his boss. The mob did not care about extenuating circumstances. Since the son had not been available for a quick lynching, his mother would do just as well.

Lynchers did not distinguish between sharecroppers in Georgia and squires in South Carolina. Owner of 427 acres of prime land and proud father of sixteen children, Anthony Crawford went to Abbeville on October 31 to sell cotton and seed to a white merchant. When he and the buyer bickered about the price, a crowd gathered and an officer arrested Crawford for disorderly conduct. He posted bail and departed. A local hothead exhorted the crowd to punish him for his audacity. A mob followed Crawford and found him at a ginning mill. A man struck Crawford, but he grabbed a hammer and leveled his assailant. The mob subdued Crawford, dragged him from the mill, and beat, kicked, stabbed, and partially blinded him. The sheriff rescued Crawford and took him into custody. Hours later the mob stormed the jail, removed the inmate, dragged him through the streets, battered and mutilated him, hanged him at the fairgrounds, and riddled his body with bullets. Whites ordered Crawford's kin to leave the county. As usual, there were no indictments and no trial. "It is appalling the lightness in which human life is esteemed all over this country," Robert Abbott of the *Chicago Defender* wrote in late 1916, "and especially in the southern portion." When the lynching total for 1916 was reported in early 1917, Abbott noted the conspicuous absence of "a protest from the powers that be" in Washington. "This country has many things to be proud of," he concluded, "and many more things to be ashamed of." The *Philadelphia Tribune*'s Chris Perry agreed. "The Solid South," he protested, "is a stench, is a stink, in the nostrils of the nation."[45]

Abbott was not alone in criticizing "the powers that be." Leaders with the NAACP urged Woodrow Wilson to condemn lynching in his second inaugural address. They acknowledged that states were supposed to apprehend and prosecute members of lynch mobs, but they thought Wilson could prod them by denouncing vigilante terror. Though a state crime, "the disgrace falls upon the nation as a whole," the NAACP petitioned. Americans could not "address the world on great moral questions" while "this stain upon our civilization" continued. Wilson used his address, however, to castigate the European belligerents and warn them of possible retaliation. "Wronged upon the seas," Americans had "despite many divisions . . . drawn closer together," he stated. They did not want war but demanded their neutral rights. "As some of the injuries done us have become intolerable," Wilson proclaimed, "we have still been clear that we wished nothing for ourselves that we were not ready to demand for all mankind—fair dealing, justice, the freedom to live and be at ease against organized wrong." Still silent on lynching, Wilson's call for "justice" and "freedom . . . against organized wrong" appeared hypocritical, another sign of his moralism in foreign affairs and his apathy toward racial injustice at home. Wilson lectured Germans on international law but chose not to remind southern whites about due process and voting rights.[46]

A month into his second term, Wilson asked Congress to declare war on Germany. Attacks by German submarines on neutral ships, he argued, were tantamount to acts of war. "The world must be made safe for democracy," he declared. "Its peace must be planted upon the tested foundations of political liberty. We have no selfish ends to serve. We desire no conquest, no dominion. . . . We are but one of the champions of the rights of mankind." Entry into the war would be "a fearful thing," Wilson admitted, but "the right is more precious than peace." He pledged that Americans would "fight for the things which we have always carried nearest to our hearts"—"democracy" and "the rights and liberties of small nations." Wilson would seek "a concert of free peoples" to ensure "peace and safety to all nations." Wilson chose war abroad rather than an offensive against racism at home. Neither Wilson nor his advisers saw any irony in his quest for "rights and liberties" abroad when black Americans lacked them in every state where his party governed unopposed. "Our entry into the war," Ambassador Walter Hines Page wired Wilson from London on April 3, "is the only proper expression of our national character, our ideals and our sympathies." Wilson had "done a great thing nobly!" Treasury Secretary William McAdoo boasted. "I firmly believe that it is God's will that America should do this transcendent service for humanity throughout the world and that you are his chosen instrument."[47]

Black Americans reacted skeptically. Wary of Wilson, his party, and his southern origin, they nevertheless wanted to do their duty to the nation. Besides, they hoped the war would spur domestic changes stymied in more mundane times. No event surpassed the Civil War, for example, in its positive impact on African Americans. Blacks had fought for the Union, and the government responded with amendments to abolish slavery, make blacks citizens, and give black men the vote. Since then, reactionaries had tried to reverse or minimize those gains. Wilson's words about "rights and liberties" suggested that United States intervention now might assist oppressed peoples at home and overseas. "The governments that are fighting in the name of democracy," James Weldon Johnson predicted, "are going to get more of it than they expected." Kelly Miller of Howard University agreed. "Political autocracy and racial autocracy will be buried in the same grave," he stated. "The divine right of kings and the divine right of race will suffer a common fate."[48]

The rhetoric of war dramatized the great gap between principles and practices. But blacks decided to pay their dues in hopes of collecting later. "With us it is America first, America last, and America forever," Ben Davis declared. "We are for war, without counting the cost." James Weldon Johnson anticipated a new world order in which old traditions, ideas, and institutions would be "broken up and melted down in the crucible of this great war." He expected the United States and its allies to defeat Germany, but "the indirect results" would be greater liberty for all, "especially the darker peoples." Calvin Chase viewed mobilization as "an exceptional opportunity" for blacks to prove themselves "the only simon-pure class of Americans." Loyalty now would help "secure a better adjustment of the relations of the races" later. "This is our nation," he proclaimed. "We helped to build it. It is our permanent abiding place. We shall eventually improve it. It means all to us."[49]

Lofty rhetoric, however, could not hide the deep schisms on the home front. The war stanched the flow of European immigrants to the United States but simultaneously multiplied the demand for American products. The sudden disruption in immigration and the movement of masses of white workers into the armed forces created an unprecedented shortage of labor in northern industry. Tired of Dixie and its ways, many blacks headed north to toil and live in the promised land, as Jack Johnson's family had done a decade before. Southern whites blamed the exodus on German propagandists and greedy northern labor agents. But W.E.B. Dubois set the record straight. "The Negro is far more loyal to this country and its ideals than the white Southern American," he argued. "He never has been a disloyal rebel. He never fought for slavery in a land of liberty." To affirm black loyalty, NAACP leaders called for a training camp for black officers, even a segregated one. Southern whites wanted to confine blacks to drudgery and deny them a chance at military distinction, DuBois protested. "Back of the German mask" was "the grinning skeleton of the Southern slave driver." DuBois thought the "real cause" of the war was "the despising of the darker races" by whites and their "fierce rivalry . . . to use darker and backward people for purposes of selfish gain regardless of the ultimate good of the oppressed." He urged his people to put their grievances aside and aid the war effort as farmers, workers, and soldiers. "This country," DuBois maintained, "belongs to us even more than to those who lynch, disfranchise, and segregate."[50]

Those hoping intervention abroad would foster racial harmony at home were disabused of that notion when whites rampaged through East St. Louis, Illinois, on July 2, 1917. Earlier that year, local meat packers had hired blacks to break a strike. Angry that some blacks remained on the job after the walkout, white workers, union organizers, and assorted ruffians clubbed, looted, burned, stabbed, hanged, and shot their way through the main black quarter with little or no interference from local police and state militia. When the smoke cleared, between 100 and 200 blacks had died, over 6,000 residents had been driven from their homes, and some $1 million in property had been destroyed. Prior to the riot, a delegation of African Americans had appealed to the governor for protection but to no avail. Unable to rely on the state, blacks had stocked guns and ammunition in their homes. When whites opened fire on some residences, occupants shot back and eight marauders died in the exchanges. Inquiries showed the whites' attack was not spontaneous. "By all accounts of eyewitnesses, both white and black," Martha Gruening and DuBois reported, "the East St. Louis outrage was deliberately planned and executed." A black woman of 65 years lost her home and belongings. "What are we to do?" she asked Gruening. "We can't live South and they don't want us North. Where are we to go?" Ben Davis echoed her plea. "If we don't work South we are jailed, if we do work North we are mobbed," he sighed. "What shall we do to be saved?"[51]

A Memphis mob also reverted to old ways during the war. Someone raped and beheaded a white girl of sixteen on the outskirts of town and dumped her body into a river. Under brutal interrogation, Ell Person, a black woodchopper, confessed. Officers planned to whisk him to Nashville, then return him to Memphis for trial. Person was seized from a train, taken by car to a predetermined site, and burned at the stake before some 15,000 people, including the slain girl's mother. The NAACP sent James Weldon Johnson to investigate. "Memphis, Tennessee, is the most murderous city on earth," he wrote. "Putting down lawlessness in the United States is about as urgent a job as fighting to make democracy safe for the world." Johnson exhorted President Wilson "to say a word, at least, against the atrocities practiced by Americans upon Americans."[52]

Blacks did not limit their protest to editorials. On July 28, some 10,000 African Americans led by children dressed in white marched to the cadence of muffled drums down Fifth Avenue in New York City. Instead of chanting and shouting the marchers carried banners and signs expressing their outrage:

WE HAVE FOUGHT FOR THE LIBERTY OF WHITE AMERICANS IN 6 WARS;
OUR REWARD IS EAST ST. LOUIS

PATRIOTISM AND LOYALTY PRESUPPOSE PROTECTION AND LIBERTY

WE ARE MALIGNED AS LAZY AND MURDERED WHEN WE WORK

RACE PREJUDICE IS THE OFFSPRING OF IGNORANCE
AND THE MOTHER OF LYNCHING

The *Freeman*'s George Knox saw "the poetry of mean conditions" in the march. To Ben Davis, this "mute petition to the American conscience was eloquence sublime." A delegation called upon Wilson on August 1 and urged him to use "his great personal and moral influence" on behalf of African Americans. They handed a petition to Joe Tumulty, noting that the states were "either unwilling or unable" to stop lynching, so the federal government had to make it "a national crime." The war necessitated this step. "No nation that seeks to fight the battles of civilization," the petition read, "can afford to march in blood-smeared garments." Wilson did not respond publicly to the plea, but he did tell a delegation two weeks later that the carnage in East St. Louis had appalled him. He promised that he and his advisers would urge prosecution of mob murderers to discourage further outbreaks. The delegates then told the press about Wilson's pledge.[53]

Events soon revealed the futility of such token gestures. In early 1918, a white mob near Valdosta, Georgia, killed eleven local blacks in retaliation for the murder of Hampton Smith, a white farmer, and the wounding of his wife. Unable to hire hands, Smith had paid fines for black inmates who then worked off their debts to him. After a dispute over wages and a beating from Smith, Sidney Johnson fired several shots into the Smiths' home, killing Hampton and wounding his wife. While searching for Johnson, a mob systematically hanged, shot, burned, and mutilated ten innocent blacks, among them Hayes Turner, who had also quarreled with Smith in the past. Turner's wife Mary viewed his death as murder and said she intended to identify his killers and seek their prosecution. She never had the chance. A mob seized her, tied her ankles, suspended her upside down from a tree limb, then splashed gasoline and oil onto her clothing and set her on fire. While Turner was burning alive, a man slashed her abdomen with a butcher knife, dropping her eight-month fetus to the ground. When the premature baby cried, a man crushed its head with his boot. Mary Turner was shot hundreds of times.

In Valdosta, Sidney Johnson, armed with a shotgun and pistol, exchanged fire with a posse and died in the fusillade. A crowd unsexed Johnson, threw his genitals into the street, hitched his body to a car, and towed it to the crime scene. Men tied Johnson's body to a tree and burned it to a crisp. This savagery made some five hundred blacks flee the area. "Hundreds of acres of untilled land flourishing with weeds and dozens of deserted farm houses," the NAACP's Walter White reported, "give their own mute testimony of the

Negroes' attitude toward a community in which lynching mobs are allowed to visit vengeance upon members of their race." Governor Hugh Dorsey attributed the bloody mayhem to rape, an "utterly mistaken" notion according to Ben Davis. "Negroes are lynched for disputing a white man's word, for jumping contracts, for attempting to leave employment, for making unwise remarks and the like," Davis countered. Not rape but "race prejudice and hate" had incited the mob. By the end of 1918, sixty-four blacks, including five women, died in lynchings, twenty more than in the previous year. Mobs also murdered four white men, two for alleged murder and two for remarks deemed disloyal to the flag.[54]

Animosity among white police and local residents in Houston toward black soldiers erupted in a shooting spree on August 23, 1917—a fracas reminiscent of the Brownsville melee in 1906. The fuse ignited when police arrested and abused a black woman, and black soldiers on the scene from Camp Logan asked the reason for the cruelty. A white police officer struck an unarmed soldier with his revolver. Other police fired at a second soldier who approached. The powder keg of black resentment against white racism was about to explode.

Outraged by frequent slurs and insults and, in some instances, emboldened by liquor, black soldiers decided to retaliate against city police. Intercepted on the way to police headquarters by Illinois militia also stationed in the area, black soldiers fought fiercely and recklessly, killing sixteen whites and wounding twelve, among them four city police, a National Guard commander, and a little white girl struck by a stray bullet in her sleep. Three blacks died in the affray. Hearings led to death sentences for twenty-nine of the black soldiers, prison terms for eighty-one, and eight acquittals. The army executed thirteen of the men on December 11. Wilson sustained the death penalty for six of the remaining sixteen and commuted the rest to life in prison. Professor Kelly Miller of Howard University objected that the troops had been "goaded to desperation" by local whites. He regretted the deaths and stiff penalties but credited the men with inverting "the usual order of perpetrator and victim."[55]

A white investigator from the Army Inspector General's office reviewed the incident. Black soldiers bristled at segregated streetcars, separate water fountains, and routine slurs by white residents and police. "This word 'nigger' appears in practically every case of disorder reported, and with the same result," the inspector noted, "a display of anger on the part of the soldier, with profane and abusive language and threats of vengeance." Soldiers resented being "punished for these troubles" when "no corrective measures were applied to the citizen offender." The shooting melee was "inherently racial" in origin, provoked by the "general treatment and attitude" of whites toward blacks and the soldiers' disdain for "Jim Crow Laws." The soldiers' desires clashed with local custom: Troops wanted "respect for the uniform" and "fairness and justice" while whites demanded conformity to racist restrictions. If whites in Texas retained "their present attitude towards the Negro," he warned, "troubles more or less aggravated and similar to the affair at Houston, are likely to occur at any time Negro troops are stationed within the boundaries of the state."[56]

The carnage at home raised doubts about the crusade abroad. After a Dixie mob burned yet another black, James Weldon Johnson wondered if the doughboys were fighting the wrong enemy. "Where in the world is democracy in greater danger than it is in these United States?" he queried. "It is high time that this country make a declaration against the Huns of Tennessee." Sylvester Russell, a newspaper columnist, parodied a popular song to point out that the races used different lyrics even when they sang the same melody. "The white man sings George Cohan's 'Over There!'" he wrote. "The black man's song is 'What About Here?'" After the army executed the first thirteen soldiers, DuBois lamented the fate of men who had "fought for a country which was never wholly theirs; men born to suffer ridicule, injustice, and, at last, death itself." They committed a capital offense and incurred the penalty, so "we cannot protest." Yet he detected a dual standard of justice:

> We . . . do protest against the shameful treatment which these men and which we, their brothers, receive all our lives, and which our fathers received, and our children await. We raise our clenched hands against the hundreds of thousands of white murderers, rapists, and scoundrels who have oppressed, killed, ruined, robbed, and debased their black fellow men and fellow women, and yet, today, walk scot-free . . . uncondemned by millions of their white fellow citizens, and unrebuked by the President of the United States.

The shootings and the executions belied Wilson's lofty rhetoric and sullied the nation.[57]

Wilson remained mum but German propagandists did not, using the racial violence to discredit the United States. Secretary of War Newton Baker and other leaders feared that federal acquiescence to mob murder and jim crow was discouraging black enlistment and civilian mobilization. Les Walton of the *New York Age* urged Joe Tumulty to pester Wilson to condemn "the wholesale lynching of Negroes" after a mob in Huntsville, Texas, killed Sarah Cabiness and her six children for her husband's threat against a white man. Lynching, Walton reminded Tumulty, "puts this country in a none too enviable light before the world." After touring the South, Robert Russa Moton,

Booker T. Washington's successor at Tuskegee, informed Wilson that blacks were feeling "more genuine restlessness, and perhaps dissatisfaction" than he had ever seen because of "recent lynchings and burnings," particularly the murder of Mary Turner. Moton urged "a strong word" from the president. Wilson replied that he awaited "an opportunity to do what you suggest and if I do not find it soon, I will do it without an opportunity."

Baker met with Moton and a delegation of black editors, then advised Wilson to send "a strong letter" to a governor of a state with a recent lynching, urging him to use all his powers "to search out and prosecute the offenders." Wilson should stress that "these acts of brutality" were "unpatriotic." Baker also urged Wilson to emphasize that the Justice Department would help states identify and prosecute suspects. Representative Leonidas Dyer of Missouri introduced an antilynching bill in the House and called upon Wilson to issue "a vigorous statement" against this "serious blot" upon the nation. The NAACP's John Shillady reminded Wilson that mobs had committed several "particularly vicious" multiple slayings since the nation entered the war. He asked him to issue "an unequivocal condemnation" of lynching.[58]

Wilson finally denounced the mobs on July 26, 1918, comparing American vigilantes to German soldiers. "Germany has outlawed herself among the nations because she has disregarded the sacred obligations of law and has made lynchers of her armies," Wilson maintained. "Lynchers emulate her disgraceful example." Loyal Americans obeyed the law, but mobs were undermining the efforts of soldiers and statesmen to make their nation the "savior" of "suffering peoples" abroad. "How shall we commend democracy to the acceptance of other peoples," he challenged, "if we disgrace our own by proving that it is, after all, no protection to the weak?" He urged governors, police, and citizens to end "this disgraceful evil. It cannot live where the community does not countenance it."[59]

The blunt message pleased black leaders. Moton called it a "wise, frank, patriotic statement on mob violence." DuBois praised Wilson for having "said strongly and well the word on lynching for which we have long waited." Ben Davis regarded the speech as "one of the bravest and ablest things" Wilson had ever done. He noted his own repeated pleas to "make our own country safe for democracy," since the "good faith" of the nation depended upon protecting American citizens at home.[60]

Despite their complaints, blacks aided the cause by working in defense industries, buying bonds, joining the army (in segregated units), and, finally, fighting in France. Military service abroad portended advances at home. "The colored soldier who fights side by side with the white American . . . will hardly be begrudged a fair chance when the victorious armies return," Robert Abbott predicted. "With tens of thousands of our Race fighting for civilization in France under the American flag, how much longer are the American people to tolerate lynchings?" Ben Davis welcomed General John "Black Jack" Pershing's praise for African American soldiers, believing it would weaken "the great wall of prejudice and hate" when they returned. DuBois urged blacks to put the war before their own needs. Then they would later be able to "vote, travel, learn, work and enjoy in peace." DuBois stressed a resolution passed by the NAACP board: "*First* your Country, *then* your Rights!" Kelly Miller agreed, urging that "just grievances" be held "in abeyance until the war is ended."

Among those wanting "a fair chance" was Jack Johnson, who hoped to parlay wartime service in Europe into leniency upon his return to the United States. At the Havana pier in 1915, Johnson had wished Willard luck and watched him depart. "My title is gone," he sighed, "but I would give it ten times over if I could just step on that boat and leave it when it hits the States and walk down the gang plank a free man." When the United States entered the war, Johnson declared his willingness to serve the cause in France. If he could not fight in the trenches, he could box exhibitions to raise money for the Red Cross. "Maybe I am getting a little too old," he mused, "but I ain't as old as Colonel Roosevelt, Hindenburg, and others. I think I can still put away a few Fritzies."[61]

Johnson worked other angles to enhance his prospects. He learned in early 1918 that Fiorello La Guardia, a captain in the army aviation signal corps and a former congressman from New York, was on assignment in Madrid. Johnson approached La Guardia in a local barber shop. "He told me his long story and claimed he had been persecuted in Chicago," La Guardia recalled. "He wanted me to help him get into the American Army. I told him to write out his whole story and state that he would accept service anywhere and perform any duty assigned to him." La Guardia promised to help. He received Johnson's written appeal the next day. "I am as good an American as any one living and naturally want to do my bit," Johnson pleaded. "I firmly believe I wasn't fairly treated at home. . . . America is my country. There's no position you could get for me that I would consider too rough or too dangerous. I am willing to fight and die for my own country. I cannot offer any more." Unfamiliar with Johnson's case, La Guardia forwarded his request to the army and added, "It would be hard to deprive any American of the right to fight." But army officials demurred, partly because the Justice Department interceded. Johnson had "forfeited bond," Raymond M. Norris, an official at the department, advised, and remained "a fugitive from justice." In a postscript, William Fitts, the assistant attorney general, added that his office "could not possibly make any order favorable to him and it should not do so even if it could." Without prospects to box for money in Spain, Johnson could not fight for glory in France. Were he to return home, he would arrive as a convicted felon, not an honored veteran.[62]

Peace came in late 1918. But demobilization brought a major recession, rampant social upheaval, a red scare, and a wave of political repression—hardly an auspicious setting for Johnson's return. Some 2 million blacks had left the South during the war, changing the composition and character of many northern cities. Tensions between races, ethnic groups, classes, and sects escalated after the war. Nothing symbolized dashed hopes more starkly than the lynching of eleven black veterans in 1919, some murdered while wearing their country's uniform. Race riots swept the country, with many deaths and extensive property damage in Longview, Texas, Chicago, Omaha, Knoxville, and even Washington, DC. Inspired by their service overseas, black veterans joined family, friends, and neighbors in striking back at white mobs. For the first time, many whites died in these clashes. Claude McKay, a Harlem poet, lauded black resistance:

> If we must die, let it not be like hogs
> Hunted and penned in an inglorious spot . . .
> Like men we'll face the murderous, cowardly pack,
> Pressed to the wall, dying, but fighting back!

Attorney General A. Mitchell Palmer blamed Bolshevik agents and the Industrial Workers of the World for the unrest. But these were convenient scapegoats. Waging righteous war abroad was easier than solving social problems at home. "One half of America denies us our right to vote; no part of America denies us our right to fight," Robert Abbott complained. "In time of peace the Southern white man wants us behind him; in time of war he wants us in front of him."[63]

Whether changed by the great war or the great migration, blacks were determined to resist what Claude McKay called "our accursed lot." Even in Georgia, notorious for recent wholesale lynchings, the spirit was unmistakable. The Reverend James Martin of Macon went to Milledgeville on May 27, 1919, to deliver a commencement address. Feelings were tense because students at both the white and black schools had chosen the same class colors, and whites resented the coincidence. Local blacks "had sworn to protect the school closing exercises to which I had to speak," Martin reported to DuBois. "Not less than 100 men were armed with rifles, pistols and shot guns" during the ceremony. The light artillery must have inspired Martin, for he used this local militancy and the legacy of black soldiers to mark the path ahead. "The Negro has earned every right and must contend for them in Georgia with as much zeal as he fought in Germany," Martin preached. "Each local community must cope with every emergency when it arises, caring more for what is right than life itself. Too many principles are too dear to be shunned by running or compromised by grinning." Whites decided that the issue of school colors did not merit a confrontation.

William Hewlett of Virginia also sensed that the days of "running" and "grinning" were over. He informed DuBois that he and other soldiers regretted having to leave France to return to the states "where true democracy is enjoyed only by white people." Blacks had not risked their lives to save jim crow. "If we have fought to make safe democracy for the white races," he noted, "we will soon fight to make it safe for ourselves and our posterity."[64]

In a manner more symbolic than substantive, Jack Johnson had fought for equality since the turn of the century. His success in the ring suggested the potential for comparable black achievement in other areas if competition were free and fair. As Johnson rose and fell, his people became more impatient with injustice and bolder in their demands for opportunity and equality. One crucial step was the formation of the NAACP in 1909. Black Americans also showed new resolve in opposing *The Birth of a Nation*. Even if they failed to block its screening, they succeeding in reminding Americans that entertainment masquerading as history could convey pernicious images that had social significance. Another impetus for change was the freedom and mobility stemming from migration and employment in northern industry. Above all, African Americans' military service inspired their resolve to attain better, freer, and safer lives. Johnson's own effort to trade boxing gloves for bayonet shows how African Americans hoped to translate sacrifice today into equality and justice tomorrow.

Yet the currents of change were erratic, their long-range impact uncertain. The great migration exposed the vast disparity between expectation and experience. Jack Johnson and his kin, for example, had joined the mass exodus from South to North, a migration that affected the nation as much as the more highly romanticized westward movement of pioneers. To both groups of migrants, the distant "frontier" beckoned as a land of new beginnings, a place to escape the past and build a better future.

As the exodus increased during the war, southern blacks deluged the *Chicago Defender* with queries about jobs, schools, and social conditions. Often too poor to buy train tickets, migrants hoped prospective employers would pay their way north and then accept reimbursement from their high wages. Eager to learn more about the unfamiliar North, they disclosed their feelings about a South they knew all too well. "There is nothing here for the colored man," a mason from Mobile, Alabama, complained, "but a hard time" from "southern crackers." Another man referred to Dapne, Alabama, as a "hard-luck place" where "15 or 20 familys" wanted to head north "but cant come on account of money . . . and we cant phone you . . . they dont want us to leave here & say if we dont go to war . . . they are going to kill us." A Texas man desperately wanted to leave because whites there were "so mean and . . . getting worse." Another writer urged the *Defender* to send a labor recruiter to Louisiana. "I am working hard in the south and can hardly earn a living," he lamented. "I have a wife and one child and can hardly feed them." He knew of "30 or 40" people eager to leave who had "to whisper this around" because whites resented the "negroes . . . going north." A Houston foundry worker pointed out that white managers always dismissed black employees first in hard times. From Macon, Georgia, a man complained that blacks had been "shot down . . . like rabbits" for the slightest "orfence."

Such travails affected all southern blacks. A minister from Newbern, Alabama, informed the *Defender* that the typical local worker was treated "as a slave" and wanted a change. "As leaders we are powerless for we dare not resent such or to show even the slightest disapproval," he wrote. "Only a few days ago more than 1000 people left here for the north and west." Whites insisted that blacks remain but offered them no incentives to stay. Himself "on the verge of starvation," the minister also wanted to leave. A teacher in Mississippi sought a new start because his white superintendent "cares less for a colored man than he does for the vilest beast."

Southern whites did take umbrage at every little "orfence" by blacks. "I want to get my famely out of this cursed south land," a father wrote from Greenville, Mississippi. "Down here a negro man is not [as] good as a white man's dog." Two men from New Orleans asked the *Defender* about the whole north, not just Chicago. "Anywhere north will do us," they explained, since "the worst place there is better than the best place here." Local hardships, not foreign agents, spurred the great migration.[65]

Chicago had promise but did not fully meet the migrants' expectations. The law allowed Jack Johnson to marry Lucille Cameron, for example, but people of all hues doubted whether what was legal was prudent or proper. Granted more rights and freedom under Illinois law and custom, Johnson had still encountered race prejudice there. Moreover, he had settled in Chicago at a time when white reformers found much of what he did repulsive—boxing, owning a nightclub, defying traffic laws, and consorting with white prostitutes. Much of the disdain whites felt for him was undeniably racial, but his lifestyle disturbed sober citizens on both sides of the color line.

Like other reformers before and after them, the progressives did more to clean up government, improve cities, safeguard workers and consumers, and regulate morals than to promote better race relations. The problems of race were far more intractable and divisive than those posed by venal politicians, avaricious railroads, white slave merchants, liquor dealers, and vendors of impure food and drugs. Johnson gained prominence at a time when his personal preferences and habits, not just his race, worked against him. Racism alone does not explain how he changed from great black hope to great black disappointment, but race was a major factor in his downfall. Johnson's initial success gratified his people but actually did little (or nothing) to improve their lot. When he lost his title and reputation, that should have also been an individual matter. But for better or worse, the peculiarities of American race relations bound Johnson and all African Americans together. It was not just; it just was. So Johnson's story reflects the intricate interplay between self and society, between private will and public weal. His significance emerges in the dialectic between his own character and conduct and the cultural complexities of his time and place. Punished for insisting on individual choice and denied differentiation from his group, Johnson found himself a crucial symbol in the struggle between the races. Neither whites nor blacks knew what to make of him, for he lived in accordance with his own wishes at a time when black folks were supposed to know better than to challenge their proscribed roles. Whether maligned on the big screen, confined to separate and unequal facilities, or lynched by southern mobs, African Americans—commoner and champion alike—lived precariously "under the white man's menace."

4

"Outcasts Asylumed"
Exile's Return and Legacy

> For never let the thought arise
> That we are here on sufferance bare;
> Outcasts asylumed 'neath these skies,
> And aliens without part or share.[1]

—James Weldon Johnson, "Fifty Years," 1917

Before earning the big purses that came with main event bouts, Jack Johnson had a problem common to those who aspire to higher status—his many wants far exceeded his meager means. Johnson was once in San Francisco, for example, when champion Jim Jeffries had a fight scheduled there. Unable or unwilling to buy tickets, Johnson and some friends schemed to get in without paying. Finding an open transom above a locked door in the arena, the intruders climbed through one by one and scrambled down the hall. Last in line, Johnson squirmed through the opening and lowered himself to the floor, only to find a policeman waiting for him. Known for quick hands in the ring, Johnson now called upon his nimble wit. "Oh, Mister Officer, chase them boys quick," he urged the patrolman. "I'm the janitor of this here pavilion and they done sneaked in through the transom. I been chasing them all over the building. Hurry, or you won't catch them." As the officer pursued "them boys," Johnson sauntered in to watch the fight. The ruse surely tickled Johnson, for he had finagled his way in and fooled "the man" in the process.[2]

This amusing anecdote is also instructive. It shows that shrewd blacks could sometimes use racial stereotypes to their own advantage, and it provides a glimpse into Jack Johnson's character. In a more subtle way, the incident suggests a peculiar relationship between Johnson and his people, between individual and group aspirations. Since whites often saw all African Americans as similar despite wide disparities, Johnson as a public figure served as a mirror reflecting one race to another. As the first black king of the heavyweights, Johnson acquired a symbolic significance that transcended boxing. In his pursuit of personal advantage, he often disappointed or betrayed others, as shown in his diversion of the police officer toward his friends. Duping the policeman had no real effect beyond the pavilion. But Johnson's violations of law and public opinion moved him from the sports pages to the front pages.

Jack Johnson and the Black Community

Less doctrinaire on matters of race and culture than whites, black journalists and intellectuals drew sharper distinctions between Johnson and his people—especially in terms of manners and morals. But they knew their efforts to separate one boxer from a race of millions would not stop whites from making broad generalizations about the group on the basis of a single celebrity's conduct. Already alarmed by rising rancor and violence, black activists wanted Johnson to help elevate the race and not embarrass it. In a society where "black champion" seemed an oxymoron to most whites, Johnson could never be his own man even if he and others thought it should be that way.

Johnson's ploy to sneak into the Jeffries' fight was one of many instances in which he resorted to dubious means to achieve his ends. Like slaves who had outsmarted masters and overseers in defiance of a hierarchy that relegated them to the level of hogs and mules, Johnson beat the white hopes and reversed the usual roles of victor and vanquished. This inversion made him a folk hero to those who dared not defy the prevailing order. As champion, Johnson fought only "white hopes" and avoided black opponents—a choice that accentuated his role as a racial avenger. Like Denmark Vesey and Nat Turner, slaves who had led revolts against their oppressors, he rebelled against a caste system based on color. "I am not a slave," he declared amid the furor over his marriage to a second white woman. His intent to live "without the dictation of any man" must have impressed even his black critics, for all African Americans chafed under a tradition of shared enslavement, submission, and deference to whites.[3] "Not a slave," Johnson was also not a master. He enjoyed certain legal rights and a measure of freedom, but he lived in a proscriptive society that sought to curtail the liberties of blacks rather than affirm or expand them. Johnson wanted a life unfettered by custom or convention and independent of any leader, organization, or race—even his own. He lived for himself, not for Tuskegee, the NAACP, the black press, and certainly not for whites.

Johnson cared primarily about himself, not group advancement or public opinion. His insistence on his "right to choose" could have been construed as a declaration in behalf of all citizens regardless of color or creed. But Johnson was no crusader for equal rights. To him, success was a ticket to personal privilege and not a lever to lift his own race or to elevate white opinion. He craved money for the pleasures it bought, and he cashed in on the white obsession to see him humbled. Some of the money that fans paid to see him lose ended up in his pockets. For Americans in his time cared about cash as well as color. His wealth and fame, for example, gave him access to white women, or at least to a certain kind of white woman, and bailed him out of jail and bought him legal counsel when he needed it.

Johnson inspired a desperate search for a "white hope," but he actually used the hysteria to his own advantage. In the contract for the 1908 title fight, for example, Johnson agreed to a purse of only $5,000 while Tommy Burns insisted on $35,000. Denying the charge he had a "yellow streak," Johnson proposed a much smaller ring only ten feet square and wagered his entire take on the outcome. "By betting the $5,000 I can double my end of the purse or quit without a nickel," he told reporters. "Burns can name the terms. As long as he doesn't demand that I wear hopples, tie my hands behind me, and wear a blindfold, I am willing to meet him on any grounds." Meeting in a regulation ring twenty-four-feet square, Johnson took command from the beginning but prolonged the white champion's ordeal for fourteen grueling rounds before dropping him. After the fight, Johnson bragged he could have knocked Burns out "in the first few rounds" but wanted him to earn his lion's share of the gate the hard way. Johnson bragged that his victory had been "even easier" than he had expected. Johnson could now mine the title as one white hope after another tried to preempt his claim.

Johnson approached Jeffries the same way, betting heavily on himself and urging friends to do so, too. He also tried to "hoodoo" the retired champion. "My young brother, Charley, is studying to be an undertaker, and he graduates July 1," Johnson observed before the fight. "I will give him his first customer. I will start a job and brother Charley will finish it." All through the bout, Johnson bantered with whites and advised telegraphic dispatchers at ringside what to transmit over the wires. Not content with the win and windfall in 1910, Johnson encouraged reporters to persuade Jeffries to try again:

> Now don't discourage Jeff if he wants to fight again. I won't hurt him, but I surely can get rich fighting him. . . . It's too bad that you ain't got a lot of good fighters, as I need a few more automobiles. I've only got six now, and I would like to own a regiment of them. But all of you fellows write and tell Jeff that I'm a wreck. Maybe he'll believe it and then I'll add a few flying machines to my collection of speedy things.

Unable to goad Jeffries into a rematch, Johnson tried to entice other white hopes to fight him. Johnson, according to Leon Pryor of the *Denver Statesman*, promised to "pay Al Palzer $2,000 for every round he stayed with him after the third." Pryor explained the gambit. "Jack is a little smarter than people give him credit for being," he noted. "He knows just how to get plenty of free advertising and notoriety."[4]

Much of Johnson's "notoriety" before his interracial marriages and liaisons came from his driving. He hardly needed "a few flying machines"—he habitually flew low in his "speedy" automobiles. His fondness for fast cars helped define him in life and legend, for he seemed to spend more time fending off judges than boxers. A New York City magistrate chided him in 1910 for repeatedly breaking traffic laws. "But, your Honor," Johnson protested, "that was done for advertising purposes." Months later he contested an arrest before a California judge. He told journalist Leon Pryor that no police officer could have seen him if he had *really* been speeding. And even if police had seen him, they never could have caught him. A popular tale captures Johnson's fondness for speed and his contempt for white authority. A sheriff in Georgia pulled Johnson over and snarled at him, "Where do you think you're going, boy, speeding like that? That'll cost you $50!" Johnson reached into his pocket, gave the sheriff a C-note, and revved his engine. "Don't you want your change?" the lawman asked. "Keep it," Johnson replied, "'cause I'm coming back the same way I'm going!" In another tale, a black man choked a southern constable into insensibility. Local folks dubbed him "Jack Johnson." In this lore Johnson symbolizes black power as he outsmarts whites, defies their laws, and flaunts his wealth. By gunning his motor and vowing to drive through the South "just as fast" on his return, he shows he is nobody's "boy."[5]

The legend of Jack Johnson depicts a bold man who refused to scrape and bow, the bottom rail elevated to the top. At the dawn of the auto age, Johnson prided himself on his fleet of these new status symbols that accentuated his social and spatial mobility. He even bought custom-made and imported cars when most whites could not afford a Model T. He lived lavishly, spared mundane labor by his servants. By crossing the color line for white prostitutes and brides, he defied the most inviolable of racial taboos. At a time when lynch mobs murdered scores of black men (and an occasional woman) for real or imagined breaches of the race code, Johnson earned a fortune beating and bloodying white opponents. As champion, he asserted himself in contract negotiations. "He is in a position to dictate terms as he deems best," Les Walton marveled in 1909, and he "refuses to be bullied into matches." Johnson derived pleasure as well as profit from his anomalous role. In one fight against a white foe, the story goes, Johnson forced his hapless opponent "around to that part of the ring at which his hopeful manager was seated." Johnson knocked him "over the ropes . . . into the man's indignant lap." Flashing his golden smile, Johnson gibed, "There's your white hope, Pop!"

Johnson's frequent brushes with the law, his brash manner, and his contempt for convention bothered some black Americans more than others. Traffic tickets and civil suits by theater owners and former managers aroused little concern. But the white slave charge was different because of the cultural connotations surrounding intimacy between black men and white women. Even if the evidence of illegality was suspect, Johnson could harm his people by flouting entrenched customs as well as by actually violating the law. His first white wife's suicide and his untimely marriage to a second white woman soon after loomed large in the declining reputation of blacks in the white mind, a nadir epitomized in D.W. Griffith's *The Birth of a Nation* in 1915. The prosecution of Johnson in 1913 was another attempt to enforce racial separation and subordination—a trend already apparent in the rise of the Klan, the Supreme Court's ruling in *Plessy v. Ferguson* that sanctioned segregation ("separate but equal") in public transportation, Tom Dixon's novels, the pogroms in Atlanta and Springfield, lynchings, and efforts to discourage interracial mixing and marriage. Johnson suffered from this repression but also exacerbated it. In Johnson's trial, the whole race seemed to stand before the bench, so many black journalists felt relieved when he jumped bail and fled abroad. Lore about his boldness still appealed to those shadowed by jim crow, but his exile and eventual defeat by Jess Willard in 1915 removed a major irritant between the races.

The bonds that tied Johnson to his people made it difficult for them to separate their future from his personal fate, since he was in a position to enhance or demean the reputation of millions. This peculiar dynamic explains why so many conflicting emotions and opinions about him emanated from the pulpit, the pressroom, and the sports desk. By the end of Johnson's trial, most black journalists considered him a dismal failure as a race ambassador. Yet they realized the inherent difficulty of his role and the odds against him. Johnson was denied "a square deal," the *Indianapolis Freeman* complained. "As a Negro, a member of a despised race, he has been meted out a terrible punishment for daring to exceed what is considered a Negro's circle of activities." Dr. Monroe Majors, a physician, poet, editor, and civil rights activist, also thought Johnson paid dearly for having aspirations beyond those that whites deemed proper. He had prestige, white women, and money—"a mansion fit for any judge, governor, or president" as well as "a $10,000 150–horsepower automobile." Like blacks of lesser fame, he had felt "the white heat of hate" kindled by bigotry. "Jack is a gentleman beside thousands of white men who will escape the horrors of the Mann Act," Majors wrote, "simply because white jurors and white courts" routinely convicted blacks and habitually acquitted whites.

Johnson had his faults, Les Walton conceded, but he had incurred penalties far exceeding his transgressions. The ban on fight films after Johnson defeated Jeffries "meant a loss of thousands of dollars" to him. Walton doubted that white police treated Johnson fairly; they arrested him "to get some publicity." Chicago officials shut down his cabaret in 1912. "We do not condone the champion's rank disregard for public opinion, for his indiscretions have done the members of his race much harm," Walton argued. "But even had he not erred in judgment his color in this country would have operated against him."[6]

Some whites also defended him. "Johnson, despite his black skin, is a good fellow at heart," wrestler Ed Dunkhorst stated in 1914. "Once I loaned him a dollar to get a place to sleep. He was down and out. The next time I met him he handed me $100. The next day he asked me the address of a Russian tailor who had befriended him. He not only paid what he owed but staked the tailor to enough coin to take his family back to Russia." Big Ed betrayed some bias in praising Johnson "despite his black skin," but on a personal level he admitted liking Johnson more than Jeffries. John Lardner later observed that Johnson's white critics held "the fundamental tenet" that any black champion was "a threat to civilization" who must be removed. "It seems to have been largely because Johnson displayed his tastes and appetites frankly, and insisted that his privileges were equal to those of any white athlete, that he was denounced," Lardner reflected. "He insisted on all his rights . . . at a time when most people believed that Negroes should know what was called their place and should live their lives as discreetly and intramurally as possible." Nat Fleischer, the founder of *Ring* magazine, considered Johnson "one of the brainiest fighters" he had known. His appreciation extended beyond boxing. "He was an arrogant man," Fleisher admitted, "but I liked him despite the many bad marks he had against him."[7]

Johnson's career unfolded amid rising nativism and racism that affected him, his people, and the nation. From Rutherford Hayes to Woodrow Wilson, presidents said little and did even less about race relations, ignoring blatant defiance of federal law in the South. Congress also neglected African Americans. Even at the peak of the Progressive movement, Congress showed more concern for pure food and drugs than for equal rights and justice. The judiciary compiled an equally dismal record, perhaps even more shameful because judges with life tenure were in a position to resist public opinion and affirm the rule of law. In the landmark cases *Plessy v. Ferguson* (1896) and *Berea College v. Kentucky* (1908), for example, the Supreme Court upheld segregation imposed by state law. Justice John Harlan dissented in each case, but his voice was out of tune with his colleagues and his time. "There is no caste here," he objected in 1896. "Our Constitution is color-blind, and neither knows nor tolerates classes among citizens." He knew that segregation subordinated blacks rather than merely separating them from whites. "The destinies of the two races in this country are indissolubly linked together," Harlan protested, "and the interests of both require that the common government of all shall not permit the seeds of race hate to be planted under the sanction of law."

Harlan realized that "the seeds of race hate" had fully sprouted by 1908— the year Johnson won the title. Having sanctioned jim crow on a public carrier in 1896, the court in 1908 upheld a state law against integrated instruction of white and black students at a private college. "Have we become so inoculated with prejudice of race," Harlan asked, "that an American government, professedly based on the principles of freedom, and charged with the protection of all citizens alike, can make distinctions between such citizens in the matter of their voluntary meeting for innocent purposes, simply because of their respective races?" To many white Americans, however, no race mixing was "innocent." For proof that "prejudice of race" permeated the land, Harlan need have looked no further than the reaction to Johnson's victory over Jeffries in 1910.[8]

Johnson viewed rights in personal rather than institutional or philosophical terms. Unlike W.E.B. DuBois, Ida B. Wells, and John Harlan, Johnson paid scant attention to law and litigation until his own Mann Act trial. Until then he spoke only of his right to marry whomever he chose. He did not challenge jim crow or take a public stand on any major issue, even lynching. The *Indianapolist Freeman*'s Charles Marshall traveled with Johnson in 1909 and noticed that he never mingled or stayed where he might be unwanted. On the train, Johnson avoided other passengers and the dining car, taking meals in his private berth. At stops, he strolled to the rear platform to get some air but then returned to his quarters rather than enter the station. Johnson, Marshall added, patronized only businesses that welcomed him.

Johnson journeyed by train through Colorado in 1911, and the dailies printed rumors that white men had chastised him and his friends for some unspecified sin. But the *Denver Statesman* denied the stories, arguing that Johnson had avoided public spaces while crossing the state. Excepting the conductor's showing him the Royal Gorge from the platform, "Johnson remained in the state room, even his meals being served him there," the *Statesman* countered. "The [white] papers find little news worthwhile when they have to pander to prejudice in such a shamelessly untruthful manner." Will Pickens, racer Barney Oldfield's manager, had watched Johnson beat Jeffries and had seen him among whites. "I never saw a negro that knew his place and kept it any better," Pickens asserted. "Johnson does not seek the society of whites. He has a white man to handle all his business deals with white men." Pickens found him "as smart and inoffensive a negro as Booker Washington."

Johnson did not see himself this way, at least not in the self-portrait he presented in his 1927 memoir. "White people often point to the writings of Booker T. Washington as the best example of a desirable attitude on the part of the colored population," Johnson noted. "I have never been able to agree with . . . Washington, because he has to my mind not been altogether frank in the statement of the problems or courageous in the formulation of his solutions to them." Johnson preferred Frederick Douglass, who had "faced the issues without compromising." He explained his own strategy: "I have found no better way of avoiding racial prejudice than to act in my relations with people of other races as if prejudice did not exist." But Johnson took other precautions, too. "I had guts," he reflected, "and was handy with my gun."[9]

But prejudice existed even if Johnson pretended otherwise. And after he beat Jeffries he triggered even more of it. If he "knew his place and kept it" in 1910, he certainly had forgotten and lost it a few years later. Johnson's decision to avoid black women for white proved a fateful one, since neither his "guts" nor his "gun" deterred those who wanted to teach him and his people a lesson about interracial sex and marriage. Harlem's black hope became Brooklyn's black horror.

But Johnson also disturbed many who shared his color but not his character. When Johnson wed Lucille Cameron the *Nashville Globe* "found nothing [in] common between the champion and the race to which he belongs," for the interracial marriage had "placed a great gulf between himself and his people." Other editors concurred. "Crime in this country is not indigenous to race," the *Bee*'s Calvin Chase argued during the investigation of Johnson. "Respectable colored men and women" viewed him "not . . . as a hero, but a pariah." Long in Johnson's corner, even the *Chicago Defender* abandoned him. He "left us a legacy . . . that has caused no end of trouble and humiliation," the *Defender* reflected in 1920, including "bills . . . to prevent intermarriage." Whites used the one to punish the many. "The lines of discrimination, already taut, were drawn tighter," the *Defender* complained. "The unfriendly press referred to him as a Race leader, insinuating that as he thought and did, so too, did the other ninety and nine. This wave of racial hatred in its most virulent form swept over the country for months." The champion's "wild escapades" spawned "the very beginning of race hatred" in Chicago, Charles Marshall asserted, and stoked tensions that sparked the awful riot of 1919.

The crusade against intermarriage was one manifestation of the furor over

Johnson. Jesse Thomas, a field director for Tuskegee from 1911 to 1916, described another. Some prospective donors to the college would "indicate that they were interested . . . and have you come back a half dozen times," Thomas recalled. Then they would "finally terminate the interview by describing some awkward conduct of some Negro . . . Jack Johnson was the ready-made exhibit."[10]

Race Hatred and Black Soldiers

This race hatred persisted during World War I. Black soldiers served in segregated units and endured insults from whites stationed in France, but their experiences abroad expanded their horizons and raised their expectations. Many whites, on the other hand, wanted no change in race matters. "On the Negroes this double experience of deliberate and devilish persecution from their own countrymen coupled with a taste of real democracy . . . was revolutionizing," DuBois observed right after the war. "They began to hate prejudice and discrimination as they had never hated it before." Professor Kelly Miller of Howard University agreed. "Regarded in America as the most alien of aliens before the war," Miller wrote of the African American, "he demands recognition today as the most loyal of loyalists."[11]

Reactionaries hoped to stymie reform in civil rights by impugning the black soldiers. Colonel Allen Greer, white chief of staff of the Colored 92nd Division, accused black troops of heinous crimes and failure in combat. "During our career, counting the time in America, we have had about thirty cases of rape, among which was one where twenty-two men at Camp Grant raped one woman, and we have had eight (I believe) reported in France with about fifteen attempts besides," Greer wrote to Senator Kenneth McKellar of Tennessee in late 1918. "There have been any number of self-inflicted wounds, among others one [by a] captain." Greer also attributed "numerous accidental shootings, several murders, and . . . several cases of patrols or sentinels shooting at each other" to these black soldiers. "They have in fact been dangerous to no one," he sneered, "except themselves and women." Only white officers had managed to restrain them. "The undoubted truth is that the Colored officers neither control nor care to control the men," Greer told McKellar. "They themselves have been engaged very largely in the pursuit of French women, it being their first opportunity to meet white women who did not treat them as servants." Greer advised McKellar to ignore the black officers' reports. "Accuracy and ability to describe facts is lacking in all," he contended, "and most of them are just plain liars."

Congressman James Byrnes of South Carolina advised black veterans to accept subordination or leave the country. "The war has in no way changed the attitude of the white man toward the social and political equality of the negro," Byrnes warned in early 1920. "If as a result of his experience in the war he does not care to live in this land without political and social equality, then he can depart for any other country he wishes, and his departure will be facilitated by the white people of this country, who desire no disturbing factor in their midst." Senator William Kirby of Arkansas opposed plans for universal military training after the war. The price tag and the specter of militarism bothered him. So did the prospect that blacks might be included. "The Negro on the whole is well disposed, industrious, peaceable, and law abiding, and makes a good farm laborer and farmer," Kirby argued. "But when he is given military training it changes his disposition and he becomes idle and arrogant, a troublesome element in the rural districts."

DuBois sailed to France to investigate complaints from black soldiers about white officers. He found "every essential statement" in Greer's letter "either false or misleading." Conceding many shortcomings among the soldiers, he stressed the obstacles they had met and their achievements against the odds. Rather than ascribe misconduct and ineptitude to race traits, DuBois blamed the War Department for failing to train black soldiers for the ordeal of trench warfare. (The War Department had initially opposed combat for black troops and had confined them to menial labor.) DuBois also thought the army had not always appointed capable white officers to command the black troops. White commanders cared more about keeping black soldiers from French women, DuBois charged, than about preparing them to confront seasoned German troops. They began "by officially stigmatizing the Negroes as rapists," admonishing them "not even to speak to women on the street," DuBois noted. They "ordered the white military police to spy on the blacks and arrest them if they found them talking with French women." White doughboys followed their commanders' cues and "spread tales and rumors among the peasants and villagers." Whites scolded black soldiers and "offending women" for socializing across the color line.

This proscription angered blacks and baffled the French. "The Negroes resented being publicly stigmatized by their own countrymen as unfit for association with decent people," DuBois reported, "but the French men and women much preferred the courtesy and bonhomie of the Negroes to the impudence and swagger of many of the whites." In many French towns, "Negro troops . . . left close and sympathetic friends among men, women, and children." The NAACP journal put a human face on these soldiers by recounting tales that circulated among them. Seasick from days of high waves on the Atlantic, one soldier lay on the deck of his ship and prayed, "Oh, Lawd, please make that ocean come to attention." A captain at the front drilling his men asked, "Suppose our company is holding the line here and the boche makes a charge at us across the field, what would you boys do?" "Well, captain," a soldier replied, "we sho' would spread the news over France." Another black soldier in the trenches sported a brand-new pair of boots. When asked where he got them he said, "from a boche." His buddy then left the trench and returned four hours later with new footgear. Anticipating the obvious question, he explained, "I had to kill twenty of dem boches befo' I got a pair to fit." One soldier loaded a big artillery gun. After firing, he would shout, "Count your men, Mr. Kaiser, count your men." Quickly reloading and directing another charge at the Germans, he jumped up and advised, "Count 'em again, Mr. Kaiser, count 'em again!" Several eminent black activists and scholars—Kelly Miller, Ralph Tyler of the Committee on Public Information, and Emmett Scott, a War Department aide formerly of Tuskegee—wrote books refuting Greer, McKellar, and others who maligned the black soldiers.[12]

Even if Jack Johnson had been allowed to join the army in 1918, he would not have been spared retribution when he returned home. "Scarcely had the armistice been signed before an honorably discharged colored soldier was lynched in Kentucky for resisting arrest by a constable," James Weldon Johnson noted in 1919. "Since then, at least four other colored soldiers have been lynched; some of them wearing their uniforms, one of them because he was wearing his uniform." Southern whites "began organizing anew the Ku Klux Klan," Johnson added, "for the openly avowed purpose of keeping the Negro in his place." The North had race problems too, as blacks "all over the country" faced "the same old and bitter fight for common justice and fair opportunity." By the end of 1919, nine black veterans had lost their lives to lynch mobs.

Race baiters attributed the lynchings to sexual assault, but statistics said otherwise. Whites used terrorism to maintain their dominance over blacks. "Dying and desperate" after losing the election of 1920, the Democratic Party, Kelly Miller argued, "clutches at the straw of race hatred as its last gasping hope." A. Philip Randolph and Chandler Owen of *The Messenger* argued that wealthy whites abetted race prejudice to divide and exploit workers. Beneficiaries of cheap child labor, bogus vagrancy and convict-lease laws, and government favoritism during strikes and lockouts, these moguls cared only about profits, not people, black or white. "Race antagonism, then," the editors concluded, "is profitable to those who own the farms, the mills, the railroads, and the banks. This economic arrangement in the South is the fundamental cause of race prejudice . . . the fuse which causes the magazine of capitalism to explode into race conflicts—lynchings." By levying a poll tax on the poor and disfranchising blacks, "the ruling class of the South" controlled politics as well as property. Politicians outside the South largely ignored these abuses because the rich "owned" them too.[13]

Whether this "race antagonism" was mainly cultural or economic in origin, it shadowed Jack Johnson throughout his career. His triumphs over white opponents provided vicarious pleasure to blacks, but this momentary psychological lift made no appreciable difference in the institutional realities of their separate and unequal lives. Besides, by the time of his conviction on the white slave charge, Johnson had done more harm than good for his people. He fled to Europe to escape his personal punishment as well as the overall opprobrium directed at his race. Other blacks who lacked the will or means to leave lived in internal exile, hoping their customary separation would shield them from the more deadly manifestations of white racism.

As Johnson won renown in mixed competition, less fortunate and more vulnerable African Americans formed all-black communities to secure and improve their lives. In Boley, Oklahoma, for example, boosters summoned black pioneers "to prove to the caucasian race and . . . the world that the Negro is a law-making and law-abiding citizen" and to do their part "[to] help solve the great racial problem that is now before us." Editor O.H. Bradley of the *Boley Progress* rebuked whites for trying to confine blacks to Dixie. "You know and I know," he wrote, "that the conditions and opportunities for the Negro to secure land, to rise in the business and social world, are growing more oppressive every day in the South." A 1911 lynching in Purcell, Oklahoma, reminded Boley's residents of their reasons for living among their own. In Purcell and across the land, blacks were "shot down like dogs, hanged without judge or jury, and burned at the stake for pleasure," the *Progress* decried. "Certainly mob violence has become a national sin."

Colonel Allen Allensworth, a former slave, Civil War veteran, and army chaplain, founded a black haven north of Bakersfield, California, in 1909. He explained what this experiment meant to the race as a whole. "A large number of our fellow countrymen have been taught for generations that the Negro is incapable of the highest development of citizenship," he observed. "This they believe and will continue to think until we show them they are mistaken. To do that we must indicate capacity." But whites seldom gave blacks a chance to prove themselves. "If we expect to be given due credit for our efforts and achievements they must be made where they will stand out distinctly and alone," Allensworth advised. "To do this people of our race must be in a community where the responsibilities of its municipal government are upon them, and them alone." Only in separate communities could blacks "show pioneer enterprise, heroic sacrifice, united effort and concentration of moral influence."[14]

Surrender and Imprisonment

Despite the disheartening trends in race relations at home, Jack Johnson tired of exile abroad and decided to return. The office of the attorney general informed Bureau of Investigation agents in 1919 "that Johnson will voluntarily return to the United States sometime in the near future, as the body of his mother, who died some time ago, is still in a receiving vault and interment has not been made." Johnson took his time, but on July 20, 1920, by prior arrangement, he met a sheriff in Tiajuana who escorted him across the border and turned him over to a federal marshal in San Diego. "I am an American through and through, and no country, however generous, can take the place of my country," Johnson announced, according to a *Defender* correspondent at the scene. "Prisons in America are preferable to thrones over there, and I am happy that my exile has come to an end." Marshals drove him to Los Angeles and made plans to return him to the federal court for Northern Illinois. Johnson, however, balked at the itinerary. "The road mapped out for the trip to Chicago was over the State of Texas," a bureau agent reported on July 23, "but the subject had some objection to this as he was in fear of being attacked by citizens of the State of Texas at some point through which they might travel." Agents revised the route to placate Johnson. In Chicago he was held without bail. Judge George Carpenter lectured him again and ordered him confined to the federal penitentiary in Leavenworth, Kansas, to complete his sentence. "If a man shows by his actions that he regrets his crime, if he is contrite in heart and wants to do right, and wants to reestablish a home and live decently among people," Carpenter explained, "that man must be shown some consideration." But Carpenter saw no more remorse or repentance in Johnson now than in 1913. "He has defied the laws of this country for six years," the judge complained. "He is in no position today to ask leniency."

The superintendent who ushered Johnson into Leavenworth was none other than Denver Dickerson, the former governor of Nevada who had allowed the Johnson–Jeffries fight to be staged in Reno. For his work assignment, Johnson became caretaker of the prison baseball field. Dickerson headed the Board of Parole in 1921 and asked the Justice Department to review Johnson's case for consideration by his panel. Bureau chief Lewis Baley complied, providing a synopsis intended to discourage Johnson's release. "He had a mania for young white girls regardless of their character or reputation," Baley noted, and along with the liaisons that had prompted the Mann Act indictment "there were at least 30 or 40 young white girls who fell victim to his vicious practices without the interstate feature." Not only had Johnson violated federal law, he had as an exile conspired against his country. "This prisoner while located in Mexico was engaged in propaganda work among the negroes of the United States, particularly in Texas and Louisiana," Baley wrote, "having for its purpose the inciting of riots among the negroes in event of trouble between Mexico and this country." If contrition and loyalty were required for clemency, Johnson seemed destined to serve his full sentence.

Eager to return to the limelight and big paydays, Johnson urged promoters to match him against champion Jack Dempsey. With characteristic bravado, he predicted he could win even without training. Jack Kearns, Dempsey's manager, immediately vetoed the idea. "Johnson is through," Kearns declared, "through with his own people; he stands discredited in the eyes of the civilized world." Kearns called him "a tremendous source of trouble" and thought boxing was better off without him. "All the money in the world," Kearns declared, could not tempt Dempsey "to dignify the Negro with a fight." Johnson had dug himself a very deep hole. It seemed unlikely he could ever climb out of it.[15]

By the time Johnson exchanged exile in Europe and Mexico for a prison cell in Kansas, his personal life was in shambles and his professional prospects dim. He had forfeited $15,000 in bond by fleeing to Europe. His mother had died in 1918, and the bank had foreclosed on her home. He could not fight for money in prison. Later, in 1924 he and Lucille divorced, ending a marriage that had been both a private pact and a public controversy. In the realm of politics and diplomacy, Americans by 1920 had lost enthusiasm for crusades at home and abroad, and the social climate made any civil rights advances unlikely. The United States had undergone a major transformation in both domestic and foreign affairs between Johnson's debut as a professional fighter in 1897 and his decision to return home in the aftermath of World War One. Warren G. Harding promised a return to "normalcy" if elected president in 1920 and won in a landslide. The conservative ascendancy during the Roaring Twenties provided a respite from muckraking, reform, and military crusades to remake the world. Race relations, on the other hand, needed no respite from rapid change, for progressives had achieved virtually nothing in this realm. With the country in perpetual motion because of constant technological, economic, social, and cultural changes, whites took some comfort in the resilience of the racial status quo. Whether from old stock or new, descendants of lords or peasants, European Americans shared "whiteness" and the race privileges premised on color. Often divided by ethnicity, religion, language, and income, they shared rights, advantages, and aspirations inherent in their preferential status. Though not rich or powerful, they at least were not black or brown. An immigrant from Europe did not have to live long in the United States to learn what that meant.

Johnson's reluctance to travel through Texas was understandable at the time. He undoubtedly had read about the horrendous lynching in Waco in 1916 and the tragedy in Houston the following year when black troops with the Twenty-fourth Infantry killed many whites—a spree that sent thirteen soldiers to the gallows for mutiny and murder. Chicago itself was reeling from a huge influx of migrants during the war, fifty-eight recent bombings of black homes and businesses, and the bloody riot of 1919 that left thirty-eight people dead, twenty-three blacks and fifteen whites. The multiracial Chicago Commission on Race Relations, appointed by the governor to investigate racial tensions in the city, contended, "Our Negro problem . . . is not of the Negro's making." The panel blamed the white press for its sensational coverage of black crime and vice. It also faulted the courts for bias in the criminal justice system and accused law enforcement personnel of "actual police participation in the rioting as well as neglect of duty." The recurring interracial violence could be traced primarily to white vigilantes who resorted to intimidation and terror to expel blacks from homes in "contested" areas and to block them from moving into "exclusive" neighborhoods. Conflict between blacks and whites, the report concluded, "is our most grave and perplexing domestic problem."[16]

Whether a champion or former champion, Johnson remained an important symbol to both blacks and whites, although in very different ways. To his people during his glory days, he was a race pioneer blazing a trail of progress others might follow. His triumphs were theirs, his punishment of white opponents a catharsis for the black masses who could not attain vengeance by any other means. As champion prior to his indictment, trial, and conviction on the Mann Act charge, he challenged many racist assumptions. "Traducers proclaimed his undeveloped capacities," Professor Kelly Miller wrote of the African American at this time. "He answered with a claim of long repressed aptitudes." For all black people and not just boxers, Miller sought nothing more and nothing less than equal opportunity and impartial justice. In a truly democratic society, some blacks would succeed while others failed, but their destiny should depend upon personal traits and not a collective handicap. This appeal for fairness and tolerance rang out in Johnson's time and continued to echo through the entire twentieth century, a reasonable plea in a society that prided itself on individualism, freedom, and getting one's just deserts.

But logic seldom prevailed in the realm of race. In a less color-conscious society, character and capacity would have mattered more than race. The Johnson–Jeffries fight, for instance, would have been nothing more than a contest between two athletes. The suicide of Etta Johnson and the marriage of Jack Johnson and Lucille Cameron would have been private concerns without public consequences. Johnson's indiscretions and alleged crimes would have been his and his alone. But Johnson, his title, his wives and consorts, his cars, his opponents, and his trial all had cultural significance that rendered them matters of public interest. Many whites interpreted Johnson's conduct as evidence of deplorable traits inherent in his people, a people in need of restraint by means of race-specific laws and customs and mob violence. Blacks rejected this view, arguing that variations within a race were more significant than purported differences between races. Nothing on the horizon seemed likely to narrow this gap. Whites and blacks seldom agreed on what the problems were, much less on how to remedy them. The races seemed to speak and hear different languages and to view life through radically different lenses.

Take, for instance, the bête noire of Johnson's harshest critics—interracial sex and marriage. Miscegenation and its origins, extent, and importance meant one thing to most whites, quite another to most blacks. To many whites, sexual intimacy between the races threatened the very survival of American civilization. Many blacks, however, viewed Johnson's private preferences as trivial in the larger context. W.E.B. DuBois addressed this disparity in 1913. "It is a question that colored people seldom discuss," he noted. "It is about the last of the social problems over which they are disturbed, because they so seldom face it in fact or in theory." They had many concerns more urgent than consensual interracial coupling. "Their problems are problems of work and wages," DuBois observed, "of the right to vote, of the right to travel decently, of the right to frequent places of public amusement, of the right to public security." Besides, "both races" had similar feelings about intermarriage. "Colored folk marry colored folk and white marry white," he noted, "and the exceptions are very few." Johnson and Cameron "proposed to live together," so DuBois thought it "better for them to be legally married." Despite the rarity of such "exceptions," DuBois opposed any ban on them. He denied that white women required special protection against black men, arguing instead that black women needed additional safeguards against white men. "Low as the white girl falls," he explained, "she can compel her seducer to marry her." Black women did not have this remedy. "This winter will see a determined attempt to insult and degrade us by such non-intermarriage laws," he warned after Johnson's wedding. "We must kill them, not because we are anxious to marry white men's sisters, but because we are determined that white men shall let our sisters alone."[17]

If white racists were not ranting about mixed marriages, they were raving about the menace of social equality, a condition that would encourage intermarriage and hasten "race suicide." Any effort by blacks to secure the vote, improve schools, gain access to public facilities, obtain better jobs, or attain due process of law was construed as a fatal first step toward a "mongrel" population lacking the better qualities of both original races. Black writers wearied of these tirades. "Like a drowning man grasping for a straw, so the white American clings to his nightmare, social equality," a *Defender* editorial complained. "Without this specter ever before him he would be at a loss for an excuse to harass us. It is so flimsy, so utterly absurd, so far fetched and idiotic." The *Defender* objected that "there is no such thing as equality, social or otherwise," since "nature abhors equality." Blacks wanted better lives, not race mixing. "We are selfish enough and particular enough to mingle with those of our own, and we would thank many of the whites to follow our example," the *Defender* counseled. "Our sole request has been for an even break, politically and industrially. We long to be let alone that we may work out our own salvation."

Sharply divided on the significance of mixed marriages and the meaning of "social equality," the races also differed on crimes by blacks. Whites considered blacks inherently disposed to deviance and crime and blamed the race for shielding its vilest criminals from the law. So whites tended to hold the entire group culpable for heinous deeds by a lone individual. DuBois objected. "There is a curious assumption in some quarters that intelligent and law-abiding Negroes like, encourage, and sympathize with Negro crime and defend Negro criminals," he protested. "They do not. They suffer more from the crime of their fellows than white folks suffer, not only vicariously, but directly; the black criminal knows that he can prey on his own people with the least danger of punishment, because they control no police or courts." This misconception led many whites to condone lynching, even if mobs killed the wrong person. "The white South," DuBois sighed, "would rather that ten innocent Negroes suffer than that one guilty one escape."[18]

In this climate of mutual suspicion, Johnson's triumphs and troubles transcended the world of sports. Whites who preferred the racial status quo dismissed his achievements. They denigrated boxing and denied any correlation between one champion's mastery and the aspirations and aptitudes of an entire race. They attributed his success to mere brawn, an atavistic trait in an increasingly cerebral age. When Johnson ran afoul of the law, however, whites often ascribed his crimes to pernicious racial characteristics. He seemed reckless, brutal, and hedonistic, enthralled with liquor, cars, diamonds, furs, and white women. He lost his title in 1915 because he failed to train properly, a weakness inherent in a lazy and lackadaisical people. Then he resorted to lies to excuse his defeat. The rumors and revelations of his promiscuity, sexual deviance, and domestic abuse confirmed crude stereotypes already pervasive because of biased ethnology, hack melodramas, a prejudicial press, and racist caricatures in kitsch culture.

Johnson largely faded from public view after fleeing to Europe in 1913 and losing his title in 1915. He made headlines with his return and surrender in 1920, but then lived in relative obscurity until the mid-1930s when a new chapter in heavyweight boxing history brought him and his era back into the public eye. For two decades after Johnson's fall, white promoters, managers, and fighters refused to give blacks a shot at the title. Not until 1937 did promoter Mike Jacobs, who had helped Tex Rickard stage the Johnson–Jeffries bout in 1910, remove the "whites only" sign from the championship ring by signing Joe Louis to fight Jimmy Braddock. The managers and trainers of Joe Louis had secured the contract by presenting their young fighter as the very antithesis of Jack Johnson. But Louis's handlers had gone beyond public relations in their quest for a title fight, first rejecting Johnson's overture to help train their fighter and then advising the former champion to stay away from their camp. Spurned by the Louis entourage, Johnson called upon other boxers to find employment in the business. He even offered to train some of Louis's white rivals, a gambit that further sullied his image among blacks. In 1936, for example, Johnson advised Max Schmeling of Germany how he could land his right over Louis's left. Herr Max handed Louis his first professional defeat. When Louis won the title from Braddock, Johnson took no pleasure in it and denigrated the new champion.

Jersey Joe Walcott, a black fighter, hoped to win the title so he could rescue his loved ones from hard times. Johnson assured Walcott that he knew how to beat Louis, but Walcott declined his help. "Johnson's background wasn't savory," Walcott explained. "I knew that whatever fame I might win would be in his shadow. I did not want to march arm in arm to success with him." Louis, like Walcott, continued to avoid Johnson's long "shadow." Unable to latch onto a winner, Johnson had to settle for lay preaching and small earnings as a sideshow attraction in New York City.

On June 10, 1946, driving from Texas to New York to attend the fight between Joe Louis and Billy Conn, Johnson lost control of his car in North Carolina and smashed it into a telephone pole. He died shortly after. Many obituaries were brief and factual, but some newspapers went beyond mere details. "Chief complaint against the former champion was his attachment to white women," the *Richmond Afro-American* observed. "Until the time of his death, however, Jack contended his marriage to each of three white girls was based on love that was strong and mutual." In reflecting on Johnson's life, Joseph Bibb of the *Pittsburgh Courier* noted that he and the ex-champion had discussed plans to revise and update his memoirs. In these conversations, Bibb recalled, Johnson discussed "how he had sinned and how he had been sinned against." He impressed Bibb with his "clever and cagey mentality." Johnson had pondered what had gone wrong. "He admitted that he got dazzled and befuddled with sudden wealth," Bibb recollected. "He confessed that he yielded when tempted by amorous sirens of all races, who became fascinated by his fame and physique." But Bibb did not blame Johnson's ordeal on his befuddlement. "Jack was no fool," he observed. "Johnson was compelled to bear the cross of color. His shortcomings were magnified because of the hue of his skin. In truth he brought no disgrace to the crown and none to his race. . . . Jack was no criminal but a victim of racial prejudice and his own understandable frailties." The passing years and the sudden death in 1946 had made Johnson less objectionable to Bibb and others than to contemporaries during the Progressive era.[19]

The rehabilitation of Jack Johnson received its greatest boost when James Earl Jones played the champion in Howard Sackler's 1968 play and then in the 1970 film *The Great White Hope*. (Boxing was not new to James Earl Jones, for his father Robert had been one of Joe Louis's sparring partners.) "I read Jack Jefferson [Johnson] as a superman, endowed with a fierce pride," Jones explained of his role, "and a man who had during his lifetime earned even more reason to be proud." Hollywood, Jones noted, was giving up Black Sambo for Black Rambo at this time. Among those who enjoyed the play and embraced the Johnson legend was Muhammad Ali, himself locked in battle with the United States government over his refusal to enter the army at the peak of the Vietnam War in 1967. Ali told Jones he viewed himself as "a clean Jack Johnson." Stripped of his title for defying the draft, Ali felt affinity for a former black champion too proud to bend or beg. "History all over again," Ali proclaimed.[20]

But in boxing history, as in royal dynasties, no two rulers are ever the same though they exhibit similar personality traits and confront recurring problems. Jack Johnson and Muhammad Ali—and Joe Louis between them—had little in common beyond their color and their exceptional skills in the ring. They faced similar obstacles because of their race, place, and prominence but responded to the challenges of a racially proscriptive society in radically different ways. An early prototype of the "ba-ad nigger," Johnson had his partisans but generally stood in low repute among both blacks and whites by the time he fled to Europe.[21] Joe Louis, on the other hand, reigned in a manner that elicited lavish praise from both sides of the color line. The rapid rise of the barefoot boy from Alabam' might have been even sweeter to black fans because of the precipitate fall of Jack Johnson. Whether because of his actual character, adept public relations, or a better racial climate, Louis became a "crossover" celebrity and national hero with an enthusiastic multiracial following. He gained respect for who he was and what he did, but perhaps more importantly he assuaged anxieties because of what he was not. A new black hope, Joe Louis would vanquish a small army of both white and black opponents as well as the ghost of Jack Johnson.

5

"Don't You Fall Now"

A New Race Ambassador Emerges

So, boy, don't you turn back . . .
Don't you fall now . . .
I'se still climbin,'
And life for me ain't been no crystal stair.[1]

Langston Hughes, "Mother to Son," 1922

Despite its powerful engine, the new Buick could not get traction on the narrow dirt road that meandered through an isolated rural area in east central Alabama. The sergeant had to abandon the car, hopelessly mired in the mud, for a mule and cart supplied by a local farmer. With wheels better suited to cotton country, the man headed for his destination in Chambers County. This area had been a historic crossroads where three distinct races and cultures met, mingled, and often fought over land, labor, and ways of life—Native Americans, mainly the Creeks; European Americans starting anew; and African Americans, usually chattel owned by land-hungry and ambitious whites.

To the northwest was Horseshoe Bend in the Tallapoosa River, where General Andrew Jackson and his white soldiers and Native American allies had crushed the Northern Creek Confederacy in 1814, thereby opening a vast and fertile domain to slave owners and yeomen who rapidly expanded the realm of cotton and servitude across Alabama. Over a century after the Creek War, cotton remained king in this region where black and white tenants and sharecroppers now toiled in the place of antebellum slaves. To the southwest lay Tuskegee, where Booker T. Washington had founded his institute for young blacks based on an accommodationist approach that emphasized economic opportunity and deference to whites while acquiescing to segregation and disfranchisement. Between the towns of Lafayette and Cusetta stood the plantation of Thomas Heflin, the congressman who had shot a black man on a streetcar in the nation's capital in 1908, the year Jack Johnson became the heavyweight champion. Heflin had represented (or misrepresented) the Alabama district where the returning sergeant was born in 1914. To the north lay Scottsboro, site of the controversial trial of eight black boys accused in 1931 of raping two young white women on a train bound for Memphis.

Guided by kin residing in the region, the soldier headed to his birthplace, a ramshackle cabin on the edge of a cotton field. He then visited the one-room schoolhouse he had attended. He squeezed his large frame behind the small desk he had occupied on those days he had been spared from hard field labor and household chores. The dirt roads, the tiny shack, the crude school, and many sharecropping and tenant kinfolk born and bred in the area had been his world until his family migrated to Detroit in 1926. Poor soil, drought, the boll weevil, and good news from relatives already relocated in the North had convinced the boy's family to join the great exodus to the promised land. Hands that chopped cotton could also butcher hogs, forge steel, and assemble cars for Henry Ford.

Nearly two decades had passed since this native son had boarded a train and left the land his ancestors and kin had worked for over a century without much hope of a better tomorrow. For many African American migrants, the North represented an ideal as well as a place. But geography alone was no elixir for all the old maladies, since newcomers often exchanged one set of problems for another. Whatever the distance between dream and reality north of the Mason-Dixon line, however, few blacks who crossed the Ohio River during the great migration between the world wars returned south to live. High wages in industry and steady though meager pay in service occupations for both men and women seemed a better bet than scanty and unpredictable returns from tilling the soil in Dixie. Despite discrimination, over-crowding, and occasional racial violence, northern blacks earned higher incomes in a wider array of jobs, voted, built churches, sent children to decent schools, created vital civic organizations, launched businesses, and generally enjoyed greater freedom and security than their brethren in Dixie. It was no coincidence that this soldier was returning to his roots for the first time in 1944. Had he not received a special government assignment, he might never have returned home.

The man in search of his past who abandoned his car for a wagon on a country road was no ordinary visitor. His reunion with kin and his search for his former home, school, and church were diversions from a mission to the Tuskegee Air Base, where he visited and entertained black pilots and technicians with the 332nd Fighter Group. Nicknamed the "Spookwaffe" because white officials hoped to keep them inactive and invisible, these pilots longed to pit their courage and skills against Hitler's vaunted flying aces. They could not prove their mettle, however, if the War Department limited them to mere training and meaningless tasks within the confines of the campus Booker T. Washington had created to reconcile the desires of southern whites, African Americans, and northern philanthropists during Jack Johnson's boyhood. Worried about declining morale and restlessness among black troops, federal officials dispatched black celebrities to jim crow bases to mollify soldiers who resented their separate and unequal status in the military. Among those emissaries was Sergeant Joseph L. Barrow, whose grandparents had been slaves on the Barrow plantation; their descendants still worked the soil tilled in bullwhip days. The Tuskegee pilots knew him by a more familiar name and title—Joe Louis, heavyweight champion of the world. Among blacks and whites alike, he was probably Uncle Sam's most recognized and respected enlisted man.[2]

Joe Louis: The People's Champion

In the context of the Great Depression, the rise of fascism, the Second World War, and the Holocaust, Joe Louis came to symbolize many things to many people. To those mired in abject poverty, he represented upward social mobility and success against great odds. To those conducting the nation's politics and diplomacy, he epitomized sacrifice in the name of turning back the sinister forces that menaced the freedom and security of peoples around the globe. In a time when the color line still deeply affected the lives and souls of black folk, Louis became a national hero who seemed to transcend geographical roots and race. In a hard-fought contest at Yankee Stadium in 1941, for example, Louis had rallied from behind and knocked out Billy Conn in the thirteenth round to retain his crown. Assessing the bout, sportswriter Bill Corum reflected on the inspiring odyssey of the champion. "It's a long, long trail from an open-faced cabin in an Alabama cotton field to where Joe Louis stands above me here tonight," Corum observed. "Only in America could a fellow so successfully negotiate such a trail . . . and only a fellow of real character could do it." To reach the summit in boxing was a daunting task for any man regardless of background, as Billy Conn now realized. To do so as a black man was doubly difficult. Louis had indeed climbed "a long, long trail" littered with stumbling blocks.[3]

Certainly an inspiring tale, the Joe Louis story affirms how Americans have wanted to see their nation and its character. For idealists, his rise exemplified the fulfillment of human potential over social proscription, a triumph of individual character over traditional prejudice. Corum and others knew, for example, that Louis could box Conn in Yankee Stadium in 1941, but black baseball players could not compete there because the Major Leagues excluded them. Black ball players had a league of their own, a metaphor for the racial divisions in much of America prior to the attack on Pearl Harbor. However satisfying the epic of Joe Louis, his fame and fortune were an anomaly among his people. In hailing his accomplishments, white writers often overlooked or underestimated the barriers to black progress both in and beyond the world of sports. More attuned to their communities, black journalists also praised Louis but reminded white Americans that his experience was the rare exception and not the general rule.

Despite being born black, southern, and poor in 1914, Louis had valuable assets in his favor. Though impoverished and uneducated, his kin were physically strong, industrious, pious, and proud. When Louis emerged as a contender in the mid-1930s, a reporter for the Associated Negro Press traveled to Alabama and interviewed Mary Turner, who was sixty-five years old, six feet tall, 190 pounds, and the aunt of the boxer. "On one farm down near Lafayette," she boasted, "I would pick two rows of cotton at one time." She moved from the farm to Birmingham, she added, where she bought a mule and wagon for peddling coal. As the city expanded with the steel industry, she supervised the clearing of land for new housing and put her hands to ax and saw. Not a woman to be trifled with, Turner was as pugnacious as the nephew she had not seen for a decade. "I was the fighter of the family long before Joe Louis ever took to fighting," she explained. "Why, when I was a child I was so strong I used to go around looking for somebody to whip. But there's one difference between me and him—he fights for money and I fought for sport!"[4]

Less bellicose but also no stranger to hard work, Joe's mother Lillie played the part of two parents after her husband Munroe entered an Alabama insane asylum when their son was still an infant. With eight children to feed from 120 acres of marginal rented land, Lillie Reese Barrow trusted in God, kin, and her labor to sustain hearth and home. "She worked as hard, and many times harder, than any man around," Joe remembered. "She could plow a good straight furrow, plant and pick with the best of them—cut cord wood like a lumberjack, then leave the fields an hour earlier than anyone else and fix a meal to serve to her family." She provided sustenance beyond simple fare. "She always told me to do the right thing," Joe noted, "to have pride in myself; she said a good name is better than money."

When Joe's family—his mother, a new stepfather, Pat Brooks, and their combined seventeen children—migrated north in 1926, ties were stretched by the distance between Chambers County and Detroit. But the Alabama kin closely followed Louis's ring career. A group of them journeyed six miles by ox-cart to Lafayette in 1938, for example, to hear the radio broadcast of Joe's rematch with Max Schmeling of Germany. (Schmeling had stunned the sports world by beating Louis in 1936.) With their native son the decisive winner this time, they returned to their homes and chores shortly before sunrise. The Barrows and Reeses continued to work the land down south while relatives worked the assembly line up north.[5]

By the time Joe Louis left Alabama, the auto industry had consolidated in and around Detroit. Nearly thirteen when his family moved, Louis entered third grade in a local school while his older brothers found jobs in manufacturing and his stepfather worked as a street sweeper. After sixth grade Louis took a job as a lathe operator for a dollar a day. The job paid better and was easier than other work he had done to earn money—delivering ice and coal with a horse and wagon beside his friend Fred Guinyard, a migrant from South Carolina whom he met at Sunday school. "Our mothers would give us enough money to buy a three-hundred pound block of ice," Guinyard recalled. Then "you'd take an ice pick and pick it down to the size you wanted—twenty five to one hundred pounds." When a customer wanted a large block, Guinyard would tell his bigger and stronger pal, "Your turn, buddy."

When not hauling ice, Louis helped his mother around the house and indulged her by playing the violin. But he soon gave up the strings for boxing gloves and trained with a friend, Thurston McKinney, under Atler Ellis at the Brewster Recreation Center. Louis competed in amateur bouts and drew attention as a promising young fighter. Brewster Center, formerly the Ginsburg Library, was located in a rapidly changing neighborhood called "Black Bottom"—as Jews moved up and out, blacks from the South moved in and stayed. William Hines, whose family left Georgia for Detroit in 1919, remembered what Brewster had meant to young males of his era. "Brewster Center here motivated a lot of young men who were headed to stay in the street," Hines reminisced. "Dave Clark, the famous fighter and stable mate of Joe Louis, had a gang called Blackstone. They were kind of rough fellows in the neighborhood. They then decided to come into the center." The gym "helped a lot of boys turn around." Brewster became a prep school for future champions. When not strolling to the gym with McKinney, Joe Barrow walked there with Walker Smith, whose family had migrated from Georgia, where Walker had been born in 1921. Walker Smith admired his older buddy and carried his duffel bag for him. Like Joe, Walker would soon box his way out of the Detroit slum. His ring style impressed a woman spectator who told his trainer he had a "sweet" prospect on his hands. Smith dropped his family name and this "sweet" boxer became "Sugar Ray" Robinson. Over the years, the paths of Joe and Ray frequently intersected.[6]

Early in 1933, Atler Ellis brought a rapidly improving Joe Barrow to the attention of John Roxborough, a prominent lawyer, real estate broker, and "numbers" man. Well-educated, community-minded, and color-conscious, Roxborough was, in the parlance of the time, an ardent "race man." He liked Louis personally and recognized his potential when he won the Detroit Golden Gloves tournament. Roxborough found Louis a job at Ford Motor Company pushing truck chassis to an assembly line for painting. He improved Joe's wardrobe, furnished his basic wants and needs, acclimated him to the manners of the black bourgeoisie, and guided him from amateur to professional. To that end Roxborough recruited his friend Julian Black, a smart, successful Chicago realtor and broker, to help manage Louis. He and Black then contacted Jack Blackburn to become trainer. A shrewd and scrappy boxer with over a hundred matches behind him, Blackburn had sparred with Jack Johnson and given the heavyweight all he could handle despite a considerable size disadvantage. The sting of Blackburn's gloves had lasted long after Johnson's welts healed. The two men despised one another.[7]

Roxborough convinced Lillie Barrow Brooks that her son could reach the top. He also persuaded her to let Joe move in with him. (He had room because he and his wife had separated and would soon divorce.) "Roxy" became Joe's legal guardian but served him even better as a trusted friend and adviser. He later sent Louis to Chicago, where Julian Black provided similar guidance while Blackburn honed the young fighter's ring skills for the big time. Louis made his professional debut on July 4, 1934, knocking out Jack Kracken in the first round. By the end of 1934, Louis, only twenty years old, had won all twelve of his professional fights over carefully chosen opponents. His final bout of the year, a match against Lee Ramage in Chicago, brought Louis a purse of $2,750. (He had recently been earning $25 a week at the auto plant.) In a return match in Los Angeles, Louis beat Ramage again, this time earning $4,000 for six minutes of fighting. For the Louis family, the money brought new consumer goods, financial security, and enhanced status. "Every time I could, I'd buy some really fine clothes. Thanks to my managers, I knew how to dress well; all I had to do was copy them," Louis reflected. "Sent my family a fistful of money and they looked fine too in new clothes. No more welfare, no more worrying about simple things like food."

Louis beat eleven more opponents in early 1935. His winning streak brought even larger gates and more income. He repaid the relief money his family had received during the darkest days of the Depression. In April 1935, Louis gave his mother a new home at 2100 McDougall Avenue on Detroit's East side. The home cost $9,000, renovations another $2,700, and furnishings, including a brand-new piano, an additional $3,000. The hands of Joe Louis had lifted his family into high cotton in the motor city.[8]

Chasing the Title

No former heavyweight had compiled so impressive a record his first year. But Roxborough, Black, and Blackburn knew that Louis faced obstacles outside the ring far greater than those within it. An all-black enterprise, the Louis entourage had to deal often with whites—promoters and managers, mob figures coveting a piece of a rising star, reporters with varying degrees of racial bias. Besides, many whites simply preferred that the heavyweight crown remain their monopoly. No black had been permitted to fight for the title since Jess Willard wrested it from Jack Johnson in 1915. For many reasons—some racist, others not—many promoters, politicians, fans, and reformers opposed interracial matches, especially in the heavyweight division. The specter of Jack Johnson hovered over the prize ring, and Louis's handlers knew that knockouts alone could not erase the color line.

Since Johnson's legacy posed a major obstacle to Louis, the handlers drilled him in the art of assuaging white anxieties. During a break in a workout, Blackburn pondered their prospects. "The heavyweight division for a Negro is hardly likely," he cautioned. "The white man ain't too keen on it. You have to really be something to get anywhere. If you really ain't gonna be another Jack Johnson, you got some hope. White man hasn't forgotten that fool nigger with his white women, acting like he owned the world." Blackburn knew Louis would need more than boxing skills. "A colored fighter's got to be lots better than the other man if he's gonna go places," he warned. "But you've got to have more than just two good hands. You gotta do the right thing. And never leave yourself open so people can talk about you."

Short on cash and hankering for attention, Jack Johnson approached Roxborough and proposed that he either replace or join Blackburn as trainer. Roxborough did not mince words. "I want to develop Joe into a great, clean living champion," he scolded him, "the exact opposite of what you've been." Roxborough "cursed Johnson out," Louis recalled, "told him how he had held up the progress of Negro people for years with his attitude, how he was a low-down, no-good nigger, and told him he wasn't welcome in my camp anymore." Roxborough asked photographers not to take pictures of Louis with Johnson. Louis recollected that he "didn't see too much more of Johnson after that."[9]

Others also helped Louis placate white boxing commissioners, promoters, reporters, and fans. Mike Jacobs, formerly an aid to Tex Rickard, advised Louis to avoid scandal to complement his rising reputation in the ring. "He told me that there was a kind of silent agreement between promoters," Louis recalled, "that there would never be another black heavyweight champion like Jack Johnson." Jacobs counseled him: "You have a chance to be the first great Negro heavyweight in boxing's history to go into the ring and through your career without the shackles of double-dealing and racial mix-ups. Keep away from the chiselers, let your project be Negro throughout, earn the respect of your own people, and remember that you can make an honest dollar faster than a crooked dime—and that you'll keep it a lot longer."

Joe Rainey, the lone black on the Pennsylvania Athletic Commission, also hoped Louis would not emulate Johnson, who had offended his own people as well as whites. "There hardly was a day during all the time this fellow was champion that the papers didn't have a story about his extravagant carryings-on," Rainey sighed in 1935. "And his flair for doing things that annoyed and offended people was astonishing. It amounted almost to genius." Even when Johnson lived abroad, "stories of his bizarre exploits . . . gave readers in this country a pain in the neck." Initially a great black hope, he instead became a heavy black burden. "He was offensive to white people, he was equally offensive to Negroes," Rainey concluded. "To the decent women of my race his name was anathema." As Louis gained in skills and stature, Johnson belittled him to make himself look better. But he only made black fans angrier, as shown when an announcer presented him to a crowd at an amateur boxing program in New York City. "Once the hero of his race, now the most despised man in it, Jack Johnson felt the full brunt of his own people's disapproval of him," the black press reported. "Johnson attempted to make a speech, but such a salvo of boos greeted him, he stood in embarrassment for five minutes while the crowd refused to give him a chance to talk." Fans had expressed their "accumulated grievances" toward him, "the capstone of which was his scathing criticism of Joe Louis."[10]

In the ring and out, Louis impressed Americans of all colors, creeds, and classes. Shy and soft-spoken in the early years, he let his fists and handlers do the talking. They spoke well. By the end of 1935 he had twenty-six wins, twenty-two by knockout, and no losses. Blackburn's advice stuck with him. "He kept telling me that the cards were stacked against me because I was a black fighter opposing white fighters," Louis recalled. "He told me that I could not win on points alone. I had to go for the knockout, so there'd be no doubt." Blackburn turned this handicap into an advantage by exhorting Louis to box harder and smarter to nullify any bias. "You've got to be good—lots better than the other man," he explained. "The surest way to win is to knock your man out." White referees and judges could not be trusted to score a mixed bout fairly. "When you get in that ring, go for the kill," Blackburn instructed Louis before his first professional fight. "Let your right fist be the referee."[11]

The handlers set other prudent guidelines. They savored victory but knew their future depended on winning (and losing) with grace. Louis showed respect for his opponents in and out of the ring and did not boast after his victories. Roxborough knew that a bare-knuckle foe who pounded the keys of a typewriter could do far more harm to Louis than a rival with a good left hook. The managers welcomed reporters to camp and supplied ample copy favorable to Louis. Most white sports writers in the 1930s, including some southerners, were quite racially tolerant for their time. But a reporter occasionally struck a low blow. "Newspaper writers put a lot of words in my mouth," Louis complained, but "Roxborough educated me not to get into arguments with writers."[12]

The Louis entourage knew the color barrier could be scaled only if they honored the arbitrary rules of race politics. Both custom and law proscribed African Americans solely because of skin color and its cultural coding. Laws in the South, for example, sought to deny all blacks the vote whether illiterate or multilingual. Jim crow relegated all blacks to separate and unequal facilities regardless of character, income, or education. The restrictive covenant denied blacks housing in certain areas whatever their individual traits or achievements. Inferior schools handicapped black children regardless of their aptitude and ambition.

Just months before Joe Louis's family had arrived in Detroit, for example, Dr. Ossian Sweet, his wife Gladys, two brothers, and some friends had confronted a mob that resented the doctor's purchase of a fine home on a previously all-white street in the city. Ossian Sweet had left Florida, where he had habitually donned a chauffeur's cap while driving his expensive car to avoid offending whites, hoping to escape racial oppression. Soon after the Sweets moved in, whites began shouting and hurling rocks and bricks through the windows of their new home. In the mayhem, someone inside the house fired into the crowd and killed a white man. The Sweets and their friends were arrested and charged with murder. To defend them, the NAACP secured Clarence Darrow as well as Charles Mahoney and Julian Perry, two black attorneys. The jury could not reach a verdict. The state then separately tried Henry Sweet, Ossian's younger brother and a student at Wilberforce University, who admitted shooting at the mob. Darrow summoned several blacks to the stand, people of learning, refinement, and affluence. One was Dr. Sweet himself. "When I opened the door," he testified, "I saw the mob and I realized that I was facing the same mob that has hounded my people throughout its entire history." Darrow's black witnesses were a cut above the prosecution's white witnesses, who seemed short on memory as well as candor.

In his summation, Darrow exhorted the jury of twelve white men to transcend "the law of hate." He thought the case pivoted on prejudice, not murder. Were it reversed and "white men had shot and killed a black while protecting their home and their lives against a mob of blacks," Darrow argued, "no one would have dreamed of having them indicted. . . . They would have been given medals instead." He defended the right of decent people to reside where they chose and to protect themselves. Henry Sweet, Darrow insisted, had done what any reasonable person would have done. "This boy went to help to defend his brother, and his brother's wife and his child and his home," Darrow observed. "Do you think the less of him for that?" Since the first slave ship had docked in the New World, Darrow noted, whites had abused blacks. "I believe the life of the Negro race has been a life of tragedy, of injustice, of oppression," Darrow told the jury. "The law has made him equal—but man has not. And after all, the last analysis is what man has done." The jurors acquitted Henry Sweet. The state then dismissed the remaining cases.

Ossian Sweet confronted jim crow again not long after this acquittal. Kelly Fritz, a black funeral director, remembered how Sweet dealt with the awful bigotry that affected the dead as well as the living: "His child died. We took him out to the cemetery, and they said, 'Go around to the back gate.' He pulled his pistol out and made them open the door. A few years later his wife died, and the same thing happened. They still wouldn't let him in. He pulled his pistol out."[13]

The white desire that blacks use "the back gate" prevailed across the nation and affected most walks of life. The United States Navy, for instance, relegated its black recruits to subordinate roles as cooks and servants for white officers. Blacks in the army did menial labor. During antiblack riots—in Louis's era as well as Jack Johnson's—white mobs invaded black neighborhoods and wantonly destroyed homes and property. They harassed, beat, and even killed people of color who had no connection whatsoever to the original incident that had triggered the disturbance. White racists believed in guilt through association, and no association mattered more to them than skin color. Lynch mobs often killed the wrong person; rioters ransacked entire black communities to punish some purported violation of racial etiquette in either deed or demeanor. These race codes had deep historical roots. Johnson had defied them a generation before, and Louis still faced the consequences.

John Roxborough and Julian Black resented this prejudice but could not ignore or evade it. They realized that whites held erroneous images of blacks, particularly black men. If Jack Johnson consorted with white women, then all black men wanted them and had to be restrained. If Johnson squandered a fortune, then his people could not manage money. If one African American in Waco, Harlem, or Memphis committed a heinous crime, then the whole race had inherent criminal tendencies. If blacks in movies shuffled along and trembled in terror at haunts and hoodoo, then all were superstitious. Knowing that these prejudices hampered both the individual and group, the handlers depicted Louis as the antithesis of the black beast. His upbringing and good instincts made the task easier, but basic decency alone could not overcome white precepts. Without his managers' acumen, Louis might have remained obscure because of the legacy of Jack Johnson. The entourage realized they had an opportunity to affect the lives of millions of black Americans and influence many white Americans as well. Louis as fighter could affect only the annals of boxing; Louis as symbol might change the history of an entire nation and diminish white fears that originated in what Afrikaners in South Africa termed the *swart gevaar* (black peril).

Crafting a Public Image

Some fans thought Louis could affect the next generation as well as his own. With vivid memories of what Johnson's victory over Jeffries had meant to her kin, Ruby Berkley Goodwin hoped Louis would win the title and defend it against all white hopes while avoiding Johnson's mistakes. Now a contributor to the *Los Angeles Sentinel*, she wrote to Louis in mid-1935 that her four sons, like "every Negro lad in America," were "bragging" about him. "Don't fail them," she urged. "Keep both your life and your fighting clean. Now, Joe, don't let us down. It's really pathetic the way we've been humiliated and sold out as a race." She had confidence in Louis but cautioned him about perils ahead. "Whenever temptation comes, whether wrapped up in a bottle or a skirt," she warned, "we hope you'll just think of the million little brown and black boys who want to be just like Joe Louis."[14]

Such admonitions might have been addressed to anyone trying to rise. But as Goodwin and others knew, this advice had a deeper meaning for black Americans. When a white person faltered or failed, whites interpreted the setback as an isolated incident reflecting individual incapacity or bad luck. But when a black person erred, whites often attributed it to group inferiority. When Goodwin mentioned how "pathetic" it had been to be "humiliated and sold out as a race," she undoubtedly had Jack Johnson in mind. So did Roxborough and Black. Johnson's affairs with white women, hints of sexual perversion and domestic abuse, frequent arrests and law suits, his cabaret, and his style in the ring had further alienated white from black, hastened his own decline, and led promoters to draw the color line. Joe Louis, however, Chester Washington and William Nunn of the *Pittsburgh Courier* wrote, "was destined to bridge the gap which Jack Johnson had opened between the races." The handlers had financial as well as social incentives for their tutelage. "My backers were not about to let their investment in me be messed up by any kind of scandal," Louis observed. "They remembered how Jack Johnson had ruined boxing for blacks, especially for heavyweights." Roxborough groomed Louis for a more constructive role, confident he could do "a lot of good" if he became champion and conducted himself in a way that "wouldn't be a discredit to Negroes."[15]

Johnson's greatest "sin" had been his penchant for white women. So the brain trust worked hard to keep Louis from places, events, and persons that might rekindle memories of the "white slave" era. Reflecting on his formative years as a professional, Louis remembered that his advisers had told him not to be photographed with a white woman, for "that would be the end of my career." They preferred he avoid white women altogether, not just pictures with them, and Louis heeded their counsel as he emerged a contender. Rumors of romance linked him to such black women as Elsie Roxborough, his manager's niece and a student at the University of Michigan, and Bennie Mitchell, a dancer. But no hint of impropriety appeared in print.

Louis visited the *Chicago Defender* office occasionally to talk with sports editor Al Monroe. There he met Marva Trotter, a staff stenographer and an organist at the Gideon Baptist Church, whose family included a number of preachers. After a brief courtship they married on September 24, 1935, just minutes before Louis went to Yankee Stadium and knocked out former champion Max Baer in the fourth round. Louis, Paul Gallico wrote, went "from a wedding to an execution . . . from tenderness to terror." The *Courier* spread the good news: JOE LOUIS WINS, WEDS! Flush with cash from his many victories, Louis gave his bride a new Lincoln car and a well-furnished six-room apartment on Chicago's south side. Joe and Marva became the storybook couple of the 1930s in the black press.

The managers welcomed the news. Julian Black "was happier than I was," Louis recalled, since he had "seen the women coming after me like Grant storming Richmond." The brain trust wanted to protect Louis's image. "Marva was pretty, intelligent, and came from a fine family—and she was black," Joe noted. "No Jack Johnson problem here." The *Afro-American*'s I.F. Coles remembered what Louis said to the press the night he wed Marva and mauled Max. "He told a number of reporters, including myself, that he would never bring disgrace to his race as Jack Johnson had done," Coles wrote, "meaning, I suppose, without saying it, that he was never going to marry a white woman." White reporters seemed "elated" with the pledge and "said a lot" about Louis's intention "to stay in his own race."[16]

Unlike Johnson, Louis had no taste for liquor, an aversion his mother attributed to his drinking too much gin when six years old and becoming violently ill. Louis promised Roxborough and Black in 1935 that he would knock out King Levinsky in the first round if they would take a temperance pledge. The wager made, Louis quickly decked Levinsky and his handlers went on the wagon for six months—at least within the confines of training camp. Nor did Louis smoke, though he tolerated Roxborough's occasional cigar. At ease only with family, friends, and handlers, Louis generally avoided nightclubs and bashes. "Louis is sincere in his policy of avoiding ballyhoo," Al Monroe confirmed in early 1936. "He does not like parties." Like his mother, Louis remained a church-going Baptist, even attending services while training and on the road. When preparing for a bout with Primo Carnera, he received a large Bible from his mother and read it regularly. He told Gene Kessler of the *Philadelphia Tribune* that he had "a mission to perform"—to win and retain the title "in a manner that will be a credit to my race." Any public disgrace "would break my mother's heart and just isn't in me." Such assurances helped clear the foul air left from Johnson's era. And Louis lived up to his words. "You see," he informed Kessler, "my mother always goes to the Calvary Baptist Church on Sundays and when I am away from home training in another city, I usually room close to a Baptist church where I can attend services. All my folks are church people." Marva confirmed Joe's piety. "I am a good Baptist and Joe is also," she told columnist P.L. Prattis. "We are going to live as simply as we can" and "not isolate ourselves but shall live the life of the normal American."[17]

Louis did not avoid all temptation. Like Johnson, he was fond of fancy cars. After beating Levinsky and drawing his winner's take, Louis "sashayed into one of the more elegant automotive parlors," Bill Cunningham of the *Boston Post* reported, "and peeled off $7,200 for a custom made job that looks like something the late Valentino used to ride in." Early in his career, Louis recalled, "I got a new Buick every Christmas." But Roxborough and Black put red roadsters in the same category as white women, so Louis avoided them. To keep him from behind the wheel and out of traffic court, Roxborough hired a chauffeur. The managers wanted to see Louis's name on the sports pages, not in the court docket.[18]

Louis spoke sparingly to the press in these early years and limited long interviews to a few trusted black reporters. "I never talked much," he explained, largely leaving that to the managers. To help Joe deal with the media, the managers and his wife hired Russ Cowans, a recent college graduate, to be a tutor, publicist, and secretary for him. A writer for the *Detroit Chronicle* and a *Defender* correspondent, Cowans supplied the press with flattering material on Louis and his family. He also taught Louis grammar, geography, history, and arithmetic and coached him in genteel manners. "I could see myself in relation to what I was doing, and in relation to what I might mean to some people," Louis reminisced. "That was the big thing Cowans did for me." Cowans did little things too—"what to do when I was introduced to important people, how to speak properly, and general etiquette." Cowans helped Louis answer his mail and continued tutoring him until 1938.[19]

Louis and his managers not only cared about their image in print, they worried about what might appear in photographs. They knew that one demeaning picture could do more damage than a thousand critical words. "One time we were talking about these little black toy dolls they used to make of fighters," Louis recalled. "Those dolls always had the wide grin with thick red lips. They looked foolish. I got the message—don't look like a fool nigger doll. Look like a black man with dignity." Louis certainly "got the message." While he trained for the Carnera fight, a white photographer tried to get him to pose with a huge slice of watermelon. He refused. On the night he defeated Baer, Louis escorted his new wife to the Cotton Club. "He had hardly arrived in the house before photographers rushed him for pictures," Al Monroe reported. "Joe consented to the photographs but kicked up terribly when one of the boys attempted to place some empty whiskey bottles on his table." Louis worried about false impressions. "We only wanted to make it look like a real cabaret," a photographer protested. "But," Louis retorted, "I am not a real cabaret man." Louis was "particular" about photographs and followed some strict rules. "He will get in an occasional picture with friends," Monroe explained, "but always sees to it that no girls are next to him. And at that most of the 'mixed' pictures Joe gets into are people of his own race." Perhaps the notorious photograph of Jack Johnson in his roadster with Belle Schreiber remained etched in the managers' minds. "Joe doesn't mind getting into pictures with admirers but the papers are so tricky," Julian Black told Monroe. "They'll take a harmless photograph and make a big fuss over it if there are women next to your fighter, so why take chances?"

In a Chicago ballroom the night Louis beat Levinsky, a film crew "tried to get him to pose for the movies with some colored bathing beauties," the Boston Post's Bill Cunningham noted. "He flatly refused. He seemed to be enduring rather than enjoying the hullabaloo." At a Newark theater in late 1935, Louis declined to pose with actress Nina Mae McKinney and the chorus girls in her show. Before the opening game of the 1935 World Series, "white celebrities tried to get Joe into a fake crap game in a stunt around the pitcher's mound before the baseball game started. Joe turned them down cold." The Philadelphia Tribune praised Louis's decorum. "He refuses to be a buffoon or a clown," an editorial observed, "to satisfy the elite who believe that all colored people must of necessity be comedians of the lower variety."[20]

Louis initially lacked the manners and tastes of striver's row, but he was no delinquent or misfit. The Brewster Center steered many boys away from crime in Black Bottom, but Louis had other influences to keep him out of trouble. His mother, despite many hardships, raised her children to "do the right thing." Others close to Louis—Roxborough, Black, Blackburn, Guinyard, Cowans, and scribes Al Monroe and Chester Washington—also mentored him and fostered his public image. They orchestrated his humble origins, stressed his affection for his mother, noted his piety, and told tales that revealed his fine character. They emphasized his personal decency as much as his hitting power. Louis might have been the best slugger since Jack Dempsey, but he had to avoid conduct often overlooked or excused in a white athlete. Only a life free of scandal could reopen the door to blacks in the heavyweight division. The handlers made Louis attractive to fans in Queens and Brooklyn as well as Harlem and the Bronx, in Evanston and Grosse Point as well as South Chicago and East Detroit.

Press coverage of Louis reveals how adeptly the handlers crafted his public image. "He remains much as he was that morning when he walked out of his mammy's door with a fiddle tucked under his arm and $2 in his trousers pocket," a *Philadelphia Tribune* story noted in 1935. "He doesn't smoke, nor does he drink. He continues to be almost fanatically religious, studying the Bible assiduously." Louis broke only one commandment—he nearly killed his opponents. "Through it all he wears the same poker face," the *Tribune* added, "although he shuns cards as being agents of the devil." In a similar vein, Al Monroe picked Joe to beat Max Baer and explained why. "Louis neither drinks, smokes, chews, nor indulges in night clubbing—a quartet of things that aid in making Baer the playboy figure that he is," Monroe observed. "And if you don't consider these things an evil to sports success, then you aren't very well up on your sports." Louis had proved himself "a genuine sportsman at all times," the *Courier*'s Chester Washington noted. "He . . . has won the respect of both races and he intends to maintain that respect by clean fighting and clean living." Others joined in the praise. Eustace Gay of the *Philadelphia Tribune* admitted that he once thought the stories about Joe's Bible reading "were so much ballyhoo," but Louis's quiet life and his refusal to be photographed with "a well known colored movie star" changed his mind. "He not only reads the Book, but tries to follow it," Gay concluded. "We are warned in the Good Book to 'shun the very appearance of evil.'"[21]

Roy Wilkins, editor of *The Crisis*, believed that Louis and track star Jesse Owens had changed whites' perceptions of blacks. Their "spectacular success" had "aided materially in altering the usual appraisal of Negroes by the rank and file of the American public," he argued. "If these two boys have done nothing more than just awaken curiosity about Negroes in millions of white minds, they have served the race well." Conceding that activists, intellectuals, and artists were probably "more important" than boxers and runners, Wilkins nevertheless contended that only black sports stars could reach the white masses. Athletes, not intellectuals, held "the solution of the race problem in their hands." Wilkins put Louis on the cover of the NAACP journal and touted him as "a yardstick" for measuring "the considerable improvement in race relations" in recent years. "The rise of this remarkable young man," Wilkins wrote in late 1935, "has been accompanied by cheers and encouragement from white and black Americans." Times had changed. When Johnson had defeated Jeffries in 1910, "Negroes hardly dared to whisper about it." Now blacks openly celebrated Louis's triumphs over white opponents, and white writers and fans usually treated Louis fairly, even fondly. "Of course, Joe Louis is not a Jack Johnson," Wilkins added, "but neither are the white folks today quite the same as the whites of 1910." Despite lingering bias, Louis's popularity showed that "America has moved up several notches since 1910."

Like Wilkins, Walter White, executive secretary of the NAACP, viewed Louis as an antidote to bigotry. After Johnson's reign, "Negro heavyweights were denied by subterfuge the opportunity to fight for the championship." Louis, however, was challenging jim crow with "great skill" and "impeccable behavior." Roi Ottley of the *Amsterdam News* overheard a telling exchange between two men in Harlem. "If we had more Negroes like Joe Louis things would be better for us," the first suggested. "Sure 'nuff," replied the second, "but if we had more white folks like Joe, things would be better still." Louis and his managers knew they must act with discretion. But they also knew whites had to change. Louis and Jesse Owens could inspire whites to think well of the race, a step advantageous to all. "When a Negro is a success, it is credited not only to him, but to the whole race," Ottley noted. "The Negro feels that achievement by a Negro breaks down the prevailing opinions of the Negro's inferiority."[22]

With just a few exceptions, white writers echoed this praise from black writers. Like their counterparts at the *Courier* and *Defender*, they argued that Louis had earned the right to rise as high as his ability would take him. "Within a year after Jack Johnson won the championship he had lost what esteem he had and his disfavor with the public started the first and only white hope era, which was the most grotesque epoch in the fight racket," Howard Freeman of the *Newark Evening News* noted. "You never can tell what will happen when a colored boy becomes the idol of his race, but Louis will have to change a lot to cause the general public to sour on him." A hometown daily made a similar point, stressing that Louis had the stature to redeem a sport long out of favor. "We should like to see as admirable a young athlete as Louis come through a bright career with something to show for his decency," a *Detroit News* editorial noted, "not merely for his own sake, but for that of the sport." *Newsweek* also urged equal opportunity: "A debauch to the

Negro hero means chewing four packs of gum a day, playing a game of pool, or studying arithmetic and history with his private tutor. He likes to read the Bible and generally does immediately before a fight." His only fault was his fondness for sleep, hardly a habit to alarm the public. "He prefers sentimental music to the hot jazz of night clubs," *Newsweek* reported, "and endorses only commercial products that he uses himself."

Sportswriter Bill Cunningham advised promoters to forget Johnson's era. "Regardless of his race or his color, Louis deserves the right to go as far as he can," he argued in 1935. "If he goes all the way, more power to his broad biceps." Cunningham did not want "avaricious buzzards" operating from "dingy offices" to keep Joe down. Columnist Bob Considine came to the same conclusion. "If Louis is good enough to win the championship," Considine declared, "he shouldn't be deprived of it by any conniving fistic bosses behind the scenes just because of color." Writer Damon Runyon marveled at the interest in Louis in 1936. "More has been written about Louis in the past two years," he thought, "than about any living man over a similar period of time, with the exception of Lindbergh."[23]

Favorable stories on Louis in white publications in New York, Boston, and Detroit suggested growing racial tolerance in the urban North. Less predictable was the level of acceptance in the white South. Jerry Bryan of the *Birmingham News* expressed pride in Joe Louis, Jesse Owens, and boxer Lorenzo Pack—all native sons of Alabama. Zipp Newman, Bryan's colleague on the *News*, called Alabama "the state of romantic athletic careers." "Alabama stars have been rising in the athletic firmament a long time," Newman wrote. "And now it would appear that Alabama will be the first Southern state to produce a heavyweight champion." (Newman either forgot Jack Johnson's Galveston origins or did not consider Texas a southern state.) Jimmy Jones at the *Richmond Times-Dispatch* pointed out that Louis "has striven to be the direct opposite of Jack Johnson . . . who came in for considerable censure during his brief and stormy reign." The rancor between them, Jones explained, stemmed from Roxborough's refusal to hire Johnson as a trainer. Louis "is not only a credit to his profession," Jones concluded, "but a credit to the South." By the time Louis met Max Schmeling in mid-1936, he had fought twenty-seven professional bouts without a loss. Jones saw no reason to draw the color line against Louis. If he won the title he "would be far less objectionable as such than some of our white champions have proved themselves."[24]

Cheered by such tributes from the South, the entourage accepted an invitation for Louis to fight an exhibition in New Orleans in late 1936. Fans welcomed Louis when he arrived. But many whites still opposed any mixed pairing, so promoters matched him against a local black boxer. Even though whites proved kind and cordial, Joe's trainer remained skittish throughout the trip. Blackburn "had his gun tucked inside his waistband with his coat over it," Louis recalled. "But he made sure everybody around saw it." Louis asked him about the pistol. "This is the South," Blackburn snapped, "and I'm not taking shit from nobody." A white police officer was aware of Blackburn's past—he had spent five years in prison for manslaughter stemming from a shooting in Philadelphia in 1909. "Everything's goin' to be all right," the officer assured him. Six thousand fans packed the coliseum three hours before the event while "as many more were on the outside clamoring for tickets." Blackburn did not need his gun. "It took exactly ten policemen to escort Joe from the ring to his dressing room," an observer noted. "He was one of the most popular celebrities to visit New Orleans, even with the whites."[25]

The entourage returned south in early 1937. Louis defeated Natie Brown in Kansas City, Missouri, then proceeded to Oklahoma and Texas. The Louis party "arrived Wednesday morning to create almost a riot at the station," the Associated Negro Press reported from Kansas City. "Fans from every walk of life were on hand to greet him, see him, touch him if possible. . . . Police had to form a cordon from the dressing room to the ring to keep gasping damsels from planting two lips against Joe's face." Okies embraced Louis but felt cheated by his passive approach to his exhibitions. Louis, a local paper complained, "did not give Enid and northwest Oklahoma fans much of a run for their money." Fans in Texas flocked to see Louis but also disliked the exhibitions. Still, a *Courier* headline accentuated the positive: LOUIS TAKES TEXAS LIKE A TORNADO. Large mixed crowds turned out for Louis in Galveston, Jack Johnson's hometown. Louis drew boos for his "listless work," Hank Rabun of the *Fort Worth Press* reported. "It looked like a wrestling playwright had been messing with the script." The Dallas papers, however, praised the entourage. "Louis is a personable young man," Red Webster observed in the *Dallas Dispatch*. "Answers questions readily, but doesn't talk too much. He talks in a low tone and his accents are those of a southern Negro." His managers, on the other hand, spoke with the "sharper, more distinct enunciation" of northerners. Louis appeared to Webster to be "pretty much the same gangling youngster who came up from a cotton plantation in Alabama." Reflecting on this trip years later, Roxborough called it a "long triumphal procession" for Louis and his friends.[26]

The reception in the Southwest suggested better race relations ahead, but Dixie's traditional ways had great staying power. Louis could do only so much, and so much had to be done. While Louis was in New Orleans, for example, a federal court convicted a white marshal, the owner of an Arkansas plantation, of holding eight blacks in virtual slavery under the convict lease system. The marshal arrested black men for vagrancy and the magistrate court quickly convicted them. The marshal paid their fines and the court released them into his custody. He then confined them to labor gangs under armed guards to work his land until they repaid their debts. Some southern blacks fared even worse. The scourge of lynching persisted in the South while Louis was gaining national acclaim. In 1936, for example, mobs killed thirteen blacks across Dixie, including a horrendous murder in Laurel, Mississippi, in December. As usual, local and state law-enforcement officers ignored evidence and made no arrests. At the time Louis boxed Natie Brown in Kansas City, Florida governor Fred Cone complained about the salary that the state paid the president of Florida A & M, an all-black university. "There's no Negro on earth that's worth $4000 a year salary—not to teach school," the governor argued. Someone asked Cone what Louis was worth. "Not worth a damn," he replied.

Cone's opinion that blacks were "not worth a damn" pervaded the South. For many whites, black folk had no value beyond their utility as cheap and docile labor. When blacks asked for better treatment and basic civil rights, whites often harassed, evicted, or eliminated them to sustain white supremacy. Nor was bias confined to one region. While Louis and his handlers traversed the South in a Pullman car attached to a jim-crow train, George Schuyler, a *Pittsburgh Courier* columnist, lamented the plight of blacks in most of the country. "Cut New England and a few isolated places out of your United States map," he suggested, "and you have left a vast torture chamber for Negroes rivaling Hitler's Germany for Jews." Across the nation blacks faced similar hardships—poor jobs, inferior schools, bad housing, police brutality, government neglect at all levels. President Franklin D. Roosevelt and his advisers had taken unprecedented steps to battle the Depression, but Schuyler doubted that the administration would use its clout to assist those who needed it most. "Extend Federal power as far as you please," he declared, "but no law offensive to white supremacy, North or South, will be passed."[27]

Proving Schuyler a prophet, Congress rejected an antilynching bill in early 1937. "The color line in the South is a permanent institution," Senator E.E. Cox of Georgia proclaimed in opposing the bill. "It will not break, and cannot be wiped out by a Federal law dictated in hate. Her people mean to maintain their racial purity and will not be mongrelized." In the same spirit, Representative John Rankin of Mississippi called the measure "a bill to encourage rape," since "its ultimate effect" would likely be "additional assaults by black men on white women." Southern whites would "never . . . submit to racial equality," he insisted. Only "complete segregation," not federal law, could regulate the races in Dixie.

As debate on the bill climaxed in the spring of 1937, news reached Washington that convinced its proponents that only federal power could ensure due process in the South. Two black men accused of killing a white shopkeeper were wrested from police by a mob and tortured with blowtorches in Duck Hill, Mississippi. One man was then burned at the stake, the other riddled with bullets and set ablaze. This grotesque lynching moved Virginius Dabney, white editor of the *Danville Register*, to reverse his stand. Formerly a typical Old Dominion proponent of states' rights, he now favored federal intervention against such brutality. "A blow torch," Dabney admitted, "is more convincing than logic."

While Joe Louis moved freely on his tour of the Southwest, the Scottsboro boys remained behind bars in Alabama. Convicted of rape in 1931 without physical evidence and on dubious testimony by two young white women (one of whom later recanted her story), the boys seemed doomed to wither away as casualties of a criminal justice system stacked against black suspects. "8 black boys," Langston Hughes sighed, "and one white lie." Attorney Loren Miller, editor of the *Los Angeles Sentinel*, saw the boys as "symbolic of the whole racketeering plantation system of the South with its oppression and exploitation of Negroes." As in the case of lynching, outsiders seemed powerless to right an awful wrong in Dixie. "They've been in jail for five years now," Miller lamented, "for a crime they didn't commit." While the white press focused on the Nazis' persecution of Jews and Catholics in Germany, the black press continued to remind Americans of rampant race prejudice and injustice at home.[28]

Joe Louis and his managers remained mum on lynching, peonage, and discrimination in the courts. They chose to keep pugilism and politics separate, not wanting to jeopardize their future in boxing by meddling in matters better suited to the NAACP. They viewed their mission in a more limited yet still significant way. Whether this approach best served the entire race is debatable, but their strategy achieved their primary goals—good press for Louis, ardent fans from all races and regions, and the prospect that the Brown Bomber would get a chance to fight for the title.

White and black observers praised Roxborough, Black, and Blackburn for their guidance of Louis, and for good reason. To make any fighter a contender was no mean feat, but for an all-black concern to do so was quite impressive. While Louis continued to show his mettle in and out of the ring, the managers proved themselves the equal if not the superior of any white entourage in the game. The New York mob bullied Roxborough for a piece of Louis in 1935, for example, but Roxborough rebuffed them. Members of the Michigan Athletic Commission leaned on the managers to include a white man in their inner circle. Roxborough and Black stood their ground, professing regret that Louis might never again fight in his adopted state but refusing to succumb to the pressure. By denying shares in Louis to grasping whites, the managers protected their own interests but also safeguarded their protégé. Black fighters with white managers, Roxborough warned Louis, "wound up burned-out and broke before they reached their prime" because such teams "were not interested in the men they were handling but in the money they could make from them." The Louis group, however, had dreams beyond dollars. Roxborough and Black both "had money before they saw Joe Louis," Al Monroe noted in late 1936. "By having their own cash" they could "direct Louis's affairs with both eyes and not with one on the purse." Floyd Calvin of the *Philadelphia Tribune* lauded these men for proving that blacks could indeed combine for a common purpose. "We see actual cooperation of grown men who came together to put over an enterprise," Calvin explained, "each contributing something vital to the success of the expedition." Louis had been "exceptionally well handled," Chester Washington agreed, particularly in terms of "physical development, matchmaking . . . [and] making provision for his future." Blackburn, the *Afro-American*'s Art Carter wrote, had "steered Joe away from the kind of errors that ruined Jack Johnson and brought disaster to Blackburn's own checkered career."[29]

The handlers deserved the accolades. Roxborough blended financial skill with basic intelligence. "I've always done all right in business, and I have done business with whites as well as those of my own race," he explained. "I find no prejudice. If we handle Joe well I don't think the public will care who manages Joe." But the black public cared, for it increasingly viewed Louis as an agent of racial redemption. "Julian Black and John Roxborough have proved beyond doubt that they are fully able to compete with their white business associates on an equal basis," Roi Ottley wrote in 1936. "They have asked no quarter because they are Negroes. . . . And while the Negro public is carried away with the racial aspects of Joe Louis, his managers are interested in smart business—and good business knows no race." Art Carter also thought the Louis team transcended sports. "If the colored race were as capably managed as Joe Louis has been," he concluded, "our future would be far more roseate."[30]

The Adopted Son of 13 Million People

More so than other peoples with longer and more tragic pasts, Americans expect happy endings. They also relish tales, factual and fictional, that validate the ideals Americans claim to hold dear. Whether in the form of Ben Franklin's how-to-succeed autobiography, William McGuffey's didactic readers, or Horatio Alger's novels celebrating upward mobility, Americans revel in tales that demonstrate the close link between morality and advancement, persistence and prominence. The story of Joe Louis exemplified many elements of this traditional American lore.

Since whites regarded blacks as inferior and destined to fail, any African American who succeeded seemed newsworthy. These apparent anomalies included individuals as diverse as Booker T. Washington, of Tuskegee Institute, singer Ethel Waters, Bill "Bojangles" Robinson, dancer and Shirley Temple's movie sidekick, and Mary McLeod Bethune, founder of Bethune-Cookman College. When Joe Louis vanquished a series of reputable white opponents, he showed promise of entering this elite circle. A crucial turning point in his transformation from mere boxer to race icon was his victory over ex-champion Primo Carnera in 1935. Subsequent triumphs over other former white champions also made him a new black hope.

The tale of Detroit's James McKnight exemplifies blacks' growing identification with Louis. Plagued by an itch to see Louis fight Carnera but short of the scratch to pay for travel, Knight jumped on his bicycle and bade farewell to his skeptical and concerned friends. Eight days later he and "his trusty two-wheeled steed" arrived in New York City. "Not only did he make it," the *Courier* bragged, "but he apparently set a new cross country bike record in doing it." McKnight joined some 20,000 other black spectators at Yankee Stadium, well over a quarter of the capacity crowd. "It is a lie that we don't stick together," Lafayette Powell protested in the *Philadelphia Tribune*, "for in the triple deck stands were about 25,000 of us, and all rooting for the same cause." In Chicago some 10,000 fans gathered at the *Defender* office where staff writer David Kellum announced the fight from dispatches sent by Al Monroe at ringside. After the fight, "a hundred newsboys" hawked *Defender* extras from Evanston to Gary.

A veritable Goliath at 6' 4" and 260 pounds, Carnera met his David in Joe. Humorist "Dr. Andrew Dobson" gave a rendition of the event that pricked whites' pretensions to race superiority:

> De bell rings. Carnera rushes in and hits Joe's glove savagely with his nose. Carnera staggers Joe Louis with a hard left eye to Joe's left fist. De bell. . . . Joe feints and Carnera wanted to. De referee cautions Carnera to quit biting Joe's glove. . . . Carnera brings blood to Joe's fist with a busted lip. . . . Joe swings and down goes Carnera and out goes [champion Jimmy] Braddock.

"Tonight Harlem is hilarious with joy," Floyd Calvin reported. "The huge and colorful crowds" savoring the win were "reminiscent of Marcus Garvey's best days." Louis, William Nunn of the *Courier* exclaimed, carried "the weight of an entire race on his shoulders!" The giddiness lasted for weeks. In mid-

July a theater in Los Angeles held over the Louis-Carnera films for three additional days "because of the tremendous crowds."[31]

The fight had another dimension beyond a black contender's defeat of a former white champion. With Mussolini's troops poised to invade Abyssinia, the last independent black nation in Africa, writers such as Arthur Brisbane had warned that the bout might provoke violence between African Americans and Italian Americans. To be safe, Lewis Valentine, New York City police commissioner, assigned a thousand of his gendarmes to the stadium and its vicinity. He also added patrols in areas where the two groups might meet. Contrary to dire predictions, the bout did not incite major disturbances between partisans of Mussolini and Haile Selassie. Common sense prevailed. Gill Holton, a former saloonkeeper in Harlem, for example, admitted paying only scant attention to the crisis in Africa and said he associated "Abyssinia" with the renowned Baptist church of that name headed by Adam Clayton Powell. Would he fight Italians in the street, a reporter asked, if the bout provoked violence? "My mama didn't raise no crazy children," Holton replied. "Let Louis do the fighting. He gets paid." Lillie Barrow Brooks, another "mama" who "didn't raise no crazy children," told John McNulty of the *Daily Mirror* that "all that talk about there being fighting outside the ring the other night when Joe beat Carnera was foolishment." "I know it was," she insisted, "because white folks been all right to me right along, and the reason was because I was right all along to white folks, and Joe I taught to do the same thing." She expected Joe to "get a chance" at the title, since "a good boy is a good boy under any skin." Like Roxborough and Black, Lillie Brooks stressed that Joe posed no threat to whites. Gene Fowler of the *San Francisco Examiner* agreed, making his point by describing Louis as "the Booker T. Washington of the prize ring."[32]

Though "hilarious with joy" in Harlem and elsewhere, blacks showed restraint around whites. Nor did Italian Americans raise a rumpus over Carnera's loss. "The race riot," the *Philadelphia Tribune* gibed, "was only in the minds of those who do not want colored people to have a chance." Harlem, one correspondent noted, was "happy, not ugly," as 500 police "stood by waiting for trouble that never came." Boxing was "brutal, worse than barbaric," Harry Smith of the *Cleveland Gazette* conceded, yet he "rejoice[d] with the rest of our people and others" over the outcome. Louis's stock also rose among those on the lookout for new celebrities. While he "was slumbering at the home of a Harlem friend" after the fight, "representatives of advertising, theatrical, and radio agencies bombarded his managers with offers totaling more than $50,000. None . . . was accepted."[33]

Louis next dropped King Levinsky in the opening round, then trained to meet Max Baer, who had dethroned Carnera in 1934 but lost the crown to

Jimmy Braddock a year later. Eager to keep Louis fit and trim, his managers considered a bout with Leroy Haynes, another black heavyweight. The prospect alarmed Ed Harris, sports editor at the *Philadelphia Tribune*. "Why should two excellent colored fighters do their best to blast each other out of the fight picture?" he protested. "Let Louis and Haynes go their separate ways and knock the stuffings out of as many chalks as possible." If Louis won the title, the managers could match him against Haynes. "Then, whoever wins," Harris added, "the championship will still be with a colored man."

Robert Abbott of the *Defender* ventured to New York to attend the Louis–Baer fight, but for fans of lesser means he again arranged for a reporter at ringside to transmit a blow-by-blow account to the paper's office in Chicago. "Two microphones have been installed," the *Defender* announced before the fight, and "expert workmen and electricians" had spent days "placing special wires in the local office for the occasion." Once again, black fans turned out in unprecedented numbers to see Louis and Baer at Yankee Stadium. Promoter Mike Jacobs told Al Monroe that over 25,000 "race fans" bought tickets. "About a fifth are Negroes," Jonathan Mitchell estimated in the *New Republic*, "more carefully dressed and more mannerly than the whites." Outside the stadium, however, "race fans" celebrated in a less "mannerly" fashion when Louis won. "There is no question but that Harlem and Chicago's South side consider Joe's every win a triumph for the Race, and that should not be," Al Monroe scolded. "The night of the fight Harlem was wild." During the mayhem taxis and buses "were snatched from drivers, and street car motormen and conductors were tossed bodily from their cars, threatening the lives of thousands." Monroe warned that such a reaction might deprive Louis of a title fight, since many whites awaited any excuse to draw the color line. He urged greater restraint.[34]

Louis also noticed that his folk were becoming more demonstrative and pesky. Black strangers, Louis recounted, often greeted him by shouting "Brown Bomber! Brown Bomber!" Others tried to shake his hand or kiss him. "Show them whites!" some exclaimed. "Joe," an occasional fan gushed, "you're our savior!" With each victory, however, the fans wanted to get closer to their hero. When Joe and Marva spent their honeymoon in New York, the growing adulation impinged on their privacy. "It was some hard job trying to show Marva the city," Joe observed. "People followed us everywhere we went. If we went to the movies, we'd have to leave before it was over; if we went to dinner, we'd have to leave before dessert. . . . The girls were still coming at me as if Marva wasn't there. They'd just push her aside; crowds would mess up her hair and clothes." Fans not only disheveled Marva's attire, they jeopardized her marriage. "Eventually you tire of it—the crowds knocking your hat off and pushing you out of the way to reach him," she explained. "Fame is the most difficult thing that can happen to a relationship. . . . Your life is just not your own."[35]

The mailbags arriving at camp were an index of Louis's growing appeal. Shortly before the fight with Baer, Russ Cowans, Joe's tutor, estimated that a thousand fans wrote to Louis each week. Six months later, Chester Washington of the *Courier* noted, the total had doubled. Some fans, such as Ruby Berkley Goodwin, simply expressed admiration and urged Louis to behave. Women sometimes sought dates or proposed marriage. Most letters, however, came from poor people needing help in hard times. The more Louis earned, the more pleas he received for money. Unable to keep up with the mail, the entourage asked Chester Washington to help. The letters "come from all races and creeds," he reported, and ranged "from the ridiculous to the sublime." A Georgia farmer begged Louis "to send him a mule to harvest his crops." An inmate at a sanitarium asked for "a loan of two bucks to bet on the Bomber." A boys' club in Berlin requested "an autographed picture to hang in their club rooms." A fan in Norway wanted a fight ticket. A "worried mother of a little Irish lad near . . . death in Brooklyn" pleaded for a signed photograph and a word of cheer for her son. (Washington discussed this one with Louis, who wrote a personal note to the boy to enclose with a picture they sent special delivery.) "A pastor of a little church in Mississippi wanted to let me know that his congregation was going to pray for my success in the Carnera fight," Louis recalled. "However, he wrote that the church roof was leaking and that members might get wet while praying." He requested "twenty-seven dollars" for repairs. Bob Murphy of the *Detroit Evening Times* thought one particular letter said it all. A man desperate for $50 to pay alimony asked for a loan. He addressed his plea to "Joe Louis Borrow."[36]

By mid-1936 Louis had attained celebrity status, holding a perfect ring record along with an impeccable reputation. Good copy on the sports pages, Louis possessed the charm needed to make the advertising pages. Although the Depression was in its sixth year by the time Louis gained renown, business still had merchandise to sell and needed new faces to pitch old products. Hard times were even harder for most blacks, yet as a tenth of the nation they constituted an important market. As Louis gained fame, he peddled hair pomade, gasoline, castor oil, and a laxative. The spots for hair tonic and fuel were straightforward. After the Carnera bout, the black press ran ads with a large photograph of a well-groomed Joe Louis. "I knew I was in a fight alright," he noted, "but thanks to MURRAY'S SUPERIOR HAIR POMADE, Carnera did not even muss up my hair." When Louis won the title, copywriters used that angle, touting Murray's pomade as "a World's Champion Hair Dressing."

By the mid-1930s Americans associated expensive cars with the rich and famous, equating mobility and high status with freedom to race across the landscape. A luxury car, of course, needed high-octane fuel. "When training, I get my relaxation in my car on the open road," Joe revealed in a pitch for premium. "The gasoline I choose has got to be smooth and full of punch. Essolene is both." Merchants also offered bonuses in the form of free gifts featuring Louis—biographical pamphlets, tin buttons, photographs, and glass coin banks modeled after him.

Most intriguing were the ads for Fletcher's Castoria. In these ads, mother and son often appeared together, preaching two recurring parables.[37] The ads reassured poor and anxious mothers that they, like Lillie Barrow, could protect their children's health and ensure their ultimate success in spite of very limited means. In addition, the upbeat messages implied that mobility was still available to all Americans regardless of origin if they only consumed the right products. In the *Defender* in 1935, for example, Louis held a pair of oversized boxing gloves that a small black boy had just removed. "Do you want to give your children the same fine start that the sensational Joe Louis had?" the text asked. "Then do as Joe's mother did!" She had given him Fletcher's Castoria, Joe revealed, "the only medicine I ever took!" Another ad featured mother and son side by side at the piano, singing the spiritual "I'm So Glad That Trouble Don't Last Always"—a song Americans might well have adopted as a new national anthem during hard times. "Joe always loved singing even in the days when we were sharecroppers down in Alabama," Lillie recalled. "All my life I've dreamed of having a nice home, and that's just what Joe bought me as soon as he made money." This new affluence, however, had not spoiled them. "We're all going to learn to play the piano," she added, "but we'll keep on singing the same spirituals we used to sing together down in Alabama when we never dreamed there'd be a piano in the family." Previous ads had already established that Lillie had given her son castor oil, so the reader only had to connect the dots between taking Fletcher's and acquiring a new home with a piano in the parlor. "My mother raised me on Fletcher's Castoria until I was 11 years old," Joe testified in yet another installment. "I can truthfully say that this is one reason why I have never been sick a day in my life."

This comforting notion that the disadvantaged could attain health and wealth as easily as the wellborn, even during the Depression, inspired another ad that pointed to "regularity" as the key to success. "Joe's mother was as poor as a church mouse. She never had the money to pay for a doctor. Yet she raised eight of the healthiest children on earth—including the great Joe Louis," the text informed readers. "How did she do it? Mainly by keeping the children regular." On the night Louis defeated Baer, he earned $217,338 and presented a new car and home to his bride. But the advertisers continued to stress his humble origins. "No matter how poor we were—and plenty of times we had only potatoes to put in the pot for supper," Joe's mother attested, "I always made sure every one of the children had their Fletcher's Castoria!" With millions of Americans living in housing akin to a sharecropper's shack, hard-pressed to put food on the table, with no money for a doctor, advertisers prescribed a spoonful of oil to cure the nation's ills.[38]

Louis provided good advertising copy for reasons beyond his remarkable mobility. Fletcher's wanted to associate his reputation for integrity with the reliability of its product. Louis "has set a new high standard for sports headliners," an ad noted. "He refuses absolutely to indorse any product unless he has actually used it himself and found that it fulfilled all advertising claims in every respect." Black journalists admired this selectivity and cited it as further proof of a fine character. This rendered his endorsements even more valuable. Such scruples, Harry Smith explained, made Louis almost entirely dependent on his fists "to bring in the cash." Smith praised him for refusing to pitch liquor and tobacco. Louis had rejected $50,000 from "a whiskey firm that wanted to use the nickname 'Brown Bomber'" and his endorsement in print. A food company had offered him $10,000 to promote an item he did not use, Smith added, but "that was turned down."

Louis earned more money than any other athlete did in 1936, an Associated Negro Press story in the *Courier* reported in early 1937. Most of that income came from fight proceeds, with small additions from "exhibitions and product endorsements."[39] Louis's success in the ring and his sterling public image made him an important symbol of sobriety and striving. He would cash in on this reputation later, when his discretion declined in proportion to his rising expenses to sustain a lifestyle quite unlike the ascetic days of the mid-1930s.[40]

The fact that Louis was the rare exception, that few Americans born dirt-poor would ever attain similar fame and riches, did not seem to deter journalists and copywriters from portraying his saga as a quintessential American story. The barefoot boy from an Alabama cotton field had become a national celebrity who earned more money in two rounds of boxing than some of the nation's largest industries earned during an entire quarter. With able guidance from his handlers, an ethic of integrity and hard work, and early help from Fletcher's Castoria, Louis had whipped the Depression as decisively as he had beaten Primo Carnera and Max Baer. As a third of the nation, "ill clad, ill housed, and ill fed" in President Roosevelt's memorable phrase, struggled to acquire the bare necessities in the 1930s, Louis purchased a closetful of tailored suits and new shoes, several automobiles, homes and apartments, and business properties. He also supported a throng of buddies and aided several charities. By dint of his payments to intimates and strangers, he acted as a private welfare agency to alleviate distress and suffering. Rich and optimistic in contrast to most Americans who were poor and anxious, Louis better symbolized the basic failure of the economic system rather than its scattered successes. But advertisers and most journalists chose the rosy lenses, spreading the gospel of free enterprise by noting how Louis had risen from rock bottom to the very top. If one obeyed the rules, lived right, and worked hard, one could thrive even in hard times.

Whatever one thinks of the way advertisers used Louis, his role as peddler had some salutary aspects. In publications aimed at whites at this time, articles, photographs, advertisements, and cartoons tended to use blacks to illustrate the superior status of the majority race. Louis's people appeared as butlers, maids, porters, and custodians. They had bad jobs and used bad grammar. "Yes, suh, Colonel, I'se comin'!" a butler, mint juleps on tray, assured his southern boss in a whiskey ad. On billboards touting Prager beer in 1938, a thick-lipped, grinning, round-faced butler assured drinkers that Prager "sho' am tops for taste." The quintessential black maid was Aunt Jemima. "Pancakes! My flavory, fragrant pancakes," she announced over the radio to an affluent white family seated at a dining room table. "That's what you is hungry for now. Happify your folks today with some fluffy, light Aunt Jemimas."[41]

The ads featuring Joe Louis deviated from this pattern. He never said "sho' am" or "happify." In the castor oil ads, both mother and son used proper grammar. To depict him as subservient or sycophantic toward whites would have been absurd, depriving the copy of credibility. Louis did not wait on white people, scratch and grin, or scrape and bow: Rather, he loomed over white men as they stretched out horizontally on the canvas. The black men around him were well educated, shrewd, refined, and comfortable. Even if Louis had wanted to earn more by selling cigarettes and whiskey, John Roxborough and Julian Black, his managers would have quashed the notion. The testimonials for hair pomade and castor oil, however, were steeped in bourgeois images and ideals. Joe and Lillie not only spoke well in the ads, they appeared amid the artifacts of affluence—the piano, the parlor, the large home, the fine clothing. The graphics and text in the Castoria ads had crossover appeal because Louis seemed worthy of emulation by Americans of all colors and classes.[42]

The Louis legend appealed to all races. But writers realized that Louis had a special relationship to blacks. That bond did not depend on the mobility stressed in advertising copy. Rather, it was more visceral, the result of a shared racial identity and a feeling that the future of all blacks depended in part on what Louis achieved. His own rise seemed to be elevating the black image in the white mind. Yet progress for African Americans was slow and littered with setbacks. Far more than the previous string of twenty-seven victories, Louis's unexpected loss to Max Schmeling in mid-1936 demonstrated the intense identification of "race fans" with "race fighter."

Roxborough and Black had concentrated on making Louis acceptable to white promoters, writers, and fans. But if the color line dating back to 1915 persisted, Louis could not compete for the title. The unexpected loss to Schmeling, however, complicated the quest because it raised doubts about Louis's boxing ability. Had black Americans again embraced a false hope? The entourage had handled success very well; it had no experience coping with failure.

Setback: Louis vs. Schmeling I

Riding an unprecedented string of victories, many over former champions, Louis internalized the belief that he was invincible. He had, the *Defender*'s Dan Burley suggested, suffered "a spell of enlarged cranium." Prior to the bout, writers had all but composed Schmeling's obituary. Sports writer Ed Hughes, for example, called his visit to Schmeling's camp "A Day With a Condemned Man." The *Chicago Daily News* on June 19, 1936, announced that Schmeling had a date with "Executioner Joe." It was not to be. After the opening bell, Louis fans watched a horrifying reversal of the predicted roles. Again and again Schmeling scored with hard rights when Louis dropped his left hand after his jab—a bad habit Schmeling and his trainer had noticed in films of Louis's previous fights. In round six, Schmeling pummeled and staggered Louis, creating some agonizing moments for his fans. Fred Guinyard escorted a tearful Lillie Brooks out of the stadium. Reeling from Schmeling's barrage, disoriented and vulnerable, Louis swung wildly and struck his opponent below the belt. Louis survived the round but could not recover, and Schmeling knocked him out with a number of punishing blows in the twelfth. For millions of African Americans, the clock struck midnight. The elegant coach had turned into a pumpkin.[43]

The outcome incited violence reminiscent of the "white hope" era. In New York City, according to the *Defender*, "thirty Race men attacked Sam Kulim . . . a white WPA worker at a subway station." At 63rd and Amsterdam, "a group of Race boys threw rocks at automobiles with white occupants until police chased them away." At 115th and Lenox, "25 men chased an unidentified white man into a drug store"; he barely escaped through a back door. Not far away, "tenement occupants showered automobiles with bricks." William Cooper, a black fan, had "bet on Schmeling" and "told a saloonful of men about it." He should have kept quiet: "An ambulance took him away unconscious." Two white men from Brooklyn went to Harlem to savor the moment. They should have stayed home, for one "lost a watch and several teeth," the other "lost $16."

Numerous coronaries and attempted suicides were attributed to the fight. "It caused twelve deaths from excitement," a *Time* story asserted. "A Negro girl [in Chicago] took the defeat so hard that she attempted to drink poison in a drug store," the *Philadelphia Tribune* reported. "She was restrained and taken to a hospital." Some 700 police roamed Harlem "to quell an outbreak of shooting, stabbing, street fighting, and other disorders." The *Philadelphia Tribune*'s Otto McClarrin saw the fans' grief. "So terrific was the shock that Harlem as a whole was dazed," he wrote. "People were weak in the knees, some nearly passed away into dead faints." Some trudged along "in funeral time." Langston Hughes watched the fight and its effects. On Seventh Avenue he saw "grown men weeping like children and women sitting on the curbs with their heads in their hands." Jack Johnson had predicted a Schmeling win and bragged that he had bet heavily on him. After he "boisterously flaunted his winnings" in Harlem, he "had to seek police escort to escape the wrath of angry Negroes."

The outcome hit Detroit fans hard, whites and blacks alike. "The blow that knocked out Joe Louis traveled 800 miles and struck deep into the hearts of those who idolized 'our Joe,'" a Detroit daily reported. "They were stunned. They walked about dazedly, blindly. . . . Even those too young to know what it was all about and those too old to care knew something was terribly wrong. It was like a sudden death in the family."[44]

For many blacks the loss remained one of their most vivid memories of the Depression years. Touring with the Noble Sissle Band in Cincinnati, singer Lena Horne joined the musicians who rushed to a radio behind the bandstand during intermission to listen to the fight. "I was near hysteria toward the end . . . when he was being so badly beaten," Horne recalled, "and some of the men in the band were crying." Demeaned by rancor and exclusion in their travels, the musicians trusted Louis to even the score. "Joe was the one invincible Negro, the one who stood up to the white man and beat him down with his fists," Horne stated. "He . . . carried so many of our hopes, maybe even dreams of vengeance." But now he was "just another Negro getting beaten by a white man."

Singer Cab Calloway and his band entertained a white crowd at a Texas Centennial event in Longview. Before the program Calloway listened to the fight. At its close he rushed down the hallway with the news. "He lost, he lost! Jesus Christ, Schmeling beat Joe!" Calloway shouted. "The guys in the band couldn't believe it." When he announced the result to the audience, "the crowd cheered and clapped while the guys in the band softly moaned and groaned." Pianist Willie "the Lion" Smith was playing a Manhattan hotel when Louis was knocked out. "Hooray, Max smashed that nigger!" an excited German-American bartender yelled. Smith pushed away from the piano, "hopped the bar," and brandished his cane "like a baseball bat" as he glared at the bartender. The startled man apologized.[45]

Far from Harlem and East Detroit, African Americans in small towns and rural areas also followed the spectacular rise and sudden fall of Joe Louis. In Stamps, Arkansas, Maya Angelou and her brother Bailey did not ring up purchases on the cash register in her grandmother's general store when the radio carried a Louis bout. Sharecroppers and farm laborers from miles around flocked to the store to lighten their loads with Joe's triumphs. Decades later, Angelou vividly described the symbolism of Louis's loss: "My race groaned. It was our people falling. It was another lynching, yet another Black man hanging on a tree. One more woman ambushed and raped. A Black boy whipped and maimed. It was hounds on the trail of a man running through slimy swamps. It was a white woman slapping her maid for being forgetful." All who bet on Louis lost their wagers, but blacks lost more than money. Louis, Jesse Owens, and Haile Selassie had comprised "a trinity of hope" for people of color, Enoc Waters Jr. noted after the fight. But Mussolini's forces had conquered Ethiopia, and now Schmeling had defeated Louis. "What the Race lost in money," Waters observed, "was as dust to diamonds compared with the loss it suffered in hope."[46]

Louis made no excuses, and his handlers denied rumors that a doctor had "doped" him before the fight. Roxborough, Black, and Blackburn knew why Louis lost: He had trained haphazardly and overestimated himself while underestimating his opponent. The setback forced Louis to take a long, hard look at himself. A few days later he talked with Murray Lewin of the *New York Mirror*. "Joe Louis realized what he meant to his race," Lewin noted. "They had put him on a pedestal as an untutored Booker T. Washington who would lead them to a better understanding with the white folks, through brawn instead of brain. Joe has lived up to the role." Louis had acted in a manner "beyond reproach," Lewin believed, and his comportment after the loss "reflects nothing but credit on him, too." He did not "belittle Schmeling's victory or excuse his own defeat." One matter, however, did puzzle him. "Some of his people have turned on him," Lewin observed, "and that's what Joe can't understand." Others shared his dismay. Musician Louis Armstrong chided black fans for acting sullen in defeat and urged them to "rally around our Joe" and encourage him. "Joe was our idol and should remain our idol," the king of swing advised. "We should be with him win, lose, or draw. We are not fair-weather people, his friends when he is winning and against him when he loses." He predicted Louis would still win the title, "and it won't be long."

Cecil Craigne, a Detroit stringer for the *Defender*, explained the burden Louis carried. A fighter of his potential, Craigne argued, "belongs to the race as a whole." Barred by law and custom from the social mingling needed to promote interracial awareness and amity, blacks depended upon celebrities to cross the color line to prove their worth to the white majority. "The unbalanced social system" made Louis "an ambassador of his race," Craigne maintained. Many whites saw him "as the sole representative of the black race's ambition, its hope, and its pride." By getting to know Joe Louis, whites indirectly familiarized themselves with millions of his people. Since so much depended on him, his setback caused "more grief among the race than any other single event," Craigne observed. He had "a double duty to perform: one to himself, the other to his race." A Louis win vindicated those denied a chance to excel. When Louis was stretched out on the canvas, however, he was a stark reminder of the insults and dangers blacks encountered daily, from the usual calumny in the white press to mob murder.[47]

Redemption

With bad bruises and a wounded ego that hurt even more, Louis disappeared for several days. His handlers housed him in a friend's apartment rather than have him recuperate at the more public Hotel Theresa. When his facial swelling subsided, he allowed Marva to come to New York. She helped tend his wounds and lift his spirits. After a few days he and Marva, "like two thieves in the night," caught a late train for Detroit, where his stepfather had suffered a stroke shortly before the fight. A limousine awaited them at the station.

Win or lose, Louis was news, so photographers and reporters hoped to intercept him. But this time Louis avoided cameras and questions. Cloaked by a large straw hat, dark glasses, and a wide upturned collar, Louis stepped off the train. But instead of walking in to the depot he hastened across the rail yard. "A member of Louis's party," Tod Rockwell reported in the *Detroit Free Press*, "threatened to destroy cameras." The group hopped over several tracks to the waiting limo, "a route comparable to the 100-meter low hurdles." For days Louis stayed in seclusion, with only his wife and close friends around him.[48]

Sobered but still sanguine, the handlers discussed ways to restore the lost luster. They found their chastened fighter more receptive to advice and training. On the public relations front, they used the setback to write another chapter in the Louis legend, stressing that the defeat would only make Louis stronger. They focused on redemption. Not only would Louis win the title, he would avenge his loss to Schmeling. To get back on track, the managers matched Louis against Jack Sharkey, another ex-champion. On the day before the fight, the *Courier*'s William Nunn talked with Louis. "You watch me, I won't let my people down," Louis assured him. "They had confidence in me, and wanted me to win the heavyweight title. . . . I'm hitting the come-back trail . . . and I don't mean maybe." Louis kept his word, knocking out Sharkey in the third round. LOUIS WINNER! declared the *Courier* in type usually reserved for presidential elections and declarations of war. In Harlem, the win touched off "a glamorous, wild, exciting, typical Joe Louis celebra-tion," reporter Otto McClarrin observed, a din of "bells, tin pans, whistles, auto horns, and everything that makes a noise" that "bounced off the side-walks until the windows shook." The reaction reminded McClarrin of a re-vival, as "a hallelujah-raving people took the streets by storm." Wezlynn Tildon of the *Defender* watched Harlem fans as they "formed parade lines" and "held up traffic beating out tin pan music . . . of triumph." Some waved Ethiopian flags. The festive mood was augmented by news from Germany that Jesse Owens had shattered the myth of Aryan supremacy right under Herr Hitler's nose by winning four gold medals at the Olympics in Berlin.[49]

After beating Sharkey, Louis knocked out three more opponents in 1936 and staged exhibitions to stay in shape. Jack Blackburn monitored him closely, hoping to remedy the flaws Schmeling had exploited while avoiding distrac-tions that could sidetrack him. Louis defeated three more opponents in early 1937. Then promoter Mike Jacobs took down the "whites only" sign and matched Louis against champion James Braddock in Chicago on June 22.

The entourage did not want the fight to become a referendum on race superiority, but the climate of the 1930s made it difficult to keep color out of the picture. Besides, Jack Johnson remained part of the fight scene and re-tained his capacity to rile fans. Rebuffed by Roxborough and Black, Johnson offered to help Braddock prepare for the fight. Braddock turned Johnson down. In a less race-conscious society, Johnson's efforts to profit from his expertise would have seemed entirely reasonable. But color sometimes mat-tered more than cash. "Why should Mr. Johnson want to train James Braddock?" Ruth Stoball protested in a letter to the *Defender*. "If I was a trainer I would never think of training a Caucasian against a Race man." Proud to be "a Race woman," Stoball called Louis "a credit to the Race" and wished "we had more young men like him." She contrasted Joe and Jack. Louis "has never gone out of his race for anything," she stressed. For a wife "he selected a very sweet, refined girl of his Race." He was "clean cut in every way" and his handlers were "cultured men." Johnson further angered fans when he called Louis "overrated" and predicted a Braddock win. "Jack . . . ought to know folks want none of him now," an Associated Negro Press writer noted. "He should go off and keep his trap shut for a while at least." Johnson "has got to have some way of getting into print," the writer com-plained, but he was "taking the wrong way as usual."[50]

Schmeling had as good a claim to a title fight as Louis. By 1937, however, boxing had become as complicated as diplomacy. The muddle in fisticuffs and foreign affairs had a common origin—Nazi Germany. If Schmeling fought and defeated Braddock, he might retire to Berlin with the most prestigious title in sports. Did Americans want the crown to pass from an Irish American to a German national, a man whose country was fast becoming synonymous with anti-Semitism, anti-Catholicism, xenophobia, and militarism? In the abstract, sports transcended international relations. But in actuality, athletics were increasingly enmeshed in the harsh realities of national, ethnic, and racial conflict at this time. Schmeling's origin was but one strand of a complex web of tribal loyalties and tensions affecting sports within nations as well as between them. While Nazis glorified the notion of a pure race, real people with mixed backgrounds and divided loyalties showed that matters of color, citizenship, and identity were far less tidy and predictable than race propagandists wanted them to be.

Promoter Mike Jacobs, for example, did not make an issue of being Jewish. Though considered "white" in the "race" hierarchy of the United States, Jews still remained out of the mainstream. Anti-Semitism persisted in the nation in the 1930s; bias and barriers continued to hamper Jews in education, employment, and politics. Perhaps awareness of such arbitrary discrimination made Jacobs more sympathetic to Louis and his managers and more determined to open a door for them. Schmeling for his part was a proud German, but his commitment to Nazi doctrine and policies remained unclear. Joe Jacobs, who managed Schmeling's affairs in the United States, was a Jew. So were some of Schmeling's closest friends in Germany. Joe Louis, of mixed African, Native American, and European ancestry, also posed a dilemma for white Americans who thought the champion should be "Caucasian." If race, however vaguely defined, mattered more than nation, then whites in the United States, including Jews, would prefer Schmeling as champion over Louis. For German Americans, the tangle was even more perplexing. Would they back Joe Louis, who shared their country and symbolized its ideals, or Max Schmeling, who shared their ethnicity and homeland? In New York City, many Americans appalled by developments in Germany—including several prominent Jews—warned Mike Jacobs they would lead a boycott against a title fight between Braddock and Schmeling. Others opposed the intrusion of world politics into boxing and insisted that Schmeling had earned a championship bout with his victory over Louis.

Mike Jacobs cared more about the box office than the color or creed of the fighters he signed. For him, boxing was a business, not a crusade, but he did realize that his work had repercussions beyond the ring. Because of the growing hostility in the United States toward the Nazi regime and all things German, Jacobs decided to match Louis and not Schmeling against Braddock.

In doing so he considered the politics of the present as well as possibilities for the future. Since Schmeling had handed Louis his sole defeat, a rematch between them would arouse enormous interest on both sides of the Atlantic. If Louis beat Braddock, then Jacobs could give Schmeling his due by matching him against the new champion. Besides, Louis had also earned a title bout, with thirty-four victories, three of them over former champions, and only one loss.

What Louis represented beyond boxing, however, had become more important than his ring record. If Americans honored their ideals, if the virtues extolled by Ben Franklin and Horatio Alger were to prevail, then Louis must not be denied through discrimination—a point made by both black and white journalists. Shortly after Jacobs signed Louis and Braddock, the *Courier*'s Ira Lewis reflected that Jack Johnson and Max Baer had treated the title "lightly, almost disrespectfully." Louis, "a gentleman," would be different, for he "would wear his honor with credit to himself, to the profession, and to his race." Chester Washington of the *Courier* concurred, describing Louis as "a fine, clean living fellow" who "still clings to those rules of right living instilled in him by his mother." On the eve of the title fight, the *Defender*'s Al Monroe urged black fans to behave so they would "not destroy in one night" what the Louis team had "built up with months of hard work." The entourage had "surmounted the most difficult of all barriers," Monroe noted, "the unwritten law in boxing that said that no Race man should fight for the championship." White writers echoed this praise and contrasted 1937 with 1910. John Lardner, for example, doubted that a Louis win would incite riots. "The Negroes of Chicago seem pretty quiet and nonchalant just now," Lardner reported from the windy city on the eve of the fight. "And besides, things have changed since the time of Jack Johnson." Sid Keener of the *St. Louis Star-Times* saw no parallel between Johnson and Louis or their eras. "Joe has been a credit to his race," he noted, "and to the fight game."[51]

On the night of June 22, 1937, Louis, just five weeks over twenty-three years old, climbed into the ring with Braddock, who was thirty-two, at Comiskey Park in the heart of Chicago's Black Belt. Among the spectators was Jess Willard, the white hope who had ended Johnson's reign in 1915. Thousands of black fans filled the bleachers while a fortunate few took ringside seats. From the cotton fields of Alabama came Albert Barrow, Louis's paternal uncle, to watch his nephew fight for the crown. Back home his wife and nine children, the *Defender* reported, "listened to a broadcast of the fight over the radio of a neighbor who purchased the set especially for the occasion." Like the Barrows in Alabama, millions of Americans turned on their radios.

With a shamrock on his trunks and the hope that the luck of the Irish would prevail, Braddock sent Louis to the canvas in the opening round with a punch that knocked one of Joe's older sisters right out of the park. She feared Braddock had duplicated Schmeling's feat. She could have remained in her seat, however, for her brother and the handicap of age proved too much for the champion. "If his chin is as hard as his arteries," a wag had joked about Braddock prior to the fight, "he'll stay the limit." But that chin caught several punches from the challenger. In the eighth round, Louis hit Braddock with a hard left to the ribs and a solid right to the jaw. The champion went down for a ten count; the reign of King James was over. LOUIS I—KING OF THE HEAVY-WEIGHTS, the *Defender* proclaimed. At a press conference after the fight, a reporter asked Louis how he felt. Gracious toward Braddock, Louis replied that he felt fine. "I had a tough fight," he remarked, "and I fought a tough man." Chester Washington called on Louis at his Chicago apartment the next day. "How does it feel being champion?" Washington asked. "I don't feel any different," Louis answered, "but I do want to beat Schmeling."[52]

In black enclaves across the country, it was a rare moment of triumph for millions mired in the longest and deepest Depression in the nation's history. When Johnson beat Jeffries in 1910 racial violence had erupted in many places, and some feared that a Louis victory over Braddock might trigger similar confrontations. Contrary to folk wisdom, however, history seldom repeats itself, and 1937 was no echo of 1910. "Now another Negro is champion of the world," Richards Vidmer wrote in the *New York Herald Tribune* right after the fight. "But there is no fear of a repetition of the incidents that marked and marred Johnson's career." Louis was "a fine fighter," Vidmer noted, "but there are other characteristics that go with greatness, and Louis apparently has them all." He was a "quiet, unassuming, healthy, and sincere" person, traits admired by all fans. "No frantic search for a white hope will be necessary," Vidmer concluded, "only a search for a better fighter, regardless of race or color, and that search may last longer than [Johnson's reign of] seven years." Kelly Miller of Howard University had closely followed Johnson, but he now expressed hope for a happier era of black rule in the ring. He quoted Rudyard Kipling: "But there is neither East nor West/ Border nor breed nor birth/ When two strong men stand face to face/ Though they come from the ends of the earth." When the Louises returned home after the fight, they met blacks dancing in the street. They stepped out several times to acknowledge the crowd. "We got another chance!" one fan shouted. "We're depending on you!" exhorted a second. "Don't be another Jack Johnson!" begged a third. Louis understood their concerns. "My conduct as champion," he assured *Defender* staffers, "will be the same as my conduct before I was champion."[53]

"We got another chance!" The fan's use of the plural pronoun was not just a rhetorical flourish. Louis realized that, for better or worse, his life was no longer his own. The managers had seen how black Americans identified with him as he emerged a respected representative of his people. But the handlers could not have anticipated the symbiosis that developed between their fighter and his fans. White fans admired Louis too, but their tie to him was fundamentally different. To whites, Louis appeared to be a great boxer with a pleasing personality; whether he won or lost had little social or psychological impact on them. To blacks, on the other hand, how Louis fared in the ring and how he behaved outside it mattered a great deal. Pundits captured this connection in a proverb: "As Joe Louis goes, so goes Harlem." The black fans' bond with Louis transcended other differences: male and female, old and young, professional and proletarian, rich and poor, northerner and southerner, urbanite and rustic—all found common ground in this Cinderella story. John Roxborough alluded to this bond when Louis enlisted in the army in 1942. "I couldn't be prouder of Joe if he was my own son," he told a *Courier* reporter. "But Joe doesn't belong to Julian or myself, or even his mother. He is the adopted son of 13,000,000 of our people."[54]

From Race Hero to National Hero

Besides wanting to avenge the one loss, the managers decided to keep Louis active so he would not be criticized for resting on his laurels. "I had to prove myself," Louis explained. "It works like this: If you're black and at the top, you gotta be superman. . . . You have to constantly show the world you're worthy. No way I could have slid by like Braddock, sitting on my championship for two years." The managers signed contracts for three quick title defenses. "We do not want either Joe or the title to get rusty," Roxborough noted. Louis and Tommy Farr, the British champion, went the distance on August 30 with Louis getting the decision. He knocked out Nathan Mann in the third round on February 22, 1938. Next came a knockout of Harry Thomas in five on April 1.

A year after winning the title, Louis again faced Max Schmeling at Yankee Stadium. Few experts thought the German could do it again. "If Max can win, they should put the guy in the Smithsonian Institute because he'll have everything against him but his sense of superiority," Paul Mickelson wrote in the *Richmond Times-Dispatch*. "He's eight years older [than Louis] and he's trying to become the first fighter to win, lose, and then regain the heavyweight crown in a city having the largest Jewish population in the world." Critics who had labeled Louis "the Brown Bummer" witnessed a remarkable turnabout, for the fighter opposite Schmeling in 1938 scarcely resembled the loser of 1936. In the shortest title fight up to that time, Louis took only 124 seconds to knock Schmeling out in the first round—a clear vindication of his right to rule. Roy Wilkins missed the knockout. He reached his seat just as the opening bell rang and was still removing his coat and draping it over his chair when Louis smashed Schmeling to the canvas. Despite missing the action, he relished the result. The knockout, Wilkins recalled decades later, was "the shortest, sweetest minute of the entire thirties."[55]

Some 20,000 African Americans watched Louis beat Schmeling, among them Jack Johnson. He praised Louis for correcting his previous errors and avenging his loss. He also pointed out advances in the racial climate since his own reign. Louis, Johnson remarked, had eased tensions between blacks and whites. "I want to say here that I think Joe's victory has done the race a lot of good and has improved race relations in every field of endeavor," he observed. "When I defeated Jim Jeffries on July 4, 1910, 10 people were killed in the resulting race riots. . . . One hour after I had won a fight a Negro was lynched in Charleston, Missouri, and a white man was fatally shot in Arkansas. Gangs of infuriated white men and delirious Negroes prowled the streets." The films of the fight had aroused additional rancor. "Several governors prohibited the showing of the fight pictures," Johnson recalled, "because of the intense race hatred that burned everywhere." He now seemed kinder to Louis. "I witnessed a great fight," he concluded, "by a great champion."

Johnson was not alone in believing Louis had "done the race a lot of good." A Chicago man quit his job and spent his meager life savings to travel to New York to watch the fight. Since Louis disposed of Schmeling in about two minutes, it seemed the fan had paid way too much for far too little. He assured a *Defender* reporter, however, that he had no regrets. "I'm willing to eat crusts of bread until I find another job," he smiled, "because I have pleasant memories to feast upon." Richard Wright, whose highly acclaimed *Uncle Tom's Children* appeared shortly before the fight, understood the basis of Joe's popularity among his people. Wright also realized how important it was for oppressed blacks to have "pleasant memories to feast upon" when sustenance in other forms so seldom came their way. Louis met basic but often unspoken needs. "Joe was the concentrated essence of black triumph over white," Wright stated, "long-nourished hate vicariously gratified." When Louis won the title, blacks grew "bold that night"—a transformation Maya Angelou also witnessed among poor blacks in Arkansas. "Their fear of property, of the armed police fell away," Wright observed. "There was in their chant a hunger deeper than that for bread as they march along. In their joy they were feeling an impulse which only the oppressed feel to the full." They craved affirmation that "the earth was theirs" too, "that they did not have to live by proscription in one corner of it."[56]

Confined to just "one corner" by white prejudice, blacks felt a rare thrill when Louis returned to his corner after punching a "chalk" to the canvas. In victory Louis turned the world upside down, punishing a white opponent for the countless times black people took their lumps and dared not strike back. The reversal of racial fortunes delighted those who knew too well the dangers of crossing a white person. Maya Angelou noticed this elation during the broadcasts of Joe Louis's fights. When a desperate white boxer clinched with Louis to save himself from a flurry of punches, a black man chortled: "That white man don't mind hugging that niggah now, I betcha." After Louis beat Braddock, black fans in Philadelphia taunted Irish police. "How do you feel about your ex-champion now? Where was his four leaf clover?" The day after the fight, singer Bill Gaither immortalized the moment in a recording studio:

> I came all the way from Chicago,
> To see Joe Louis and Max Schmeling fight.
> Schmeling went down like the *Titanic*
> When Joe gave him just one hard right.

Ostracized, insulted, sometimes even lynched by whites, blacks longed for "just one hard right" to even the score. The punch that decked Schmeling was even sweeter, for Nazi Germany now symbolized the doctrine of white supremacy run riot, race arrogance carried to its tragic extreme. White Europeans and Americans not only took pride in their supposed race superiority, they also exalted their technological genius. Gaither suggested a common thread between the sinking of the *Titanic* in 1912 and Schmeling's defeat in 1938: Whites must learn that technology could not fully reduce nature to human will, nor could whites permanently keep blacks down. (The legend that Jack Johnson's life was spared because a white captain denied him passage on the *Titanic* further linked the 1912 disaster to Schmeling's loss to Louis. The skipper, lore had it, told Johnson, "I ain't haulin' no coal.") In Gaither's song, the white man, not the black, becomes the desperate supplicant:

> It was only two minutes and four seconds,
> Poor Schmeling was down on his knees,
> He looked like he was praying to the Good Lord
> To have "Mercy on me please."

Blacks welcomed any challenge to white arrogance, but they also knew that whites could not abide an "uppity nigger." Maya Angelou, for example, remembered how cautious blacks were in Stamps after Louis whipped a white man. Many stayed overnight with kin or friends in town rather than return to their rural homes after dark. "It wouldn't do," Angelou observed, "for a Black man and his family to be caught on a lonely country road on a night when Joe Louis had proved that we were the strongest people in the world."[57]

Despite pleas from both whites and blacks for restraint, the Louis–Schmeling rematch produced more fighting outside the ring than within it. Each race had perpetrators as well as victims in the altercations. In New York City, Washington, DC, Richmond, Cleveland, and Gary, violence erupted between blacks, white police, and white bystanders. Ralph Matthews of the *Afro-American* took Harlemites to task. "Going around punching everybody in the nose who happens to be of a different race simply because a black man beat an Aryan is not a legitimate exhibition of race pride," he scolded. "That to me is savagery at its worst, primitive lack of restraint, and evidence of racial adolescence." Roy Wilkins warned that "hoodlum demonstrations" by fans might destroy the "good will" spread by Louis and other athletes and jeopardize civil rights advances. But the "racial adolescence" Matthews deplored had its troubled teens on both sides of the color line. In Richmond, for example, a white man drove his car into a jubilant black crowd. He knocked down five people and sent two to the hospital. Several scuffles followed, with white police ordering black fans to desist and go home. "When colored people are filling streets and having their own celebration, in their own community, it is no time for Nazi-minded sympathizers to interfere, call them names, and order them indoors," the *Afro-American* protested. If police suppressed such demonstrations, then the nation "is not a democracy any more, but something akin to what now exists in Germany and Italy." The comparison was more valid, at least in terms of race relations, than whites wanted to believe. "America," Langston Hughes lamented in 1936, "never was America to me."[58]

Such extreme reactions to interracial contests revealed the deep fissure between the races—blacks unhappy with the status quo, whites resistant to change. Louis tapped into deep and seldom spoken feelings. "No one in the United States," Langston Hughes contended, "has ever had such an effect on Negro emotions, or on mine." Louis had "smashed into smithereens the false prophets of racial inequality," the *Afro-American*'s James Reid wrote after Schmeling's defeat. "This if no more will furnish wells of inspiration for generations yet unborn." Louis had "never coveted honor or distinction," Reid argued, only "right and justice as a servant of his race." Don Deleighbur, Reid's colleague at the *Afro-American,* believed that Louis captivated people of color overseas as well as at home. "Willingly and unwillingly, the rest of Joe's race has been taken along with him," Deleighbur noted. "The hope that Louis inspired in the millions of colored people all over the world by his ability to knock out white men and with them the cockeyed notion" of "white supremacy" had provided the race "its greatest boost in morale."

John Killens, who worked for the National Labor Relations Board in Washington, DC, had watched Louis batter Schmeling and then joined the celebration in Harlem. Louis was "our Joe, not your Old Black Joe," he boasted. "Each time he whipped another white man black hearts overflowed with joy." A bloody win avenged a long history of hurt. "Every triumph he experienced, we experienced," Killens explained. "Yes, we were finally fighting back. We were fighting back against Mr. Charlie in a way we had never been allowed to fight. Joe was the embodiment of our deepest wish fulfillment. He was black manhood redeemed forevermore."

Russell Baker, later a Pulitzer prize-winning columnist for the *New York Times*, lived in a mixed neighborhood in Baltimore during the late 1930s, though he recalled little actual race mixing there. Among other whites, Baker witnessed "blatant racism candidly expressed daily" within a separate and unequal system "in place so long it seemed to have been divinely ordained." Yet Providence took a strange turn in 1937. "Joe Louis was a living, breathing mockery of the natural order of things," Baker wrote, and when he defeated a white rival "shouts, cheering, clapping, a tumult of joyous celebration" emanated from blacks across the alley. Whites, on the other hand, reacted with "the silence of the tomb." The rematch between Louis and Schmeling dramatized the racial divide in southwest Baltimore. Whites on Lombard Street viewed Schmeling's loss as "the ultimate anticlimax" that was "paralyzing in its brutal suddenness." Baker went to his kitchen window to see the other side: "Doors were being flung open down there. People were streaming out into the alley, pounding each other delightedly on the back, and roaring with exultation. Then I saw someone start to move up the alley, out toward white territory, and the rest of the group, seized by an instinct to defy destiny, falling in behind him and moving en masse." Baker ran to the front of the apartment to see if the blacks were bold enough to invade "white territory":

> They were. They seemed to have been joined by other groups pouring out of other neighborhood alleys, for there was a large throng now coming around into Lombard Street, marching right out in the middle of the street as though it was their street, too. Men in shirtsleeves, women, boys and girls, mothers carrying babies—they moved down Lombard Street almost silently except for a low murmur of conversation and an occasional laugh. Nervous laughter most likely.

"Nervous laughter" perhaps, but blacks had turned a corner in more ways than one. "Joe Louis had given them the courage to assert their right to use a public thoroughfare, and there wasn't a white person down there to dispute it," Baker realized. "It was the first civil rights demonstration I ever saw, and it was completely spontaneous, ignited by the finality with which Joe Louis had destroyed the theory of white superiority."[59]

Charles Johnson, a sociologist who studied the attitudes of black boys in the rural South during the late 1930s, found that "racial superiority in the field of athletics has contributed more to race pride than any other single factor in recent years." Although his subjects mentioned Jesse Owens, they especially identified with Joe Louis and Henry Armstrong, a black welterweight champion. Johnson knew why. Unable to "resent insults, or pit their strength fairly" against whites, "or resist malicious aggression without incurring the danger of wholesale reprisals from the white community," these boys "are more than normally thrilled and vindicated when the special racial handicap is removed and a Negro reveals his superior physical quality."

Decades later, black Americans still vividly remembered how they had reveled in this new black Joe's dominance over the "ofays." When Louis defeated Braddock, Malcolm X recalled, "all the Negroes in Lansing, like Negroes everywhere, went wildly happy with the greatest celebration of race pride our generation had ever known. Every Negro boy old enough to walk wanted to be the next Brown Bomber." Fame and fortune went with the title, but the desire to emulate Joe Louis involved more than celebrity and riches. "The ring," Malcolm X reflected, "was the only place a Negro could whip a white man and not be lynched."[60]

Black women also derived vicarious satisfaction from Joe Louis's victories over white opponents. Seated at ringside when Louis fought Max Baer, Julia Jones of the *Courier* estimated that 15,000 women attended the fight. "The modern woman," Jones stated, "takes her fighting as serenely as grandmother did her knitting." Lena Horne, however, did not take fighting serenely. Her mother chided her for "getting hysterical" when Louis lost to Schmeling, especially since he was a total stranger. "He belongs to us," Horne replied. Maya Angelou studied the older black women who gathered around the radio at her grandmother's store. When Louis knocked out a white man, "even the old Christian ladies who taught their children and tried themselves to practice turning the other cheek would buy soft drinks," she recalled. "And if the Brown Bomber's victory was a particularly bloody one they would order peanut patties and Baby Ruths also." Lillie Barrow Brooks thought her son did the Lord's work. "Yes, indeed, I tell those ladies out in my church, Joe can do plenty good by fighting," she told John McNulty of the *Daily Mirror*. "And that makes it religious if you can do good for people by it." Mary McLeod Bethune, an aid to President Roosevelt, saw the joy in black Washington when Louis beat Schmeling. "It did something important to every Negro in this land," Bethune observed. Louis symbolized "the will to achieve, to overcome every handicap, to come back when we're down, to make good." Edgar Pitts, founder of a booster club in Detroit, counted "as many females as males" in the group. These women viewed Louis as a symbol of redemption whose race trumped his gender.[61]

From the cotton rows of Alabama to the paved streets of Chicago, from poverty to opulence, obscurity to celebrity—no wonder the Joe Louis story captivated Americans. Writers searched for the right analogy to describe his odyssey. He was the "Black Moses" leading the children of Ham out of bondage; he was the Booker T. Washington of boxing. Suggestive but simplistic, these analogies could not capture the complexity of the meaning of Joe Louis to Americans during the Depression. Booker T. Washington, for example, had urged blacks to stay in the South. "Cast down your bucket where you are," he had declared in Atlanta in 1895. "Cast it down in making friends in every manly way of the people of all races by whom we are surrounded." John Roxborough, Jack Blackburn, and Joe Louis certainly hoped to make friends "of all races," but all three had abandoned the South to cast down their buckets in the urban North. None had prospered from farming or the trades Washington had recommended to his people. Nor was Louis a black Moses, for he and his people intended to stay in and improve the country of their bondage rather than flee to another land. In a society less preoccupied with race, Louis would have meant no more (and no less) than the white hero in the rags-to-riches tales—a plucky person who attained individual and not group goals. But the long history of prejudice and proscription, the legacy of Jack Johnson, and the determination of Louis's managers to make him an agent of change all meant that "the Brown Bomber" had to bear a burden far greater than most Americans of his time. His achievement seems even more remarkable when his origins, age, and calling are taken into account. Few ever assume such responsibility and fewer still ever meet or exceed such high expectations.

Louis possessed the talent and acquired the training to keep "a-climbin' on" to the top of the stairs in boxing. But leading an entire nation into uncharted territory "where there ain't been no light," as Langston Hughes had noted in his 1922 poem, "Mother to Son," turned out to be a fight that would have to go many more rounds, a battle royal that would continue indefinitely into the future. By the time Louis vindicated his title with his decisive victory over Max Schmeling in 1938, growing numbers of white Americans—especially sports writers—seemed less concerned with race than their predecessors in Jack Johnson's era. Louis had earned his place in sports history. He had become a figure whose craft and character had begun to transcend color. But black Americans wanted more than tokenism, more than wealth and fame for a few while most remained destitute and outcast. Joe Louis and his handlers had fought on several fronts to uplift millions whose lives had been, in Hughes's words, "no crystal stair." They had reached a new landing, but the races remained "in the dark" on the eve of World War II, with many additional steps to climb.

Champion Jack Johnson in a classic fighting pose. *(Otto Sarony, Library of Congress)*

The house Johnson bought for his mother at 3344 South Wabash in Chicago. (*Chicago Daily News, Chicago Historical Society*)

Johnson and Tiny, his mother, in July 1910. (*Chicago Daily News, Chicago Historical Society*)

Johnson and Jim Jeffries, black hope versus white hope, July 4, 1910. (*Bob Pace Boxing Memorabilia*)

Johnson marries Lucille Cameron in late 1912. *(National Archives)*

Johnson in 1912. *(Samuel A. Marrs, Chicago Daily News, Chicago Historical Society)*

Johnson's reign ended by Jess Willard on April 5, 1915. (*Bob Pace Boxing Memorabilia*)

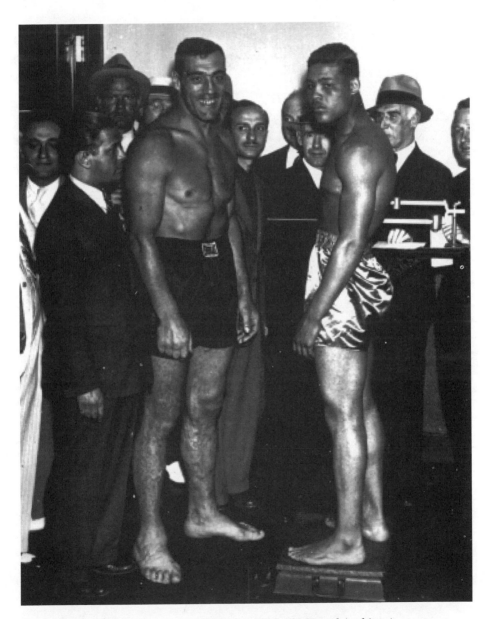

Joe Louis and Primo Carnera at weigh-in, 1935. *(National Archives)*

Joe, his wife Marva, and his mother Lillian Barrow Brooks. *(National Archives)*

Champion Joe Louis knocks Max Schmeling to the canvas on June 22, 1938. *(Associated Press, Library of Congress)*

Louis puts Schmeling (and racist theory) on the ropes. *(Photographs and Prints Division, Schomburg Center for Research in Black Culture, The New York Public Library, Astor, Lenox and Tilden Foundations)*

Sketch of Louis, Schmeling, and Hitler by Tom Webster, *The Daily Mail* (London), October 12, 1939. *(Caroline and Erwin Swann Collection, Library of Congress)*

GI Joe. *(Office of War Information, Library of Congress)*

The Brown Bomber inspects an allied bomber during World War II. *(National Archives)*

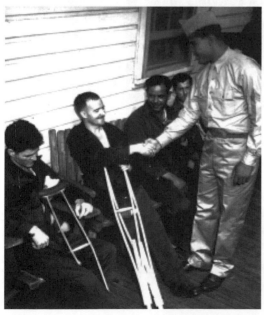

Louis visits wounded soldiers at a Boston Hospital. *(National Archives)*

Louis and Billy Conn at an army awards ceremony in 1945. *(National Archives)*

Marva Louis at home at the piano, beneath Joe's image—her music was more harmonious than their marriage. *(Chicago Historical Society)*

6

"No Other Dream,
No Land But This"

Black Americans and the Enemy Within

> Better our seed rot on the ground
> And our hearts burn to ash
> Than the years be empty of our imprint,
> We have no other dream, no land but this.[1]

> —*Pauli Murray, "Dark Testament," 1942*

On the day Joe Louis won the title—June 22, 1937—Senator Arthur Vandenburg of Michigan warned colleagues about chronically high unemployment, soaring deficits, and Franklin D. Roosevelt's failure to revive the economy. Government expenses had grossly exceeded income for seven consecutive years, he complained, and the national debt had reached "staggering" proportions. "Federal relief outlays" were now "eight times as high" as in 1933, "while state and local expenditures are twice as high." Yet hard times persisted, as the nation was "'in the red' in more than one sinister meaning of the phrase." Vandenburg and other Republicans railed against New Deal programs, mounting public debt, and militant unions allegedly tied to the White House. To reduce federal spending and power, Vandenburg recommended "a restoration of State decisions, more substantial local contributions, and a complete restoration of basic State responsibility for relief administration." He urged senators "to quit talking about balancing the Federal budget and actually . . . do something about it."

Backlash

Sharing Vandenburg's preference for states' rights, Senator Theodore Bilbo of Mississippi proposed another solution to the economic crisis. "Two questions can be solved at one time," he promised, "the race problem and the unemployment problem." Bilbo urged federal officials to create a program for "the repatriation of the Negro" to Africa. "We could buy all the territory needed to colonize 12,000,000 Negroes," he assured colleagues. "In fact, we could get almost as much territory in Africa as we have now in the United States." Since Britain and France were "considerably in arrears on their war debts," they could meet "their just and honest obligations" by ceding to the United States "as much territory [in Africa] as the Negro race would need for the next several hundred years." Slaves "brought to America" had converted to Christianity, so their descendants could now become missionaries for "Christianizing and civilizing . . . the African race in Africa." All present relief payments to blacks, Bilbo advised, should be diverted to colonization. As blacks resettled in Africa, unemployed whites could take their land and jobs, curtailing the need for public aid. Spared the burden of its unwanted black population, white America could achieve renewed prosperity, internal security, and sectional harmony.

Bilbo believed that all Americans should embrace his plan. Only northern politicians who coveted black votes and civil rights leaders who misrepresented their race opposed his scheme. "The Negro knows that he has no place in this country," Bilbo observed. "He knows that, as time moves on and competition between the whites and the blacks becomes keener and keener, the Negro is going to be discriminated against." Bilbo knew that bias against blacks was widespread, since "the Negro . . . is discriminated against in the North and the South alike" and was denied "an equal chance." Such prejudice persisted because it stemmed from immutable causes. "The Negro is inferior," Bilbo asserted, "when it comes to creative genius . . . intellect . . . any mental powers."

> His head is not suitably built, and it does not grow in such a manner as to permit intellectual development, because, as the scientists and ethnologists tell us, the bones which make up the skull are joined together by sutures; and in the case of the Negro, by the time he has reached the age of puberty, these sutures have become ossified and solidified, and there is no room thereafter for the brain to expand.

Drawing on a century of "scientific" racism, Bilbo attributed the blacks' condition to inherent genetic defects. He feared that the more tolerant race policies in the North encouraged mingling and intermarriage, spawning a new generation of mixed offspring inferior to its progenitors. Since northerners rejected strict segregation and laws against mixed marriages, only removal and geographical distance could ensure the integrity of the races.[2]

Bilbo reintroduced his repatriation plan not long before Joe Louis fought Max Schmeling in 1938. While many white fans favored Louis, Bilbo remained adamant that the champion's people had no future in the United States. "In the South," Bilbo proclaimed, "society is protected from horrors unspeakable and worse than all the ravages of war only by maintaining an eternal sentinel upon every doorstep." Efforts to elevate the African American had been futile. "Nature has endowed the Negro with ethnic characteristics, primal instincts, [and] hereditary values," Bilbo argued, that "cannot be eradicated either by education or social contact."

Naive Americans ignored this biological fact, but whites in other places accepted it. "The Germans appreciate the importance of race values" and "understand that racial improvement is the greatest asset that any country can have," Bilbo contended. They had written "more books on heredity, genetics, race culture, and the principles of inheritance and the science of biology than have almost any other people." Americans should emulate them. "They know, as few other nations have yet realized," he added, "that the impoverishment of race values contributes more to the impairment and destruction of civilization than any other agency."

By denying "race values," Americans risked a precipitate decline. "Never before has a nation deliberately invited the horrible specter of race mixture to its very vitals as the United States . . . is doing at the present time." All states should ban mixed marriages and impose segregation. If all barriers between the races fell, Bilbo warned, "miscegenation becomes inevitable and complete amalgamation inescapable." Past mistakes must be avoided. At the time of Reconstruction, "carpetbaggers" had blocked colonization by promising forty acres and a mule to former slaves. Now a small number of northern zealots, Bilbo complained, thwarted black removal once more by advocating equal rights. With millions of ex-slaves and their descendants resettled in the North since 1900, the sectional problem of the nineteenth century had become the national peril of Bilbo's era. Yet the solution remained the same. To end economic distress, sectional rancor, and racial strife, the federal government must devote its full diplomatic and financial resources to relocating the entire black population beyond American borders.[3]

Like any counsel, Bilbo used evidence selectively to make his case. Whatever the bias in his ethnological sources, he firmly believed that three centuries of American experience validated his racial determinism. Much of American history did indeed revolve around the importation of millions of

Africans to do the most arduous and demeaning labor. In addition, the conquest and dispossession of Native American peoples had provided whites with ample territory and resources to transform into private property and personal wealth. "Manifest destiny" had been a rallying cry for acquiring a continental empire as well as a celebration of "whiteness" and all it implied by the 1840s. The Civil War ended slavery but not racism. However suspect Bilbo's genetic theories and inane his plan to ship some 12 million blacks to Africa, his point that the black American was "discriminated against now" and "does not get an equal chance" could well have emanated from W.E.B. DuBois. But DuBois and others rejected racist ethnology and colonization schemes. They viewed Bilbo as an aberration, a remnant of a resilient yet declining order. One black pundit saw colonization as a symptom of "Bilbonic plague"—a common malady among whites, especially in the South. Perhaps Bilbo was an anachronism, but "race values" had undeniably loomed large in American history and they remained important in the 1930s.

While Bilbo worked to keep whites and blacks apart, Joe Louis and his managers tried to bring them closer together. As Bilbo outlined his expatriation plan, Jack Blackburn and Louis spent long hours training to even the score with Max Schmeling of Germany. No one in Louis's entourage wanted his title to go to the nation Bilbo extolled for its devotion to "racial improvement." Still hesitant to comment on politics and policy, Louis and his handlers said nothing about Bilbo's scheme to ship American blacks to Africa. But Louis later revealed his strong feelings on the topic. "We've been here a long time," Louis reflected. "God bless Africa, but I never saw it. I am an American. I want me and all black Americans to have the same chance in this country."[4]

Bilbo might have spoken for ardent racists, but he did not speak for most white sportswriters. Not entirely free of racial bias, these writers nevertheless favored equal opportunity for black boxers, especially Joe Louis. Black journalists viewed this new tolerance as a harbinger of better days to come. "The trend of the times . . . is vastly different than back in the days when Harry Wills tried in vain to get a crack at Dempsey's crown," Chester Washington of the *Pittsburgh Courier* observed. "A fair-minded sports-writing fraternity" supported by "a liberal public" had contributed greatly "toward tearing down racial prejudices in boxing." Washington praised white sportswriters Hype Igoe, Jimmy Powers, Dan Parker, Bill Corum, Bill Farnsworth, and Walter Stewart for challenging the color line. Complimenting Woody Woodhouse of the *Durham Sun*, Washington added that "even Southern sports writers have rallied to the crusade for a square deal for all in sports." Louis deserved much credit for this new tolerance. So did Jesse Owens, the hero of the 1936 Olympics, and Henry Armstrong and John Henry Lewis, boxing champions in the lighter divisions. Jimmy Powers had joined Wendell Smith and other black writers in their call to abolish jim crow in major-league baseball. An irate white fan scolded Powers for his stance. "How would you like your sister to marry one?" the fan sneered. Powers parried the snide remark. "Are we discussing ball players," he asked, "or brothers-in-law?"[5]

Some whites, however, did suffer mild symptoms of "Bilbonic plague." Subtler than the senator, white writers sometimes relied on racist notions to describe the new black hope. "There isn't anything funny about fighting to Louis," the *New York Sun*'s Frank Graham observed in mid-1935. "To him it is an expression of an instinct . . . he obeys not so much because it is a means to a comfortable, even opulent, living, but because it is impossible for him to ignore it." Others also stressed instinct over intelligence and training in assessing Louis. Any "fairly smart" opponent "can make Louis look very bad," Joe Williams wrote in the *New York World-Telegram*, "can, in fact, just about make him beat himself." Schmeling had figured out how to whip Louis, and others would too. "Louis does most things aimlessly," Williams argued before the title fight in 1937. "Thought and design have little part in his life." *Life* invoked similar images: "In the ring, Louis is lithe, shuffling, and stolid. Outside he is lethargic, uncommunicative, unimaginative." These authors overlooked Joe's reticence among white reporters and his habit of showing different sides of himself to different people. Jack Miley watched him prepare for the fight against Jimmy Braddock. Louis appeared "slow and lazy"; his black sparring partners were "halt, lame, and lazy," so weak they could hardly "lick their lips." Miley doubted Louis could win it all. "A natural fighter," he would "never be any better than he was the day he first pulled on a glove. He performs by instinct and nobody will ever be able to pound anything through his kinky skull."

Louis had "a freak mental condition," Fred Digby of the *New Orleans Item* suggested, being "more like a machine than a human, as far as thinking is concerned." The *Sun*'s Grantland Rice watched Louis train for his rematch with Schmeling and expected the same result. "I don't believe Joe has any plan of battle—not the slightest," Rice wrote. "Louis is a natural, instinctive fighter. I don't think he can be taught anything that is even slightly new." Besides insulting Louis, these sportswriters underestimated trainer Jack Blackburn.

When Louis vindicated himself by knocking out Schmeling in the first round, some writers still denied he had learned anything from his previous loss. They reiterated his reliance on instinct and emotion. "He is a jungle man, as completely primitive as any savage, out to destroy a thing he hates," columnist Henry McLemore wrote after the bout. "Even the style of fighting he had been patiently taught was abandoned. He fought instinctively and not by any man-made pattern." McLemore might have been describing Louis as an individual, but by choosing terms like "jungle man" and "savage," he reduced Louis to the level of cinematic African bushmen who boiled missionaries in big pots and of wild Indians who scalped white pioneers. Had Schmeling not been associated with the Nazis by mid-1938, others might well have joined McLemore in seeing Louis primarily through a racial lens.[6]

Life magazine went a step beyond McLemore. Its editors in early 1939 furnished anonymous writing samples from a few famous Americans to Dr. Artur Holz of Vienna, a renowned graphologist. A former student of Sigmund Freud and Karl Jung, Holz had worked with the juvenile court in Vienna and had served as a consultant on matters of criminal evidence. Without knowledge of authorship, Holz was asked to analyze handwriting from President Roosevelt, Chief Justice Charles Evans Hughes, Helen Hayes, Ginger Rogers, and others. Of his samples, just one disturbed him. "This writer is a dangerous man," Holz warned. "He cannot be overestimated as an opponent, because he is willing to pursue his brutal course ruthlessly, regardless of consequences either to himself or to others, until he finally succeeds in winning what he wants." He would relentlessly seek "profit or other form of satisfaction," Holz added. "Interested in no one except himself," he possessed "a personality . . . entirely unconcerned with spiritual things." Had the editors tricked Holz by slipping in a sample from *Der Führer* himself? No. The handwriting of Joe Louis—reputed for his good sportsmanship, kindness, and piety—had prompted his alarm.

Life's editors might not have meant to malign Louis or his race, but they routinely used words and images reminiscent of old minstrel days. In 1937, for example, the magazine featured Huddie Ledbetter, a musician and convicted felon, in an article entitled LEADBELLY: BAD NIGGER MAKES GOOD MINSTREL. Later that year, *Life* ran a photo essay on harvesting watermelons. In one picture, a young black woman nursed her baby while eating a large slice of melon. "Nothing makes a Negro's mouth water like a luscious, fresh-picked melon," the caption read. "Any colored 'mammy' can hold a huge slice in one hand while holding her offspring in the other." In another photograph, a farmhand showed the next step in the process. "The watermelon," *Life* explained, "starts its journey to market in an ordinary wheelbarrow pushed by a grinning Negro." *Time*, another Henry Luce publication, described Joe Louis in 1936 as "impassive as a baby and equally susceptible, enormously pleased with the sleek clothes and large automobiles which changed circumstances" had brought him. Many blacks in Luce's journals grinned and grunted their way through a carefree life. Music, melons, slick clothes, and big cars preoccupied them. These hackneyed images annoyed the *Courier*'s George Schuyler, who labeled *Life* and *Time* "organs of Luce thinking."[7]

By arguing that Louis fought by instinct, writers linked him to "primitive" peoples living close to nature. To the same end, some reporters traced his speech to unlettered rural folk. Quite shy among whites in his early years, Louis spoke sparingly if at all, leading observers to suggest that his vocabulary consisted largely of mumbles and nods. To prepare for the rematch with Schmeling, Louis and his handlers studied films of the first fight as well as footage of other bouts. Havey Boyle of the *Pittsburgh Post-Gazette* "quoted" what Louis said to John Roxborough, his manager, after watching these reels: "John, is dat de fellah what whip me? That fellah ain't got no right whippin' me. I mussa been somewheres else dat night." When Louis kicked his bad habit and thumped Schmeling, the *Birmingham News* ran a large photograph of him and his reaction to the win—"Ah'm sho 'nuff champeen now!" Just what these papers intended with this dialect is unclear, but their usage says more about the whites who composed the copy than it does about Louis and his actual speech.[8]

Black writers criticized whites for hanging this usage on Louis. "Joe makes no more grammatical errors than the average person," Harry Webber protested in the *Afro-American*. He was simply "extremely economical in the use of words." Art Carter, the *Afro-American* sports editor, suspected racial bias in stories that portrayed Louis as inarticulate and stolid. "To give Louis credit for displaying even the slightest cleverness and mental brilliance in defeating an opponent," Carter grumbled, "would be too much for the majority of Nordic writers." Too many white journalists, a *Chicago Defender* editorial complained, "carry their pen in one hand and a bucket of mud in the other." Rather than depict Louis as dim and dull, black writers explained his mien in terms of regional and cultural variations that had little to do with his race or personality. "Before he got into the important money he had had little contact with white people and was very shy of them," Roi Ottley of the *New York Amsterdam News* noted. That shyness made Louis shrink into "impenetrable silence" among white strangers. But after whites left, he "expanded among his Negro associates," Ottley revealed. "He was alert to what was happening about him and possessed a sense of humor expressed in Negro idioms." Ottley spoke from personal experience. He had often lingered at Joe's training camp to enjoy the company of the entourage.[9]

The Migration Experience

Ottley realized that migration and mobility had created both obstacles and opportunities for Joe Louis. An adolescent migrant from a world of traditional, poor, and oppressed rural black folk, he entered an adult world of educated, affluent urbanites of both races. His career required frequent contact across racial and class lines, a mixing rarely experienced by most black migrants and new immigrants confined to separate urban enclaves. Whether from Mississippi or Montenegro, migrants in the Jack Johnson and Joe Louis eras usually arrived in the North with little formal education, few assets beyond their backs and hands, and a worldview molded by old-time religion, folklore, and preindustrial habits and values. In many ways, the transition from rural Alabama to Detroit and Chicago was not much different than the change from Russian *shtetl* to lower Manhattan, or from Poland to Pittsburgh. Northern cities offered novel opportunities as well as new problems to urban pioneers. White reporters who covered Louis seldom understood the magnitude of these challenges.

Louis's family had deep roots in Alabama, but familiarity with southern ways failed to keep them in Dixie. Relatives of Patrick Brooks, Joe's stepfather, ventured to Detroit to find work during the Roaring Twenties. Some of them returned South in early 1926 to tell kin about the good life in the Motor City. They talked "about cars, factories, jobs, and money," Louis recollected, "and stone sidewalks, movies, and electricity." They made a good living without worrying about "rainfall or the boll weevil." Even as a child, Joe had "worked in the fields, sunup to sundown," with little "a sharecropper's boy could do for pleasure." Patrick and Lillie Barrow Brooks left Joe and his sixteen siblings with kin and ventured north to see Canaan for themselves. Finally convinced, they retrieved the children and moved in with relatives on Detroit's East Side. "It was kind of crowded there, but the house had toilets indoors and electric lights," Louis recalled. "Down in Alabama we had outhouses and kerosene lamps."[10]

Plumbing and lights provided convenience and comfort, but at a price. Laborers earned more money up north, but higher expenses depleted larger incomes. The frigid winters brought big bills for fuel and clothing. The landlord, coal vendor, grocer, butcher, and utility company all had long fingers in the workers' pockets. As a blues singer lamented, "Starvation in my kitchen, rent sign's on my door, / And if my luck don't change, I can't stay at my home no more."[11] For many, the promised land became a land of broken promises.

The decision to move divided those who stayed behind. Some approved, doubtful that blacks would ever be free in the South. Others remained ambivalent, preferring Dixie's familiar if fatalistic ways to the unpredictable and untried prospects of the North. The train trip young Joe Barrow took from Alabama to Michigan in 1926 dramatized the regional differences. The women prepared their own food for the journey, since jim crow laws barred blacks from the dining car. Besides, the family could not have afforded the meals on board even if allowed to dine there. Black passengers rode in separate, inferior coaches. From his window, Joe glimpsed a chain gang at work along the tracks. As the train headed north, the cotton fields and shacks vanished, and "cities kept getting bigger, the houses were taller." Across the Ohio River, laws did not require segregated seating. Nor did Louis see convict lease gangs in the fields.[12]

Not just a border between states and regions, the Ohio River often split the country in attitudes and folkways. Of the South left behind by Joe Louis Barrow, Langston Hughes wrote:

> The lazy, laughing South
> With blood on its mouth. . . .
> Scratching in the dead fire's ashes
> For a Negro's bones. . . .
> And I, who am black,
> Would give her many rare gifts
> But she turns her back upon me.
> So now I seek the North. . . .[13]

Nothing had prepared Joe for his new home. "You can't imagine the impact that city had," he recalled. "I never saw so many people in one place, so many cars at one time; I had never even seen a trolley car before." He discovered "other things that I had never heard of—parks, libraries, brick schoolhouses, movie theaters." He noticed that "people dress[ed] different" and he "wasn't dressed right" for this setting. Still, "Detroit looked awfully good." His stepfather cleaned city streets and the older boys worked at Ford. "I remember when a relative drove us around the town and showed us the Ford plant," Louis reminisced. "My God, it was bigger than a cottonfield and a cornfield combined, bigger than some cities we had passed by on the train." The family did well until the Depression. Among the last hired before the crash, the Brooks and Barrow men were also among the first fired. They moved from assembly line to breadline along with thousands of other jobless workers.

Henry Biggs, born in Detroit in 1911, contrasted the boom of the twenties with the bust of the thirties. "Everybody wanted to get to Detroit where the big money was," he recalled. "People were renting out their basements, their attics. They were putting in partitions and sleeping two people in the same room." As one man awakened to work afternoons, another coming off the day shift went to sleep in the same bed. Born in South Carolina but bred in Detroit, Frederick Cureton recalled how southern kin packed his parents' home. "They had two or three families, or more, living in that house," he reminisced. "I had an aunt downstairs. I had an uncle; I had cousins started coming in from the South." There were "twelve people in the house" until "they got money enough" to buy their own. Katherine Reid and her family left an Arkansas town for Detroit in 1923. Like the Brooks and Barrow men, her father worked for Henry Ford. "It was difficult to find a place to stay," she remembered, "so we ended up on the east side" in a rented room. The bubble soon burst for the folks crowding Black Bottom. "For three years as a young man I walked the streets of Detroit," Biggs recalled, "and couldn't find a job, couldn't buy a job."[14]

Hard times in northern cities posed problems that could not be solved with old southern methods. Even the poorest tenant farmers and sharecroppers grew fruits and vegetables, raised hogs, cattle, or chickens, and hunted, fished, and foraged the woods and streams. But a packed tenement surrounded by pavement made self-sufficiency impossible. City dwellers competed for scarce jobs and many had to seek aid from relief agencies. Joe Louis's family was no exception. Richard Wright, familiar with both South and North, sighed that his people had switched masters by leaving "the lords of the land" for "the bosses of the buildings."

The Barrow and Brooks clan struggled in the early 1930s, but Joe turned the family finances around with his able fists. By late 1934 he was able to keep his whole family comfortable with his ring earnings, and family pride rose with improving fortunes. Now much better off than most blacks and whites in Detroit, Louis in 1935 repaid the $270 in public assistance his family had drawn since the crash of 1929.[15]

Strange customs perplexed black migrants. "In . . . Alabama I never knew anything about race or anything like that," Louis reflected. "No one talked about it, as I can remember." His family "seemed to get along with the white people" there. In hindsight, however, he realized that this amity depended on well-defined spheres and roles. Moreover, he had lived in Alabama only when young, precluding any deep understanding of racial mores in Dixie. In Detroit a wider array of racial, ethnic, religious, and class variations complicated relations between peoples. That customs often violated the laws also compounded the confusion. Michigan statutes did not mandate segregation, for example, but residential separation prevailed because white desires and real estate practices confined blacks to certain neighborhoods. When the races met, sparks often flew. "Nobody ever called me a 'nigger,'" Louis recalled, "until I got to Detroit."[16]

The Dream Deferred: The Mean Streets of the Modern Metropolis

A year after Louis moved to Detroit, Richard Wright left Memphis for Chicago. Employed as a dishwasher on the north side but still steeped in the racial code of the South, Wright panicked when a busy white waitress brushed against him. Such contact in Dixie violated the ultimate taboo, a stricture aimed at enforcing both a racial and gender barrier. Wright knew that white mobs had lynched black men for less in the South. The waitress, unfazed by the contact, went on with her work.[17]

Detroit's "Black Bottom" and Chicago's "Bronzeville" shared many features of emerging northern ghettos. Populations soared but employment, housing, schools, recreational facilities, and police protection lagged behind. Prejudice further complicated urban problems. Often complicit with white landlords and merchants who profited from rapid population growth, city officials ignored the needs and complaints of blacks enmeshed in a web of urban decay and its customary ills—poverty, disease, substance abuse, violence, and family disorganization. Bias in employment, housing, education, and public aid often confined blacks to slums and made mobility virtually impossible. Poor upon arrival, black migrants struggled to hold their own. The Depression magnified problems that had originated decades earlier with mass industrialization and urbanization.

Robert Abbott and his *Chicago Defender* staff kept a wary eye on Dixie, but they found much that disturbed them closer to home. Like other northern metropolises, Chicago had well-defined and sharply divided neighborhoods and a notorious vice district within a predominantly black section of the city. "The South Side is completely dominated by the vice element," the *Defender* grumbled in 1936, and its residents wanted "a new deal in decency." These residents included Joe Louis, who had moved to Chicago from Detroit, and his wife Marva, among the lucky few with comfortable quarters on Forty-seventh Street. Few South Side inhabitants, however, could afford such housing and the safety this particular area provided. The *Defender* reiterated its plea later that year, bemoaning that "vice lords" had surpassed "preachers" in influence. Sharing a room of his aunt's small apartment with his mother and brother, Richard Wright saw the stultifying effects of slum life. While he immersed himself in books and magazines, others pursued more dangerous diversions. "The most valued pleasure of the people I knew was a car," Wright noted, "the most cherished experience a bottle of whisky, the most sought-after prize somebody else's wife." As a social worker he counseled local boys who depressed him—"a wild and homeless lot, culturally lost, spiritually disinherited," they were destined "for the clinics, morgues, prisons, reformatories, and the electric chair of the state's death house."

Besides good jobs and safe streets, blacks wanted decent and affordable housing. Those with means demanded the right to rent or buy anywhere without harassment. In black Chicago many structures were congested, decrepit, and dangerous, yet "the bosses of the buildings" collected high rents.

With housing already in short supply during the 1920s, the problem worsened in the 1930s because builders lacked incentive to construct new projects during hard times. Blacks welcomed public housing programs, but funds flowed mainly into white neighborhoods closed to them. Local politics, not need, drove the housing agenda. Even wealthy blacks found that realtors and bankers directed them toward particular areas. The restrictive covenant "is not to restrict against undesirables, against lawbreakers, against ugliness or against depreciation of property," the *Defender* objected. "It is a covenant against Race people, no matter how good they are, no matter how wealthy they are, no matter what if they are black." In early 1938 the *Defender* blamed the housing crisis on "34 years of cumulative criminal negligence" by city officials. Two weeks later the paper noted that blacks comprised 8 percent of the city's population but constituted 40 percent of its public aid recipients. "Black people were the first to be fired," the *Defender* noted, "and have not, in many instances, yet been rehired."

Hardship seemed chronic and inescapable. "A depression is nothing new to a black man," Lucius Harper, a *Defender* columnist, quipped. "He's been under one ever since he was brought to America" and wears it "like a tailor-made suit." Langston Hughes reflected on being "black in a white world" where his people had endured "Three hundred years / In the cotton and the cane, / Plowing and reaping / With no gain." The blues singers, many of them migrants like Joe Louis, joined the refrain: "My burden's so heavy, I can't hardly see. / Seems like everybody is down on me." Down south blacks rented poor land; up north they rented poor housing. Many ghetto problems stemmed from the fact that too many people chased too few private and public resources.[18]

Nor was poverty the only culprit. Blacks faced a criminal justice system that was often unfair and occasionally deadly. White police and judges treated the races differently. "The Chicago police have enjoyed for some time the reputation of being ruthless to a point of bestiality, particularly to unarmed and helpless people," the *Defender* observed. "They use neither wit or sticks on roving gunmen" but resorted to excessive force "when arresting defenseless, timid individuals." When police themselves became "law breakers," they posed "a far more dangerous menace to society than unapprehended criminals." The problem was, the *Defender* suggested, "too many morons" getting a badge. White officers seemed more concerned with color than crime. They treated white suspects one way and blacks another; they cared more about white victims than black. "Most of the brutal crimes committed within the race of late years in the North," the *Defender* noted, "have been instigated by newcomers from the South who have been exposed to lax law enforcement" and assumed "that murder is not strictly murder if it does not cross the color line." Often easy on blacks who preyed upon their own, police and judges reacted harshly toward blacks who targeted whites. What Frank Marshall Davis, a columnist for the *Atlanta World*, called "the unwritten code" of southern justice seemed to apply to Chicago as well: "If a nigger kills a white man, that's murder and automatically means the death penalty. If whitey kills a nigger that's justifiable homicide; and if one nigger kills another, that's good riddance."[19]

Bias meant more arrests and prosecutions on minor infractions for blacks, skewing crime statistics. "These reports do not tell the public that black people are picked up in large numbers for the most trivial offenses, often illegally, nor that their ignorance often opens wide the prison doors for them," the *Defender* noted, nor that "rank prejudice is the cause of their arrests and is frequently the direct or indirect cause of their convictions." Not all black suspects were innocent, of course, but the *Defender* argued that most whites presumed blacks were guilty.[20]

In Philadelphia similar conditions prevailed. The *Tribune*'s Harry Webber investigated real estate practices, machine politics, and housing there in the mid-1930s. "The slums of Philadelphia are no accident," he argued. "They are planned slums." The great migration greatly increased demand for housing. Shrewd realtors responded by selling property to a few black customers in certain neighborhoods that had been exclusively or overwhelmingly white. When these blacks entered the old ethnic enclaves, many whites panicked and sold out at depressed prices—a scheme called "blockbusting." Realtors then peddled these properties at inflated prices to eager blacks able to afford them, or owners partitioned their buildings and levied high rents. As additional blacks arrived more whites departed, and the composition of the area changed rapidly. Since white landlords often had connections at city hall, inspectors ignored housing code violations in the ghetto. With demand high and supply low, even bad buildings were profitable, so owners seldom had to maintain or improve deteriorating properties to attract buyers or tenants. Lacking political power, slum dwellers got short shrift in city services.

These "planned slums" awarded realtors and developers twice. Not only did they profit from turnover in the city, they sold new houses to whites in the burgeoning suburbs. Business and industry often followed their customers and workers, depriving the inner city of good jobs, a viable tax base, and political clout. The suburbs spread rapidly and prospered; the central city did not. The ghetto expanded slowly into adjacent areas but remained congested because white businesses, city leaders, and mobs devised methods to confine blacks within proscribed limits. Whites owned the ghetto and usually collected its money and votes. In a pattern typical of northern cities, Philadelphia had few truly mixed neighborhoods by World War II. When blacks, whatever their character or class, moved into an area, whites usually fled. Whites paid dearly for their prejudices, further straining race relations.

"Housing conditions in Philadelphia are rotten," editor E.W. Rhodes wrote in response to Webber's study. He blamed "heartless landlords and crooked politicians who refuse to enforce the law." Bad housing "in congested areas with no sanitary facilities" led to "ill health" and "crime." Rhodes called for slum clearance, new construction, and better schools and jobs. "Crime, delinquency, disease, and death walk hand in hand through the slums of Philadelphia," he warned. "The economic standard of those who dwell in slums must be raised and . . . instruction must be given in the art of decent living."

Rhodes faulted "partisan politics, grafting real estate owners, and boundless red tape" for blocking "any federal funds from being spent in Philadelphia for better housing." So the ghetto decayed and crime increased apace. "Comparatively few colored criminals are vicious," he argued. "The majority of colored defendants are petty larceny crooks." Blacks turned to "petty" crime only when they found it "impossible . . . to earn a decent living because of discrimination." Rhodes denied that the Roosevelt administration had given blacks "a New Deal." With "the third largest Negro population in America," the city had been "sadly neglected" by Washington. After two slum buildings collapsed in 1937, city hall finally launched an investigation. Rhodes recommended bold initiatives to change "the damnable system" that reduced poor residents to "stealing a bottle of milk or an automobile tire."

Rhodes urged blacks to agitate for better jobs, arguing that workers must not "leave their fate" to Henry Ford or John L. Lewis. "It is a fight for existence, a fight to work," he argued, "a fight to eat, a fight to live." To slay "the grim monster prejudice," blacks in 1937 picketed and boycotted white-owned ghetto businesses that refused to hire them. City police arrested the marchers, a move Rhodes viewed as "unlawful" and "stupid." Unemployment and scant relief left no alternative to theft, for desperate people would "either get jobs or snatch pocketbooks." The lid nearly blew in Central Philadelphia in 1938. ANGRY CROWD DEFIES POLICE IN NEAR RIOT, the *Tribune* reported. Bootblacks had set up shop in front of a white-owned restaurant. The manager ordered them to move, then tossed their boot box into the street and brandished a knife. Black men nearby confronted the manager and struck him. Police arrived and dispersed the crowd, but Rhodes knew that his city—like many others—sat "on a powder keg."[21]

Harlem, Joe Louis's home away from home, was the largest and best-known black metropolis. Regarded as a black Mecca earlier in the century, Harlem by the mid-1930s faced problems like those in Chicago and Philadelphia. Even before the Depression, over half of Harlem's black women were a part of "the Bronx slave market," toiling as domestics for white families at low wages, sometimes for no pay at all. By the time Joe Louis refunded the relief money his family had received in Detroit, nearly half of Harlem's families were on public aid. Some with decent incomes resided in a few select enclaves, but most Harlemites dwelled in unhealthy tenements. "Fully ten thousand . . . now live in cellars: dark, damp, cold dungeons," the Reverend Adam Clayton Powell, Jr. of the Abyssinian Baptist Church wrote in 1935. "Here they exist in squalor worse than that of the sharecroppers." Powell detected "a new social 'odor'" that should have bothered the property owners. "Crime," Roi Ottley of the *Amsterdam News* observed, "was the bitter blossom of poverty."

Desperate men in Harlem "fled into the service" or moved "to other ghettos," writer James Baldwin, who grew up in Harlem during the Depression, recalled. Those who stayed "went on wine or whiskey or the needle" or, like him, sought refuge in the church. Baldwin saw decay all around him. "The wages of sin were visible everywhere," he reflected, "in every wine-stained and urine-splashed hallway, in every clanging ambulance bell, in every scar on the faces of the pimps and their whores, in every helpless, newborn baby being brought into this danger, in every knife and pistol fight." White police officers had initiated Baldwin into race politics in his neighborhood when he was only ten. "Two white policemen amused themselves with me by frisking me," Baldwin recalled, "making comic (and terrifying) speculations concerning my ancestry and probable sexual prowess, and for good measure, leaving me flat on my back in one of Harlem's empty lots." Hoping that education would enchance his prospects, Baldwin defied his father and stayed in school, but the odds were against him. At thirteen he crossed Fifth Avenue to visit the public library on Forty-second Street. A white policeman scolded him: "Why don't you niggers stay uptown where you belong?"[22]

The daily grind gave poor blacks little cause to cheer. Often down and out, they embraced Joe Louis and turned his triumphs over white opponents into public celebrations. "The Brown Bomber's ring victories," the *Atlanta World*'s Frank Marshall Davis noted, "made it easier for the slum dweller to live among his rats and roaches." But not much easier for James Baldwin, who realized he could not follow in the Brown Bomber's footsteps. Nor could he do what others had done to escape the ghetto. "I could not become a prize-fighter—many of us tried but very few succeeded," he sighed. "I could not sing. I could not dance."

Many decent people called Harlem home, but Harlem did not get its reputation from them by the late 1930s. Even Joe Louis and his fans sometimes lost money and blood amid hustlers and thugs. "Ask many Chicagoans who attended the Louis-Schmeling fight if they do not now wish that they had tied a cow bell or hitching post to their purses," the *Defender*'s Lucius Harper wrote. "Thirty or more yelled 'stop thief' in Harlem night clubs when it was a bit too late. . . . The best place to find sympathy in Harlem is in the dictionary at the 135th and Lenox Avenue library. We marvel at them not having to nail the books to the center table." After Louis defeated Joe Walcott at Yankee Stadium, he reached the Hotel Theresa to find "10,000 hysterical admirers crowded around his car" who "kept him prisoner at the curb for half an hour." The delight turned ugly. "They tore off the car hood, broke the windows, ripped off the tires, danced on the car roof," *Time* reported. "It took a balcony speech from Joe to disperse them." Douglass Hall, an *Afro-American* correspondent, watched Harlem "go mad with joy" after the fight. People danced outdoors, hoisted a car into the air, and "crush[ed] other cars by standing on them." Hall feared for Louis. "The mob would have taken him apart piece by piece," he shuddered, had "thirty or more cops" not escorted him into the hotel. An officer asked fans why Louis stayed in Harlem. "This is Joe's home," a man smiled. "He ain't above his people!"[23]

By the time Louis beat Schmeling, Harlem's image had evolved from the literary mecca of the twenties to the crime-infested ghetto of the late thirties. Prior to the New York World's Fair in 1939, for example, some white publications expressed concern about the safety of visitors who would have to pass through Harlem to reach the fairgrounds. The NAACP staff worried about Harlem's reputation and addressed crime there in a long article in *The Crisis*. "The Harlem Negroes' diagonal position, high in crime, low in income, is not unique," Michael Carter argued. "The identical diagonal position has been previously held by each racial group of immigrant whites before their final acceptance or absorption into the scheme of things." Unlike earlier groups, however, blacks had not been "fully integrated into American life." Destitution in Harlem made its residents prone to petty crime of a "spontaneous, disorganized, nature," unlike other parts of the city where "organized gangsters" terrorized the people. Carter admitted that prostitution flourished in Harlem but denied the bugaboo that blacks raped in disproportionate numbers. Excepting prostitution, he argued, "other forms of criminal sexual behavior are as unknown to Harlem as good housing." Echoing other black writers, Carter contended that white police and judges treated black suspects differently. "An attitude of indifference to Negro versus Negro crime has been in existence for many years," he observed. "As a result, such offenders may get off easily." But when victims were white, "the Negro may expect maximum penalties."

Whites in New York City also preferred that blacks reside within certain limits. Cab Calloway, swing sensation and an avid Louis fan, preferred to live in Harlem, but his wife Betty found her dream home in 1937 in Fieldston, "an all-white section of the north Bronx." On the day they moved in, Calloway recalled, NIGGER GO HOME signs appeared on their lawn. He feared they had made a dreadful mistake. "I loved Harlem," he explained. "I loved being with my people." Torn by the move and other disputes, the Calloways divorced. Cab knew the rules of race in the city and the nation. "In New York at that time there were a lot of hotels where Negroes were not welcome," he noted. "And anywhere south and west of New York was just hell."

Jack Schiffman, whose father Frank had established Harlem's renowned Apollo Theater, noticed that jovial interracial mixing became less common toward the end of the Louis era. "Despite an increasingly sinister reputation, the Harlem of the Depression years and early forties was popular with whites," Schiffman recalled. "Whole generations of Columbia University students . . . knew the theater intimately." The Schiffmans featured Louis at the Harlem Opera House before his first fight in New York. Comedian George Wiltshire played promoter Mike Jacobs, Jack Schiffman remembered, "and Joe boxed, punched the bag, jumped rope, and chased George around the stage."

Talent, not pigment, impressed the Schiffmans. "Not only were Apollo audiences mixed," Jack recalled, "but the artists as well." The mixing ended when a wall replaced the bridge between the races. In retrospect, Schiffman realized that "much of the good relations between blacks and whites" had been premised on a "patronizing attitude" among whites and "an emasculated submissiveness" among blacks. Still, he missed the days when mixed audiences had shared song, dance, and comedy too infectious to be confined by color. "It's a shame, because for all its faults there was an enriching interaction between blacks and whites in Harlem in the heyday of the uptown scene," Schiffman concluded, "an interaction that has almost disappeared in a welter of mutual suspicion and recrimination."[24]

The "new social odor" Powell sniffed in Harlem also wafted over Los Angeles. Loren Miller, editor of the *Sentinel*, crusaded against biased unions, jim crow grand juries, police brutality, and prejudice in Hollywood. Fred Davis, a fifty-year-old veteran of the Tenth Cavalry, headed to a city park to drill with his old company in late 1934. The police reprimanded him for carrying a weapon, one officer yelling at him, "Where in the hell, nigger, did you get authority to carry a rifle?" Davis explained his purpose but they called him a "black son of a bitch" and beat him so badly he lost vision in one eye. With an unblemished record of eighteen years in the army, Davis had "never been arrested in this city." Despite protests, the brutality continued. As tension mounted, a committee of the grand jury agreed to examine allegations of police misconduct, "a tremendous victory," Miller declared. He hoped a full inquiry would "curb police lawlessness once and for all." But he rejoiced too soon. The grand jury dropped the matter.

Like other slums, East Los Angeles had a housing crisis. "Rent is too high in this community," Miller complained in 1936. The problem was "two-fold." "Artificial limits, growing out of racial restrictions," blocked any "normal expansion." Second, "almost no building has been done here for six years and the community has outgrown present housing." Charlotta Bass, the feisty editor of the *California Eagle*, had long opposed restrictive covenants in Los Angeles. Back in 1914, the year Joe Louis was born, Mary Johnson had made a down payment on a house just four doors off Central Avenue on East Eighteenth Street, where only whites had resided. When Johnson left her new home for a few hours, whites entered and piled her furniture, kitchen utensils, clothing, and bedding on the front lawn. They nailed the door shut and left a sign: NIGGER IF YOU VALUE YOUR HIDE DON'T LET NIGHT CATCH YOU HERE. Police did nothing. Bass and the NAACP could not interest public prosecutors in the case.

Bass remained committed to open housing and led another protest against residential jim crow thirty years later. The setting was more auspicious this time, for the plight of the Laws family became front-page news and a national embarrassment. In 1945 Mr. and Mrs. Henry Laws and Pauletta Fears, their married daughter, defied residential segregation in Los Angeles by obtaining a home in a "whites-only" area. Police arrested them. While the three waited behind bars, son Alfred Laws and son-in-law Antone Fears returned home on military leave. Laws served in the army, Fears in the navy. Fears, a mess attendant, wore a Purple Heart for bravery at Pearl Harbor. Badly wounded in the initial bombing, he had helped save several men trapped in the hold of his ship. Not only were Alfred and Antone in the military, the Lawses and their daughter worked in defense plants. The case dramatized the distance between principle and practice during the war: Neither valor abroad nor labor at home entitled the family to live where they chose in Los Angeles.[25]

Angered by such injustices, blacks often attacked each other. "More than six times as many Negroes as whites are murdered," the *Pittsburgh Courier* noted in 1935. "Most of the murderers of these Negroes are Negroes." The *Courier* blamed white neglect and black apathy for rising crime in Pittsburgh. "Poverty and lack of proper recreational facilities" had spawned "high crime and delinquency," but "civic indifference" also played a part. Blacks had acquiesced as city officials permitted "vice in our sections . . . to spare other parts" of the city "while continuing to collect their tribute off human degradation."

A similar pattern prevailed in Dallas. "Killing a Negro is far less likely to cause trouble than killing a white man's dog or standing up for one's rights against a white man," the *Dallas Express* protested in 1941. "Negroes who carry knives and pistols . . . do so as a rule because they know that they can use them and get away with it." The year was marked by "a record-breaking number of Negroes killing other Negroes." To stem the tide, the *Express* advocated "the death penalty for anybody who is guilty of first-degree murder of a Negro." When the court convicted a man of killing his former sweetheart and imposed the death penalty, the *Express* approved. In the spring of 1942, the *Express* observed that black assailants had already murdered nine local blacks. The *Express* demanded "rigid prosecution" of all killers and urged those with "inside facts on such homicides" to testify in court. Without these changes, "Negro lives will continue to be practically worthless." As if to prove the newspaper a prophet, a husband, enraged that his new wife put too little sugar in his lemonade, shot her and her father. Like Dallas, Houston experienced rampant black-on-black crime. "Negroes in Houston seem to be taking undue advantage of the privilege of killing one another without too much fear of punishment," the *Express* grumbled. "Lives of Negroes must become a little dearer lest we exterminate ourselves in the near future."

Dismayed by a bloody weekend of "intrafraternal warfare" in Atlanta, Frank Marshall Davis of the local *World* urged readers to do more to bring black criminals to justice. He recommended an ordinance banning switchblades, an opinion that provoked many irate calls and letters. "Some writers were so incensed," Davis recollected, "they promised to come down to the *World* office and personally carve me into souvenir strips if ever the police tried to prevent their carrying those trusty switchblades." Davis understood why blacks feared lynch mobs and "hair-trigger cops," but he doubted that the knives saved any blacks from whites. Evidence showed Atlanta's blacks to be "far more proficient at injuring and decimating our numbers than were Caucasians": "What depressed me most about Dixie in the early 1930s," Davis admitted, "was the wantonness with which we maimed each other as well as the mass acceptance of racism."[26]

Vulnerable to ghetto predators, blacks also suffered abuse from white vigilantes and police. The *Express* noted "a reign of terror" in South Dallas prior to American intervention in World War II. "Seventeen bombings have taken place," the *Express* reported, "with Negro homes being the targets in all of the cases." Several vicious beatings also alarmed residents. If city leaders and the police did not "curb the crazed criminals of South Dallas," the *Express* warned, "Dallas will find itself covered with the blood of innocent people." As police brutality mounted "by leaps and bounds," no real progress against crime in Dallas or any other city seemed likely because "a wave of prejudice and discrimination" was sweeping the nation. "Negroes are being brutalized by city police [and] by the sheriffs of counties," and even black soldiers found that "the military police are filled with hatred toward them." Lest people dismiss these protests, the editor detailed recent incidents of extreme cruelty. "Two of the cases . . . involved the beating and kicking of Negro women—one of them ill," the *Express* noted. "Another was the battering of a young Negro so badly that even his mother could not recognize him." Police had to learn how to do their jobs "without whipping Negroes' heads with blackjacks and pistol butts."[27]

Black citizens knew that pleas for law and order cut both ways. Confined to enclaves inhabited by the entire gamut of black society, law-abiding residents desperately needed the police and courts to stop predators of all races. But white police often knew little about inner-city life and lacked discretion in sorting out perpetrators, bystanders, and victims. Moreover, police sometimes met even the slightest offense or objection with excessive force. They often carried a cavalier attitude into black areas, as a 1938 incident revealed. In a pregame interview, a radio reporter asked Yankee outfielder "Jake" Powell how he kept in shape during the off-season in Dayton, Ohio. "Oh, that's easy," Powell replied. "I'm a policeman and I beat niggers on the head with my blackjack while on my beat." Unable to convince mayors and police commissioners to restrain rogue cops like Powell, African American fans, ignoring this apology, threw bottles, apples, and litter at him when the Yankees played the Senators. The Yankee front office suspended Powell for ten days, and he sat in the stands as his team took on Detroit. A spectator yelled to him, "Say again what you said over the radio, Powell, then look two rows behind you." Joe Louis, an avid Tigers fan, was sitting not far from Powell.[28]

By the time Louis beat Schmeling in 1938, ghettos from coast to coast shared similar problems. Except for a smattering of black entrepreneurs and professionals who catered to their own people, inner-city residents were poor with dim prospects. Unemployment was high even when the wider economy prospered, and recessions hit ghettos particularly hard. A high percentage of black women and children worked for meager wages to supplement the low pay of husbands and fathers in marginal jobs. Women's labor as domestic employees often provided a family's only reliable income. Adolescents left school and entered a bleak job market. Employers and unions often excluded blacks or relegated even skilled and reliable workers to menial jobs. The Committee for Industrial Organization (CIO) backed integration, but resistance remained strong among many American Federation of Labor affiliates.[29]

Other aspects of the urban jungle also puzzled black newcomers. Cities had much to offer but imposed hardships unknown in rural areas. Some observers doubted that the exodus from field to factory had helped the race. James Boggs left Alabama with a friend and a dollar between them and "hoboed up north" on a freight train in 1937. "We had nothing but what we had on our backs, that's all," he reminisced, not even "a change of clothes." He found work with the Works Progress Administration, but most did not. Conditions appalled him. "They . . . had a lot of soup kitchens in Detroit in those days," he recalled. "That's the first time I ever saw white people who were hungry. Down South nobody was hungry, not even black folks. . . . Down South people were ragged. We didn't have no shoes, no clothes much; but you had food." Misery loved company, for the soup lines "weren't segregated." Walter Rosser, a Detroit native, never forgot the bad times. "I have seen people foraging in garbage cans," he recollected. "As a little fellow" he had "almost been trampled to death" while scrounging at "the packing house." Meat packers dumped "a heart, kidneys, lungs, or chitterlings or the intestines" into a tub "and threw them out to hungry people."[30] A local blues singer wailed:

> Detroit's a cold place, and I ain't got a dime to my name.
> I would go to the poorhouse, but Lord you know I'm ashamed.
> I been walking Hastings Street, nobody seems to treat me right.
> I can make it in the daytime, but Lord these cold cold nights.[31]

George Schuyler, a native of Syracuse, doubted that most migrants found milk and honey north of the Ohio. "Two-fifths of our workers are farmers," he noted in 1937. "Agriculture was once our economic backbone but now it clamors for a chiropractor. Our landless laborers increase faster than fleas in a flophouse." Richard Wright agreed. "Our people have fled from farm to flat and now have nothing to flee back to," he wrote. "The city heaps too much responsibility upon us and gives us too little security in return." Urban blacks had become "a folk imprisoned in steel and stone." Across the land, "life for us is daily warfare," Wright concluded, "and . . . we live hard, like soldiers." Shaped by rural roots and urban experience, singer Roland Hayes also sensed greater losses than gains from the migration. "When all is said and done, we are more at home with our feet in the furrow," he argued. "We Negroes were not meant to congregate in cities. Whenever the machine has brought us together so that we have had to live in large numbers in city tenements, we have gone against nature."[32]

Other groups—the Irish, southern Italians, Lithuanians, Poles—had arrived mostly poor and powerless but had experienced some upward mobility over a generation or two. So humble origins alone did not explain persistent poverty in the ghettos. Unlike the immigrant slum, the ghetto offered its residents fewer ladders to climb because racist public policies and personal discrimination intentionally minimized spatial and social mobility. Restrictive covenants, realtors' and bankers' practices, zoning laws, and white mobs circumscribed blacks regardless of their character, education, or income. Though numerically preponderant in some wards, blacks had only token political representation and consequently received poor municipal services in sanitation, schools, parks, and police. Ghetto vice districts thrived because city officials often looked the other way. And the criminal justice system took ghetto crime seriously mainly when white victims filed complaints.

How could blacks trust the law when police themselves seemed at war with the race? During the Detroit riot of 1943, for example, police often ignored whites' crimes but used excessive, even deadly, force against unruly blacks. Kelly Fritz remembered the riot well because he married in the midst of it, with National Guard troops posted outside the church. "People [were] killed like flies," he recalled. "It was all over the city." Fritz saw the body of a black man cut in two by officers' automatic weapons. Even though whites took the offensive, over 90 percent of those arrested were black. Of thirty-four deaths, twenty-five were blacks—seventeen of them killed by police. No white rioter died that way. Ten days after the mayhem in Detroit, a riot rocked Harlem, triggered by a rumor that a white policeman had shot and killed a black soldier. Six died in the outbreak. Unlike in Detroit, however, blacks largely initiated the carnage in Harlem. To calm angry crowds, Walter White of the NAACP rode the streets and denied the rumor. White hoped to recruit Joe Louis to help restore peace, but time was too short to bring him to Harlem. Writer Chester Himes had a lesson for his people. "The first thing to do in case of a race riot," he scoffed, "is not to call the police but to shoot them." The joke had a long life in the ghetto.

Such protest did not seem to faze the Detroit police. In 1946 they shot and killed Leon Mosely in an alley in his neighborhood for no apparent reason. Carl Winter, a white engineer active in the Civil Rights Congress and the Communist Party, led demonstrations against the killing. "Police shoot first and ask questions afterwards," Winter stated. "They often didn't ask any questions in the case of black youth in particular." Police "without warrant" and with "no excuse whatsoever" routinely stopped and frisked blacks and searched their cars. Winter suspected that such policies originated at the top of the command and said so at a rally after Mosely's funeral. He saw the murder as "part of an effort to terrorize the community, and to prevent it from joining in any demand for equal treatment, whether in employment or in housing opportunities or in welfare." Winston Lang, who was deprived of his eighth-grade graduation because of restrictions imposed on large gatherings during the riot, did not trust white police either. "The policeman's word was law," he explained. "Whatever a police officer said happened against a black person, that was law."[33]

One Nation Divisible: With Liberty and Justice for Some

Blacks who toured frequently met jim crow. Negro League baseball players, for example, endured many slights and hardships from whites who wanted nothing to do with them. "When we traveled through the South, a lot of places we couldn't get a decent meal," Othello Renfroe recalled. "We ate out of grocery stores, sardines and cheese and cinnamon buns." George Giles remembered the doors of white hotels and restaurants being closed to them. The game against jim crow always went extra innings: "If we were in Nebraska, we'd ride all night to Lincoln or Omaha. In some of those small towns we couldn't stay, and sometimes we'd just ride all night and sleep in the bus." On barnstorming tours, whites suited up in hotels; blacks used barns or stables. In Shelby, Montana, locals would not even sell take-out food to the players. "Colorado was just as bad as Mississippi," Giles concluded. "New York was just as bad as Alabama." The Homestead Grays toured and slept in big cars Giles dubbed "Hotel Buicks." John "Buck" O'Neil of the Kansas City Monarchs remembered sleeping in black funeral homes. "Usually the undertaker would have space," he explained, "and they would put down cots."

When hotels did admit them, players were often denied basic necessities and comforts. "Many's the night I've stayed at hotels so cold," Paul "Jake" Stephens recalled, "I wore my baseball uniform in bed." Ted Page relished having played against Babe Ruth and Lou Gehrig. But off the field black players were very much alone. "Conditions were horrible then," Page noted. "You couldn't buy a hamburger on the highway between Akron and Youngstown." Yet an empty stomach was not the worst of his worries: "I carried a pistol all through my baseball days."[34]

Singer Ethel Waters, who began her vaudeville career under Jack Blackburn's wing, learned that her northern ways did not play well in Dixie. "The white people I encountered in the South," she complained, "never overlooked a chance to put me in my place, as it is called." When Waters appeared at a theater in Macon, Georgia, a mob threw the corpse of a black boy accused of talking back to a white man into the lobby. Waters argued with a stage manager in Atlanta who refused to tune the piano for her. He called her a "Yankee nigger bitch"; she called him a "cracker sonofabitch." After the tiff, police kept her under surveillance. Knowing they were not there to protect her, Waters feared for her life. When the police left for a moment, she and her friends abandoned their costumes and pay, sneaked out a side door, hailed a wagon, and caught a train to Nashville. When she became a star, agents urged her to perform for white audiences in white-owned theaters. But she did not like whites she met. She demurred, crossing the color line only later in her career. "White people generally bored me, and we didn't speak the same language," Waters observed. "If whites bored me, it was because they bored themselves. They seemed to get little fun out of life and were desperately lonely."

Like Joe Louis, Ethel Waters had fans of all races. She performed at the Cotton Club in Harlem, where black stars usually entertained white patrons. Its grand stage resembled the veranda of the "big house" on a Dixie plantation. Indeed, club managers replicated the magnolia myth of kind masters and grateful slaves. Waters continued to scale barriers on stage and screen. In the widely acclaimed Broadway show *As Thousands Cheer*, Waters earned $1,000 per week and became the first black entertainer to costar with white players when the show later toured below the Mason-Dixon line. To her surprise, "the people who came to see the show always received me warmly." In 1939 she brought her signature film role as Hagar in *Mamba's Daughters* to the stage. After one show, first lady Eleanor Roosevelt approached Waters, hugged her, and praised her performance. Still leery of whites, Waters relished the compliment.

Other white-owned clubs also invoked nostalgic images of the Old South. "You can be up to your boobies in white satin, with gardenias in your hair and no sugar cane for miles," singer Billie Holiday griped, "but you can still be working on a plantation." She and accompanist Teddy Wilson performed at the Famous Door. "There was no cotton to be picked . . . but . . . it was a plantation any way you looked at it," Holiday recalled. The two entertainers "were not allowed to mingle" with whites. When Holiday broke the rule and had a drink with a white millionaire fan, the manager fired her and sacked Wilson besides. "We got our asses fraternized right off the street," she mused. The fan, however, pulled strings to place Wilson with a local radio studio band. Another club hired Holiday. The fan was Charlie Barnet, who later formed his own mixed band and hired Lena Horne as his vocalist.[35]

Horne also played the midtown clubs and discovered the bigotry beneath the glitz and glamour. "The Cotton Club had no difficulty whatever in getting the pick of the nation's colored talent," Horne observed. "It paid the highest salaries, and it was the one place in the United States which offered Negro performers year-round employment." Yet artists who appeared there answered to white owners and patrons. "There were bouncers at the door to keep out Negroes," she recalled. "Even the parents of the kids from the show couldn't get in." They sat "in the booth near the kitchen door" to catch "final dress rehearsals." Popular on stage, Horne learned that her appeal did not extend beyond the club. "With all this applause and critical acclaim," she wondered, "how could it be that these people didn't want us to get a cup of coffee between shows in the restaurant next door?" Touring with Noble Sissle's band, Horne encountered the usual indignities—unreceptive hotels, closed restaurants, even jim crow elevators. In Cincinnati she conducted the band the night Louis lost to Schmeling, the first time a black group had played the city's Moonlight Gardens. But walls came tumbling down just one at a time. The band entertained an all-white audience. The tension took its toll. "You wrap the monotony and the misery around you like a blanket," she sighed, "and you pray no one will yank the covers off."

Seething at the bias, Horne suffered in silence early in her career. Her reticence stemmed from her sense of mission as an "ambassador of good will." Blacks with a large white following, she believed, "had a duty" to their people. "We were to remember during every waking moment that we were on exhibit and . . . must keep our conduct above reproach," she explained. "If we could prove by our deportment on the stage and by our appearance and manner when we walked down the street or entered any public place that we were ladies and gentlemen, people would learn to have a higher opinion of Negroes. And, by degrees, life would become easier for our people." John Roxborough, Julian Black, and Joe Louis held a similar belief, avoiding conduct that might reflect poorly on the race as a whole.[36]

To later generations, this ambassadorial approach to race relations appeared servile, even sycophantic. But crossover artists and athletes had little choice but to pocket their pride and political beliefs. They thought they could do more for their people by honing their talents, behaving discreetly, mollifying whites, and leaving protest to a more auspicious time. Speaking out was quite difficult, but keeping quiet was not easy, either.

Joe Louis and Racial Diplomacy

Joe Louis epitomized the race diplomat. "Negroes have placed a big trust in me," he observed in 1935. "I feel that I have a mission to perform and I sure am determined to carry it through until the championship is won. Then I want to defend the championship in a manner that will be a credit to my race." An emerging contender, he joined his mother and sisters for services at their church in Detroit. The Reverend J.H. Maston included him in his sermon that day. "He talked about how God gave certain people gifts and that these gifts were given to help other men," Louis recalled. "My gift was fighting, and through my fighting I was to uplift the spirit of my race. I must make the whole world know that Negro people were strong, fair, and decent. . . . I was also supposed to show that the Negroes were tired of being muddled around in the ground."

Writers of both races embraced the idea that popular black celebrities could promote tolerance and advance civil rights. A 1935 *Courier* editorial, for example, hailed Louis and Jesse Owens as "ambassadors . . . spreading good will while they achieve." Louis, William Nunn suggested, carried "the weight of an entire race on his shoulders." The *Philadelphia Tribune* also labeled Louis and Owens "ambassadors of good will." Chester Washington praised Louis for "say[ing] the right thing at the right time." Louis had excelled as an envoy to the white race, he added, "and it will be a long time, if ever, before his equal comes along."

Louis took his role "as a representative of the Negro race" seriously, Steve Hannagan wrote in the *Saturday Evening Post*. "He insists that it is his aim to do nothing which will bring other than credit to his people." More skeptical than most, Joe Williams of the *World-Telegram* suggested that the Louis camp had spilled "much heroic bilge" in Joe's behalf. But Williams conceded that Louis possessed "something approximating a religious zeal" in seeking the crown "for the pride and glory of the colored race." Jack Johnson had "left a smudge on the escutcheon" that "Louis hoped to erase." After Louis won the title, avenged his loss to Schmeling, and defended his crown against all comers, *Time* called him "a living legend to his people" and "a black Moses."[37]

Writers had good reason to borrow metaphors from diplomacy and theology to describe Louis's role. Like hostile nations sharing a precarious border, the races had to find ways to promote peaceful coexistence. The riots in Detroit and Harlem dramatized the high risks to life, property, and national prestige when interracial tensions erupted in violence. If the animus persisted, a single incident or inflammatory rumor might again lead to bloody streets and smoky skies over America's cities.

Unlike most blacks who lacked his fame and money, Joe Louis could usually shield himself from extreme manifestations of racism. But an incident in New Orleans after he became champion reminded him and Leonard Reed, a close friend who was black but who could have passed for white, that the South remained steeped in old ways despite signs of progress. Reed phoned a club in New Orleans on Joe's behalf and explained that he and Joe wanted to golf there during their visit. Waiving the jim crow rule, the club managers assented. Reed looked forward to eighteen holes and some friendly wagers, since Louis punched much better than he putted. At the New Orleans airport, they loaded their clubs and baggage into a limousine and, as Reed remembered, "waited—and waited—and waited." Reed approached three uniformed white drivers nearby and asked about the delay. "It's against the law," one advised Reed, "for us to carry colored passengers in our limousines." He explained that, personally, he and the others would "be happy to take the Champ, but we can't." Reed told Louis about the problem. "To hell with it!" Joe exclaimed. "Let's take our stuff and go over in a cab." So Reed tossed the luggage and golf bags into a nearby taxi, slid inside, "and waited—and waited—and waited." Reed found the white driver, who politely said he could not transport "colored people" in his car. Not to be denied their game, Reed carried their gear to "another cab, a colored one this time, and Joe and I get in." The black driver glanced over his shoulder and shook his head. "Sorry, Mister," he sighed to Reed. "I ain't allowed to carry white people in my cab." Louis now joined in the farce. "Leonard," he lectured his pal, "you know white folks ain't allowed in this cab. Better get in another one!" Reed found a "white" cab. "Mine follows Joe's to the golf course, where we finally get our game in."

Each then rode a separate cab to a hotel "in the middle of the colored section." Reed approached the desk. "You want to stay here, sir?" the clerk queried. Reed said yes. "Sorry, sir," the clerk replied. "We ain't allowed to have white folks here." By this time Reed's white driver and cab had departed, so he had no way to reach another hotel. Louis in the meantime registered with the clerk. By now Reed was exasperated. "We compromise," he recalled, "by getting in a colored cab with me on the floor!" As Reed "cramped down" to avoid detection for violating a law based upon an imprecise color line, Louis rode in comfort between black and white New Orleans. Louis saw humor in their predicament. "Leonard," he chortled, "it's a pain in the ass to have white folks around all the time."

After the long and uncomfortable ride, Reed checked into a "white" hotel, showered, and dressed. He heard a knock at the door. "Mr. Reed," the manager inquired, "are you colored?" "Hell no!" Reed answered. "Well, there's a dark-skinned colored lady down in the lobby," the manager continued. "She's got three kids with her and claims her husband is staying here and his name is Leonard Reed." If Louis had lost on the links, he won by several strokes in the practical joke competition. He had paid the black woman to pose as Reed's wife.[38]

John Roxborough, a migrant from Louisiana to Detroit, wanted to limit Louis's southern exposure. When white promoters wanted the champion to box exhibitions in Memphis and Miami, Roxborough declined, seeing "no point" in the offers. "If those white southerners want to see Joe fight," he told a *Courier* reporter, "let them come north." But some black celebrities did venture deep into Dixie. Lucky Millinder's orchestra, for example, performed in Jacksonville, Florida, in 1938. During the show, white women gathered near the bandstand to watch the musicians. At intermission, friendly fans requested songs and autographs. After the last number, Millinder and his bus driver, a white man he had employed for years, reviewed bookings and travel plans. These signs of interracial amity angered a city policeman. As the musicians loaded the bus, the officer chided Millinder for mingling with whites. When Millinder tried to mollify the man, the officer called him "a cocky nigger" and struck him with a blackjack.

A similar incident marred a successful tour of the Southwest by the Benny Goodman Quartet in 1937. Goodman, on clarinet, and Gene Krupa, drummer, were white; Lionel Hampton, on vibraphone, and Teddy Wilson, on piano, were black. After shooting musical scenes for the film *Hollywood Hotel*, the quartet left California for a fair in Dallas. At their concert, young whites addressed Hampton and Wilson as "mister" and requested autographs. Two city police officers, Goodman recalled, "didn't like the attention that Lionel and Teddy were getting." After the show, a white fan sent a waiter with a bottle of champagne to Hampton's quarters. One of the officers intercepted him. "The hell with that stuff!" he yelled at the waiter and knocked the tray, bottle, ice, and glasses to the floor. But Goodman regarded this incident as an aberration. In most places, crowds were "wonderfully responsive to Lionel and Teddy," he observed. "When we go out to play, nobody cares much what colors or races are represented just so long as we play good music." Goodman yearned for the day "when any band can play anyplace" and be judged on musical merit alone.

Black musicians might be applauded as performers, but their talent did not ensure safe passage through enemy terrain. Stars often toured for the Theatre Owners' Booking Association—TOBA for short. To Cab Calloway and others, however, TOBA stood for "Tough On Black Asses." These performers often played venues for white owners who wanted black talent but not black patrons. One nasty circuit that stuck in Calloway's mind included Richmond, Baltimore, Pittsburgh, Columbus, and Detroit. "Negroes weren't allowed to stay in any of the main hotels in the places we played," Calloway recalled, "so everywhere we went the company had a list of Negro families that would rent us rooms." Twenty-five musicians had to "spread out all around town" for lodging and meals. In the same week that Joe Louis became champion, Calloway and his wife Blanche came face to face with "the law" in Mississippi. After getting a tank of gas at a local station, Blanche Calloway and a friend entered the women's restroom. Two police officers asked Cab where the women had gone. Unsure of their whereabouts and confused by the query, he replied, "What did you say?" The police answered by clubbing him with pistols and arresting all three for disorderly conduct. A magistrate fined them each $7.50. "That incident is an ordinary occurrence in the South," a *Philadelphia Tribune* writer complained. "Colored people are beaten and forced to pay for the pleasure of having their heads cracked."

Police in Rome, Georgia, operated in much the same way. Mrs. Roland Hayes, wife of the world-famous tenor, passed through the city with her husband in 1942 and decided she needed new shoes. A white clerk insisted she sit in a designated part of the store. When she objected, he called the police. In an attempt to restore law and order, officers beat Roland Hayes, punishing him in their chivalrous way for his wife's impertinence. They then cuffed him and heaved him face-first onto the floor of a patrol wagon. The local jailer locked up husband and wife and detained their daughter nearby. "America is indignant over this latest disgraceful incident," the *Courier* noted, "because a citizen of international fame is involved." Yet "thousands of Negroes" suffered such "humiliations and indignities" regularly without protest because of their anonymity. The attack on Hayes, *The Crisis* agreed, proved that "no Negro is safe unless all Negroes are safe." The NAACP urged that federal authorities compel the South to obey the Constitution. But Hayes doubted whether "new laws by white legislators" could prevent abuses in view of such pervasive prejudice. "Stones have been thrown through the windows of my house in Brookline," he noted. "I have been refused a bed in a hotel in Tucson; a chair in a Seattle lobby, a meal in a restaurant in Duluth . . . I was beaten and thrown into jail." These trials did not rob Hayes of his humor. "Tragedy may stalk our houses," he mused, "but Comedy lives handily around the corner. We could not be sane if we had not made his acquaintance."

Hayes realized that humor often provided the only balm for the wounds of injustice. Whether blacks mocked pretentious whites or made fun of themselves, they found laughter sweet music for their souls. Laughing at people of all hues reaffirmed their humanity and placed them on a level with their supposed superiors, perhaps above them. Whatever their education or calling, blacks saw the absurdity of racism and realized that wit offered a safer outlet for their rage than revolt. Cab Calloway, for example, explained how rich black doctors drove through Dixie in their expensive cars while chuckling at "the man." "They put on a chauffeur's cap," he noted, "so the troopers would figure the car was owned by a white man and not some uppity Negro"— Ossian Sweet was not the only physician in the South who donned a token of servility to disguise his eminence. Jackie "Moms" Mabley, a comic and satirist who moved from the TOBA circuit to top billing at the Apollo, quipped that Louisiana's Crescent City would be called "*Old* Orleans" before she played there: "The Greyhound ain't goin' take me down there and the bloodhounds run me back." On her way to "*They*-ami" (not "*My*-ami"), Moms drove her Cadillac through a small South Carolina town and ran a red light. "One of them big cops" asked her why. "'Cause I seen all you white folks goin' on the green light," she replied. "I thought the red light was for us!"[39]

J. Saunders Redding, a scholar intrigued by southern life, traveled from Virginia to Mississippi in 1940. He picked up Bill Perry, an itinerant musician, in Rockwood, Tennessee, and the two black men chatted their way through the Cumberland Valley. The local mines were idle, with owners and laborers locked in struggle. "In the villages guards with automatic rifles stood about the company buildings," Redding noted. "The guards were about the only men we saw." One stopped Redding and Perry and asked them their business. Perry replied that they were merely heading for Kentucky. "Go'n," the guard advised with a grin. "But don' stop nowheres. Don' even breathe hard." Reading the guard posed a riddle—was he issuing a stern warning or toying with them? Perry sensed trouble and tried to defuse it. "No suh, Cap'n," he assured the guard. "I ain't much of a breever noway. Jus' 'nough ter live on. No, suh. I don't want no mo' o' white folks' air den I jus' got ter have." Now the guard had to do the translating. Had Perry bowed to white authority or lampooned it? Was he hiding behind a mask? Nodding toward his guitar, Perry apologized for not having time to play the guard a song. Redding and Perry drove on. At a safe distance Perry "doubled up with laughter" and confessed, "I kin lie when I has ter." These "peckerwoods," he grumbled, were always making some kind of trouble.

As he continued his travel, Redding learned about other blacks who made a sport of puttin' on or puttin' down whites. In Missouri, Redding talked with a man whose father, a former slave, had just died. "Pa'd ruther fool a white man," his son smiled, than "own a hundred dollars." Blacks often viewed white folks as crazy and had a hard time taking them seriously. "There was a big deficit between what we thought of ourselves and how white folks treated us," Charles Evers recalled of his home town, Decatur, Mississippi, in the 1930s. "To fill that gap, we stole from whites." The Evers brothers even attended Senator Bilbo's rallies. "Medgar and I went to watch Bilbo clown, and we ignored all the nigger baiting," Charles recollected. "Northerners can't appreciate a southern rascal. I always could." An assassin shot and killed Senator Huey Long on the steps of the Louisiana statehouse in 1935. A champion of poor whites, Long as governor of Louisiana had also provided token aid to blacks, but he insisted they did not deserve the same rights as whites. Someone asked a black man if he planned to attend Long's funeral. "No, I'm not going," he replied. "But I'm in favor of it."[40]

Long's racial attitudes were as cryptic as the guard's in the coal country. Appalled by the chasm between the classes and the masses, Long was aware of the dire poverty among blacks and he genuinely wanted to help them. But his aid came with strings. Gross disparities between rich and poor angered him, but glaring inequities between whites and blacks did not. Roy Wilkins had interviewed Long in early 1935, a day after an awful lynching near Franklinton, Louisiana. "That one slipped up on us," Long admitted. "Too bad, but those slips will happen." Such "slips" reawakened interest in a federal antilynching law, but Long preferred that the South be left alone. When Wilkins asked if Long would pursue and prosecute the mob, he replied that the NAACP did not really want him to do that. Such a step "might cause a hundred more niggers to be killed," he warned, because whites believed an occasional lynching kept them secure. No governor dared take that away from them. Long changed the subject to his record as governor, stressing that his aid to schools would help future black sharecroppers negotiate fair contracts with white landlords. Long urged adequate relief for blacks but defended the racial status quo. "I'm not working for equality or anything like that," he told Wilkins. "Don't say I'm working for niggers. I'm not. I'm for the poor man—all poor men." Long later repeated his view on mob murder. "We just lynch an occasional nigger," he remarked.[41]

Lynching exposed deep fissures in American society, multiple rifts caused by racial, sectional, cultural, and philosophical differences. To complicate matters further, opinions varied within each region, party, and gender. Politics shadowed the debate on mob murder. Even some who deplored vigilante killings felt uneasy about expanding federal power. Since blacks voted in the North but cast few ballots in the South, northern legislators had to consider black constituents while southerners could ignore theirs. Diplomacy also intruded. American leaders could hardly condemn persecution and atrocities abroad when southern whites killed blacks with impunity.

Louisiana had the first two "slips" of 1935. In the case Wilkins broached with Long, a mob entered the Franklinton jail on January 11 and killed Jerome Wilson, convicted of killing a deputy sheriff after an argument over a mule. Attorneys for the NAACP had appealed and the state supreme court ordered a new trial. The mob rejected the ruling. With no sentries at the jail and no resistance from the sheriff, the mob shot at Wilson through his cell window as he screamed for help. Vigilantes sawed the bars, bludgeoned Wilson with a hammer, and dumped his body on a road. Six weeks later, a mob hanged Anderson Ward at Maringouin. Ward had bickered and grappled with a white man who tried to shoot him. But the man's pistol did not fire, so Ward used his knife to prevent a second attempt. A black man nearby interceded, probably saving the white man's life. The town marshal arrested Ward, but a mob stormed the jail and killed him, hanging his body from a tree, "his mouth bandaged, his body riddled by bullets."

In southwest Tennessee, vigilantes abducted Ab Young, charged with killing a white highway worker. They crossed the border into Mississippi, hanged him at sundown and peppered the body with bullets—a lynching announced in advance by a Memphis daily. Despite the publicity and presence of a newspaper photographer, a coroner's jury ruled that Young died "by hanging at the hands of parties unknown." A local attorney called Young's death a suicide. Ten days later, a Mississippi mob killed R.J. Tyronne, too proud and prosperous a farmer for area whites. In a third lynching within eighteen days, whites killed the Reverend T.A. Allen of Marks, an advocate of due process

and higher incomes for all sharecroppers and tenants. Allen endorsed Huey
Long's "share the wealth" program and wore a button bearing Long's slo-
gan, EVERY MAN A KING. His body was wrapped in chains and dumped into
a river.

Three days before Joe Louis beat Primo Carnera in 1935, a mob of 400
hanged R.D. McGhee of Wiggins, Mississippi, before trial for an alleged
assault on a girl. Vigilantes in Bilbo's state struck again in July. A group of
thirty-five white men in Lowndes County removed from custody two men
accused of assault on a white woman and hanged them in a black church-
yard. Later that summer, a white woman accused two blacks of assault and
they were jailed. A mob removed one and killed him, then returned for the
other. "No effort was made by 'peace' officers to defend their prisoners," *The
Crisis* noted. "No one has been arrested for the lynching or the abduction.
No one will be." Mississippi completed its bloody summer in September.
Elwood Higginbotham, a sharecropper, disputed a debt with a white planter.
Both men went for their guns, but Higginbotham was faster. He went on trial
for homicide, but whites decided the jury was taking too long to convict him.
Over 100 people swarmed the jail and lynched him near Ole Miss in Oxford
on September 17—a week before Joe Louis defeated Max Baer. By year's
end, eight blacks in Mississippi had died "at the hands of parties unknown."

In Vienna, Georgia, an inebriated Lewis Harris allegedly threatened the
sheriff with a gun. A mob hanged him. Some 700 whites near Columbus,
Texas, wrested two black boys, age fifteen and sixteen, from local officers
and killed them. The boys faced charges of raping and drowning a white
woman. A county judge excused the mob that "meted out justice to the rav-
ishing murderers" because the minors "could not be adequately punished by
the law because of their ages." But mobs resorted to rope and rifle for lesser
crimes as well. Near Deerfield, Florida, Reuben Stacey robbed a white woman
and cut her arm with a small knife. After she identified him, law enforcement
officers decided to transport Stacey to Miami for safekeeping. Five carloads
of masked men overtook their vehicle and seized the suspect without resistance from the guards. They took Stacey to the victim's home, hanged him in
her yard, then shot him repeatedly. In White Bluffs, Tennessee, lynching
became a family affair when four white brothers and their cousin killed Baxter
Bell in late 1935. Bell had supposedly insulted the wife of one of the brothers "in a Negro drinking place." The lynchers turned themselves in and stood
trial, but a white jury acquitted them. "I am astounded at your verdict," the
judge told the jurors. By year's end, mobs had killed twenty men, including
a white man in California.[42]

Lynchings declined to nine in 1936. In one case, blacks made the mob
pay. For years, city officials in Gordonsville, Virginia, had pressured Will-

iam Wales, sixty, and his sister Cora, sixty-two, to sell their land and home so a cemetery might expand. They refused. The city condemned their property, but they defied orders to vacate. The sheriff secured a warrant to arrest William for "lunacy." When he arrived with the warrant, Wales shot him. An army of some 5,000, including sheriffs, deputies, constables, and state troopers, surrounded the house. For six hours, brother and sister exchanged shots with the mob, wounding five and giving others pause. At sunset, whites threw a burning torch into the wood house. Flames quickly engulfed the building and the roof collapsed. Aided by the firelight, the mob mowed down Cora Wales with machine guns. When William ran to the door, he, too, met a barrage of bullets.

Drawing on reports from Virginia, Roy Wilkins noted that the mob had not stopped with burning the house and slaughtering its owners. As the embers cooled, "killers rushed in and chopped up the two bodies for souvenirs to carry home." Rumors spread that William Wales had threatened a white woman who scolded him for being obstinate. Wilkins doubted it. The bloody siege had made "the colored people in the vicinity who might know something . . . sensibly mute," he wrote. Besides, "the trick of involving a white woman with a Negro . . . is an old one," a common "preliminary to a lynching." Wilkins saw no "lunacy" in William and Cora Wales. "It was the five thousand outside who were mad."[43]

The *Crisis* edition that told the Waleses' story also carried a photograph of Lint Shaw of Royston, Georgia—killed, burned, and mutilated by a mob "eight hours before . . . trial on a charge of attempted assault." The *Defender* ran the grisly print as well. "Clip this picture," the *Defender* urged, and "mail it to your congressman." Another Georgia mob at Pavo lynched John Rushin, who had confessed to a killing. In September a mob in Dalton in northern Georgia hanged A.L. McCamy for an "attempted attack" on a white woman. "What Georgia leads in for 1936 is lynching," the *Courier* complained. No vigilantes had been "sought or apprehended." In protest, the NAACP unfurled a large banner from its Manhattan office that read A MAN WAS LYNCHED TODAY. The stark black and white banner contrasted sharply with the stars and stripes in many places along Fifth Avenue. The owner of the building threatened to cancel the NAACP's lease if the banner was not removed. Mobs murdered with impunity, but the NAACP could not even display a flag of protest. As Congress debated an antilynching bill, killers struck again. In Laurel, Mississippi, a mob executed seventeen-year-old J.B. Grant. Shot more than a hundred times, he was "dragged through the streets" as "thousands of white men, women, and children cheered madly," an eyewitness reported. "Along the route the car dragging the body halted so that little children using their parents' firearms could pump lead into the inert form."[44]

Additional lynchings in 1937, the year Joe Louis won the title, convinced some southern whites, even a few prominent ones, that their states would not move against mob murder. Reformers hoped that federal agents might at least help uncover evidence to bring vigilantes to justice. But Attorney General Homer Cummings kept his federal department aloof when lynchings occurred. While Congress talked, the mobs murdered. Acting on vague rumors of an assault in Abbeville, Alabama, a sheriff arrested Wesley Johnson on February 1. Some 100 men removed Johnson from jail and killed him. In this instance, however, Albert Carmichael, the state attorney general, recommended that the sheriff be impeached for negligence. "We will be able to prove, beyond all reasonable doubt," Carmichael told the state supreme court, "that the mob got the wrong Negro." The victim's white boss, he noted, would testify that Johnson had been washing a car four miles from the crime scene. To mollify whites, the sheriff had arrested a black man, but even he had known that Johnson was innocent. Despite these arguments, four of six jurists voted to exonerate the sheriff. A grand jury refused to indict anyone in the mob. Yet Roy Wilkins saw some sign of hope. "Here for the first time in many years," he wrote, "the highest law enforcement official of a state, before the state's highest court," admitted that "the wrong man was lynched."[45]

The mayhem in Alabama, however, paled before the savagery in Mississippi. In Duck Hill on April 13, a mob seized two homicide suspects, "Boot Jack" MacDaniels and Roosevelt Townes, from a sheriff and deputies as they left the courthouse in broad daylight. The mob took the two men out of town to a spot where more than 300 whites waited. Men chained the suspects to trees and used blowtorches on them. They were tortured, hanged, shot, and burned as a photographer snapped pictures. Senator "Champ" Clark of Missouri obtained the photographs and posted them in the Senate while the Southern Democrats filibustered the antilynching bill. Joseph Gavagan of New York read a related news report to the House. BLOW TORCH LYNCHINGS SHOCK U.S., the *Courier* proclaimed. The barbarity aroused an outcry even in Dixie, but the stalwarts remained unmoved. Led by Senators Tom Connally of Texas, "Cotton Ed" Smith of South Carolina, Walter George of Georgia, and Claude Pepper of Florida, they blocked a vote on the bill. Southern mobs took five more lives that year after Duck Hill.[46]

Revulsion at the blowtorch murders did not deter mobs in 1938. The first victim was Wash Adams of Columbus, Mississippi. Three white men beat him to death with an iron bar because he had failed to pay a $10 balance due on funeral expenses for his wife. A month later, some 300 Mississippians shot and burned Tom Green, a blacksmith accused of killing a white planter in a dispute over ownership of a rifle. Within seventy-two hours, vigilantes killed John Dukes, who had resisted arrest for drunkenness and exchanged shots with a marshal in Arabi, Georgia. Two weeks later in Canton, Mississippi, a crowd stopped Claude Banks even though he was not their target. Terrified by the mob, Banks bolted from his car and a white man shot him. Otis Price of Perry, Florida, also died because of bad timing. Walking to a well used by both races, Price passed a white family's cabin where the wife was bathing in a tub in the doorway. She screamed, and Price was arrested on suspicion of rape. A mob seized and shot him several times. In Ruston, Louisiana, someone clubbed a white man to death and beat his companion at a local lovers' lane. Whites grabbed R.C. Williams and tormented him with a red-hot poker until he confessed. They hanged him. Two southern white men who investigated concluded that the mob killed the wrong man. There were no indictments.

In Smyrna, Georgia, police apprehended and secreted for trial a man suspected of killing a white farmer and his daughter. Unable to locate him, a mob went on a rampage. They "ran amuck for three days, beating and burning to their hearts' content," the *Courier* reported. "Fifteen Negroes were stoned or beaten and the Negro school was burned; white mobsters boarded . . . street cars and beat Negro passengers with sticks." The mob ransacked homes and businesses and attacked black motorists. "The entire Negro group," *The Crisis* noted, "was made to suffer for the wrongdoing of one of their number." This was nothing new, since whites often held all blacks responsible for one's crime. No white vigilantes were prosecuted for arson, assault, or murder.

In the final lynching of the year, a Wiggins, Mississippi, mob killed twenty-four-year-old Wilder McGowan, on suspicion of robbing and raping a seventy-four-year-old white woman. Blacks suspected that he actually died because of his independence and pride. Without fair trials, of course, the innocence or guilt of McGowan and all other lynch victims could not be ascertained. But vigilantes did not care, since due process was not their concern.[47]

By Any Means Necessary: Maintaining the Color Line

Southern Democrats insisted that they alone knew what was best for blacks, but they made their case in confusing and contradictory terms. They exhumed old ethnological theories about African Americans to defend their stand on lynching and the law. They also invoked grievances dating back to the Civil War and Reconstruction—Union tyranny, "carpetbagger" avarice, black insolence, and antisouthern prejudice everywhere outside Dixie. They vowed to resist "Yankee rule." Their motives were usually ignoble, but their arguments were not always wrong. They noted, for example, that lynching had declined dramatically over the past half-century. They also argued that southern lawmen had done relatively well in protecting suspects awaiting trial; the awful exceptions made the news. Even some prominent civil rights figures conceded this point. "The law-abiding element in the South was active, and its efforts, sometimes heroic, were shown in many preventions of lynching," Mary White Ovington observed. "In one year, 1935, our annual report showed nineteen lynchings prevented."[48] Moreover, the Southern Democrats noted, the North had urban riots and rising street crime as well as notorious gangsters who plundered and murdered at will. While lynching appeared on the path to extinction, gangland violence and urban crime seemed worse each passing year. Such statistics and ingrained racist precepts made it hard for southern lawmakers to grasp what the fuss was all about. The nation had many urgent problems, but an occasional lynching hardly seemed foremost among them.

Proponents of an antilynching bill wanted to put more pressure on law enforcement officers to protect suspects before, during, and after trial. Courts, not mobs, should determine guilt on evidence and not skin color. The NAACP and black journalists implored southerners to comply with the Fourteenth Amendment's provision that no state could "deprive any person of life, liberty, or property, without due process of law; nor deny to any person within its jurisdiction the equal protection of the laws." Southern lawmakers countered that private citizens, not the states, defied the spirit of the amendment. Others warned that federal intrusion would jeopardize recent progress because black men would interpret any bill from Washington as a license to commit heinous crimes. Representative John Rankin of Mississippi called himself "a far better friend to the Negroes than any man who sponsors or supports this measure," which was sure to upset "the peaceful relationship" between the races in Dixie. "The Negro is a tenant at sufferance wherever he comes in contact with the white man," Rankin told his colleagues. "He is no longer an economic asset to the South, if he ever was. If you stir dissension between the whites and blacks, the Negro must move on." The bill would not protect the innocent, Rankin advised, since it would "encourage the more vicious element of the Negro race to attack white women and to perpetuate other crimes for which the innocent Negroes will be made to suffer." He recalled a horrible crime when Congress had debated a similar bill on lynching. A hotel telephone operator had been walking home at midnight near the Library of Congress. "A brutal Negro," a "vicious brute," stalked her and "dragged her into the underbrush, choked and beat her to insensibility, outraged her, and left her lying there, a living example of the consequences of the legislative perfidy you are about to perpetuate." Whites in the House gallery applauded.

Rankin alluded to past race riots in northern cities and cited a rash of sex crimes in urban centers, particularly Detroit. The problem there was not lynching but opposition in Michigan to convict labor and the death penalty. "The worst these criminals can get is a term in the penitentiary, which is something on the order of a sit-down vacation, since they have about succeeded in outlawing every kind of work that a convict can do in that state," he argued. Detroit would soon feel "the flames of a race riot" because whites there would not continue "to sit supinely by and let these brutes outrage defenseless women in this manner, law or no law." The antilynching bill was "just the beginning" of efforts to impose "race amalgamation" on whites and sink them into "the mire of mongrelism." White southerners, however, would "never . . . submit to racial equality." Northern traders had imposed slavery on the South, Rankin argued, benefiting Yankee merchants and African slaves at the expense of southern whites. "At no time in all history has one race ever done so much for another as the white people of the South have done for the Negro race," he professed. Slavery had "elevated the Negro" from "savage to . . . servant" and introduced him to "Christian civilization." Rankin assessed the various solutions to the race problem. Intermarriage and race mixing were unthinkable, "too horrible to even consider." Colonization, Bilbo's panacea, seemed "out of the question." The only answer remained that chosen by "the people of the South for more than 300 years—a complete segregation of the races." Applause again filled the chamber.

Other southern legislators agreed. Edward Cox of Georgia objected that the bill contained "just as much malice" toward the South as the earlier Reconstruction laws. "The color line in the South is a permanent institution," he insisted. "Her people mean to maintain their racial purity and will not be mongrelized." Emmett Owen, another Georgian, agreed that federal intrusion would make matters worse. "Knowing the colored man as I do, I think this bill will encourage him to commit the unspeakable crime," Owen warned. No law could prevent a white man "from wreaking his vengeance on the brute" guilty of rape. Shortly after the blowtorch lynching, Aaron Ford—who represented the district where those murders occurred—advised that passage of the bill would "encourage the Negroes to commit the crime of rape" and "other heinous crimes." These crimes would then prompt more lynchings.[49]

Informed lawmakers could have done more to discredit this tactic of linking lynching to rape. The NAACP had published ample evidence that rape (or allegations of rape) accounted for only a fifth of all lynchings. The bill's sponsors should have exposed the illusion that southerners alone understood and cared for "the Negro." Masters had sung the same tune about their happy and loyal slaves. If the southern politicans were right, why had millions of blacks fled the South over the past half-century?

Southern lawmakers resumed the filibuster in early 1938, invoking states'-rights doctrine and old arguments about black inferiority. They reviewed the evolution of white attitudes toward Africa and its people. To southerners, the issue was not an occasional lynching but rather the very survival of the white race. "What I fear is that political equality will lead to social equality," Louisiana's Allen Ellender told the Senate, "and social equality will eventually spell the decay and the downfall of our American civilization." In a familiar refrain, Ellender stressed that no one had "greater compassion" or a more "sympathetic understanding for the colored race and its problems" than he. But that empathy did not compromise his devotion to "white supremacy."

The next day Theodore Bilbo predicted disaster if Congress passed the bill. It would "open the flood-gates of hell in the South," he warned. "Raping, mobbing, lynching, race riots, and crime" would increase "a thousand-fold," and those behind the bill would be "responsible for . . . the blood of the raped and outraged daughters of Dixie." Bilbo instead urged the removal of all blacks to Africa. Until then, whites must enforce separation. "To maintain our civilization there is only one solution," he counseled, "and that is either segregation within the United States or . . . deportation or repatriation of the entire Negro race to . . . Africa."

Critics of the bill impugned its sponsors' motives. They cited figures on violent crime in the North and taunted colleagues, especially Joseph Gavagan and Robert Wagner of New York, to look at their own cities. Senator Tom Connally of Texas, for example, asked Bilbo if he found "anything in this bill . . . which would deal with these 1,460 flagrant cases [of sex crimes] in the city of New York?" Bilbo said no. "They are indifferent to that," Connally sneered, "but are very much concerned about the eight lynchings." The South had spontaneous lynch mobs; the North had career gangsters. "If we offer an amendment designed to bring within the terms of the bill the 462 killings in Chicago, that is a smoke screen," Senator Richard Russell of Georgia objected. "But if there are eight lynchings, that is a matter to which the statesmen of the Senate should address their time and efforts."

Connally and others chided colleagues who left the chamber while southerners denounced the bill. John Bankhead of Alabama saw only crass motives in his opponents. Senator Joseph Guffey, Bankhead gibed, "has 277,335 reasons for being for this bill, and they are all colored persons in Pennsylvania over 21 years of age." Senator Wagner had Harlem voters on his mind. Bankhead contended that even southern blacks opposed the bill. "The thoughtful, intelligent Negroes of the South know that we are better friends to them than are those northern Senators who are using the race question to stir up strife," he asserted. "In my judgment, its passage would lead to the lynching of more colored persons than would be lynched if it were not passed." Since the bill held law officers liable for the safety of their suspects whatever their crime, southern police would realize it was better to leave a black suspect alone than risk prosecution for failing to stop a mob. The anti-lynching leaders "do not understand much about the psychology and processes of reasoning of many colored people, especially those who have not reached the proper point in the development of their mental processes," Bankhead argued. "Ignorant members of the colored race" would assume that federal officials would "stand behind them" and "come to their rescue" whatever their crime. Senator Ellender spoke for many of his southern colleagues when he declared that he trusted paternalistic southern whites more than federal laws. "We know the Negro and we sympathize with him," he maintained. "And we have taken care of him ever since he was brought to our shores centuries ago." The South had served all Americans by defending its traditional racial beliefs and habits. "But for the fact that the white woman and the white man of the South fought for the supremacy of the white race," Ellender argued, "today this nation of ours might be nearer a mongrel race than otherwise."[50]

These arguments were deceptive, even devious. Southern white men, so devoted to race purity, had sired a substantial number of mixed-race children on the old plantations. White women saw through the denial and hypocrisy, and so did slaves. Mary Boykin Chesnut, a mistress in South Carolina, had confided to her diary: "Like the patriarchs of old our men live all in one house with their wives and their concubines, and the mulattoes one sees in every family exactly resemble the white children—and every lady tells you who is the father of all the mulatto children in everybody's household, but those in her own she seems to think drop from the clouds, or pretends so to think." Frederick Douglass, a runaway slave who became a leading abolitionist, suspected his master was also his father. The slave masters had passed laws stipulating that all children born of slave women would "follow the condition of their mothers," Douglass observed, making "a gratification of their wicked desires profitable as well as pleasurable." At age fifteen, Harriet Jacobs, whose pen name was Linda Brent, began to fend off crude advances from her master who was "the father of eleven slaves." She was not the first of her kin to encounter lecherous whites. Her grandmother had "once chased a white gentleman with a loaded pistol because he insulted one of her daughters." Such strange unions created bizarre personal relationships. "I once saw two beautiful children playing together," Jacobs recalled. "One was a fair white child; the other was her slave, and also her sister."[51]

Southern Democrats seemed stricken with historical amnesia. Their ancestors had imported Africans to exploit their labor to produce profitable commodities, not to convert them to Christianity. In fact, many owners opposed making the Gospel available to slaves, fearful that it might serve as a manual of resistance and liberation. Many planters actually viewed slaves much like mules, as tools to transform their land into money. Owners varied in how they treated their slaves, of course, but ledgers usually mattered more than the slaves' physical and mental well-being.

The Democrats from Dixie had a point when they contrasted the decline in southern lynching with the rise in northern crime. Despite the hardships blacks faced in the South, the odds of dying by mob violence had dropped sharply over a generation. When James Corbett beat John Sullivan for the heavyweight title in 1892, for example, 230 people, 161 blacks and 69 whites, lost their lives in lynchings, according to Tuskegee Institute figures. In 1908, when Jack Johnson became champion, mobs killed 97 people, 89 blacks and 8 whites. When Johnson lost the title in 1915, 56 blacks and 13 whites perished in lynchings. In 1926, when Joe Louis moved to Detroit, 23 blacks and 7 whites were lynched. When Louis won the crown in 1937, lynch mobs killed 8 people, all blacks, among them the blowtorch victims. In 1939, when Louis defended his title four times, only 3 people, 2 blacks and 1 white, fell victim to lynch mobs, the lowest total up to that time.[52]

Black voters did influence northern legislators. But the opponents of a federal antilynching bill did not mention who proceeded upon the most brazen of political calculations—Franklin D. Roosevelt. To advance the New Deal, the president placated southern Democrats on race matters. He expressed his dilemma to Walter White of the NAACP in 1935. "I did not choose the tools with which I must work," he explained:

> Had I been permitted to choose them I would have selected quite different ones. But I've got to get legislation passed by Congress to save America. The Southerners by reason of the seniority rule in Congress are chairmen or occupy strategic places on most of the Senate and House committees. If I come out for the anti-lynching bill now, they will block every bill I ask Congress to pass to keep America from collapsing. I just can't take that risk.

White understood Roosevelt's dilemma but still regretted his course. Roosevelt always changed the subject, White noticed, when lynching was mentioned. White admitted being "very annoyed" with him for not denouncing lynch mobs and their apologists in Congress.[53]

Black leaders split on Roosevelt. But they could not abide demagogues who repeatedly slandered an entire race. However flattering the image of chivalrous white patriarchs guarding their females in the South, the historical record suggested that they cared mainly about their own power and privilege. If racial "amalgamation" imperiled the nation, white men, not black, were mainly to blame. If blacks remained ignorant, poor, and prone to petty crime, white politicians need only glance in the mirror to see the primary cause. Blacks offered a radically different viewpoint on southern history and lynching, refuting the notion of the black man as incipient rapist. By challenging old clichés, they helped sow the seeds of a new civil rights movement that germinated during World War II and blossomed after it.

Blacks did not interpret lynching statistics as Tom Connally did. They saw lynching as the final arbiter in the interracial struggle in the South. To note that only eight lynchings occurred in 1937 was correct, but numbers could not tell the full story. Even one lynching was one too many for activists. When mobs executed eight victims, they sent a message to some 8 million southern blacks. So long as lynching went unprosecuted and unpunished, whites retained the ultimate weapon to perpetuate inequality and injustice. Whites held all the cards in Dixie, since they monopolized elective office, ran the criminal justice system, owned the industries, held virtually all the land, and controlled education and the major media. This dominance surfaced in two remarkable court cases during the 1930s. Blacks who followed Joe Louis also watched the many rounds fought by the Scottsboro boys and Angelo Herndon.

Justice or Just Us? White Courts and Black "Crime"

The Scottsboro boys' ordeal commenced when white and black hoboes scuffled while riding the rails between Tennessee and Alabama in 1931. A white boy tried to eject Haywood Patterson, one of the black boys, from the train, but he fought back. "The Scottsboro case began," Patterson noted, "with a white foot on my black hand." Near Paint Rock the blacks forced the whites off the train. The whites complained to a storekeeper who also served as deputy sheriff. Through a station master he contacted county authorities, who formed a posse and arrested nine black "boys," ranging in age from 13 to 20, on the train. They were charged with "inciting a riot" and vagrancy. The sheriff also arrested three whites. In a strange twist, however, lawmen discovered that two of the white vagabonds were young women, later identified as Victoria Price and Ruby Bates. Price and Bates conferred with police and accused the black boys of rape. The suspects were jailed in Scottsboro. An all-white grand jury quickly indicted them for rape. "It was a miracle," Roy Wilkins wrote, "that all nine weren't lynched on the spot."

Local whites wanted to play judge, jury, and executioner. But the women were not entirely convincing. The medical examiner, for example, found no evidence of sexual assault and said so a few days later at the boys' hasty trial.

Sheriff M.L. Wann also doubted the allegations. He phoned the governor and asked for help from the National Guard. Wann averted a bloody lynching by a mob, but he could not prevent a legal lynching by the jurors. The judge appointed an elderly attorney to represent the boys but gave him little time to prepare a defense. In slipshod proceedings that produced no evidence beyond the "victims'" testimony, white jurors found all nine defendants guilty. The judge ordered eight to die, only fourteen-year-old Roy Wright being sentenced to life in prison. "The people in the court cheered and clapped" at the harsh sentences, Patterson recalled. "That courtroom was one big smiling white face."

Ruby Bates, a reluctant and reticent witness, later recanted her testimony and admitted that the rape charge was false. Moreover, investigators learned that Price and Bates were prostitutes, not Bilbo's delicate "daughters of Dixie." For years the NAACP and the International Labor Defense League filed appeals and sought acquittals. The United States Supreme Court ruled the Scottsboro proceedings unconstitutional, and the Alabama Supreme Court ordered a new trial in 1935. But the lower court again convicted the boys. Even some Alabama officials had doubts, though, and in 1937 the state dropped rape charges against five of the defendants and released four of them. This belated admission of error did not satisfy the NAACP. "The state now declares, in effect, that Victoria Price's story is not sufficient to convict four boys and therefore it sets them free," Roy Wilkins observed. "If the story is not strong enough in the case of four, it is not strong enough in the case of five, and all the defendants should be released." The case epitomized racial injustice in Dixie. That black boys were guilty of "criminally assaulting two white girls on a freight trains in Alabama loaded with prejudiced white male vagrants," Frank Marshall Davis of the *Atlanta World* observed, "was too preposterous to be believed by anybody but a confirmed irrational racist." The defendants, the *Los Angeles Sentinel* stated, had become "living symbols of all that is rotten and disgraceful about racial relations". in the South. "The tragic Scottsboro case drags on," a "football of race prejudice, class prejudice, and rabid sectionalism," the *Courier* complained. "It continues to disgrace Alabama and America." The state ordered new trials, but the rape convictions stood in the interim and the boys remained on death row.

Roy Wilkins demanded justice. "Alabama continues the tragic farce of the Scottsboro cases by denying the application for parole of the five defendants still in prison," he wrote in 1940. "If all nine were convicted on the same evidence and the state subsequently released four as innocent, how can the remaining five be held as guilty?" Indeed, southern whites had to ponder the unthinkable: two white women who had lied under oath were free; nine black males were innocent yet five remained in prison. For another decade the "tragic farce" continued as politicians and the parole board bumbled along. Not until June 9, 1950, did Andy Wright, the last defendant, receive parole and walk out of Kilby Prison. Wright wasted nineteen years behind bars in Alabama, longer than Joe Louis's career as an amateur and professional boxer.[54]

Georgia matched Alabama in the realm of trials gone awry. Angelo Herndon of Atlanta alarmed Georgia authorities for three reasons—his color, his class consciousness, and his activism. After cuts in aid payments and removal of thousands of destitute people from relief roles in 1932, Herndon rallied needy people of all races against the retrenchment. A mixed crowd of some 1,000 people gathered at the county courthouse to demand a restoration of public assistance. The rally remained peaceful, despite dire warnings from white editors and provocation by white police. Officials found funds and resumed the aid. The protest "caused alarm and consternation," Herndon noted. "It meant that the end of the world was at hand. . . . Never had such a huge gathering of black and white workers taken place in all the South."

A police officer arrested Herndon at the post office the next day. Besides being a labor organizer, Herndon was a Communist. At the city jail, a detective interrogated him. "Now out with it and confess!" the detective snapped. "We know that you are not smart enough to be the head of this Red outfit in town. No nigger is." Only "some slick white guy, a Yankee from up North" could have initiated "all this plotting and stirring up of trouble among the workers in this town." The idea was a familiar one—unrest always originated from an alien source. Failing to browbeat Herndon into a "confession," police led him to another room. "We have brought many niggers in here," an officer warned, "and . . . those who refused to talk never left here alive." Herndon spent three weeks in jail without formal charges, then learned he had been indicted for inciting an insurrection against the government of Georgia. The law dated back to 1861, when nervous lawmakers had enacted it to discourage rebellion and flight by slaves. After the war, the assembly had amended the bill to maintain "the lawful authority of the State" by mandating the death penalty for anyone found guilty of inciting revolt. Only if a jury found a compelling reason for mercy could the sentence be reduced to a prison term. The state delayed its prosecution, letting Herndon languish in Fulton Tower, the notorious lockup, for several months. Lawyers finally gained his release on bail pending trial.

The case mixed elements of tragedy and farce. To prove Herndon guilty of sedition, the prosecutor showed an all-white jury communist literature seized at his home. Among the incriminating documents was a copy of the fashion magazine *Redbook*, resplendent in its scarlet cover. The scene, Herndon thought, was "too comical for words." The prosecutor conceded that citizens had acted within their rights to protest relief cuts but contended that the trial was not about the freedom to assemble. It concerned the safety of Georgia and the survival of the South. "This is not only a trial of Angelo Herndon," he told the court, "but of Lenin, Stalin, Trotsky and Kerensky, and every white person who believes that black and white should unite for the purpose of setting up a nigger Soviet Republic in the Black Belt." Georgia whites certainly did not want to become a Soviet satellite, particularly one ruled by a "nigger" minority. The prosecutor urged the jury to "send this damnable anarchistic Bolsheviki to his death by electrocution." Jurors found Herndon guilty but recommended eighteen to twenty years in prison rather than execution, a move that surprised Herndon because he expected a death sentence. But Herndon could take little comfort in the prison term, for long confinement of a black inmate was often tantamount to an execution, albeit a slower one. Slated for hard convict labor, Herndon knew no black man survived two decades of ball-and-chain brutality. Whether strapped in the electric chair or sweated and beaten on a chain gang, Herndon would never live free again.

The judge allowed Herndon to address the court. In a ringing denunciation of class and race oppression, he proclaimed:

> You may do what you will with Angelo Herndon. You may indict him. You may put him in jail. But there will come other thousands of Angelo Herndons. If you really want to do anything . . . you must go out and indict the social system. But this you will not do, for your role is to defend the system under which the toiling masses are robbed and oppressed. You may succeed in killing one, two, even a score of working-class organizers. But you cannot kill the working class.

Herndon recited the party line, but his indictment of "the social system" was not just red rhetoric. This system robbed black boys of their youth for crimes they did not commit while sheltering white mobs who slaughtered innocent blacks with impunity. When the judge announced the sentence, a black woman in the courtroom shouted, "It's a damn shame! If they ever get him on that chain gang, they will sure kill him." The state returned him to Fulton Tower. A white inmate who came to know Herndon wrote a song for him, a song equating forced labor with lynching:

> There's a chain gang down in Georgia,
> That's where they are keeping me.
> It makes me sick to swing a pick,
> It's misery!
> Hallelujah! How I hate this job!
> And this dirty, rotten lynching mob!

For over two years state authorities rejected appeals for bail. Then they granted the application but demanded $15,000 within twenty-three days. To Herndon's amazement, workers and radicals across the nation raised the money. His lawyers petitioned for review by the Supreme Court, but the justices declined.

The persecution of Herndon for organizing interracial protests troubled progressives but did not arouse the same indignation as the Scottsboro case. Herndon was black but also red, and the African American press had qualms about defending him. Yet editors knew that all blacks, not just "Bolsheviki," got short shrift in southern courts. The *Courier* printed a commentary on the case by John Spivak, the white author of a provocative book, *White Nigger*, and a correspondent who had covered the Scottsboro trial for the Associated Negro Press. Were Herndon permitted "to be sent to the chain gang, it means that he will live in a cage like a wild animal," Spivak warned. "He will be worked on the Georgia roads from sunrise to sunset at a pace which will kill anyone not inured to it by years of back-breaking toil as a sharecropper on some white man's farm." He awaited "Spanish inquisition tortures" in prison. When the high court declined to intercede, the *Courier* depicted Herndon as a reformer and not a revolutionary: He had "committed the unforgivable sin (in Georgia) of wanting a New Deal" for all workers.

The *Sentinel* defended Herndon and denounced the proceedings. "Herndon was sent to jail because he had the temerity to organize Negroes and whites and lead them to the court house to ask for an increase in relief," the *Sentinel* stated. "Regardless of Herndon's political convictions such activities must not be classified as crimes." Bolder in its defense, the *St. Louis Argus* compared Herndon to abolitionists and rebellious slaves. Georgia stayed mired in the past as the world moved ahead. "The protest of Herndon has resounded the world over," the *Argus* maintained. "No doubt it has been heard in every language in the civilized world."

Rejecting advice that he forfeit bail and relocate beyond the jurisdiction of the court, Herndon and his attorneys appealed the conviction and waged a five-year battle for his acquittal. Finally in 1937—a week after the blow-torch lynchings and two months before Joe Louis won the title—the Supreme Court in a 5 to 4 ruling declared Georgia's antisedition law unconstitutional and ordered Herndon released. After watching many black inmates trudge the corridor to the death chamber, Herndon walked out the front door. He left the South and settled in Harlem. In the meantime, his brother Milton had joined the Lincoln Brigade while fighting fascist troops in Spain and died trying to rescue a wounded white comrade.[55]

Whether whites lynched blacks from trees or jury boxes, they intended to maintain white supremacy. So long as the lynch rope and bench stood behind the old order, there was little hope for real change in Dixie. Friendships across the color line did exist in the South, but overall conditions belied Representative John Rankin's argument that he and his colleagues were "the best friend" of blacks. A true "friend" would have publicly condemned lynching, the Klan, convict-lease labor, and the Scottsboro travesty. Blacks refuted the white's rhetoric in deeds that spoke louder than words. Barred from the polls, they voted against Dixie with their feet.

No one, including Joe Louis, expected change to be rapid or easy in the South. The Democrats from Dixie held undue power in Congress, where their seniority and parliamentary tactics stymied progressive legislation. "The South is America's spoiled child," the *Courier* complained. "Because she was spanked seventy years ago, she must be permitted to have her way at all times." After six lynchings within three days in 1936, the *Defender* grumbled that the former Confederacy remained unreconstructed. "The South is still in a state of rebellion against the laws of the United States," the *Defender* fumed. "Insofar as its respect for the Constitution, it is still out of the Union."

The denial of basic rights was but one of many grievances. Most people suffered during the Depression, but southern whites made sure blacks suffered more. In the North "there has been a minimum of discrimination in the administration of relief funds," the *Philadelphia Tribune* noted in 1936. "But in the South . . . gross discriminations have been practiced." When tenant farmers and industrial workers organized, southern conservatives blamed Bolsheviks and not labor conditions. But the *Defender* countered that "injustice, not the Reds" was "stirring up" labor. Challenged by the interracial Southern Tenant Farmers' Union and the CIO, the "lords of the land" and the "bosses of the buildings" fought back to divide the races and keep wealthy whites on top. Scholar J. Saunders Redding watched this confrontation in 1940. "The old South," he sighed, "is as active a ghost as there ever was."[56]

So "active a ghost" hovered in a miasma of racial myths and shadowed the entire nation. Rape had never been the chief cause of lynching—not in Jack Johnson's era and not in Joe Louis's. Following yet another lynching of a black man in 1936, the *Defender* refuted the customary excuse: "Assaulting a white woman in the South could have consisted of not removing his hat when he passed her; refusing to get off the street when he saw her coming; disputing his grocery bill, or insisting upon being paid for his work." Black editors welcomed a southern antilynching movement led by Will Alexander and Jessie Daniel Ames. "Southern white women," the *Philadelphia Tribune* observed, "are determined that white mobs will no longer hide behind their skirts." Statistics, the *Tribune* stressed, showed that the desire to exploit and oppress blacks, not sex crimes, caused most race killings. "The prevention of lynching will do more for the progress of colored Americans than any other single thing," the *Tribune* argued. "Lynching makes disfranchisement possible. Remove the fear of death from the colored citizens of the South and they will move forward as never before." The *Tribune* later reiterated the view that southern whites lynched blacks "to prevent them from obtaining civil rights," the ballot, and decent schools.

Roy Wilkins concurred. "Lynching is not for the protection of much-maligned southern white womanhood, but for the control of the Negro population," he wrote. "It is to keep them terrorized, obedient, tractable; to keep them from agitating for the ballot, for education, for employment at decent wages." The South, however, held firm to its myth of demure belles and chivalrous gents, white purity and black sin. Bilbo, Connally, and Rankin did not really want to know what investigators had learned about the Scottsboro "victims." Victoria Price and Ruby Bates had toiled for low wages in a Huntsville cotton mill and supplemented their meager pay through prostitution with men of both races. They chewed snuff. Price used language usually heard in vice districts and prisons and had prior convictions for vagrancy, bootlegging, and adultery. These gentle flowers had dropped off the vine well before their famous train ride in 1931.[57]

Unable to rely on cops and courts, blacks had to consider other means of defense. After three successive lynchings in Mississippi in 1935, the *Defender* exhorted blacks to strike back. "Mobs are both cowardly and criminal at heart," the *Defender* argued. "If you must go, then take somebody with you. Answer terror with terror; you can die only once." During another filibuster in 1936, the *Defender* repeated its call to arms: "Congress has failed to enact laws to curb lynching. Sheriffs and police officials in some sections of the South are leaders of the mob. Grand juries will not indict lynchers and Southern judges have openly expressed sympathy with their activities." If white mobs had the right to possess "ammunition and guns," so did "law-abiding black citizens." The *Defender* doubted that whites wanted to stop lynching or bring vigilantes to justice. "Lynchers must be fought with the same instruments they use," the *Defender* advised. "When black American citizens of the South make up their minds to stop lynching, it will be stopped." After the blowtorch murders, the *Defender* repeated that "firearms are used for other purposes than hunting."[58]

FDR and the Race Question

Urban disorder and violence disturbed President Roosevelt, who urged Americans to desist because the bloodshed distorted the nation's true character and besmirched its image. Roy Wilkins disagreed. "Violence is *not* un-American," he insisted. "It is distinctly American." In urging restraint, Roosevelt failed to mention lynching, an omission that offended blacks of all parties. Roosevelt's mixed messages perplexed blacks. He appointed African Americans to important federal posts, for example, but his administration also sanctioned bias in federal housing, public works projects, and the dispensing of federal relief. Black critics of the NRA (National Recovery Administration) said the initials stood for "Negroes Ruined Again." The Social Security Act did not include farmers and domestics, so millions who most needed a public pension did not qualify for one. Interior Secretary Harold Ickes boasted in 1935 that the administration had achieved "a New Deal in American life" for blacks. Most citizens of color, the *Tribune* countered, were "receiving the same old rotten deal." After several lynchings, a virtual war against sharecroppers trying to organize in Arkansas, and more police brutality, the *Sentinel* chided both major parties in 1936 for ignoring civil rights. "New Dealers and Old Dealers," the *Sentinel* lamented, "are both double dealers in this respect." "Knock, knock. Who's there? The *Tribune* joked in 1936. "F.D.R. F.D.R. who? F.D.R. sensible they'll vote for Landon." Yet some critics understood Roosevelt's quandary. If he sided with blacks, Mississippi might "secede from the Democratic party," David Cartwright noted in *The Crisis*. All the president could do was mimic a kind master. Had he owned slaves in the Old South, Cartwright suggested, "Roosevelt would have probably had the leaks repaired in the servants' cabins." That was faint praise indeed.[59]

As the administration shifted its focus to foreign affairs, blacks urged that domestic issues not be ignored. "Fascism is *already* in America and has been here for centuries, so far as colored people are concerned," Columnist George Schuyler of the *Pittsburgh Courier* maintained in late 1938. "Our problem is not how to keep it from coming in but how to get rid of it." When Roosevelt sought a large appropriation in 1940 to prepare the country for war, the *Courier* admonished him to look within. "The president has found words to condemn race prejudice and persecution abroad," the *Courier* noted, "but will not even whisper against the same thing at home."

Roosevelt was suspect for reasons beyond his silence on lynching. His nomination of Senator Hugo Black of Alabama, a former Klansman, to the Supreme Court in 1937 worried many African Americans. The Senate quickly confirmed him. Black "is now about to throw off a white robe stained with murder and ravishment for a black one christened with honor and dignity," the *Defender* warned. He could not "serve two masters." The *Tribune* also doubted Black's integrity, fearing the Klan's white robe would overshadow "the black robe of the Bench." Cartoonist Jay Jackson sketched Black wearing Klan garb and burning the Constitution at the stake with others in the Supreme Court plaza. Another cartoon depicted a Klansman hovering over the White House, a flaming cross in one hand and pistol in the other, with BLACKKK stitched on his robe.

Walter White dismissed Black's past, however, and urged that he be given a fair chance. Their previous contact had convinced White that Black had little in common with the South's habitual race baiters. His advice proved sound. In the case of *Chambers v. Florida*, for example, Justice Black excoriated lawmen who had isolated and beaten several young black tenant farmers until they "confessed" to a crime. The courts, Black declared, must act as "havens of refuge for those who might otherwise suffer because they are helpless, weak, outnumbered, or . . . victims of prejudice and public excitement." The Supreme Court reversed the convictions.[60]

For Joe Louis, the robe he wore into the ring was a more immediate concern than the white or black robe worn by Hugo Black. His reading confined mostly to Scripture, the sports pages, and comics, Louis lacked both the knowledge and inclination to comment on current events. From his professional debut in 1934 to his defeat of Max Schmeling in 1938, Louis remained mum on matters that engaged the NAACP. As he said, he let his fists do the talking. John Roxborough was a proud "race man" but said little in public on divisive issues. "Joe does what he is told," Heywood Broun observed in *The Nation* in 1937. "Generally he dodges questions such as those bearing on his attitude toward the Scottsboro case and other vital problems affecting the Negro." Broun understood and did not fault Louis. But he criticized others who were obsessed with sports. Editors assigned their "brightest workers" to baseball and boxing, Broun complained, while "second stringers" covered "floods and strikes." John L. Lewis of the CIO, Broun argued, not Joe Louis, fought the greatest fight of the 1930s. The labor struggle would affect the daily lives of many millions, black and white alike. To Broun, Lewis was "a far more interesting figure than Louis" and "the greatest heavyweight of our time."[61]

Broun had a point. Many blacks agreed that people cared too much about Louis and too little about other matters. Yet Louis fulfilled vital psychological needs for his fans while challenging stereotypes and discriminatory practices. When Louis fought in Philadelphia in 1936, for example, the exclusive Warwick Hotel welcomed him as a guest—"almost unbelieveable news," the *Tribune* remarked. The hotel had spurned black customers and instructed black visitors to use the freight lift instead of the elevator. Like other posh hotels, it tried to keep blacks out of the main lobby and dining room. "The Warwick management would go into hysterics when a colored person called on one of the Warwick's guests," the *Tribune* observed. "But the manager of the Warwick went to the station to meet Joe Louis." Yet breaking barriers was never simple. Some blacks criticized Louis for choosing a "white" hotel over a "race" business. Journalist Frank Marshall Davis defended him. "He can get better service and accommodations, can afford it, is acceptable as a guest, and probably wants to," Davis maintained. "It's silly to segregate one's self when it isn't necessary and especially when a person is a member of a race always yelping about jim crow." Louis won a similar victory when he was admitted to the golf course in New Orleans. Once Louis entered, others might follow. Despite the stay at the Warwick, the Louises generally patronized black enterprise. Prior to her wedding, Marva had "set an example of fidelity to racial business institutions" by purchasing clothing "at a colored store" in Chicago. When Joe injured his ankle playing softball, he "chose Provident [Hospital] for treatment because he was convinced, he said, that the surgical attention he would receive at the South Side institution was as fine as any to be obtained at any other Chicago hospital." The couple made the Hotel Theresa in Harlem their home away from home.

Louis and his managers accepted invitations from whites willing to suspend jim crow, but they did not openly protest segregation. For the trip to Texas in 1937, for example, Mike Jacobs rented a plush Pullman car, the one used by presidential candidate Alf Landon during the recent campaign. The Pullman spared them problems other black travelers experienced. "Real fancy set up," Louis recalled. "I felt like a king." The entourage mollified whites by being apolitical but probably squandered an opportunity to do more. No black American was better situated than the Brown Bomber to use personal popularity to promote greater awareness and to challenge jim crow. But Louis was no crusader, and even black observers did not press him to make a soapbox of the boxing ring.[62]

Yet Louis was not apathetic. John Dancy, head of the Detroit Urban League, remembered his buying gifts for 300 poor children at a league Christmas party in 1936. Louis gave Dancy $1,100 in 1937 so he could meet his United Fund goal. Then Louis invited Dancy along on the trip to New Orleans. "Joe is a very fine man," Dancy noted, "generous to a fault, kind, unassuming, a man of unswerving honesty." At a train depot Dancy saw Louis tip a redcap $20. When Joe joined his family for worship, church members saw him drop a hundred-dollar bill into the collection plate. After beating Schmeling, he donated $2,500 each to the NAACP and the Urban League. His sponsorship of the "Brown Bombers" softball team in Detroit boosted local pride and provided desperately needed income for players— Louis estimated he lost $50,000 on the venture its first year. Concerned about the expense and the risk of injury when Louis played with the team, the managers persuaded him to disband it. "I felt real bad," Louis admitted. "Those guys were my friends. . . . I got them jobs at Ford and the Sanitation Department. Those I couldn't get jobs for, I helped support until they could do better." Coleman Young, another migrant from Alabama to Detroit, remembered how Louis shared his good fortune. Louis would return to Black Bottom "after a big payday" and hand out bills on a street corner. He made money beyond his wildest dreams and redistributed some of it to folks with far more dreams than money.

Louis lavished favors on his family and friends. He paid his sister Vunies's expenses at Howard University, then helped her earn an advanced degree at the University of Michigan, John Roxborough's alma mater. When a reporter asked him to name his proudest moment, he cited his sister's graduation from Howard. Along with Sunnie Wilson and Leonard Reed, he opened the Chicken Shack in Detroit, agreeing to be a partner only when Wilson pledged to hire some "old friends . . . having a tough time." In 1942 Louis paid Mike Jacobs $1,200 for tickets to Louis's upcoming fight, then distributed them free to black soldiers and others unable to pay. He financed many projects and most lost money.[63]

While Louis aided family, friends, and strangers, the federal government continued to expend vast sums to help the needy and revive the economy. The high expenditures and massive debt alarmed conservatives; the failure to revamp modern capitalism dismayed radicals. The long Depression baffled people whatever their ideology. With his domestic programs under attack and developments abroad growing more ominous, Roosevelt felt even more compelled to placate the southern Democrats. He said little about civil rights, nothing about lynching. He continued to lose favor with African Americans, among them Joe Louis. Emmett Scott, a former aid to Booker T. Washington and a member of the Republican National Committee, encouraged Louis to endorse Wendell Willkie for president in 1940. Louis agreed, a deviation from his past. "This country has been good to me. It gave me everything I have," he noted in a telegram that Scott passed on to the media. "I have never come out for any candidate before but I think Wendell L. Willkie will give us a square deal." For eight years Roosevelt had watched the antilynching crusade in silence. Willkie, on the other hand, proclaimed that murder in the South should be treated like murder in the North. "So I am for Willkie because I think he will help my people," Louis stated, "and I figure my people should be for him, too." At a rally in New York City, Louis heard that Jesse Owens, a Roosevelt supporter, wanted to debate him. "At last," Louis joked, "the Democrats found somebody to work for them who could make a good run." In Cleveland, Jesse's hometown, Louis stumped for Willkie at Baptist churches. "Most of us were born down South and came here to get away from southern Democrats," he remarked. "If you weren't good enough to be Democrats down South, how come you are good enough to be Democrats up here?"[64]

Louis lost this contest when Roosevelt won. His third term, however, would be vastly different from the first two. Less than a year into the third term,

Americans had to respond to the Japanese attack on Pearl Harbor. The country went to war, a war that redefined the federal government, transformed American society, ushered in the atomic age, and raised issues of race and national identity that could not be ignored. The war changed the life of Joe Louis and made him a living legend. Like other peoples in other places, Americans discovered that a common front against enemies abroad could be achieved more easily than a unified campaign against undemocratic forces within. For Sergeant Joe Louis and other black Americans who had, in Pauli Murray's words, "no other dream, no land but this," the war against fascism and imperialism in Europe and Asia became entwined with the battle against racism and discrimination in the United States.

7

"Another World Be Born"

In Search of Victory at Home and Abroad

Let a new earth rise. Let another world be born.
Let a bloody peace be written in the sky.
Let a second generation full of courage issue forth;
Let a people loving freedom come to growth.[1]

—Margaret Walker, "For My People," 1942

Major Edward Gierring led his company of twenty-five soldiers from California to Camp Shelby, Mississippi, in 1945. At Jackson, Gierring, a white officer, entered a "white" downtown grill with his mixed unit. With two black GIs seated near him, he asked the manager to serve his men, and the manager complied. This breach of jim crow outraged local whites who taunted and threatened the group. Police arrived and arrested the black soldiers. When Gierring objected and complained about the crowd, police also arrested him and took him and the black soldiers to city hall. A magistrate booked the grill manager for defying segregation laws. Police escorted the white GIs to the train station in hopes that the company would quickly move on to its destination. In Jackson and around the nation, Americans faced a dilemma: would the black soldiers' recent sacrifices in war exempt them from customary discrimination?[2]

The surrender of Germany and Japan in 1945 left empires in shambles, the vanquished at the victors' mercy, and a globe haunted by the Holocaust and ominous new weapons. Americans had escaped the ravages of war in Europe and Asia, but the advent of the atomic age complicated international relations and made Americans far less complacent and confident. Despite the triumph over foreign adversaries, the nation faced a domestic menace left largely untouched by the bombing of Dresden, Hiroshima, and Nagasaki. By helping to defeat fascism abroad, troops like those under Major Gierring had changed history. Their service overseas had introduced them to peoples with different racial attitudes and practices. They had witnessed the carnage wrought by racial, ethnic, and religious chauvinism and militarism. Still, at war's end, many Americans yearned for old values and habits amid the profound changes reshaping the globe. Domestic racism would prove a more tenacious foe than Nazi storm troopers and Japanese soldiers on Iwo Jima.

For Americans, the rise of Germany, Italy, and Japan posed a challenge beyond calculations of moral right and wrong and how a realignment of global power would affect national interests. Several factors complicated the equation. In historical hindsight, the national experience seemed to validate the belief that whites had been predestined to conquer and rule other peoples. American expansionism, for example, had often violated the principle of self-determination—as shown in the cases of the conquest of the Mexican borderlands in 1846 and the development of the reservation system for Native Americans during the last half of the nineteenth century. As the United States expanded and prospered, American custom and law often assigned peoples of Native, African, Asian, and mixed ancestry to a separate and unequal status. The slave codes and the Chinese Exclusion Act of 1882, for example, exemplified the white ambition to control, proscribe, and exclude. Not only did "Anglo-Saxons" possess a genius for self-rule, they had a duty to govern "lesser breeds." Nations, like disparate species, advanced or declined largely because of genetics and the operation of natural laws of competition. Whether progress was measured by a nation's economic growth, political stability, or military power, Americans from Thomas Jefferson to Theodore Roosevelt had come to link the destiny of races and nations to biology (or "blood" in the nomenclature of the time).[3]

Migrants from all parts of the globe had resettled in the United States, not just "Anglo-Saxons" and "Teutons." But racists and nativists, imbued with a romantic image of whiteness and all it implied, ignored a complex mosaic of color and creed and expressed nostalgia for a homogeneity that had never existed. Moreover, they blamed the marginalized and dispossessed for their own fate and often denied the impact of prejudice on the relative ranking of various peoples. W.E.B. DuBois had pondered this sensation "of measuring one's soul by the tape of a world that looks on in amused contempt and pity." Promised equal rights during Reconstruction, black Americans instead faced rampant discrimination that gave them a peculiar sense of "two-ness." DuBois exhorted whites to change their ways, taking issue with Booker T.

Washington's idea that separatism and self-help alone could bridge the racial divide. The Tuskegee ideal, DuBois complained, "tended to make the whites, North and South, shift the burden of the Negro problem to the Negro's shoulders and stand aside as critical and rather pessimistic spectators." DuBois, however, thought "the burden belongs to the nation," and all had a stake in "righting these great wrongs."[4]

Whites had indeed become "critical and rather pessimistic spectators" of racial ills. The Roosevelt, Taft, and Wilson administrations had done little, Congress and the Supreme Court even less, to right the "great wrongs" DuBois described. When the United States had entered the world war in 1917, DuBois sensed an opportunity to improve race relations despite the apathy in the nation. He urged blacks to defer their own needs to the demands of the state. But the war and its aftermath had instead augmented nativism, racism, and reactionary politics. DuBois and other blacks would change tactics during World War II, supporting United States policy but demanding equality for black soldiers and citizens. They hoped for the best, though experience tempered their expectations. Ruth Fisher of the Library of Congress wrote DuBois about race relations in the capital in 1943. "I hate Washington with an intense hatred," she confided, but added that her attitude "as a whole is rather detached." She discerned "no difference between the Japanese and Prussian military caste and the Southern oligarchy here. They are all convinced of their race superiority, and they control the army and navy. The Ku Klux Klan is like the Storm Troopers." Fisher worried that racists at home and abroad intended to make their views "the predominant and powerful ones in their respective countries and the world with all else subservient to them." She thought prospects "for a Hitler to arise here" seemed "as likely . . . as in Germany."

Well aware of "race superiority" feeling, DuBois did not deny that bigotry ruled in Washington. Yet Fisher's views disturbed him. "There is no use of your trying to be detached from America," he advised. "You are permanently attached and you had better learn to like it." He admitted "certain resemblances between America and Germany" but thought it best "not [to] emphasize them just now." DuBois saw flaws in Fisher's analogies. Despite his long crusade against racism, he did not regard white Americans as mere Nazis who spoke English. Moreover, he knew that war often brought unexpected changes. The war to defeat secessionists had become a war to free slaves. The war against fascists might become a war to liberate colonial subjects and to equalize the races at home.

DuBois stressed these issues when he proposed two articles to the *Atlantic Monthly* in the fall of 1941. "To the trite truths that a nation cannot exist half-slave and half-free and a culture cannot survive half democratic and half totalitarian," he wrote, "we must add . . . the modern world cannot survive with democracy among white Europeans and colonial imperialism rampant in Asia and Africa." Blacks could rise "to or above the average level" of whites if only their "deliberate hindrances" were removed. To grant equal opportunity at home would mark "the beginning of the end of domination," DuBois predicted. "There is no moral question facing the Americas of greater and more pressing importance than this question of racial tolerance in the Western Hemisphere." Editor Edward Weeks rejected DuBois's proposal, finding it "deeply penetrating in certain passages and equally intemperate in others." Weeks preferred not to denounce colonialism, since the British were "allies in a fight for survival." Nor did he agree that black degradation resulted primarily from discrimination. Weeks wondered "whether it is strictly true that all barriers to the Negro's advancement are social and political," since "a biological handicap" could well be the major factor. Erudite and proud, DuBois resented the editor's rejection of his articles. Even more galling was his suggestion that racial proscription resulted from ineradicable genetic causes.[5]

DuBois was right to stress the global reach of racism even if editors disputed him. The onslaught by Germany and revelations of Nazi persecution of Jews dramatized the results of racist and nationalist dogma run riot. When the United States entered the war, Americans again confronted the disparity between noble ideals and ignoble practices. From the president to the White House maid, from southern planters to sharecroppers, Americans pondered what their nation stood for in a world shaken by a long depression and a savage war. The stunning losses at Pearl Harbor dramatized the vulnerability of all peoples in a world made suddenly smaller by new and deadlier weapons. The uncertainties went beyond this stark challenge to global order. Not only did Germany and Japan threaten American interests, they were the homelands of many immigrants who now had to measure their blood ties to the old country against their affinity for the new. Americans of recent or distant British, Irish, Polish, Italian, African, and Chinese ancestry also watched to see how the war affected places once their own or still home to relatives and friends.

Joe Louis in a Global Context

In this era of bitter global conflict and mixed allegiances, international sporting events became important political and diplomatic contests as well. Boxing in particular had drawn competitors from many lands, races, and ethnic groups. Coveted at all times, the heavyweight crown acquired even greater symbolic meaning between 1935 and 1945. Joe Louis dominated the sport during that decade, a time of rising expectations for black Americans. His victories over Primo Carnera of Italy in 1935 and Max Schmeling of Germany in 1938 suggested the vulnerability of the Axis powers and foreshadowed their ultimate defeat. When Louis entered the army in early 1942, he exemplified the joining of blacks and whites in a vital common endeavor. From his professional debut in 1934 to his military induction in 1942, sportswriters called him "a credit to his race." As a soldier he became "a credit to his country." Initially an inspiration to his own people, he became a national hero during the war.

Louis's reputation was closely linked to global events. In 1935 he headed to training camp to prepare for Carnera, just as Mussolini mobilized his imperial forces in Eritrea and Somaliland to invade Ethiopia. Marcus Garvey's movement a generation earlier had reawakened interest in Africa, and Haile Selassie's Ethiopia (or Abyssinia) remained the only independent black nation on the continent. To accentuate the symbolism of the fight, Princess Heshla Tamanya of Abyssinia ventured to Pompton Lakes to wish Louis good luck against Carnera. The black press ran photographs of Louis and Tamanya to link the black hope to the black kingdom. Louis learned about the crisis in Africa. "Mussolini had started threatening Ethiopia," he recalled. "So here you had a black man and an Italian man having a fight. The whole world was looking." Black visitors told him he "represented Ethiopia" and that European imperialism violated Garvey's ideal of Africa for Africans. "Now, not only did I have to beat the man," Louis realized, "but I had to beat him for a cause."

Louis did beat Carnera, his first win over a former champion and a major step up the heavyweight ladder. The triumph also inspired black Americans and Africans to envision a future free of white oppression and exploitation. Louis, the *Chicago Defender* noted, had won "the year's most sensational sock exchange with Mussolini's pride and joy." Along with fight pictures, the *Defender* ran a photograph of two black women chained to a lamppost near the Italian consulate in Chicago. They wore blouses lettered HANDS OFF ETHIOPIA. "Al Monroe was wrong when he sed dat Joe's knockout punch just traveled six inches," humorist Andrew Dobson mused. "It traveled plum to Italy." Louis had alarmed both Mussolini and Mississippi whites. "De referee stops de fight and raises Joe's right hand," Dobson chuckled. "Mussolini raises his army and de 'crackers' down home raise a fever." The *Philadelphia Tribune*'s Ed Harris joked that Louis risked greater injury during the Harlem celebration than during the bout. "The first Italian-Ethiopian War started and ended" on June 25, Harris wrote. "Victory went to the Ethiops."[6]

Louis had made the last first, and they relished his victory. In Stamps, Arkansas, young Maya Angelou watched poor sharecroppers mingle in her grandmother's store for over an hour to savor the triumph. "Joe Louis," Angelou observed, "proved that we were the strongest people in the world." Clifton Taulbert did not recall seeing many radios "in the colored section" of his Mississippi town, but his great aunt owned "an old battery-operated one" she played on Sundays and "for special occasions" like Louis fights. She set the radio in a window, and soon "her front porch was filled to capacity and there were grown men sitting on the ground" to listen. Louis "made us proud," Taulbert recalled, and his fights became "subjects of sermons" and added "sizzle" to conversations. Like Angelou, Taulbert thought Louis inspired people of color from Mississippi to Mozambique, from Carolina to the Congo.

Chester Washington of the *Courier* regaled readers with a yarn celebrating black over white. After Carnera lost, he toured the United States. As his train entered Missouri, the conductor yelled "St. Louis!" But Carnera thought he said "Joe Louis" and jumped out the window and broke his leg. The victory entered the realm of legend and lore. On the night of a Louis fight years later, a New York cab driver reminisced about that magical night. "I remember when he fought Carnera," the cabby told A.J. Liebling. "The celebration in Harlem. They poisoned his mind before that fight, his managers and Jack Blackburn did. They told him Carnera was Mussolini's man and Mussolini started the Ethiopian War. He cut that man down like he was a tree."[7]

Black journalists shared the elation but warned fans not to goad Italian Americans. Writers realized the limitations of symbolism in sports— Mussolini's army invaded Ethiopia and crushed its poorly equipped soldiers. "We can do Ethiopia no good as long as we only talk and remain in America," the *Defender* counseled. "It is not within the bounds of proper sense to stir up any discord among American citizens of different races because of a foreign controversy." In Philadelphia a large Italian American population competed for jobs with a rising black population, a pattern common in northern cities. A brawl between the two groups in Newark in August reminded a *Tribune* editor of "what can happen when two races permit their racial feelings to surmount common sense." Americans should not allow their passions about events abroad to affect how they treated one another at home. "Bad blood between Italians and colored Americans will not help either Ethiopia or Italy," the *Tribune* advised. Both groups had "a common cause in the United States." Multiple lynchings that summer reminded a *Courier* writer of the primacy of internal matters. "Much as we all sympathize with Ethiopia . . . our burdens here are sufficiently heavy without assuming those of Negroes over 7,000 miles away," the *Courier* noted. "We have fought our battle alone and they will have to do likewise."[8]

The conduct of Mussolini's soldiers in Ethiopia portended later atrocities by troops loyal to Franco and Hitler. But when Britain, France, the United

States, and the Soviet Union opted not to assist Ethiopia, black Americans could do precious little to save the beleaguered Africans. Britain allowed Italy to use the Suez Canal, and western corporations continued to supply steel and petroleum to Italy despite Roosevelt's call for a "moral embargo" against the nation. "Appeasement" actually began when the West allowed Italy to take Ethiopia, three years before Britain and France agreed to Germany's seizure of the Sudetenland at Munich in 1938. Britain and France permitted Italy's aggression in order to retain firm control over their own empires and subjects, the *Courier* maintained: "Ethiopia is black, and when you are sitting on the backs of hundreds of millions of black and brown slaves in Africa and Asia, you do not want any black people triumphing over any white people. It's a bad example." Fear of colonial unrest influenced how European leaders reacted to Joe Louis. England, France, and Holland had sent "secret suggestions" to American leaders "hinting that it would be disagreeable if Louis should win the title," Ted Benson wrote in 1936. "These nations own extensive colonies peopled by colored races and fear riots and the development of anti-imperialist, pro-national feeling." No promoter in London responded when Louis's managers suggested a return bout with British champion Tommy Farr. Louis had beaten him badly in 1937, Chester Washington observed, and the "lords and squires" preferred that Farr fight "the Huns" and not Louis.[9]

As global tensions rose, sports became more political on both sides of the Atlantic. The bouts between Louis and Max Schmeling in 1936 and 1938 and the 1936 Olympics in Berlin revealed the growing entanglement between national, racial, and religious matters and professional and amateur athletics. Jesse Owens and Joe Louis became national heroes for their triumphs over foreign opponents, yet their achievements did not shield fellow blacks from customary bias. As Owens and Louis became the nation's favorite sons, their folk remained Uncle Sam's stepchildren.

Six months after Louis beat Carnera, promoter Mike Jacobs signed him to fight Schmeling, another ex-champion. This marquee match pitted a hard-hitting newcomer against an aging former champion trying to regain a title lost in 1932. But the boxers' personal stories were only part of the drama. Jacobs, a Jew, pitted Louis, the son of sharecroppers, against Schmeling, a German with close personal ties to high officials in the Nazi regime. In addition, Jacobs booked the fight for Yankee Stadium, an icon of Americanism since the days of Babe Ruth and Lou Gehrig. Louis had a large black following in the Bronx, and nearby Harlem regarded him as one of its own. The five boroughs of New York were home to more Jews than any city in the world. To complicate matters further, an enclave of German Americans resided in the city, and its mayor, Fiorello La Guardia, was probably the nation's most prominent Italian American. Never had a fight tugged the heartstrings of so many people in so many directions.

Nazism and the Schmeling Fights

The politics of the match surfaced in many ways. Realtor Abe Alpert, a Jew, offered Louis his "well appointed house" and yard in Lakewood, New Jersey, for a training camp. "A great admirer of the Brown Bomber," Alpert hoped "to see Joe give Schmeling, the Nazi-man, a good trouncing," Robert Pelham reported in the *Tribune*. Ed Harris also wanted Louis to knock out "Hitler's pet and pride." Schmeling, one source noted, would leave "Hitler's concentration camp, Germany," on April 15 and arrive in New York on April 21. A *New York Times* correspondent saw Schmeling get "a shabby send-off" in Berlin. "Race-conscious Germany cannot forgive Max for fighting a Negro and letting himself be paid therefore," the wire stated. Besides, boxing had "never really been popular" in Germany. But recent developments gave him "more incentive" to win. "The semi-religious attitude toward sport" among "Nazi youth" and the "propaganda which endows the coming Olympics with an almost sacred character, has made the path of the professional athlete even more rocky than heretofore."

Animus toward Germany preceded news of the Nazis' rearmament and persecution of its peoples, for Americans remembered the deadly attacks on neutral ships by the kaiser's submarines before the United States entered the war in 1917. "With veterans, it is still the 'Hun' when war is discussed," Harry Edwards noted in the *Atlanta Journal* the day of the Louis-Schmeling fight, "just as among the old Confederates a northerner is still a Yankee." Southern whites, he wrote, "will quietly pull for Joe." The "Solid South" was, perhaps, not so solid after all. For every Theodore Bilbo who admired the land of "Aryan supremacy," there were others who deplored Nazi ideas and practices. Like Edwards, some favored a fellow southerner despite the color line. Actress Tallulah Bankhead, the daughter of William Bankhead, former Speaker of the House, and niece of Senator John Bankhead of Alabama, ranked Louis the second greatest American (behind Roosevelt) and said so publicly. She sent him a good luck charm. "I . . . carried an emotional banner for Joe Louis," she declared.[10]

Jews debated the wisdom of matching Louis against Schmeling. Disturbed by Nazi repression abroad and anti-Semitism at home, some welcomed the prospect that Louis would humble Schmeling and, by proxy, his rulers in the Third Reich. But others feared that Schmeling might take a small fortune back to Germany. Some Jews threatened to boycott the fight, putting a damper on ticket sales. Five days before the bout, Mike Jacobs told Louis that only

50,000 tickets had sold, far below the expected 85,000. "We found out later that some Jewish organization had sent out a big batch of flyers to storekeepers asking them to boycott the fight because Schmeling 'represented' Nazi Germany," Louis recalled. "The whole thing made me uneasy."

As Louis worried about the protest, Schmeling distanced himself from the Nazis. "What has Hitler to do with me?" he asked Frank Graham of the *New York Sun*. "He is a politician. I am a sportsman." Schmeling assured a *Courier* correspondent that Germans would treat African Americans kindly at the Olympics. "It's ridiculous to even talk about American Negro athletes not receiving anything they want when they compete against us in Berlin this summer," he protested. "Personally, I wish them luck." When not surrounded by reporters, Schmeling trained for the fight, getting tips from none other than former champion Jack Johnson.[11]

Louis spent too much time on the golf course and too little in the gym. He argued with his handlers and squabbled with his wife, Marva, not long before the fight. In the house that Ruth built, Schmeling took some mighty swings of his own on June 19. Louis, disoriented and desperate, hit his opponent below the belt. In the twelfth round Schmeling knocked Louis out, a stunning blow for him, his loved ones, and fans. When told about his fouls, Louis sent John Roxborough to apologize for him. "I let myself down," Louis lamented. "I let a whole race of people down because I thought I was some kind of hot shit." The defeat rankled even more because Schmeling had injected race into the contest. "He made cracks that no Negro could stand up against a superrace man like him," Louis complained. "The sportswriters would come down from his training camp and tell me things like that."[12]

Nazi officials who had largely ignored the fight suddenly took great interest in it. "I won this one for Germany," Schmeling gushed. "I will win back the title for Germany." Writer James Farrell predicted that the Nazis would "make political capital of the fight," defining it as "a triumph for Hitler" and the Teutons. Schmeling flew home on the *Hindenberg*, and Hitler hosted a reception for him and his wife, actress Anny Ondra, in Berlin. Joseph Goebbels, the regime's information minister, noted Hitler's pride in the boxer: "*Ist begeistert über Schmeling. Erläßt ihm die Steuern.*" [He is very enthusiastic about Schmeling, exempting him from taxes.] Schmeling emerged a national hero as masses of people flocked to see him as well as the films of his victory: "*Schmeling unter großem Jubel in Frankfurt und Berlin empfangen.*" [Schmeling drew large and jubilant crowds in Frankfurt and Berlin.][13]

Black journalists took offense at the German reaction. "Hitler and the rest of his Jew-baiting, Negro-hating gangsters have advanced the Schmeling-Louis film to a place of honor in German theaters," the *Los Angeles Sentinel* grumbled. "They claim it proves the superiority of the Aryans." The Germans' "superiority racket is due for a fall this summer," the *Sentinel* predicted, "when ten Negro athletes invade Nazi-land with the American Olympic team." These stars would "trounce German track and field men in their events." The *Sentinel* advised readers not to misinterpret its prediction, for race was irrelevant to sports no matter what the Nazis said. "Race has nothing to do with superiority—physical or mental," the *Sentinel* argued. "We await with interest the alibis that Hitler is going to need." The *Courier*'s George Schuyler wondered what Hitler and his cohorts would think when these black track stars "force[d] the 'superior' Nazi athletes to eat dust." Jesse Owens and his teammates would deliver "a rebuke" to racists everywhere who "made a fantastic religion out of skin pigment." The African American athletes lived up to their advanced billing and dazzled the crowds in Berlin. Owens won four gold medals, a feat that shattered the notion of Aryan physical supremacy. Still reeling from the Louis debacle, black journalists embraced Owens as a new black hope. He "has been deadly poison to white supremacy," a *Cleveland Gazette* correspondent reported from Berlin, "not only by his victories but by the greatest form and smoothest style that coaches from all over the world have ever seen." Roy Wilkins, editor of *The Crisis,* featured Owens on the cover of the NAACP journal and captioned his photograph TOO FAST FOR HITLER. "Jesse's winged feet have speeded interracial understanding and appreciation in this country," Wilkins argued. "We are several notches above where we were before he sailed away July 15."

White writers praised these athletes for winning honors not just for themselves and their race but for all Americans. "Every tape broken by Owens," the *New York Post* declared, "is an answer to Hitler that burning of a thousand books cannot wipe out." Editors at *The Nation* rejoiced that the black sprinters had "sent Hitler scurrying" from his seat to find seclusion "under his own Olympic propagrandstand." The black athletes, *The Nation* added, "put several painful knots in the myth of white supremacy."[14]

Lines were not so easily drawn, however, for among those who hailed Jesse Owens was Max Schmeling. He visited him at the Olympic village. "I've heard lots about you!" he exclaimed. Days later, Schmeling returned to the United States and called upon Joe Louis at his training camp, where they discussed the Olympics, not boxing. A *Courier* reporter asked Schmeling what he thought of the black Olympians. "They are great and Mr. Owens is the most perfect athlete I have ever seen," he effused. "He flies like the Hindenburg." A year later, Max visited Joe again. Joe introduced him to Marva, and Joe, Max, and Mike Jacobs posed for a photograph around the pool table. "Max and I were talking about things I'd read in the paper about Nazi Germany and the Aryan race being the only pure race," Louis recalled. "Shoot! Max told me he never said those things and wouldn't think them."

Schmeling, at least in Louis's company, divorced sports from race. But ardent Nazis viewed athletics as an arena for political manipulation and a lab for comparative genetics. Hitler, for example, left the stadium to avoid congratulating Jesse Owens. (His spokesman excused his absence by saying he had left early to avoid a traffic jam.) Nazi officials regulated filming. "All American newsreel companies were compelled to sign a contract with the Nazi government which limited newsreel coverage to what the Nazis wanted covered," a *Defender* correspondent cabled. "As the sensational performance of the Race athletes would torpedo the Nazi doctrine of 'Aryan' superiority, Leni Riefenstahl, German motion picture actress, an intimate of Hitler and newsreel censor for the games, kept the coverage of the events in which Race boys ran away with the honors down to a minimum." Robert Vann, editor of the *Courier*, went to Berlin. "The Germans," he noted upon return, "controlled all the releases both by press and by telegraph." Spectators had cheered the black stars but Hitler had snubbed them. "My seat was directly behind Herr Hitler . . . and I could look right down upon him," Vann added. "And I did look down upon him almost every moment of the time he sat in his seat."

Others also resented the Nazis' tactics. Hitler's pettiness led the *Sentinel*'s Loren Miller to denounce fascists on both sides of the Atlantic. "Hitler and the rest of his gangsters must fan race prejudice because it serves to hide their own war plans and their inability to solve Germany's domestic problems," Miller contended. "Every American Negro knows plenty about race prejudice. . . . Many Southern governors, judges, senators, and lesser fry . . . would go to the same lengths as Hitler has gone." Some wanted "an American Hitler." But Owens had "exploded Hitler's race superiority racket." Eddie Cantor, former vaudeville star with a popular radio show, told a *Sentinel* reporter that Jews owed Owens "a debt of gratitude" for his success in Berlin. Jews and African Americans had a common interest in deflating bigots at home and abroad.[15]

Roy Wilkins also cited Nazi rudeness as a common characteristic linking German fascists and American racists. "Germany knows that millions of Negroes are not allowed to vote," he noted, and "that mobs make sport of black men upon the slightest pretext, without the government lifting a hand to apprehend lynchers." Jesse Owens attended Ohio State, yet there were "hundreds of colleges . . . where a Negro had better not try even to walk across campus." Besides, Germans knew that blacks were "humiliated and insulted" in virtually all forms of "public accommodation." The excesses in Germany showed why Americans had to change. "Jesse and his people,"

Wilkins concluded, "deserve to be given all the rights and privileges of American citizens."[16]

While Owens basked in the accolades after his triumphs in Berlin, Joe Louis resumed his climb, beating former champion Jack Sharkey and then Al Ettore. "You watch me," Louis assured the *Courier*'s William Nunn. "I won't let my people down." With Louis a winner again, a *Defender* correspondent saw Harlemites "waving Ethiopian flags, blowing horns, ringing cowbells, and setting off flares." After Louis beat Ettore in Philadelphia, the *Tribune*'s Otto McClarrin reported "fun galore" on "the sepia side" of town. Jesse Owens attended the fight, and black newspapers ran photographs of him and Louis together. Louis fought a few exhibitions in the North and then headed south to New Orleans.

No Berlin, New Orleans was also no New York. "In 1936," Louis noted, "Louisiana wasn't the kind of place a black man would go for a vacation." Brothers John and Charles Roxborough had left the state for Detroit and were uneasy during the trip, and Jack Blackburn made a revolver his constant traveling companion. Even though whites treated the men kindly, promoters would not allow a white boxer to spar with Louis. "The idea of a white man being knocked around by a black man," he reflected, "was more than they could take."[17]

Like the Bilbos in Dixie, Nazis took interracial competition seriously. In the August issue of *Der Weltkampf* (reprinted in *The Crisis*), George Spandau, a German writer, assessed Schmeling's victory over Louis in geopolitical terms. Spandau repeated that Louis had fouled during the fray. Not only had Schmeling won, Spandau observed, but "German honesty [had] conquered brutality and want of discipline." Through Schmeling, "the white race, Europe and white America, defeated the black race." Spandau maintained that "the Negro world considered this fight at the very outset a racial struggle." He now viewed the event the same way. "We know how much the Negro of North America and Africa resents white domination," he admitted, a fact of imperial rule no "white" nation dared ignore. During the Great War, England and France had resorted to the deployment of colonial African troops to subdue Germany, Spandau recollected, a tactic that had made Africans lose "respect and fear for the white race." Echoing the apologists for lynching, Spandau said "the Negro" possessed "a slave nature" and warned that "if this slave nature is unbridled . . . arrogance and cruelty show themselves in the most bestial way." In relying upon African auxiliaries, England and France had "unbridled the Negro," but Schmeling had now reimposed vital psychological restraints. "He checked the arrogance of the Negro and clearly demonstrated to them the superiority of white intelligence," Spandau argued. "He restored the prestige of the white race and in doing so accomplished a cultural achievement." Schmeling had duplicated Mussolini's triumph. "What would have happened if Abyssinia had won?" Spandau queried. "The whole black world would have risen up against the white race in arrogance and bestial cruelty."[18]

Spandau alluded to a primal fear among whites ruling over dark subjects, a feeling reminiscent of the old antebellum masters' obsession with rebellious slaves. Mussolini and Schmeling had served the same purpose as the slave patrols and the Klan. The film of Schmeling's triumph and the pages of Spandau's essay spread the same message as Tom Dixon's novels and D.W. Griffith's *The Birth of a Nation*. In these parables of races at war, civilized whites had no choice but to subdue the dark savages prone to rebellion and rape among them. Writer Paul Gallico discussed the fight with Schmeling, who accused Louis of "deliberate" punches below the belt. Between the early rounds, Schmeling recalled, his trainer Max Machon had blamed Louis's handlers for instructing him to foul to salvage the fight. Under New York rules, Louis could lose a round for fouling but could not be disqualified. As Louis continued to foul, however, Schmeling agreed with his trainer that his opponent was intentionally breaking the rules to buy time to recuperate and rally. "Joe Louis is a good boy, and clean," Schmeling told Gallico, "but he does what he is told in his corner." Gallico also wondered about the low blows, since Louis had previously "seemed as though he could drive his fists through a knot-hole and never touch the sides." But Gallico added that fatigue, not malice, might have made Joe careless. Infuriated by these accusations, Roxborough and Julian Black considered a lawsuit against those behind the article. They did not sue but did deny the charges. They could dismiss racist ranting by Nazi shills in Berlin, but they could not fathom why Schmeling, Gallico, and the *Saturday Evening Post* would suggest they had stooped so low. "Schmeling has lied on Louis, attacked him in the press and magazines, and we are sick and tired of it," Black fumed to Al Monroe, sports editor of the *Defender*. "We will fight him any time . . . and eliminate him from the picture." Louis felt the same way. He blamed Schmeling for taking a cheap shot in the press after having taken one in the ring. "The bell rang ending the fifth," Louis recalled. "Naturally, I dropped both hands the way fighters always do at the bell. But just after I dropped my guard another one of those crashing rights hit me on my jaw. . . . That was the punch that made me mad." The blow nagged Louis for a long time. "In all my fighting I never got a real hate on another fighter," he reminisced years later. "But I didn't like that Schmeling." Long after retiring, Louis claimed he and Max had been friendly rivals whose mutual regard survived the two epic fights of the 1930s. But time had healed some very painful wounds.[19]

Schmeling hoped his win would earn him a shot at champion James

Braddock. But the German reaction to Schmeling's victory angered many Americans. With evidence mounting of the Nazis' persecution of internal "enemies" and their ambitions for a greater Germany, Mike Jacobs hesitated to sign Schmeling for a title fight. Journalists, promoters, and fans feared that Goebbels and his staff would use a German champion as a propaganda weapon for the regime. Schmeling's earning potential as champion would also enrich government coffers in Berlin. Schmeling, sportswriter Dan Parker muttered, "has never pretended to be interested in anything American except our currency." Even if Schmeling wanted to be apolitical, he still had to answer to German leaders. If he won the title, they would never permit him to risk it against Louis.

Jews warned that they would boycott any Schmeling fight in the United States, a threat that split the black press. Chester Washington of the *Courier* understood their concerns. "You can't blame them for not wanting to spend their dollars for Maxie to take back to Germany to help persecute their brothers," he explained. The prospect of a small gate would lead promoters to give "that Nazi man . . . one of the greatest run-arounds" in boxing history. The *Sentinel* had backed a boycott of the Berlin games to protest persecution in Germany. A year later, the *Sentinel* urged that any boycott of Schmeling "ought to be supported by American Negroes." But others opposed such protests. "I'm not pro-Hitler," the *Courier*'s Rollo Wilson objected. "Neither have I any sympathy with the movement which has started to boycott the Braddock-Schmeling fight." To deny the German his due seemed "un-American and indefensible from any viewpoint." Another *Courier* writer agreed. The Nazis "are as opposed to Negroes as they are to Jews," George Schuyler observed, but he doubted that protest against Schmeling would do any good. "Negroes have been the victims of too many boycotts based on prejudice for them to start doing the same thing to others," Schuyler advised. "The best way to fight Hitlerism in Germany is to get rid of Hitlerism in America. The Negro has worse enemies than Schmeling and Hitler in every city and town in the United States."[20]

Joe Gould, Braddock's Jewish manager, entered the fray. "If a boycott is on, I will not let Jimmy into the same ring with Schmeling," Gould announced. "Jim is not going to defend his title for peanuts." Braddock, at thirty, had few lucrative fights left in him, and Gould wanted to make the most of them. While protecting their financial interests, Gould also proved himself the uncrowned champion of chutzpah. In an interview with writer Budd Schulberg, Gould described a particularly memorable conversation at this time. Just about to sit down to dinner, Gould answered the telephone. From Berlin, Max Schmeling asked Gould if he had signed Braddock to fight Louis. Gould said no, but admitted that the parties had talked and were close to an agreement. This news upset Schmeling as well as Goebbels, who was listening in on the line. Schmeling implored Gould to end the talks with promoter Mike Jacobs and the Louis camp. "Max says if we come to Berlin and fight him instead we c'n do even better," Gould reminisced. "I sez for a Jew to bring his champion to Germany and face all them anti-Semites they gotta do a lot better." Schmeling replied that he was calling from Goebbels's home and would put him on the line because the regime was eager to finance the fight. "Just tell 'im what you want."

Schmeling handed over the receiver. "Goebbels is very polite," Gould recalled. "He says the Germans are great sports fans and we will be treated like royalty when we come to Germany." He also wanted them "to meet *Der Fuehrer* himself." Goebbels urged Gould to state his terms. Picturing the two Germans "all smiles on the other end," Gould proceeded:

> Gould: Well, for openers I want three hunnert t'ousand in dollars here in the Chase National Bank before we get on the boat.
>
> Goebbels: Ya, you haf it.
>
> Gould: An' another hunnert thou when we get to Berlin.
>
> Goebbels: Ya, you haf it.
>
> Gould: An' first class travel and hotel accommodations for six people.
>
> Goebbels: Ya, you haf it.
>
> Gould: An' twenty-five thousand trainin' expenses.
>
> Goebbels: Ya, ya, you will haf that also. If you come to Berlin right away we will sign the contract.

Gould took a deep breath. "Only one more clause, Mr. Goebbels," he added. "Before we enter the ring we want every Jew let out of your concentration camps." The line went dead.[21]

Dead too were Schmeling's chances for a title fight against Braddock—in Berlin or the Bronx. Mike Jacobs viewed boxing primarily as a business and he, like Gould and Braddock, realized that the risks of a title fight with Schmeling outweighed any possible rewards. Rather than sign Schmeling and Braddock, Jacobs persuaded Braddock to fight Louis. He offered him a cut of his own future proceeds from Louis's fights if Joe won the title.

Despite the loss to Schmeling, Louis and his handlers believed he could beat Braddock. Joe needed little prodding to prepare for the fight. "There ain't been none of that hi-de-ho stuff" that had distracted Louis before the loss in 1936, trainer Jack Blackburn assured the press. Louis defeated Braddock at Comiskey Park in the heart of Black Chicago on June 22, 1937. Chester Washington of the *Courier* talked with Louis afterward. "How does it feel being champion?" he asked. "I don't feel any different," Louis replied. "But I do want to beat Schmeling." A week later Blackburn told Washington that Louis "wants to beat Schmeling for the sake of all the people who have stuck by him."

Jacobs now hoped to pit Schmeling against Louis, giving him his due and Louis a chance to avenge his only loss. But this match had complications too. Jacobs hesitated "to gamble on the large Jewish population in New York," the *Defender*'s Al Monroe suggested, and he considered a Chicago venue because protest against the first fight "certainly did tell at the box office." Fewer Jews lived in Chicago, and the city had a less vocal anti-Nazi movement. Besides, since Chicago lay "in the thick of German settlements" in the Midwest, Schmeling might draw German Americans from Milwaukee, Kenosha, and St. Louis as well as Chicago and its suburbs. To gauge public sentiment, Jacobs first matched Schmeling against Harry Thomas in New York City. The bout "should have drawn more than $100,000 because of the excellent publicity it received," Jacobs complained. "But the anti-Nazi boycott kept away a lot of fans." He did not want "the same thing happening to the big fight." Harry Thomas then fought Louis in Chicago, but the gate was the smallest for a title fight since Jack Johnson's era. Jacobs gave up on Chicago, even though he remained anxious about the mood in New York City. He decided Louis and Schmeling should return to Yankee Stadium.[22]

The bout loomed large for millions, particularly blacks, Germans, and Jews. Rising tensions abroad increased resentment against Schmeling. Persistent prejudice, lynchings, and lack of progress on civil rights had made Louis an even more significant symbol to his people. Fans of all hues generally did not want Schmeling to board the *Hindenberg* with the crown and a large check in his pocket. "If Schmeling wins the title goes to Germany," Dan Parker of the *New York Daily Mirror* fretted, "and this time, it would remain there for a long spell . . . with Max defending it only in Hitler's domain and against opponents who can pass the test for pure Aryanism, whatever that is." Were Schmeling to prevail, *The Nation* warned, he would become Hitler's director of youth physical education "to make them fit for the next fascist aggression." Fans in droves flooded Louis's training camp. "Spectators crowded the grounds, the trees, and fences that give clear view into the ring," the *Afro-American*'s Levi Jolley noted. "Scores of others observed from the tops of automobiles and nearby buildings, weathering a scorching sun and flies." Louis knew this contest meant more than the first. "Germany was tearing up Europe, and we were hearing more and more about the concentration camps for the Jews," he recollected. "A lot of Americans had family in Europe and they were afraid for their people's lives. Schmeling represented everything that Americans disliked, and they wanted him beat and beat good." When Louis traveled to Washington, Roosevelt invited him to the White House and sent a car for him. "Joe," the president quipped as he squeezed his bicep, "we need muscles like yours to beat Germany."[23]

Mayor La Guardia and Samuel Untermyer of the Anti-Nazi League urged fans not to spend dollars that might end up as deutsche marks. People picketed ticket outlets. To mollify protesters, Jacobs pledged 10 percent of his cut to a fund to assist refugees. Boycott leaders welcomed the gesture but demanded that Schmeling commit at least half his purse to assist those fleeing the Nazis. Only then would they suspend their protest. Demonstrators met Schmeling when he arrived in New York, and others marched against him when he called on Mike Jacobs at his office. Dan Daniel of *Ring* magazine attended a meeting between Jacobs and the dissidents. The delegates urged the promoter to cancel the fight. Jacobs replied that his plan would better serve their purposes. "The Germans insist they have the greatest heavyweight in the world, and that we have been giving him the runaround," Jacobs explained. "Right now, Schmeling is a martyr, even with many boxing fans in this country. Max knocked out Louis, and Germany says he can do it again." He thought otherwise. "I can assure you," Jacobs told them, "that if you desist in your protests Louis will murder him."

Jacobs found it hard to be impartial in 1938. He liked Louis and his handlers and loathed the Nazis. Jacobs goaded Louis during his training, warning that another loss to Schmeling might drive both of them from boxing. "Murder that bum," Jacobs pleaded, "and don't make an asshole out of me." Louis reciprocated "Uncle Mike's" affection and did not want him forced into early retirement. But Louis hardly needed the prodding. He resented Schmeling's charge of intentional fouls and wanted to vindicate his title by beating the only man who had knocked him out. Moreover, Louis found Hitler's stateside quislings repugnant. "Swastikas on their arms," American Nazis watched him train "and sat around laughing like jackasses," Louis recalled. He also heard that Max Machon, Schmeling's trainer, strutted around camp in "a Nazi uniform" spouting that Germans were "a superior race." Dan Parker confirmed that *Herr* Max's camp resembled "a miniature Nazi state." More discreet than Machon, Schmeling still irked Louis and his advisers. "The black dynasty of pugilism must come to an end," Max announced before the fight. "I am going to stop this black domination by regaining the crown."[24]

People expressed strong feelings about the fight, even to complete strangers. On a European tour in 1938, musician Clyde Bernhardt and his fellow members of the Edgar Hayes band found themselves sharing a railroad car with Nazi soldiers who spoke English, liked jazz, and wanted to converse with them. One "very blond" soldier blurted out a prediction. "That Max," he exclaimed, "he going to knock him out in the first round this time. Joe Louis not fight all that good." Trombonist Robert Horton disagreed. "Goddamn, you just wait," Horton snorted as he pointed at the man. "Old Joe get him this time." Bernhardt urged his friend to be calm when *der Soldat* persisted. "Someday we will be in America," the soldier warned. "We going to take your country, and the first thing we will do is send all you *schwarzes* back to Africa." Now Horton was on his feet, shouting that if Hitler attacked the United States he would be stopped "before he even get started." Bernhardt tried to restrain Horton but to no avail. "The only damn way you come to America," Horton yelled, shaking his fist, "will be as a prisoner of war!" This time Bernhardt jerked his sleeve: "You damn fool, keep quiet. You in Germany now. Put the soft pedal on it. Won't take much for them to pull us all off the train and toss us in a concentration camp." The soldier then declared that Americans were soft, lazy, and ill prepared for war. "We will whip the world!" he proclaimed as he sauntered out of the car. No brawl ensued, but Bernhardt was shaken. "There was a lot of military activity going on," he recalled. "Soldiers everywhere—coming, going, marching, lining up." His train passed "long rows of rifles all stacked like corn stalks" and "pretty little towns with dozens of Army trucks just standing around, waiting." The "waiting" would not last much longer.

Amid the anxiety, Louis and his handlers remained serene. Walking along the Harlem River before heading to Yankee Stadium, Blackburn, Louis, and Freddie Wilson, Joe's friend, mulled over the occasion. "How you feel, Joe?" Wilson asked. "I'm scared," Joe answered. "Scared?" Freddie replied. "Yeah," Joe growled. "I'm scared I might kill Schmeling tonight." In the locker room, Blackburn taped Joe's hands. "Keep cool," he advised. "It's going to be alright." Mike Jacobs poked his head in the door. "Joe, I told these folks you're gonna knock that German out," he reminded him. "Don't make a sucker out of me, and make it a quick knockout."[25]

Some 70,000 spectators packed the stadium despite the protest. The German press had virtually ignored Schmeling in 1936 until he won. Now, according to journalist Bob Considine, the German media gave the fight "plenty of publicity." Four correspondents at ringside stood ready to spread the good news to *Deutschland*. A small army of American reporters clambered to their seats. Rollo Wilson of the *Courier* heard "hisses and boos" as Schmeling walked to the ring. As "the friend of Hitler, the playmate of Goebbels . . . a passive exponent of the Jewish purge, Fascism, and the mailed fist," Max now realized "his type had few sympathizers in the crowd." "All hell broke loose," Schmeling recalled, as cigarette packs, cigars, apple cores, paper cups, and banana peels greeted him. The worst was yet to come.

Immediately after the opening bell, Louis took the offensive. "Kill that

Nazi, Joe!" a ringside fan yelled. "Kill him!" Only a minute into the round,
Louis tagged Schmeling with a barrage of hard punches. Schmeling staggered and swayed, unable to ward off the furious attack. "Murder him, Joe!"
a white woman shouted. "Let him have it on the kisser!" Louis complied,
striking Schmeling several times. "Hit 'im again," another fan screamed.
"Give 'im one to take back to his boss!" As Schmeling slumped to the canvas, Tallulah Bankhead leaped up and glared at several members of the German-American *Bund*, a group of Nazi sympathizers, sitting nearby. "I told
you so!" she chortled. "You sons-of-bitches!" Louis knocked out Schmeling
at 2:04 in the first round, the shortest heavyweight title match up to that time.
Frank Young, sports editor of the *Defender*, had predicted that Louis would
demolish Schmeling and German newspapers would lie about it. As Louis
fulfilled the prophecy, Young felt relief and elation. "I did a war dance," he
admitted. "I yelled some more. It is two days later and I am still hoarse."
Louis heard that the German wire service had stopped the broadcast of the
fight to Berlin. "They didn't want the German people to know," Louis wrote,
that "a Negro was getting the best of a fight with a superman." At his press
conference, he mentioned nationalism and the title. "I just couldn't let that
crown get out of this country, and I aim to keep it here for many years," he
promised. "It wasn't just Joe Louis . . . against Max Schmeling. It was international, like the Olympic games." He looked back on this moment as "the
top" of his career. "I had the championship, and I had beaten the man who
had humiliated me," Louis reflected. "America was proud of me, my people
were proud of me, and . . . race relations were lightening up."[26]

Enemies on Many Fronts: Racism, Nationalism, and World War II

Louis exaggerated the progress in race relations but accurately conveyed
how Americans felt about his triumph. German propagandists had defined
Schmeling's earlier win as proof of biological and cultural superiority; now
Americans had to interpret just what Louis's victory meant. The fight had
posed a dilemma for whites who combined prejudice with their patriotism,
for they had to choose between common race and common nationality. Did
they want a white German to hold the title, or a dark American who shared
their flag but not their race? Sportswriter Dan Parker scolded fellow whites
for putting color before country. "That a colored boy can get to the top of his
profession in America is a much better advertisement for Joe's country than
that a Jewish lawyer or doctor can't even practice his profession in Germany
is for Max's native land," Parker argued. "Of course, it isn't fair to blame
Hitler on Schmeling. But quite blameworthy . . . are those Americans who

are rooting for Max to bring the title to Germany!" Royce Brier of the *San Francisco Chronicle* saw Louis's triumph as a salutary lesson to fascists. "Nazi philosophy is founded upon racial pride," Brier observed, "and this pride has reached such explosive force that it has become a world scandal in its anti-Semitic phase, and blows up time and again at the slightest jostle from a 'non-Aryan.'" Louis had hurt Nazi pride, Brier noted, so Germans would vent their anger with "the moody conviction that Schmeling betrayed his race."

To writer Heywood Broun, the Louis win gave "the tiniest hint that the Nazi bark is more than the Nazi bite." Louis had "exploded the Nordic myth with a boxing glove." The *Birmingham News* boasted that Louis had "knock[ed] Max back into Hitler's lap." Louis not only "knocked out Max Schmeling," *The Nation* bragged, but "Adolf Hitler, [Nazi propagandist] Julius Streicher, Benito Mussolini, and Jim Crow as well." Russell Baker, the future *New York Times* columnist, listened to the fight on the radio in his Baltimore boyhood home and knew the blacks across the alley were listening too. "Louis . . . appraised Schmeling the way a butcher eyes a side of beef," Baker recalled, "then punched him senseless." Blacks hit the streets in "the first civil rights demonstration" Baker had seen, a "completely spontaneous" act "ignited by the finality with which Joe Louis had destroyed the theory of white supremacy."[27]

Black Americans saw even greater significance in the event. When Louis triumphed, the Reverend Ralph Abernathy recalled, blacks "crowded around their radios shouting, cheering, and then laughing at Hitler and the Nazis." To Roy Wilkins of the NAACP, the knockout was "the shortest, sweetest minute" of a difficult decade. Louis "is a Negro," the *Philadelphia Tribune* boasted, "but he was fighting for America." Americans "both black and white" depended on Louis "to keep the title away from Nazi Germany," the *Sentinel*'s Harry Levette noted. "And he did the miraculous, ending it all in less than a round." When the opening bell rang, "never before in American history were so many black voices silent," Frank Marshall Davis of the *Atlanta World* observed. "It was more than the victory of one athlete over another, it was the triumph of a repressed people against the evil forces of racial oppression and discrimination condensed—by chance—into the shape of Max Schmeling." Louis "smashed into smithereens the false prophets of racial inequality," the *Defender*'s James Reid wrote, making him "a servant of his race." Dan Daniel of *Ring* magazine thought Louis had washed away "the scarred marks of the shackle" and transformed "a subservient attitude into one steeled with a belief in equality." In Philadelphia, Jews also "had their fingers crossed" that Louis would "blast the Nazi," the *Tribune*'s Kent Jackson reported. Jews and blacks comprised "a united front" for Joe. The

Defender's Frank Young believed "every Jew in New York was solidly behind Joe Louis," hoping he would prove that "Hitler could rule Germany, but not America." One particular Jew savored vindication. "Thrills?" Mike Jacobs mused. "I never will forget how Louis belted Schmeling almost to death in one round, and took me off the hook with those people who had protested against letting the German fight in New York."[28]

After the first fight, Louis had accepted defeat graciously. "I forgot to duck," he joked to reporters. He told Wendell Smith of the *Courier* that Schmeling had beaten him "fair and square." To trainer Max Machon and Schmeling, however, Louis's win this time was neither fair nor square. Trying to evade Joe's flurry of punishing blows, Max had leaned on the ropes and turned away. Louis hit his kidney area with a solid right, and Schmeling wound up at a city hospital where x-rays revealed fractured vertebrae. However painful the injury, the punch that caused it was not a foul. Many blows had weakened Schmeling before the hard right to the back. But some Germans blamed the loss on a sneaky kidney punch. "Only a graduate of one of Hitler's universities," Arthur Fauset, a black folklorist, joked, "could explain how the Teutonic kidney could float up to where the jaw should be!" The "ballyhoo" was "an alibi to take back to Germany," the *Defender's* Al Monroe argued, so Aryan supremacy would be spared "an international flop." A German language newspaper in New York City echoed the charge of foul play by alleging a Semitic conspiracy. "A Jewish monopoly" ran American boxing, the paper maintained, and Jews controlled "nearly all other public institutions . . . at least in New York." Promoters and press alike had decided the title "was never to be allowed to go to Germany." "Politics" and "prejudice," not fair play, had "determined the result."[29]

Not content to rely on charges of cheating, Machon resorted to blatant fraud to excuse the loss. With deft use of scissors and tape, he fabricated a fantasy film of the recent bout. Machon lifted several feet of film from the 1936 contest that showed Schmeling firmly in command. Besides splicing in earlier film, Machon deleted footage from the second, cutting scores of frames in which Louis pummeled Schmeling and weakened him for the knockout. In Machon's fanciful rendition of the rematch, the only solid punch Louis threw hit Schmeling in the lower back and crumpled him to the mat. Some sixty feet of film remained frozen on this scene as the narrator explained the treachery that had doomed Schmeling.[30]

Whatever the technical flaws of Machon's splicing, Germans exposed to a steady litany of racist and ethnocentric harangues were predisposed to accept his version. In texts such as Hitler's *Mein Kampf*, Goebbels's *"Die verflüchten Hakenkreuzler"* [The Damned Nazis]; and Professor Hermann Gauch's *Neue Grundlagen der Rassenforschung* [New Frontiers of Racial

Research], Nazis had forged a racist ideology exalting a resurgent Germany and its superior "Nordics" and relegating Jews, Gypsies, Africans, Asians, and mixed "races" to an inferior status and an inevitable demise. These texts blamed "the Jewish peril" for Germany's problems. "The Jew is the ferment of the decomposition of people," Hitler wrote. "It is in the nature of the Jew to destroy, and he must destroy, because he lacks altogether any idea of working for the common good." Jews believed in racial equality, Hitler stated in *Mein Kampf*, a delusion that imperiled western civilization. The African, he countered, was "born half ape." Goebbels also lashed the Jews. "He takes on the mask of those whom he wants to deceive, pretends to be the friend of his victim, and before the unfortunate one knows it, he has his neck broken," Goebbels warned. "The Jew is uncreative. He does not produce anything. . . . Who ever saw a Jew work and not plunder, steal, sponge [*schmarotzen*] and live from the sweat of the other man's brow? . . . THE JEW IS OUR GREAT-EST CALAMITY." Hermann Gauch assigned humans to two groups—superior Nordics and inferior others. "If non-Nordics are more closely allied to monkeys and apes than to Nordics, why is it possible for them to mate with Nordics and not with apes?" he pondered. "The answer is this: it has not been proved that non-Nordics cannot mate with apes." With Jews stigmatized as the main "peril" and "calamity" plaguing "Nordics," no great leap of imagination was needed to blame Jews everywhere for plotting against Germany. So promoter Mike Jacobs and manager Joe Gould had schemed to deny Schmeling a chance to win the crown jewel of sports. The Jewish media had demonized Schmeling. Nazi leaders, of course, soon learned that Louis had clobbered Schmeling and the punch to the back was incidental to the outcome. After Goebbels watched the actual film, he realized his duty to his government and its people: *"Dann Filme geprüft: Schmelings Boxkampf. Er Wird dabei furchtbar zusammengeschlagen. Nicht aufführbar."* [I scrutinized the films of the Schmeling fight. He was terribly beaten. The films must not be shown.][31]

Machon's film flam outraged Louis's handlers and the black press. John Roxborough cabled the American ambassador in Berlin to protest the "deleted, cut, and combined" film of the fight. German fans deserved "the truth," Roxborough insisted. "They are not getting it with . . . this patched-up picture." The real film "would be humiliating to German pride," the *Afro-American* observed. "Hitler . . . can't account for the fact that Joe Louis beat the pride of the German race into submission in two minutes." Louis resented the deception. "The movies show I didn't foul," he noted, "but they didn't show those fight movies in Germany."[32]

Blacks and those whites committed to civil rights realized that Hitler's snub of Jesse Owens and Machon's film caper revealed a Nazi malady likely to turn global and deadly. Much of what the Nazis said about race and culture expressed in extreme form biases common among white Americans. Some Americans admired the Nazis and shared their anti-Semitism and Negrophobia. The German-American *Bund*, for example, attracted zealots with biases typical of Klansmen and Coughlinites, the anti-Semitic, anti-New Deal followers of radio priest Charles Coughlin. The *Klansman's Manual* of 1925, for example, had instructed Klan members to "maintain forever the God-given supremacy of the white race" and avoid "the polluting of Caucasian blood through miscegenation." The words could well have been Hermann Gauch's.

Blacks found Nazi beliefs and practices reprehensible but initially insisted that their chief enemies lived in Dixie, not *Deutschland*. As Germany augmented its military power and increasingly menaced its neighbors, however, many black observers realized their nation might soon face a war unlike any other. In addition, Asia appeared poised for a major upheaval as Japan set out to dominate or destroy those who resisted its hegemony. The United States stood fast in Hawaii and the Philippines. With growing perils abroad, Uncle Sam continued to face sharp racial divisions at home and a lingering depression that left little revenue for increases in military spending. The house divided against itself might not stand.

A *Philadelphia Tribune* editorial in 1937 argued that the Japanese marauders guilty of the "rape" of Nanjing regarded the Chinese much as southern whites viewed blacks. "The only difference between the Japanese murdering defenseless Chinese and the lynching of Negroes by their fellow Americans is one of degree," the *Tribune* maintained. The Japanese engaged in "wholesale slaughter" while Americans "pick their victims off one at a time." The *Tribune* hoped that the indignation over German and Japanese persecution of weaker peoples might make Americans "stop and think" about their own prejudices. Arthur Fauset denied that the world had gone "mad" with the rise of fascism. "Thanks to Mussolini and Hitler the world is just beginning to get some common sense," he wrote after Louis beat Schmeling. "The old Southern adage that 'the worst white man is better than the best black man' is being exploded." Like European Jews, blacks in the United States were "segregated, humiliated, and terrorized," Roy Wilkins of the NAACP observed, and he urged Americans to desist from "Hitlerism on every side directed against citizens who happen not to be white." The *Courier's* George Schuyler ridiculed self-righteous southerners who denounced Nazis for persecuting Jews but defended lynchers for killing blacks. Nor could he countenance calls for sacrifice in the name of assisting Great Britain and France, colonial empires with millions of dark subjects. "I am much too selfish to love those who mistreat me and mine," he confessed in 1940, "and too little of a hypocrite to pretend that I do." Lofty ideals simply vanished along the color line. "I could never forget that black people everywhere were pariahs in the land they had helped build," Schuyler lamented. "Behind the Declaration of Independence I saw ravished black women and families parted at the slave block. Through the noble Constitution, I spied the endless ranks of the disfranchised and disinherited. Above the sound of the Star Spangled Banner I could always hear the yell of the mob victims."[33]

When Germany invaded Poland in the fall of 1939, Britain and France declared war and sought assistance from the United States. Leaders in London and Paris justified intervention by noting their antiaggression pact with Poland. But these officials also depicted their nations as bulwarks of freedom. African Americans wondered. Britain and France had enlisted African subjects in the previous war but had retained their colonies despite Woodrow Wilson's call for self-determination. Now the rhetoric about liberty reappeared as imperial leaders exhorted subjects to rally behind the home governments. This hypocrisy angered George Padmore, an expert on Africa. "What do black folks know about democracy?" he asked. "There is as much democracy for Negroes in Mississippi as in Africa, especially in . . . Kenya, the Congo, Rhodesia and South Africa. The natives have as much liberty and freedom in their own countries as the Jews enjoy in Hitler's Germany." Whites showed incredible "impudence" in asking Africans "to line up with their slave masters as they did in 1914-1918." Wary of the imperial line, Roy Wilkins backed Mohandas Gandhi's demand that Britain grant concessions to Colonial India in return for his support of British foreign policy. (Gandhi used passive resistance to agitate for a free, united India.) "The time to drive a bargain," Wilkins agreed, "is when the other party needs aid, not when he has won his point."

When the war began, blacks were "politically disinherited, economically exploited, socially ostracized, [and] educationally underprivileged," the Reverend Adam Clayton Powell Jr. noted. If they were to furnish labor and lives to the cause, they would do so "determined to make the world safe for democracy and doubly determined to make America safe as well." On a tour to study southern life, scholar J. Saunders Redding discussed the war with local blacks in Memphis. "These niggers don't want to go to no army!" one man told Redding. "An' I don't blame 'em neither. Damn it, there ain't no point!" What had "Uncle" given blacks in 1918 when the fighting stopped? "The same old crap, all the time the same old crap." At Alcorn College, Redding met students Willie and Ike Midgett, whose father was the largest black landowner in Mississippi. "This war is li'ble to open up things for the colored," one son predicted. "It's a got-dawg shame," the other added, "it takes a war to do it."

As Redding toured a South redolent of bullwhip days, American politicians, among them southerners who had filibustered federal antilynching legislation, grew increasingly nervous about the violence engulfing Europe. They expressed hope for a quick end to the war and restoration of free governments there. At the same time, however, southern Democrats continued to oppose any advances in civil rights. "The hysterical cries" for democracy in Europe "leave us cold," Roy Wilkins protested. "We want democracy in Alabama and Arkansas, in Mississippi and Michigan, in the District of Columbia—**in the Senate of the United States**."[34]

Harsh colonial rule in Africa and Asia and persistent prejudice in the United States and Europe complicated the diplomatic picture for African Americans. Past experience led them to weigh carefully the relative risks of new threats abroad and chronic perils at home. They also reflected upon black sacrifices in previous wars and wondered if yet another would help vanquish the enemy within. Whether for or against committing Americans to combat overseas, black activists expected major domestic reforms to follow any costly intervention abroad. By repeatedly drawing parallels between Nazi policies and American practices, black observers insisted that only a nation and a people at peace with themselves could successfully wage a war against fanatical enemies abroad.

Ralph Matthews of the *Afro-American* advised his readers as early as 1938 to watch Europe closely. "Hitler is most definitely our business," he argued, "because any individual who becomes a world menace on a doctrine of racial prejudice, bigotry, and oppression of minorities—and rises to power through threat of force—is our concern." Though disgusted by Nazi doctrine and practice, Matthews did not lose sight of the marginalized at home. He advised Martin Dies of Texas, chair of the House Committee on Un-American Activities, for example, to leave unions and New Deal agencies alone and instead investigate bigots who defied the Constitution in his own state. "Excluding colored taxpayers from . . . primary elections in Texas" was clearly an "un-American activity," as was denying them "social, civic and economic rights because of color," Matthews protested. So were "lynching, exclusion from jury service [and] jim crow . . . un-American activities." He hoped the House Committee and other federal agencies would compel the South to provide "the equal protection of the laws" promised by the Fourteenth Amendment.

The *Courier* also had doubts about Dies. "The worst menaces to Americanism are not Fascism, Nazism, and Communism," an editorial asserted in 1938, but rather "Negrophobism." Dies and others should worry less about subversion and instead make the Fourteenth Amendment "more than a scrap of paper." Fascism had existed "for centuries" for most blacks, the *Courier* objected, so Americans should destroy the domestic strain and worry less about European imports. The *Defender* raised similar objections, accusing Dies of "hiding behind the cloak of Congress" to carry out a reactionary agenda. "If given enough time, money, and latitude," the *Defender* warned, Dies would make his committee "a Fascist agency, capable of aping all the sadistic practices and antiracialisms of Hitler and Mussolini." Later that year, the *Defender* repeated that "what is happening in Germany may yet happen here." Dies hid behind his committee and wasted federal funds "to better persecute the New Deal and its friends, and advance his own political cause." The *Defender* urged Dies to look into the Klan, the Silver Shirts, and the *Volksbund*, groups that defied the law and were truly "un-American" in their beliefs and practices. Sympathetic toward wage workers, sharecroppers, and reformers, many black observers feared that Dies and his ilk intended to defeat all who challenged the status quo—labor organizers, unionists, and advocates of civil rights, world peace, and intellectual freedom. Americans should have heeded these warnings, for the broad cloak of anticommunism could cover many reactionary ends. "I was repeatedly referred to as being a Communist or a fellow traveler," President Benjamin Mays of Morehouse College recalled. "How else could a self-righteous white South explain my opposition to segregation and the exploitation of the Negro?" One blunt editor urged the House to abolish the committee. "The Dies Committee," L.D. Williams wrote, "should be permitted to do just that."[35]

The Nazis officially declared Jews a menace and enacted laws to proscribe them and then policies to eliminate them. The Roosevelt administration and Congress did not actively oppress or persecute blacks, but all branches of the federal government sanctioned prejudice in their own domains and largely ignored it elsewhere. Federal officials, for example, acquiesced in virtual apartheid in the nation's capital, the so-called arsenal of democracy. Blacks "are barred from almost all public places of recreation and accommodation, and some colored artist or tourist is constantly being insulted by . . . jim crow regulations," the *Courier* complained in 1939. "If there is any place in the country where a strong civil rights law could and should be operative, it is in the District of Columbia, and yet Congress permits inequality to flourish and no president, at least in recent years, has ever voiced one word of criticism." District police had a reputation for abusing local blacks and visitors. In the shadow of the Capitol blacks lived in decrepit housing, sent children to poor schools, and earned low wages if they could find work at all.

As Europe plunged into war, the *Courier* retained its domestic focus. "Our immediate concern," the *Courier* advised, "should be the war in which we ourselves are engaged and have been engaged for some time." Blacks should pursue their own goals and ignore the whites' hollow claims to advanced civilization. "Europe . . . is slowly committing suicide," the *Courier* suggested, "and yet the Europeans consider themselves superior to all other peoples." When Roosevelt called for a major increase in military spending in 1940, the *Courier* pointedly reminded him that the armed forces remained segregated and minorities still lacked security at home. Roosevelt eloquently denounced "race prejudice and persecution abroad" but did "not even whisper" about bigotry where he could actually resist it. The *Courier* remained ambivalent. "Negroes could more wholeheartedly applaud this great expenditure of tax money to get ready to fight Nazism," an editorial explained, "if the policies of the United States government were not so similar to those of *Herr* Hitler where we are concerned."

George Schuyler, an iconoclastic *Courier* columnist, labeled the allies "democ(k)racies" because their actual practices belied their professions of benevolence. "There isn't enough idealism involved to jam under a gnat's finger nail," he protested. "The beds of French railroads and highways in Africa are paved with the bones of hapless Negroes, as even French writers admit." The British record was no better. "Let England, the mother of race prejudice, and America, its father, fight the Nazi Negrophobes without our aid," he advised. "If we have any spare dollars to help anybody, let us aid our landless, voteless, and jobless black millions, and not help pull England's chestnuts out of the fire." Schuyler hoped the imperial powers would bleed each other dry, for only then would their subjects gain autonomy or advantages from their overlords. The war should remain a white man's fight. "Our war," he explained, "is . . . against the dominant American spirit of Bilboism." President Wilson had fooled blacks in 1917, but President Roosevelt should not be allowed to do so now. That war had not changed whites; neither would this one. "Colored folk cannot defend democracy because they have none to defend," Schuyler argued. "No people confined to ghettoes, barred from the ballot, forbidden by law or custom from free association with other citizens and kept on the economic fringes by industrial discrimination can claim that they are enjoying democracy."[36]

The legacy of colonialism and racism made *Courier* writers suspicious of the belligerents' real objectives, a skepticism that annoyed interventionists. After Japan attacked Pearl Harbor, Roosevelt warned Walter White of the NAACP that some powerful players in Washington were pressuring him and the Justice Department to indict some black editors for "sedition" and "interference with the war effort." Roosevelt did not specify which papers had aroused their ire, but the *Courier* was undoubtedly at the top of the list.[37]

Other black publications also premised their support for American policy on progress in civil rights. "The black people of today, no less than those of 1860 and 1917, stand ready to defend America," the *Defender* declared. But they expected "progressive and democratic people" to stand with them. The

Defender pitied the Poles who faced the onslaught by the *Wehrmacht* but reminded readers that their "stake in this war" was the same one they "did not get out of the war to end wars." Roy Wilkins thought blacks were "not very enthusiastic about going to war" because the federal government had not met its obligations in regard to "lynchings" and "denial of the ballot . . . decent education . . . employment" and "exploitation on plantations." "Negroes find when they do prepare to serve their country," he added, "that most branches of the army and the entire navy (except work as mess attendants) are closed to them." As the nation prepared for war, the high command indicated it would retain segregation in the armed forces, a further insult to African Americans.[38]

World War II

Blacks already in the military faced outrages similar to those among their civilian kin. The body of Private Felix Hall was found hanging from a tree within the confines of Fort Benning in 1941. "America is marching to war for the purpose of stopping brutalities overseas," Roy Wilkins observed, "but apparently our government does not choose to stop lynching within its own borders, or even within the borders of its army camps, which are wholly under its jurisdiction." After Pearl Harbor, Wilkins proclaimed that blacks would "fight for a world" free of "lynching, brutality, terror, humiliation . . . segregation and discrimination . . . either here or there." He later reiterated that pledge. "This is their native country," he vowed, "and they are going to defend it."

In Dallas a rash of bombings and beatings convinced the *Express* staff that the nation was too divided to vanquish an external foe. "A wave of prejudice and discrimination . . . is sweeping the entire nation," editor Lawrence Brockenbury warned before Pearl Harbor. "Negroes are being brutalized by city police, by the sheriffs of counties, and even our soldiers wearing Uncle Sam's uniform find that the military police are filled with hatred toward them." The "war within" required immediate action. "America must do some housecleaning at home," Brockenbury advised, "before she too busily engages herself in such a task abroad." When Congress declared war, the *Express* proclaimed that "Negroes will fight and be loyal," but added that they wanted voting rights, an end to police brutality, "the right to work freely and on equal terms," equitable funding for "decent schools," and "opportunities for training in civilian and military defense."[39]

While some blacks linked their support to better race relations, others pledged unconditional allegiance—among them the heavyweight champion. "Every colored man I've ever known has been 100 per cent American and

I'll always be loyal to my country and to my race," Louis told Chester Washington. "I'd never let either down." Louis thought he could best help his people by serving without conditions, and he expected others to do the same. "All my people stick by America," he declared. "Even in the South where they are pretty tough on my race sometimes, they're still loyal to America. They respect the Federal government and its flag and they have always been willing to fight for Uncle Sam just like they did in the last war." Having been allowed to compete for the title, Louis felt obliged to the nation. "I knew I'd be glad to help defend America," he explained. "No place else in the world could a onetime black cotton picker like me get to be a millionaire. I love this country like I love my people." He registered for the draft.

Mary McLeod Bethune, an aid to Roosevelt and president of the National Council of Negro Women, waved the flag with the same fervor. "For America, it must be all-out or it is all over," she stated prior to Pearl Harbor. "In spite of the discrimination against Negroes in America, we feel that the fight against fascism is our fight, too." After Congress declared war, Bethune insisted that blacks would "stand straight up without reservations" for the cause. "No blood more red, more loyal penetrates the veins of mankind than that which flows through the body of the Negro," she exclaimed. "America can depend upon us." Bethune drew upon the past to define the stakes in the present. "Victory must be ours," she concluded, "or worse than slavery will be."[40]

Louis answered the call in other ways. A month before Pearl Harbor, promoter Mike Jacobs asked him to consider a title fight to benefit Navy Relief, a civilian agency that assisted dependents of navy personnel killed or disabled in service. Not only would Louis risk his crown, he would donate his own proceeds to the cause. Louis agreed and signed to fight Buddy Baer. Blacks split on whether Louis should give either direct or indirect aid to the jim-crow navy. The *Afro-American*'s Art Carter reported that many fans preferred he not assist "an institution which daily discriminates against Joe's colored brethren in its branch services and in its training centers." An *Afro-American* editorial grumbled that Louis was supporting a fund linked to a service branch that relegated black men to positions as "cooks, waiters, and flunkies." The *Courier*'s Randy Dixon saw Louis's gesture as tantamount to the NAACP "donating half of the funds it collects to the Ku Klux Klan." Dan Burley, a *Star News* correspondent, complained that black sailors shined white officers' shoes, made their beds, and cooked and served their meals, enduring "vile discrimination and abuse" daily. Besides, the Naval Academy refused to compete against college football teams with black players. Burley thought Louis "dead wrong" in aiding a relief fund associated with the navy, a branch of service "against him, against us, and against everything we hope to do." At the very least, Burley added, Louis should have wrung some concessions from the War Department. From Camp Claiborne in Louisiana, Private James Reid advised Louis to fight a benefit for the NAACP instead.[41]

But others expected Louis's generosity to spur changes in the navy. Mike Jacobs defended the bout, just as he had justified the Louis-Schmeling fight. "I am just as much against racial discrimination as anyone in America," he insisted. "I deplore it and have constantly worked to improve interracial relations ever since I started to promote fights." He predicted Louis would earn "the gratitude of the nation and the warm goodwill of every man in our uniform" by fighting for the relief fund. Jacobs reminded the press that three black seamen had just died in a German submarine attack on the *Reuben James*. He urged fans to attend the benefit fight on January 9. A large mixed crowd would be "the kind of demonstration which Hitler most fears."

Still wary of the bout, the *Afro-American* hoped Louis's gesture would "dramatize . . . navy's jim crow." The *Courier* staff was split; some columnists opposed the match but a November 22 editorial endorsed it. "Rigid and exasperating discrimination," especially the exclusion of blacks from the Marines, was inexcusable, the editorial conceded. But in "one grand and dramatic gesture" Louis would shine "the white light of justice on the forces of racial hate and prejudice" in the navy and expose its "meanness." Mean it was. J. Earle Mason, a former sailor, compared the black seaman to "an indentured servant" and noted the dismal retention rate. "Most Negroes find," he observed, "that four years in the navy is much too much for them." Only 1 percent reenlisted. But the turn of events validated Louis's decision. Not long after the contract was signed, Japanese pilots attacked Pearl Harbor. The horrible loss of sailors and ships reconciled many critics to the relief fight, for seamen of all hues perished on December 7. Black journalists still objected to bias in the armed forces, but they tempered their criticism with calls for unity to punish the aggressors and avenge the losses. "Joe Louis cannot now turn his back to the United States Navy," Wendell Smith wrote on December 13. "Louis has an obligation to the Navy, just as the Navy has an obligation to the people of this nation." Randy Dixon changed his mind and backed the bout. Art Carter explained that race fans had objected because of the navy's "persistent bar" against them. But Louis had shamed the high command and emerged "without question . . . the country's most unselfish patriot." Bob Gregory of the *Dallas Express* agreed, calling Louis "a grand patriot."

The initial criticism disturbed the entourage. Manager John Roxborough argued that Louis would have appeared "un-American" had he said no. Art Carter asked Louis to reveal his ring strategy for the fight. "I'm fighting for nothing," he replied, "so I don't expect to fight long." Ever conscious of his image, however, Louis used different words a week later so no one would misconstrue his point about "fighting for nothing." "This is a country that's been good to me," he told Carter. "It's worth fighting for." Fred Guinyard, the champion's good friend and secretary, informed Carter that seventy percent of Louis's mail supported him. Writers later downplayed the initial disagreement and stressed the champion's loyalty. Roi Ottley of the *Amsterdam News* quoted Louis as having said, "I'm not fighting for nothing. I'm fighting for my country."[42]

Louis and Baer fought in a flag-draped Madison Square Garden on January 9, 1942. Before the bell Wendell Willkie, the Republican presidential candidate in 1940, addressed the crowd. "How, in view of such a magnificent example of generosity," he asked in referring to Louis, a black Baptist, and Baer, a white Jew, "can there be any discrimination on the grounds of race, color, or religion?" Louis thought Willkie gave "a great speech." Willkie's remarks must have seemed longer to fans than the fight itself. With 2:54 expired in round one, the referee stopped it because Louis had already smashed Baer to the canvas twice. (Baer later quipped that he felt no shame in the short bout. Fans had paid to see a fight, not an execution.) By winning quickly, Louis kept a promise to Jack Blackburn, who had said that severe rheumatism and arthritis would prevent his climbing into the ring. "You got to," Joe pleaded. "If you get up those stairs with me, I'll have Baer out before you can relax." The ailing trainer consented and made the painful ascent just once.

Louis gave $49,000 to Navy Relief, Jacobs added $37,000, and Baer pitched in $4,000. Three days after the fight, Louis, dressed in red tie, white shirt, and blue suit, reported for induction at Camp Upton, New York. The army made the most of it. Photographers snapped pictures and reporters asked leading questions. "I wanted to go in quiet, like all the other boys," Louis later explained, "but Army Public Relations said it was good for morale to let them write all about me going in the service." Louis did not disappoint. "I used to do my fighting for Uncle Mike Jacobs," he announced. "Now I'll do my fighting for Uncle Sam." Louis mulled over the nation's prospects in East Asia. "Them Japs is all lightweights," he gibed. "They don't have any heavyweights." The *Courier's* James Boyack asked Louis afterward about jim crow in the navy. "I sure hope our boys will get their opportunity in the Navy equal with the other boys," Louis answered. "I think we deserve the chance because our country is united now, and those Jap bullets don't have any prejudice in 'em. Those shells never stop to ask whether you're white or colored." He hoped the war would "put an end to all this foolish discrimination." Before reporting for basic training, Louis was a guest on Eddie Cantor's radio show. "Did you see the motion pictures of the fight?" Louis asked. "With Buddy Baer?" Cantor joked. "Joe, that's a snapshot!" Louis had defeated Buddy's brother Max in 1935. "Yes, sir," Louis grinned, "I took care of the Baers—I'm going after the snakes!"

The charity bout and the induction transformed Louis into a symbol of color-blind patriotism. "Each time Joe Louis struck Baer," the *Afro-American* contended, "he also struck Navy Jim Crow." At a dinner in New York City, former mayor Jimmy Walker hailed Louis. "You took all your personal and business assets, your present and your future," Walker marveled, "and you bet them all on patriotism and love of country." And Americans would do well, Walker added, to mimic Joe's style in waging the war—"more punching and less gab!" Columnist and friend Billy Rowe called Louis "the most outstanding symbol of colored America which . . . has fought to make the world safe for a democracy he has never known." Louis "inspired the imagination of both the humble and mighty" to a greater degree "than any Negro in history," the *Courier*'s Wendell Smith stated. He "tugged at the heartstrings of the ruling whites with greater effect than any of the others." His sacrifices guaranteed his name would "go down in history in capital letters."[43]

Besides joining the army, Louis pitched and purchased war bonds along with other celebrities. The black press ran ads with two images of him—he wore boxing trunks in one and appeared in army uniform on horseback in the other. The text read: HELP KO THE AXIS! INVEST 10% OF YOUR INCOME IN WAR BONDS. Louis signed to fight Abe Simon in a benefit for Army Relief, the counterpart of the navy fund. Louis bought $3,000 worth of tickets for the fight and distributed them to poor black soldiers. Two weeks before the event, Louis attended a bond rally in Madison Square Garden. Master of ceremonies Walter Winchell, a syndicated columnist, praised him for his efforts and the crowd clamored for him to speak. "I'm really happy that I'm able enough to do what I'm doin', what I have done, and what I'm going to do," Louis responded. "I'm only doing what any redblooded American would. We're all goin' to do our part and we'll win 'cause God is on our side."

The remarks made quite an impression, inspiring Carl Byoir, a public relations expert, to write the poem, "Joe Louis Named the War." Louis spoke truly, Byoir noted, for "freedom" was "part of God's plan" and Americans aimed "to fight through to glorious victory / On God's side / In God's War." Past patriots had declared that the United States fought on God's side, Byoir added, but Louis had come closer to the truth by saying God actually favored the stars and stripes. President Roosevelt, Louis recalled, sent his compliments on the speech. Billy Rowe, Joe's friend and a *Courier* columnist, however, maintained that a nervous Louis had actually muffed his lines. He had intended to repeat the refrain that Americans fought on God's side but had inverted the terms. If he erred, the slip was fortunate because the remark added luster to his legend.

In the second relief bout, Louis knocked out Simon to retain his title. He and Mike Jacobs donated $75,000 to Army Relief. As Louis trained for the fight, composer Irving Berlin made plans to transform the Broadway hit *This Is the Army* into a feature film. Louis and a veritable regiment of soldiers appeared with actor Ronald Reagan in the movie. In his cameo, the champion predicted that the United States would triumph "'cuz we're on God's side." He also punched the overhead bag in rhythm to a rousing song and dance number. The curtain closed with Louis at attention in uniform, saluting, at center stage.[44]

The government found other uses for Louis. The Office of War Information (OWI) released a recruiting poster featuring him in army khaki, bayonet drawn, with the celebrated line from the bond rally. In 1943 Chandler Owen of the OWI authored *Negroes and the War*, a pamphlet designed to convince blacks that the war abroad was their war too. Owen argued that the New Deal had been a boon to African Americans. As proof, he included a panorama of the Ida B. Wells housing project in Chicago. Seeking money and men from black neighborhoods, Owen argued that the nation had recently made great strides in race relations and would continue to advance if victorious in the war. "Germany backed up Mussolini in the rape of Ethiopia," Owen wrote, and Hitler might make the United States the next Poland, with black workers "turned into slaves or turned into the street." Nazis would repress or expunge the black press, the churches, fraternal orders, and artists. "Race prejudice, from the first," Owen argued, "has been Hitler's stock in trade." If Germany prevailed, "Bill Robinson's dancing feet would be heard no more."

Owen stressed notable contributions already made by blacks. Dorie Miller, a messmate from Texas, had fired antiaircraft guns at Japanese planes bombing Pearl Harbor. He had risked his life to help drag a wounded white officer to safety. "Some Americans say that it makes no difference who wins the war," Owen observed. "Dorie Miller doesn't say that. Joe Louis doesn't say that." A snapshot showed a black woman stitching a parachute for "our intrepid combat fliers." Eddie "Rochester" Anderson, the "Negro radio star," owned the factory. Other photographs featured many black service men, including air cadets training at Tuskegee, a statue of Booker T. Washington shadowing them.

Also pictured were Jesse Owens, trumpeter Louis Armstrong, pitcher Satchel Paige, and Joe Louis, rifle and bayonet poised, reminding Americans how to knock out foreign foes. "One cool summer night in 1938 . . . our champion knocked out the German champion in one round," the text noted. "Sergeant Joe Louis is now a champion in an army of champions. Joe Louis doesn't talk much, but he talks truly." He spoke for all Americans when he proclaimed the United States would win "'cause we're on God's side."[45]

Owen quoted Louis correctly but oversimplified how blacks felt about the war. The *Afro-American* praised Owen for "a masterful job in editing" a "beautifully illustrated" pamphlet. However, noting that the OWI planned to circulate it widely, the *Afro-American* still doubted that Owen could move the masses because "100 million propaganda pamphlets" could not "undo the harm that Congress heaps up by filibustering against poll tax repeal and anti-lynching bills." As *Negroes and the War* began to circulate, Roy Wilkins scolded the Roosevelt administration for leaving black soldiers at the mercy of hostile southern whites, Dixie law enforcement personnel, and military police. "Off the military reservations our fighting men have been treated so viciously by their own fellow Americans," Wilkins complained, "that many of them have wondered whether the enemy is really across the seas or here at home."

The War Department not only refused to integrate the military, it further angered blacks when it ordered the Red Cross to label and separate blood by the donor's race. Officials admitted there was no medical reason for doing so. "The Red Cross, a jim crow outfit if there ever was one, passes the buck to the Army-Navy reactionaries, who in turn blame the masses for the existence of racial blood banks," the *Courier*'s George Schuyler fumed. "It is simply a lie that the racial blood banks were established because of pressure from those who would be saved by the blood plasma." Had the Red Cross and War Department not raised the issue, "nobody would have given a damn as long as the blood saved his life." Surgeon General James Magee ascribed the policy to "psychologically important" but "not biologically convincing" reasons that made it unwise "to collect and mix Caucasian and Negro blood indiscriminately for later administration to members of the armed forces."

Ample evidence suggested that the same old deal would prevail in race matters. Major-league baseball retained the color line, even though white stars insisted that many Negro Leaguers could excel in the majors. Police brutality persisted. White police in Detroit shot several blacks during the 1943 riot—many victims had bullet wounds in their backs. In Beaumont, Texas, a police officer killed a black soldier in the back seat of a patrol car. A riot followed, just days after the mayhem in Detroit. Defense contractors and unions blocked the hiring and promotion of minority workers. Mobs continued to lynch blacks, six in 1942, three the next year. President Roosevelt did nothing. Americans wanted "to stamp out racial bigotry and intolerance as practiced by Hitler," Don Davis noted in the *Dallas Express* 1943, yet they continued to coddle "the heathen who lynch and brutalize and carry on the most vicious propaganda of race hatred" at home.[46]

Louis said Americans were "on God's side," but he soon learned that white soldiers and civilians were seldom on the black soldiers' side. He toured bases and hospitals around the country to boost morale and met thousands of ordinary black men who proudly wore their nation's uniform but lacked the celebrity to shield them from malice. By 1945 over a million black men and women had entered the armed forces along with the Brown Bomber. Their experiences varied, but they learned a common lesson: Government leaders and white citizens generally cared little about civil rights regardless of what black soldiers, sailors, and pilots did for their country.

The War Department understandably built most of its large bases in the temperate South. Had the military been exclusively white, the preponderance of training camps in Dixie would not have mattered. But many blacks in uniform had fled the South to seek refuge in the North—among them Joe Louis, Sugar Ray Robinson, and Coleman Young. Migrants and their offspring had seldom returned to Dixie, and southern whites did not want them back. Claude Barnett, head of the Associated Negro Press, feared trouble between black soldiers and white police and civilians in the South. "South Carolina is such a lousy hole," he wrote to Truman Gibson, a black civilian aide in the War Department, "and Mississippi [is] equally bad." He doubted black trainees would receive the respect they deserved. As early as April 19, 1941—almost eight months before Pearl Harbor—the *Courier* reported that southern Democrats led by Senator John Bankhead had objected to the training of northern blacks in Dixie. The army acquiesced to local jim crow. "The South is more powerful than Hitler," the *Courier* protested. The nation risked war with Germany by aiding England but would not "antagonize the South by abolishing racial segregation and discrimination" in the armed forces and federal departments. Moving toward righteous war abroad, Roosevelt remained an isolationist on race at home. "Hitler is unable to scare the United States government into neutrality," the *Courier* stated, "but the South has forced this government to surrender on every front."

On August 6, 1941, a black private at Fort Bragg, North Carolina, objected to segregated seating on an army bus, arousing the ire of the white driver and a white military policeman. In the ensuing fracas, both private and MP were shot and killed. The incident provoked a clash between blacks and whites in nearby Fayetteville, a great embarrassment to federal authorities. "The U.S. Army is a jim-crow institution wedded to color discrimination," George Schuyler complained. "It is bad enough to serve under such circumstances in the North. It is terrible to have to do so in the South." If the army could not protect black soldiers in Dixie, "it should station them elsewhere." After learning about conditions in the area, a *Courier* writer blamed the War Department for the bloodshed. "Far from insisting that Negro soldiers must be treated as other soldiers," the *Courier* noted, "it has cooperated with the traditional Ku Klux spirit of the unreconstructed South until discrimination and segregation have become military law." Roy Wilkins demanded an investigation of the initial shootings and prosecution of those guilty of the subsequent attacks on black GIs. The fatalities stemmed from "the Army policy of segregating and humiliating Negro soldiers," Wilkins charged, "and then placing military police duty over them largely in the hands of ignorant, prejudiced, white southern soldiers."

Only days after the Fort Bragg incident, black soldiers on maneuvers with the 94th Engineers Battalion came face to face with local whites and police near Gurdon, Arkansas. "A group of mounted farmers came out of nowhere" and approached the soldiers and their white officers, Duane Simons, a sergeant from Michigan, recalled. "Get those god-damned niggers off of the white highway and march 'em in the ditch," a local man told the commander. The officer objected and warned that the entire area could be placed under martial law. The locals "rode him down with their horses" and beat him; his injuries necessitated a medical discharge. "They damned near killed him," Simons recalled, "one of their own color!" Sergeant Eugene Gaillard remembered a state trooper who called a white officer a "niggah lover" and ordered the men off the road. When the officer hesitated, a deputy hit him and dislodged his glasses. The officer "retaliated with a few well thrown punches" before the whites "almost beat him to death." The soldiers resumed their march, slogging through the ditch or beating the bush behind it, "forbidden to put our black feet on the white man's highway." Nothing had prepared these northern GIs for this "antebellum mentality." Later, in Italy, fragments from a wired bazooka sent Gaillard to a military hospital. "I came in contact with some of the meanest white people the good Lord ever created," Gaillard reminisced. "And for my country that disavowed me I got some metal in my body and lost an eye." Simons tired of the abuse in the army and went AWOL whenever he could. He served overseas where "the only people . . . who went out of their way to create trouble for us were our good old brethren in uniform, American whites."[47]

At the time Joe Louis enlisted, another news story also drew front-page coverage. Two headlines in the *Afro-American* conveyed the good news and bad news for the military. JOE GIVES $50,000 TO NAVY, THEN JOINS ARMY, one read. 28 HURT IN ARMY RIOT, noted another. In Alexandria, Louisiana, a white bus driver and black soldier triggered a riot in early 1942. The driver threatened to "brain a black soldier" for "not moving back in the bus," E.J. Wells of the 365th Infantry Regiment recalled, but the GI could not comply because the vehicle was "jammed to capacity." When the driver reached under his seat for a gun, "another soldier hit him and the riot was on." Gunshots rang out during the scuffle. City police went after the black soldiers suspected in the shooting. A white patrolman tried to arrest a black MP who refused to abandon his post. The patrolman shot and killed him. Black soldiers became more belligerent toward white military police. With tensions high, state troopers arrived to assist the city and military police. The white forces shot twelve black soldiers. In retaliation, black troops "turned the town upside down." Wells knew the cause of the trouble. "The military did not want black combat units," he observed, and "certainly did not want black officers." The *Courier* labeled the shootings a "massacre," the result of "an almost studied plan to terrorize Negroes." No pamphlet from the OWI could undo the harm caused by trigger-happy military and civilian police who killed black soldiers with impunity.

Except for lynching, nothing angered the NAACP's Walter White and Roy Wilkins more than discrimination against blacks in uniform. They also denounced bias in defense employment. White and A. Philip Randolph of the Brotherhood of Sleeping Car Porters took these issues to President Roosevelt at a meeting arranged by the first lady. Earlier in New York City, Randolph had disclosed a plan for a mass march on Washington to protest jim crow in the armed forces and bias in defense employment. In favor of the goal, Eleanor Roosevelt expressed some qualms about the means. "You know where I stand," she assured Randolph and White. "But the attitude of the Washington police, most of them Southerners, and the general feeling of Washington itself are such that I fear that there may be trouble if the march occurs." The threat of a mass demonstration, however, caught the president's attention. At the White House, Randolph and White implored him to integrate the armed forces and outlined how to do it. The military, White argued, was "handicapped with inefficient and prejudiced Southern officers in the higher ranks" who held "more than fifty per cent of the top-ranking positions in the armed services." Some were fit and fair, White conceded, but "the majority were neither able nor racially democratic in spirit or attitude." Roosevelt asked Assistant Secretary of War Robert Patterson and Secretary of the Navy Frank Knox if White was correct. Patterson said yes; Knox admitted the ratio was even higher in the navy. Roosevelt compromised and issued Executive Order 8802 banning racial, ethnic, and religious discrimination in defense industry employment but leaving jim crow untouched in the military. Randolph did not want half a loaf. "If the president wants us to stop our agitation, then let him stop discrimination," he declared at a mass meeting in Harlem. Blacks were "all-out for the war to lick Hitler in Europe," but they also wanted to go "all-out . . . to lick the hell out of Hitlerism in America."[48]

One of millions who had abandoned southern field for northern factory,

Joe Louis knew that manufacturing jobs paid better than agricultural labor and menial service. At a bond rally in Detroit in 1942, Louis received a plaque presented by dancer and film star Bill Robinson for his contributions to the war effort. Jesse Thomas, on leave from the Urban League to sell bonds, attended the event. When Louis accepted his award, "the audience demanded through their applause that he make a speech." Louis bowed but sat down. "The applause became thunderous," so Louis rose, bowed again, and took his seat. The cheers persisted until Louis strolled to the microphone. "Yes, we are going to buy bonds," he promised. "What we want is to be given some jobs so we can make some money with which to buy bonds."

Louis remained attentive to defense employment throughout the war. When Lockheed Vega Aircraft announced it would comply with Roosevelt's directive, Louis traveled to one of its plants to be present as the first black workers arrived. Louis "introduced the one hundredth," Roi Ottley of the *Amsterdam News* reported, "with much cheering by the white workers." He also toured Eddie Anderson's parachute factory. Louis realized that blacks' job performance now would affect their opportunities later. They had to work hard to help win the war, but they also had to work well to help themselves when peace returned. After several months of boxing exhibitions and mingling with troops in Africa and Europe, Louis visited war plants in Pennsylvania, New Jersey, and Delaware in late 1944. He urged workers to avoid absences and be productive. "Over there they can't quit fighting for eight hours, not even five minutes," Louis reminded them. "They have to stay in there every minute, and you should likewise be on the job every working hour so that we can have them back with us real soon." If even a tiny portion of black workers proved unreliable, the whole race would pay. "When one Negro is absent from his job due to excessive drinking, all Negro workers suffer," the *Express* warned. "Unfortunately, most of the generalizations which are made about us as a racial group are unjustly based upon a case or so rather than upon the behavior of Negroes as a whole." Blacks' dependability now would greatly affect their opportunities later, "especially in those plants where we were not hired extensively before the war."[49]

War Within a War: Double Jeopardy for Black Soldiers

Louis cared a great deal about his fellow GIs. He traveled around the nation and overseas to entertain, console, and inspire them, particularly black soldiers. The dramatic deaths at Fort Bragg and Alexandria made the news, but most blacks in uniform suffered in silence. Nothing symbolized so starkly the tension between nationalism and racism than the recurring problems plaguing black soldiers on or near army bases. Louis remained loyal and optimistic, but other soldiers grew disillusioned and defiant. And even the champion learned he could run but not hide from the enemy within.

Black soldiers never knew just how white officers, soldiers, and civilians would receive them. The response might be a sincere welcome, an awkward hello, a reluctant handshake, slurs and snubs, or a loaded gun. Sergeant Frank Penick thought officers at Fort McClellan, Alabama, "on the whole were fairly decent," except for "one real bigoted bastard" and some who joked that blacks "would make good soldiers for night fighting." But white civilians were "vicious," white troops not much better with their habitual "name-calling and obscene remarks." At Camp Rucker, in Alabama, Private Latrophe Jenkins admitted feeling more vulnerable there among "anti-Negro MP's and Nazi-minded Southern whites" than in the jungles of the South Pacific. "We studied our enemy there, and knew his methods of attack before he came, but here we know NOTHING!" he wrote to P.L. Prattis of the *Courier* in 1944. "We are attacked with our hands tied, and why, we never know."

Conditions were similar in Louisiana. Black GIs resided on "swampland" at Camp Claiborne, Sergeant Eddie Donald recalled, while whites occupied "good ground with the highway nearby and bus facilities to take them to town." The base was "completely segregated," and so was the closest city. What irked Donald most were the contrasting conditions between black GIs and German prisoners of war at Claiborne. The POWs lived "in a special area, not swampland" and enjoyed "freedom of movement and . . . access to facilities denied black American soldiers." The captives could get "passes to town" while black GIs were "confined to the area" without the prisoners' "privileges." Camp Livingston drew similar complaints. Private James Pritchett called it "a hell hole" where German captives had "more rights and freedom" than he did.[50]

In most places soldiers pocketed their pride, but some struck back. Usually at a considerable disadvantage against whites, one group of black GIs remembered a particular day when they had the last laugh. A Louisiana farmer brandishing a shotgun approached soldiers on maneuvers and ordered them off his property. A radio operator called in reinforcements. "A tank arrived promptly and without even stopping it ran right over Shotgun Joe's henhouse," leaving "feathers . . . everywhere," Sergeant David Cason Jr. chuckled. "Old Joe withdrew quietly to the rear." Cason suspected "our Uncle paid for a new chicken coop." A diner and its white patrons might have suffered the same fate as the henhouse. After maneuvers on a hot summer day, black troops in a jeep and armored personnel carrier spotted a roadside ice cream sign and stopped. "Just as the first fellows off of the truck reached the door somebody inside hooked the screen, stepped back, and stood looking at us," Cason recalled, and an armed "cracker" appeared. No one spoke. The soldiers headed back to their carrier. One climbed aboard and lifted the canvas from the machine gun. Soldiers loaded it, and "the trigger man swung that machine gun around" and aimed it at the doorway. Others slapped full clips into their rifles. They knew what that gun could do. "It would cut it and everybody in it in half," Cason noted. "We knew every white regiment and division in the state, plus their police at every level would be called down upon our heads. Without a word we had decided to make our stand." The "shotgun totin' cracker" vanished and a woman unhooked the door. With teary eyes and trembling hands she scooped ice cream for the men. Several women and children huddled inside, "crying and shaking like leaves." All served, the men departed. No reprisals came.

Texas was no better than Louisiana and Arkansas. Private Bert Babero informed Truman Gibson, a civilian aide to Secretary of War Henry Stimson, about Camp Barkeley. On local buses, Babero reported, white drivers ordered black soldiers to the rear. The army also ran buses to town, "but we aren't allowed to ride them." Black GIs lived in "terrible" quarters, former Civilian Conservation Corps barracks near "the camp cesspool." When Babero arrived, their sector "looked like a garbage dump." The men cleaned the area for three weeks before they could drill. Babero had glimpsed the captives' quarters and thought them better than his own. "Here," Babero sighed, "the tyrant is actually placed over the liberator."

Joe Louis visited Barkeley to boost morale, and troops there needed it. Camp Stewart was similar, maybe worse, with rampant "segregation and prejudice," according to Major William Shelton. "Instead of Americans against Germans it was black Americans versus white Americans. . . . There were three soldiers killed, two or three MPs killed, and a large number of troops hospitalized." Black GIs complained to the *Courier* that Stewart was "nothing but a slave camp for the colored." Camp Hood was "frightening," Harry Duplessis, a second lieutenant, recalled. "Segregation there was so complete" that outhouses were marked *White, Colored, and Mexican*. Black soldiers are "treated worse than . . . German prisoners here," Private John Rivers wrote to the *Afro-American*. "We in the camp stockade are being beaten every day until we can't stand up; drilled all hours of the night." The MPs jailed blacks for the slightest infraction; army doctors ignored their pleas of illness or injury. "Are we free Negroes," Rivers challenged, "or still slaves?"[51]

The army sometimes hid the truth. At a base in Texas, commanding officers refused to investigate the suspicious deaths of black GIs. They attributed strange fatalities to accidents, suicide, or the men's own recklessness. "One of their suicides," Sergeant Floyd Jones protested, "was hanging from a tree with his hands tied behind his back." Claude Barnett accused white MPs at Fort Benning of "turning Negro soldiers over to the civilian police who beat them up." He conceded that the army had to maintain discipline, but he thought "racial bias" came into play. "When the army is wrong, it is wrong," he insisted to Truman Gibson, "and it needs to be made right." Travel through the South vexed many blacks in uniform. Soldiers bound for Alabama from Virginia by train had to sleep in a jim crow car, and the railroad provided one meal in two days. Lieutenant Lacey Wilson remembered having to walk down an alley to the back door of a restaurant in Texas to get food while "white MPs with German prisoners of war [sat] inside enjoying each other's company over a steak dinner." Wilson's experience was not unusual. "Proudly wearing the uniform of the United States Navy I traveled from the East Coast to San Diego on a train carrying German prisoners of war into the western interior of the country," C. Eric Lincoln recalled. "The Germans had the run of the diner, but because I was black, whenever I went there to eat I had to be seated behind a curtain lest my presence . . . offend the honor and spoil the appetites of our Caucasian guests from Nazi Germany, whose mission and whose intention was to destroy us." Ray Carter, a navy steward, survived "a long swim" in the Pacific but saw many die after a Japanese cruiser sank his ship off Guadalcanal. When Carter and his shipmates returned to the states, whites repeatedly refused to serve them while German prisoners had "a ball." Like Floyd Jones, Carter accused the army of concealing the extent of interracial violence during the war.[52]

The South lacked its legendary hospitality when black soldiers arrived, but other regions were not much better. From New Mexico, Private John Lyons wrote to the *Courier* about an Alamogordo base "rotten with prejudice and discrimination" where officers from Dixie seemed determined to "retard colored soldiers' morale." Coleman Young, a second lieutenant from Joe Louis's old neighborhood in Detroit, tired of the army's "plantation attitude." At Fort Huachuca, "an open rebellion" nearly erupted over jim crow. That plantation mentality seemed as evil to Young as the fascists in Europe. "I had enlisted in a private war that was being fought on a different front," Young reminisced. "My sights were trained on Jim Crow, and I dug my foxhole wherever my orders took me." Young also remembered "several race riots" at Fort Dix in New Jersey and a comrade "killed in cold blood" there. Dix reminded Duane Simons of southern camps. "Fort Dix might be above the Mason-Dixon line," he noted, "but it is strictly an accident of geography." Blacks dubbed it "Fort Dixie."

Corporal William Lee thought Oregon's Camp Adair was "worse . . . than being way down South." Black soldiers had no recreational outlets or friendly local blacks, and military police discouraged them from talking with white women in nearby Corvallis. "This is strictly a white camp," Lee wrote, with "plenty of down dixie boys to enforce Jim Crow laws." At Fort Lawton,

Washington, black soldiers rebelled at the preferential treatment given to Italian captives. One man died in the outbreak. The army convicted twenty-eight black soldiers on various charges. Sailor Norman McRae, whose "only black heroes were Joe Louis and Paul Robeson," reflected on the irony of race, place, and nationality during the war. German and Italian prisoners in the states "had more rights than the black guys guarding them," he recalled. "They could go to the white PX" and "the white base movies."[53]

Even in the nation's capital, a military uniform did not shield its black wearer from bias. Captain Lee Rayford and Lieutenant Walter Lawson, pilots with the 99th Pursuit Squadron, returned to the states after flying their quota of missions in Europe. Shot down over Austria, Rayford had received the Purple Heart and a Distinguished Flying Cross. Though both pilots were eligible to complete their hitches as flight instructors at home, they opted to return to war. They waited at a bus stop to catch a ride to the Pentagon to make arrangements. Gordon Parks, a photographer with the OWI seeking permission to tell the pilots' story, waited with them. The bus arrived. "We took seats behind the driver" who "flushed with anger" and demanded they "go to the back of the bus," Parks recalled. "We looked at him in disbelief." The men did not budge, and senior white officers on board chose not to order them to the rear. "Don't you move!" an elderly black woman shouted from the back. "Pull out, man," a major advised the driver. "Can't you tell when you're licked?" The driver headed across the Potomac. How ironic, Parks thought, that these pilots chose "to defend a country which, at that precise moment, was harshly offending them." Having confronted Hitler's vaunted *Luftwaffe*, they had no intention of capitulating to a white bus driver.

Six black soldiers entered a district cafeteria in 1944 in the midst of picketing and a sit-in by students from Howard University. A placard asked, WE DIE TOGETHER—WHY CAN'T WE EAT TOGETHER? The manager refused to serve the soldiers or students. Pauli Murray, one of the protesters, thought that the capital "epitomized the great gap between official United States war propaganda and racial practices within our own borders." A major source of this "great gap" was the War Department. It initially excluded blacks from the marines and air corps and balked at enlisting them in the army. It delayed promotions for black officers and confined recruits to labor and service. It sanctioned jim crow blood banks. Under southern pressure in early 1944, it withheld a pamphlet, *The Races of Mankind,* written by anthropologists Ruth Benedict and Gene Weltfish of Columbia University, aimed at countering intolerance in the military. The department barred black nurses and delayed admitting black women to the Women's Army Corps. It sanctioned separate and unequal treatment and often ignored complaints from black soldiers. "Although a military reservation is federal property where the laws of states do not obtain," George Schuyler observed, "Roosevelt and Stimson permitted the setting up of remarkably accurate replicas of civilian ghettoes in every military and naval reservation."[54]

William Hastie, a black civilian aide in the War Department, repeatedly protested these military "ghettoes." "The traditional mores of the South," Hastie objected to Secretary of War Henry Stimson, "have been widely accepted and adopted by the army as the basis of policy and practice in matters affecting the Negro soldier." This policy caused many problems. "It is impossible to create a dual personality," he stressed, "a fighting man toward the foreign enemy" on the one hand and "a craven" willing to "accept treatment as less than a man at home" on the other. Discrimination could "not be changed overnight," he conceded, but he detected "no apparent disposition" to try "any different plan." When the high command balked at basic changes, Hastie resigned in 1943. Chief of Staff George C. Marshall rejected integration. The army could not solve "a social problem which has perplexed the American people throughout the history of this nation," he advised. Nor should the army "be charged with the undertaking." The high command faced a "tremendous task" and nothing must "jeopardize discipline and morale." Correct about the "vexing" nature of racism, Marshall overlooked the fact that existing policies already damaged "discipline and morale" among blacks. Moreover, he surely knew that the chain of command provided some leverage for change so long as the top brass exerted strong leadership.[55]

Journalists and NAACP investigators publicized the travails of black GIs, earning them the enmity of federal officials, biased commanders, and southern politicians. The *Pittsburgh Courier*, for example, waged a "double victory" (VV) campaign during the war, demanding an end to racism at home as well as fascism abroad. To that end, the *Courier* and other publications exposed jim crow in the military, urged the dismissal of Henry Stimson, chided Roosevelt for ignoring injustice, and compared the South of Bilbo, Bankhead, and Ellender to Nazi Germany. "Wherever the flag has gone in this war," George Schuyler protested in 1945, "jim crow has been carrying it." Federal officials took issue with the black press. Assistant Secretary of War John McCloy advised Hastie to persuade editors "to lessen their emphasis upon discriminatory acts and color incidents" in daily life. "If the United States does not win this war, the lot of the Negro is going to be far, far worse than it is today," McCloy warned. "Yet . . . an alarmingly large percentage of Negroes" did not seem "vitally concerned about winning the war." He blamed "some forces . . . at work misleading the Negroes." Bias in the military, McCloy added, had nothing to do with "the basic issues" of the war or "the basic issues of freedom." Blacks would do well to give "greater out-and-out support of the war." Roi Ottley of the *New York Amsterdam*

News recalled efforts to squelch the black press. Archibald MacLeish, director of the Office of Facts and Figures, "called an informal conference of Negro editors," Ottley noted, and urged them "to lay off the rough racial stuff—for the duration of the war, at least." Frank Marshall Davis remembered frequent calls from the Office of Censorship that followed a familiar script. The caller would complain that recent news about race problems in the military impeded the war effort. Davis would reply that if the War Department would just abolish "the two-army system, one white and one black," then "the stories will stop themselves."

Black editors resented these tactics. Carter Wesley of the *Dallas Express* argued in 1945 that reticence had not worked during World War I. Now blacks waged two offensives—"one on the battlefront and the other on the home front against demagogy and intolerance." The previous decision to "drop all differences at home and fight the war abroad" had not served the interests of "Negroes and Americans generally," Wesley argued. "This time the Negro leadership refused to be befuddled and insisted that they were fighting under two Vs instead of one." The black press stood its ground. In one cartoon an American soldier thrust a bayonet toward the chest of a hooded knight, whose real identity is revealed when a Klan hood flies off the head of Hitler. "You tell me that hitler / Is a mighty bad man," Langston Hughes wrote in 1943. "I guess he took lessons / From the ku klux klan." After the defeat of Germany, the *Afro-American*'s Josephus Simpson urged continuing vigilance, since no foreign regime had ever "affected us so gravely and so intimately as have Fascist governments in America." The NAACP publicized the plight of black soldiers and demanded justice for those facing charges. Roy Wilkins, for example, blamed the army for treating allegations of rape by black and by white soldiers differently. Blacks so accused were likely to receive "the minimum defense required by law" and to incur "the maximum penalty." Before the 1944 election, Wilkins complained that federal officials had done "absolutely nothing" for black soldiers, "a disgrace which stinks to heaven." Wilkins printed a telling eyewitness account by Grant Reynolds, an army chaplain for almost three years. Reynolds agreed that white soldiers gave "better treatment" to Nazi prisoners than to their black comrades. One recruit told Reynolds that his base was reminiscent of slave days, with a "red-neck" officer from Tennessee who acted like "a plantation boss." The War Department, Reynolds added, found the legal authority to uproot and confine Japanese American civilians to concentration camps but pleaded helplessness in providing "elementary protection" to blacks in uniform.[56]

Dixiecrats resisted efforts to translate the black soldiers' service into civil rights advances. Senator James Eastland of Mississippi began a vendetta against black troops in mid-1945. "The Negro soldier was an utter and dismal failure in combat in Europe," he declared in the Senate. "I was told in any number of cities that decent white girls could not go out on the street because they would be accosted by groups of drunken Negro soldiers." The black GI had "disgraced the flag of his country. He will not fight. He will not work." Such reports seemed to validate southern racial mores. "The doctrine of white supremacy," Eastland proclaimed, "is one which, if adhered to, will save America."

When Harry Truman succeeded Roosevelt in 1945, he appointed James Byrnes, a South Carolina segregationist, secretary of state. "Jim Crow, Jim Byrnes, and Jim Eastland," Harold Preece, a columnist for the *Express* gibed, "are jims of the same feather." Roy Wilkins feared a reversal of recent minimal gains. "We suffered a million casualties to defeat the master race theory," he noted, "but we continue to follow the race superiority line at home and abroad." Congress abolished the Fair Employment Practices Commission and blocked a bill to abolish the poll tax. To Wilkins, southern blacks still seemed "little better off" than "Indonesians or the Nigerians."[57]

Persistent white prejudice amid black sacrifice baffled Joe Louis, whose own contributions were considerable. He did not box professionally between early 1942 and mid-1946, prompting black writers to contrast his conduct with Jack Dempsey's avoidance of military service during World War I. His exhibitions to entertain troops earned him a basic soldier's pay, small change compared to the big peacetime purses. He ran up huge debts, but the burdens were not just financial. He seldom saw John Roxborough, Julian Black, or his wife Marva and their new daughter. Jack Blackburn, his trainer and counselor, died in 1942.

Removed from his former mentors, Louis spoke and acted with a new autonomy that proved a mixed blessing. In basic training at Fort Riley, Kansas, he met fellow soldier Jackie Robinson, who complained of being excluded from the camp baseball and football teams. Ability was not the issue—Robinson had lettered in four sports at UCLA, baseball and football included. Louis took the matter to the base commander, who ordered white soldiers to admit Robinson to the teams. Then the army rejected Robinson for Officer Candidate School despite his obvious qualifications, so Louis again approached the commander. Unhappy with their meeting, Louis contacted Truman Gibson in Washington. The army admitted Robinson to OCS and accepted other black candidates as well, another victory for Louis. Robinson continued to challenge army jim crow after he was commissioned. When he objected to limited and segregated seating at the post exchange, commanders added seats but retained separation. Robinson moved on to Fort Hood, Texas. Before going into town one day, he stopped to cash a check at the officers' club, where whites turned him away at the door. A few days later, boarding a bus he recognized an African-American woman with light skin, an officer's wife, and sat with her. The driver objected and ordered Robinson off the bus, but he remained. The driver summoned help. When Robinson refused to obey the order of noncommissioned MPs, they found a major who commanded him to leave the bus. Mimicking the slave and mocking the master, Robinson bent low, swept his cap in a wide arc, and replied, "yessah!" The army charged him with being disrespectful to a superior officer. Ivan Harrison, another black officer at Hood, watched "the shortest court-martial" ever. At the hearing, someone hastily read the dubious charges. "On his last word" the presiding officer banged the gavel and declared Robinson not guilty.[58]

"I'll Fight with My Gloves"

Louis met with army officials in Washington in mid-1943 and reaffirmed his loyalty. "I'll fight with my gloves or my gun," he announced, "anywhere, anytime." The military decided to use his gloves. At Walter Reed Army Hospital, he joked that he wanted to box Hitler in Berlin while Sugar Ray Robinson fought Japanese Prime Minister Tojo in Tokyo. "I have already met one of Hitler's men and he was not bad at all," Louis quipped. "I am sure that I can take Hitler in the first." In a recurring gag on his tour, Louis saluted a sparring partner who outranked him, then proceeded to belt him around the ring. Soldiers loved it. Mixing with greater ease, Louis delighted both black and white GIs. But the tour was not all quips and gags, for Louis set rules for his engagements. "I told the Army I wouldn't appear anywhere to segregated Army audiences," he recalled. "Whites and blacks were all fighting the same war, why couldn't their morale be lifted at the same theater?" The army complied, so he performed for mixed audiences across the country. Yet much remained undone. "There was," Louis realized, "a lot of racism in the service."

When the War Department finally established a black air station at Tuskegee, Louis traveled there in 1944 to meet its trainees. White commanders and local civilians had devised plans to confine the men to their station, making it "the equivalent of a prison camp for black servicemen and their families," according to General Benjamin O. Davis Jr., the senior black officer there. White residents snatched a black officer from his car, insulted him, knocked out his driver's tooth, then told them to get back where they belonged. Whites wanted trainees to know they "were not welcome in their town," Corporal Ralph Jones recalled. Coleman Young remembered a merchant in nearby Union Springs who alerted the local sheriff to the men's liquor runs. "The sheriff would arrest us in town," Young remembered, "hold our booze and our cars, and charge us the exact amount of money we had in our wallets to buy our cars back." But Young remained focused on the airmen's mission. "I quickly grew enamored of the idea of flying a B-25 over Germany," he recalled, "and dropping bombs on those superior Aryan motherfuckers."

Corporal Ambrose Nutt witnessed a dramatic example of the racial divide at Tuskegee. A white flight instructor crashed his plane and bled profusely. He knew the base had ample plasma on hand, but while still conscious he told doctors not to give him a transfusion of "black" blood. Doctors informed his wife he would die before they could get "white" blood from another base. She told them to use the available plasma and saved her husband's life. The town of Tuskegee "demanded and got from the war department humiliating restrictions" on the airmen, Roy Wilkins noted. City police "cursed them and beat them and made the army take away their sidearms." In addition, Commander Frederick von Kimble chose to reside in the city and not on base. He "yielded completely to the town pattern and enforced galling segregation on the men." To Kermit Bailer, a pilot trainee from Detroit, his year at Tuskegee was "a shocking experience" despite his having traveled in the South before the war. "I was shocked at hearing whites call blacks 'nigger' to their faces and at the rigorously enforced segregation laws and customs."[59]

After visiting Tuskegee, Louis headed for his boyhood home and then joined Ray Robinson at Camp Sibert. But Louis would not leave Alabama with only fond memories of his youth. When a bus to Birmingham failed to arrive, the two soldiers strolled through the station to the only available phone to call a cab. Someone was using the phone, however, so they sat down on a bench nearby. More familiar with Detroit than Dixie, they had unknowingly selected a "white" phone near a "white" bench. A white MP approached and ordered them to the "colored" area. "We ain't moving," Louis replied. Sugar Ray feared the MP might use force against them. "He drew back the billy club as if to swing it at Joe," Robinson recalled. "When I saw that, I leaped on the MP. I was choking him, biting him, anything to keep him away from Joe." More MPs rushed in and broke up the fight. They "might really have roughed us up," Robinson thought, but some soldiers nearby recognized the champion and shouted, "That's Joe Louis, that's Joe Louis!"

After the scuffle, Louis went to headquarters. An officer chided him for contesting the order to move. "Listen, I'm an American," Louis told him, "and I expect to be treated like anybody else." He pointed out that he complied with segregation laws off base but could not see why he should bow to jim crow on army property. The officer let Louis and Robinson go, but the champion realized that only his fame had saved him from stern punishment or injury. "If I was just an average black GI," Louis admitted, "I would have wound up in the stockades." From other soldiers, Louis and Robinson learned that the South was a law unto itself. At Keesler Air Base, blacks informed Robinson that the commander had reserved Robinson's show for whites. "Isn't this the United States?" Sugar Ray asked. "No, man," a GI replied. "This is Mississippi." The feisty boxer informed the officer he would leave unless all personnel were admitted. After a call to Washington, the commander acquiesced and a mixed audience happily watched Robinson. Other black celebrities also chafed at this bias. Singer Lena Horne left the stage at a base in Arkansas when she noticed German prisoners of war seated in front of black soldiers. She walked over to the black men, sang to them, and left. She split with the USO over jim crow and toured on her own. Lucky Millinder's band entertained black GIs at the Harlem USO and had "VV" painted on their bus, a rolling reminder of the dual nature of the war. The *Courier* ran a photograph of Millinder standing proudly in front of his "double victory" banner on wheels.[60]

The War Department sent Louis to the British Isles, Italy, and North Africa. At a theater in Britain, an usher told him and his black comrades to sit in a designated section. Louis went to the manager, who explained that American commanders had told him to impose segregated seating—jim crow had crossed the Atlantic with the screaming eagle. Other American officers in Europe discouraged locals from being friendly to black GIs, lest whites take offense. And white soldiers abroad sometimes acted like lynch mobs. Chester Jones, a driver with the Red Ball Express, a GI trucking outfit, for example, remembered the 29th Division. "It was an all-cracker division that had a real 'thing' about blacks," Jones explained. "In Bremen Negro soldiers did not go out on the streets alone at night because they not only got stomped but members of the 29th enjoyed killing them." At a Paris nightspot Jones had a drink with a French woman. A drunken white soldier glared at him and snarled, "You black-sons-of-bitches don't sit with white women at home, and I'll be damned if you'll do it here while I'm around." He pushed a gun between Jones's shoulder blades and marched him out of the club. Corporal Jonathan Welch accused officers in the British Isles of replicating the atmosphere at Fort Hood. "That old Southern principle of keeping Negroes as slaves is still being practiced," Welch observed, "working from sunrise to sunset and in some cases into the middle of the night." Commanders also controlled the soldiers' off-duty time: "We are practically imprisoned at the present." Whites had cautioned locals that blacks were "direct descendants from monkeys." Welch wondered if President Roosevelt understood their frustration when he declared that the nation fought for freedom.

In response to frequent complaints from black soldiers overseas, Walter

White of the NAACP went abroad in early 1944 to investigate. "What are we fighting for over here?" an angry soldier asked White in Great Britain. "Are we sent to the E[uropean] T[heater of] O[perations] to fight the Nazis— or our white soldiers?" White soon learned the cause of the strife—"an appalling number of men who put their prejudices above their patriotism," particularly officers who "used every device, official or personal . . . to make the lot of the Negro soldier as unpleasant as possible." Matters were even worse in the Pacific. In Hawaii, whites demanded that black servicemen "be excluded from restaurants, hotels, dance halls, and other such places." He found "a persistent campaign of anti-Negro propaganda" in the islands. The War Department kept blacks out of combat in the Far East, confining them to sanitation, dock work, service, and construction. In Guam, this policy angered soldiers of both races. Whites threw grenades into the blacks' camp and shot some of them. "Combat troops . . . looked with either indifference or contempt on noncombat troops," White observed, "particularly if they were Negroes." An interracial shoot-out in Guam led to the conviction of forty-four black GIs. Upon appeal, however, the army commuted the sentences.[61]

As Walter White continued his investigation, Joe Louis went to Italy to renew his acquaintance with the 99th Pursuit Squadron. The unit had aroused great excitement among blacks, for the Pentagon had finally authorized its pilots to fly combat missions. 99TH BLASTS NAZIS, the *Courier* exclaimed. The "spookwaffe" hit several Nazi aircraft over Anzio, Italy, in early 1944. 99TH DOWNS 12 GERMAN PLANES, the *Courier* crowed. These strikes vindicated the pilots and undermined the notion that blacks could not fly modern aircraft or stand up to the Nazis. At Ramitelli, the Brown Bomber mixed with the black bombers. "Several of our men had their pictures made with the champ," Commander Benjamin Davis Jr. recalled. "He was mobbed by hundreds of admirers who were thrilled to be in his presence, shake his hand, and explain to him what we were doing in Italy." What Louis learned impressed him. Max Johnson, an *Afro-American* correspondent, talked with him. "I think these fellows overseas know now that the world is not meant to be ruled by one color," Louis remarked. "They know that is why we are beating Hitler." Upon returning home, southern whites would bring with them "a different feeling" about blacks, for by "fighting and working together" they had learned "that a lot of stuff they have been taught before is not right."[62]

In his homespun way Louis captured what black activists and intellectuals had been saying for decades—"a lot of stuff" was "not right" in race matters. The nation had an opportunity and an obligation to live up to its better ideals and impulses. Americans had weathered the long Depression and intervened to turn the tide in Europe and Asia. Now the time had come to assess what they had learned about themselves, their institutions, and their role in the world. "The depression has taught America that most of its problems are more economic than racial or emotional," the *Afro-American*'s Ralph Matthews had argued in 1940. "Even the ignorant masses of the South have learned that poor white trash and poor colored people are all in the same boat, and that merely burning a defenseless 'n——r' does not put one more meal under their belts." A black speaker made this point to Boston Yankees in 1945. "Your ancestors came to the United States on the Mayflower," he observed. "Mine came on a slave ship. But we're all in the same boat now." With the return of peace, the *Express* boasted that blacks had "again proved themselves to be thoroughbred Americans." The nation owed them "their well-earned status of full citizenship."[63]

To recognize wrong was one matter, to rectify it quite another. Joe Louis thought that mutual service in war had narrowed the gap between the races. On his discharge from the army, he had cause for both optimism and despair. Over the preceding decade, industrial workers and southern tenant farmers had formed unprecedented interracial unions to pursue common interests. The war had opened new doors in industry to black workers. And federal officials had finally taken bold steps against bias in the military during the last months of the war. The navy began to integrate its advanced officer training classes in 1944. The army authorized deployment of "colored units" in combat, then later ordered the desegregation of post exchanges, recreational facilities, and base transportation. Black pilots shifted from escort duty to assaults; black soldiers moved from labor to combat. The Supreme Court in *Morgan v. Virginia* declared segregated seating in interstate transportation unconstitutional in 1946. The ruling signaled an important shift to a court less tolerant of states' rights and more concerned with equal protection of the laws.

Progress appeared on other fronts as well. Movie producers began to portray blacks in more realistic ways, moving from crude stereotypes of mammies and mountebanks to characters of greater complexity and appeal. MGM, for example, announced in 1944 that it would not proceed with *Uncle Tom's Cabin* because of black opposition. Prospects for the film, the *Afro-American* gloated, were "gone with the wind." Hollywood and the army collaborated on *The Negro Soldier*, a 1944 film that sought to reduce white bias and improve black morale by tracing the military service of African Americans back to 1776. The film included a scene with Joe Louis leading several army trainees over an obstacle course, the narrator reminding viewers that before the war the champion had knocked out Max Schmeling, now a paratrooper for *Herr* Hitler. In a move of symbolic as well as substantive significance, owner Branch Rickey signed Jackie Robinson, an army veteran, to the Brooklyn Dodger organization in 1945, a vital step toward the integration of major-league baseball.

Every positive action, however, seemed to have a negative reaction. Hollywood made less biased films—*Stormy Weather, Pillow to Post, Cabin in the Sky*—but censors in Dixie cut the footage showing interracial friendships or equality. In early 1945 Theodore Bilbo reintroduced his bill to send blacks to Africa, and James Eastland maligned black American and Liberian soldiers to impugn all peoples of African origin. Southern white mobs resorted to violence to terrorize blacks. In Columbia, Tennessee in early 1946, for example, a mob of lawmen and local residents shot, slashed, and burned their way through a black neighborhood. That summer, vigilantes in Monroe, Georgia lynched two sisters and their husbands. One, George Dorsey, had fought in North Africa during a five-year hitch in the army. Just hours after discharge from Fort Gordon in Georgia, veteran Isaac Woodard argued with a bus driver who thought he had loitered too long in a restroom. The driver told police that Woodard was drunk and unruly and demanded his arrest. But Woodard did not drink. When Woodard protested his arrest, the police chief of Batesburg, South Carolina, pummeled him with a blackjack, struck his eyes and blinded him, then tossed him into a cell. An all-white jury acquitted the chief. Woodard met Walter White in New York City. "I saw you, Mr. White, when you visited my outfit in the Pacific," Woodard recalled. "I could see then." White and others complained to President Truman about these outrages. The vicious assault on Woodard "made me sick to my stomach," Joe Louis noted, and he made a speech at a benefit for him in New York City. "Me and a whole lot of black guys went out fighting for the American cause," Louis told the crowd. "Now we're gonna have to get America to give us our civil rights too. We earned them."[64]

Blacks surely had "earned" their rights, but many whites did not intend to pay them. By war's end, Joe Louis had become a national icon. Early in his career, writers had labeled him "a credit to his race." When he defeated Max Schmeling and joined the army, writers shifted their emphasis from color to country, proclaiming Louis a credit to his nation. The charity bouts for Navy and Army Relief further enhanced his reputation. After the war, a white writer reiterated that Louis was "a credit to his race," but he explained that he meant that Louis was a credit to "the human race." This was not mere semantics. The more inclusive usage portended a new current in politics and society. Even if only a small fraction of whites became more aware and tolerant during the war, they could help the whole nation confront the internal foe. What Louis achieved outside the ring cannot be tallied as readily as his record within it. But he scored all wins and no losses in his standing among Americans by 1945. No single ambassador of goodwill could normalize race relations, but Louis performed his mission remarkably well from 1935 to 1945. He emerged a true national hero by the end of the war, perhaps the first African American to attain that distinction.

With the "bloody peace" predicted by writer Margaret Walker in 1942 came "a second generation full of courage" to seek "another world" unfettered by the racist precepts of the past. More familiar with that "second generation" that waged the civil rights crusade of the 1950s and 1960s, Americans should not forget Joe Louis and those of his generation who emerged from the war determined to create a nation with liberty and justice for all.

8

"The Harder They Fall"

A Champion's Life and Legend

> Joe Louis is a two-fist fighter,
> And he stands six feet tall,
> And the bigger they come,
> He say the harder they fall.[1]

—Memphis Minnie McCoy, "He's in the Ring," 1935

You Can't Take It With You won the Oscar for best picture in 1938, but a different film that year intrigued African Americans. With an all-black cast, *Spirit of Youth* brought Joe Louis to the big screen in a rendition of his rise to world champion. The film "is not designed for an exclusive appeal" to black viewers, Loren Miller of the *Los Angeles Sentinel* noted, for its producers had sought "to make a talkie which will have a Negro cast and yet appeal to all theater-goers as 'good entertainment.'" Studio insiders had assured Miller that this movie (and others to follow) would portray black people in radically different ways. "Uncle Tom plays no part in them," Miller added. "Consciously, or unconsciously, these producers are making their films in response to widespread criticism of Hollywood's habit of casting the Negro as clown, a fool, or an underling."

A man fond of humor and practical jokes, Joe Louis liked to laugh. But he was no "fool" or "underling." His conduct as a contender had defied many racist stereotypes. In the lead role as "Joe Thomas" in this film, Louis symbolized the universality of human striving. He triumphed over temptation and earned honors consistent with his effort and character—a plot not specific to any race. A quintessential American story, the script for *Spirit of Youth* could have been written by Horatio Alger.

295

A far better boxer than actor, Louis managed to play his role without hint of the buffoon or bushman. He demonstrated traits consistent with the best in American character—noble ambition, generosity, perseverance, and modesty. ("I wanna get ahead and be somebody," Joe tells his sweetheart before leaving his southern home, "and do things for mama and papa.") He wins the title without losing his integrity. On screen Louis appeared stiff and scripted, but the inclusion of actual fight footage and the refreshing roles for several black characters meant more to his fans than his acting. The film "packs a punch that isn't always in the ring," the *Sentinel* observed, "for it boasts a simple yet interesting story based on the life of the champ" that would appeal to audiences beyond "the fight fans."

Miller welcomed this trend but wanted even more from the studios—films that revealed the stark realities of daily life for his people. "The Negro's place on stage and screen has been fixed for so many years," he complained, "that the tradition sways the judgment of Negroes themselves and honest whites." Producers feared that racial realism would "spoil the entertainment value" of their films and be dismissed as "propaganda." Miller praised the studios for "good intentions" but urged them to go further: "The truth is that every time a Negro steps outside the black belt of his home town to buy a hot dog, select a school for his child, ride a train, look for a job or get married, divorced, or buried, he runs into problems arising out of his Jim Crow status in society." The industry needed to address this "truth" of black life. To show "the Negro actor on the screen with his hat on his head instead of in his hand" was, Miller concluded, only a first step.[2]

A *Life* photographer covered the premiere of *Spirit of Youth* in the nation's capital. "The audience was enthusiastic," *Life* reported, "despite the hero's stolid, dead-pan acting." Blacks packed theaters to see the film. The *Courier*'s Louis Lautier found it "entertaining" despite its "hackneyed" plot. Critics of both races thought the picture lacked artistry, yet *Time* predicted it would "not be duplicated for many a moon." Its creative flaws aside, the movie gratified black viewers because it avoided the usual racist clichés. For over two decades the stock cinematic black character had been a reflection of the screen names of two marquee stars—Stepin Fetchit and Willie "Sleep 'n' Eat" Best. "With one or two exceptions, the Negro in pictures must dance, shoot craps, make faces, 'get hot,' run from ghosts, eat watermelons or steal chickens," the *Chicago Defender*'s Lucius Harper protested. "This applies with equal force to the stage." A *Courier* critic agreed, charging Hollywood with "the great crime" of casting Africans and African Americans "only as clowns, servants and savages," roles that would "flatter the egos of white people and bolster the international propaganda of white supremacy."

Americans went to see *Spirit of Youth* as Germans watched the fabricated film of Louis's recent win over Max Schmeling. Manager John Roxborough had denounced the spurious fight film, knowing that the big screen magnified images and impressions whether the reel came from a Hollywood studio or a Berlin cutting room. Louis realized that producers could be as pernicious as Max Machon had been in his celluloid smear against him. "Stepin Fetchit was a funny man," Louis reminisced. "Those black actors who bugged their eyes and acted stupid were funny, and that's alright, to be funny.... But when that's the only side of a race of people you see, that's bad. When you think of the influence of the movies on black people and white people, it can scare you." Louis noted that white directors habitually cast black women as maids and mammies. "Most times you had to be big, fat, talking with a heavy Southern accent, bug your eyes, and act stupid," he recalled. "It must have been hard on those actors."[3]

"Hard" indeed, leading some performers to join the protest against the unflattering images and trite parts for blacks in the usual studio fare. If not confined to the kitchen or nursery, black women sang or danced but did not play leading roles. "It happened again and again and again," singer and actress Lena Horne recalled. "Before I knew it, I'd been in Hollywood almost three years, I had appeared in more pictures than I liked to count, and I hadn't been part of a single story. I was just singing a song in a night club setting." She realized that producers preferred movies with the races in a relationship "of master and servant." More outspoken than Horne, singer, actor, and activist Paul Robeson detected duplicity as well as prejudice. "I thought I could do something for the Negro race on the films: show the truth about them—and about other people too," he explained in 1937. "I used to do my part and go away feeling satisfied." But his scenes "were twisted and changed—distorted." He realized "the Negro artist" had to think beyond "individual interests," for he and others had "a responsibility to his people" to resist "the traditional stereotyped portrayals of Negroes." Like Joe Louis, Robeson knew that black celebrities' personal choices had public consequences.

Despite the industry bias, many blacks held steady jobs in the studios during the Depression. Some, such as Stepin Fetchit and Hattie McDaniel, even prospered. When McDaniel won an Oscar for best supporting actress in *Gone With the Wind*, activists implored her to boycott the ceremony to protest the film's nostalgia for the Old South and slave days. Routinely cast as mammy or maid, McDaniel defended her roles. "I'd rather play a maid," she explained, "than be one." On a personal level, her response made sense; politically, she seemed naive. "Stepin Fetchit made a fortune portraying a slothful, lazy, anti-social character which has been accepted as a stereotype of the American colored man all over the world," Ralph Matthews of the *Afro-*

American observed. "Should colored artists put race above cash, or should they feather their own nests and let the devil take the hindmost?" Matthews hoped other black celebrities would follow Louis's lead in not exchanging dignity for dollars.[4]

The Joe Louis portrayed in *Spirit of Youth* confirmed the image his handlers had promoted since his first professional fight in 1934, an image contrary to the pernicious depiction of blacks in popular culture. Two years prior to Louis's acting debut, for example, Willie "Sleep 'n' Eat" Best played the stock horror film "coon" in *The Monster Walks*. As Louis gained prominence, Stepin Fetchit endeared himself to director John Ford for his role as a dutiful servant in *Judge Priest*, a nostalgic tale set in an 1890 Kentucky town where whites and blacks join voices in a wistful rendition of "My Old Kentucky Home." In *Spirit of Youth* black characters did not wait on the master, dance for the white folks, tremble with fright at "haunts," or sing sentimental songs about the good old days in Dixie. Instead, the Louis biopic told a credible story that reflected well on him and his people.

When Louis vowed "to get ahead and be somebody," he spoke for millions of his people who found white attitudes and actions a barrier to their own aspirations. "Who can say," columnist George Schuyler of the *Pittsburgh Courier* queried, "how many Joe Louises there will be in every walk of life in the America of the future?" Wendell Smith, a critic of the color line in major-league baseball, also hailed Louis as a symbol of striving. "As long as Louis is champion," he wrote in the *Courier* in 1940, "this race can point to him with pride and say that there is one man who exemplifies what a Negro can do if given the opportunity." He was "our best model . . . showing the average white man something about the Negro he never knew before." The *Dallas Express* praised Louis for mitigating harm done by others who lacked his discretion. "He is a symbol of all the things Negroes have wanted to convince the world that members of the race hold dear," the *Express* declared. Louis had "done more for interracial relationships than any other single individual or agency in the last several years." This impression was the accepted wisdom in the black press by the time the United States entered World War II.

White writers echoed the praise. "The fists of Joe Louis are the megaphones and microphones of his race on the nights that he defends his championship," sportswriter Ed Sullivan wrote after Louis beat Billy Conn in 1941. "Never an individual—he is all the sorrows and joys, and fears and hopes, and the melody of an entire race." Louis became Detroit's favorite son. "There may have been more spectacular champions, but we doubt they were greater," Leo Macdonnell argued in the *Detroit Times*. Louis's conduct "in or out of the ring" had been impeccable. "Detroit . . . may well be proud of the fabulous Negro boy who once worked at Ford's."[5]

Few people graduate from cotton row and assembly line to Madison Square Garden and the Hollywood studio. Fewer still attain the fame and fortune Louis enjoyed for over a decade at the peak of his career. From the Gilded Age through World War II, millions of southern blacks migrated north and west, among them Jack Johnson, Ida B. Wells, Louis Armstrong, Billie Holiday, Richard Wright, and Maya Angelou. Even though these well-known migrants comprised just a tiny portion of the exodus, they symbolized enhanced freedom and opportunity for all blacks. Joe Louis did not mirror his people's attainments but he reflected their ambitions. Drew "Bundini" Brown, later known as a cornerman for Muhammad Ali, recalled how his neighbors in Florida gravitated to radios when Louis fought. "The quietest our people ever got was listening to Joe Louis," Brown remembered. "He gave them some gladness . . . some glorious feeling." Ernest Dillard, a native of Montgomery, Alabama, remembered borrowing a satchel from a friend as he prepared to leave the South for Detroit the day Louis fought for the title. Dillard and his pal "didn't have radios," but those who did "had a public service in mind: they played them loud." Dillard could "follow the fight" as he "walked across town." Blacks in Montgomery remained calm when Louis knocked out a white opponent, but Dillard knew they welcomed the reversal of customary race roles.[6]

Louis also gave fans "some glorious feeling" with his stature beyond the ring. His enlistment in the army made him a symbol of black unselfishness and sacrifice. When he risked his title while fighting for the military relief funds, he dramatized the paradox between his own color-blind generosity and the blatant discrimination in the armed forces. When he gave up a champion's purses for a common soldier's pay, he put country before career and challenged Americans to embrace equality over exclusion. In pitching bonds, urging enlistment, entertaining troops, and encouraging defense workers, Louis summoned the nation to apply its wartime fervor for freedom and self-determination abroad to vital changes on the home front.

By war's end, Louis had decided that blacks should not only give but receive. At a dinner sponsored by the Southern Conference for Human Welfare in late 1946, he stated his intention to become more involved in the organization's causes. "Lots of people think that I'm doing all right as a fighter and that I should stick to my business," he told the guests.

> They mean all right, but they don't understand that fighting prejudice, disease, and second class citizenship is my business, too. I hate jim crow. I hate disease. I hate the poll tax. I hate seeing people kept down because

they are colored. I am not going to let this hate stay in my system, but I am going to help people fight jim crow and try to make this a better America. I am going to try to keep my punch in the ring as well as out of the ring.[7]

A New Star Rises

Unfortunately for Louis, his pledge to become more involved came just as his "punch in the ring" diminished. By the time Louis spoke to the Southern Conference in late 1946, Jackie Robinson had completed a successful season in the Brooklyn Dodgers farm system and anticipated joining the parent club in the spring. In both substantive and symbolic terms, Robinson's big league debut quickly eclipsed the Louis story. Jackie's wife, Rachel, for example, realized that the torch was being passed from fading icons to a new generation of race pioneers. "In the 1930s, we had witnessed the stunning achievements of Jesse Owens, Joe Louis, Marian Anderson, and many other outstanding black Americans, and their experiences had seemed to promise broad advances," she recalled. "But the social order that denied opportunity to black Americans didn't change. Breaking baseball's color barrier was another chance to chip away at ingrained racist attitudes."

Fans and writers alike shifted their attention from boxing to baseball—by 1947 Louis was old copy and Robinson the breaking news. After Jackie's rookie year, the *Afro-American*'s Ralph Matthews paid tribute to Joe, but the slant was all past and no future. "When he walked into the ring the nation's ears were glued to the radio and when he was in difficulty some weak hearts collapsed and died," Matthews recalled. "When he met a challenger or defeated an ex-champion it was necessary to call out the police in a hundred cities to maintain order. But today . . . nobody seems to care." Louis defeated Jersey Joe Walcott in a split decision in late 1947. "For the first time in his brilliant and great reign," Louis left the ring "under a salvo of boos," Art Carter of the *Afro-American* reported. "Generally speaking Louis looked bad. . . . At 33, the champion has lost much of what he had." Louis redeemed himself when he knocked out Walcott in a rematch and announced his retirement in 1948. But huge tax bills and foolish pride brought him back into the ring. He defeated some mediocre opponents but lost to champion Ezzard Charles in 1950. Rocky Marciano knocked Louis out of boxing for good in 1951. By the time Louis ended his career sprawled on the ring apron at the Garden, Jackie Robinson had been named rookie of the year (1947), led the National League in hitting (1949) and stolen bases (1947, 1949), and won the Most Valuable Player award (1949). The Dodgers won league pennants in 1947 and 1949. While Robinson flourished, Louis lost round after round to the Internal Revenue Service. Fans of all races cheered him against this hard-hitting and relentless opponent.[8]

An avid baseball fan and Robinson's army buddy, Louis also followed the big story. If Joe resented the attention lavished on Jackie, he never showed it. Louis later noted that Branch Rickey, the owner of the Brooklyn Dodgers, had asked him to help prepare Robinson for his rookie season. But Louis declined, confident that this new black hope could put out jim crow unassisted. As Robinson proved his mettle on the field, Louis realized that the burden of carrying the race now belonged to an athlete who wore a different kind of glove. "Fame is fickle and for that reason I don't think much about it at all," Louis had once said. "I know that I may be a hero today and just another fighter tomorrow." Spectators "yell for you today and at you tomorrow." Fans and fair-weather friends sought "other heroes" to replace familiar idols. "They are with you when you are up," Louis sighed, "and easily forget you when you start down."[9]

Louis and his handlers had adeptly overcome the resistance to his fighting for the title, but that precedent did not shield Jackie Robinson from fierce opposition to the reconstruction of major-league baseball. Led by Fred "Dixie" Walker from Birmingham, a clique of Dodgers had circulated a petition in training camp urging Rickey to keep Robinson off the roster. Manager Leo Durocher heard about it and called a team meeting for one in the morning. He obliquely told the players they knew what to do with their appeal. When they looked puzzled, he spoke more bluntly. "Take the petition and, you know, wipe your ass." In the season opener, the Phillies taunted Robinson and his teammates. "Hey, nigger," one shouted, "why don't you go back to the cotton field where you belong?" Manager Ben Chapman insisted that Robinson wanted to integrate more than baseball. "Hey, snowflake," he yelled, "which one of those white boy's wives are you dating tonight?" He went further, asking the "black boy" if he liked "white poontang." The Phillies spouted old plantation attitudes. "Hey, you carpetbaggers!" one snarled. "How's your little reconstruction period getting along?" Even Dodgers not keen on Robinson resented the baiting. At Ebbetts Field, an opponent's infielder pretended not to know Robinson was standing on base. He swung his arm and slapped the runner's face with his mitt, the impact audible in the Dodger dugout. Following Rickey's advice, Robinson kept quiet. But he stole third base on the next pitch. Pee Wee Reese, the Dodger's shortstop, from Louisville, showed that the South was not solid on race matters. He spurned Dixie Walker's petition and welcomed Robinson aboard. When an opponent asked Reese how he liked playing with a "nigger," Reese walked over and placed his hand on Jackie's shoulder at second base. Besides the insults, Robinson ducked beanballs and high spikes. Targeted for abuse on the field, he also received hate mail—including death threats—at his Brooklyn home.

In his second season, Robinson was hit by more pitches than any player in the league. The team did well with him in the lineup, and the victories and the prospects for a pennant and the World Series reduced racial tensions in the clubhouse. Pee Wee Reese realized that baseball's black hope brought more to the team than clutch hitting, fielding, and speed on the bases. "People tell me that I helped Jackie," Reese later reflected to Roger Kahn. "But knowing my background and the progress I've made, I have to say he helped me as much as I helped him."[10]

Louis and Robinson inspired black folks while giving all other groups two remarkable athletes to admire. Yet black observers knew the limits of sports symbolism, for breakthroughs in athletics did not necessarily bring general advances in civil rights. Besides, many blacks who earned their living at a desk or pulpit doubted that athletic success represented the pinnacle of race achievement. "Truly we are not only a child race, but a race little removed from the savage," the Reverend Francis J. Grimke complained in 1936, "if Joe Louis is the ideal that we wish to lift up before our young people." Before Louis fought for the title, the *Philadelphia Tribune* joined NAACP leaders in urging calm if he prevailed. "After all, if Joe Louis wins the championship it will not prove anything more than the fact that Louis is a better boxer than Braddock," the *Tribune* observed. "It will naturally set in motion a certain pride in accomplishment among colored Americans. But a Louis victory will not settle any of the fundamental problems which face colored America." The *Afro-American*'s I.F. Coles chided black journalists and fans for their preoccupation with Louis. Jews would never elevate Max Baer over Freud or Einstein, and whites held Washington and Lincoln in higher repute than John L. Sullivan and Jim Jeffries. Folklorist Zora Neale Hurston denied any "single Negro" or "single organization" could "carry the thirteen million in any direction," even though Louis "comes nearer to it than anyone else at present." An outspoken individualist, she chafed at notions of group identity and solidarity. "Negroes want a variety of things and many of them diametrically opposed," she wrote in 1942. "Why should Negroes be united? Nobody else in America is."

"All God's chillun may have shoes," Joseph Bibb mused in the *Courier*, "but they can't have Golden Gloves." Blacks had "tremendously overemphasized" boxing. "Social, economic, and political problems," he warned, would "not be settled" in the ring. With the radio on in her grandmother's general store, Maya Angelou witnessed Louis's effect on Arkansas sharecroppers, but she realized that only a lucky few would make it in professional sports. She bristled when a white speaker flattered her graduating class in 1940 by praising former students from her school who had achieved athletic success. "The white kids were going to have a chance to become Galileos and Madame Curies and Edisons and Gauguins, and our boys (the girls weren't even in on it) would try to be Jesse Owenses and Joe Louises," Angelou recalled. "We were maids and farmers, handymen and washerwomen, and anything higher that we aspired to was farcical and presumptuous." She wondered about those too slow, too small, too clumsy, or too female to be sports stars. How would the race produce engineers, doctors, judges, and scientists? "Owens and the Brown Bomber were great heroes in our world," she conceded, "but what school official in the white-goddom of Little Rock had the right to decide that those two men must be our only heroes?"[11]

Objects of great public acclaim, black stars also felt the burden of high group expectations. Black fans anticipated gains from their Olympians' victories in 1936, for example, but the *Courier* urged them to be realistic. "There is an unfortunate disposition in Aframerica," the *Courier* noted, "to want every Negro of prominence to fight the race problem" in behalf of those "who sit back doing nothing." Lucius Harper of the *Defender* also lectured readers about lack of perspective and proportion. "You can get ten thousand black people on the side of a river bank to chant hymns during a baptizing," he grumbled, "but you can't get 100 to go to Washington to form a lobby against lynching." Louis and Robinson knew they competed in behalf of an entire race. "I was the black grandson of a slave, the son of a black sharecropper," Jackie Robinson reflected, "part of a historic occasion, a symbolic hope to my people." Rachel Robinson also sensed this connection. "Jack and I began to realize how important we were to black America," she reflected on that first season, "and how much we symbolized its hunger for opportunity and its determination to make dreams long deferred possible."

Such expectations troubled certain celebrities. Singer Marian Anderson thought the DAR erred in denying her Constitution Hall for a concert in 1939, for example, but she wanted the issue to be her talent and not her lineage. She did not see herself as a "fearless fighter" for civil rights. "I have been in this world long enough to know that there are all kinds of people," she observed, "all suited by their own natures for different tasks." When Secretary of the Interior Harold Ickes invited her to perform at the Lincoln Memorial instead, she felt uneasy. The controversy cast her in a role she did not relish. "I had become, whether I liked it or not, a symbol, representing my people," she observed. "I had to appear." Sensitive to her discomfort, the *Courier* called for a mass movement to relieve the few famous athletes and artists from their burden. "It has always seemed shameful to us that Negroes in various communities should sit supinely amid discrimination and segregation, doing nothing except grumble," the *Courier* scolded, "until some prominent Negro visits the city, and then expect him or her by courageous action to undo the evil which we have permitted to flourish unchallenged." A large mixed audience heard Anderson at the memorial on Easter Sunday 1939, a poignant rebuke to jim crow in the district. "Genius," Ickes declared when he introduced her, "draws no color line." The DAR opened its hall to Anderson for benefit concerts during the war and later leased it to her on the same terms that white artists received. Discrimination is "no longer an issue" at Constitution Hall, she noted in her 1956 memoir, "and that is good."[12]

Ickes spoke nobly in divorcing genius from race, but he did not express the prevailing opinion among whites. Nor did actual practice conform to his lofty principle. So long as whites believed race to be the chief determinant of character and capacity, blacks would need means beyond exhortation to gain equality. Joe Louis, Jackie Robinson, and others had talents that transcended color, and they built bridges to opportunity that all might eventually cross. The *Courier*'s William Nunn noted this role when he labeled Louis an "ambassador of good will" who bore "the weight of an entire race on his shoulders." Chester Washington, Nunn's colleague, similarly praised Louis for saying "the right thing at the right time" and for giving hope to those who needed it most.

Louis won and lost with equanimity. He acted discreetly in public, avoiding settings that might reinforce racist notions. By doing so he assuaged white anxieties. Even if white reporters sometimes found him inarticulate and uninformed, they usually treated him fairly. His story was irresistible— the grandson of a former slave and his wife who was half Cherokee, the son of sharecropping parents, the mother a pious and overworked woman with a husband confined to a state mental asylum when Joe was only two. For most fans of Joe Louis, the man seemed entirely consistent with the image that prevailed from his professional debut in 1934 to his discharge from the army in late 1945.[13]

The Champ in Decline

At times, however, rumors hinted at discrepancies between the life and the legend. Louis possessed the fine qualities ascribed to him, but the iconic image was somewhat misleading. Success brought many temptations his way. Under his handlers' watchful gaze, he managed to resist most of them until he won the title in 1937. Idolized by millions and dazzled by a single fight purse that often brought more money than a sharecropper's lifetime income, Louis found his fame incompatible with family ties and preparations for a future after the cheering and big paydays stopped. Luckily for him and his image, the press knew little or nothing about his other side or chose to keep its knowledge to itself.

Louis found it easier to retain his title than to hold on to his wife and money. His managers kept him active in the ring, so he remained confined to training camp for extended periods of time. The long and frequent separations strained Joe's marriage to Marva. Becoming champion fulfilled a common dream but it proved a mixed blessing. As Joe devoted more time to public appearances, business ventures, and charitable causes, he gave less attention to his family. Joe and Marva gained the public's affection but lost their privacy. Joe's special bond with his race often interfered with the bonds of matrimony.

Other factors besides training, travel, and lack of privacy estranged the couple. A columnist in early 1938, for example, linked Joe to Marian Egbert, a New York City dancer. Marva stood by her man. "But I am happy!" she insisted to the *Courier*'s Julia Jones. "I don't think Joe is interested in any other woman. I have heard this Miss Egbert is a very nice person. Suppose she and Joe are friends? That doesn't mean he doesn't love his wife." Egbert denied the rumors. "I wish you would tell everybody that I am engaged, and that I am not trying to break up Joe's home," she pleaded to Edgar Rouzeau of the *Courier*. "Joe and I are good friends. Nothing more." The press accepted the denial, but gossip persisted. Louis trained hard to avenge his loss to Schmeling. He kept his spouse at a distance, no easy matter for Marva. "Yes, I like children," she told an *Afro-American* reporter in late 1938. "We both want them. We are waiting until Joe has some time. My life is spent waiting for Joe."

But when Joe had "some time" he often spent it far from home. Marva tired of waiting. Columnist Walter Winchell reported that she intended to file for divorce in 1941. Billy Rowe, Joe's close friend at the *Courier*, denied it. "Joe," Rowe assured readers, "says it ain't so." This time the gossip was true. "He didn't come home for two months," Marva complained. "Even a champ should come home sometime." Julia Jones of the *Courier* understood her frustration but did not take sides. "I love them both," she sighed, "and have known for some time that a break was imminent." Marva filed papers but promised to wait until she and Joe could talk it over. "Just think," Rowe wrote, "Joe [is] in training so much he knows less about what's going on in his household than Walter Winchell" does. As talk of a serious rift spread, friendly columnists tried to dispel the rumors by hinting that Marva was pregnant. But Lulu Garrett of the *Afro-American* ridiculed that notion. "The temperature in the Louis household," she scoffed, "would have kept an ice cube in its original solid state." The couple reconciled, but Joe entered the army in early 1942. For almost four years Uncle Sam kept him busy and distant from Marva. She still waited.[14]

The prospect of a divorce saddened fans, but when Marva accused Joe of cruelty and domestic violence as well as negligence, that disturbed them even more. In the divorce papers, Marva stated that Joe hit her during arguments, conduct entirely at odds with his image. "Marva says Joe did his boxing against her," Carter Wesley wrote in the *Dallas Express*. "Frankly, we don't believe it." Wesley regarded the allegation as an attempt "to embarrass Joe and keep him from fighting the suit much, lest she go through with more of that type of charge." Wesley could not picture Louis "as a wife-beater" and urged a reconciliation. If they failed, he hoped they would part "without destroying the reputations of either one of them." Lawrence Brockenbury, the *Express* editor, doubted Marva's charge and depicted her as an ingrate. "Joe has done enough for her not to have said that," he objected. "She was just another stenographer when Joe started draping her in togs galore. That's what I call biting the hand that feeds (or slaps?) you."

Ralph Matthews of the *Afro-American* blamed the rift on the couple's peculiar status and not on personal flaws. "Not many girls of our group," he noted, "have ever had to adjust themselves, suddenly, without previous experience, to the trying exactions of being married to the race's most popular idol and still maintain emotional equilibrium." Idolatry was just part of the problem, for boxing always strained a marriage. The ring "is a man's world, from which women are excluded," Matthews argued, an exclusion more troublesome to Marva than to Joe. "Men turn love on and off like a spigot," he added, "but women . . . must maintain an even flow." Whatever the source of the "trying exactions," Matthews urged press and public to leave them alone. "What Joe does in the prize ring is everybody's business," he concluded, "but what he does with his wedding ring is his private affair."

The managers accepted some blame for the rift but saw no alternative to their strategy. Without steady exercise and a strict diet, Louis gained weight quickly. Besides, the managers wanted him to be an active champion. Louis blamed his marital woes on this regimen. "Marva sued me for divorce," he recalled. "I was surprised because I had been in training so much that I hadn't had much time to spend at home." Louis later made the same excuse and revealed that his wife had "wanted me to give up fighting."[15]

The couple stayed together and had a baby girl in early 1943. They named her Jacqueline for Jack Blackburn, who had died the year before. Then they split again. "I am reluctantly doing my duty to my publication," Julia Jones wrote, "but I personally regret having to write any pronouncement of their separation." Marva moved to New York City to study voice and drama. "During my six years of married life," she lamented, "Joe and I have really spent less than a full year together due to training schedules and now the war." Both regarded their marriage as "a flop" and would decide what to do after the war. "It's definitely the end of the road for Marva and Joe, America's story-book couple!" the *Courier* announced in 1944. While interviewing Marva at the Hotel Theresa, two *Courier* correspondents saw a note she had scribbled on a program marking her debut as a club singer: "Joe vs. Marva . . . 8 years' bout . . . Winnah?" After appearing in Philadelphia, she seemed optimistic. "Why should Joe and I get a divorce?" she asked a reporter. Neither wanted to marry anyone else, and they had Jacqueline. "I've just one aim—to be good at this. Maybe if I'm good Joe will think me the most glamorous woman he's ever met when he comes home from the war."

Marva played some fine clubs, the Zanzibar in New York, the Orpheum in Los Angeles, and the Three Sixes in Detroit's Paradise Valley, not far from the Brown Bomber Chicken Shack, John Roxborough's office, and a bowling alley in which he and Joe had an interest. Manager Richard King of the Three Sixes never forgot her run at his club. "We made more money with her appearance than we made with any of the other performers," he recalled. "She was there for three weeks, and we carried a packed house during her entire engagement." She promised an agent she would not wear the same gown twice and kept her word. "Many women came to see what she was wearing," King reminisced. He paid her $800 a week, but she brought in so many customers that the club made enough money the first week to cover her full engagement. Weeks two and three were pure profit. While Marva played the nightspots, Joe visited black fighter pilots in Italy. Had he toured their barracks he would have seen a familiar face. MARVA PIN-UP PICK OF GIs IN ITALY, the *Courier* declared in 1944.[16]

The war outlasted Marva's patience, and she refiled for divorce in 1945. Joe returned to Chicago for the hearing but, the press reported, he showed "more concern for a game of golf than the divorce case." Marva told reporters she and Joe had never spent more than thirty-two consecutive days together. She also complained that Joe squandered money far beyond his meager soldier's pay. He gambled, dropping as much as $100 a hole on the golf course. "People seem to feel like Joe and I go together like ham and eggs," Marva sighed. "The greatest difficulty seems to be being apart so much." She denied that other women were a problem. "The glamorous Mrs. Louis does not think any of Joe's girl friends are serious rivals," the story noted, "because he has had many of them." The couple divorced, then quietly remarried the next year. Son Joseph arrived in 1947, but a new child did not solve the old problems. In 1949 Marva divorced Joe yet again and won custody of their children. The long fight was over, neither the "winnah" when the match ended.

Journalists were kind to Louis. They separated his private and public lives, not wanting bad press to sully his image, embarrass his people, and impede their progress. Other black celebrities also protected his reputation, among them Lena Horne, who first met him at the Cotton Club. She moved from stage to studio, where she worked on *Cabin in the Sky* while Louis did his bit for Irving Berlin's *This Is the Army* in 1943. Like Paul Robeson, Horne hoped to bring a more nuanced picture of her people to the big screen. The established black stars snubbed her, and the tension between her and Ethel Waters was palpable. "In a large part of the Hollywood Negro community," she complained, "I was never warmly received." Confused by the hostility, Horne took solace in the company of another outsider. "About the only friend I made was Joe Louis, who was in the Army and stationed out there for a while," she noted. "He was a good and gentle man, he became my friend."

But Louis was more than a "friend" to Horne, although he hardly fit the role of "a good and gentle man." By mid-1943 Joe, Lena, and Marva found themselves in a love triangle worthy of a blockbuster movie. Marva found a letter to Joe from Lena and confronted him with it. "I wanted to marry Lena," Joe admitted years later, "[but] didn't want to leave Marva, especially now with my new baby." His divided affections and indecision led to a nasty fight with Horne. "Lena started cursing me like nobody ever had," Joe recalled. "Before I knew it, I hit her with a left hook and knocked her on the bed. Then I jumped on her and started choking her. The thing, thank God, that saved her was that her aunt was in the apartment." Louis left and then phoned to apologize, but Horne hung up on him. Without the proverbial happy ending, Louis and Horne were lucky to end the romance with hurt feelings rather than broken bones and an awful scandal.[17]

Late in life, Louis confirmed the old rumors about his many romances and escapades. He confessed to a long affair with Marian Egbert, whom he had met when still single. "I went with her for years," he admitted. "I was crazy about her. Later on, she'd meet me all over the country when I was fighting." Louis also disclosed a discreet affair with Sonja Henie, a Norwegian gold medalist in figure skating, "a smart woman" who "kept everything 'undercover.'" Other chorus girls turned his head. He met Ruby Dallas at the Cotton Club. "She was something else," Louis reminisced. "Fell in love with her, and we saw each other as much as we could." Louis had good looks, fame, lots of money, and little will power. "I was the weaker sex," he conceded. "I didn't resist one pretty girl who had a sparkle in her eye."

Close friends knew that the bonds of matrimony did not restrain Louis. "One, three or four girls he'd have after a fight, each going in and staying fifteen to twenty minutes," Joe's friend Leonard Reed recalled. "I don't know what they were doing, but I know that I went around the hotel picking up the tabs. He supported women around the country." Reed sent money to "a list of women," getting them apartments and paying rent "so he could go there when he was in town." Louis told the truth, but not the whole truth, when he said training kept him from home. He often chose to be away. Sunnie Wilson, Joe's close friend and business partner, remembered their "good time[s] together." One trip soon after Louis won the title stuck in his mind. "We drove to Toledo, Ohio, to see a big show with a lot of pretty girls," Wilson recollected, then "followed the show to Cleveland." They went on to Pittsburgh, returned to Cleveland ("where we borrowed money from friends"), then proceeded to Buffalo. The men tracked the show for "a good two weeks."

Louis also toured with Sugar Ray Robinson. They traveled to Washington, DC, in mid-1943 to confer with War Department officers who were planning their schedule for entertaining troops at home and abroad. When they arrived, their arrangements had not been finalized, so they did some scheduling of their own. "We had met a couple of girls the day before," Robinson recalled. "The adultery commandment was about to lose a decision." The women booked hotel rooms down the hall from the men. But Sugar Ray's wife, the former Edna Mae Holly, a dancer at the Cotton Club, arrived a day early and foiled the scheme.

The *Courier*'s Billy Rowe knew plenty about Louis's personal life but kept it to himself until after World War II. "Yes, the Champ has plenty [of] feeling for the beauties of the opposite sex," Rowe confirmed in 1946. "So what?" Louis had been an exemplary boxer, citizen, and soldier, Rowe stressed, and he had avoided scandal for well over a decade. "Since he won the championship he has been in a position to do so much damage," Rowe observed.

> Young and good looking for a fighter, to him it has always been an open field in whatever direction he wanted to go. On all sides of the ledger his record is great. He has always said the right thing and said it when saying it meant most. He has done no visible wrong and kept out of the rough stream down which flows all flesh. Win, lose, or draw, Joe Louis has been a superb fighter and, better yet, a great man, a credit to people and country.

Most journalists, black and white, agreed. They ignored or excused what Louis did privately ("no visible wrong") so long as he behaved well publicly. Journalists like Julia Jones and Lulu Garrett treated him kindly in print. Mary McLeod Bethune stressed his role as a symbol of striving and achievement. Lena Horne remained mum about their tempestuous affair. Marva Louis spoke discreetly to reporters, saving her serious charges for legal proceedings. Common race, not uncommon gender, moved these women to extol Louis's virtues and ignore his vices.[18]

The most embarrassing disclosures about Joe Louis came from the man himself in his 1978 memoir. Perhaps Louis sought to confirm rumors about his sexual prowess for a more permissive generation obsessed with the private lives of public people. Long out of the limelight, he might have found solace in a happier time when he had enjoyed considerable fame and fortune. Or maybe he simply wanted to "tell it like it is" in the parlance of the era of full disclosure and ruined reputations. Whatever his reasons, Louis misjudged the impact of his personal revelations. He had stood high on a pedestal for well over a generation, but the urge to discredit and debunk was strong in the wake of the Vietnam War and the Nixon White House scandals. Even though the sexual revolution had extended the boundaries of permissible private behavior, the feminist movement had exposed the double standard and raised awareness about gender bias in the past and present. By the time Louis's memoir appeared, journalists no longer drew such sharp distinctions between the personal and public spheres. For them, private conduct was quite relevant to assessing moral character and public reputation. Some reviewers found the Joe Louis of the 1978 memoir a relic of a distinctly unliberated age that was best forgotten. "The man is a classic male chauvinist and he attempts to exculpate his constant lechery and infidelity by claiming that as a 'big man' he had a 'big appetite,'" Barry Amis wrote in *Freedomways:*

> The only thing "big" about Louis was his ego. . . . Louis seems to have spent the greater part of his career as a boxer whoring after pretty women. He especially liked beautiful movie stars but apparently almost any woman with a sparkle in her eye would do. The names of several well-known personalities are mentioned but, rather than enhancing his own stature, it only seems to confirm the criticism of him that he was all body and no brain.

Amis also faulted Louis for "hypocrisy," a "disturbing" level of "financial incompetence," and "social naiveté." "Completely devoid of sociopolitical sagacity," Louis owed "any contributions that he made to improved racial conditions . . . to circumstance [rather] than to political commitment." Little more than "a hedonist," Joe Louis seemed "a sorry, pathetic figure" to Amis, "and not a person that anyone would want to remember."

A reviewer in *Ebony* was kinder, stressing Louis's humble origins and achievements: "He grew up poor, the son of struggling sharecroppers in Alabama, and later was a ghetto teenager in Detroit who dabbled at boxing between violin lessons and vocational school." His life changed dramatically when he won the title. Only twenty-three, "he had it all—money, fame, glamour, and a host of beautiful women." He fell victim to "insurmountable financial problems," and his glamour "slowly wane[d]." Yet "Louis always loved—and had—his women." To illustrate his "passion for beautiful women," *Ebony* made the review a pictorial on Joe's many "loves." The lead photograph showed him and Lena Horne sitting side by side at a piano. Another featured Joe and Marva strolling down a city sidewalk. Others included Sonja Henie on skates, Ruby Dallas jumping rope in short shorts and a tight top, and Lana Turner in a standard studio pose. *Ebony* included photographs of Joe's wives after he retired from the ring—Rose Morgan, "an important figure in Black beauty culture during the 1950s," and Martha Malone Jefferson, "a California lawyer." Joe and Rose wed in 1955 but the marriage was annulled in 1958; Joe and Martha married in 1959 and remained together despite recurring tensions over his restlessness and detachment. To explain the failed marriages, *Ebony* quoted Louis: "I tried to get domesticated, but old habits are hard to get rid of." The review praised Joe for being "frank." *Ebony* had finessed the matter of his infidelity before. In an article inspired by the film *The Joe Louis Story* in 1953, *Ebony* referred to the former champion as "perhaps the most lied-about, slandered and maligned Negro in the world today." To rebut rumors of Louis's marital and money problems, *Ebony* listed "the ten biggest lies" about him. "Although Louis has had a number of affairs of the heart," *Ebony* maintained, "these are not considered excessive in light of his prominence." Not all readers appreciated *Ebony*'s special pleading for Joe Louis. Robert Thorpe of the Bronx wrote to protest a "new low" in "the caliber and content" of recent articles, including one devoted to "the sordid 'achievements' of a San Francisco hooker" and the other on "Joe Louis on the bimbo circuit." Thorpe planned to let his subscription expire.[19]

Herb Gluck in the *New York Times* called Louis's memoir "classy" and said he was "rooting for it to do well." He appreciated that Louis did "no whimpering" about his troubles, including his fight with the folks at Internal Revenue who "almost shook his pockets clean." Even more persistent than tax collectors were the women who had "buzz[ed] around him like flies." Gluck found "the total effect" of the book "marvelous." In a review in *Newsweek,* James Baker acknowledged Louis's "trials and tribulations" but denied that he was "the victimized chump people often like to think he is." "His biggest weakness was women," Baker explained, extravagance a close second. Despite blowing a fortune he had "saved . . . his dignity." It hardly seems possible that Amis, Gluck, and Baker read the same book.[20]

The text was the same, but readers approached it with varying sensibilities and agendas. None of the reviewers, for example, brought much historical perspective to the analysis of Louis and his era. That limitation made it hard for them to assess Louis's character and conduct in terms of beliefs and values prevalent in his time. In addition, no reviewer appreciated the inherent problems in a work so dependent on an old boxer's reminiscences about specific events, people, and feelings from decades before, often some forty years or more past. These issues aside, the autobiography pleased many readers and reviewers even if parts of it repulsed others. In many ways Louis embodied the triumphant American spirit, a symbol of a simpler time as well as a happy reminder of past wrongs righted and perils at home and abroad overcome. This aspect of the legend also informed the memoir, but it was an old story and less titillating than intimate details about sex, infidelity, gambling, drugs, and money. Glamour shots of Lena Horne and Ruby Dallas sold more magazines than a keen analysis of what the sensational knockout of Max Schmeling had meant in 1938.

Often perceptive and provocative, Barry Amis was also unduly harsh in judging Louis. The Brown Bomber had undeniably damaged his reputation by admitting his many affairs, gambling problems, and, after his retirement, drug abuse. The gist of his financial and tax woes had been told before. His sexual exploits, however—and his tone in relating them—startled many readers who now had to reconcile the man with the myth. Since blacks had long borne the stigma of excessive id and nonchalance about family ties, the sordid details of Louis's domestic failings fit the racists' pernicious theories about stunted moral and cognitive development among African Americans. Critics understandably worried that the memoir would provide more grist for the bigots' mill. But the point that Louis lacked "sociopolitical sagacity" and had fostered better race relations only by "circumstance" and not "commitment" is erroneous. John Roxborough, Julian Black, and Jack Blackburn understood racial totems and taboos, and they adeptly steered Louis away from impropriety early in his career. Nor was Louis himself ignorant of these codes. As he aged and became more prominent, he drifted away from close kin, mentors, and friends, making him more susceptible to temptation in many forms. Yet his foibles should be measured against his many public achievements—an unprecedented record in the ring, exemplary sportsmanship, innumerable acts of kindness and charity, and service and sacrifice to the nation unrivaled by any celebrity of his era. Louis and his advisers thought their approach to the color line was the best for their time. He did not lobby against lynching, protest police brutality or judicial misconduct, walk picket lines, speak on the stump, or risk a court martial and discharge by defying jim crow in the army. Nor did most of his black contemporaries who also understood the perils of overt resistance and rebellion. Rather, Joe Louis and other black celebrities found themselves in roles that transcended their personalities and professions—symbols in a struggle older than the nation against an enemy that often exiled, imprisoned, maimed, or even murdered its adversaries. When the DAR denied its hall to Marian Anderson, reporters pressed her for a reaction. "I knew too little to tell an intelligent story about it," she reminisced. "There were occasions, of course, when I knew more than I said. I did not want to talk. . . . I did not feel that I was designed for hand-to-hand combat, and I did not wish to make statements that I would later regret." She wanted to keep her music from becoming a pawn in race politics.[21]

Louis, Anderson, and others knew the price that black militants paid for seeking social justice—the Reverend T.A. Allen (lynched for organizing agricultural workers); Angelo Herndon (locked in Fulton Tower and sentenced to the chain gang); Paul Robeson (denied venues because of his anti-imperialist and pro-labor views); Elbert Williams (lynched for voter registration activity). Well equipped for "hand-to-hand combat" in the ring, Louis pulled his punches outside of it. Though not a Frederick Douglass or an Ida B. Wells, neither was Louis an Uncle Tom or a Stepin Fetchit.

From the vantage point of 1978, Amis was justifiably skeptical, even cynical, about the "ambassador of good will" approach to race relations. Forty years had passed since Louis knocked out Schmeling, a symbol of Aryan pride and pugnacity, yet blacks still waited for full equality. The history of the postwar struggle for racial justice is written in blood—in assaults on black veterans, beatings of protestors, bombings of homes and churches, assassinations of revered leaders, murders of many people, even children, guilty of being black and in the wrong place at the wrong time. Advances came sporadically and at great cost; racial attitudes and arrangements that had evolved over three centuries were repellent to reason and resistant to change. Ironically, the movement won its greatest political victories in the mid-1960s, just as economic and social conditions worsened for blacks in the ghetto. As memories of the reign of "King Joe" faded in the tumult of the 1960s and 1970s, Americans could see a glass half full or half empty. Race remained the national dilemma.

After World War II, activists had sensed a new day dawning in race relations. Many developments—the desegregation of baseball, the integration of the armed forces, court rulings against segregation in interstate transportation and public education, the rise of a mass movement in the South, the civil rights laws of the 1960s—all pointed to a better future. But the second Reconstruction lasted no longer than the first, the casualty of American escalation in Vietnam, urban riots, rising crime, high taxes, growing resentment against the federal government, and a white backlash against mass protest and public policies to assist and uplift the poor. Even some African Americans raised doubts about the old liberal orthodoxy and debated the relative merits of integration and public assistance versus separation and self-help.

The publication of Louis's autobiography coincided with rampant confusion and frustration following the American withdrawal and defeat in Vietnam, revelations of deceit and law breaking in the White House, the resignations of Vice President Spiro Agnew and President Richard Nixon, the first energy crisis, and persistent "stagflation." Like many events of the

1970s, the Louis memoir exposed another national icon who had been less than what he had appeared to be. In his time he had exemplified black pride and portended better race relations, a chance to exorcise the ghost of Jack Johnson and move beyond the extreme tribalism of the era of the great white hopes. His confessions in the memoir, however, suggested a charlatan whose private life belied the legend, not unlike the recent revelations about national leaders who espoused law and order but violated statutes and the public trust. Louis also appeared to be a man behind the changing times. In disclosing details about his extramarital affairs, he reinforced a racist notion as detrimental as any perpetrated on the big screen by Stepin Fetchit or Willie Best. By admitting sexual intimacy across the color line, Louis touched another raw nerve. Many whites remained opposed to interracial sex and marriage, and Malcolm X and other black nationalists had condemned mixed unions, arguing that race pride and solidarity precluded sleeping with the enemy. Louis had defied the old taboo, but his motive was purely personal rather than political—not unlike Jack Johnson's a generation before. Parts of the Louis story still tugged on Americans' heartstrings, but the memoir overall seemed unlikely to be an asset in the ongoing struggle for equality.

Oblivious to the effect his disclosures would have on black activists, Louis also seemed indifferent to the impressions his memoir would make on feminists. To him, women were much like golf and horses, diversions to break the monotony of intense training followed by long periods of relative inactivity. Louis traveled far and wide to find women, but only a certain kind of woman—glamorous and beautiful by cabaret and studio standards. In recounting his "loves," Louis stressed appearance. He had resumed the affair with Lena Horne, he confessed, because she seemed "more beautiful than she'd ever been." Sonja Henie was "one of the cutest gals" he ever met, "a pug-nosed blonde with bright blue eyes" who was "smart" because she kept secrets. He "fell in love" with Ruby Dallas because she "was something else." A pattern emerged. Joe would fall for a woman, disappear from his home, try to make it up to Marva with a lavish gift, vow to stop, then do it again. Marva complained that "she felt more like a kept woman," Joe recalled, "than a wife." But he shifted the blame. "My God," he exclaimed, "the women, the starlets, White and Black, came at me." They viewed *him* as a sex object: "A big movie star would see me . . . and wonder how I am in . . . bed. I'd see a big beautiful movie star and wonder how she is in . . . bed. We would find out very easily." An intriguing alibi, it did not placate Marva.[22]

Louis largely sat out the civil rights movement, though he did appear in Birmingham at Martin Luther King's request in 1963. He cared deeply for his people, but politics and protest bored him. Too complacent or hidebound to grapple with sexism, he approached women in a distinctly cavalier manner all his life. Nor did Louis fully comprehend his own place in black history. Barry Amis expected more from him. But Amis made a common error in his *Freedomways* review: He used only one yardstick to measure Louis, not two. Some principles transcend time and place; many values ebb and flow with the tides of history. When judged by the radical protest agendas of the 1960s and 1970s, Louis shrinks in stature, his limitations and failings often overshadowing his virtues and achievements. By the standards of a previous generation, however, he stands taller. He ended the white hope era and erased the color line in boxing. His triumphs over Carnera, Braddock, and Schmeling had considerable symbolic importance in a decade of persistent prejudice and economic hardship at home and rising fascism and militarism abroad. This political context helped transform Louis into a public figure transcending sports. His enlistment in 1942 further enhanced his stature and reminded his fellow citizens of the preponderance of "American" in African American. The recurring national and international crises during Louis's heyday magnified his virtues and minimized his vices. Finally, some of his habits that drove those closest to him to distraction endeared him to others.

Money Blues

Louis earned and spent a lot of money. Generous to both intimates and strangers, he helped a small army of needy people survive the Depression. In addition to direct aid to individuals, he donated money or time, sometimes both, to a wide array of organizations and institutions. "His heart," Jack Blackburn told a reporter, "is as big as a watermelon." Spoiled by a long string of big paydays, Louis acted as if the money spigot would never run dry. His managers steered him to annuities and real estate, but the return on his investments never matched his expenses. The allure of big money, like women, proved irresistible. "A champion's life is no longer normal after he becomes champ," Louis reflected. "There's a lot of fast living—hopping from one place to another—and there's a lot of people hanging around and living off him and leading him into a lot of temptation. . . . Everybody want[s] to take him for a soft touch." This "fast living" provoked many arguments. "The more fights he won and the more important he became, the more sycophants he attracted," Marva reflected. "To me, they were just leeches." "I was always too generous when it came to my money," Joe admitted. "Marva always complained about it."[23]

Reporters who covered Louis early in his career expected him to avoid the usual pitfalls of his profession. He had astute managers, a pious mother, a mature wife, and a sense of mission. Other signs also portended a bright future. "The best thing about Joe is that he has saved most of his money," a

Defender writer noted in 1935. "He is not . . . a free spender" even though he had "everything he wants" and gave his wife "the best of everything." Roi Ottley of the *Amsterdam News* agreed, labeling Louis "one of the thriftiest of the Negro boxers." Writers warned Louis about the spendthrift stereotype. Whites expected any black man with "big money" to "toss it away in public," the *Chicago Defender*'s Lucius Harper noted when Louis won the title. "He becomes popular with them through such silly capers. But Joe has a yen to save and invest for the future, and that's where the rub comes." Harper urged him not "to put hundred dollar bills on the noses of race horses." The *Courier*'s Ira Lewis observed that fans had expected Louis to repeat "some of the public escapades of Jack Johnson," but he had avoided them. When news of his tax liability and heavy debts surfaced during the war, many writers struggled to reconcile the reports with the prevailing image. "We have come to think of Joe as being a man of sober habits and homespun thrift," the *Dallas Express* countered in 1944. "We have come to believe that the sporting idea of 'easy come, easy go' just somehow did not apply to Joe Louis."[24]

Reporters had either missed the money problems or had decided to keep them quiet—not unlike their response to Louis's extramarital affairs. Like others suddenly standing at rainbow's end, Louis acquired a taste for big cars, tailored suits, purebred horses, fine cuisine, and the best accommodations at home and on the road. He invested in clubs and restaurants, notoriously risky ventures. He bought lavish gifts, paid tabs for friends, and gave generously to many causes. Louis could afford such habits as long as his fights continued to attract large crowds willing to pay high prices. By 1939, however, the premier division was long on pretenders and short on contenders. Writers dubbed Louis's opponents "the-bum-of-the-month club." Gate receipts dropped as the caliber of the challengers declined.

The hitch in the army ended the bonanza for over four years. Louis ran up debts with an equally rash Ray Robinson beside him. They spent "maybe $30,000 in six months . . . as easy as if it was thirty cents," Sugar Ray recalled, "by picking up tabs, buying presents for chicks, tipping big." Their credit was good because Mike Jacobs "would always stake" them, confident that he could collect when they resumed boxing. By late 1945, Louis owed about $150,000 to Jacobs, at least $40,000 to Roxborough.

If Louis did not have his hands in his pockets, someone else did. Art Carter of the *Afro-American* was a regular at training camp and often followed Joe on the road. He watched a steady parade of gold diggers. "He is constantly worried by salesmen, scamps, scoundrels, and just plain scum of society," Carter reported in 1940, "all eager to fashion some way to get some of the champion's money or to engineer the subject into a deal that will profit nobody but themselves." These deals invariably left Louis poorer but no wiser.

While scam artists took a share, Louis threw away plenty on his own. He lost a small fortune on his Brown Bombers softball team. Coleman Young, the future mayor of Detroit, recalled how Louis "came back to Black Bottom and passed out dollar bills on the street corner." When Louis fought the military relief bouts in 1942, he bought tickets to distribute to poor black soldiers. "The champion not only contributed his purse to the Army Emergency Relief Fund," Wendell Smith reported, "but treated 3,000 of his comrades with free ducats." Louis had a hard time saying no. "Once when a crony told Joe that he wanted to put on an all-Negro show," *Time* noted, "Joe reached mechanically for his checkbook [and] asked his friend, 'Will $1,000 do?'" His wallet seemed to have a string attached to his big heart. Mail for Louis arrived by the bagful at training camp. Between 1937 and 1942, John Roxborough estimated, Louis received requests for some $72 million from strangers seeking aid. The pleas continued throughout the war and after.[25]

Louis also took bad advice from accountants and ran up an enormous tax bill. When discharged from the army, he owed the IRS $115,000 in deferred taxes. In his final years in the ring, he did not earn enough to pay his back taxes and interest, much less his living expenses and current taxes. By 1950, he owed the federal government $208,000. His money woes prompted the comeback that ended with the humiliating loss to Rocky Marciano in 1951. He stooped to advertising cigarettes, violating his old rule of pitching only products he actually used. "I still didn't smoke then," Louis explained, "but now Uncle Sam was breathing down my back." He and Leonard Reed promoted "Joe Louis Punch" with hopes of high sales. A radio announcer in St. Louis asked Louis, "What's your favorite drink?" Perhaps tired from travel or too honest for his own good, Joe replied, "Coca-Cola." Louis lost his stake in several cabarets and restaurants. "Everything he has touched," a *Time* story noted in 1947, "seemed to turn to red ink." Louis worked as a promoter, wrestler, and referee. Watching him wrestle, Rose Morgan, his second wife, sighed, was "like seeing President Eisenhower wash dishes." Later he greeted gamblers at a Las Vegas casino—a fitting finale for a man who faced long odds all his life.[26]

The back taxes haunted Louis for years, but the debt had some advantages. The massive IRS bill—$1.3 million in back taxes and charges by 1957—seemed grossly unfair in view of his large payments during the 1930s and his many contributions to the war effort. Now in his lean years the government kept demanding more. "The story of Joe's adventures with the Bureau of Internal Revenue, in which he lost every round, is almost too melancholy to read," John Lardner, a *Newsweek* columnist, observed. "Not that it won't be, and hasn't been, read widely. A tax story like this one has the same kind of appeal that the death of Little Nell had, when Dickens was making them cry."[27]

Louis did not put big bills "on the noses of race horses," but he did bet them on golf balls. Sportswriter and friend Hype Igoe saw Louis shirk his training to play golf before his loss to Schmeling. Louis and Igoe were on a course when Jack Blackburn drove up and told Louis to return to camp. Louis refused. "Of course, I was glad that Joe did buck over the traces," Igoe admitted, "because I was playing him a dollar a hole at the time and I had him four down." The wagers increased over the years. Friend Billy Rowe reported in 1941 that Louis had recently lost some $5,000 on the links. He could not stop. "For a long time," Sam Lacy of the *Afro-American* wrote in 1948, "it has been whispered that the champ bets heavily on golf (sometimes as high as $1,000 a round), a practice which reportedly has gotten him deep in the red." Marva confirmed the gambling problem. "Golf contributed to his downfall," she explained. "In one summer he lost $90,000 gambling on the course." The reckless betting split the couple. "I play 36 holes almost every day," Louis admitted in 1948. "Marva don't like that. I spend a lot of money on golf, too." But Louis had no regrets and remained unrepentant until he died. "I had a ball spending money," he reflected, "I danced, I paid the piper, and left him a big fat tip."[28]

The Brown Bomber remained the major sports story in the black press for over a decade until Jackie Robinson took center stage. Plaudits came from white writers as well as black, and his popularity endured despite many setbacks after the war. Louis emerged a national hero during the halcyon days between his victory over Max Schmeling in 1938 and his knockout of Billy Conn in 1946, leading contemporaries and later commentators to view him as a great champion who transcended race, region, origin, and profession. He was a pioneer who cleared the way for African American dominance in professional sports in the United States within a generation of his winning the title. Without Joe, would there have been a Jackie? Louis also served as a harbinger of the civil rights movement, since his own service during the war (and contributions made by other African Americans) seemed a reasonable down payment toward full equality when peace returned. He might have done more, but most Americans of his time did very much less.

Only two decades separated Jack Johnson's loss to Jess Willard in 1915 and Joe Louis's win over Primo Carnera in 1935. While Louis served in the army in 1943 one of the worst riots in United States history ravaged East Detroit, where his family had settled after leaving Alabama in 1926. Southern mobs still resorted to lynching, not just to punish criminals but to enforce inequality and exploitation. Even if Senators Bilbo and Eastland and Phillies manager Ben Chapman did not speak for most whites, they spoke for too many of them. Painfully aware of the tenacity of prejudice, the Louis entourage hoped that Joe's public conduct would change attitudes and discredit discriminatory policies and habits. Louis embodied achievement in a more open society, suggesting that his people had similar untapped potential for distinction in other endeavors. As a boxer and a soldier, Louis played a vital role in the drama of a nation compelled by domestic and foreign events to begin anew the task of creating a more perfect union. At war with Hitler overseas, Americans had to confront what one journalist called the "hatelers" at home. How ironic that boxing and the armed forces (both in the bloody business of knocking out opponents) should lead in promoting opportunity and integration while residential neighborhoods, schools, churches, businesses, and clubs remained segregated and intransigent.

Joe Louis gave vicarious satisfaction to people who dared not strike back against the white foe. For all Americans, his rise from sharecropper's son to world champion served as a parable of promise in a society too preoccupied with race. Even if his calling seemed atavistic to some, his popularity proved that no race, sect, class, or region had a monopoly on traits Americans claimed to cherish. Stark in its simplicity and finality, boxing has clear rules, obvious risks and rewards, and in many instances a climactic knockout that leaves no doubt about the rightful winner. In Joe Louis, black editors and columnists saw living proof that bias, not inherent incapacity, kept the race from similar distinction in other walks of life. That lesson had the power to transform a nation.

Those who opposed the integration of baseball, for example, argued that black players lacked the skills to compete in the big leagues. In the decade after desegregation, however, Jackie Robinson, Larry Doby, Roy Campanella, Don Newcombe, Willie Mays, Hank Aaron, Ernie Banks, and others proved beyond a doubt that intolerance, not inability, had kept black players out. The National League's Most Valuable Player award went to a black star fourteen seasons out of twenty in the two decades after Robinson broke the color barrier. That statistic alone reveals more truth than multiple tomes of Senator Bilbo's speeches.

Symbolic significance is elusive and not easily measured, but that does not mean the impressionistic or anecdotal is less important than the quantifiable. Since clear thought and candor have rarely characterized the American conversation about race, symbols have often provided vital clues for unraveling the mystery of the color line in the national experience. Louis was something more than he appeared, as John H. Johnson, founder of *Ebony* and *Jet*, realized. "Although he'd been denied a formal education by the Old South, he was one of the most educated and thoughtful men I ever met," Johnson reflected. "He could be mesmerized by a golf ball or a pretty leg, but he was also capable of great eloquence." Martin Luther King Jr. realized that Louis had attained mythic status among his people. In a book written at the high tide of the civil rights movement in 1964, King told the story of "a young Negro" sent to the gas chamber in a southern state. As the gas pellet vaporized, the man pleaded, "Save me, Joe Louis. Save me, Joe Louis." These final words, King noted, showed "the helplessness, the loneliness and the profound despair of Negroes in that period." How does one measure helplessness and despair? How does one ascertain the psychological and social impact of a black man repeatedly beating white men and making a fortune doing so within a nation whose senior members of Congress defended lynching? In a society obsessed with statistics and polls, people lose sight of other social and cultural signifiers that bring the dark to light, especially in the lives of the poor and marginalized.

When Joe Louis died of cardiac arrest on April 12, 1981, two prominent men defined his special place in Americans' hearts and minds. Representing different races, generations, parties, and ideologies, these two leaders disagreed sharply on the major issues of their day. Yet they agreed that Louis had been a national asset while becoming a true American hero. "Out of the ring, he was a considerate and soft-spoken man; inside the ring, his courage, strength, and consummate skill wrote a unique and unforgettable chapter in sports history," President Ronald Reagan observed. "But Joe Louis was more than a sports legend—his career was an indictment of racial bigotry and a source of pride and inspiration to millions of white and black people around the world." Reagan waived the rules for burial at Arlington National Cemetery so Louis could be interred there.

From the other end of the political spectrum came even higher praise. "When we were vulnerable, the stench of the Depression still in our clothes, lynching mobs threatening our existence, we were defenseless and without legal, political, economic, or military protection," the Reverend Jesse Jackson declared in his eulogy for Louis. "He was our Samson, our David fighting Goliath." Yet Louis was more—he was probably the first African American to transcend race in a nation long obsessed with it. "God sent Joe from the black race," Jackson proclaimed, "to represent the human race." In a time of crisis at home and abroad, Louis stood for decency, democracy, and dreams of a better future. "Usually the champion rides on the shoulders of the nation and its people," Jackson reflected. "But in this case the nation rode on the shoulders of its hero, Joe." The requiem also had a personal meaning for the preacher. In 1941, his mother had named him Jesse *Louis* Jackson.[29]

Skeptics understandably complained that Joe Louis and other black celebrities received too much attention. But they did not seem to grasp the subversive potential of gifted people whose transcendent talents challenged racist precepts and thereby undermined the legitimacy of segregation and subordination. Bill "Bojangles" Robinson danced his way into many hearts. Jesse Owens ran and jumped as no one before him ever had and thereby validated himself, his people, his country, and an ideal not popular in Berlin in 1936. Louis Armstrong blew down barriers of race and place with his golden trumpet. Marian Anderson and Lena Horne sang for crowds of many colors. Jackie Robinson thrilled fans of all shades with his spectacular play on the baseball field. Yet none of them gave more to the nation and its people in a troubled time than the Brown Bomber. Joe Louis beat the odds and did more for racial tolerance than anyone might have expected from a poor black boy born in a sharecropper's cabin whose claim to national attention originated with the dynamite he packed in his two fists. Those fists hammered away at white opponents and white prejudice, fighting for the same rights and recognition that black militants demanded with their clenched fists in the black power salute of the late 1960s. Long after Louis retired, Martin Luther King, Maya Angelou, Richard Wright, Malcolm X, Jesse Louis Jackson, and other African Americans recalled how important the champion had been to a struggle that had originated in the distant past and seemed likely to persist into the indefinite future. In this long, hard fight that still awaits the final gong, Joe Louis fought many memorable rounds, and he fought them well.

Epilogue

On the day after Christmas in 1908, champion Tommy Burns and challenger Jack Johnson climbed into a ring outside Sydney, Australia. The heavyweight title conferred many benefits on its holder, but the stakes on December 26 went far beyond the ambitions of two boxers coveting one prize. Like the politics and diplomacy of the time, boxing was suffused with the issue of color. Johnson had chased Burns around the globe and goaded him into a title fight—a fight that former champion John L. Sullivan opposed because he wanted only whites to compete for the crown. Burns had made an issue of race as well by contending that Johnson's skin made him both inferior and "yellow." Writer Jack London set the scene. "Twenty thousand men were at the ringside," he reported, "and twice twenty thousand lingered outside." Burns entered the arena and received "a heartier greeting" as the obvious "favourite with the crowd." "It promised to be a bitter fight," London noted. "There was no chivalry nor good will in it."

Johnson provided his own intriguing account of the event. Firmly in command from the opening bell, he sometimes turned his attention to the large crowd. Just a few fans of African descent attended the fight, but one of them remained vivid in Johnson's memory almost two decades later. "As my gaze wandered out into the surrounding territory," he recalled,

> I saw a colored man sitting on a fence watching the fight with open mouth and bulging eyes. My glance returned to him again and again. He was one of the very few colored people present, and he became a sort of landmark for me. I . . . soon discovered that mentally, he was fighting harder than I was. Whenever I unlimbered a blow, he, too, shot one into the air landing it on an imaginary antagonist at about the same spot where I landed on Burns.

> When I swayed to avert a blow from Burns, the fighter on the fence also swayed in the same direction and at a similar angle. When I ducked, he also ducked. But his battle came to an inglorious end when it was necessary for me to make an unusually low duck. He attempted to follow the movement and fell off the fence. . . . I laughed heartily, and Burns and the spectators were at a loss to know what had so aroused my mirth.

That "fighter on the fence" symbolized the bond between the lone black man in the ring and millions of his people beyond it. Deemed inferior by whites and proscribed by discriminatory customs and laws, African Americans felt immediate joy and lasting hope when Johnson vanquished a white opponent. "When I was a little boy that early heavyweight boxing champion was one of the most admired underground heroes," Ralph Ellison, renowned author of *The Invisible Man*, recalled some sixty years after Johnson won the title. "He was rejected by most whites and by many respectable Negroes, but he was nevertheless a hero among veterans of the Spanish-American War who rejoiced in the skill and élan with which Johnson set off the now-outrageous search for a 'White Hope.'" A generation later, Joe Louis filled Johnson's boxing shoes. "He was, to black folk," author John Killens wrote, "the Magnificent Vicarious Experience."[1]

This connection between African Americans and their champions crossed class, gender, generational, religious, and regional lines. The psychological lift that Johnson and Louis provided stemmed from the peculiar status of former slaves and their progeny after the end of Reconstruction, when the sections and political parties opted for reconciliation and economic development over civil rights. The confusion that blacks felt during the sudden transition from bondage to freedom was expressed by George King, who recalled his life as a slave on "two hundred acres of Hell" in South Carolina, where the plantation mistress had laughed gleefully as the whip lacerated her servants. King did not know what to expect when the Civil War ended. "The Master he says we are all free, but it don't mean we is white," King recalled. "And it don't mean we is equal." Frederick Douglass pondered the liminal status of his people after emancipation. "It is true that we are no longer slaves, but it is equally true that we are not yet quite free," he declared in 1869. "We have been turned out of the house of bondage, but we have not yet been fully admitted to the glorious temple of American liberty." The future was "shrouded in doubt and danger." Douglass did all he could to alleviate this "doubt and danger," but he knew that weapons beyond words were needed to attain full freedom. In the study of his home in Anacostia with its splendid view of Capitol Hill, Douglass displayed a photograph of boxer Peter Jackson. He would point to the picture, writer James

Weldon Johnson recollected, and tell visitors, "Peter is doing a great deal with his fists to solve the Negro question."[2]

Symbols of "bottom rail" aspiration and accomplishment, black champions often contrasted their new status with that of their forbears. Jack Johnson's father, for example, had been a slave in Maryland before migrating as a free man to Galveston, Texas. Pilloried for marrying a white woman, Jack Johnson distanced himself from antebellum days by insisting he was "not a slave" and was free to select a mate "without the dictation of any man." Joe Louis traced his family origins to the slave cabins of Alabama and, like millions of other southern migrants, left the soil irrigated by the sweat and tears of generations of field hands and sharecroppers to seek a better life in the promised land. Louis purchased Spring Hill Farm in 1940 for a training camp, dude ranch, and eventual retirement home. Some twenty miles north of Detroit, the site had been a stop on the underground railroad that transported fugitive slaves to freedom in Canada.

The wounds of the lash healed slowly if they healed at all, but the psychological burden of slavery persisted for generations. After winning the title in 1964, Cassius Clay told reporters he now had a new name. "I will not be identified as an Uncle Tom," he explained. "I will be known as Cassius X. I am waiting for my name. Clay was undoubtedly a Kentucky slave master." To distance himself further from the slave past, he also rejected the master's religion, joining the Nation of Islam and becoming Muhammad Ali. Joe Frazier, Ali's archrival, remained a Christian and retained his name, but he too was haunted by the old order. He purchased a plantation near Yemassee, South Carolina, that dated back to 1732. The estate, according to local lore, had been owned during the Civil War "by a white man named Frazier, who might have been the master of my ancestors, who had been slaves in this part of the country." When the remodeled big house was ready for occupancy, Frazier wanted to torch his humble boyhood home at Laurel Bay as "a kind of gesture—a way of burning away all the hardships and troubles we'd known." But Dolly, his mother, refused, for old shacks, like old ways, had a habit of surviving. Shortly after Frazier earned $2.5 million for beating Ali, his mother "had gone into the fields to pick tomatoes for twenty-five cents a bucket." Settled into the big house of the old plantation, she and her kin planted beans in the yard and raised hogs, goats, and chickens. Asked about the symbolism of owning the land where his progenitors had toiled under the lash for whites, Joe Frazier replied, "It means a lot because I don't know of any other Black man in the United States who has a plantation."[3]

For a people steeped in hallowed racial myths and illusions, precepts and symbols have often prevailed over evidence and reason. Had Americans been less obsessed with race and all it implied, the lives of Jack Johnson and Joe

Louis would have had little or no social impact. But the American fixation on race transformed the prize ring into a bully pulpit, blurring lines between individual and group, private and public, sports and society, biography and allegory. Major events in these champions' lives served as defining moments in American cultural history. For Johnson, these events were both positive and negative: His victories over Burns and Jeffries; his ties to white women; his "white slave" trial and conviction; his loss to Jess Willard. Louis left a more favorable legacy, partly because his own story became so entwined with the struggles of the entire nation during the Depression and World War II. In his role as an "ambassador of good will" between the races, Louis retained the affection of blacks while gaining favor among whites. His victories over Primo Carnera and Max Schmeling and his enlistment in the army put Louis (and the race he "represented") on the right side of the battle against deadly enemies. The night before leaving Cleveland to cross the Atlantic to cover the Spanish Civil War, Langston Hughes celebrated this new black hope. "I had ridden around for hours in a car full of folks shouting and yelling after the news of Braddock's defeat came over the radio," Hughes recalled. "I do not believe Negro America has ever before or since had a national hero like Joe Louis." On his way to New York, Hughes "could hardly speak above a whisper" because he had nearly lost his voice cheering the Brown Bomber's redemption from his prior defeat. "When Joe Louis had lost his first fight to Schmeling," Hughes reminisced, "I had been a part of the hush and the sadness that fell over darker New York." New York's "darker" residents seldom faced the more brutal forms of racial oppression, but Hughes knew their lives were no crystal stair. Louis fulfilled needs that went beyond bread and basic rights. Whether northern or southern, urban or rural, African Americans had yet to attain full equality in the 1930s. When Louis knocked out a white opponent, it was some compensation for a dream long denied.[4]

Reformers knew that equitable laws and due process were needed to protect and advance African Americans. But statutes and courts could be only as effective as officials and citizens chose to make them. Besides, laws could not prevent the more casual forms of condescension and proscription. Less violent and deadly than the lynch rope and revolver, these more subtle expressions of prejudice also took their toll, as Mary Church Terrell, the first president of the National Association of Colored Women, attested. "Assault and battery committed upon a human being's soul," she reflected, "often leave wounds which are deeper and more painful than those inflicted upon the body, while they are harder to heal and do greater harm." In American race relations, particularly in the South, custom was king and played the tyrant. Jack Johnson, for example, did nothing illegal in marrying a white woman. His victory over Jim Jeffries was no crime. Joe Louis would have

broken no laws had he gloated about beating white rivals, posed for photographs with white women, driven a luxury car through Dixie, or challenged
jim crow in the army. Discriminatory laws denied people basic freedoms, but
public opinion served the same purpose. Lena Horne, for example, married
Lennie Hayton in Paris in 1947 because California law prohibited mixed
marriages. The couple decided to keep their marriage a secret. "Isn't it ironic?"
Horne mused. "For three years I preferred to let the world think I was a
woman living in sin rather than admit that I had married a white man."[5]

White Americans have defined "race" in a far more arbitrary and unscien-
tific way than they have cared to admit. The "color line" has been and remains a spectrum that lacks a clear or consistent demarcation point between
"black" and "white." James Weldon Johnson, for example, explored the ambiguity of racial categorization in his novel *The Autobiography of an Ex-
Coloured Man*, first published in 1912—the year Jack Johnson was indicted
for violating the Mann Act. Born as a result of the "unsanctioned love" between a black mother and white father in Georgia, the main character in this
fictional memoir learns the politics of prejudice when very young. His absent father, his mother assures him, had been "all to us that custom and the
law would allow." "She loved him; more, she worshipped him, and she died
firmly believing that he loved her more than any other woman in the world,"
Johnson wrote. "Perhaps she was right." But their love was no match for the
tyranny of tradition. Southern whites "are not yet living quite in the present
age," Johnson contended. "Many of their general ideas hark back to a former
century, some of them to the Dark Ages." Taken for white in Europe, the
narrator of mixed origin chooses to pass when he returns to the states because he wants to avoid the "unbearable shame" of "being identified with a
people that could with impunity be treated worse than animals." His "passing" troubles him when he falls in love with a white woman and wonders if
he should tell her his secret and risk losing her for a reason both profound
and petty—his lineage. In this work and others, James Weldon Johnson blamed
blacks as well as whites for the national racial psychosis. But he held whites
primarily responsible for the problems of color and caste and expected them
to do more to make matters right.

While Langston Hughes covered the civil war in Spain, he exchanged
letters with Elsie Roxborough, the niece of John Roxborough, Joe Louis's
manager. Hughes admitted being "in love" with this "lovely-looking girl" of
"ivory-white" skin, with "dark eyes and raven hair." She had staged one of
his plays and conveyed her ambition "to become a director in the professional theater, radio, or motion pictures." In their long conversations, she
pondered "whether or not it would be better for her to pass" to pursue her
goals. Since she "was often mistaken for white in public places," she would

have "no trouble at all" crossing the color line, Hughes noted. "While I was in Spain she wrote that she had made up her mind to do so." Her letters dwindled, then stopped. When Hughes returned home, "Elsie had disappeared into the white world," and neither he nor her other old friends saw her. "But every Christmas for several years she sent me a carefully chosen little present," Hughes recalled, "with no return address on the packet."

Walter White, an NAACP leader for decades, also faced the conundrum of color. "I am a Negro," he explained. "My skin is white, my eyes are blue, my hair is blond. The traits of my race are nowhere visible upon me." Rather than reside and work among whites, however, he passed only to investigate riots and lynchings. White's experiences made him philosophical on race matters. "I am white and I am black, and know that there is no difference," he concluded. "Each casts a shadow, and all shadows are dark." More recently, Anatole Broyard, an advertising copywriter and literary critic for the *New York Times*, blurred the margin between light and shadow. Not sharing Walter White's views, Broyard thought that race defined and divided Americans. Born in 1920 in a "Negro" neighborhood in the French Quarter of New Orleans and raised in the Bedford-Stuyvesant area of Brooklyn, Broyard moved his family to Connecticut in 1963 to live amid the Anglo-Saxon gentry. "Society had decreed race to be a matter of natural law, but he wanted race to be an elective affinity," Henry Louis Gates Jr. noted. "So here is a man who passed for white because he wanted to be a writer and he did not want to be a Negro writer."[6]

Perhaps Walter White sensed "no difference" between blacks and whites, but his was not the prevalent view among Americans. The lives and times of Jack Johnson and Joe Louis reveal the persistence of race politics in the first half of the twentieth century and the great disparity between ideals that supposedly were not race specific and actual practices that were. Confined to a separate and unequal sphere by a society so often described as free, fair, and individualistic, African Americans lived as a people apart, relegated by group association and custom to the slave cabin, sharecropper's shack, ghetto flat, back of the bus, and "buzzard's roost" (the balcony in a segregated theater). For over two centuries, "the American way" has been synonymous with rapid change, but blacks for several generations have encountered surprisingly resilient racist attitudes and practices. On rare occasions when barriers fell, only one race pioneer at a time gained admission to "the glorious temple of American liberty." This token individual then attained a significance far beyond any personal goals because collective aspirations claimed precedence over private ambitions. Such a symbiosis explains the inordinate attention paid to African American "firsts"—the first black senator, the first heavyweight champion, the first major-league ball player, the first Supreme Court justice, the first student at Ole Miss, the first star on a prime-time television show, the first Miss America—the list goes on and on. The lives of black champions and other race pioneers illustrate the joy of breaking barriers as well as the frustration about the slow and uneven progress for the race as a whole.

The race question remains perplexing. Why has a society with such racial and ethnic diversity throughout its history been so presumptive and proscriptive about color and character? The first Africans, after all, arrived in Jamestown a decade before the Pilgrims landed at Plymouth Rock. Native Americans confounded the predictions of their eclipse and extinction and remain a part of the national mosaic. In California, *las familias* Peralta, Berreyesa, and others ruled the province before the conquest of 1846 and the era of the Stanfords and Hearsts. With abundant lands and burgeoning industries creating a voracious demand for cheap labor, immigrants and sojourners arrived from places near and far—some crossed rivers, others sailed the seas. Others became Americans when the stars and stripes replaced the flags of distant European empires and Mexico. For over two centuries, slave ships delivered Africans to ports stretching from Brazil to Barbados and Charlestown to Narragansett Bay. The notion of the United States as "a white man's country" is a racist illusion and fantasy, not a past or present reality.

From Phillis Wheatley (whose first collection of poems was published in 1773) to Maya Angelou, Frederick Douglass to Martin Luther King Jr., Ida B. Wells to Representative Barbara Jordan of Texas, Jack Johnson to Muhammad Ali, the black minority has challenged the white majority to think differently about race and to translate democratic ideals into daily practice. The roots of prejudice run deep and resist easy or rapid removal, and the burdens of the past weigh heavily upon the nation and its people. Since the reigns of Jack Johnson and Joe Louis, bigotry has become less fashionable yet never seems to go entirely out of style among whites who continue to see life primarily through the lens of color. With "skin . . . as light as that of the average white person," author Shirlee Taylor Haizlip has, like most of her kin, "lived as, worked as and mostly married black people." Yet some in her mixed family chose to "crossover" so "their light skins would give them the privileges, status and entitlements of white people, a state of grace that clearly meant more to them than their connections to the black community." Haizlip found ambiguity in both the substance and shadow of race identity. "All in all, I have grown a great deal less certain about the vagaries of race," she reflected in 1994, "and know that I am ambivalent about its implications."[7]

Americans should acknowledge and learn from these "vagaries of race." "Even today America remains an undiscovered country," Ralph Ellison wisely observed. "We are at once very unified, and at the same time diversified. On many, many levels we don't know who we are, and there are always moments of confrontation where we meet as absolute strangers."[8] Americans whose ancestors came from different shores have not yet fully explored their "undiscovered country," nor have they completely mapped the historical landscape they have shared as "absolute strangers." This process of discovery and redefinition is often contentious and divisive, even dangerous, for, in the words of the old spiritual, freedom is a constant struggle. If people deny responsibility for the past, they remain strangers even to themselves. The fight against race prejudice might well be the most difficult battle ever waged in American history. Against the odds, it can be won.

Notes

Key to Abbreviations

AC	*Atlanta Constitution*	NYA	*New York Age*
AI	*Atlanta Independent*	NYAN	*New York Amsterdam News*
BP	*Boston Post*	NYT	*New York Times*
CBA	*Chicago Broad-Ax*	PC	*Pittsburgh Courier*
CD	*Chicago Defender*	PPL	*Philadelphia Public Ledger*
CG	*Cleveland Gazette*	PT	*Philadelphia Tribune*
DE	*Dallas Express*	RAA	*Richmond Afro-American*
DS	*Denver Statesman*	SEP	*Saturday Evening Post*
IF	*Indianapolis Freeman*	TEP	*Toronto Evening Post*
LAS	*Los Angeles Sentinel*	WB	*Washington Bee*
NG	*Nashville Globe*	WS	*Wichita Searchlight*

Introduction

1. Richard Wright, *Black Boy: A Record of Childhood and Youth* (New York and London: Harper, 1942), 198–201, 221, 224–27. For other instructive works by Wright, see the following texts: *Native Son* (New York: Harper, 1940); *Uncle Tom's Children* (New York: Harper, 1940); *12 Million Black Voices: A Folk History of the Negro in the United States* (New York: Viking, 1941); *American Hunger* (New York: Harper, 1944); *The Richard Wright Reader*, ed. Ellen Wright and Michel Fabre (New York: Harper and Row, 1978).

2. Richard Wright, *American Hunger* (New York: Harper & Row, 1977 [1944]), 13–14. Most black activists in the Johnson and Louis eras saw no alternative to a cautious and conciliatory approach on civil rights. With minimal results from this gradualist strategy by the mid-1950s, however, new leaders and organizations emerged and launched the more radical massive nonviolent resistance campaigns between the Montgomery bus boycott and the Selma-to-Montgomery march a decade later. Whatever the thrust of the movement at any given time, individual African Americans who

331

attained distinction provided important symbols in the struggle. These race pioneers ranged from Jack Johnson to Thurgood Marshall, from Mary McLeod Bethune to Fannie Lou Hamer. Boxing champions attained a unique status among race heroes, for they achieved fame and fortune by bloodying and beating white opponents. This reversal of customary race roles had great symbolic significance beyond the ring.

3. Fannie Barrier Williams, "The Club Movement Among Colored Women of America," *A New Negro for a New Century* (New York: AMS Press, 1973 [1900]), 383; Mary Church Terrell, *A Colored Woman in a White World* (Washington, DC: Ransdell, 1940), 149; Booker T. Washington, *Up From Slavery* (New York: Doubleday, Page, 1901), 314–315; W.E.B. DuBois, *The Souls of Black Folk* (Chicago: A.C. McClurg, 1903), 108; *Pittsburgh Courier*, December 9, 1911; "Joe Louis and Jesse Owens," *The Crisis*, August 1935, 241; *Chicago Defender*, June 26, 1936. The reputations of Johnson and Louis have fluctuated over time, and these changes in opinion often signify important turning points in race relations.

4. *Congressional Record*, 78th Cong., 3d sess., June 28, 1945, vol. 91, pt. 5, 6887. Bilbo and his ilk deplored any display of black ascendance and took particular exception to black men who trespassed upon white turf in matters of sex and marriage. Such racial fears had a profound impact on American culture, customs, laws, and public policy. The chapters to come explore how these racial anxieties shadowed Jack Johnson and Joe Louis and how the black champions, in turn, affected race relations in their time.

Chapter 1. "A Retribution Seeks": Repression and Black Redemption

1. Lizelia A.J. Moorer, "Retribution," 1907, in *Collected Black Women's Poetry*, ed. Joan R. Sherman (New York: Oxford University Press, 1988), vol. 3, 38.

2. Ruby Berkley Goodwin, *It's Good to Be Black* (Garden City: Doubleday, 1953), 74–79, 193.

3. *Cleveland Gazette* (hereafter *CG*), September 29, October 6, 1906; W.E.B. DuBois, "A Litany of Atlanta," *The Book of American Negro Poetry*, ed. James Weldon Johnson (New York: Harcourt, Brace, 1931), 90–94. Editor J.C. Battle blamed Hoke Smith's "dirty campaign" as well as racist "yellow journalism" for what he called "the Atlanta massacre." *Nashville Globe* (hereafter *NG*), June 19, 1908.

4. *Atlanta Independent* (herafter *AI*), February 23, August 17, October 12, November 16, 1907.

5. "Hard to Be a Nigger," in John A. and Alan Lomax, *American Ballads and Folk Songs* (New York: Macmillan, 1934), 233–234.

6. *AI*, October 31, 1908; *NG*, April 26, May 17, August 16, September 6, 1907, January 3, April 3, 1908; *Congressional Record*, 61st Cong., 2d sess., 1909, 45, pt. 1: 180; 62d Cong., 2d sess., 1911, 48, pt. 1: 59.

7. *Wichita Searchlight* (hereafter *WS*), February 16, 1907, July 28, September 25, 1906, July 27, 1907, June 13, 1908.

8. *NG*, August 21, 1908; *CG*, September 12, 1908.

9. *The Booker T. Washington Papers*, ed. Louis R. Harlan and Raymond W. Smock, vol. 9 (Urbana: University of Illinois Press, 1980), 611–613; *AI*, August 22, 1908; *New York Age* (hereafter *NYA*), December 3, 1908, *Crusade for Justice: The Autobiography of Ida B. Wells*, ed. Alfreda M. Duster (Chicago: University of Chicago Press,

1970), 47–66, 299–300; *Selected Works of Ida B. Wells-Barnett*, comp. Trudier Harris (New York: Oxford University Press, 1991), 79–85, 191–200, 219–220.

10. Thomas Dixon Jr., *The Clansman: An Historical Romance of the Ku Klux Klan* (New York: Grosset and Dunlap, 1905), 46–47, 289–292, 303–308, 325, 327–328, 374.

11. William A. Dunning, *Reconstruction Political and Economic, 1865–1877* (New York: Harpers, 1907), 58, 213–214, 340–341.

12. Robert Bennett Bean, "The Negro Brain," *Century Magazine*, September 1906, 778–784. For scholarly works on pseudoscientific racism in this era, see George Fredrickson, *The Black Image in the White Mind: The Debate over Afro-American Character and Destiny, 1817–1914* (New York: Harper & Row, 1971); I.W. Newby, *Jim Crow's Defense: Anti-Negro Thought in America, 1900–1930* (Baton Rouge: Louisiana State University Press, 1965).

13. Howard W. Odum, *Social and Mental Traits of the Negro: Research into the Conditions of the Negro Race in Southern Towns* (New York: Longmans, Green, 1910), 39, 259–261, 278–286.

14. Roosevelt's Special Message to the Senate, December 19, 1906, *A Compilation of the Messages and Papers of the Presidents*, ed. James D. Richardson (New York: Bureau of National Literature, 1907), vols. 16, 17, 7329–37; Booker T. Washington to Charles W. Anderson, "Personal and Confidential," November 7, 1906, *Booker T. Washington Papers*, vol. 9, 118–119. See also Washington to Roosevelt, "Personal," November 2, 1906; Washington to Oswald Garrison Villard, "Personal," November 10, 1906; Washington to William Howard Taft, "Personal and Confidential," November 20, 1906; Washington to Roosevelt, "Personal," November 26, 1906, *Booker T. Washington Papers*, vol. 9, 113, 122–123, 141, 147–148. "There is no law, human or divine," Washington told Villard, "which justifies the punishment of an innocent man." For the president's views, see Roosevelt to Curtis Guild Jr., November 7, 1906; Roosevelt to Silas McBee, "Personal," November 27, 1906; Roosevelt to Ray Stannard Baker, "Personal: Private," March 30, 1907, *The Letters of Theodore Roosevelt*, ed. Elting E. Morison (Cambridge: Harvard University Press, 1952), vol. 5, 489–490, 509, 634–635.

15. "Discipline: The Brownsville Affray," Annual Report of the Secretary of War, 1906; Washington to Taft, November 20, 1906, *Blacks in the Military: Essential Documents*, ed. Bernard C. Nalty and Morris J. MacGregor (Wilmington: Scholarly Resources, 1981), 60–62.

16. *NYA*, November 29, 1906; *WS*, November 17, 1906, January 19, May 18, 1907, April 18, 1908; *CG*, August 24, September 28, November 2, November 16, 1907. William Ferguson, a *Gazette* correspondent in Washington, assisted Senator Foraker and his committee in their investigation.

17. The Mann White Slave Traffic Act of 1910, for example, codified the belief that only white women merited federal protection when it criminalized the interstate transport of *white* women for immoral purposes. The Justice Department indicted Jack Johnson in 1912 under the law, but only because the evidence revealed that he had transported white women across state lines for sexual relations.

18. Roosevelt's Sixth Annual Message to Congress, December 3, 1906, *Messages and Papers of the Presidents*, vol. 16, 7029–31; Roosevelt to Silas McBee, "Personal," November 27, 1906, *Letters of Theodore Roosevelt*, vol. 5, 509. See also Roosevelt to Lyman Abbott, "Confidential," May 10, 1908, vol. 6, 1026. Roosevelt told Abbott that some critics of his disciplinary action were agents of "the great capitalistic reactionaries" who opposed his policies. Roosevelt regretted the Brownsville affray because it gave "the greatest possible impetus" to the idea that "negroes as a

race always stand by their own criminals." He accused his critics of "put[ting] a premium on murder and perjury among the enlisted men" by insisting that "murderers and perjurers" be reinstated regardless of their guilt. But no one argued that all the soldiers were innocent. The critics simply wanted the innocent cleared and the guilty punished.

19. Fortune to Washington, December 8, 1906, *Booker T. Washington Papers*, vol. 9, 156–157; W.E.B. DuBois, "The President and the Soldiers," *Voice of the Negro*, December 1906, 552–553.

20. *Jack London Reports: War Correspondence, Sports Articles, and Miscellaneous Writings*, ed. King Hendricks and Irving Shepard (Garden City: Doubleday, 1970), 258–259, 261, 263–264.

21. *NYA*, December 31, 1908; *Indianapolis Freeman* (hereafter *IA*), January 23, 1909. For a similar argument, see the *Wichita Searchlight*, October 23, 1909.

22. *IF*, January 23, 1909; *Chicago Broad-Ax* (hereafter *CBA*), March 27, 1909 *NYA*, April 1, 1909, January 27, 1910; Scott to Wheaton, March 23, 1909, *Booker T. Washington Papers*, vol. 10, 75.

23. *NYA*, December 30, 1909; *IF*, April 9, 1910; *Chicago Defender* (hereafter *CD*), May 21, 1910.

24. W.E.B. DuBois, *The Souls of Black Folk* (Chicago: A.C. McClurg, 1903), 13, 39–40; "Niagara Movement Address to the Nation," August 16, 1906, "The Evolution of the Race Problem," June 1, 1909, "Race Prejudice," March 5, 1910, *W.E.B. DuBois Speaks: Speeches and Addresses, 1890–1919*, ed. Philip S. Foner (New York: Pathfinder, 1970), 170, 173, 208, 217.

25. *IF*, January 30, February 6, March 13, 1909; *Atlanta Constitution* (hereafter *AC*), July 2, 1910; *New York Times* (hereafter *NYT*), July 2, 1910 *AC*, July 3, 1910.

26. *Jack London Reports*, 266, 267, 268; *CD*, July 30, 1910.

27. This description of the scene in Reno stems from several eyewitness accounts. See Arthur Ruhl, "The Fight in the Desert," *Collier's*, July 23, 1910, 12–22; Harris Lyon, "In Reno Riotous: Being Various Snap Shots of the Little City That Had the Big Fight," *Hampton's Magazine*, September 1910, 387–396; *Harper's Weekly*, July 9, 1910, 7–8; *AC*, July 2, 3, 4, 5, 6, 1910; Rex Beach, *Personal Exposures* (New York: Harpers, 1940), 84–88; *NYT*, July 1, 2, 3, 4, 5, 1910; *Jack London Reports*, 264–301; *IF*, July 9, 1910; *NYA*, July 7, 1910; *CG*, July 9, 1910.

28. *IF*, July 2, 1910; *NG*, July 1, 1910; *Philadelphia Tribune*, January 2, 1915; *CBA*, January 16, 1915; *NG*, July 8, 1910; Goodwin, *It's Good to Be Black*, 76; *AC*, July 3, 1910; *NYA*, June 9, 1910; *NYT*, July 3, 1910; *Collier's*, July 23, 1910, 22.

29. Jack Johnson later referred to rumors that he would be shot if he beat Jeffries, but he contended he "took little stock" in them. John Arthur Johnson, *Jack Johnson Is a Dandy: An Autobiography* (New York: Chelsea House, 1969 [1927]), 62. A June 30 dispatch from a *Times* correspondent noted, "Precautions against gun men are being taken . . . at Johnson's camp. Deputy Sheriff Hammel is always on guard there, wearing his cartridge belt and big .44 in full view. Two lookouts are always at the foot of the stairs leading to Johnson's apartments. No one is allowed to ascend unless he is known to be harmless." *NYT*, July 1, 1910.

30. For details on the action, see *Harper's Weekly*, July 9, 1910, 7–8; Lyon, "In Reno Riotous," 393–396; Ruhl, "The Fight in the Desert," 22; *Jack London Reports*, 293–301; *NG*, July 8, 1910; *CG*, July 9, 1910; *IF*, July 9, 1910; *AC*, July 5, 1910; *NYT*, July 5, 1910; Johnson, *Jack Johnson Is a Dandy*, 63.

31. Beach, *Personal Exposures*, 85; *AC*, July 5, 6, 1910; Goodwin, *It's Good to Be*

Black, 74–79, 193; *IF*, July 9, 1910; Johnson, *Jack Johnson Is a Dandy*, 183–84; Lyon, "In Reno Riotous," 390; *NYT*, July 5, 1910.

32. *NYT*, July 5, 1910. The *Atlanta Constitution* on July 5 carried this report dated July 4: "Three negroes were killed in a race riot here yesterday afternoon at a cross-tie camp on the Georgia and Florida railroad. No specific reason is assigned for the clash between the races, except that a number of the blacks had been drinking heavily . . . [and] began to get unruly and obstreperous."

33. *NYT*, July 5, 1910; *Current Literature*, August 1910, 130–131; *IF*, July 9, 1910.

34. *Washington Bee* (hereafter *WB*), July 9, 1910; *CG*, July 9, 1910; *AI*, December 30, 1911; Benjamin E. Mays, *Born to Rebel* (New York: Scribner, 1971), 19; Larry Neal, "Uncle Rufus Raps on the Squared Circle," *Partisan Review*, 1972, 46; Finis Farr, *Black Champion: The Life and Times of Jack Johnson* (London: Macmillan, 1964), 116.

35. *WB*, July 9, 1910; *NYA*, July 7, 14, 1910, July 6, 1911.

36. Theodore Roosevelt, "The Recent Prize Fight," *Outlook*, July 16, 1910, 550–551; *AC*, July 6, 1910; *Jack Johnson Is a Dandy*, 228.

37. *CG*, July 9, 1910; *CD*, July 30, 1910; *WB*, July 9, 1910; *IF*, July 9, 1910; *NYA*, July 9, 1910.

38. *IF*, July 9, 1910; *NYA*, July 9, 1910; Nat Fleischer, *50 Years at Ringside* (New York: Fleet, 1958), 75–76; *Pittsburgh Courier* (hereafter *PC*), June 22, 1946 *NG*, July 15, 1910; Goodwin, *It's Good to Be Black*, 75, 79.

39. *PC*, June 7, 1912; *CG*, June 15, 1912; *NYA*, July 14, 1910.

Chapter 2. "A Tempest of Dispraise": From Black Hope to Black Burden

1. Paul L. Dunbar, "Douglass," *Lyrics of Love and Laughter* (New York: Dodd, Mead, 1903), 339.

2. George Jean Nathan and H.L. Mencken, *The American Credo: A Contribution Toward the Interpretation of the National Mind* (New York: Knopf, 1920), 13, 111, 120, 123, 130, 137, 145, 154, 157, 174, 179, 189.

3. *The Outlook*, July 16, 1910, 541–542, 551; *Vigilance*, August 1910, 3; O. Edward Janney, *The White Slave Traffic in America* (Baltimore: Lord Baltimore Press, 1911), 82, 97–98.

4. *Atlanta Constitution*, July 12, 16, 1910. See the editorials of July 6 and 11 as well. The July 11 issue noted that the mayor of Memphis had just decreed that local blacks could no longer box for money because whites needed them to pick their cotton.

5. *New York Age* (hereafter *NYA*), July 14, 1910; *Nashville Globe* (hereafter *NG*), July 8, 1910; *Chicago Broad-Ax* (hereafter *CBA*), July 16, 30, 1910; *Indianapolis Freeman* (hereafter *IF*), July 30, 1910, December 23, 1911. For similar arguments in the black press, see *Washington Bee* (hereafter *WB*), July 9, 1910; *Cleveland Gazette* (hereafter *CG*), July 23, December 17, 1910; *Wichita Searchlight* (hereafter *WS*), August 6, 1910. In a cartoon by Fon Holly in the *Chicago Defender* of July 30, a constable resembling Uncle Sam pushes a "fight picture promoter" into a patrol wagon while three men labeled "lyncher" run away.

6. Nat Fleischer thought Jeffries had hung up his gloves to avoid these black contenders. "There really wasn't a white man who could be classed with this dusky

quartet," Fleischer noted, "and that was the real reason why Jim Jeffries retired." Nat Fleischer, *50 Years at Ringside* (New York: Fleet, 1958), 78.

7. Ethel Waters with Charles Samuels, *His Eye Is on the Sparrow* (Garden City: Doubleday, 1951), 109, 154–155, 240–241. "The heartaches which Mary Austin and Clara Kerr had caused me," Johnson wrote in his memoir, "led me to forswear colored women and to determine that my lot henceforth would be cast only with white women." John Arthur Johnson, *Jack Johnson Is a Dandy: An Autobiography* (New York: Chelsea House, 1969 [1927]), 76.

8. Johnson, *Jack Johnson Is a Dandy*, 76–78; *NG*, March 12, 1909; *IF*, March 20, 27, 1909; *CBA*, March 20, 1909.

9. *AI*, March 27, 1909, August 29, 1908.

10. *IF*, March 20, 1909, March 12, 1910. These details about Johnson's relationships with women were disclosed in Bureau of Investigation reports about his personal life, stories in several black and white newspapers, and Johnson's own selective memoir.

11. *IF*, August 13, 1910.

12. *WB*, November 6, 1909; *NYA*, January 27, 1910; *Chicago Defender* (hereafter *CD*), February 12, 1910; *IF*, February 12, 1910; *CG*, March 19, 1910; M. Madeline Southard, *The White Slave Traffic versus The American Home* (Louisville: Pentacostal Publishing, 1914), 58; "Report from the Immigration Commission on the Importation and Harboring of Women for Immoral Purposes," December 10, 1909, *Senate Documents*, 61st Cong., 2d sess., no. 196 (Washington, DC: GPO, 1910), 3–36 (text), 37–64 (appendix).

13. Taft's First Annual Message to Congress, December 7, 1909, *A Compilation of the Messages and Papers of the Presidents*, ed. James D. Richardson, vol. 17 (New York: Bureau of National Literature, 1913), 7438. See also Janney, *White Slave Traffic in America*. Janney chaired the National Vigilance Committee for the Suppression of the White Slave Traffic.

14. *Congressional Record*, 61st Cong., 2d sess., January 11–12, 1910, appendix 5–8 (Burnett); January 12, 1910, 546 (Gillespie); 548 (Mann); 551 (Sabath); January 19, 1910, 821 (Russell); January 26, 1910, 1041. The Senate did not debate the bill, but its Committee on Immigration reviewed it and issued a favorable majority report. A minority report questioned the constitutionality of the bill but praised its intent. *Congressional Record*, 61st Cong., 2d sess., June 25, 1910, 9037–9042.

15. Edwin W. Sims to the Immigration Commission, February 3, 1909, "Report on the Importation and Harboring of Women for Immoral Purposes," December 10, 1909, *Senate Documents*, 61st Cong., 2d sess., vol. 63, no. 196 (Washington, DC: GPO, 1910), 5–7. The law against importation of alien women for immoral purposes, Sims noted, "was being violated on an extensive scale" in Chicago. See also Janney, *White Slave Traffic in America*, 131–139.

16. *CD*, September 14, 1912; *CBA*, September 14, 1912; *New York Times* (hereafter *NYT*), September 12, 1912; *Philadelphia Tribune* (hereafter *PT*), September 14, 1912; *CG*, September 21, 1912; *Denver Statesman* (hereafter *DS*), September 14, 1912.

17. *CD*, October 26, 1912; *IF*, October 26, 1912; *NYT*, October 19, 20, 21, 1912.

18. Lins Report, October 21, 1912; Meyer Report, October 20, 1912, U.S. Department of Justice, Bureau of Investigation, Record Group 60, File 506, National Archives; *NYT*, October 19, 1912. Washington officials then shifted their focus from abduction to white slavery. Attorney General George Wickersham wired United States Attorney James Wilkerson on October 19, advising "great care in investigating

Johnson" so the government could develop a case on matters "within scope of evils sought to be reached by white slave act" rather than on the "mere question of abduction." See also *NYT*, October 27, 1912.

19. Lins Report, October 24, 1912; Meyer Report, October 25, 1912; Meyer Report, October 26, 1912; Lins Report, October 29, 1912; Meyer Report, November 1, 1912; Murdock Report, October 29, 1912; Murdock Report, November 2, 1912.

20. *DS*, October 19, 1912; July 29, 1911; November 2, 1912; *NYA*, October 24, 1912; *Pittsburgh Courier* (hereafter *PC*), December 9, 1911, October 25, 1912; *NG*, October 25, 1912; *IF*, October 26, November 2, 1912. See similar disapproving editorials in the *Philadelphia Tribune*, October 26 and November 2, 1912.

21. *CD*, October 26, 1912; *CBA*, October 26, 1912; *IF*, November 2, 1912; *CD*, November 2, 16, 1912.

22. "Chicagoan" to U.S. District Attorney, Chicago, Illinois, October 28, 1912; Meyer Report, November 4, 1912; Marshall Report, November 9, 1912; "Jack Allen" (Belle Schreiber) Sworn Statement, October 31, 1912, Department of Justice, RG 60.

23. Lins to A. Bruce Bielaski, acting chief of the Bureau of Investigation, November 4, 1912; Lins to Bielaski, November 7, 1912; Lins Report, November 10, 1912; Offley (New York) to Bielaski, November 20, 1912; Offley Report, November 23, 1912; Lins Report, December 6, 1912.

24. Meyer Report, November 18, 1912; Agent Pigniulo to Chief Bielaski May 27, 1913; Belle "Calvert" [Schreiber] to "My Dear," no date; Calvert to Miss Grace, no date; Offley to Bielaski, November 20, 1912; Offley Report, November 23, 1912; Rosen Report, November 29, 1912; Raymond Horn to Belle Schreiber, December 3, 1912; Rosen Report, November 29, 1912; Offley Report, December 16, 1912; Poulin Report, December 19, 1912; Craft Report, December 19, 1912; Grgurevich Report, December 19, 1912; Bielaski to Grgurevich, December 31, 1912; Offley Report, December 5, 1912, RG 60.

25. *CBA*, February 8, 1913; *IF*, March 15, 1913; *NYT*, December 4, 5, 6, 1912.

26. *CD*, December 14, 1912; *The Crisis*, February 1913, 194–195; March 1913, 220–221; April 1913, 296–297.

27. *Congressional Record*, 62d Cong., 3d sess., December 11, 1912, 502–503. Roddenbery had also tried to amend a recent pension bill to require segregation in veterans' homes and hospitals.

28. *PT*, February 24, 1912; *DS*, February 22, 1913; *AI*, April 19, 1913; *The Crisis*, November 1912, 28; December 1912, 76–77.

29. Charles Anderson to Booker T. Washington, April 4, 1913, *The Booker T. Washington Papers*, ed. Louis R. Harlan and Raymond W. Smock, vol. 12 (Urbana: University of Illinois Press, 1982), 161; *PT*, April 26, December 20, 1913; Eddie Cantor with Jane Kesner Ardmore, *Take My Life* (Garden City: Doubleday, 1957), 280–281; Waters, *His Eye Is on the Sparrow*, 159–169.

30. *NG*, December 6, 13, 1912; *NYA*, December 12, 1912; *IF*, December 14, 1912, January 11, 1913; *PT*, December 14, 1912, January 4, 1913. For related editorials on Johnson's conduct and its impact, see *CD*, December 14, 1912; *DS*, December 14, 1912; *CG*, December 7, 21, 1912; *WB*, December 21, 1912.

31. *Crusade for Justice: The Autobiography of Ida B. Wells*, ed. Alfreda M. Duster (Chicago: University of Chicago Press, 1970), 358–359; *CG*, November 30, 1912; *CBA*, January 4, 1913; *IF*, January 11, 1913; *CG*, January 18, February 8, 22, 1913.

32. Fowler to James Wilkerson, December 28, 1912; Charles DeWoody to Bielaski, April 28, 1913; Garbarino Report (Atlantic City), February 24, 1913; Garbarino Re-

port (Philadelphia), February 28, 1913; Sterling Report (Chicago), March 6, 1913; Bielaski to Garbarino, March 18, 1913; Scully Report (New York City), March 19, 1913; Gordon Report (Philadelphia), May 5, 1913, RG 60.

33. "Surely if the facility of interstate transportation can be taken away from the demoralization of lotteries, the debasement of obscene literature, the contagion of diseased cattle or persons, the impurity of food and drugs," the Court argued, "the like facility can be taken away from the systematic enticement to and the enslavement in prostitution and debauchery of women, and, more insistently, of girls." The Court declared the Mann Act "a legal exercise of the power of Congress." *United States Reports*, October Term 1912, vol. 227 (New York: Banks Law Publishing Co., 1913), 322, 323.

34. DeWoody Report, March 11, 1913, RG 60.

35. *United States Reports*, 227, 327–333. The Court maintained that the men had intended to debauch the plaintiff: "The plan might have succeeded if the coarse precipitancy of one of the defendants and the ribaldry of the habitués of the place had not shocked the modesty of the girl."

36. Bragdon Report, May 7, 1913, RG 60. Bragdon probably said nothing more about Ullrick's racial bias because he seemed typical of most white jurors in 1913, and Bragdon likely shared his views on property, race, religion, and family.

37. In a sworn statement on December 12, 1912, Julia Allen, who had traveled with the couple, noted, "While at Boston Jack Johnson and Belle Schreiber had a quarrel and Johnson struck her with some tool belonging to his automobile, inflicting a severe bruise on her side. She asked him for fifty dollars and left him." DeWoody quizzed Schreiber about domestic violence. Kenna's recollections appear in Bert Meyer's report on November 15, 1912, RG 60.

38. Charles Sterling Reports, May 8, 9, 1913, RG 60.

39. The testimony and details of the trial are drawn from the official transcript in the Justice Department files, RG 60. See Transcript of Record, *United States v. John Arthur Johnson*, United States Circuit Court for the Seventh District, October Term 1912, Case #2017.

40. Lins Report, May 17, 1913, RG 60.

41. *CBA*, June 7, 1913; *CD*, May 17, 1913.

42. *IF*, May 24, 1913.

43. W.A. Byrd, "Doings of the Race," *CG*, May 24, 1913; *IF*, May 24, June 14, 1913; *NYA*, May 22, July 3, 31, 1913.

Chapter 3. "Under the White Man's Menace"

1. *Selected Poems of Claude McKay* (New York: Bookman Associates, 1953), 41.

2. *New York Times* (hereafter *NYT*), April 8, 9, 1915; *Philadelphia Public Ledger* (hereafter *PPL*), April 8, 9, 11, 18, 1915; *Philadelphia Tribune* (hereafter *PT*), April 24, 1915.

3. *Indianapolis Freeman* (herafter *IF*), May 24, 1913; *Chicago Defender* (hereafter *CD*), May 24, June 7, 1913; Wilkerson Statement, United States Circuit Court of Appeals for the Seventh Circuit, Case 2017 (Chicago, 1914), Justice Department Files, Record Group 60, National Archives.

4. *The Crisis*, June 1913, 74; Newlands to Governor Denver Dickerson of California, February 3, 1909, *The Public Papers of Francis G. Newlands*, ed. Arthur B. Darling, vol. 1 (Boston: Houghton Mifflin, 1932), 297–298.

5. Washington to Villard, "Personal," August 8, 10, 1913, *The Booker T. Washington Papers*, ed. Louis R. Harlan and Raymond W. Smock, vol. 12 (Urbana: University of Illinois Press, 1982), 246, 248; *The Crisis*, September 1913, 232–233. For additional complaints, see *The Crisis*, August 1913, 181, 184; October 1913, 298–299.

6. *IF*, May 17, 24, June 14, October 18, 1913.

7. *CD*, May 17, 24, 1913; *Cleveland Gazette* (hereafter *CG*), May 24, 1913; *New York Age* (hereafter *NYA*), May 22, July 3, September 4, 1913. On the Caminetti case, see *The Crisis*, August 1913, 176–178; September 1913, 221; *NYA*, July 3, 1913. Secretary of the Navy Josephus Daniels recalled that Attorney General McReynolds "was treating the matter rather cavalierly." A spate of critical editorials and telegrams on the case moved President Wilson to bring the case before his full cabinet. McReynolds "sneered at the Mann Act," Daniels noted, and so did Secretary of War Lindley Garrison, who called it "a bad law" that "made possible the blackmailing of men by women who were not forced to immoral practices but willingly accompanied men out of state." Wilson ordered McReynolds to prosecute Caminetti. Josephus Daniels, *The Wilson Era: Years of Peace, 1910–1917* (Chapel Hill: University of North Carolina Press, 1944), 141–142.

8. John Arthur Johnson, *Jack Johnson Is a Dandy: An Autobiography* (New York: Chelsea House, 1969 [1927]), 83–85; *Chicago Broad-Ax* (hereafter *CBA*), May 17, 24, June 7, 1913.

9. Bielaski to DeWoody, June 27, 1913; McReynolds to Wilkerson, June 27, 1913; Wilkerson to McReynolds, June 27, 1913; DeWoody Report, June 28, 1913, Justice Department Files, RG 60.

10. *Chicago Examiner*, January 19, 1914; Wilkerson to McReynolds, January 31, 1914; Depositions by Rhodes, Tiny Johnson, and Kritzinger; Wilkerson to McReynolds, March 9, 1914; William Brady, United States consulate general, Montreal, to Secretary of State William J. Bryan, June 30, 1913; Lins Report, January 23, 1914, RG 60; *CD*, January 31, 1914.

11. Phil Dixon with Patrick J. Hannigan, *The Negro Baseball Leagues: A Photographic History* (Mattituck, NY: Amereon Ltd., 1992), 71; *IF*, July 5, August 23, 1913; *CD*, August 9, 1913, April 26, 1919, July 17, 1937; *Denver Star*, July 12, 1913; Johnson, *Jack Johnson Is a Dandy*, 85–87. Johnson relished fooling whites by posing as Gatewood while another black man passed for him. If whites thought all blacks looked alike, why not use that impression to one's advantage? Whatever the merits of Johnson's story, he played a role typical of black heroes when he turned white racism against the whites themselves. Other examples of Johnson's "puttin' on the man" appear in Chapter Four.

12. These Justice Department records were not declassified until 1981, sixty-eight years after Johnson's trial. The long delay left ample time for the removal and destruction of incriminating or embarrassing documents.

13. DeWoody Reports, January 15, 16, 1913, RG 60; *IF*, July 6, 1912; *PT*, July 4, 1914.

14. *CD*, August 9, 1913.

15. *Witness for Freedom: African American Voices on Race, Slavery, and Emancipation*, ed. C. Peter Ripley (Chapel Hill: University of North Carolina Press, 1993), 34, 36; "Address to the Emancipation League in Boston," *Afro-American History: Primary Sources*, ed. Thomas R. Frazier, 2d ed. (Chicago: Dorsey Press, 1988), 127.

16. *CD*, July 12, August 9, 1913; *CG*, July 19, August 2, 1913; *IF*, July 19, 1913; *NYA*, August 14, 1913; *CD*, August 30, October 4, November 15, 1913, March 14, June 27, July 4, 1914; *PT*, July 4, 1914.

17. *CD*, August 8, 29, 1914; *NYA*, August 13, 1914; *IF*, September 26, 1914; *CD*, January 9, 1915, June 7, July 12, 1919.

18. *PT*, January 16, February 27, March 13, 1915; *IF*, January 23, February 27, 1915; *CD*, March 13, 1915.

19. Guy Report, January 26, 1915; Wheeler Report, February 20, 1915; Clabaugh to Bielaski, "Personal and Confidential," February 19, 1915; Bielaski to Clabaugh, February 23, 1915; Barnes to Bielaski, "Personal and Confidential," March 4, 1915; Assistant Attorney General to Secretary of State Bryan, March 1, 1915; Lansing to McReynolds, March 9, 1915; RG 60. See also *IF*, February 13, 27, 1915; *CD*, March 13, 1915; *PT*, January 16, February 27, 1915.

20. *Atlanta Constitution*, July 5, 1910; *IF*, February 20, March 20, 1915; *Toronto Evening Telegram* (hereafter *TET*), December 25, 1914; *CD*, April 3, 1915.

21. *NYT*, April 4, 6, 1915; *PPL*, April 6, 1915; *PT*, April 10, 1915; *IF*, April 10, 1915; Grantland Rice, "After That Million," *Collier's*, May 1, 1915, 11, 24; John Lardner, "That Was Pugilism," *New Yorker*, June 25, 1949, 56–65, July 2, 1949, 36–46; Nat Fleischer, *50 Years at Ringside* (New York: Fleet, 1958), 89–92; *PPL*, April 6, 1915.

22. *PT*, April 10, 1915; *NYT*, April 7, 1915; *PPL*, April 6, 1915.

23. *The Great White Hope*, the 1970 film starring James Earl Jones, accepted as fact Johnson's claim that he had sacrificed his title for a pledge of leniency from federal agents. In one scene, Jack's white manager informs him he can earn $100,000 and a reduced sentence of six months if he throws the fight. Later, in Mexico, a federal agent offers a suspended sentence for a fall. The movie also shows Johnson's slipping surveillance by posing as a member of a baseball team that gathers at his mother's home. He swaggers right past agents parked outside. The film begins with the message, "Much of what follows is true." A disclaimer would have been more accurate: "Most of what follows is false." *The Great White Hope*, Martin Ritt, director, screenplay by Howard Sackler, CBS/Fox Video, 1970.

24. *PT*, July 24, 1915; *CD*, July 31, August 14, 1915; *IF*, July 31, 1915; *TET*, April 3, 6, 1915; Fleischer, *50 Years at Ringside*, 89; *IF*, July 24, 1915. See also Johnson, *Jack Johnson Is a Dandy*, 24, 100–102, 197–202. Johnson's nose must have grown longer while he wrote his memoir. He described his condition as "fair" for the match. But "stirred by the irresistible desire" to see his mother again, he "permitted the title to pass to Willard."

25. *PT*, August 7, 1915; *NYA*, April 8, 1915. Black editors noted, for example, that Presidents Roosevelt and Wilson had pressured white Californians not to discriminate against Japanese Americans because these leaders feared possible reprisals from Japan. The presidents challenged white westerners in behalf of Asian Americans but would not confront white southerners in defense of black Americans. See the *Nashville Globe*, February 12, 19, 1909; *CBA*, February 13, 1909; *CG*, March 27, 1909; *CD*, April 26, May 3, 1913; *Muskogee Cimiter*, May 5, 1913; *PT*, May 10, 1913; *CBA*, May 24, 1913; *The Crisis*, June 1913, 74–75. "The wonderful progress of the Japanese people" and the "sudden rise" of Japan, Booker T. Washington wrote to a Japanese editor, "has nowhere been studied with greater interest or enthusiasm than by the Negroes of America." Washington to Naoichi Masaoka, December 5, 1912, Washington to J. Harada, November 10, 1913, *Booker T. Washington Papers*, vol. 12, 328–329.

26. *CG*, April 15, 1915; *CBA*, April 15, 1915; *PT*, April 10, 1915; *CD*, April 17, 24, 1915.

27. *NYA*, April 8, 1915; *TET*, April 8, 10, 13, 1915; *IF*, April 17, 1915. See also *NYA*, May 1, 1913.

28. *PT*, August 7, April 17, November 27, 1915. Perry and others omitted that Johnson had also ducked able black rivals. Johnson argued that intraracial matches lacked the appeal of a fight with a "white hope" angle. Whatever his rationale, he had, like Willard and others, drawn the color line.

29. *IF*, August 21, 1915; *NYT*, April 5, 6, 7, 1915; *Billy Sunday Speaks*, ed. Karen Gullen (New York: Chelsea House, 1970), 52–73, 112–113; *American Issue*, February 8, 1913.

30. Dixon to Wilson, July 27, 1913; Dixon to Tumulty, January 27, 1915, *The Papers of Woodrow Wilson*, ed. Arthur S. Link (Princeton University Press, 1966-1994), vol. 28, 88–89; vol. 32, 142; Dixon to Tumulty, May 1, 1915, 142; Dixon to Wilson, February 20, 1915, 267; Griffith to Wilson, March 2, 1915, 310–311; Margaret Damrosch to Tumulty, March 27, 1915, 455; White to Tumulty, April 5, 1915, 486; *NYA*, March 4, 1915; *The Crisis*, June 1915, 88; *The Survey*, June 5, 1915, 209; *The Man Who Invented Hollywood: The Autobiography of D.W. Griffith*, ed. James Hart (Louisville: Touchstone, 1972), 24–27. On April 5, the day Johnson fought Willard, Chief Justice Edward White had instructed a New York agent to stop using his name to promote the film. White stated that he was "so situated" that further claims that he "sanctioned the show" would necessitate his public denial: "I do not approve the show ... if the owners were wise they would stop the rumors." A Confederate veteran, former Klansman, and Supreme Court justice since 1894, White did not specify his objections.

31. William Pickens, *The Heir of Slaves: An Autobiography* (Boston: The Pilgrim Press, 1911), 14–15; *Atlanta Independent* (hereafter *AI*), February 3, March 23, October 12, 1912; January 4, 8, October 18, December 6, 1913; February 14, 21, May 9, July 25, 1914.

32. Schneider to DuBois, May 23, 1914; DuBois to Schneider, June 2, 1914, *The Correspondence of W.E.B. DuBois*, ed. Herbert Aptheker (Amherst: University of Massachusetts Press, 1973), vol. 1, 196–197.

33. Karl Brown, *Adventures with D.W. Griffith* (New York: Farrar, Straus and Giroux, 1973), 31–33, 86–96.

34. *The Survey*, April 3, 1915, 4–5, June 5, 1915, 209–210; Francis Hackett, "Brotherly Love," *New Republic*, March 20, 1915, 185. In terms of "technical mastery," another reviewer noted, "this film is one of the best yet produced by a modern director." The rub was that Dixon, "a purveyor of history," was "not a historian." He was, rather, "a partisan, and a dangerous one." The film denied "the power of development within the free Negro" and amounted to "an exultation of race war." *The Outlook*, April 14, 1915, 854.

35. *Autobiography of D.W. Griffith*, 89–97; Brown, *Adventures with D.W. Griffith*, 98–99, 103, 128.

36. Brown, *Adventures with D.W. Griffith*, 78; *The Crisis*, April 1915, 311, May 1915, 87–88; *The Survey*, June 5, 1915, 209–210; Courtney to Washington, April 19, 1915, *Booker T. Washington Papers*, vol. 13, 274; Mary White Ovington, *The Walls Came Tumbling Down* (New York: Harcourt, Brace, 1947), 127–130.

37. *NYT*, April 15, 1915; Benjamin E. Mays, *Born to Rebel: An Autobiography* (New York: Scribner, 1971), 60; Washington to Thompson, June 3, 1915, Washington to Florence Sewell Bond, June 30, 1915, *Booker T. Washington Papers*, vol. 13, 317–318, 335.

38. D.W. Griffith, *The Man Who Invented Hollywood*, 88–89.

39. *PT*, April 10, 1915; *CG*, April 10, May 8, 29, 1915; *IF*, May 29, 1915; *CD*, May 22, June 12, 1915; *Washington Bee* (hereafter *WB*), June 5, October 16, 1915.

See also *IF*, April 17, May 1, 8, August 28, 1915; *NYA*, March 4, 11, 1915; *CG*, May 13, 1915. Griffith thought the protests boosted his film. After its raucous opening in New York City, Griffith went to the box office the following day and saw "a serpentine line about a block long trying to buy tickets" for the next show. *Autobiography of D.W. Griffith*, 96.

40. Tumulty to Wilson, April 24, 1915; Wilson to Tumulty, April 24, 28, 1915, *Papers of Woodrow Wilson*, vol. 33, 68, 86. Of the freed slaves Wilson wrote, "They had the easy faith, the simplicity, the idle hopes, the inexperience of children. Their masterless, homeless freedom made them the more pitiable, the more dependent, because under slavery they had been shielded . . . [and] had never learned independence or the rough buffets of freedom." They expected the government to assist them. Some northerners went south on "an errand of mercy and humanity," but most who arrived were "bitter" and "intolerant" toward local whites. The Klan arose to shield whites "from some of the ugliest hazards of a time of revolution." Woodrow Wilson, *A History of the American People* (New York: Harper and Brothers, 1902), vol. 5, 18, 46, 60, 63–64.

41. *NYA*, August 19, 1916; *The Crisis*, October 1916, 268; Alexander Walters, *My Life and Work* (New York: Revell, 1917), 195–196; *CG*, November 4, 1916.

42. *The Crisis*, February 1917, 195–196, April 1916, 302–304; *AI*, January 29, 1916; *IF*, January 29, 1916; *AI*, February 26, 1916. See also February 5, 1916.

43. *The Crisis*, July 1916, 1–8, 135; National Association for the Advancement of Colored People, comp., *Thirty Years of Lynching in the United States, 1889–1918* (New York: Negro Universities Press, 1969 [1919]), 23–24; *PT*, May 27, 1916; *NYA*, June 8, 1916.

44. M[ason] A. H[awkins], "Another Lynching," *The Crisis*, October 1916, 275–276; *NYT*, August 20, 21, 1916; *Thirty Years of Lynching*, 24.

45. *NYT*, October 5, 1916; *The Crisis*, January 1917, 112–113; December 1916, 67; Ovington, *Walls Came Tumbling Down*, 150–152; *Thirty Years of Lynching*, 24–25; *CD*, December 30, 1916, January 6, 1917; *PT*, December 23, 1916.

46. Moorfield Storey et al. to Wilson, February 13, 1917, *Papers of Woodrow Wilson*, vol. 41, 217–218; *The Crisis*, April 1917, 284; Wilson's Second Inaugural Address, March 5, 1917, *The Messages and Papers of Woodrow Wilson*, ed. Albert Shaw (New York: Doranic, 1924), vol. 1, 369–371.

47. *Messages and Papers of Woodrow Wilson*, vol. 1, 381–383; Page to Wilson, "Personal," April 3, 1917; McAdoo to Wilson, April 3, 1917, *Papers of Woodrow Wilson*, vol. 41, 538, 541.

48. *NYA*, May 24, 1917; Kelly Miller, *An Appeal to Conscience* (New York: Arno Press, 1969 [1918]), 83.

49. *AI*, April 7, 1917; *NYA*, May 3, 24, 1917; *WB*, October 20, November 17, 1917. Even before the declaration of war, Davis had contrasted German American and Irish American ambivalence with the blacks' uncompromising loyalty. "No hyphen divides his patriotism," Davis bragged, "no double allegiance." *AI*, March 31, 1917.

50. *The Crisis*, May 1917, 8; April 1917, 270–71; William Pickens, *Bursting Bonds* (Boston: The Pilgram Press, 1923), 217–219; *The Crisis*, June 1917, 60. Advocating a training camp for black officers, Pickens conceded that "it would not make the world safe for democracy, but it would make the United States army much less dangerous for the Negro."

51. Martha Gruening and W.E.B. DuBois, "The Massacre of East St. Louis," *The*

Crisis, September 1917, 219–238; *AI*, July 7, 1917. See also *Crusade for Justice: The Autobiography of Ida B. Wells*, ed. Alfreda M. Duster (Chicago: University of Chicago Press, 1970), 383–395.

52. *The Crisis*, July 1917, 133–135, supplement 1–4; August 1917, 185–188; NAACP, *Thirty Years of Lynching*, 25–26; *NYA*, June 21, July 5, 1917. In a move worthy of a D.W. Griffith film, detectives disinterred the victim and photographed her eyes in hopes of finding the killer's image on her retinas. When magnified, the pictures showed an indistinct but apparently convincing visage of Ell Person. The forensic expert in the city crime lab, however, found no trace of blood on Person's ax, shoes, or pants—rather strange if he had decapitated the girl and tossed her corpse into the river.

53. *NYA*, August 2, 1917; *The Crisis*, September 1917, 241–244; *The Negro in New York: An Informal Social History*, ed. Roi Ottley and William J. Weatherby (New York: New York Public Library, 1967), 199–203; James Weldon Johnson, *Black Manhattan* (New York: Atheneum, 1972 [1930]), 236; Ovington, *Walls Came Tumbling Down*, 180–181; *IF*, August 11, 1917; *AI*, August 11, 1917; Tumulty to Wilson, August 1, 1917, Wilson to Tumulty, August 1, 1917, Tumulty to Wilson, August 3, 1917, Alfred Cosey to Wilson, August 9, 1917, *Papers of Woodrow Wilson*, vol. 43, 342–343, 359, 412–413.

54. *The Crisis*, August 1918, 180–182; Walter White, "The Work of a Mob," *The Crisis*, September 1918, 221–223; *Thirty Years of Lynching*, 26–27; Ovington, *Walls Came Tumbling Down*, 152; Oswald Garrison Villard, *Fighting Years: Memoirs of a Liberal Editor* (New York: Harcourt, Brace, 1939), 339–340; *AI*, June 1, 8, 1918; *The Crisis*, February 1919, 180–181.

55. *The Crisis*, October 1917, 284–285; Martha Gruening, "Houston: An NAACP Investigation," *The Crisis*, November 1917, 14–19; *The Crisis*, January 1918, 130–131, February 1918, 187–189; Wells, *Crusade for Justice*, 367–371; Charlotta A. Bass, *Forty Years: Memoirs From the Pages of a Newspaper* (Los Angeles: 1960), 43–46; Ovington, *Walls Came Tumbling Down*, 137; Miller, *An Appeal to Conscience*, 46.

56. Memo of Colonel G.E. Gross, assistant inspector general, to Brigadier General James Parker, commanding general, Southern Department, September 13, 1917, *Blacks in the Military: Essential Documents*, ed. Bernard C. Nalty and Morris J. MacGregor (Wilmington: Scholarly Resources, 1981), 68-71. See also Major General James Parker to Secretary of War Newton Baker, August 24, 1917, Congressman Joe Eagle to Wilson, August 24, 1917, Baker to Wilson, August 28, 1917, *Papers of Woodrow Wilson*, vol. 44, 41-42, 62-64, 77-78. Congressman Eagle, whose district included Houston, advised Wilson that the uprising "conclusively proves [the] tragic blunder committed in ordering negro troops to Southern camps. . . . Unless all these negro troops are sent away quickly my opinion [is] that last night's tragedy is but a prelude to a tragedy upon [an] enormous scale." He advised "prompt removal of all negro troops who are here and rescinding any order for others to come." In Chicago, Ida B. Wells organized protest against the executions and the soldiers' burial in nameless graves, a dissent that brought two secret service agents to her door who threatened to prosecute her for treason. When told blacks did not agree with her, she replied, "Maybe not. They don't know any better or they are afraid of losing their whole skins. As for myself I don't care. . . . I would consider it an honor to spend whatever years are necessary in prison as the one member of the race who protested, rather than to be with all the 11,999,999 Negroes who didn't have to go to prison because they kept their mouths shut." *The Autobiography of Ida B. Wells*, 361-370. See also *AI*, September 1, 1917; *NYA*, Au-

gust 30, 1917; *The Crisis*, October 1917, 285. A useful account is Robert V. Haynes, *A Night of Violence: The Houston Riot of 1917* (Baton Rouge: Louisiana State University Press, 1976).

57. *NYA*, December 8, 1917; *IF*, December 15, 1917; *The Crisis*, January 1918, 114.

58. Walton to Tumulty, June 12, 1918, Moton to Wilson, June 15, 1918, Wilson to Moton, June 18, 1918, Baker to Wilson, July 1, 1918, *Papers of Woodrow Wilson*, vol. 48, 302, 323–324, 346, 475–476; Dyer to Wilson, July 23, 1918, Shillady to Wilson, July 25, 1918, *Papers of Woodrow Wilson*, vol. 49, 61–62, 88–89.

59. *Papers of Woodrow Wilson*, vol. 49, 97–98.

60. Moton to Wilson, July 27, 1918, *Papers of Woodrow Wilson*, vol. 49, 113–114; *The Crisis*, September 1918, 227; *AI*, August 10, 1918.

61. *CD*, May 18, June 1, 1918; *AI*, May 25, 1918; *The Crisis*, August 1918, 164–165, September 1918, 216–217; Miller, *An Appeal to Conscience*, 79; *IF*, July 27, October 27, 1917.

62. Fiorello La Guardia, *The Making of an Insurgent: An Autobiography, 1882–1919* (Philadelphia: Lippincott, 1948), 192–193; *CD*, June 15, 1918; *IF*, June 22, 1918; Raymond Morris to W.C. Fitts, July 11, 1918, Department of Justice Files, RG 60. Taking advantage of a gullible *Chicago Defender* staff, Johnson and his nephew Gus Rhodes spread fantastic tales of heroism in Europe. A "report" from Gibraltar in 1917, for example, noted that Johnson had been "captured by an Austrian submarine. Jack, single-handed, subdued the Austrian captain and blew up the submarine, and was rescued, after drifting three days." In early 1919, the *Defender* referred to Johnson as a "special aid" in Spanish naval intelligence. The *Defender* later repeated that Johnson had "rendered valuable services in detecting German submarine bases" and acted as "a special courier for the American embassy." In his memoir, Johnson said he had investigated "German submarine operations off the coast of Spain." Why Johnson failed to mention these exploits to La Guardia is unclear. Johnson might have lost his punch, but he still had his imagination. *CD*, February 24, 1917, April 19, 1919, July 31, 1920; Johnson, *Jack Johnson Is a Dandy*, 108–109.

63. *The Crisis*, February 1920, 183–186; *NYA*, June 7, 1919, January 3, 1920; *CD*, January 3, 1920; *Selected Poems of Claude McKay* (New York: Bookman, 1953), 36; *NYA*, November 8, 29, 1919, August 21, 1920; *IF*, December 4, 1920; *CD*, October 30, 1920.

64. Martin to DuBois, May 30, 1919; Hewlett to DuBois, August 26, 1919, *Correspondence of W.E.B. DuBois*, vol. 1, 233–235. DuBois printed Martin's letter anonymously in *The Crisis* for October.

65. Emmett J. Scott, "Letters of Negro Migrants of 1916–1918," *Journal of Negro History*, 4 (1919): 304, 329, 417, 419–20, 425, 438, 442, 451, 452.

Chapter 4. "Outcasts Asylumed"

1. James Weldon Johnson, "Fifty Years," *The Book of American Negro Poetry*, ed. James Weldon Johnson (New York: Harcourt, Brace, 1931), 131.

2. *Philadelphia Tribune* (hereafter *PT*), December 6, 1913.

3. *Chicago Defender* (hereafter *CD*), October 26, 1912 *Chicago Broad-Ax* (hereafter *CBA*), October 26, 1912 *Indianapolis Freeman* (hereafter *IF*), November 2, 1912.

4. *Nashville Globe* (hereafter *NG*), February 28, 1908; John Arthur Johnson, *Jack Johnson Is a Dandy: An Autobiography* (New York: Chelsea House, 1969 [1927]),

165–166; *IF*, February 12, 1910; Johnson, *Jack Johnson Is a Dandy*, 63; *PT*, March 9, 1912; *Denver Statesman* (hereafter *DS*), February 3, 1912.

5. *CD*, July 23, 1910; *DS*, April 5, 1911; *PT*, September 8, 1938; *Richmond Planet*, September 17, 1938; William H. Wiggins Jr., "Jack Johnson as Bad Nigger: The Folklore of His Life," *The Black Scholar*, January 1971, 35–46; H.C. Brearley, "'Ba-ad Nigger,'" *Mother Wit From the Laughing Barrel: Readings in the Interpretation of Afro-American Culture*, ed. Alan Dundes (Jackson: University of Mississippi Press, 1990), 583.

6. *New York Age* (hereafter *NYA*), July 1, 1909, Wolcott Gibbs, "He Didn't Have a Thing," *New Yorker*, June 29, 1946, 45; *IF*, May 17, 1913; *CD*, July 5, 1913; *NYA*, September 4, 1913.

7. *Cleveland Gazette*, October 3, 1914; John Lardner, "That Was Pugilism," *New Yorker*, June 25, 1949, 63, July 2, 1949, 36; Nat Fleischer, *50 Years at Ringside* (New York: Fleet, 1958), 77, 83, 84.

8. *Plessy v. Ferguson* 163 U.S. 210 (1896); *Berea College v. Commonwealth of Kentucky* 211 U.S. 12 (1908).

9. *IF*, November 27, 1909; *DS*, February 18, 1911; *Atlanta Constitution*, July 31, 1910; Johnson, *Jack Johnson Is a Dandy*, 238–239; *New York Amsterdam News*, June 26, 1965.

10. *NG*, October 25, 1912; *Washington Bee*, December 21, 1912; *CD*, April 24, 1920; *IF*, February 7, 1920; Jesse O. Thomas, *My Story in Black and White* (New York: Exposition Press, 1967), 79. Like many editors, Robert Abbott objected that white journalists portrayed Johnson as "a leader . . . expressing the views and sentiments of the rest of his group, a conclusion that was absolutely false and unjustified." Instead, Johnson occupied "the same position" among blacks as Willard did among whites. *CD*, February 20, 1920.

11. W.E.B. DuBois, "An Essay Toward a History of the Black Man in the Great War," *The Crisis*, June 1919, 72; Kelly Miller, *The World War for Human Rights* (New York: Negro Universities Press, 1969 [1919]), 477.

12. Colonel Allen Greer to Kenneth D. McKellar, December 6, 1918, "Documents of the War," *The Crisis*, May 1919, 19–20; *Congressional Record*, 66th Cong., 2d sess., April 8, 1920, vol. 59, pt. 5, 5319; *The Crisis*, June 1919, 87; "The Saving Grace," *The Crisis*, May 1919, 28–29. Some white legislators defended the black soldiers, among them Julius Kahn of California and Edward King of Illinois. *Congressional Record*, 65th Cong., 3d sess., March 1, 1919, App. 176; 66th Cong., 2d sess., June 2, 1920, 9138. DuBois wrote that Greer's letter to McKellar and other important documents "have come into the hands of the editor," but he did not reveal how. *The Crisis*, May 1919, 16.

13. *NYA*, June 7, 1919; *IF*, December 4, 1920; *The Messenger*, August 1919, 11–12.

14. *Boley Progress*, March 9, 1905, February 1, 1906, August 31, 1911, July 8, 1909. The race towns emerged after the federal government quit enforcing the Reconstruction amendments and left ex-slaves to the mercy of former masters. Before the founding of Boley (1903) and Allensworth (1909) came Nicodemus, Kansas (1877), Eatonville, Florida (1886), Mound Bayou, Mississippi (1887), and Langston, Oklahoma Territory (1891). These separatist experiments deserve more attention from scholars.

15. H.B. Allen Report (Chicago), April 1, 1919; Connell Report (Los Angeles), July 23, 1920, Record Group 60, National Archives; *CD*, July 24, 1920; Lewis J. Baley to D.S. Dickerson, January 20, 1921, RG 60; *CD*, September 18, October 2, 1920; *NYA*, July 24, 31, September 18, 1920; *IF*, July 24, August 14, September 18, October 2, 1920; *IF*, February 28, 1920; Frank Marshall Davis, *Livin' the Blues: Mem-*

oirs of a Black Journalist and Poet, ed. John Edgar Tidwell (Madison: University of Wisconsin Press, 1992), 122–123.

16. Chicago Commission on Race Relations, *The Negro in Chicago: A Study of Race Relations and a Race Riot* (Chicago: University of Chicago Press, 1922), xxiii, 33–34, 122, 343–354, 490, 520–535, 596, 599.

17. Miller, *World War for Human Rights,* 438; DuBois, "Intermarriage," *The Crisis,* February 1913, 180–181.

18. *CD,* January 31, 1920; DuBois, "Crime," *The Crisis,* February 1920, 172–173.

19. Jersey Joe Walcott with Lewis Burton, "I'll Lick Joe Louis Again," *Saturday Evening Post,* June 19, 1948, 28, 119; *Richmond Afro-American,* June 15, 1946; *Pittsburgh Courier,* June 22, 1946.

20. James Earl Jones and Penelope Niven, *Voices and Silences* (New York: Charles Scribner's Sons, 1993), 191, 210–211, 335–336; Mark Kram, "He Moves Like Silk, Hits Like a Ton," *Sports Illustrated,* October 26, 1970, 16; George Plimpton, "Watching the Man in the Mirror," *Sports Illustrated,* November 23, 1970, 82. Feelings about interracial relationships remained strong when *The Great White Hope* appeared on stage and screen. Jane Alexander, Jones recalled, "received numerous obscene letters about her role as my mistress." Jones and Niven, *Voices and Silences,* 199.

21. In addition to the 1970 film, biographies demonstrate major shifts in Johnson's historical reputation. See Finis Farr, *Black Champion: The Life and Times of Jack Johnson* (London: Macmillan, 1964); Al-Tony Gilmore, *Bad Nigger! The National Impact of Jack Johnson* (Port Washington, NY: Kennikat Press, 1975); Randy Roberts, *Papa Jack: Jack Johnson and the Era of White Hopes* (New York: Free Press, 1983).

Chapter 5. "Don't You Fall Now": A New Race Ambassador

1. *Collected Poems of Langston Hughes,* ed. Arnold Rampersad (New York: Knopf, 1995), 30.

2. For details on Louis's trip to Alabama, see the *Pittsburgh Courier* (hereafter *PC*), January 15, 1944, *Dallas Express* (hereafter *DE*), January 22, 1944, *Life,* November 15, 1948, 146. The background on Louis and kin appears in Chester Washington and William Nunn, "The Life Story of Joe Louis," *PC,* February 2, 9, 16, 23, March 2, 9, 16, 23, 30, April 6, 13, 1935; Gene Kessler, "Joe Louis' Own Story," *Philadelphia Tribune* (hereafter *PT*), July 25, August 1, 8, 15, 22, 29, September 5, 12, 19, 26, 1935; Joe Louis, as told to Meyer Berger and Barney Nagler, "My Story," *Life,* November 8, 1948, 126–151; November 15, 1948, 126–146; Joe Louis, *My Life Story* (New York: Duell, Sloan and Pearce, 1947); Joe Louis, with Edna and Art Rust Jr., *Joe Louis: My Life* (New York: Harcourt Brace Jovanovich, 1978); Joe Louis Barrow Jr. and Barbara Munder, *Joe Louis: 50 Years an American Hero* (New York: McGraw-Hill, 1988).

3. *PC,* June 28, 1941; *DE,* July 5, 1941.

4. *PT,* February 27, 1936.

5. *Joe Louis: My Life,* 4–5; Caswell Adams, "Introducing—the New Joe Louis," *Saturday Evening Post,* May 10, 1941, 107.

6. Interviews with Rosa Lee Kirkman Wheeler, William Hines, and Fred Guinyard in *Untold Tales, Unsung Heroes: An Oral History of Detroit's African American Com-*

munity, 1918–1967, ed. Elaine Latzman Moon (Detroit: Wayne State Press, 1994), 31, 77, 111–112; Louis, *My Life Story,* 19–26; *Joe Louis: My Life,* 18–24; Coleman Young and Lonnie Wheeler, *Hard Stuff: The Autobiography of Coleman Young* (New York: Viking, 1994), 27; Sugar Ray Robinson with Dave Anderson, *Sugar Ray* (New York: Viking, 1970), 7–8, 13–14. "Joe Barrow was the big hero of the neighborhood" and "little kids used to tag along behind him," Robinson recalled. "He lived a couple of blocks away from me. . . . When he'd come out, I'd grab the little bag he carried . . . and carry it for him."

7. "The breach between Jack Johnson and Jack Blackburn," sportswriter Al Monroe explained, "was opened when Blackburn, a light-weight, beat Johnson up in a gymnasium workout. Johnson had brought several girl friends to watch his workout and Jack spoiled the setting by tanning the later heavyweight champion to a frazzle." *Chicago Defender* (hereafter *CD*), April 10, 1937. See also *PC,* May 2, 1942.

8. *Joe Louis: My Life,* 40–52; Louis, *My Life Story,* 36–43; John Roxborough, "How I Discovered Joe Louis," *Ebony,* October 1954, 64–76; *PC,* February 16, 1935; Louis, "My Story," 128, 137–141; *PT,* September 5, 12, 1935; *Time,* September 29, 1941, 60; *Newsweek,* July 6, 1935, 23; Edwin R. Embree, *13 Against the Odds* (New York: Viking, 1944), 232; Julia Jones interview with Lillie Barrow Brooks, *PC,* April 27, 1935; *CD,* April 13, 1935.

9. *Joe Louis: My Life,* 35–36, 39, 68–69; Joe Louis, "Why I Won't Marry Again," *Ebony,* November 1952, 45; *Time,* September 29, 1941, 60–64; *Ebony,* October 1954, 67; *DE,* April 5, 1941. Only in 1941 did Louis finally pose for a photograph with Johnson. "No love was lost on the champion's part," the *Courier* noted. "This is believed to be the first time Louis and 'Lil' Artha' have been pictured together." *PC,* November 15, 1941.

10. Louis, *Joe Louis: My Life,* 50–51; *Philadelphia Record,* June 28, 1935 (Julian Black Collection, Smithsonian Institution); Steve Hannagan, "Black Gold," *Saturday Evening Post* (hereafter *SEP*) June 20, 1936, 78; *PC,* March 13, 1937.

11. *Joe Louis: My Life,* 37–38; Louis, *My Life Story,* 33; *New York Sun,* June 11, 1936 (Black Collection).

12. Louis, "My Story," 127.

13. Young and Wheeler, *Hard Stuff,* 23–25; Clarence Darrow, *The Story of My Life* (New York: Scribner's, 1932), 304–311; Mary White Ovington, *The Walls Came Tumbling Down* (New York: Harcourt Brace, 1947), 198–213; Langston Hughes, *Fight for Freedom: The Story of the NAACP* (New York: Norton, 1962), 42–45; interview with M. Kelly Fritz in Moon, *Untold Tales* 82–84.

14. *CD,* July 13, 1935.

15. *PC,* February 23, 1935; *Joe Louis: My Life,* 38–39; Louis, *My Life Story,* 196–197.

16. *Joe Louis: My Life,* 38–39, 66, 69–73; *CD,* July 13, August 24, September 7, 28, 1935, March 21, 1936; *SEP,* June 20, 1936, 78; *PC,* June 8, July 13, 20, 1935; interview with Marva Trotter, *PC,* September 14, 1935; *PC,* September 28, October 5, 17, 1935; *PT,* October 3, 1935; *Cleveland Gazette* (hereafter *CG*), September 7, 28, 1935; Louis, "My Story," 148; *Richmond Afro-American* (hereafter *RAA*), July 2, 1938.

17. *Joe Louis: My Life,* 5–6; *CD,* April 18, 1936; *PT,* January 10, August 8, September 19, 1935; *CD,* December 28, 1935, March 7, 21, 1936; *Literary Digest,* May 4, 1935, 35, July 6, 1935, 33; *Newsweek,* July 6, 1935, 22–23, August 17, 1935, 24, October 5, 1935, 25; *PC,* September 14, 1935.

18. *Boston Post* (hereafter *BP*), August 16, 1935 (Black Collection); *Joe Louis:*

My Life, 66–67; *Newsweek*, July 6, 1935, 23; *Time*, September 29, 1941, 62–63.

19. Louis, "My Story," 141; *Joe Louis: My Life*, 67–68; Louis, *My Life Story*, 53; *CD*, June 15, July 13, August 24, September 14, 1935, January 25, June 27, November 7, 1936. By early 1936 Louis was receiving over 2,000 letters a week, most asking for donations or loans or giving advice. Louis grumbled to Al Monroe that people should "think more and write less."

20. *Joe Louis: My Life*, 39; Louis, "Why I Won't Marry Again," *Ebony*, November 1952, 45; *CD*, January 25, March 7, 1936; *BP*, August 16, 1935 (Black Collection); *DE*, April 5, 1941; *PT*, October 10, December 26, 1935. An eyewitness described Louis's gesture to the *Defender* and its effect upon the crowd: "When news of his refusal to pose with women gradually spread about the theatre, ladies expressed . . . approval of this fine consideration shown to his wife. News of it will add another high tribute to the great fighter." *CD*, December 7, 1935.

21. *PT*, January 10, 1935; *CD*, April 20, 1935; *PC*, April 20, 1935; *PT*, December 26, 1935.

22. *The Crisis*, June 1935 (cover), August 1935, 241, November 1935, 337; Walter White, *How Far the Promised Land* (New York: Viking, 1955), 183; Roi Ottley, *New World A-Coming* (Boston: Houghton Mifflin, 1943), 189, 193–194.

23. *Newark Evening News*, June 27, 1935; *Detroit News*, June 27, 1935 (Black Collection); *Newsweek*, July 6, 1935, 22–23, October 5, 1935, 25; *BP*, July 8, 1935; *New York American*, June 13, 1937, May 13, 1936 (Black Collection). See also *Boston Transcript*, June 26, 1935; *Cleveland Press*, June 27, 1935; *Syracuse Journal* (cartoon), July 6, 1935; *New York Evening Journal*, June 22, 1936 (Black Collection).

24. *Birmingham News*, June 26, 27, 1935; *Richmond Times-Dispatch*, June 19, 1936 (Black Collection).

25. *Joe Louis: My Life*, 97–98; *CD*, November 14, 28, 1936; *PC*, November 28, 1936; John C. Dancy, *Sand Against the Wind: The Memoirs of John C. Dancy* (Detroit: Wayne State University Press, 1966), 186. Dancy directed the Urban League in Detroit. He and Charles Roxborough, John's brother and a state legislator, also made the trip to New Orleans.

26. *PT*, February 25, 1937; *Enid Daily Eagle*, March 18, 1937 (Black Collection); *PC*, April 3, 1937; *Forth Worth Press*, March 24, 1937; *Dallas Dispatch*, March 21, 1937 (Black Collection); *Ebony*, October 1954, 74.

27. *PC*, December 5, 1936; *New York Times* (hereafter *NYT*), November 23, 25, December 11, 1937; *The Crisis*, January 1937, 17; *CD*, February 20, 1937; *PC*, March 20, 1937.

28. *Congressional Record*, 75th Cong., 1st sess., April 15, 1937, vol. 81, pt. 3, 3547–3550; *CD*, April 17, 24, May 1, 8, 1937; *PC*, April 24, 1937; *The Crisis*, May 1937, 145; "Scottsboro," *Collected Poems of Langston Hughes*, 142; *Los Angeles Sentinel* (hereafter *LAS*), April 9, 1936.

29. Louis, "My Story," 146; *Joe Louis: My Life*, 32, 41; *CD*, December 26, 1936; *PT*, July 15, 1937; *PC*, February 19, 1938; *RAA*, February 3, 1940. For Louis's own praise for his handlers, see *PT*, September 26, 1935; *PC*, February 16, April 13, 1935, May 2, 1942; Louis, *My Life Story*, 29, 159; *Joe Louis: My Life*, 176; Louis, "My Story," 127, 137.

30. Quentin Reynolds, "Dark Dynamite," *Collier's*, June 22, 1935, 34; *New York Amsterdam News* (hereafter *NYAN*), June 20, 1936; *RAA*, August 3, 1940.

31. *PC*, June 29, 1935; *PT*, June 27, 1935; *CD*, June 29, July 6, 1935; *LAS*, July 11, 1935.

32. *New York World Telegram*, June 25, 1935; *New York Daily Mirror*, June 28, 1935; *San Francisco Examiner*, June 27, 1935 (Black Collection).

33. *PT*, July 4, 1935; *Literary Digest*, July 6, 1935, 32; *CG*, June 22, 1935; *Cleveland Plain Dealer*, June 27, 1935 (Black Collection).

34. *PT*, August 1, 1935; *CD*, September 21, 28, 1935; Jonathan Mitchell, "Joe Louis Never Smiles," *New Republic*, October 9, 1935, 239; *CD*, October 5, 1935.

35. *Joe Louis: My Life*, 48–49, 73–74; interview with Marva Louis Spaulding in Barrow and Munder, *Joe Louis*, 202–203.

36. *CD*, July 13, August 24, 1935; *PC*, September 14, 1935, February 29, 1936, October 30, 1937; Louis, *My Life Story*, 109; *Detroit Evening Times*, June 18, 1936 (Black Collection).

37. On recurring "parables" in advertising during the 1920s and 1930s, see Roland Marchand, *Advertising the American Dream: Making Way for Modernity, 1920–1940* (Berkeley: University of California Press, 1985). In magazines for white readers, Marchand notes, blacks almost always appeared as janitors and maids. The Louis advertisements, however, utilized radically different images to appeal to black consumers.

38. For the ads cited here, see *CD*, August 10, September 7, October 26, 1935; *PC*, August 31, September 14, 21, October 19, 1935; *PT*, June 20, August 15, October 10, 1935; *The Crisis*, February, March, April, May, June, August, September, October, November, December, 1938.

39. *PT*, August 15, 1935; *CG*, January 9, 1937; *PC*, January 2, 1937. See also *Newsweek*, October 5, 1935, 25; Adams, "Introducing—the New Joe Louis," 105–106.

40. This change in Louis and his later struggles with marriage, money, taxes, and women figure prominently in Chapter Eight.

41. *Time*, August 26, 1935, 57; *CD*, December 17, 1938; *Life*, February 6, 1939, 42.

42. The black press emphasized Joe and Marva Louis's high income and refined tastes. After the victory over Max Baer, the Louises returned to Chicago to inspect their new apartment. Marva and interior decorators had chosen the décor. A local reporter toured the flat with the newlyweds. The residence, the *Defender* observed, was "as complete in detail and taste as any model home shown at any exhibit." Joe "was all smiles" and gave Marva "a big kiss for what he called perfect taste in the selection of the household furnishings." *CD*, September 28, October 5, 1935.

43. *CD*, June 27, 1936; *Brooklyn Daily Eagle*, June 10, 1936; *Chicago Daily News*, June 19, 1936 (Black Collection); *Joe Louis: My Life*, 86–89; Louis *My Life Story*, 67–73; Nat Fleischer, *50 Years at Ringside* (New York: Fleet, 1958), 80–81; *Max Schmeling: An Autobiography*, trans. and ed. George B. von der Lippe (Chicago: Bonus Books, 1998 [1977]), 111, 113–114, 119–128; Max Schmeling, as told to Paul Gallico, "This Way I Beat Joe Louis," *SEP*, August 29, 1936, 40–41, September 5, 1936, 32–34. Further analysis of this fight and its significance for German–American relations appears in Chapter Seven. ·

44. *CD*, June 27, 1936; *Time*, June 29, 1936, 35; *PT*, June 20, 25, 1936; Langston Hughes, *I Wonder As I Wander* (New York: Hill and Wang, 1956), 315; Ottley, *New World A-Coming*, 195; *Detroit Evening Times*, June 20, 1936 (Black Collection). See also Frank Marshall Davis, *Livin' the Blues: Memoirs of a Black Journalist and Poet*, ed. John Edgar Tidwell (Madison: University of Wisconsin Press, 1992), 257.

45. Lena Horne with Richard Schickel, *Lena* (Garden City: Doubleday, 1965), 75–76; Cab Calloway and Bryant Rollins, *Of Minnie the Moocher & Me* (New York:

Crowell, 1976), 140; Willie "the Lion" Smith with George Hoefer, *Music on My Mind: The Memoirs of an American Pianist* (Garden City: Doubleday, 1964), 247.

46. Maya Angelou, *I Know Why the Caged Bird Sings* (New York: Random House, 1969), 129–132; *CD*, June 27, 1936.

47. *New York Sunday Mirror*, July 5, 1936 (Black Collection); *PC*, July 4, 1936; *CD*, June 27, 1936.

48. *Joe Louis: My Life*, 89–92; Barrow and Munder, *Joe Louis*, 73–74; *Detroit Free Press*, June 22, 1936 (Black Collection).

49. *PC*, August 22, 1936; *PT*, August 6, 13, 20, 1936; *CD*, August 22, 29, 1936; *CG*, August 8, 15, 22, 29, 1936; *LAS*, August 27, 1936.

50. *CD*, March 14, 1936; *PT*, May 28, 1936, July 1, 1937.

51. *PC*, February 27, May 22, 1937; *CD*, June 19, 1937; *Syracuse Post-Standard*, June 22, 1937; *St. Louis Star-Times*, June 22, 1937 (Black Collection). See also *Richmond Times Dispatch*, June 19, 1936; *New York Evening Journal*, June 18, 1937; *New York Herald Tribune*, June 23, 1937 (Black Collection).

52. *CD*, June 26, 1937; *PC*, July 3, 1937; *Brooklyn Daily Eagle* (cartoon by Ed Hughs), June 20, 1937 (Black Collection); *CD*, June 26, 1937; "Boxing's Best: Joe Louis," HBO Sports and Big Fights, Inc., 1990; *PC*, July 3, 1937.

53. *New York Herald Tribune*, June 23, 1937 (Black Collection); *PC*, July 10, 1937; *Joe Louis: My Life*, 118–19; *CD*, June 26, 1937.

54. *PC*, January 17, 1942. Roxborough underestimated the fondness for Louis on both sides of the color line. When Louis enlisted in the army, perhaps before, he became an *American* hero, not just a black hero—a theme addressed in Chapter Seven.

55. *Joe Louis: My Life*, 125; *NYT*, June 23, 1937; *Richmond Times-Dispatch*, June 21, 1938 (Black Collection); Roy Wilkins with Tom Mathews, *Standing Fast: The Autobiography of Roy Wilkins* (New York: Viking, 1982), 164.

56. *PC*, June 25, 1938; *CD*, June 25, 1938; "Joe Louis Uncovers Dynamite," *New Masses*, October 8, 1935, in *The Richard Wright Reader*, ed. Ellen Wright and Michel Fabre (New York: Harper and Row, 1978), 32–35; *The Negro in New York: An Informal Social History*, ed. Roi Ottley and William J. Weatherby (New York: New York Public Library, 1967), 291. Wright learned the risks of interracial confrontations at an early age. In the opening scene of *Uncle Tom's Children*, black boys throw cinders at white boys who fight back with bottles. The narrator suffers a head wound that requires three stitches. When he explains the cut to his mother, she spanks him with a barrel stave and recites "gems of Jim Crow wisdom," advising him "never, never, under any conditions to fight *white* folks again." This scene was based on an actual incident from Wright's Arkansas boyhood. See *Black Boy: A Record of Childhood and Youth* (New York: Harper and Brothers, 1942), 72.

57. Angelou, *I Know Why the Caged Bird Sings*, 129, 132; *PT*, June 24, 1937; Bill Gaither, "Champ Joe Louis," Decca, 1938; Charles Wolfe and Kip Lornell, *The Life and Legend of Leadbelly* (New York: Harper Collins, 1992), 247–248; Paul Oliver, *Aspects of the Blues Tradition* (New York: Oak Publications, 1970), 157; Paul Oliver, *Songsters and Saints: Vocal Traditions on Race Records* (Cambridge: Cambridge University Press, 1984), 224; Bruce Jackson, *Get Your Ass in the Water and Swim Like Me* (Cambridge: Harvard University Press, 1974), 37. See also David Margolick, "Only One Athlete Has Ever Inspired This Many Songs," *NYT*, February 25, 2001.

58. *RAA*, July 2, 1938; *The Crisis*, August 1938, 265; *CG*, June 25, 1938; *PT*, June 23, 1938; *PC*, July 2, 1938; "Let America Be America Again," *The Collected Poems of Langston Hughes*, 189–91. On the postfight mayhem, see also *NYT*, June 23, 24,

1938; Louis, *My Life*, 143; *Time*, July 4, 1938, 19; *New York Daily Mirror*, June 23, 1938; *New York World Telegram*, June 23, 1938; *Boston Post*, June 23, 1938 (Black Collection).

59. Hughes, *I Wonder As I Wander*, 314; *CD*, June 25, 1938; *RAA*, April 29, 1944; John O. Killens, *Black Man's Burden* (New York: Trident, 1965), 114; Russell Baker, *Growing Up* (New York: Congdon and Weed, 1982), 203–206.

60. Charles S. Johnson, *Growing Up in the Black Belt* (Washington, DC: American Council on Education, 1941), 246; Malcolm X with Alex Haley, *Autobiography of Malcolm X* (New York: Grove, 1964), 23–24. See also Claude Brown, *Manchild in the Promised Land* (New York: Macmillan, 1965), 165; Ottley, *New World A-Coming*, 189–190; *PC*, September 7, 1940, July 5, 1941; Floyd Patterson, "It Was a Victory For Us!" *Ebony*, August 1960, 117.

61. *PC*, September 28, 1935; Horne, *Lena*, 75–76; Angelou, *I Know Why the Caged Bird Sings*, 130; *New York Daily Mirror*, July 12, 1936 (Black Collection); *PC*, July 2, 1938; *RAA*, June 22, 1946.

Chapter 6. "No Other Dream, No Land But This": Black Americans and the Enemy Within

1. Pauli Murray, *Dark Testament and Other Poems* (Norwalk, CT: Silvermine, 1970), 27.

2. *Congressional Record*, 75th Cong., 1st sess., June 22, 1937, vol. 81, pt. 6, 6117–18; 75th Cong., 3d sess., February 7, 1938, vol. 83, pt. 2, 1533–1562.

3. *Congressional Record*, 75th Cong., 3d sess., May 24, 1938, vol. 83, pt. 7, 7248–70.

4. *Richmond Afro-American* (hereafter *RAA*), June 29, 1946; Joe Louis, with Edna and Art Rust Jr., *Joe Louis: My Life* (New York: Harcourt Brace Jovanovich, 1978), 159.

5. *Pittsburgh Courier* (hereafter *PC*), February 13, 1937; *Philadelphia Tribune* (hereafter *PT*), July 30, 1936. The *Chicago Defender* praised the *Chicago Tribune* for its treatment of Joe Louis. *Chicago Defender* (hereafter *CD*), June 29, 1935. Louis golfed with Hype Igoe and Walter Stewart after Ed Sullivan of the *New York Daily News* introduced Louis to the game. (Sullivan not only promoted equality in sports, he later helped open prime-time television to blacks as host of a popular weekly variety program. Louis was a guest on his show in its first season in 1955.)

6. *New York Sun*, June 25, 1935; *New York World-Telegram*, June 10, 1937; *New York Daily News*, June 15, 1937; *New Orleans Item*, June 25, 1937; *New York Sun*, June 14, 1938; *Baltimore News-Post*, June 24, 1938 (Julian Black Collection, Smithsonian Institution).

7. *Life*, June 21, 1937, 21–22; March 27, 1939, 7; April 19, 1937, 39; August 9, 1937, 51–52; *Time*, June 29, 1936, 36; *PC*, June 27, 1942. But Luce's journals sometimes feted prominent blacks as well, among them Marian Anderson, Ethel Waters, George Washington Carver, and Satchel Paige. *Life* quoted white baseball stars who believed Paige had "more than proved his ability to play in the big leagues." *Life*, February 22, 1937, 20; March 22, 1937, 37; January 23, 1939, 49; December 9, 1940, 63; June 2, 1941, 91–92.

8. *Pittsburgh Post-Gazette*, June 21, 1938; *Birmingham News*, June 23, 1938 (Black Collection).

9. *RAA*, June 17, 1939, February 8, 1941; *CD*, June 12, 1937; Roi Ottley, *New World A-Coming* (Boston: Houghton Mifflin, 1943), 199.

10. *Joe Louis: My Life*, 10–12; Joe Louis, *My Life Story* (New York: Duell, Sloan, and Pearce, 1947), 14–19; Joe Louis, as told to Meyer Berger and Barney Nagler, "My Story," *Life*, November 8, 1948, 128–130; Chester Washington and William Nunn, "The Life Story of Joe Louis," *PC*, February 9, 1935.

11. Big Bill Broonzy, "Starvation Blues," Yazoo, Belzona Records, 1928; Michael Taft, *Blues Lyric Poetry: An Anthology* (New York: Garland, 1983), 2236.

12. *Life*, November 8, 1948, 129-130; *Joe Louis: My Life*, 11-15; PC, February 9, 1935.

13. "The South," *The Collected Poems of Langston Hughes*, ed. Arnold Rampersad (New York: Knopf, 1995), 26–27.

14. *Joe Louis: My Life*, 13–16; interviews with Henry Biggs, Frederick Cureton, and Katherine Reid in *Untold Tales, Unsung Heroes: An Oral History of Detroit's African American Community, 1918–1967,* ed. Elaine Latzman Moon (Detroit: Wayne State Press, 1994), 44, 58–59, 92–93.

15. Richard Wright, *12 Million Black Voices: A Folk History of the Negro in the United States* (New York: Viking, 1941), 48–56; Louis, *My Life Story*, 16–17; Louis, "My Story," 128–141; interview with Fred Guinyard in Moon, *Untold Stories* 111–112.

16. *Life*, November 8, 1948, 129; *Joe Louis: My Life*, 9.

17. Richard Wright, *American Hunger* (New York: Harper and Row, 1977 [1944]), 11–12.

18. *CD*, August 15, October 24, 1936; Wright, *American Hunger*, 21, 88; *CD*, March 20, July 3, 1937; January 1, 15, July 9, 1938; "The Black Clown," *Collected Poems of Langston Hughes*, 151; Julio Finn, *The Bluesman: The Musical Heritage of Black Men and Women in the Americas* (New York: Interlink, 1992), 201.

19. *CD*, July 16, September 24, 1938; Frank Marshall Davis, *Livin' the Blues: Memoirs of a Black Journalist and Poet*, ed. John Edgar Tidwell (Madison: University of Wisconsin Press, 1992), 192.

20. *CD*, December 31, 1938.

21. *PT*, February 14, 28, March 14, 28, November 7, 1935; March 5, November 26, December 31, 1936; March 4, April 22, August 19, 1937; April 21, June 2, 1938. Walter White, who investigated many riots over a long career, blamed "blockbusting" for straining race relations and often inciting violence. Walter White, *A Man Called White* (New York: Arno, 1969 [1948]), 44–45.

22. Ella Baker and Marvel Cooke, "The Bronx Slave Market," *The Crisis*, November 1935, 330–331, 340; *New York Post*, March 28, 1935; *The Negro in New York: An Informal Social History*, ed. Roi Ottley and William J. Weatherby (New York: New York Public Library, 1967), 273–275; James Baldwin, *The Fire Next Time* (New York: Dial, 1963), 27–38.

23. Davis, *Livin' the Blues*, 255; Baldwin, *The Fire Next Time*, 38; *CD*, July 2, 1938; *Time*, July 5, 1948, 40; *RAA*, July 3, 1948.

24. Michael Carter, "Crime in Harlem," *The Crisis*, December 1939, 366–367; Cab Calloway and Bryant Rollins, *Of Minnie the Moocher and Me* (New York: Crowell, 1976), 116; Jack Schiffman, *Uptown: The Story of Harlem's Apollo Theatre* (New York: Cowles, 1971), 3–4, 49–50; 100–101. Earnest Hooten, an anthropologist at Harvard, also found rape rare among blacks, less common than among foreign-born whites, native whites of foreign parentage, and old stock whites. Hooten denied that

"frequent lynchings" were needed to protect white women from black men. Earnest Hooten, *Crime and the Man* (Cambridge: Harvard Press, 1939), 296–302.

25. *Los Angeles Sentinel* (hereafter *LAS*), October 18, 25, 1934; February 21, 1935; January 2, February 20, July 30, December 22, 1936; March 4, 1937; Charlotta A. Bass, *Forty Years: Memoirs From the Pages of a Newspaper* (Los Angeles: Bass, 1960), 95–113.

26. *PC*, March 16, 1935, September 17, 1938; *Dallas Express* (hereafter *DE*), November 8, 1941, January 17, March 7, April 11, July 25, September 5, 1942; Davis, *Livin' the Blues*, 191–193.

27. *DE*, May 24, August 2, 9, September 6, 20, 1941.

28. *CD*, August 6, 13, 20, 1938; *PC*, August 6, 20, 27, 1938.

29. The Committee for Industrial Organization split from the American Federation of Labor in 1938 and became known as the Congress of Industrial Organizations.

30. Interviews with Walter Rosser and James Boggs in Moon, *Untold Tales*, 139, 149–151.

31. Victoria Spivey, "Detroit Moan," 1936, *The Victoria Spivey Recorded Legacy of the Blues,* Spivey Records; Taft, *Blues Lyric Poetry*, 559.

32. George Schuyler, "Reflections on Negro Leadership," *The Crisis*, November 1937, 327; Wright, *12 Million Black Voices*, 105, 117–123; MacKinley Helm, *Angel Mo' and Her Son, Roland Hayes* (Boston: Little, Brown, 1942), 288–289.

33. "The Riots," *The Crisis*, July 1943, 199; Thurgood Marshall, "The Gestapo in Detroit," *The Crisis*, August 1943, 232, 247, 281; White, *A Man Called White*, 226, 235; John Dancy, *Sand Against the Wind: The Memoirs of John C. Dancy* (Detroit: Wayne State Press, 1966), 195–223; *PC*, August 7, 1943; *DE*, August 7, 1943; *New York Post*, August 2, 1943; *New York Times* (hereafter *NYT*), August 30, 1943; "The Harlem Riot," *The Crisis*, September 1943, 263; Chester Himes, "Negro Martyrs Are Needed," *The Crisis*, May 1944, 174; interviews with Carl Winter, M. Kelly Fritz, and Winston Lang in Moon, *Untold Tales*, 69–70, 83–84, 293.

34. Interviews with Othello Renfroe, George Giles, Paul O'Neil, John Stephens, and Ted Page in John Holway, *Voices from the Great Black Baseball Leagues* (New York: Dodd, Mead, 1975), 158–161, 345; Holway, *Black Diamonds: Life in the Negro Leagues from the Men Who Lived It* (Westport: Meckler, 1989), 15, 59–60, 64, 98–99.

35. Ethel Waters with Charles Samuels, *His Eye Is on the Sparrow* (Garden City: Doubleday, 1951), 92, 109, 159–160, 169–175, 194, 220, 224, 277; Ethel Waters, *To Me It's Wonderful* (New York: Harper, 1972), 77, 135; Calloway and Rollins, *Of Minnie the Moocher & Me*, 82–88; Billie Holiday with William Dufty, *Lady Sings the Blues* (Garden City: Doubleday, 1956), 95–97; Schiffman, *Uptown*, 58.

36. Lena Horne, as told to Helen Arstein and Carlton Moss, *In Person* (New York: Greenberg, 1950), 38–47, 78, 86; Lena Horne with Richard Schickel, *Lena* (Garden City: Doubleday, 1965), 47–59, 70, 75–76, 231.

37. *PT*, September 5, 19, 1935; *Joe Louis: My Life*, 62–63; *PC*, June 8, 29, 1935; *PT*, June 27, 1935; *PC*, July 13, 1940; Steve Hannagan, "Black Gold," *Saturday Evening Post*, June 20, 1936, 78; *New York World-Telegram*, April 21, 1936 (Black Collection); *Time*, September 29, 1941, 62. See also Joe Louis, "Why I Won't Marry Again," *Ebony*, November 1952, 45–48.

38. Jack Schiffman, *Harlem Heyday* (Buffalo: Prometheus, 1984), 216, 236–237; interview with Leonard Reed in Joe Louis Barrow Jr. and Barbara Munder, *Joe Louis: 50 Years on American Hero* (New York: McGraw-Hill, 1988), 507. Schiffman noted that Reed, like most black comics in the 1930s, "blackened up" for the stage with

burnt cork. Reed later pondered the riddle of race and identity in terms of his own liminal position on the color line: "The black performers hated me because they thought I was white; the white performers shunned me because I was black. Hell! I couldn't please nobody!"

39. *PC*, January 29, 1938; *PT*, September 8, 1938; *CD*, September 10, 1938; Benny Goodman and Irving Kolodin, *The Kingdom of Swing* (New York: Ungar, 1961 [1939]), 228–231; John Hammond, "King of Swing," *The Crisis*, April 1937, 110–111, 123–124; James Lincoln Collier, *Benny Goodman and the Swing Era* (New York: Oxford Press, 1989), 205–206; Calloway and Rollins, *Of Minnie the Moocher and Me*, 54–55; Count Basie, as told to Albert Murray, *Good Morning Blues* (New York: Random House, 1985), 3; *PT*, June 24, 1937; *PC*, July 25, 1942; "Hayes, Waller, and Democracy," *The Crisis*, August 1942, 247; Helm, *Angel Mo' and Her Son,* 283–286, 289. See also Schiffman, *Harlem Heyday*, 43–45.

40. Calloway and Rollins, *Of Minnie the Moocher & Me*, 123; Mel Watkins, *On the Real Side: Laughing, Lying, and Signifying* (New York: Simon and Schuster, 1994), 391–392; J. Saunders Redding, *No Day of Triumph* (New York: Harper, 1942), 210–211, 269; Charles Evers and Andrew Szanton, *Have No Fear: The Charles Evers Story* (New York: John Wiley & Sons, 1997), 26, 29-31; *PC*, November 8, 1941. On humor as an antidote to oppression, see Lawrence Levine, *Black Culture and Black Consciousness: Afro-American Folk Thought from Slavery to Freedom* (New York: Oxford Press, 1977); Watkins, *On the Real Side*; William Schechter, *The History of Negro Humor in America* (New York: Fleet, 1970); *Mother Wit from the Laughing Barrel*, ed. Alan Dundes (Jackson: University of Mississippi Press, 1990); Langston Hughes, "Jokes Negroes Tell on Themselves," *Negro Digest*, June 1951, 21–25.

41. Roy Wilkins, "Huey Long Says," *The Crisis*, February 1935, 41, 52; *Congressional Record*, 73d Cong., 2d sess., June 16, 1934, vol. 78, pt. 11, 11941; *Washington Post*, May 5, 1935.

42. "Can the States Stop Lynching?" *The Crisis*, January 1936, 6–7, 18; *The Crisis*, February 1935, 55; April 1935, 119; *NYT*, January 12, March 13, June 23, July 16, 20, 21, 31, August 6, September 19, 29, November 5, 13, 14, 15, 1935; *PC*, April 27, June 29, August 10, November 23, 1935; *CD*, January 19, July 6, 13, 1935. Publications in Germany printed photos of lynching victims to counter American protests against Nazi persecution of Jews and Catholics. See *Without Sanctuary: Lynching Photography in America*, ed. James Allen (Santa Fe, NM: Twin Palms, 2000).

43. Roy Wilkins, "Two Against 5,000," *The Crisis*, June 1936, 169–170.

44. *The Crisis*, June 1936, inside front cover; *CD*, April 10, 1937; *NYT*, May 4, September 7, 9, 1936; *PC*, January 9, 1937; Roy Wilkins with Tom Mathews, *Standing Fast: The Autobiography of Roy Wilkins* (New York: Viking, 1982), 174–175; *CD*, December 12, 1936.

45. "Any Negro Will Do," *The Crisis*, July 1937, 209; "Can the States Stop Lynching?" *The Crisis*, January 1938, 12; *NYT*, February 5, 7, March 10, June 5, 6, 1937.

46. "Can the States Stop Lynching?" *The Crisis*, January 1938, 12–13; *CD*, April 17, 1937; White, *A Man Called White*, 123–124; *The Crisis*, September 1937, 278–280; *PC*, April 24, 1937; "Virginia Dailies on Lynching," *The Crisis*, May 1937, 145; *NYT*, July 21, August 18, September 4, October 5, 1937; Mary White Ovington, *The Walls Came Tumbling Down* (New York: Harcourt, 1947), 258–266. NAACP leaders urged Clark to display the photographs taken at Duck Hill in the Senate because they deemed them "too horrible" to print in the black press.

47. "Can the States Stop Lynching?" *The Crisis*, January 1939, 9; *The Crisis*,

October 1938, 334; *PC*, July 16, 1938; *CD*, July 9, 1938; *NYT*, July 10, 1938; *The Crisis*, November 1938, 366; *NYT*, October 14, 18, 20, 1938; *PC*, October 22, 1938; *CD*, October 15, 29, 1938; *PC*, December 3, 1938; *NYT*, October 18, November 20, 1938; Layle Lane, "Land of the Noble Free," *The Crisis*, July 1939, 208; *NYT*, November 22, 1939; *The Crisis*, January 1939, 22.

48. Ovington, *Walls Came Tumbling Down*, 265.

49. *Congressional Record*, 75th Cong., 1st sess., April 15, 1937, vol. 81, pt. 3, 3546–49, 3550, 3552, 3553.

50. *Congressional Record*, 75th Cong., 3d sess., January 12, 14, 19, 20, 21, 1938, vol. 81, pt. 3, 374, 503, 753, 764, 813, 873, 881, 883, 894; February 8, 1938, vol. 83, pt. 2, 1626–31, 1639, 1641–42.

51. *Mary Chesnut's Civil War*, ed. C. Vann Woodward (New Haven: Yale Press, 1981), 29; *Narrative of the Life of Frederick Douglass*, ed. Benjamin Quarles (Cambridge: Belknap, 1960), 24, 25–26; Linda Brent [Harriet Jacobs], *Incidents in the Life of a Slave Girl*, ed. L. Maria Child (San Diego: Harcourt Brace Jovanovich, 1973), 26–28, 34–35.

52. See Robert L. Zangrando, *The NAACP Crusade Against Lynching, 1909–1950* (Philadelphia: Temple University Press, 1980), 6–7.

53. White, *A Man Called White*, 169–170.

54. Haywood Patterson and Earl Conrad, *Scottsboro Boy* (New York: Doubleday, 1950), 3–14; Ovington, *Walls Came Tumbling Down*, 231–236; Wilkins, *Standing Fast*, 157–160; White, *A Man Called White*, 125–133; Harry Jones, "The Negro Before the Courts During 1932," *The Crisis*, September 1933, 206; *The Crisis*, September 1937, 273; *LAS*, March 18, 1937; Davis, *Livin' the Blues*, 190-191; *PC*, February 1, 1936; *The Crisis*, April 1940, 113. For full accounts of this case, see Dan Carter, *Scottsboro: A Tragedy of the American South* (Baton Rouge: Louisiana State University Press, 1969); James Goodman, *Stories of Scottsboro* (New York: Pantheon, 1994).

55. Angelo Herndon, *Let Me Live* (New York: Arno, 1969 [1937]), 188–332, 345–346; Harry Haywood, *Black Bolshevik: Autobiography of an Afro-American Communist* (Chicago: Liberator Press, 1978), 380–382; Davis, *Livin' the Blues*, 194–196; *PC*, July 14, 1934, June 1, 1935; *LAS*, December 12, 1935; *St. Louis Argus*, January 27, 1933; Langston Hughes, *I Wonder As I Wander* (New York: Hill and Wang, 1956), 372–77. The NAACP virtually ignored Herndon. "God knows it was hard enough being black," Wilkins wrote. "We certainly didn't need to be red, too." *Standing Fast*, 210. See Charles H. Martin, *The Angelo Herndon Case and Southern Justice* (Baton Rouge: Louisiana State University Press, 1976).

56. *PC*, December 22, 1934; *CD*, May 16, 1936; *PT*, January 9, 1936; *CD*, January 18, 1936; Redding, *No Day of Triumph*, 317.

57. *CD*, March 28, 1936; *PT*, March 12, September 3, 1936, January 3, 1938; *The Crisis*, February 1940, 49; Carter, *Scottsboro*, 78–84, 206–210; Goodman, *Stories of Scottsboro*, 42–43, 57, 125–27, 131.

58. *CD*, May 11, 1935, October 17, December 19, 1936, May 18, June 5, 1937.

59. "Reason for Lynchings," *The Crisis*, December 1935, 369; *PT*, March 5, 1936; *LAS*, July 2, 1936; *PT*, October 1, 1936; David Cartwright, "Political Futures and the Negro," *The Crisis*, June 1937, 171.

60. *PC*, December 31, 1938, January 13, 1940; *CD*, September 18, 1937; *PT*, October 7, 1937; *CD*, September 25, October 9, 1937; *PT*, October 21, 1937; White, *A Man Called White*, 177–179; A. Leon Higginbotham Jr., *Shades of Freedom: Racial*

Politics and Presumptions of the American Legal Process (New York: Oxford Press, 1996), 163–164. Roy Wilkins endorsed Roosevelt for reelection in 1940 but remained ambivalent about him forty years later, believing he had been "overrated as a champion of the Negro." A "patrician" both "distant" and "aloof," Roosevelt had "no natural feel for the sensibilities of black people, no compelling inner commitment to their cause." Wilkins, *Standing Fast*, 127–128.

61. Heywood Broun, "Louis and Lewis," *The Nation*, February 6, 1937, 156.

62. *PT*, October 1, 8, 1936; *PC*, September 28, 1935; *PT*, September 22, 1938; *CD*, September 17, 1938; *Tulsa Daily World*, March 18, 1937; *Dallas Journal*, March 22, 1937 (Black Collection); *PC*, March 13, 20, 1937; *Joe Louis: My Life*, 108–110, 129.

63. Dancy, *Sand Against the Wind*, 186–190; *PT*, October 3, 1935, June 30, 1938; *Joe Louis: My Life*, 65, 101–102, 131–132; Coleman Young and Lonnie Wheeler, *Hard Stuff: The Autobiography of Coleman Young* (New York: Viking, 1994), 27–28; Louis, *My Life Story*, 191–193; *Time*, September 29, 1941, 63–64; interview with Vunies Barrow High in Joe Louis Barrow Jr. and Barbara Munder, *Joe Louis: 50 Years an American Hero* (New York: McGraw-Hill, 1988), 113–114.

64. *Cleveland Gazette*, November 2, 9, 1940; *Joe Louis: My Life*, 158–159.

Chapter 7. "Another World Be Born": In Search of Victory at Home and Abroad

1. Margaret Walker, *This Is My Country: New and Collected Poems* (Athens, GA: University of Georgia Press, 1989), 11.

2. *Pittsburgh Courier* (hereafter *PC*), November 17, 1945.

3. For analyses of these intellectual currents see Paul F. Boller Jr., *American Thought in Transition: The Impact of Evolutionary Naturalism, 1865–1900* (Chicago: Rand McNally, 1969); I.A. Newby, *Jim Crow's Defense: Anti-Negro Thought in America, 1900–1930* (Baton Rouge: Louisiana State Univerity Press, 1965); Robert F. Berkhofer Jr., *The White Man's Indian: Images of the American Indian from Columbus to the Present* (New York: Knopf, 1978); Gerald F. Linderman, *The Mirror of War: American Society and the Spanish-American War* (Ann Arbor: University of Michigan Press, 1974); Frederick Hoxie, *A Final Promise: The Campaign to Assimilate the Indians, 1880–1920* (Lincoln: University of Nebraska Press, 1984); Stuart C. Miller, *The Unwelcome Immigrant: The American Image of the Chinese, 1785–1882* (Berkeley: University of California Press, 1969).

4. W.E.B. DuBois, *The Souls of Black Folk* (New York: New American Library, 1969 [1903]), 94.

5. Ruth A. Fisher to W.E.B. DuBois, March 17, 1943, DuBois to Fisher, March 29, 1943, DuBois to Edward Weeks, October 2, 1941, Weeks to DuBois, January 26, 1942, *The Correspondence of W.E.B. DuBois*, ed. Herbert Aptheker (Amherst: University of Massachusetts Press, 1976), vol. 2, 302–306, 325, 358–360.

6. *Philadelphia Tribune* (hereafter *PT*), June 20, 1935; Joe Louis, with Edna and Art Rust Jr., *Joe Louis: My Life* (New York: Harcourt Brace Jovanovich, 1978), 58; *Chicago Defender* (hereafter *CD*), June 29, July 6, 1935 *PT*, June 27, 1935.

7. Maya Angelou, *I Know Why the Caged Bird Sings* (New York: Random House, 1969), 132; Clifton L. Taulbert, *Once Upon a Time When We Were Colored* (Tulsa: Council Oaks Books, 1989), 51–52; *PC*, July 27, 1935; A.J. Liebling, "Boxing With the Naked Eye," *New Yorker*, June 30, 1951, 38.

8. *CD*, June 22, 1935; *PT*, August 15, 1935; *PC*, July 20, 1935.

9. *PC*, January 25, February 29, 1936, April 13, 1940.

10. *PT*, June 11, 1936; Louis, *Joe Louis: My Life*, 83; *PT*, April 2, 1936; *New York Times* (hereafter *NYT*), April 16, 1936; *Atlanta Journal*, June 19, 1936 (Julian Black Collection, Smithsonian Institution); *PC*, February 21, 1942; *Richmond Afro-American*, (hereafter *RAA*), February 28, 1942; Tallulah Bankhead, *Tallulah: My Autobiography* (New York: Harper, 1952), 21–22; George Frazier, "Tallulah Bankhead," *Life*, February 15, 1943, 46-47.

11. *Joe Louis: My Life*, 85–86; *New York Sun*, April 22, 1936 (Black Collection); *PC*, May 9, 1936; Nat Fleischer, *50 Years at Ringside* (New York: Fleet, 1958), 80–81.

12. *Joe Louis: My Life*, 87–90; *Time*, June 29, 1936, 36; Max Schmeling, as told to Paul Gallico, "This Way I Beat Joe Louis," *Saturday Evening Post* (hereafter *SEP*), August 29, 1936, 6, 40–41, September 5, 1936, 32–34; Joe Louis, as told to Meyer Berger and Barney Nagler, "My Story," *Life*, November 15, 1948, 129.

13. *Detroit Evening Times*, June 20, 1936 (Black Collection); *The Nation*, June 27, 1936, 836; *Die Tagebücher von Joseph Goebbels*, ed. Elke Fröhlich (Munich: K.G. Saur, 1987), June 26, 27, 1936, vol. 2, 633–635; *Max Schmeling: An Autobiography*, trans. and ed. George B. von der Lippe (Chicago: Bonus Books, 1998 [1977]), 129–131; interview with Max Schmeling in Joe Louis Barrow Jr. and Barbara Munder, *Joe Louis: 50 Years an American Hero* (New York: McGraw-Hill, 1988), 19.

14. *Los Angeles Sentinel*, (hereafter *LAS*) July 16, 1936; *PC*, July 25, 1936; *Cleveland Gazette* (hereafter *CG*), August 8, 1936; "Black Auxiliaries," *The Crisis*, September 1936, 273; *New York Post*, August 13, 1936; *The Nation*, August 8, 15, 1936, 142, 170. See also *The New Republic*, August 17, 1936, 29.

15. *CG*, August 1, 1936; *CD*, August 15, 1936; *Max Schmeling: An Autobiography*, 135–136; *PC*, August 15, 1936; *Joe Louis: My Life*, 124–25; *CD*, August 29, 1936; *PC*, September 5, 1936; *LAS*, August 6, 20, 27, 1936. See also Eddie Cantor, with Jane Kesner Ardmore, *Take My Life* (Garden City: Doubleday, 1957), 280-282.

16. "Black Auxiliaries," *The Crisis*, September 1936, 273; Roy Wilkins with Tom Mathews, *Standing Fast: The Autobiography of Roy Wilkins* (New York: Viking, 1982), 163–164.

17. *PC*, August 22, 1936; *CD*, August 29, 1936; *PT*, September 24, 1936.

18. George Spandau, "Schmeling's a Cultural Victory," reprinted in *The Crisis*, October 1936, 301, 309.

19. Schmeling and Gallico, "This Way I Beat Joe Louis," *SEP*, September 5, 1936, 32–34; *CD*, September 19, 1936, February 13, 1937; *Joe Louis, My Life Story* (New York: Duell, Sloan and Pearce, 1947), 71; Louis, "My Story," 129; *Joe Louis: My Life*, 143.

20. *New York Daily Mirror*, June 18, 1938 (Black Collection); *PC*, December 12, 1936; *LAS*, December 5, 1935, January 14, 1937; *PC*, January 16, 23, 1937. See also *Newsweek*, May 29, 1937, 19.

21. Budd Schulberg, *Loser and Still Champion: Muhammad Ali* (Garden City: Doubleday, 1972), 23–24.

22. *PC*, July 3, 10, 1937; *CD*, July 17, December 18, 1937; *PT*, December 23, 1937, April 7, 1938; *PC*, November 13, 1937; *Newsweek*, May 29, 1937, 19, 22.

23. *New York Daily Mirror*, June 21, 1938 (Black Collection); I.Q. Gross, "'Yussel' Jacobs Okays the Nazis," *The Nation*, June 18, 1938, 698; *RAA*, June 18, 1938; *Joe Louis: My Life*, 137; Louis, "My Life Story," 133.

24. Gross, "'Yussel' Jacobs," 698; *CD*, December 4, 1937; Daniel M. Daniel, *The Mike Jacobs Story* (New York: Ring, 1950), 76; *Joe Louis: My Life*, 138–140; *PC*, June 11, 1938; *New York Daily Mirror*, June 18, 1938 (Black Collection); *LAS*, June 16, 1938.

25. Clyde E.B. Bernhardt, as told to Sheldon Harris, *I Remember: Eighty Years of Black Entertainment, Big Bands, and the Blues* (Philadelphia: University of Pennsylvania Press, 1986), 133–134; *Joe Louis: My Life*, 141.

26. *Denver Post*, June 21, 1938 (Black Collection); *PC*, June 25, 1938; *Max Schmeling: An Autobiography*, 153–156; interview with Schmeling in Barrow and Munder, *Joe Louis: 50 Years an American Hero*, 10–11; *PC*, June 25, 1938; *New York Post*, June 23, 1938 (Black Collection); *Tallulah: My Autobiography*, 22; *CD*, May 28, July 2, 1938; Louis, "My Life Story," 134; *St. Louis Post-Dispatch*, June 23, 1938 (Black Collection); *Joe Louis: My Life*, 143–144. According to a *New York Times* dispatch from Berlin, the entire broadcast of the fight did reach Germany. *NYT*, June 23, 1938. "After this defeat, I no longer existed for Hitler and Goebbels," Schmeling wrote in his autobiography. "For quite a while my name simply disappeared from the newspapers."

27. *New York Daily Mirror*, June 18, 1938; *San Francisco Chronicle*, June 23, 1938; *New York World-Telegram*, June 24, 1938; *Birmingham News*, June 23, 1938 (Black Collection); *The Nation*, July 2, 1938, 4; Russell Baker, *Growing Up* (New York: Congdon and Weed, 1982), 205–206.

28. Ralph David Abernathy, *And the Walls Came Tumbling Down: An Autobiography* (New York: Harper and Row, 1989), 33; Wilkins, *Standing Fast*, 164; *PT*, June 30, 1938; *LAS*, June 23, 30, 1938; *PC*, July 2, 1938; *CD*, June 25, 1938; *PT*, June 23, 1938; *CD*, June 25, 1938; Daniel, *The Mike Jacobs Story*, 113.

29. *CD*, July 18, 1936; *PC*, January 15, 1938; *Joe Louis: My Life*, 143; *PT*, July 7, 1938; *CD*, June 25, 1938; *Deutscher Weckruf und Beobachter*, June 30, 1938 (Black Collection); *Time*, July 4, 1938, 19. Even before the fight, Goebbels suspected Jewish treachery: "*Juden suchen wieder Schmelings Kampf zu sabotieren.*" [The Jews are trying once again to sabotage Schmeling's match.] *Die Tagebücher von Joseph Goebbels*, May 18, 1938, vol. 3, 445.

30. *CD*, July 30, 1938; *PT*, August 4, 1938; *PC*, August 13, 1938; *NYT*, July 27, 31, 1938.

31. *Hitler's Third Reich: A Documentary History*, ed. Louis L. Snyder (Chicago: University of Chicago Press, 1981), 27–30, 54–55, 162–163; *Die Tagebücher von Joseph Goebbels*, July 13, 1938, vol. 3, 479. On Nazi racialism, see Michael Burleigh and Wolfgang Wipperman, *The Racial State: Germany 1933–1945* (Cambridge: Cambridge University Press, 1991); Gerald Fleming, *Hitler and the Final Solution* (Oxford: Oxford University Press, 1986); Karl Schleunes, *The Twisted Road to Auschwitz: Nazi Policy towards German Jews 1933–1939* (Urbana: University of Illinois Press, 1972); Leon Poliakov, *The Aryan Myth: A History of Racist and Nationalist Ideas in Europe* (New York: Basic Books, 1974).

32. *NYT*, July 27, 31, 1938; *CD*, July 30, 1938; *PT*, August 4, 1938; *RAA*, August 20, 1938; Louis, "My Story," 134; Louis, *My Life Story*, 98.

33. *Klansman's Manual*, 1925, in *America Firsthand*, ed. Robert D. Marcus and David Burner (New York: St. Martin's, 1989), vol. 2, 239–240; *The Nation*, July 23, 1938, 81; *PT*, October 14, 1937, October 20, 1938, July 7, 1938; *The Crisis*, September 1938, 301; *PC*, August 24, 1940.

34. George Padmore, "The Second World War and the Darker Races," *The Crisis*, November 1939, 337; *The Crisis*, December 1939, 369; Adam Clayton

Powell Jr., *A Rising Tide* (New York: Dial, 1945), 2–4; Adam Clayton Powell Jr., *Marching Blacks* (New York: Dial, 1945), 3–4; J. Saunders Redding, *No Day of Triumph* (New York: Harper, 1942), 189, 327; "Lynching and Liberty," *The Crisis*, July 1940, 209.

35. *RAA*, October 8, August 20, 1938; *PC*, October 1, December 31, 1938; *CD*, September 10, November 19, 1938, February 11, October 7, 1939; Benjamin E. Mays, *Born to Rebel* (New York: Scribner's, 1971), 209; *Nashville Globe-Independent*, February 3, 1939.

36. *PC*, February 4, September 9, November 25, 1939, January 13, May 25, 1940, March 25, 1939, March 2, July 13, October 26, December 21, 28, 1940.

37. Walter F. White, *A Man Called White* (New York: Arno Press, 1969 [1948]), 206–208; "We Are Accused of Inciting to Riot and Being Traitors," *The Crisis*, June 1942, 183; Frank Marshall Davis, *Livin' the Blues: Memoirs of a Black Journalist and Poet*, ed. John Edgar Tidwell (Madison: University of Wisconsin Press, 1992), 268–73.

38. *CD*, September 9, 16, 1939; *The Crisis*, May 1938, 145.

39. *The Crisis*, June 1941, 183; January 1942, 7; March 1942, 79; *Dallas Express* (hereafter *DE*), September 6, 20, 1941, March 14, 1942.

40. *PC*, August 24, 1940; *Joe Louis: My Life*, 156; *PC*, November 22, 1941; *CD*, February 4, 1939; *PC*, December 13, 1941, January 17, 1942.

41. *Joe Louis: My Life*, 169–171; *RAA*, November 22, 1941; *PC*, December 6, 1941; *DE*, November 29, 1941; *PC*, November 29, 1941. See also Louis, *My Life Story*, 144–146; interview with Thomas H. Bowles Sr., in Elaine Latzman Moon, *Untold Tales, Unsung Heroes: An Oral History of Detroit's African American Community, 1918–1967* (Detroit: Wayne State Press, 1994), 237–238.

42. *PC*, November 22, 1941; *RAA*, November 22, 1941; J. Earle Mason, "The Negro in the United States Navy," *The Crisis*, July 1940, 200–201; *PC*, December 13, 20, 1941; *RAA*, December 27, 1941, January 3, 1942; *DE*, January 3, 1942; *RAA*, December 27, 1941, January 3, 10, 1942; Roi Ottley, *New World A' Coming* (Boston: Houghton Mifflin, 1943), 201.

43. *NYT*, January 10, 1942; *RAA*, January 17, 1942; *Joe Louis: My Life*, 170–171; Louis, *My Life Story*, 145–146; *RAA*, January 17, 1942; Louis, "My Story," 136; *RAA*, January 24, 1942; *Life*, January 26, 1942, 24; *PC*, January 17, 24, 31, 1942.

44. *DE*, February 14, 1942, January 23, 1943; *RAA*, June 6, 1942; Jesse Thomas, *My Story in Black and White* (New York: Exposition Press, 1967), 153; *PC*, January 23, 1943; *RAA*, January 23, 1943; *DE*, January 23, 1943; *Joe Louis: My Life*, 173–74; Carl Byoir, "Joe Louis Named the War," *Collier's*, May 16, 1942, 14; Barrow and Munder, *Joe Louis*, 139–140; *This Is the Army,* 1943; *PC*, June 27, 1942; *DE*, June 27, 1942.

45. Chandler Owen, *Negroes and the War* (Washington: Office of War Information, 1942), OWI Files, National Archives.

46. *RAA*, January 30, 1943; *The Crisis*, January 1943, 8; *PC*, April 17, 1943; Magee Memo to John McCloy, Assistant Secretary of War, September 3, 1941, *Blacks in the Military: Essential Documents*, ed. Bernard C. Nalty and Morris J. MacGregor (Wilmington: Scholarly Resources, 1981), 116–117; *DE*, August 21, 1943.

47. Barnett to Gibson, April 23, 1941 (Barnett Papers, Chicago Historical Society); *PC*, April 19, May 3, August 16, 23, 1941; "The Army Must Act," *The Crisis*, September 1941, 279; interviews with Eugene Gaillard and Duane Simons, *The Invisible Soldier: The Experience of the Black Soldier, World War II*, ed. Mary Penick Motley (Detroit: Wayne State Press, 1975), 41–44, 44–49.

48. *RAA*, January 17, 1942; interview with E.J. Wells, *Invisible Soldier*, 73; *PC*, February 14, 1942; Gibson to Barnett, November 14, 1942 (Barnett Papers); *The Crisis*, June 1942, 183; White, *A Man Called White*, 189–193; Powell, *A Rising Tide*, 149–150; *New York Age*, September 19, 1942.

49. Thomas, *My Story in Black and White*, 153; Ottley, *New World A' Coming*, 299; Owen, *Negroes and the War*, 15; *RAA*, June 26, 1943, November 4, 1944; *DE*, April 17, 1943.

50. Interview with Frank Penick, *Invisible Soldier*, 50; Jenkins to P.L. Prattis, September 12, 1944, *Taps for a Jim Crow Army: Letters from Soldiers in World War II*, ed. Phillip McGuire (Santa Barbara: ABC-Clio, 1983), 198–199; interview with Eddie Donald, *Invisible Soldier*, 162; James Pritchett to James Evans, January 12, 1944, *Taps*, 23.

51. Interviews with E.J. Wells and David Cason Jr., *Invisible Soldier*, 311, 264–265; Bert Babero to Truman Gibson, February 13, 1944, *Taps*, 50–51; interview with William P. Shelton, *Invisible Soldier*, 57; "A Group of Soldiers" to the *Pittsburgh Courier*, February 10, 1943, *Taps*, 13; interview with Harry Duplessis, *Invisible Soldier*, 328; John Rivers to Carl Murphy, President, *Afro-American*, November 24, 1943, *Taps*, 218.

52. Interview with Floyd Jones, *Invisible Soldier*, 179; Claude Barnett to Truman Gibson, July 6, 1943 (Barnett Papers); "Three Hundred Soldiers" to the Editor, *Baltimore Afro-American*, November 23, 1942, *Taps*, 11; interview with Lacey Wilson, *Invisible Soldier*, 61; C. Eric Lincoln, *Coming Through the Fire: Surviving Race and Place in America* (Durham: Duke University Press, 1996), 5; interview with Ray Carter, *Invisible Soldier*, 107–111.

53. Private John Lyons to the *Courier*, December 14, 1943, *Taps*, 122; Coleman Young and Lonnie Wheeler, *Hard Stuff: The Autobiography of Coleman Young* (New York: Viking, 1994), 54–58; interview with Duane Simons, *Invisible Soldier*, 49; *RAA*, February 23, 1946; William Lee to William Nunn, July 28, 1943, *Taps*, 171; *PC*, December 23, 1944; Roy Wilkins, "The Old Army Game?" *The Crisis*, May 1945, 131; interview with Norman McRae, Moon, *Untold Tales*, 183.

54. Gordon Parks, *Voices in the Mirror: An Autobiography* (New York: Doubleday, 1990), 88–89; Pauli Murray, "A Blueprint for First Class Citizenship," *The Crisis*, November 1944, 358–359; Pauli Murray, *Song in a Weary Throat: An American Pilgrimage* (New York: Harper and Row, 1987), 200–228; *PC*, March 11, 18, April 22, 1944.

55. Hastie to Stimson, September 22, 1941; Marshall to Stimson, December 1, 1941, *Blacks in the Military*, 112–114, 114–115.

56. *PC*, September 29, 1945; Motley, *Invisible Soldier*, 243; Roi Ottley, *Black Odyssey: The Story of the Negro in America* (New York: Scribner's, 1948), 287; Davis, *Livin' the Blues*, 271–272; *DE*, April 28, July 14, 1945; "Beaumont to Detroit," *The Collected Poems of Langston Hughes*, ed. Arnold Rampersad (New York: Knopf, 1995), 281; *RAA*, October 30, 1943, August 25, 1945; *The Crisis*, July 1944, 217, August 1944, 249; Grant Reynolds, "What the Negro Soldier Thinks About This War," *The Crisis*, October 1944, 316–317, 328, November 1944, 353.

57. *Congressional Record*, 78th Cong., 3d sess., June 29, 1945, vol. 91, pt. 5, 6994–7005; *DE*, December 15, 1945; *The Crisis*, December 1945, 345. See also Wilkins, *Standing Fast*, 178–191; Walter White, *How Far the Promised Land* (New York: Viking, 1955), 167; White, *A Man Called White*, 242–261, 271–293; Young and Wheeler, *Hard Stuff*, 65–69; Langston Hughes, *The Big Sea* (New York: Hill and Wang, 1940), 243.

58. *Joe Louis: My Life*, 177–179; Louis, "My Story," 139; Jackie Robinson as told to Alfred Duckett, *I Never Had It Made* (New York: G.P. Putnam's, 1972), 24–35; interview with Ivan Harrison, *Invisible Soldier*, 163; Rachel Robinson with Lee Daniels, *Jackie Robinson: An Intimate Portrait* (New York: Abrams, 1996), 31–32.

59. *RAA*, July 17, September 4, 1943; *PC*, August 26, 1944, Benjamin O. Davis Jr., *American: An Autobiography* (Washington: Smithsonian, 1991), 74–77; Young and Wheeler, *Hard Stuff*, 59–62; interviews with Ralph Jones and Ambrose Nutt, *Invisible Soldier*, 201–202, 248–249; "Hastie Resigns," *The Crisis*, February 1943, 41; interview with Kermit Bailer, Moon, *Untold Tales*, 175–176.

60. *DE*, January 22, 1944; *PC*, January 15, 1944; *Joe Louis: My Life*, 184–185; Louis, "My Life Story," 139; Sugar Ray Robinson with Dave Anderson, *Sugar Ray* (New York: Viking, 1970), 122–123; *PC*, April 8, 1944; *DE*, April 8, 1944; *RAA*, April 15, 1944; *Sugar Ray*, 120–122; *Time*, June 25, 1951, 64; "Hastie Resigns," 41; *PC*, February 6, 1943; *RAA*, February 6, 1943; Ottley, *New World A-Coming*, 261; White, *A Man Called White*, 87; Lena Horne, with Richard Schickel, *Lena* (Garden City: Doubleday, 1965), 174–175; *DE*, December 30, 1944; *RAA*, May 7, 1945; *PC*, April 4, 1942.

61. *Joe Louis: My Life*, 186; Louis, *My Life Story*, 169; interview with Chester Jones, *Invisible Soldier*, 191–192; Corporal Jonathan Welch to Howard Murphy, *Afro-American*, December 19, 1943, *Taps*, 118–120; Walter White, *A Rising Wind* (Garden City: Doubleday, 1945), 18; White, *A Man Called White*, 242–245; Poppy Cannon, *A Gentle Knight: My Husband, Walter White* (New York: Rinehart, 1956), 27–28.

62. *PC*, December 18, 1943, February 5, 1944; White, *A Rising Wind*, 86-96; Davis, *American*, 107–108, 124; Ottley, *Black Odyssey*, 297–300; *RAA*, September 9, 1944. See also Ruby Goldstein, as told to Frank Graham, *Third Man in the Ring* (Westport: Greenwood Press, 1972 [1959]), 133–138; *Joe Louis: My Life*, 189–190. Louis served for forty-six months, traveled "over 70,000 miles," gave ninety-six boxing exhibitions, "and was seen by close to 5,000,000 servicemen."

63. *RAA*, February 12, 1944; *PC*, April 8, 1944.

64. Thomas Cripps, *Making Movies Black: The Hollywood Message Movie from World War II to the Civil Rights Era* (New York: Oxford, 1993), 102-110; *PC*, June 23, July 7, 27, August 3, 10, 17, 24, 31, October 5, November 16, 1946; *DE*, July 27, August 24, 1946; *RAA*, July 20, August 3, 10, 24, 31, October 5, November 9, 1946; White, *A Man Called White*, 325-328; Cannon, *A Gentle Knight*, 30-31; Wilkins, *Standing Fast*, 187-188; *Joe Louis: My Life*, 196-197.

Chapter 8. "The Harder They Fall"

1. Memphis Minnie McCoy, "He's in the Ring (Doin' the Same Old Thing),'' Vocalion Records, 1935.

2. Loren Miller, "Hollywood's New Negro Films," *The Crisis*, January 1938, 8–9; *Spirit of Youth*, National Pictures, 1938; *Time*, January 31, 1938, 35–37; *Los Angeles Sentinel*, May 19, 1938. See Thomas Cripps, *Slow Fade to Black: The Negro in American Film* (New York: Oxford, 1977), 339–340; Donald Bogle, *Toms, Coons, Mulattoes, Mammies, and Bucks: An Interpretive History of Blacks in American Films* (New York: Viking, 1973), 108; Henry T. Sampson, *Blacks in Black and White: A Source Book on Black Films* (Metuchen, NJ: Scarecrow Press, 1977), 149–150.

3. *Life*, February 7, 1938, 17; *Pittsburgh Courier* (hereafter *PC*), January 29,

1938; *Time*, January 31, 1938, 36; *Chicago Defender* (hereafter *CD*), November 28, 1936; *PC*, September 20, 1941; Joe Louis with Edna and Art Rust Jr. *Joe Louis: My Life* (New York: Harcourt Brace Jovanovich, 1978), 81.

4. Lena Horne, as told to Helen Arstein and Carlton Moss, *In Person* (New York: Greenberg, 1950), 218; *Paul Robeson Speaks: Writings, Speeches, Interviews, 1918–1974*, ed. Philip S. Foner (New York: Brunner-Mazel, 1978), 120; Paul Robeson, *Here I Stand* (Boston: Beacon, 1988 [1958]), 31–32; Eileen Landay, *Black Film Stars* (New York: Drake, 1973), 76; *Richmond Afro-American* (hereafter *RAA*), October 5, 1940.

5. *PC*, December 2, 1935, September 7, 1941; *Dallas Express* (hereafter *DE*), June 28, 1941; *Toledo Blade*, June 25, 1941; *Detroit Times*, June 20, 1941 (Julian Black Collection, Smithsonian).

6. Edwin Shrake, "Bundini: Svengali in Ali's Corner," *Sports Illustrated*, February 15, 1971, 34; interview with Ernest Dillard Sr., *Untold Tales, Unsung Heroes: An Oral History of Detroit's African American Community, 1918–1967*, ed. Elaine Latzman Moon (Detroit: Wayne State Press, 1994), 157.

7. *PC*, December 28, 1946.

8. Rachel Robinson with Lee Daniels, *Jackie Robinson: An Intimate Portrait* (New York: Henry N. Abrams, 1996), 66; *RAA*, October 11, December 13, 1947; *Time*, December 15, 1947, 48, July 5, 1948, 40; Louis, *My Life*, 202–212, 219–224.

9. Louis, *My Life*, 200–201; *CD*, April 11, 1936.

10. Jackie Robinson, as told to Alfred Duckett, *I Never Had It Made* (New York: G.P. Putnam's, 1972), 71–73; *Chicago Tribune*, March 31, 1997; Robinson and Daniels, *Jackie Robinson*, 70–75; Roger Kahn, *The Era 1947–1957: When the Yankees, the Giants, and the Dodgers Ruled the World* (New York: Ticknor and Fields, 1993), 34–36, 47.

11. *Philadelphia Tribune*, November 19, 1936, June 17, 1937; *RAA*, July 2, 1938; Zora Neale Hurston, *Dust Tracks on a Road: An Autobiography*, 2d ed. (Urbana: University of Illinois Press, 1970 [1942]), 328; *PC*, August 2, 1941; Maya Angelou, *I Know Why the Caged Bird Sings* (New York: Random House, 1970), 174–175.

12. *PC*, August 31, 1935; *CD*, September 24, 1938; Robinson and Duckett, *I Never Had It Made*, 12; Robinson and Daniels, *Jackie Robinson*, 66; *PC*, April 22, 1939; Marian Anderson, *My Lord, What a Morning* (New York: Viking, 1956), 187–193.

13. *PC*, June 29, 1935, July 13, 1940; Joe Louis, as told to Meyer Berger and Barney Nagler, "My Story," *Life*, November 8, 1948, 127.

14. *PC*, January 22, 1938; *RAA*, October 29, 1938; *PC*, July 5, 12, August 30, 1941; *RAA*, July 5, 12, 1941.

15. *DE*, July 12, 19, 1941; *RAA*, July 12, 1941; Joe Louis, *My Life Story* (New York: Duell, Sloan and Pearce, 1947), 139; Louis, "My Story," 140.

16. *PC*, September 25, 1943; *RAA*, October 9, 1943; *PC*, February 5, 12, 1944; *DE*, January 8, 1944; interview with Richard King in Moon, *Untold Tales*, 166–167; *PC*, July 22, 1944.

17. *DE*, March 31, April 7, 1945; Horne and Schickel, *Lena*, 138, 140–141; *Joe Louis: My Life*, 182–84.

18. *Joe Louis: My Life*, 56, 81, 155, 159; "The Loves of Joe Louis," *Ebony*, November 1978, 43–46, 50; interviews with Leonard Reed and Sunnie Wilson in Joe Louis Barrow Jr. and Barbara Munder, *Joe Louis: 50 Years an American Hero* (New York: McGraw-Hill, 1988), 201–202, 205; Sugar Ray Robinson with Dave Anderson, *Sugar Ray* (New York: Viking, 1970), 117; *PC*, June 15, 1946.

19. *Freedomways*, vol. 3, 1978, 172–174; "Loves of Joe Louis," 43–46, 50; "The

Ten Biggest Lies About Joe Louis," *Ebony*, August 1953, 52, 56; Robert Thorpe to *Ebony*, February 1979, 20. John H. Johnson, the publisher of *Ebony*, might have been trying to make amends. In 1946, in an early issue of the magazine, Johnson had printed an article, "How Joe Louis Spent $2,000,000," a story based largely "on the charges of his estranged wife." Louis became "fighting mad," according to Johnson, and sued him. Johnson phoned Louis, apologized, urged him to drop the suit, and agreed to pay his attorney's fees. See John H. Johnson, with Lerone Bennett Jr., *Succeeding Against the Odds* (New York: Warner, 1989), 166-167. See also *PC*, May 25, 1946.

20. *New York Times Book Review*, July 23, 1978; 13; *Newsweek*, July 17, 1978, 83-84.

21. Anderson, *My Lord, What a Morning*, 188–189.

22. *Joe Louis: My Story*, 81–82, 132, 152, 154–155; "Loves of Joe Louis," 43–46, 50. See also Barrow and Munder, *Joe Louis*, 196, 200.

23. Quentin Reynolds, "Dark Dynamite," *Collier's*, June 22, 1935, 34; Joe Louis, "Why I Won't Marry Again," *Ebony*, November 1952, 47–48; interview with Marva Louis Spaulding in Barrow and Munder, *Joe Louis*, 150; Louis, *My Life Story*, 191.

24. *CD*, December 28, 1935; Roi Ottley, *New World A-Coming* (Boston: Houghton Mifflin, 1943), 200; *CD*, September 25, 1937; *PC*, July 15, 1939; *DE*, January 29, 1944.

25. Robinson and Anderson, *Sugar Ray*, 126; *Joe Louis: My Life*, 190–191; *RAA*, September 26, 1942; Barrow and Munder, *Joe Louis*, 148–149, 173; *RAA*, February 3, 1940; *Joe Louis: My Life*, 65; Louis, "My Story," 134–136; Coleman Young and Lonnie Wheeler, *Hard Stuff: The Autobiography of Coleman Young* (New York: Viking, 1994), 27–28; *PC*, January 17, April 4, 1942; *Time*, March 3, 1947, 52; John Roxborough, "How I Discovered Joe Louis," *Ebony*, October 1954, 76.

26. Barrow and Munder, *Joe Louis*, 151, 174; *New York Times*, May 20, 1950, July 29, 1950; December 7, 1951; *DE*, May 17, 24, 1947; *RAA*, May 17, 1947; *Joe Louis: My Life*, 215–216; *PC*, August 31, 1946; interview with Leonard Reed in Barrow and Munder, *Joe Louis*, 246; *Time*, March 3, 1947, 52; *Joe Louis: My Life*, 233.

27. *Ebony*, January 1957, 42; John Lardner, "The Pathos of Taxes," *Newsweek*, January 16, 1956, 73.

28. Hype Igoe, *The Ring*, July 1937 (Black Collection); *PC*, December 6, 1941; *RAA*, September 25, 1948; interview with Marva Louis Spaulding in Barrow and Munder, *Joe Louis*, 186; Louis, "My Story," 142; Louis, *My Life Story*, 102; *Joe Louis: My Life*, 268.

29. Johnson, and Bennett, *Succeeding Against the Odds,* 166–167; Martin Luther King Jr., *Why We Can't Wait* (New York: Harper and Row, 1964), 119; Ronald W. Reagan, *Public Papers of the Presidents* (Washington, DC: GPO, 1982), vol. 1, 351; Jesse L. Jackson, *Straight from the Heart*, ed. Roger D. Hatch and Frank E. Watkins (Philadelphia: Fortress Press, 1987), 168–173.

Epilogue

1. *Jack London Reports: War Correspondence, Sports Articles, and Miscellaneous Writings*, ed. King Hendricks and Irving Shepard (Garden City: Doubleday, 1970), 260–61; John Arthur Johnson, *Jack Johnson Is a Dandy: An Autobiography* (New York: Chelsea House, 1969 [1927]), 166–167; Ralph Ellison, *Going to the Territory* (New York: Random House, 1986), 215; John O. Killens, *Black Man's Burden* (New York: Trident Press, 1965), 114–115.

2. *The American Slave: A Composite Autobiography*, ed. George P. Rawick (Westport: Greenwood Press, 1977), vol. 7, 165, 167; "We Are Not Yet Quite Free," August 3, 1869, *The Frederick Douglass Papers*, ed. John W. Blassingame and John R. McKivigan (New Haven: Yale Press, 1991), vol. 4, 231; James Weldon Johnson, *Along This Way* (New York: Viking Press, 1933), 208.

3. *Chicago Defender*, October 29, 1912; *Chicago Broad-Ax*, October 26, 1912; *Cleveland Gazette*, February 17, 1940; *Pittsburgh Courier*, March 30, August 17, 1940; Joe Louis, *My Life Story* (New York: Duell, Sloan and Pearce, 1947), 117; Edwin R. Embree, *13 Against the Odds* (Port Washington: Kennikat Press, 1968 [1944]), 241; *New York Amsterdam News*, March 7, 1964; Huston Horn, "The First Days in the New Life of the Champion of the World," *Sports Illustrated*, March 9, 1964, 27; Joe Frazier with Phil Berger, *Smokin' Joe: The Autobiography of a Heavyweight Champion of the World* (New York: Macmillan, 1996), 119–120; *Black Sports*, October 1975, 29.

4. Langston Hughes, *I Wonder As I Wander: An Autobiographical Journey* (New York: Hill and Wang, 1956), 314–315. Hughes labeled Louis "a man for any man to imitate." *Collected Poems of Langston Hughes*, ed. Arnold Rampersad (New York: Knopf, 1995), 423, 575.

5. Mary Church Terrell, *A Colored Woman in a White World* (Washington, DC: Ransdell, 1940), 423; Lena Horne with Richard Schickel, *Lena* (Garden City: Doubleday, 1965), 226.

6. James Weldon Johnson, *The Autobiography of an Ex-Coloured Man* (New York: Knopf, 1928 [1912]), 43, 189, 190–191; Hughes, *I Wonder As I Wander*, 328–329; Walter F. White, *A Man Called White* (New York: Arno, 1969 [1948]), 3, 366; Henry Louis Gates Jr., *Thirteen Ways of Looking at a Black Man* (New York: Random House, 1997), 180–214.

7. Shirlee Taylor Haizlip, *The Sweeter the Juice* (New York: Simon and Schuster, 1994), 15, 71–72, 267. On racial liminality, see also Gregory Howard Williams, *Life on the Color Line* (New York: Penguin, 1996). As a boy in Richmond, Williams learned that his father was not "Italian": "My father was a Negro! We were colored! After ten years in Virginia on the white side of the color line, I knew what that meant." Later, in Muncie, Indiana, he was too black for some but too white for others. "My very existence made people uncomfortable," he noted, "and shattered too many racial taboos." *Life on the Color Line*, 33–34, 165–166.

8. Ellison, *Going to the Territory*, 317–318.

Index

About the Author

Thomas R. Hietala is professor of history at Grinnell College. Born on the Mesabi Iron Range in Minnesota, he attended Gustavus Adolphus College and earned his doctorate at Yale University. He previously taught at Yale and Dartmouth College. His first book, *Manifest Design*, examines the myths and realities of American expansionism in the 1840s. Excerpts from this widely cited text appear in several recent anthologies in the fields of foreign relations, the western frontier, and the Jacksonian era. Committed to making history more enticing and accessible to a wider audience, Professor Hietala has been a consultant to KERA television for its documentary on the Mexican-American War, a Walter Prescott Webb lecturer at the University of Texas Arlington, and a reviewer for the National Endowment for the Humanities.